# THE WORLD OF THE FLORENTINE
# RENAISSANCE ARTIST

MARTIN WACKERNAGEL

# The World of the Florentine Renaissance Artist

## PROJECTS AND PATRONS, WORKSHOP AND ART MARKET

TRANSLATED BY

ALISON LUCHS

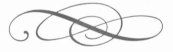

PRINCETON UNIVERSITY PRESS

PRINCETON, N.J.

The original edition appeared under the title
*Der Lebensraum des Künstlers in der florentinischen Renaissance:*
*Aufgaben und Auftraggeber, Werkstatt und Kunstmarkt*
im Verlag E. A. Seemann, Leipzig
© 1938 Verlag E. A. Seemann, Leipzig

English translation © 1981 by Princeton University Press
Published by Princeton University Press, Princeton, New Jersey
IN THE UNITED KINGDOM:
Princeton University Press, Guildford, Surrey

Library of Congress Cataloging in Publication Data will be
found on the last printed page of this book

This book has been composed in Linotron Sabon

Clothbound editions of Princeton University Press books
are printed on acid-free paper, and binding materials are
chosen for strength and durability

Printed in the United States of America by
Princeton University Press,
Princeton, New Jersey

# CONTENTS

# TRANSLATOR'S

# ACKNOWLEDGMENTS

This translation of Wackernagel's *Lebensraum des Kunstlers in der florentinischen Renaissance* could not have appeared without a great deal of help that deserves grateful mention here. The libraries and their staffs at the National Gallery of Art, Syracuse University, and Johns Hopkins University were indispensable, particularly Candida Allenbrook of Johns Hopkins. A grant from the Syracuse University Senate Research and Equipment Fund helped with production expenses. Valuable suggestions affecting the prefaces, editing and the new bibliography came from Caroline Elam and Richard Goldthwaite. Jürg Dedial, Margery Ganz, Father Al Hennelly, Bess Hormats, George Nugent, and Elaine Stanis helped me to obtain rare publications and track down some specialized terms.

The author's son and daughter, Martin Wackernagel, Jr. and Marlis Ruban-Wackernagel, kindly shared recollections of their father with me. Ulrich Middeldorf, who enthusiastically reviewed the original work in 1939, opened the way to fruitful contacts with others who knew Wackernagel. Werner Hager and Hilda Maria Martin have been unfailingly generous, sensitive, and articulate in their reminiscences of Wackernagel himself.

H. W. Janson's support for the idea of a Wackernagel translation helped make publication possible. Christine Ivusic, fine arts editor, and Rita Gentry, manuscript editor, at Princeton University Press provided invaluable aid and encouragement. Essential help and indeed, much of the inspiration for the project came from my friends the Verheyens—Egon, who trained me in Italian Renaissance art history and historiography at Johns Hopkins University and proved for years the most constructive of advisors; Hanne, whose careful and patient help cleared up many of the linguistic problems involved in translating Wackernagel's work; and Peter David, Gero, and Esther, who also gave a share in one of the best gifts I ever received—their language.

My mother, Barbara Baer Luchs, contributed many sensitive editorial solutions and also carried out the monumental task of typing the translation. My father, Wallace Luchs, Jr., gave advice, support and encouragement, and helped me time and again by asking the right questions. The only shadow over the happy outcome is sorrow that he did not live to see it.

To them and all the friends of Florence who shared enthusiasm for this translation project:

The imperfections to be found in it are mine. The credit for its completion is yours.

*Washington, D.C.*
*1980*

# TRANSLATOR'S

# INTRODUCTION

## APPROACH AND THEMES IN *The World of the Florentine Renaissance Artist*

"It is not too daring," Ulrich Middeldorf declared, "to prophesy an especially good reception in this country for Dr. Wackernagel's studies."[1] He was writing in the United States in anticipation of the original publication of the present book, entitled *Der Lebensraum des Künstlers in der florentinischen Renaissance: Aufgaben und Auftraggeber, Werkstatt und Kunstmarkt* (Leipzig, 1938).

The word *Lebensraum* as Wackernagel used it comes from a biological term meaning roughly habitat or environment. He intended it to denote "the whole complex of economic-material, social and cultural circumstances and preconditions which in any way affected the existence and activity of the artist." It corresponds closely to the French term *milieu* characterized in Hippolyte Taine's writings as one of the essential determining factors for the nature of a work of art.[2]

The approach to art history represented in Wackernagel's book made it a pioneering work in what has since become a major trend.[3] Wackernagel sought to focus attention on the relationship between Florentine art and the immediate conditions under which it was created. In detailed,

[1] Ulrich Middeldorf, review of *Vier Aufsätze über geschichtliche und gegenwärtige Faktoren des Kunstlebens* (Wattenscheid, 1936) in *Art Bulletin* 20, 1938, pp. 123-24. Some important writings since 1938 that either develop Wackernagel's approach or contribute significantly to the study of his principal topics are discussed in notes 3ff.

[2] For the several meanings of *Lebensraum* see *Brockhaus Enzyklopädie*, 17th ed. (Wiesbaden, 1970), 11; 237. Wackernagel's own discussion of the term appears on page 5 of *Vier Aufsätze*, which was the initial volume of a series of art historical studies he edited, *Lebensräume der Kunst*. See also his "Der Lebensraum der bildenden Kunst im älterer und gegenwärtiger Zeit," *Schweizer Rundschau*, 35, 1935-36, 1, pp. 42-55. He refers there (p. 52) to "the concept 'Lebensraum,' more frequently evoked today in another context," and goes on to discuss his own (quite apolitical) use of the term to denote the artist's environment.

For Taine's theories on art see his *Lectures on Art*, trans. John Durand, 2 vols. (New York, 1875), and the introduction to his *Histoire de la Littérature Anglaise* (Paris, 1863).

[3] For Wackernagel's place in art historiography see W. Eugene Kleinbauer, ed., *Modern Perspectives in Western Art History* (New York, 1971), p. 83, and Peter Burke, *Culture and Society in Renaissance Italy 1420-1540* (London, 1972), pp. 16-17. The Burke book deals with many of the themes that concerned Wackernagel, such as patronage, taste, subject matter, the functions of art, and the art market. The opening chapter on historiographers of the Renaissance is especially valuable.

richly documented examinations he explored the impact of patronage and function, of widespread demand, of workshop techniques, and business practices on the lives of artists and on the results they achieved. His aim was nothing less than to reconstruct the context of Florentine artistic life from about 1420 to 1530.

Wackernagel's principal predecessors in this orientation toward Italian Renaissance art were Jacob Burckhardt and Aby Warburg. Wackernagel himself acknowledged debts not only to Burckhardt's *Civilization of the Renaissance in Italy*, but also to his studies on Renaissance collectors and on various types of commissions. Wackernagel also cited Warburg's comments on the importance of demand as a stimulus to Renaissance art and in his book itself develops the concentration on the patron and his needs that characterized Warburg's essays on donor portraits and on Francesco Sassetti's chapel at Santa Trinita. Another forerunner in terms of scope, factual detail, and sensitivity to the whole Renaissance environment (including the economic aspect) was the monumental survey of Renaissance art in its many variations by Eugene Müntz (see Wackernagel's notes and his original bibliography for these).

But Wackernagel's contextual approach was not simply the result of adherence to any particular school of art history or theory (he himself was a pupil of Heinrich Wölfflin who is best known for his studies of style development and contrasts). Nor does Wackernagel's study aim to promote any one particular conception of the Renaissance. Rather, it reflects Wackernagel's personal, lifelong concern with the art and artists of his own time, a concern that made him keenly interested, as a historian, in the external conditions that affected artists and their work in the past. In a respectful acknowledgment of his teacher, Wackernagel stated that his aim was not to challenge Wölfflin's approach, but "to supplement from another point of view the insights gained from a style-historical standpoint . . . to establish them in general historical terms and build them into the complex of all the . . . circumstances that defined . . . the world in which the Florentine artist lived."

In evoking that world, Wackernagel meant also to provide an antidote for "the many misguided conceptions that could not help but result from the currently predominant, fundamentally antihistorical display" of art works from churches and domestic settings in museums. From their present isolation against museum walls and from the pages of inventories and old sources that record the numerous vanished examples, he strove to restore works of Florentine art "at least mentally" to their original settings and meanings in a living, developing society.

His book has three main sections that focus in turn on the commissions, *die Aufgabe* (the tasks and problems for which artists were needed), the patrons, *die Auftraggeber* (the employers of artists and commissioners of art works), and the artists and their market. Each section is essentially a well-organized, carefully documented survey of its topic. As has sometimes been noted, Wackernagel exercised considerable caution about drawing generalizing conclusions.[4] Nevertheless, a number of important wider observations emerge from the surveys. Later studies have qualified, elaborated, and deepened but rarely refuted them.

In the section on commissions Wackernagel stresses the change from the early fifteenth century, when communal efforts played a major role in the large-scale development of the chief Florentine monuments, to the more private, small-scale emphasis in the culture of the late Quattrocento under Lorenzo de' Medici. In the process, the history and changing appearance of a few specific monuments are traced through the century— the Duomo, Baptistery and Santa Maria Novella as religious centers, the Palazzo Vecchio as a secular one. These surveys call attention not only to style changes but also to the development of certain specifically Florentine themes. Wackernagel, for example, was one of the first historians to point out the special Florentine political significance of David, reflected in the city government's acquiring no less than four of the life-sized or larger statues of him produced in Florence by 1504. In the study of the Palazzo Vecchio he also notes the interlocking political and artistic significance of the Hall of the Great Council and its decoration by Leonardo and Michelangelo.[5]

[4] See for instance Creighton Gilbert, "The Earliest Guide to Florentine Architecture," *Mitteilungen des Kunsthistorischen Institutes in Florenz*, 14, 1969, p. 34, and Burke, *Culture and Society*, p. 17.

[5] On art and architecture for Florentine churches in general, the basic, exhaustive though dated catalogue is Walter and Elisabeth Paatz, *Die Kirchen von Florenz*, 6 vols. (Frankfurt am Main, 1940-54). A later treatment, less detailed but splendidly illustrated, organized by quarters of the city, is Alberto Busignani and Raffaello Bencini, *Le Chiese di Firenze* (Florence, 1974 ff.). Interesting studies by Marcia B. Hall on the Quattrocento state of major Florentine churches and their subsequent alteration (see Translator's Bibliography, section V, part, B1.) have culminated in a book, *Renovation and Counter-Reformation: Vasari and Duke Cosimo in Santa Croce and Santa Maria Novella, 1565-1577* (Oxford University Press, 1978).

On the David theme in Florentine sculpture see especially Charles Seymour, Jr., *Michelangelo's David: A Search for Identity* (Pittsburgh, 1967); on the political connotations in particular see recently Saul Levine, "The Location of Michelangelo's David: The Meeting of January 25, 1504," *Art Bulletin*, 56, 1974, pp. 31-49; the critique of Levine's argument by N. Randolph Parks, "The Placement of Michelangelo's David: A Review of the Documents," *Art Bulletin*, 57, 1975, pp. 560-570; and H. W. Janson, "La signification politique du 'David' de Donatello," *Revue de l'Art*, 39, 1978, pp. 33-38.

A detailed study and reconstruction of the Hall of the Great Council, including the Leonardo and Michelangelo murals, is Johannes Wilde's "The Hall of the Great Council in Florence," *Journal of the Warburg and Courtauld Institutes*, 7, 1944, pp. 65-81; reprinted in *Renaissance Art*, ed. Creighton Gilbert (New York, 1970), pp. 92-132. Wilde's interpretation has been discussed and criticized by Hans Werner Grohn, "Die Schule der Welt:

With the increasingly aristocratic concentration of power in the Medici family during the latter half of the fifteenth century, Wackernagel notes the growing importance of private commissions for luxury items to satisfy the taste of patricians intent on enhancing the splendor of their own domestic surroundings. The objects in question were not only paintings and sculpture but also household utensils, jewelry, armor, furniture, and decoratively enriched utilitarian objects of all sorts. At the same time, he traces a corresponding stylistic development in painting and sculpture toward increasing elegance and refinement, "a pronounced luxuriousness and lavish splendor of detail" that characterized the taste of Lorenzo the Magnificent and his period.[6]

In reference to the style change occurring around 1500, with the simplicity, monumentality, and emotional depth that Wölfflin described, Wackernagel discusses the "at least indirect" influence of Savonarola's

---

Zu Michelangelos Karton der Schlacht bei Cascina," *Il Vasari*, 21, 1963, pp. 63-79, and "Michelangelos Darstellung der Schlacht von Cascina: Versuch einer Rekonstruktion," *Jahrbuch der Hamburger Kunstsammlungen*, 17, 1972, 23-42; and by C. A. Isermeyer, "Die Arbeiten Leonardos und Michelangelos für den grossen Ratsaal in Florenz," *Studien zur Toskanischen Kunst. Festschrift für Ludwig Heinrich Heydenreich*, ed. Wolfgang Lotz and Lise Lotte Möller (Munich, 1964), pp. 83ff.

[6] Creighton Gilbert and Ernst Gombrich have since noted a preference for a gothicizing, decorative style in secular painting commissions through much of the Quattrocento, with the more austere, profound and monumental style of the early Renaissance associated principally with religious subject matter. While Wackernagel never went this far, he did allude to the extraordinary fact that a revolutionary painting style like Masaccio's should have emerged in ecclesiastical settings in particular. See Gilbert, "Earliest Guide," pp. 33-46; "The Archbishop on the Painters of Florence, 1450," *Art Bulletin*, 41, 1959, pp. 75-87; and E. H. Gombrich, "Apollonio di Giovanni: A Florence *Cassone* Workshop through the Eyes of a Humanist Poet," *Journal of the Warburg and Courtauld Institutes*, 18, 1955, pp. 16-34, reprinted in *Norm and Form* (London, 1966), pp. 11-28.

On the late Gothic "international style" of the early Quattrocento and its social significance see Richard Krautheimer and Trude Krautheimer-Hesse, *Lorenzo Ghiberti* (Princeton, 1956), pp. 76 ff.

Wackernagel made only brief reference to the heroically individualized style, inspired, as he noted, at least partly by Roman realism, in sculpture before 1420 as it appeared especially in the statues by Donatello, Nanni di Banco, and even Ghiberti at Or San Michele. Frederick Hartt has since written an exciting essay on the connection between the antique style of these works of public sculpture and the political thought of Florentine civic humanism in the early fifteenth century. See Hartt's "Art and Freedom in Quattrocento Florence," in *Essays in Memory of Karl Lehmann*, ed. Lucy Freeman Sandler (New York, 1964), pp. 114-31; reprinted, abridged, in *Modern Perspectives in Western Art History*, ed. W. Eugene Kleinbauer (New York, 1971), pp. 293-311.

For a recent development of the Burckhardt theme of the "secularization" of high culture in the early Renaissance in particular, see John Larner, *Culture and Society in Italy 1290-1420* (New York, 1971). Larner stresses the influence of the urban and governmental nature of much early Renaissance patronage (in which he includes patronage by the Church). Though brief, Larner's chapters on "the artist in society" are a highly useful counterpart to Wackernagel for the earlier period.

criticism of Laurentian art. He suggests Savonarola was giving voice to what must have been a more widespread uneasiness about the blatantly worldly character of much late Quattrocento religious painting, in which "the actual subject matter and meaning are almost completely overshadowed by the panoply of rich architectural or landscape scenery and by the patron's purely worldly, egotistical desire to introduce all possible portrait figures from his circle of friends and relations." He seems to divide responsibility for the mundane character of much Laurentian art equally between patrons' demands and the "purely artistic striving for truth to reality."[7]

In discussing the rich style of the late Quattrocento, Wackernagel does not dismiss it as reflecting an abandonment of religious for secular interests. He sees private domestic patronage as a new competitor but by no means a replacement for church patronage, and a recurring theme in Wackernagel's study is the inextricable interweaving of religious and secular values in many aspects of Florentine life throughout the fifteenth century. In particular, Wackernagel calls attention to the impact of chapel patronage for combined motives of piety and personal fame on the design of fifteenth-century Florentine churches.[8]

Patronage and its development from about 1420 to 1530 are traced in *Der Lebensraum des Künstlers in der florentinischen Renaissance* through various types of commissions, organizations, and personalities, including several generations of Medici. In this evolution, Cosimo il Vecchio and his generation represent an early type of enterprising, large-scale builder, donor to pious foundations, and cosupervisor of public projects. Wackernagel sees an evident contrast to these early pioneers in

[7] On Savonarola and art see most recently Ronald M. Steinberg, *Fra Girolamo Savonarola, Florentine Art and Renaissance Historiography* (Athens, Ohio, 1977). Steinberg tends to play down the idea of Savonarola's influence on artists in all but a few specific cases, suggesting that such influence was too willfully sought and found by later romanticizing historiographers. On the targets of Savonarola's criticism see also David Friedman, "The Burial Chapel of Filippo Strozzi in Santa Maria Novella in Florence," *L'Arte*, 9, 1970, pp. 108-331.

On the question of the adherence of artists, particularly Botticelli, to Savonarola, see especially the careful and skeptical article by Jacques Mesnil, "Connaissons-nous Botticelli?" in *Gazette des Beaux-Arts*, ser. 6, vol. 4, 1930, pp. 80-99 (evidently unknown to Wackernagel) and Mesnil's *Botticelli*, Paris, 1938.

[8] On art works for Florentine churches in general see Paatz, *Die Kirchen*; on late Quattrocento chapel patronage, its forms and motivations, see Alison Luchs, *Cestello: A Cistercian Church of the Florentine Renaissance* (New York, 1977), pp. 37 ff.

On the interplay of religious and secular, that is, Christian and humanistic themes in both thought and artistic style see especially E. H. Gombrich, "Botticelli's Mythologies: A Study in the Neo-Platonic Symbolism of his Circle," *Journal of the Warburg and Courtauld Institutes*, 8, 1945, pp. 7-60, reprinted with a new introduction in the author's *Symbolic Images* (London, 1972), pp. 31-81.

their descendants: consumers of art with a collector-connoisseur's mentality, lavishing inherited wealth on art works for private enjoyment and valuing such objects for their own sake or for the special mastery of a known creator more than for an immediate function or destination.

In the late Quattrocento attention falls on the unique role of Lorenzo the Magnificent. Wackernagel points out his significance for reasons other than direct employment of artists (although he did participate moderately in patronage in that sense also). Lorenzo, as Wackernagel was one of the first to stress, stood out less as a patron than as a collector of exquisite taste (chiefly of antique gems and rare objets d'art), as a widely acknowledged authority on art, and as one with the reputation of a friend to artists. For Wackernagel the culminating point of Lorenzo's involvement with art and artists was the legendary garden of San Marco where a new generation of artists was supposedly trained by Bertoldo di Giovanni in a school set up by Lorenzo amid a splendid antique collection. The nature and even the existence of this school, which so fascinated Wackernagel, are admittedly more controversial today. Likewise, Lorenzo's actual participation as a designer in the competition for a facade for the Duomo, repeatedly mentioned by Wackernagel, has no firm basis in early documents. But Lorenzo today still receives the credit given him by Wackernagel and earlier historians for his support and encouragement of the young Michelangelo.[9]

[9] Medici patronage, its nature and limitations are discussed in André Chastel's *Art et humanisme à Florence au temps de Laurent le Magnifique* (Paris 1959), especially with reference to Lorenzo and his circle; on the garden of San Marco see *Art et humanisme*, pp. 19-25, and Chastel's more detailed discussion, "Vasari et la légende médicéenne: l'école du jardin de Saint Marc," *Studi Vasariani* (Florence, 1952), pp. 159-167. Chastel's analysis, based on a careful examination of early evidence, has reduced this proto-academy to a study collection of a few ancient works of sculpture, opened occasionally to visitors, with the aged Bertoldo as a sort of honorary curator. The rest, according to Chastel, would be Vasari's elaboration, as a Medici propagandist and promotor of the Florentine artists' academy, of this relatively humble nucleus. John Pope-Hennessy, on the other hand, has defended at least the original concept of Michelangelo's training under Bertoldo's influence and Medici auspices. See his *An Introduction to Italian Sculpture: Italian High Renaissance and Baroque Sculpture* (London, 1963), pt. 1, pp. 4-5.

Chastel's *Art et humanisme*, a major compendium on late Quattrocento patronage and thought, may be classed with Wackernagel's work in the thoroughness of its documentation. It also provides a good balance to Wackernagel's brevity on humanist themes in the arts.

An important briefer study is E. H. Gombrich's "The Early Medici as Patrons of Art: A Survey of Primary Sources," in *Italian Renaissance Studies: A Tribute to the Memory of the Late Cecilia M. Ady*, ed. E. F. Jacob (New York, 1960), reprinted in Gombrich's *Norm and Form* (London, 1966), pp. 35-57. Gombrich acknowledges that "in many places this essay merely follows up and expands Wackernagel's references to see how far they lead towards an interpretation." He examines the early Medici as three types of patrons: Cosimo, chiefly a builder and grand-scale donor to pious foundations for the goods of his reputation and his soul, who was closely involved in the planning of the architecture he

In demonstrating the range of social levels represented by purchasers of art works, Wackernagel notes the correspondingly wide range of quality that existed. He does not propose any neat formula equating the style of works with the social class of their commissioners.[10] But he does provide a healthy reminder that just as Renaissance patrons were not all Medici, so Renaissance artists were not all Masaccio and Michelangelo. Repeatedly he points out that of all the Florentine artists whose names are recorded in the Quattrocento, only about one-fourth to one-third are represented by securely attributed works. And he calls our attention to the pervasive mediocrity of taste that alone could account for the "broad and unremitting productivity" of a workshop like Neri di Bicci's.[11] Yet the point of these observations is not so much to deromanticize the Renaissance as to stress all the more the extraordinary character of art like that of Masaccio, Castagno, or Uccello, the open-mindedness of patrons who would employ them, and the freedom that church authorities must have permitted to both.

---

commissioned; his son Piero, an avid collector of precious books and other objects, a devotee of the rich and ornate, whose taste in painting clung to the late Gothic "international style"; and the "elusive" Lorenzo, a collector of precious ancient gems, the commissioner of a few buildings and major art works (mostly lost now), but active especially as a learned arbiter of taste in and out of Florence and as a promotor of a new antiquarian art in his association with Bertoldo and Michelangelo. See also Gombrich's "Renaissance and Golden Age," *Journal of the Warburg and Courtauld Institutes*, 24, 1961, pp. 306-309, reprinted in *Norm and Form*, pp. 27-34; and A. D. Fraser Jenkins, "Cosimo de' Medici's Patronage and the Theory of Magnificence," *Journal of the Warburg and Courtauld Institutes*, 33, 1970, pp. 162-170.

The account of a design by Lorenzo for a Duomo facade, carried out in a temporary wooden version by Jacopo Sansovino for the entry into Florence of Lorenzo's son Pope Leo X in 1515 is cited repeatedly by Wackernagel. It appears to have no foundation earlier than Vasari's life of Andrea del Sarto. See Luigi del Moro, *La Facciata di Santa Maria del Fiore* (Florence, 1888), pp. 21-22.

[10] Such formulas, proposed without sufficient evidence or firm class definitions, were a principal basis for criticism of Frederick Antal's *Florentine Painting and its Social Background* (London, 1948). The Antal book provides a copious and informative discussion of Florentine political, economic, and social history, religion, philosophy, patronage, and iconography in the fourteenth and early fifteenth centuries. Antal set out to explore the question of how a single society could foster the contrasting styles of Gentile da Fabriano and Masaccio at the same time. He sought answers in an association between each style and a particular class outlook. See reviews by Theodore Mommsen, *Journal of the History of Ideas*, 9, 1950, pp. 369-379, and Millard Meiss, *Art Bulletin*, 31, 1949, pp. 143-150.

Arnold Hauser's *Social History of Art* (New York and London, 1951), vol. 2, deals with Renaissance art in an even more generalizing manner as the outgrowth of broad social forces. See the review by E. H. Gombrich, *Art Bulletin*, 35, 1953, pp. 79-84, reprinted in his *Meditations on a Hobby Horse and Other Essays in the Theory of Art* (London, 1963), pp. 86-94.

[11] Neri di Bicci's copious and informative workshop records are now published in a comprehensive new edition. See Neri di Bicci, *Le Ricordanze (10 marzo 1435-24 aprile 1475)*, ed. Bruno Santi (Pisa and Leiden, 1977).

In the section devoted to artists, Wackernagel discusses their professional organization and the step-by-step details of their training and working procedure. Citing the fundamental study by his student, Hanna Lerner-Lehmkuhl, *Zur Struktur und Geschichte des florentinischen Kunstmarktes im 15. Jahrhundert* (Wattenscheid, 1936), he examines the economics of art as reflected in contracts and prices. The relevance of precious materials like gold and lapis lazuli as well as such factors as complexity of composition in determining the price of a work is noted. If prices for paintings in a simpler, grander style after 1500 did not rise much above late Quattrocento prices, Wackernagel suggests that at least a greater proportion of the payment was now going for the artist's mastery once the "external price-boosting factors" of rich materials were removed.[12]

The artists themselves, as Wackernagel notes, might work as specialists like the della Robbia. Yet even the best known painters might also be prepared to take on commissions ranging from murals to market baskets. As the author surveys the economic and social status and the public reputation and behavior of artists, he points to a few, admittedly infrequent instances of proud or rebellious behavior by artists that might be taken as concrete evidence of the growing self-esteem of a group "nourished on Renaissance theory." He does not lose sight of the fact, however, that well into the lifetime of Michelangelo himself, artists were still regarded essentially as craftsmen.[13]

[12] On the Florentine artists' academy and earlier organizations of Florentine artists see Mary Ann Jack, "The Accademia del Disegno in Late Renaissance Florence," *The Sixteenth Century Journal*, 7, 1976, pp. 3-20. For additional material on the earlier organizations see her dissertation, Mary Ann Jack Ward, "The Accademia del Disegno in Sixteenth Century Florence: A Study of an Artists' Institution" (University of Chicago, 1972).

On the economic and legal aspects of the artist-patron relationship, with particular reference to their application to Leonardo da Vinci's *Madonna of the Rocks*, see the valuable study by Hannelore Glasser, *Artists' Contracts of the Early Renaissance* (New York, 1977); based on the author's doctoral dissertation, Columbia University, 1965. The more than 200 examples considered are primarily Tuscan. Larner's *Culture and Society* also deals with the artist's place in society and the public consciousness in Italy up to about 1420, with an appendix of notes on contracts and payments to artists.

Michael Baxandall, in *Painting and Experience in Fifteenth Century Italy* (London, 1972), pp. 1-23, also examines the economics of artistic commissions. In a study of the language of contracts, he notes a changing emphasis from the purchase by a client of rich materials to the purchase of the artist's skills as the century progressed.

[13] The artists' social position, behavior, and personality are examined, with special reference to the question of the "artistic type" in history, in Rudolf and Margot Wittkower's *Born Under Saturn. The Character and Conduct of Artists. A Documented History from Antiquity to the French Revolution.* (London, 1963).

Vasari was naturally one of Wackernagel's principal sources for stories about artists. For Vasari's accounts in light of subsequent historiography see especially the commentary in the edition prepared by Paola Barocchi and Rosanna Bettarini: Giorgio Vasari, *Le Vite de'*

In particular, two related factors seem to have fascinated Wackernagel, who was in frequent, sympathetic contact with artists. These are the widespread demand for art in the Renaissance and the functional role of most of the works, even while the idea of art as a collectible and marketable commodity was developing. In the pages of his study Renaissance art, in its multitude of media and variations, emerges as a constant and necessary presence for Florentines of all classes as they worshipped, worked, celebrated, and conducted their government and diplomatic relations. It confronted them, Wackernagel reminds us, as they went about the business of daily life in their homes and walked the streets of their city. It played a fundamental role in the rituals and observances of birth, marriage, and death.[14]

For Wackernagel, the factors of function and demand had an evident relevance to the high level of artistic achievement even at a time when artists remained primarily craftsmen, setting out from tradition to wend

---

*piu eccellenti pittori, scultori e architettori, nelle redazioni del 1550 e del 1568* (Florence, 1966 ff.).

For Michelangelo, often cited by Wackernagel as an atypical but richly documented artist, see especially Giorgio Vasari, *La Vita di Michelangelo nelle redazioni del 1550 e del 1568*, ed. Paola Barocchi, 5 vols. (Milan and Naple, 1962). In this extensively annotated work, Vasari's accounts are analyzed in light of some four hundred years of subsequent studies.

For a discussion of the wage scale for manual workers and its meaning see especially Richard Goldthwaite, "The Building of the Strozzi Palace: the Construction Industry in Renaissance Florence," *Studies in Medieval and Renaissance History* 10, 1973, pp. 168 ff. On fifteenth-century Florentine monetary systems and prices see Raymond de Roover, *The Rise and Decline of the Medici Bank 1397-1494* (Cambridge, Mass., 1963), pp. 31-34 and Richard Goldthwaite, *Private Wealth in Renaissance Florence* (Princeton, N.J., 1968), pp. 289-290.

[14] On the functional, especially the didactic, role of art and painting's communication with observers by means of gestures and actions familiar from other public sources, see Baxandall, *Painting and Experience*, pp. 40 ff. On the role of art in fifteenth-century private devotion, with many references from contemporary sources, see Sixten Ringbom, *Icon to Narrative* (Acta Academiae Aboensis, ser. A, vol. 31, no. 2, Abo, 1965).

The relationship between the demand for art and the Florentine economy has been examined in particular by A. Krey, *A City that Art Built* (Minneapolis, 1936), reprinted in his *History and the Social Web* (Minneapolis, 1955), and by Robert Lopez in "Hard Times and Investment in Culture" in *The Renaissance: A Symposium*, ed. Wallace K. Ferguson (New York, 1953), reprinted as *The Renaissance: Six Essays* (New York, 1962). Krey considers the importance of Florence's artisan traditions for the widespread appreciation of art there. Lopez speculates on the relationship between economic slowdown and artistic patronage in Renaissance Florence.

In a lecture on "The Investment in Architecture in Renaissance Florence" to be published in a forthcoming book on the Florentine building industry, Richard Goldthwaite examines the vast market for luxury goods in late Quattrocento Florence and the appetite for them that Wackernagel described. Goldthwaite discusses ways in which the artists themselves may deliberately have stimulated demand.

their way between inventive freedom and customer instructions, rarely able to aspire realistically to more than a middle class economic position. Wackernagel's work ends on a note of hope that wider public awareness of Renaissance conditions might work to the benefit of present-day art and artists. What Wackernagel had in mind is spelled out more emphatically in his writings elsewhere concerning church art in the twentieth century (see below).

Many of the topics touched on by Wackernagel have been studied in greater detail since 1938, as the notes here and the new bibliography should attest. Certain subjects, such as humanist thought, perspective theory, or architecture, are only barely mentioned. Opinions on some matters have changed or grown more controversial, and occasional slips or omissions of a source will be found even (or especially) in a work of documentation as thorough and wide-ranging as Wackernagel's. But the study, more than forty years after its initial publication, remains a factual foundation unsurpassed in its breadth and firmness. It has value for students of art history at all levels and of various approaches: critics and connoisseurs who deal with attribution, style development, and quality; iconologists concerned with subject matter; and other historians dealing with the meaning of art works in a broader intellectual or social context. The author surely meant it also for artists themselves who might be concerned with the living and working conditions of predecessors in their profession. And it should offer a special satisfaction to any layman whose interest in Florence and its art demands well-supported and balanced information.

## The Translation: Form and Changes

No attempt has been made here to bring Wackernagel's study completely up to date by tracing each object to its present location, noting all new opinions for attributions, dates, and artists' biographies or annotating each page with references to every publication bearing on its contents since 1938. Such an updating would constitute a second book longer than the first. And even unrevised, the usefulness of the 1938 original is such that the importance of making the English edition available relatively soon seemed to outweigh the potential value of withholding it for as long as a complete annotation would take.

A few typographical errors have been corrected, an occasional minor factual error or newly pinpointed date noted, and some attribution controversies discussed when they involve major or frequently mentioned works. The author's footnotes, which originally appeared as sections set in small type interspersed with the text, have been numbered and set at the bottoms of the pages. References given in summary form in the original notes have been completed as far as possible, and a list of shortened titles has been devised for frequently cited sources. A new bibliography organized by topics (including architecture, which Wackernagel largely omitted) follows the original bibliography at the end of the book. Otherwise, this edition adheres as closely as possible to the style and content of the original.

It is essential, however, to devote some attention to a few important changes involving Florentine art works since World War II.

One major change, tragic and complex in nature, involves the reorganization of the Berlin museums and their contents as well as the loss of a number of their works since the war. Most of the major works of Italian Renaissance painting and sculpture from the Kaiser Friedrich Museum on the Museumsinsel (rechristened the Bode Museum in present day East Berlin) were hidden in shelters in what later became West Berlin. With a few exceptions, they are now under the jurisdiction of the Staatliche Museen in the West and are housed at the time of this writing in the Berlin-Dahlem Museum in a suburb of West Berlin. Objects from the Kunstgewerbemuseum (Decorative Arts Museum) and the Kupferstichkabinett (Print Cabinet) are divided between the East and West.[15]

The tragic losses in the 1945 fire at the Friedrichshain bunker in Berlin have been chronicled in a number of articles.[16] The most unique Florentine Renaissance work lost was Signorelli's *Court of Pan*, probably painted for Lorenzo the Magnificent. Others included a Fra Bartolommeo *Assumption*, Botticelli's *Madonna and Child with Angels Carrying Candelabra*, Lorenzo di Credi's *Madonna Worshipping the Child* and *Ma-*

---

[15] On the Berlin collections in general, for West Berlin see Peter Krieger, ed., *Berlin. Staatliche Museen. Short Guide* (Berlin, 1964); Peter Metz, *Das neue Skulpturensammlung in Berlin-Dahlem* (Berlin, 1966); Rudiger Klessmann, *The Berlin Museum: Paintings in the Picture Gallery, Dahlem-West Berlin* (New York, 1971); Staatliche Museen, Preussischer Kulturbesitz, Gemäldegalerie, *Katalog der ausgestellten Gemälde des 13.-18. Jahrhunderts* (Berlin, 1975), and for publications up to 1970, the works catalogued by Horst-Johs Tümmers, *Kataloge und Führer der Berliner Museen*, (Berlin, 1975). For East Berlin see Peter H. Feist, *Florentinische frührenaissance Plastik in den Staatlichen Museen zu Berlin* (Leipzig, 1959); Lore Börner and Martin Ohlsberg, *Italienische Renaissance-medaillen* (Berlin, 1962); *Art Treasures of the Berlin State Museums*, intro. by John Russell (New York, 1965; translation of *Staatliche Museen zu Berlin*, ed. Kurt Schifner, Leipzig, 1963; a later edition entitled *Museumsinsel Berlin* was published in Munich, 1965); Sabine Schulz, *Staatliche Museen zu Berlin. Gesamtführer* (Berlin, 1966), and Hannelore Nützmann, *Italienische Bildnisse* (Berlin, 1969).

[16] On the Berlin losses see "Verzeichnis der im Flakturm Friedrichshain verlorengegangenen Bilder der Gemäldegalerie," *Berliner Museen*, 2, 1952, pp. 61-28; "Verzeichnis der im Flakturm Friedrichshain verlorengegangenen Bildwerke der Skulpturen-Abteilung," *Berliner Museen*, 3, 1953, 10-24; Christopher Norris, "The Disaster at Flakturm Friedrichshain: a chronicle and list of paintings," *Burlington Magazine*, 94, 1952, pp. 337-47; "Italian Sculpture in the Berlin Museums: Losses and Survivals," editorial, *Burlington Magazine*, 96, 1954, p. 69; and Georges S. Salmann, "Masterpieces of Sculpture Lost in Berlin," *Connoisseur*, 166, September 1957, pp. 22-27.

*donna and Child*, Domenico Ghirlandaio's *Madonna and Child in Glory Worshipped by Four Saints* and two wing panels of Saints Anthony and Vincent Ferrer, Benozzo Gozzoli's *Madonna and Child with Two Saints*, Filippino Lippi's *Christ Crucified with the Madonna and Saint Francis* and a Madonna and Child, Fra Filippo Lippi's *Madonna of Mercy with Worshippers*, Lorenzo Monaco's *Madonna and Child Enthroned with Two Saints and Angels*, Piero di Cosimo's *Adoration of the Child*, Andrea del Sarto's *Madonna and Child Enthroned with Saints*, and Sodoma's *Charity in a Landscape*.

Lost sculptures included a relief of the scourging of Christ and a bronze John the Baptist, both attributed to Donatello, a bust of the young John the Baptist assigned to Donatello or Desiderio da Settignano, Luca della Robbia's stucco Frescobaldi Madonna, and an Antonio Rossellino Virgin and Child relief.

A change of a happier order is the creation of the National Gallery of Art in Washington, D. C., which opened in 1941. It contains a number of important Florentine works in private collections when Wackernagel was preparing his book (especially the collections of Andrew Mellon, Samuel H. Kress, and the Widener family of Philadelphia). Prominent among the works now in Washington are a Fra Angelico Madonna of Humility; the "Cook tondo" of the Adoration of the Magi, most recently attributed to Fra Filippo Lippi and a Fra Angelico follower (see p. 164); the *David* painted by Andrea del Castagno on a leather shield; a Madonna by Domenico Veneziano, as well as two predella panels (one of Saint Francis receiving the Stigmata, one of John the Baptist in the desert) from the Saint Lucy altarpiece by the same painter; Leonardo da Vinci's portrait of Ginevra dei Benci; a half-octagonal Annunciation lunette by Fra Filippo Lippi; a Masolino Annunciation; an Adoration of the Child tondo and the *Visitation* altarpiece from Santo Spirito, both by Piero di Cosimo. Sculptures include busts of Pietro Talani and a Florentine statesman by Benedetto da Maiano; busts of the Christ Child and other small boys, "Marietta Strozzi" and another lady, and several reliefs, all attributed to Desiderio da Settignano; the Martelli David, controversially attributed to Donatello (see p. 99); a bust of Astorgio Manfredi by Mino da Fiesole; two busts of the young John the Baptist by Antonio Rossellino; a Verrocchio bust of Giuliano de' Medici and a bust of Lorenzo de' Medici, more controversially attributed to Verrocchio, as well as a Verrocchio workshop marble relief of a warrior. The National Gallery also received major collections of Renaissance medals and small bronzes.[17]

[17] For objects now in the National Gallery of Art in Washington see the following: United States, National Gallery of Art, *Summary Catalogue of European Paintings and Sculpture* (Washington, 1965); *European Paintings and Sculpture: Illustrations* (Washington, 1968); and *European Paintings: an Illustrated Summary Catalogue* (Washington, 1975); Fern Rusk Shapley, *Paintings from the Samuel H. Kress Collection: Italian Schools*, 3 vols.

A number of works in Florence itself have also changed location due to museum reorganizations, the 1966 flood, and the need for settings better protected from air pollution. Many paintings have moved from the Accademia into the Uffizi—including Fra Bartolomeo's *Vision of Saint Bernard* and Botticelli's Cestello *Annunciation*. Frescoes like Castagno's *Uomini Famosi* from the Villa Carducci-Pandolfini at Legnaia and Botticelli's *Annunciation* from San Martino alla Scala are also now in the Uffizi. Statues from the niches at Or San Michele and the Duomo Campanile, including many by Donatello, have been replaced by casts. The Campanile figures entered the Opera del Duomo Museum, as did Donatello's *Magdalen* from the Baptistery. His Or San Michele *Saint George* is housed now in the Bargello (soon, it is hoped, to be followed by the *Saint Mark*). Verrocchio's *Putto with a Dolphin* from the Medici villa at Careggi now resides in an upper room of the Palazzo Vecchio with a copy replacing it on the fountain in the Palazzo courtyard. The Fra Bartolommeo-Mariotto Albertinelli *Last Judgment* fresco from Santa Maria Nuova is now in the San Marco Museum.

Works that Wackernagel knew as lost or misplaced have since been rediscovered or relocated. Botticelli's *Adoration of the Magi* with Medici portraits, noted as lost from Santa Maria Novella, is in the Uffizi; the predella panels of Gentile da Fabriano's Quaratesi altarpiece, mentioned by Wackernagel as lost, are now generally recognized as the four Saint Nicholas panels in the Vatican and the one in Washington. Masaccio's *Trinity* was restored in 1952 to its original position on a nave wall in Santa Maria Novella, where it was rejoined with its lower portion, the skeleton on a sarcophagus. A strong contender for identification as Michelangelo's lost Santo Spirito crucifix was found at that church in the early 1960s and installed in Casa Buonarotti. As this translation goes to press there is even talk of a rediscovery by means of ultrasonic scanning of remains of Leonardo's *Battle of Anghiari* under the Vasari frescoes in the Salone dei Cinquecento (the former Hall of the Great Council) in the Palazzo Vecchio. In general, works in Florence can be traced through the most recent edition of the Guida del Touring Club Italiano for Florence. Recent catalogues for various Florentine collections are listed in Section IX of the Translators' Bibliography.[18]

(London and New York, 1966-73; including works in many institutions besides the National Gallery of Art); Fern Rusk Shapley, *Catalague of Italian Paintings in the National Gallery of Art*, 2 vols. (Washington, D.C., 1979); John Pope-Hennessey, *Renaissance Bronzes from the Samuel H. Kress Collection* (London, 1965); Graham Pollard, *Renaissance Medals from the Samuel H. Kress Collection* (London, 1967; based on the catalogue of Renaissance medals in the Gustave Dreyfus Collection, by G. F. Hill, revised and enlarged by Graham Pollard); Ulrich Middeldorf, *Sculptures from the Samuel H. Kress Collection: European Schools XIV-XIX Century* (New York, 1976).

[18] On the Botticelli *Adoration* see recently Rab Hatfield, *Botticelli's Uffizi "Adoration":*

## Martin Wackernagel

*Der Lebensraum des Künstlers in der florentinischen Renaissance,* in all its scope and detail, still represents only a fraction of the life's work of Martin Wackernagel (1881-1962). His scholarly interests and publications ranged from Cima da Conegliano to Cezanne and Manet, from Apulian Romanesque sculpture to German Baroque architecture, from Raphael to Italian painting of the nineteenth and twentieth centuries. He published guides to his native city of Basel, Switzerland and his adopted city of Münster, Germany and prepared the first section of the Gronau-Gottschewski German edition of Vasari's *Lives of the Artists* (Strasbourg, 1916).[19]

This scholarly output shares the stage with another side of Wackernagel's character also reflected in this study of Florentine art. Throughout his life he was drawn to and fascinated by artists and their personalities, problems, way of life, and creative activity. Werner Hager, his friend and colleague who later succeeded him in the Münster University art history chairmanship, wrote: "His study of art history drew rich nourishment from his active involvement with the artistic life of his own time. He himself sensed that his calling as an art scholar grew out of his own innate artistic instincts. The unique character of his thought and work, crowned by his most successful book, stemmed from this unconstrained interplay of the present and history in his consciousness."[20]

Born in Basel, Wackernagel was a Burckhardt on his mother's side

*A Study in Pictorial Content* (Princeton, N. J., 1976); on the Gentile panels see Luigi Grassi, *Tutta la Pittura di Gentile da Fabriano* (Milan, 1953), pp. 63 ff. On Masaccio's *Trinity* see Luciano Berti and Paolo Volponi, *L'Opera Completa di Masaccio* (Milan, 1968), p. 97. On the Michelangelo crucifix see Margrit Lisner, "Michelangelos Kruzifixus aus S. Spirito," *Münchner Jahrbuch der bildenden Kunst,* 15, 1964, pp. 7-36: on the Leonardo fresco see Herbert R. Lottmann, "Digging for the Lost Leonardo," *Art News,* 74, December 1975, pp. 66-68. The most recent Touring Club Italiano guide to Florence is *Guida d'Italia; Firenze e Dintorni* (Milan, 1974).

[19] A bibliography of Wackernagel's writings from 1905 to 1957 is published in *Festschrift Martin Wackernagel zum 75. Geburtstag,* prepared by the Kunstgeschichtliche Seminar, Münster University (Cologne, 1958), pp. 212-16.

[20] Werner Hager, *Martin Wackernagel, Gedenkrede* (Münster University, February 24, 1962), privately printed. The quotations here from Hager are freely translated from this commemorative address, which is my main published source of biographical information. I owe a great debt of gratitude to Professor Hager and to Mrs. Hilda Maria Martin, who each shared recollections of Wackernagel in long and eloquent letters. Professor Hager was a younger colleague of Wackernagel at Münster, a successor in the chairmanship there, and a devoted friend. Mrs. Martin, originally from Soest, Germany and now living in De Kalb, Illinois, was a close friend of Wackernagel and his family for over forty years. Her daughter Denise Heilbronn also shared reminiscences. In addition, I am grateful for the recollections of the author's son and daughter, Martin Wackernagel, Jr. and Marlis Ruban-Wackernagel.

(although his mother Elisabeth came from a different branch of the Burck-hardt family than the Renaissance historian Jacob) and the grandson of Wilhelm Wackernagel, a renowned German philologist from Berlin who had settled in Basel in 1835. His father, Rudolf, was a university professor in Basel and director of the state archives. Wackernagel began early the humanistic education that was a birthright in his city and family. He studied in Basel, Geneva, Göttingen, and Berlin with such teachers as Adolph Goldschmidt and Arthur Haseloff before completing his doctoral dissertation (on the representation and idealization of court life in Emperor Maximilian I's woodcuts) under Heinrich Wölfflin in Berlin in 1905.

His long and fruitful affection for Italy began soon afterward with an assistantship at the Prussian Historial Institute in Rome. The Institute sent him south to study and write on Apulian Romanesque sculpture. One result was his *Die Plastik des XI. und XII. Jahrhunderts in Apulien* (Leipzig, 1911), a ground-breaking study at the time and still a fundamental work in the field. But the Apulia project also provided him with a joyfully embraced opportunity to roam the Italian countryside, to live among the people, and to record his observations on both.

In Rome, increasingly fascinated with contemporary art and artists, Wackernagel frequented the German artist colony at the foot of the Spanish steps and even did some drawing of his own. When he wrote about the work and the Bohemian lifestyle of his artist friends, it was both as an observer and a participant.

His character, with its divergent instincts of a methodical scholar and a peripatetic artist, showed yet another element in his conversion to Roman Catholicism in 1911. This was just before his marriage to Ilse von Stach (1879-1941), a religious poet and playwright and a women's movement activist. She had joined the church in 1908. Wackernagel had evidently felt an attraction for Catholicism since a meeting during his student days in Geneva with the Catholic painter and writer Alexandre Cingria (1879-1945). Later he also came to share Cingria's intense concern for the revival of a high quality, moving religious art, and to campaign in writing for its creation.

After his Italian years, Wackernagel served as a reserve officer in the Swiss army during World War I, participating in the defensive occupation of the Swiss border. His teaching career began in Halle and Leipzig. In the latter city, where he made his inaugural lecture on Italian Renaissance artistic life in 1917, he also took on the directorship of the local art association (Kunstverein).

The pattern of historical scholarship and involvement in modern artistic life continued in Münster, where he accepted a professorship in art history in 1920. During his tenure there from 1920 to 1948, much of it as chairman, that university's art history department rose to a widely respected status in Germany. Wackernagel also became chairman of the Westphalian Art Association, a post he held from 1921 to 1954. When he was not teaching and writing, he was organizing exhibitions, tours, artistic competitions, and celebrations, sometimes involving theatrical productions. One thinks, as he surely must have done, of the festivities arranged by Florentine artists that he discusses in *Der Lebensraum des Künstlers in der florentinischen Renaissance*.

This work was published in Leipzig in 1938, at a time when the darkness in Wackernagel's personal life corresponded to the grim conditions in the world around him. As the alienation between Switzerland and Germany grew, he was torn between ties to his Swiss homeland and his professional and family responsibilities in Germany, where he had lived for decades and where his children were born. His beloved wife was seriously ill, paralyzed and nearly helpless for years before her death in 1941. The continual, devoted care that she received from her husband and children in those last terrible years is recalled almost with awe by friends who witnessed it.

These are the circumstances that surrounded Wackernagel's decision to remain in Münster and go on with his work as best he could during the Hitler years. His writings from 1933 to 1945 are detached by all but total silence from their immediate political environment, even the aspects of it that affected art.[21] But nothing that is known about his character or his work suggests any sympathy with Nazi policies. And a Jewish friend recalls the loyalty of Wackernagel and his family who continued to visit her home and invite her to theirs long after other Gentile friends had turned away.

In the first months after the war Wackernagel opened his house to shelter younger colleagues and their families and gradually began to hold makeshift seminars there for his students until the university could func-

---

[21] Wackernagel did touch, briefly and guardedly, on official artistic policy under Hitler in "Der Lebensraum der bildenden Kunst in älterer und gegenwärtiger Zeit," *Schweizer Rundschau*, 35, 1935-1936, vol. 1, p. 54 (reprinted almost verbatim in his *Vier Aufsätze über geschichtliche und gegenwärtige Faktoren des Kunstlebens*, Wattenscheid, 1936, pp. 37-38). Here, in a discussion of the gulf that had grown up between artist and public in recent years, he referred to a speech given by his fellow Swiss, Cingria, at a conference in Venice in 1934. The conference, sponsored by the "Coopération intellectuelle" organization of the League of Nations, had as its theme "Art and Reality, Art and the State." Cingria discussed modern alienation between the artist and public, state measures to support artists, and the need to regain for art its roots in daily life and closeness to the people. "Certainly without suspecting it, probably without wishing it," Cingria had expressed ideas closely paralleling the general aims of Third Reich cultural policy, Wackernagel observed. He remarked that the practical means for achieving these goals were still to be discovered and went on to devote the rest of the article to his favorite theme, church art.

tion again. Hager recalls how the now venerable scholar could be found on cold early mornings, reading some Latin author at his lectern, dressed to keep warm in the academic gown and velvet beret he had salvaged— "the very image of the old Erasmus." (That visual evocation was enhanced by a particular sympathy that Wackernagel had once expressed for qualities in Erasmus that friends saw clearly in Wackernagel himself— "a wide-open versatility of mind and intimate involvement with life, combined with a humane, warmhearted religiosity.")[22]

After his retirement, Wackernagel settled in Begnins, Switzerland with his second wife, Erika Schlössin, a sculptor whom he had met at an exhibition and married in 1954. The couple rented space in a small castle called Schloss Cottens in a vineyard overlooking Lake Geneva. He continued to publish, to travel, and to put in an appearance in Münster every summer. At the beginning of his eighty-second year in 1962, he was in the midst of work on a manuscript on Italian Ottocento painting when death overtook him one Sunday morning on his way to church.

The devout Catholicism that directed his last steps on earth is also a crucial factor underlying Wackernagel's attitude toward art and its history. Churches, the great artistic centers of the middle ages and Renaissance, were for him first of all places of prayer. A travelling companion in Italy recalls that when visiting a church he would sometimes withdraw quietly behind a pillar to pray his breviary before continuing his art historical itinerary. He had a strong interest in the potential of art to inspire faith and took an active part in the Kirchliche Kunstbewegung, a movement to promote modern ecclesiastical art. Many of his writings from 1920 to 1938, inspired by those of the Genevan painter Cingria, ring with a crusader's zeal to sweep away the mass-produced, banal, spiritless images that he felt had lately monopolized the churches and to introduce fresh, individual works born of "equally strong religious and artistic impulses."

If modern churches lacked vital art, Wackernagel wrote, it was not for want of capable artists, but rather of determined and enlightened patrons. One of the aims of *Der Lebensraum des Künstlers in der florentinischen Renaissance,* which he cited in a 1938 article discussing church patronage, was to point out the generative role of the donor at a time when original and moving works were being produced precisely for churches. In the enthusiasm of his faith, Wackernagel felt that religious art, which was still functional art, could once again become a major source of both

---

[22] "Der ideale Landsitz eines christlichen Humanisten in der Renaissancezeit," in *Festgabe für Alois Fuchs zum 70. Geburtstage* (Paderborn, 1950) pp. 159-171; newly published as "Der ideale Landsitz eines christlichen Humanisten. Aus den Colloquia des Erasmus," *Schweizer Rundschau,* 51, vol. 5, 1951-1952, pp. 274-282.

economic support and creative stimulus for artists, so that the Church, the Faith, the artist, and art itself could all benefit.

He envisioned a process whereby church donors, individually and collectively, would bestow commissions only on the basis of guidance from generally recognized, honorably disinterested experts on art (a suggestion perhaps intentionally reminiscent of Florentine *Operai*). While subject matter would be assigned, as is traditional for church commissions, the artist would be free to interpret it without interference from his patrons. It was precisely such freedom, Wackernagel suggested in this work on the world of the Florentine artist and elsewhere, that had allowed the powerful and revolutionary works of Donatello and Masaccio to take shape in ecclesiastical contexts.[23]

The nature of Wackernagel's personal taste in contemporary art remains elusive. His writings on church art dwell more on the ideal faith-inspiring effect than on specific stylistic means. The best known German artist among his contemporaries on whom he wrote is perhaps the impressionistic painter, printmaker, and illustrator Max Slevogt (1868-1932).[24] The Westfälische Kunstverein commissioned a portrait of Wackernagel by the Münster painter Carl Busch (born in 1905) in 1942. In the 1950s, Wackernagel responded with enthusiastic praise to le Corbusier's pilgrimage chapel at Ronchamp. Otherwise, his name does not seem to be associated, as promotor or critic, with any twentieth-century artist familiar to a broad public today (in Hitler's Germany the choices would in any case have grown increasingly limited).

Some light on Wackernagel's preferences in contemporary art is shed, however, by his sympathetic writings on the sculpture of his friend Kurt Kluge (1886-1940), whose works included a cast-iron portrait mask of Ilse von Stach. Kluge, who had restored the bronze *quadriga* on the Brandenburg gate in Berlin, was a veritable Renaissance man of the twentieth century. Better known today as a novelist, he was also a poet, printmaker, professor of metal casting at the Berlin Akademie für bildende Künste, and a sculptor dedicated to meticulous craftsmanship. The illustrations of his work suggest he could carve marble with a Desiderian delicacy as in his bust of Klara Kluge and cast bronze figures into a sleek and sinuous grace reminiscent of Giambologna (Schildkrötenbrunnen, Marburg). His style varied considerably, but his sculpture until 1930 (illustrated in a book with an introduction by Wackernagel) is almost exclusively naturalistic, generally contemplative in mood, often with an idealizing, classically reserved tendency. Wackernagel clearly approved

---

[23] See Wackernagel's "Die Kunst der Kirche," *Hochland*, 17:2, 1920, pp. 88-93 (including a discussion of Alexandre Cingria) and "Vom Stiftertum in der kirchlichen Kunst," *Hochland*, 35:2, 1938, pp. 476-487.

[24] *Max Slevogt* (Munich-Gladbach, 1926).

of his choice of themes with "universal human, even markedly religious significance." The language of his discussion on Kluge foreshadows themes encountered later in *Der Lebensraum des Künstlers in der florentinischen Renaissance*. The description of Kluge's creative process stimulated by constant personal handling of his materials at every stage contains an unexpressed parallel to what Wackernagel knew of Michelangelo. And as he discusses Kluge's research on ancient sculpture, a leitmotif of so much of Wackernagel's writing sounds: the idea of the mutual benefits that arise from interaction between modern artistic creation and art historical study.[25]

Qualities and eccentricities that made Wackernagel a sort of legend as a public figure in Münster fill the recollections of his friends. An enthusiastic musician, he often made visits to play his violin in duets and chamber music groups. He insisted on surrounding himself with old weathered things, like the ancient family automobile, christened Remigius after a particularly eloquent saint, with which he refused to part. He liked to wear embroidered, delicately patterned, velvet vests of a kind that had long been out of fashion.

Several who knew Wackernagel comment on what he himself liked to call jokingly his "Hang nach unten," his delight in the company of ordinary, working-class people who led lives remote from a sophisticated scholarly environment. On train rides, especially in Italy, he preferred the relaxed conversation with peasants and marketwomen in a second-class compartment to the sterile atmosphere of first class, where people sat facing each other in silence. In Germany he liked to frequent small neighborhood pubs and village inns where he could sit and talk at length with the workers or country people at the next table.

A student remembers that he spoke just as he wrote, in long, drawn-out sentences, clause upon clause, to the astonishment of new students who only later came to realize how much they were learning from him. His ready hospitality, loyal friendship, and ironic sense of humor were accompanied by a quiet insistence on respect in scholarly matters and a determined adherence to what he felt was right.

Hager recalls the fragile old gentleman conducting a seminar as late as 1961, speaking "in a soft voice, in flowing unconstrained speech, in that charmingly ornamental German of his old age style . . . and then one might well tell himself that this man, who every year in his lecture

---

[25] *Der Bildhauer Kurt Kluge* (Berlin and Leipzig, 1930); this slim volume has an introduction by Wackernagel and photographs of works by Kluge, but no dates or locations. Wackernagel also wrote a moving essay on Kluge and his art, this time voicing the parallel with Michelangelo, after Kluge's death in 1940 at the battle front on a poetry-writing journey. See "Kurt Kluges bildkünstlerisches Werk," *Deutsche Rundschau*, 67, 1941, pp. 20-23.

hall summoned forth, as though from a great distance, an era already vanished for our youth, in his own youth might still have seen Jacob Burckhardt step across the Basel Cathedral square toward the university. Thus the tradition of a whole century was speaking to us, embraced in this long human life, and moreover in a language, with a culture, a humanity which still came from that very tradition, in which we ourselves, even the oldest of us, are no longer rooted."

A scholarly historian and artistic entrepreneur, a restless wanderer who lived for nearly forty years in the same city, a devout Catholic with a shrewd consciousness of the worldly motives involved even in religious art patronage, a cordial host and beloved teacher who "required human companionship" and yet accorded few "a glance into his inner being," Martin Wackernagel is no more easily summed up than his book. "In all the seriousness and learnedness of his scholarly work," Hager writes, "he remained the 'dilettante' " in the Renaissance ideal sense of the word, "the free-spirited admirer of the beautiful and remarkable in the past and present."

The few lines in an occasional German encyclopedia that sum up Wackernagel's life for the public record make a sharp contrast with the warm, vivid and detailed memory his friends keep twenty years after his death. And his unmatched contribution to Italian Renaissance studies has up to now been accessible only to relatively few specialists. With the centennial of his birth at hand, it seems fitting that Wackernagel and his work should at last be given back to a new and enlarged audience of students.

# ABBREVIATIONS

| | |
|---|---|
| AS | *Arte e Storia* |
| ASA | *Archivio Storico dell'Arte* |
| BA | *Bolletino d'Arte* |
| BM | *Burlington Magazine* |
| KJBH | *Kunstgeschichtliches Jahrbuch der Bibliotheca Hertziana, Rome* |
| JfK | *Jahrbuch für Kunstwissenschaft* |
| JPK | *Jahrbuch der (Königlich) Preussischen Kunstsammlungen* |
| MA | *Miscellanea d'Arte* |
| MJ | *Münchner Jahrbuch der bildenden Kunst* |
| MK | *Monatshefte für Kunstwissenschaft* |
| MKIF | *Mitteilungen des Kunsthistorischen Institutes in Florenz* |
| RA | *Rivista d'Arte* |
| Rass. A. | *Rassegna d'Arte* |
| Rep. | *Repertorium für Kunstwissenschaft* |
| ZBK | *Zeitschrift für bildende Kunst* |
| ZKG | *Zeitschrift für Kunstgeschichte* |

# THE WORLD OF THE FLORENTINE
## RENAISSANCE ARTIST

# AUTHOR'S PREFACE

The present book has grown out of more than ten years of preoccupation, even if frequently interrupted, with the viewpoints and questions considered here. And its basic premise has attracted me as an object of study for much longer.

Impetus in this direction came also from certain writings in the literature of the field that took a similar approach. But what led me above all toward the projected investigation of the conditions of art and artists in the historical past was my early association with artists, which I constantly sought to renew, and the insights I gained into their living and working conditions and the situation of the art market in our time. This experience came from years of activity in art criticism, as well as from management of exhibitions for artistic societies. Thus, with the help of testimony from contemporary sources, I hoped to gain the clearest possible conception of the general artistic circumstances of a particular civilization—to determine how the conditions and relationships familiar to us in contemporary society (such as the artist's work process, the structure of the art market, the interrelations between artist and public) might have manifested themselves in an earlier time.

My choice of an area for research, however, was decided by the fact that hardly any early, artistically important cultural setting besides the period of the Florentine Renaissance is so richly documented by its surviving monuments as well as by relevant documents and other information. For Florence, so extraordinarily many documents and other literary source materials have been published, even if in widely scattered and sometimes inaccessible places, that a sufficient basis for the desired depiction of general practices and conditions was possible even without recourse to further unedited archival material.

My work, then, need not focus on reports of information newly culled out or isolated findings of research presented in exhaustive detail. What I propose is the first attempt at a preliminary, rough, and certainly in many respects incomplete sketch of certain types of questions and relationships which, up to the present, have not been systematically examined. My book is not directed only toward a narrow circle of experts in the field and readers otherwise informed on art history. Its general ideas and goals have their roots in the atmosphere of the artist's studio and other arenas of artistic life today. In its execution it keeps this counterpart of modern artistic production constantly in view. Thus, this exposition of the components of an enviably healthy, individual and highly productive artistic period of the past seeks to gain art historical insights through a particular approach, insights that might also serve as indirect points of reference and comparison for the solution of cultural and economic problems of current artistic life—problems which are again of great concern to all of us today.

Münster, August 1938

Martin Wackernagel

# AUTHOR'S INTRODUCTION

The object and purpose of this book is to present the most multifaceted possible exploration and description of the concrete conditions and factors of Florentine artistic life and its development and changes during the fifteenth century, up to the full maturity of the High Renaissance. We are inquiring, therefore, into premises and preconditions of a spiritual and cultural as well as a sociological and material-economic nature, into whatever attitudes, institutions, and customs exercised any influence on the extent and organization of general artistic activity, and also, perhaps, on many qualitative peculiarities in the artistic production of the period.

Such an investigation into the cultural- and economic-historical foundations from which the entire complex of the artistic life developed has to date been pursued only sporadically and never in a systematic and comprehensive manner. The sections immediately following will attempt to demonstrate in detail how such a study can bring to light new knowledge directly related to art history and the history of style.

Here, first of all, a general overview will be provided on the questions and viewpoints to be considered and closely examined.

In the first place we must, at least mentally, and on the basis of available primary source information, transfer the concrete factual material—the monuments, some widely scattered, which have come down to us from the whole artistic output of the Florentine Renaissance—back into its original spacial setting and function. That is, we must place this remnant of the original output, together with all the products of Florentine artistic workshops that are no longer preserved but are in some way noted in old accounts, into the context of the causal preconditions from which the works originated. To this end we must first of all free ourselves from our customary assumption, deriving from recent and present conditions, that the first and decisive stimulus to the production of an art work is the personality of the artist and his own spontaneous creative impulse. In the organization of the artistic life of all earlier epochs, even the Italian Renaissance, the artist's personal desire to create determined only the final touches, and in some cases a more or less perceptible modification. The primary, fundamental factors lay outside the artist's studio. One element was the commission—the demand, the need for a work of art which an artist was called on to fulfill. The other was the patron—the commissioner and user, who had to be present and active in order to set artistic ingenuity in motion and make the work of art materially possible. Thus the work of art did not simply originate from artistic initiative and, theoretically, as an end in itself. It did not take on its material value and function by way of the supply process (through exhibitions and art dealers). Rather, the constant and exceptionally powerful demand emerged as the decisive stimulus to production and even dictated its extent and intensity. Only with rare exceptions was art produced, throughout the whole fifteenth and early sixteenth centuries, without such concrete needs and stimuli; that is, without the order of a patron.[1]

The consumers of art, the primary initiators, however, were not necessarily members of the educated and wealthy upper class, of special patrons of the arts, connoisseurs, and collectors. To a certain extent they included all levels of the population including the petty bourgeois artisans with whose wishes and ability to pay most artists—themselves traditionally members of the artisan class—were directly in touch. To be sure, from the mid-Quattrocento on, certainly in the period of Lorenzo Magnifico, there arose a group of patrons and purchasers of finer aesthetic cultivation, pronounced taste, and a connoisseur's interest in collecting. Members of this group emerged in the art market with higher demands but also with correspondingly generous expenditures. But as a rule, even their commissions were motivated and modified by particular, practical religious as well as secular artistic needs. We are seeking, first of all, to gain a mental image of that first, elementary, instigating factor expressed by the term "need for art." This is that desire, constantly present and in some measure manifested in the whole population with its wide range of tasks and demands, that made the work of artists and artisans recurrently necessary.

What then, are the precise motives and general preconditions for such a need for art, as we see it asserted in the private, familiar existence of all classes, in the corporate associations, and in the organs of public life?

In the first place, the self-evident point of departure for all architectural and figural art work of a religious character, then as now, was the religious impulse, the conviction that expenditures for the foundation, advancement and rich furnishing of church buildings and art work would be pleasing to God and eternally ascribe merit. A universal need, a distinct element of the old Catholic mode of feeling, called for the best possible contributions to the glory of God and His saints, and even for the opening

[1] Aby Warburg already emphasized this point in the introduction to his *Bildniskunst und florentinisches Bürgertum* (Leipzig, 1902): "It is a fundamental fact of the civilization of the Florentine Renaissance that works of art owe their origin to the mutually sympathetic cooperation between patron and artist, and thus must be regarded at the outset, in some measure, as the product of an agreement between the customer and the master who executes his order." For the interrelation between artist and public in general see my *Vier Aufsätze über geschichtliche und gegenwärtigen Faktoren des Kunstlebens*, vol. 1, Lebensräume der Kunst (Wattenscheid, 1936).

of one's own house to the immediate objects of reverence and sources of blessing through the display of some kind of devotional image.

Closely bound up with this religious urge in a great many cases, however, was a worldly motive. This was the overriding desire, already perceptible during the Trecento, but later becoming more and more pronounced, to make the most imposing and impressive appearance possible, even in religious commissions. It was directed at posterity as well as contemporary society and based on the ideas of self-representation and of fame after death. It is true that we see these two impulses of devotion on the one hand and desire for fame on the other still effective today in private and public art commissions. But the third, more deeply underlying factor, closely related throughout to the first mentioned motive, is by comparison present today in such a narrowed and weakened degree that its former significance and effect is hardly conceivable to us. This is the powerful need to look at images that was alive in all levels of the population as an elemental, instinctive drive. It is somewhat comparable to present-day humanity's desire for the daily consumption of literature. In this connection we might observe that it is evidently just this spread of printing and growth of the ability and habit of reading that was chiefly responsible for diverting the eye from its natural receptivity to and desire for pictorial representation.[2]

As long as written material could be directed at the small upper class that could pay attention to reading matter—still the case, Gutenberg notwithstanding, well into the sixteenth century—pictorial representation persisted as the universal concern as well as the medium of religious, historical, and other educational content. Images could also claim to be the most effective and lasting manifestation, homage, and glorification for the persons or events depicted, as well as for the patron who had instigated such a portrayal.

Only in the last place do we speak in this context of the directly artistic aspect of the work of art, of form's powers of aesthetic stimulation and attraction. The desire and taste for elegant, ornamental splendor, for forms significant in their beauty or individuality, forms in which reality is artistically reshaped, are initially only a hardly conscious, undefined impulse. In a sense they are a side effect, and not always an absolutely

[2] Admittedly, the improvement and cheapening of mechanical reproduction processes has strongly rekindled the desire for illustrations and contemplation of images in recent times (illustrated newspapers, cinema, etc.). General art historical education has been greatly advanced by this. But on a broader scale, the eye's receptivity to figural impressions has grown increasingly shallow due to the massive availability of nonartistic material for observation. The characterless productions of stereotype plates enfeeble, exhaust, and deaden the observer's sense of form that could once be enriched in some measure even by graphic illustrations of the most primitive kind.

necessary one, of the aforementioned general need for pictorial demonstration. Only in scattered cases in the circles of the educated and wealthy does there already appear in the Quattrocento an occasional conscious appreciation of the work of art for its own sake and of important artistic personalities with their aesthetic peculiarities and accomplishments. In this context there is also an interest in older—ancient or medieval—as well as foreign, especially Netherlandish art. And therewith the patron—for whom the work of art is immediately significant for the fulfilment of a particular extraartistic function—is joined for the first time by the collector and connoisseur for whom the impetus to commission or acquire a work stems from its particular formal excellence or the individual mastery of certain prominent artists.

As to precise characteristics of the general artistic taste of the period, let us mention only the demand for and special appreciation of a meticulously ornate execution of detail, even in large-scale sculpture and painting. The workshops of goldsmiths, first training grounds of so many subsequent sculptors, painters, and architects, and the art of book illuminators, which flourished into the beginning of the sixteenth century, were the principal areas where painstaking splendor of detail was cultivated. At the same time they stimulated and set standards for a corresponding execution of all details deserving consideration in monumental art works. And we shall only do justice to these qualities of Quattrocento art work if we surrender our accustomed impressionistic mode of observation and seek to adapt ourselves to a more leisurely tempo of absorption, savoring objects bit by bit in close observation as is only appropriate to the manner of execution of images of that time.

All of this will be discussed in detail in the following sections of this book. Here, however, certain general socioeconomic and cultural preconditions for the state of Florentine art in the Quattrocento remain to be considered.

The organization, behavior, and importance of artists as a class will be discussed in detail in the third main section. At this point, let it only be noted that all branches of the fine arts through the fifteenth century and into the sixteenth remain classified in the general economic life as crafts. Their exercise, like that of all other trades, was subject to the long traditional guild regulation, even in cases of distinguished masters.[3]

Thus it follows that the work even of famous, especially esteemed artists was fundamentally no more honored than that of other artisans,

[3] Even in the linguistic usage of the time, the designation *arte* is not understood as art or even fine art, but rather, simply as handicraft, manual skill, or special trade and trade organization (such as Arte della Lana, Arte della Seta, etc., as the guild names of wool workers and silk manufacturers, respectively).

that is, according to the standard of expenditure of time and productive energy in each case. Working time, however—this is also of some consequence—was cheap, for the general tempo of life was still untouched by the haste and nervousness of the present industrial era, and so the uncommonly intricate procedure of executing a painting, for example, brought no marked appreciation of the market price of pictures. The contracts that patrons and artists customarily drew up for all major works almost always set fixed time periods for completion. Yet we may observe that in a great many cases these were exceeded by months or years without the patron remonstrating much about it. The extraordinarily wide circle of commissioners and purchasers on the art market saw to it that under these conditions the original work of art, the richly decorated furnishing or utensil represented no luxury object.

It need only be mentioned here how much the democratic organization of the city-state and the constantly fluctuating stratifications of the whole class structure, without particularly sharp social and cultural separation of classes, correspond with an equally multilevelled production in arts and crafts. Certain general claims to education and a practically instinctive formal culture were not essentially remote even from the lowest levels of the population. On the other hand, the wealthy upper class was accustomed to respond to the aforementioned stimuli to art patronage as a duty of class and could regard the expense for the most imposing possible artistic undertaking as a distinguished privilege of rank. Under such circumstances, artists and artisans of all kinds had no need to worry about the likelihood of employment.

If we inquire further, however, into the various types and provinces of tasks for whose execution the wishes and ability of the patron constantly interacted with the creative activity of the artist, we may begin with the religious and secular spheres as two great parallel main areas, developing nearly equally in the course of the Quattrocento, for the classification of the immeasurably vast mass of material, though not without observing how constantly and in how many ways these two spheres interpenetrated. It has already been mentioned that in many great enterprises of church decoration and even church construction, the transcendental-religious and worldly-egotistical intentions of the patron were indissolubly linked. This, however, is more readily understandable if we consider that in daily life in general the sacred and profane elements were not separated by any sharp boundaries. Church rooms served not only for worship, but for all possible gatherings and councils of a secular, cultural, and even purely political nature, sometimes of a none-too-peaceful character. Furthermore, the church interior, Santa Croce for example, seems to have served through the proud construction of tomb monuments, the banners, colorful coats of arms, weapons, and draperies readily displayed in it as a kind of hall of honor and fame for important personalities and families. Certain ecclesiastical feast days also took on strongly secular implications through all manner of purely worldly productions, entertainments, and theatrical performances. Conversely, on important political anniversaries, the saint of the day would understandably also be honored through some sort of religious ceremonies, offerings of sacrifice, processions of the temporal authorities and corporations, etc.

In the first rank of localized and typological groupings of all the concrete inducements and stimuli to artistic production we must place the churches and public secular buildings of the city, in many cases inherited from the Trecento, but now also being newly built. The architectural adaptation and development, sometimes even the complete renovation of these, along with their rich furnishing of liturgically necessary objects of all kinds became, in consequence of the attitudes and ways of thinking mentioned above, a continuing, constantly renewed concern of obvious importance and an ever-pressing responsibility for the civic officials and corporations, as well as for the wealthy private citizen.

Above all stood the Cathedral and Baptistery as the focal points of citywide interest and ambition. The most financially powerful guilds, Calimala and Arte della Lana, as the administrative organs of these buildings, had the time-honord responsibility to attend to the material as well as artistic needs of these two most important construction projects.

After this, however, came the incalculably vast area of private patronage activities in the field of church and convent complexes. One aspect that recurred with particular frequency was the construction and furnishing of private altars or whole family chapels by families belonging to a parish or closely associated with a particular order.

Indeed, the desire for such private precincts in public church spaces in the fifteenth century made possible the undertaking and execution of individual new church buildings and even had evident effects on the plan formation (for example the chapel rows in San Lorenzo and Santo Spirito). On the other hand, the private zeal of individual donors not infrequently also took over the execution of comprehensive expansions and supplementary buildings for a church and convent or the construction of whole great convent complexes.

Besides all this, artistic skill was invoked for the construction, embellishing alterations, and in particular for the whole interior decoration of important residences, as well as for the buildings for guilds or confraternities and the palace of the city government.

Most of the important secular buildings of the Quattrocento survive today; but almost none of their original, contemporary interior appointments are still in their old places. And all of the great quantity of paintings and sculpture, of artistically decorated furnishings and implements from the former stock of Florentine bourgeois houses and palaces, now in museums, private collections, and art dealer shops scattered throughout the world—all this yet represents only a relatively small and random section of all that once existed. The rooms of the old Palazzo Davanzati, restored a few years ago—admittedly more according to the viewpoints of amateurs and art dealers—with their murals and woven wall hangings of religious or worldly subject matter, their wall tabernacles and other household devotional images, painted chests, and other richly decorated furniture offer at least an intimation of the endlessly broad and varied fields of activity open to artists and art tradesmen through the constant need for such household furnishings and utilitarian objects. Only one branch, admittedly important and charming, of this secular and domestic world of the Renaissance was made clearly visible by Schubring's great work on cassoni. Even in this area, just as for figurally painted panelling and large-scale wall painting in private houses, individual masters of rank and reputation were not infrequently called upon, in addition to the multitude of more craft-oriented specialists. This shows clearly that all these applied arts are by no means regarded essentially as arts of the second rank. And this is also apparent in the participation of artists in decoration, apparatus, costumes, and the like for festivities and processions, tournaments, the theater, etc.

It is true that precisely from these last categories, but also from many other types of commissions for painting and small-scale sculpture, hardly a single example has survived until today. But a hoard of contemporary reports, inventory notices, and other evidence, even certain old illustrations of especially important and fine single objects, come to our aid.

On the basis of these sources, it will be attempted further on to reconstruct hypothetically the original interior decoration of the Palazzo Vecchio and certain rooms of the Palazzo Medici, as well as some of the most important churches of Florence. We shall try to see how their stock of furnishings might have grown up and what their general appearance might have been during the Renaissance centuries.

Thus it will become possible to demonstrate how the three factors of artistic life—commissions, patrons and artists—worked together in the context of such complexes of ecclesiastical and worldly monuments. This must appear all the more necessary, given that only parts and fragments of the former inventory are still extant in situ at these focal points of patron and artist activity. A great deal has been altered or completely destroyed in later times.

Here, incidentally, we should remember the remodellings, transformations, destruction, and alienations, sometimes quite radical, through which the stock of monuments in Florence has repeatedly suffered great losses and partitionings.

To begin with, the whole region in front of the fortifications was ruthlessly cleared at the time of the siege of 1529. At that time a multitude of old monasteries and church buildings in this zone were completely destroyed and razed to the ground.[4] To this may be added more famous churches within the city that in early or later times were destroyed by fire or other damage or secularized and cleared out.[5] Finally in the 1880s came the destruction of a great number of old domestic buildings and smaller churches at the time of the reorganization of the city center around the former Mercato Vecchio, now Piazza Vittorio Emanuele.

Also not to be forgotten is the decimation of the artistic contents of many old convent churches in the systemization carried out partly by Vasari himself at the order of the grand duke, in accordance with the taste of that time. Choir screens were destroyed, and many altars, tombs, and wall paintings attached to the choir screen or placed elsewhere in the church interior were eliminated.

The attempt below to reconstruct certain formerly existing spacial ensembles will perhaps also in some measure counteract certain misconceptions that could not help but result from the present manner of exhibition and appearance of most old artistic monuments in museums. We must at least mentally transfer these scattered "irredenta," generally arranged didactically in academic stylistic groupings, back into the old setting of their origin and function. Only then can we more correctly and completely visualize the original context in which the individual work had its roots and by which it was in many ways conditioned and modified in detail.

A declaration of principle should be made at this point: art history will be understood and treated in this book neither simply as style history—history of form creation and of vision—nor simply in the context of intellectual history; rather it will be considered as the history of the whole life of art, with the inclusion of all possible material as well as intellectual-cultural factors that had any bearing on it.

[4] Vasari and Richa in his source material, among others, have left information—unfortunately all too brief—about these establishments and their sometimes significant artistic furnishings.

[5] Thus in particular the old church of Santo Spirito, which burned in 1471; San Piero Scheraggio, which had to make way for Vasari's Uffizi building; the church of the Carmine, destroyed by a fire in 1771 and then rebuilt; San Piero Maggiore, destroyed in 1783 except for the Baroque portico; the convent church of San Pancrazio, secularized after the suppression of 1808, with the sole exception of the adjoining chapel of the Holy Sepulcher.

And with this object in view we shall also finally have to examine artists as a group in the atmosphere of the workshop and the art market and generally the whole economy of art. Relevant material for this is not only the more-or-less accidental remnants of preserved monuments and the relatively small and incomplete groups of Florentine artists immediately illustrated by them. Rather we must attempt, with the help of the unusually numerous and sometimes fairly detailed written references from documents and other contemporary sources, to survey as far as possible the whole artistic harvest from Florentine soil. We must do so with a universal, purely objective interest similar to that of the botanist, who finds not only the blossoms and fragrant fruit, but the whole structure of the tree, the humble tufts of grass and even the weed worthy of scientific observation. The widely branching development of the need for art outlined above encompassed commissioners and consumers of art from virtually all social levels. And the great multitude of art producers responded to this need and consumption with a correspondingly extensive range of activity on a great variety of levels. Consequently, even a fundamental separation between fine and applied arts in the modern sense does not come into consideration. Thus if certain artists specialized by preference in particular saleable articles for the art market—for example, chest painting or cloth painting for wall hangings and the like—nevertheless each great workshop certainly accepted and worked on commissions of any and all kinds, including those just mentioned.

The third main section of this book will provide a documentary survey. This will involve, on one hand, the concrete conditions and customs of the art market—the material costs and artists' fees, type and method of payment (through installments and final completion payments), etc. On the other hand, it will consider the artists' economic and social position, standard of living, and class standing. Thus the great master's emergence from the average level of artistic life and skilled craftsmanship can also become discernible.

The number of artists mentioned in documents who at any given time were active during the same period in Florence is surprisingly large—even in proportion to the status of other trades. Yet this is thoroughly understandable considering what has been said about the scope and variety of the need for art. Thereby it also becomes evident that from the membership, so readily ascertainable, of the painters' guild, for example, or the sculptors, the names illustrated by verified or otherwise reliably attributed works make up only a fairly small percentage—a quarter or a third of all the artists whose names have been handed down. Incidentally, although this state of affairs was always open to observation, it has up to now been the practice to attribute unassigned works, probably all too quickly, on the basis of any kind of similarity, to one of the few masters known in another connection. A secure historical basis is also lacking for the improvised label, freely used in our attribution practice, "Workshop of Master X," since as yet only isolated facts can be established concerning the customary manner of division of labor between master and studio personnel. Consequently it will also be attempted on the basis of extensive reference to relevant indications and testimony to sketch the pervading customary organization of the artist's studio and its working operation and in the process also to examine closely the work procedure as it is revealed by a study of the work itself with the help of evidence from primary sources.

For all these points of inquiry, however, we shall have to look over the whole development of the Renaissance period in Florence, that is, the rich century from the beginning of the 1420s up to the end of the 1520s.

With the exception of isolated instances, the first two decades still essentially belong together with the previous period of the late Trecento in terms of the history of style as well as in their whole artistic and cultural behavior. On the other hand, the end of the republican system in Florence in 1530 signifies the final end of the formal world of the High Renaissance and thus the chronological concluding point for our exposition. The course of development from the second to the last third of the Quattrocento and toward high classicism has hitherto almost always been pursued only with relevance to the formal nature of the work and to some extent also to its general aesthetic conception. In our study it will become clearly evident how this progression finds its natural counterpart, and perhaps even its partial basis, in the parallel development of the aforementioned factors of the general life of art. These factors— organization as a group, attitude of the patron, etc.—can be seen to undergo gradual modification and sometimes even marked transformation over this hundred-year period. Or, in other words, we shall find the progressive changes in the formal structure of the work of art, as well as in the whole artistic behavior of the period, strongly illuminated and firmly founded in the structure of general artistic conditions and their gradual course of development.

The method of research and observation followed here is in no way meant to set itself in opposition to the Renaissance research of Wölfflin to whose teaching the author is indebted for the foundation acquired during the greater part of his own student days and far beyond. It seeks rather to supplement from another point of view the insights gained from a style-historical standpoint in a Wölfflinian sense and to establish them in general historical terms and build them into the complex of all the preconditions and circumstances that defined and determined the world in which the Florentine artist lived, a world from which the formal as well as the spiritual nature of his creations in a certain sense derives.[6]

[6] The preceding introduction corresponds in its essentials to the contents of a lecture at the Kunstgeschichtlichen Institut of Florence (published in the *Schweizerischen Rundschau*, 1928).

From an early study, not limited to Florence, of the area of investigation handled here, the author took the theme of his inaugural lecture at Leipzig (July 1917): "Das italienische Kunstleben und die Künstlerwerkstatt der Renaissance" (published in the Swiss monthly *Wissen und Leben*, 1918).

German artistic conditions in the fifteenth and sixteenth centuries are treated (on the basis of source material which, in this case, is admittedly far more scarce) by Hans Huth's small book *Künstler and Werkstatt der Spätgothik* (Augsburg, 1923), and subsequently, most recently, in a systematic examination of all pertinent questions, the Giessen dissertation of Heinz Schwarzmann, *Kunst und Gemeinschaft in der Dürerzeit*, which will appear shortly as volume 6 of the Münster study series Lebensräume der Kunst (Wattenscheid).

See also the programmatic article by von Einem, "Aufgaben der Kunstgeschichte in der Zukunft," *ZKG*, 1936, pp. 1 ff., which, with its discussion of the "functional tasks of the artist" and of certain "extra-artistic factors" in artistic creation, comes repeatedly into close contact with the points of view pursued in the present book.

PART I

# The Commissions

The material for the work of art comes from life;
Art gives the form.

GEORG DEHIO

# CHAPTER 1

# GREAT PROJECTS AND
# WORK ON THEM
# FROM 1420 TO 1530

The artist's work was repeatedly in demand for certain continuing and recurrent needs. This is most clearly evident in the great projects represented by every major public building with a religious or secular function. Each presented a multitude of the most varied special problems for the different figurative and decorative arts.

Accordingly we shall begin by tracing, in a monographic presentation, the artistic undertakings which, considered desirable for certain of the most important projects during the period from about 1420 to 1530, were planned and begun, but not necessarily brought to full completion.

As the most important and productive centers of such diverse artistic problems, we must consider the symbolic focal points of ecclesiastical and political life. These were on the one hand the Duomo and Baptistery and on the other the Palazzo della Signoria. The further construction and constantly enriched artistic furnishing of these were pursued throughout the whole Renaissance century, partly out of functional necessity and partly as an honorable duty of the commune and the most prestigious corporations. As the most valid example of prevailing private or family patron activity, we have the development of the whole artistic complex of the church and convent buildings of Santa Maria Novella through the competitive cooperation of many families, confraternities, etc. with some close interest in it. As far as these main arenas of continuous artistic undertaking are concerned, they are certainly still extant today and only partially altered in their architectural substance, but not too much of their former stock of furnishings has remained in place.

Thus, if we wish to gain a mental image of all that was undertaken at these places during the Renaissance and of how the works of art within the architectural setting might have fit together and looked, we must seek to draw up a hypothetical reconstruction of the original stock of articles and their placement on the basis of contemporary statements and old reports. This can be attempted without too farfetched fantasizing, since a very great number of documentary points of reference are still available and for the most part have even been published. Among these are various old descriptions and the references to be gathered from Vasari and other sources.

Such a reconstruction, then, will be attempted in the following sections. Its basis, to emphasize it once more, will be not so much an antiquarian point of view as the conviction, already expressed in the introductory chapter, of the general art historical necessity of placing each individual monument as far as possible back in its original context and functional setting. By this means also we seek to correct many misconceptions that could not help but result from the current predominant and fundamentally antihistorical preservation and disposal in museums of works of art stemming from churches and domestic buildings.

## THE DUOMO AND BAPTISTERY

The Duomo and Baptistery in the setting and scale of their surroundings even in the sixteenth century presented a far more dominating appearance than they did later, and, surely, than within the present cityscape. In order to be able to imagine the former situation, one must walk from the Palazzo Vecchio through the section of the city which is still preserved somewhat in its old architectural state with its little twisting streets and small crowded middle-class houses, and approach the Duomo by Via dello Studio. Thus the whole extraordinary dimensions of the major ecclesiastical buildings and their material and decorative splendor can be appreciated. How they must have towered above the more modest and diminutive building types of the town even during the High Renaissance!

Besides this, however, these buildings were distinguished as the most important centers of Florentine religious devotion and civic self-consciousness. Accordingly the concern for the cathedral building stood continuously from the beginning at the center of public, city-state, and general citizen interest. The two most important, financially powerful guilds—the woolworkers (Arte della Lana) for the Duomo since 1337 and the merchants (Calimala) for San Giovanni since even earlier—administered the construction and furnishing as a most honorable obligation. This ancient preoccupation can only be called to mind here, since we now have to pursue the continuation of this arrangement in its particular effects during the Renaissance century. An old ordinance of 1294 that set aside before all other expenditures a bequest of at least three lire in every will for the Duomo building fund as a sort of inheritance tax remained constantly in force. In addition, all important questions of the architectural or figurative artistic development of the Duomo and Baptistery were decided at any given time by a public competition in which anyone could participate, and the whole citizenry was invited to express opinions. Both these facts are unambiguous testimony to the immediate and continuous interest in these concerns of the whole population of the city.

The Duomo as cathedral of the diocese was, of course, first of all the focal point and pinnacle of the ecclesiastical system, but this greatest and most imposing church of the city also played a conceptual as well as practical role in the general public life of the townspeople through the great events of both an ecclesiastical and a secular nature that could find a setting appropriate to their significance only here. Such were the great ceremonies for the Council of Florence and other papal and princely visits, the readings from Dante organized by the civic authorities in the fifteenth century and the sermons of Savonarola when not rarely more than twelve thousand listeners assembled.[1]

At the same time the ancient Baptistery, San Giovanni, was no less deeply rooted in the hearts of all Florentines as the sole baptismal place of everyone born in the city for centuries. With its finely decorated outer exterior, "bel San Giovanni" was the pride and joy of the citizens already in Dante's time. In addition, it was the shrine of the city patron and had risen here on the foundation walls, supposedly still surviving, of an ancient Roman temple of Mars, supplanting the former pagan patron of Florence. Accordingly, this saint's day of June 24 had been celebrated since distant times as the most splendid of all church and popular festivals, and this date is still prominent, with a somewhat reduced significance, even in present-day Florentine life.[2]

The piazza between the Duomo and Baptistery and especially the step-terrace around the former seem also to have been a favorite meeting place and forum for discussion for the citizens. An author of the mid-Cinque-cento, Antonio Doni, gives a most charming picture of the evening amusements of Florentine youth on these terraces, enjoying the coolness given off by the marble.[3]

We must imagine all these conditions and assumptions that underlay the unique significance of the Duomo and San Giovanni in the consciousness of the Florentine people at that time, in order to conceive of

[1] Dante readings, for example, were held from 1430 on by the humanist Filelfo and from 1483 by the Dominican Fra Domenico da Corella. In 1441 a poetic "academy," that is, a poetry competition, on the theme Praise of Friendship was held here, etc. See Alfred von Reumont, *Lorenzo de Medici, il Magnifico*, 2nd ed. 2 vols. (Leipzig, 1883), 1:590-91; Joseph Schnitzer, *Savonarola*, 2 vols. (Munich, 1924), 1:254.

[2] For the spectacles of the St. John's festival, see below. The captured war trophies and the *carroccio*, the city's war chariot, were formerly also kept in San Giovanni.

[3] From this also comes the title of his book of stories, *I Marmi*, (Venice, 1552); see p. 6. We should probably picture this step structure during the Renaissance as still almost as high and broad as the present-day ones at the cathedrals of Pisa and Siena. On this see especially Francesco Bocchi, *Le bellezze della citta di Fiorenza* (Florence, 1591), new ed. Giovanni Cinelli (Florence, 1677).

the extraordinary zeal for artistic enterprises with which officials and citizens repeatedly exerted themselves for these two edifices and their furnishing up to the end of the Florentine republic.[4]

The chronological starting point of our presentation, about 1420, can be clearly recognized as a decisive juncture in the development of the Duomo and San Giovanni. For the work of the first two decades appears here simply as the last pursuit of projects begun earlier. Ghiberti's bronze doors and the marble work of Nanni di Banco and the young Donatello, including sculpture for the Porta della Mandorla and the first statues for the niches of the facade and the Campanile, remained until about 1420 as isolated advances in the midst of an otherwise almost unshaken conventionality of plan and form. All these works were going on in the Duomo construction workshop alongside the great building project, also inherited from the Trecento, the completion of the three tribunes around the crossing and the dome drum rising over them. Now, however, when it became necessary to solve the formidable static problem of vaulting the cupola, all decorative furnishing work stopped almost completely as if at one stroke. In 1420 the risk was taken, and Brunelleschi's construction model went into execution; on this alone all the energy and interest of the workshop focussed. For the rest, a sort of breathless tension lay on all minds. And so during the whole decade of the 1420s, there was nothing to note down in the annals of the Duomo besides the dome construction, except certain statues by Donatello and Rosso for the Campanile, the painted tomb monument for Cardinal Corsini by Bicci di Lorenzo (1423), some designs for stained glass in the upper nave windows, and some private donations of pictures and tombs.

Not until 1432, when the giant dome-shell neared its closing and its successful completion appeared assured—in 1434 came the fitting in of the closing-ring under the lantern—did the activity of sculptors and painters suddenly begin anew; for now it became important to prepare the main liturgical part of the cathedral for use for services and to furnish it appropriately.[5]

---

[4] Giovanni Poggi published the documents for the Duomo construction project in *Italienische Forschungen herausgegeben vom Kunsthistorisches Institut in Florenz*, vol. 1 (Berlin, 1909); volume 2 was not published. For the Baptistery see the extract from Carlo Strozzi in Giorgio Vasari, *Le vite* . . . , ed. Karl Frey (Munich, 1911), 1:328-78. For the rest, all documentary and other evidence is now being brought together with the utmost completeness in the comprehensive inventory work on the churches of Florence, compiled by Dr. Paatz on behalf of the Florentine Institute. With this publication forthcoming, we can for the most part dispense with the enumeration of sources in this and the following chapter. [*Translator's note*: See Walter Paatz and Elisabeth Paatz, *Die Kirchen von Florenz*, 6 vols., Frankfurt am Main, 1940-1954.]

[5] See the boastful description of the Duomo in a 1432 letter from the Signoria to Pope Eugene IV in Giovanni Gaye, *Carteggio inedito d'artisti dei secoli XIV, XV, XVI*, 3 vols. (Florence, 1839-1840), 1:129.

So indeed the following enterprises are crowded into the next five years from 1432 to 1436 and were commissioned and begun at the same time or one after the other, although admittedly only a small fraction of them were completed in this span of time:

(1) The stained glass for the three groups of five chapels in the tribunes and one of the great round windows of the drum (the latter after a design of Donatello's, while Ghiberti designed other stained glass);

(2) The great Ghiberti bronze shrine for the head of St. Zenobius, which held an important place of veneration in the middle chapel of the choir arm;

(3) The marble organ tribunes by Donatello and Luca della Robbia on the east pair of piers, completed in 1438 and 1439 (in 1668 they were set up below in the choir precinct for easier visibility and in 1872 brought into the Museo dell' Opera; the 1610 engraved view of the interior by Matthäus Greuter shows them in their original position; see Hans Kauffmann, *Donatello* [Berlin, 1935], n. 224);

(4) The octagonal psalm choir of the canons under the dome; at first, admittedly, only in a modest wood rendition intended as temporary, after Brunelleschi's design.

When the consecration of the Duomo took place amid festive cere-monies on 25 March 1436, all these works were still in production.[6]

Yet forthwith even more tasks were taken on, which had to do chiefly with the arrangements in the fifteen chapels around the choir. Brunelleschi designed their marble altar tables, while Luca della Robbia and Donatello prepared the first parts of their relief decoration.[7]

For the paintings on the chapel walls they also thought immediately about "bonos et optimos magistros," but they settled for the trusty Bicci di Lorenzo, who did the underpainting for the whole series of titular figures over the fifteen altars in one campaign through 1440, and, with two assistants, immediately afterwards also executed the great individual figures of the twelve apostles in the aisles and the passages to the tribunes (which in the sixteenth century had to make way for the marble apostles).

The furnishing of the two sacristies was also pursued; work began around 1440 with the first parts of their intarsia panelling by Antonio Manetti and others, and Buggiano, Brunelleschi's adopted son, carved

[6] F. P. Luiso published a very detailed description by an eyewitness of the act of con-secration in a Per-Nozze publication of 1904. The hymn "Nuper rosarum flores" composed for the occasion by Guillaume Dufay, with which the description just mentioned agrees in rapturous wording ("ut angelici ac divini cantus"), can be found with music reproduced, for example, in Heinrich Martens, *Musikalische Formen*, 20 vols. (Berlin, 1930-1937), vol. 5.

[7] Granted, only the two not altogether complete marble reliefs by Luca with scenes from the life of Peter now in the Bargello were executed.

the two wall fountains with putti. For the entrances, however, Donatello was to produce relief-decorated bronze doors. The commission for these, already assigned in 1436—and to which the clay sketches surviving in the Bargello can perhaps be related—would be again conferred ten years later on Luca della Robbia who in the period from 1443 to 1448 had just supplied the two great terra-cotta reliefs over the sacristy doors. But the execution of the bronze doors still dragged on for a long time. On the other hand, in 1447 Luca's charming candlestick angels were produced as part of a marble sacrament tabernacle by Buggiano that had been set up a short time earlier in the middle chapel of the north transept at the behest of Bishop Antoninus. They are now in one of the sacristies. Another liturgical object probably created in the later 1440s is the great bronze paschal candlestick that is still used at Easter in the Duomo today.[8]

The new organ, whose execution was the object of long effort, was also finished in 1448. It received its place above Donatello's cantoria as a counterpart to the old organ set up over the Robbia balustrade and was framed with a decoration constructed by Giovanni da Gaiuole, for which Castagno furnished certain painted ornamental figures and Michelozzo carved putti.[9]

But certain works of nonliturgical purpose, some of which belong to the time shortly after the Duomo consecration, also deserve mention. They include the two painted monuments to the university teacher Luigi Marsili by Bicci di Lorenzo of 1439 and the equestrian monument to the mercenary leader Acuto (John Hawkwood), painted by Uccello, which was already erected on one aisle wall in the summer of 1436 and only later transferred to its present place.

Uccello was also entrusted in 1443 with the painting of the great clock face high up on the inner facade wall, of which at least the four powerful prophet heads survive in their original position. In addition, in 1443 to 1444 Uccello supplied the cartoons for three of the great round windows in the dome drum (of which the stained glass Nativity and Resurrection of Christ executed from them are still preserved), while Ghiberti drew the designs for the other three oculi, and Castagno took charge of the last part of this series in 1444 (see below).

[8] It stands then near the high altar on the left on a marble base decorated with the Florentine insignia in the style of Antonio Rossellino. The candelabra itself, however, whose decorative motifs accord with the external architecture of Brunelleschi's model of the dome lantern (see below), can probably be attributed to Michelozzo. At that time Michelozzo had certainly also gotten the assignment to do both the smaller metal work for the sacristy and the grillwork for the new sacrament altar (completed only in 1462 and still in existence at the altar in the north tribune).

[9] Soon thereafter, in 1453, the Duomo received the pax now in the Bargello and the niello scene of the Deposition from the Cross. See Giorgio Vasari, *Le vite de' piu eccellenti pittori* . . . , ed. Gaetano Milanesi, 9 vols. (Florence, 1878-1885), 9:280, s.v. Pollaiuolo.

Certain works for the exterior of the Cathedral can also be added to all these for the interior: on the Campanile, the last missing niche statues, including Donatello's Habakuk (*Zuccone*) and the five marble reliefs by Luca della Robbia (executed between 1437 and 1440), which were still lacking in the lower story of the series begun one hundred years earlier. Shortly after the completion of the dome about 1438, however, its builder erected the semicircular exedrae on the four exposed sides of the drum, as the first pieces of pure Renaissance architecture to appear on the Duomo. The second section in the new style, the crowning lantern, was begun according to Brunelleschi's model just before his death and brought very slowly to completion. The erection of Brunelleschi's tomb monument after his death in 1446 with relief portrait and inscription tablet in the right aisle should be noted as the last event of this period (see document in *RA*, 1930, pp. 535ff.).

Now we leave for a while the province of commissions for the Duomo—for which a certain lull set in immediately following the intense industriousness of the 1430s and 1440s—and turn our attention to projects undertaken for the Baptistery in the second quarter of the century.

The successful completion and installation of Ghiberti's first bronze portals in 1424—which differed from their Gothic prototype, Andrea Pisano's doors, only in certain Renaissance details—moved the building commission of the Calimala to the resolution to provide another such door for the third entrance to San Giovanni and to entrust this commission also to Ghiberti. Now, however, the new outlook triumphed and led to a work of completely different form in overall design with only ten large panels for scenes between figured borders.[10] Ghiberti had been free from the cosupervision of the dome since 1426, but he was so frequently distracted by many sculptural works going on at the same time that the execution of these doors also dragged on for a full twenty-five years.[11] They finally received a place of honor as a much admired masterpiece in the main portal of the Baptistery, facing the Duomo facade, where the Andrea Pisano doors had stood up to that time.[12]

In the meantime it was considered sufficient for Ghiberti's son and

[10] This project was not, however, established from the very beginning; for in 1425 Leonardo Bruni was still working at the Operai's request on a program of scenes which, like the two doors existing at that time, contained twenty narrative reliefs and eight individual figures (Vasari-Frey, 1: 357ff.).

[11] In the house with a casting studio near Santa Maria Nuova, placed at his disposal by the Signoria, ten relief scenes were first of all finished by 1436 and 1437 in rough cast. The chasing took ten more years, the execution of the borders, etc. five, so that the gilding of the finished doors and their installation could not take place until 1452.

[12] These were transferred to the south side entrance; the plan was considered, however, to replace them with a third pair of doors by Ghiberti, for which Vasari in his youth claims to have seen some sort of sketches by the master.

coworker Vittorio to enrich the frame of the south portal with bronze relief borders, as at the two other entrances.

Only after the conclusion of this last work could the commission appointed by the guild for the bronze doors be dissolved. These *provveditori* (Niccolò da Uzzano, Matteo and Filippo Villani, Palla Strozzi, and others) had carried on the duties of their office for more than half a century, from the beginning of work on the first Ghiberti doors. Enormous sums had passed through their hands—partly as salary funds and advance payments for the master and his many assistants, partly for the supply of materials—before this important matter was brought to its conclusion.

It is understandable enough that not much else could be undertaken along with such a costly enterprise. Nevertheless, during the last work on the bronze doors in the years from 1425 to 1428, the great tomb monument for the *quondam Papa*—the antipope John XXIII, deposed by the Council of Constance, who died in Florence in 1419—was also begun. The executors of his will, headed by Cosimo de' Medici, had obtained for him the rare honor of burial in San Giovanni and arranged for the construction of a most imposing tomb monument by Donatello and Michelozzo. The Baptistery had at that time also acquired from his legacy the highly prized relic of a finger of St. John the Baptist, as well as a bequest for the production of an appropriate container for it, which was therefore also executed during the 1420s by the goldsmith Antonio del Vagliente. A reliquary for an arm bone of the apostle Philip and a third reliquary, hexagonal and resting on lion's feet, were also produced by him. Furthermore, the treasury of San Giovanni received a silver-gilt bust of the Baptist in 1430 from Giovanni Portinari's widow, and in 1442 Rinuccio Farnese donated the golden rose conferred on him by the pope, which was mounted on a gilded pedestal. The documentary references reported here are all that has survived of the last-named treasures.

Through these donations from third parties the guild that was managing the building incurred no noteworthy expenses; their only other expenses, though these recurred constantly later, were for all sorts of works improving the building itself and older parts of its decoration, the new painting of the Gothic Holy Cross Tabernacle by Uccello carried out about 1450, and the like.

However, after the exceptionally important task of the bronze portals was essentially finished during the beginning of the 1450s, the Calimala was free to turn its initiative to another more considerable enterprise, the long-due completion of the silver altar, that is, to that particularly splendid adornment of the high altar of San Giovanni, on which work had begun in the last third of the Trecento with eight relief scenes of the legend of St. John in the middle of an extremely rich decorative frame on the broad front side of the altar structure following a widespread practice of the early middle ages. Thus now, after a pause of more than fifty years, this enterprise was taken up again, first of all with a commission in 1452 to Michelozzo for the almost half life-size silver figure of the titular saint for the middle niche of the antependium. At the same time Pollaiuolo and two other goldsmiths began the execution of the mighty silver altar cross—in which a relic of the cross recently received from Constantinople was to be inserted. It was completed in 1459, at a total expenditure of over three thousand florins. At that time the socle step and crowning cornice in richly profiled woodcarving were probably also attached to the antependium in order that the precious object, none too stable in itself, could be set up on the altar on high feast days.[13]

The final completion of the whole altar frontal occurred twenty years later, after further interruptions. On the other hand, certain valuable individual pieces for San Giovanni were produced in the 1450s. The first of these, completed in 1452, was the famous pax of Maso Finiguerra, the silver tablet with the niello image of the Coronation of the Virgin for the faithful to kiss, now in the Bargello, as well as two other paxes which Vasari saw there and attributed to Pollaiuolo. On the other side, Donatello's great wooden figure of Mary Magdalen still has its place in a wall niche. There are also reports of a Madonna tabernacle which a private donor was allowed to set up in San Giovanni in 1459 with the injunction that the insignia of the Commune and the Calimala should appear on it. Finally during the period of 1453 to 1455, with a mosaic by Baldovinetti in the lunette of the main portal—the same one in which Ghiberti's Gates of Paradise were installed—this long-forgotten, most costly medium of monumental art was taken up anew.

The intense enthusiasm of the 1450s for projects emerged again at the end of the following decade, after a pause, but with greater intensity and willingness to spend. First of all, for the appropriate furnishing of the high altar, two silver candlesticks with rich enamel decoration were commissioned from Pollaiuolo and completed in 1470. Above all, however, a new, unusually costly enterprise began in 1466: the preparation of a particularly magnificent set of chapel furnishings for the high feasts, that is, a set of mass vestments in white damask including copes, a chasuble, two dalmatics, and accessories, for whose figural trimming (now in the Duomo museum) Pollaiuolo once again furnished designs. Although at any given time five to seven embroiderers were at work on this minute needlework, the completion of the objects extended to the end of the 1470s and consumed endless sums.

This was a matter that kept all else in the background for a long time.

[13] The antependium, exhibited in the Duomo museum, will now for its safety no longer be returned to its original place of exhibition and function on St. John's day, as was still customary until a few decades ago.

So also was the completion of the silver altar, to which the lacking short sides with the four reliefs and corresponding decorative frames were first added in the years 1476-1480 by Pollaiuolo, Verrochio, Antonio di Salvi, and Bernardo Cennini. With this, more than one hundred years after its inception, the magnificent object finally reached its definitive completion.

Small individual pieces from this period remain to be noted: the marble holy water basin by Benedetto da Maiano installed in the sacristy in 1477 and a silver *ex-voto* bust of Lorenzo Magnifico—a donation probably occasioned by his escape from the Pazzi conspirators in 1478—which was then melted down in 1500 for other use of the precious metal. San Giovanni also had Lorenzo to thank for the donation of two new organs during the period from 1482 to 1484. Their appearance we may probably imagine as similar to their counterparts in the Duomo (see above).[14]

The main task that the 1480s presented to the Calimala was the thorough-going restoration of the medieval mosaic decoration of the dome and choir chapel, for which Baldovinetti, who had already proved himself earlier in such work, was engaged with a fixed annual salary for the rest of his life. The necessary suspended scaffolding for this work was so ingeniously constructed by Francesco la Cecca that in consequence he was appointed foreman of works at San Giovanni.

With the provision of a bronze crucifix in 1488, which was then also gilded, the series of works executed for the Baptistery in the time of Lorenzo Magnifico comes to a close.

Now let us see what had happened at the Duomo since the middle of the century.

To begin with architecture, the execution of the dome lantern, according to Brunelleschi's model, was first of all a matter that dragged on through the whole decade of the 1450s to be completed in 1461, and again, not until ten years later could the highest, ultimate crowning detail be set in place—a hollow gilded copper ball with a cross rising from it produced in Verrocchio's workshop. Thus the project that had been pursued through a full half century finally reached a conclusion.

Another highly important part of the building's exterior had remained in a shamefully fragmentary condition: the decorative facade of the great west front, of which only the lowermost third of the whole height had been provided with a decorative marble covering since the late Trecento. Countless pieces of statuary had been produced for its niche frames during the first two or three decades of the Quattrocento.[15] It could now

---

[14] The organ frame with Calimala arms in the Duomo Museum—thus presumably for San Giovanni—is perhaps one of these donations of Lorenzo's.

[15] In 1428 the Opera acquired a figure of St. Stephen, which was no longer needed at Or San Michele, for use on the Duomo facade. In the following year, however, certain

no longer be resolved, however, to carry on the whole facade project in accordance with the inherited system, and already in 1429 Brunelleschi and Ghiberti were invited to submit designs for a "facies de novo edificanda." Thus the eventual destruction or reworking of the existing parts was already under consideration at that time.

Such a solution must have appeared all the more as the only one possible, since the construction of Alberti's Renaissance-style facade at Santa Maria Novella in 1470 had meanwhile taken place. The enormous dimensions of the front of the Duomo, of course, made the formal as well as material problem of an appropriate articulation much more difficult. And finally, since the fronts of several principal churches of the city, Santa Croce, San Lorenzo, and Santo Spirito still showed the same unfinished condition, there was always the comforting thought that the weighty matter of the Duomo should in any case not be rushed.

At various times during the late Quattrocento the Opera was certainly offered designs, drawings, and models for a new facade structure.[16] In 1490 and 1491 a public competition was announced in which countless artists and nonartists, among others even the Magnifico himself, took part; yet no decision was reached, so that Lorenzo himself subsequently recommended a postponement until a later time.*

Two sculptural enterprises for the exterior of the Duomo also occurred in the 1460s: on the one hand the resumption of the plan already pursued at the beginning of the century to crown the corner piers of the three tribunes with colossal statues. Donatello's marble *David* was indeed originally intended for this, and a second still larger clay figure (which later perished) was executed in 1421-1422 by Donatello. As a counterpart to this statue, called *Joshua*, Agostino di Duccio provided in 1463-1464 a Hercules, which has also vanished since then.[17]

And soon thereafter another giant was commissioned from the same master; but in marble, and this time in the specified size of nine *braccia* (5.30 meters). However, the block was immediately so sadly hacked by the preparatory worker in its beginning stages that Duccio gave up the work, and a new commission to Antonio Rosselino in 1476 also remained

---

statuary commissions were withdrawn from Ciuffagni because too much surplus material had already collected in the store of the construction workshop. See Giovanni Poggi, *Il Duomo di Firenze; Documenti sulla decorazione* . . . Italienische Forschungen herausgegeben vom Kunsthistorischen Institut in Florenz (Berlin, 1909), pp. 296-97, 300.

[16] Such a model was even referred to in the testament of Mino da Fiesole (1484). See *RA*, 1904, p. 44.

* *Translator's note*: On Lorenzo's alleged entry in the Duomo facade design competition see the Translator's Introduction, p. xviin.

[17] Bocchi-Cinelli (*Le bellezze della citta*, p. 572) still record this or the Donatello figure standing on one of the *speroni* toward Via de' Servi. [*Translator's note*: full bibliographic information for titles shortened in the notes can be found in the author's bibliography.]

without results. Finally in 1501 and 1502 Michelangelo formed the *David* from it.*

On the Campanile, however, in 1464, the medium-sized niche statues of the late Trecento displayed on the front side were exchanged for Donatello's figures, which had hitherto stood, much to their disadvantage, on the Cathedral side of the Campanile and only now were appraised as more valuable.

Now to the works in the interior of the Duomo.

In 1455 the Operai were directed by the city government to have a painted monument erected to honor the deserving condottiere Niccolò da Tolentino in the style of the Acuto picture executed by Uccello twenty years earlier. Castagno received the commission, which was completed the following year.[18] Thought was also given to the renewal of the old commemorative picture of Dante. This plan did not take effect until 1464, and then only with the insignificant panel by Domenico di Michelino.

Otherwise, for the 1450s we know only of small decorative works. Thus an old picture of the Madonna near the Porta dei Canonici, which had recently attracted special veneration, was set off with a carved gilded tabernacle by Antonio Manetti; a baldachin enriched with painting and gilding was set up over the high altar, and Manetti, who had succeeded Michelozzo in 1452 as Duomo construction master, was commissioned to prepare designs and trial sections of a new choir installation. The matter, however, was not followed up for the time being, and at the beginning of the 1460s interest turned primarily to the furnishing of the sacristy. The specialist Giuliano da Maiano and Giovanni da Gaivole carried out the panelling all around with cabinets and wall benches from 1463 to 1464 in a noble decorative articulation and with the richest figural intarsia decoration, for which the goldsmith Finiguerra, as well as Baldovinetti, was called in for the preliminary designs of figural compositions and certain heads.

In addition, the old plan for the erection of bronze doors was taken up again, and Luca della Robbia, who had already in 1445 taken over this commission in Donatello's place, was now in 1456 engaged more specifically with a new contract, still limited to a single door.[19]

* *Translator's note*: For more recent literature on Michelangelo's *David* and the David theme in Florentine art see Translator's Introduction, p. xiii.

[18] Both equestrian images stood next to each other on the north aisle wall but were transferred to canvas in 1842 and moved to their present places.

[19] The frame portions and two of the ten reliefs were cast at that time; all the rest were completed in Verrocchio's foundry in 1467. The last stage, the gilding of individual parts and the installation of the doors, dragged on until 1474. The account notations about all sorts of occasional purchases of small quantities of metal, of melted-down mortars, brass basins, and the like (*l'Arte*, 1918, pp. 199, 201) show how much circumstances determined the supply of suitable casting materials.

Other costly objects for liturgical use were created at that time. Zanobi Strozzi and Francesco del Chierico illuminated two great antiphonals from 1463 to 1470 and about the same time Verrocchio was working on some morses for choir robes, which Vasari cites as youthful works of this master (Vasari-Milanesi, 3:358).[20]

Finally, after the conclusion of work on the dome in 1471, a definitive, appropriate development was desirable for the canons' choir under the dome, which still remained in the first temporary stage. Various consultations were taken, which also led to commissions to Giuliano da Maiano for the woodwork and to Verrocchio for decorative elements in bronze and marble. But this resolution was left unfulfilled, and it was considered enough, under pressure from the canons, at least to raise and enrich the outer surrounding enclosure in 1477 and 1478 by means of a tapestry running around it from the workshop of the weaver Giovanni d'Alemagna, who had established himself in Florence.[21] When the attack of the Pazzi conspirators took place in front of this choir enclosure shortly afterward on 26 April 1478 during the Sunday high mass in the Duomo, the bronze sacristy doors installed a few years earlier offered Lorenzo Magnifico shelter from the assailants who were closing in, and saved his life.

Besides this, the accounts of the Duomo authorities note for long years only a few insignificant items, such as the painting of four wooden candlesticks by Ghirlandaio and decorative work by Andrea della Robbia in the administrative offices of the construction workshop.[22]

Thereupon, however, the restoration of the mosaics of the Baptistery, initiated in the 1480s, also spurred the Opera of the Duomo to competitive efforts in this artistic medium. In 1487 an old mosaic over the central portal of the facade was repaired; shortly thereafter, however, Ghirlandaio was commissioned to decorate the tympanum of the Porta della Mandorla, up to then occupied by an old sculptural Annunciation group, with a mosaic composition of the same theme (completed 1490). This was a first attempt—after Baldovinetti's lunette mosaic on the Baptistery, mentioned above—with this technique, so well suited to the increased love of splendor of the late Quattrocento. Its success inspired the Opera immediately to set off effectively the St. Zanobius chapel in the interior of the Duomo with similar decoration. Four artists were to share

[20] Later, in 1476 (or perhaps 1456) we hear of a bronze reliquary ordered from Vittorio Ghiberti. In 1476, however, a stone case (*cassa di pietra*)—possibly a sort of safe—was ordered for the relics of Santa Maria del Fiore (Gaye, *Carteggio*, 1:109; Vasari-Milanesi, 2:244n.).

[21] Thus the choir installation appears in a fresco view of the choir area by Vasari. See the illustration in Poggi, *Duomo*, p. 123.

[22] Could the candlesticks mentioned perhaps be identified with two richly carved candelabra of about 1480 in the Duomo museum (Vasari-Milanesi, 2:180n; 3:276, 279; *l'Arte*, 1918, p. 205)?

the task: Ghirlandaio, the miniaturists Gherardo and Monte di Giovanni, and Botticelli. However, the death of Lorenzo Magnifico, who in this case also had been the soul of the enterprise, and the bad financial circumstances of the 1490s did not for the moment allow the designs to be carried out at all. Even later it was possible only in a small part.

On the other hand, a few individual works of sculpture were installed in the Duomo in these years. First of all, an especially magnificent piece of goldsmith's work, the reliquary still in the Duomo treasury today for an arm bone and the jawbone of St. Jerome was donated in 1487 by a canon Manetti.[23]

Then a strange popular devotional object was provided in 1491 by the Opera for the vesper devotions of Holy Week: a small image of the Mother of God, the head and limbs modelled in wax and painted by Benedetto Buglione, the clothes made of genuine precious cloth (l'Arte, 1919, p. 107).

Finally in 1490 a new series of monuments to honor important Florentine personalities was begun. The first of these were the monuments to Giotto and the Duomo organist Squarcialupi, who had died recently. Both were fashioned by Benedetto da Maiano as simple portrait-epitaphs, similar to that of Brunelleschi (see above), in a design that thereupon also set the pattern for later pieces of this kind.

We have traced the art history of the Duomo and Baptistery up to the end of Medici supremacy. Its collapse and the following years, dominated by Savonarola's influence, mark the end of the early Renaissance in the narrower sense and the transition from which the mature classical art was soon to come forth.

Before we turn our attention to this epoch, let us review the whole production and the general attitude of the early Renaissance in the sphere of the Duomo and Baptistery.

First of all, the lack of stability and continuity here in the handling of the individual problems appears noteworthy. We saw how certain projects were repeatedly planned but never set in action or long remained half-finished, while work on some other object interceded (as with the Duomo choir installation and facade or the silver altar of the Baptistery). Also, the intensity and tempo of production are very different for one and the same project in successive decades (such as the building of the dome and its lantern). Throughout, however, the length of time for the execution of all traceable works is disproportionately drawn out; almost incomprehensible is the delay, sometimes for years, of the final stages and installation of virtually completed works (the bronze doors of San

[23] Its first exhibition in the Duomo was also noted by Landucci in his diary: Luca Landucci, *Ein florentinisches Tagebuch 1450-1516*, ed. and trans. Marie Herzfeld, 2 vols. (Jena, 1912-1913), p. 79-80.

Giovanni and the Duomo sacristy). All these are explainable only through the special situation of the patrons as well as the artists. First of all, private persons are not—or only exceptionally—in question here. Rather there are committees and subcommittees delegated by the two great guilds—multi-membered groups—which certainly underwent many changes in their composition and with it in their interests.[24]

Also incumbent on these commissions was the problem, always more or less difficult, of obtaining money for projects newly begun or to be continued. Since, however, most undertakings and projects waited impatiently for completion, there had to be constant discussions and new decisions on which object should be pursued first at any given time. But for the artists also, it was often not easy to do justice to all the different instructions issued simultaneously or in rapid succession. In spite of an often numerous staff of assistants, many projects proceeded much more slowly than might already have been expected on account of a work procedure that was in itself highly intricate because more objects, including many immediately pressing small works of applied arts, were almost constantly having to be executed.

The disparity between what was planned and what was actually completed, between the length of working time and the volume of production, shows itself at its strongest in the second half of the early Renaissance. This, however, corresponds to the observation, also relevant in other contexts, that the general, powerful, bourgeois impulse, which from the 1420s through the 1440s made possible the completion of the giant dome structure in one campaign and the addition of a stately series of monumental furnishings to the newly dedicated Duomo, was almost completely paralyzed after about 1460. Thus, for example, the execution of the dome lantern took more than two years longer than the construction of the dome itself; and neither the pressing matter of the facade nor the definitive choir installation was realized, nor is there any other significant addition to the Duomo furnishings recorded from the time of Piero and Lorenzo de' Medici.

The interest of the time shows itself in fact almost exclusively in small decorative works, sometimes, it is true, of the most luxurious splendor. This holds true for the Opera of San Giovanni as well as for the Duomo, where during the first half of the century the bronze portals of Ghiberti and the papal tomb were installed, but from 1450 through 1490 only those costly luxury items of the silver altar and the feast vestments were added. Now let us see how the succeeding, final span of time, from about

[24] Occasionally the city Signoria or perhaps even the Parte Guelfa also came forward to assign a commission directly, in the face of which the bishop and cathedral chapter of canons, although they had the primary responsibility for the Duomo, asserted themselves only with admonitions, wishes, and suggestions.

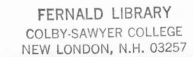

1495 to 1530, expressed itself in the context of our complex of commissions.

The late 1490s were marked by general want, trouble, and high prices. In addition, Savonarola in his sermons was repeatedly exhorting the offering of generous alms in such a difficult time rather than fame-seeking, luxurious donations for church buildings and decorations.[25] Thus little was immediately planned and almost nothing of consequence executed for the Duomo and San Giovanni.

A valuable acquisition for the treasury of San Giovanni does, it is true, fall into these years and still exists there today. In 1494 the Calimala bought from the Cardinal of Siena an old ornamental reliquary, called "il libretto," which had once belonged to the king of France and more recently to Lorenzo Magnifico. Subsequently in 1500 a silver gilded tempietto was ordered from Paolo Sogliani for the effective framing and exhibition of the small, magnificent object. However, the precious metal for the setting was obtained by melting down the *ex-voto* bust of Lorenzo mentioned above, whose memory, after 1494, there was admittedly no longer reason to respect. In addition, also in 1500, the Magdalen statue by Donatello, which had for some years been set aside for safety reasons, was provided with a silver diadem on the occasion of its installation; and the silver bust of the titular patron received a similar one.

In the Duomo, however, the baldachin over the high altar was renovated by Cosimo Rosselli with painting and gilding and fitted with a curtain of ornamented pennants. Thereafter a more imposing marble tabernacle for the host was to be provided, for which a wooden model, crowned with a carved bambino by Andrea di Piero, was set up first in 1496 for a trial period on the high altar, "ad ostendum utrum placeat populo." In spite of public interest presupposed and stimulated by this, it never came to realization. And a new campaign in 1504 in the same direction led again only to a trial model, this time by Andrea Sansovino.

In the meantime from 1495 to 1500 the altars of the tribune chapels were furnished with benches (predelle) for candlesticks in intarsia work and the predella of the sacrament altar with paintings by Cosimo Rosselli; a multicolored patterned marble pavement, such as had up to now existed only in the central chapel of each tribune, was begun according to Cronaca's designs for the other chapels also.

Then in the first decade of the new century, various old devotional images and individual altars of the nave received new frames and decorative furnishings.[26]

---

[25] Savonarola in his stern consistency went even so far as to recommend, in case of need, the melting of valuable altar utensils for the benefit of the hungry (Schnitzer, *Savonarola*, 1:199, 228).

[26] For this, Nanni dell'Unghero was employed for carved work, the famous miniaturist

In addition, the plan for mosaic decoration of the St. Zenobius chapel, which had come to a standstill in 1492, was taken up again. In 1504 two of those commissioned earlier, Monte di Giovanni and Davide Ghirlandaio (as his brother's successor) were each invited to execute a trial mosaic, the half-figure of St. Zenobius. The jury, which also included Perugino and Lorenzo di Credi, decided in favor of Monte, whose work was bought for 100 florins and afterwards set up in the chapel (now in the Museo dell' Opera). Nothing further for the covering of this whole vault surface was executed, even after the specific assignment of commissions in 1510, except for the ornamental decoration of the ribs.

All these enterprises still belong, in conception and formal character, completely to the late Quattrocento; the spirit of the new century is more clearly to be recognized in certain projects, also partially realized, in the province of monumental sculpture.

First of all the contract for the unlucky old "Gigante" block, renewed in 1511 and only then brought to a happy result with the assignment to Michelangelo, once again deserves mention. His David figure, completed in 1504, certainly appeared then as such an extraordinary creation that even before final completion the highest civic authorities, passing over the heads of the Duomo building supervisors, took over the decision concerning the installation of the colossus itself. Its subsequent fate will be described along with the art history of the Signoria palace.

For the Duomo, however, there was the ready consolation that in the previous year the consuls of the wool guild believed they had already won to their purposes, through a new, much more extensive commission, the master so suddenly risen to fame. Through the contract of 23 April 1503 Michelangelo was engaged to execute a whole cycle of apostles in over life-size marble statues within twelve years. But already in 1505 Michelangelo withdrew from the contract with the Opera on account of other more pressing claims on his time, leaving the Opera as value for the advance payments he had received only the roughed-out figure of a St. Matthew, which afterwards remained standing for more than three hundred years in the storeroom of the workshop and finally came into the Accademia.

In 1512 and 1513 the execution of the marble apostles for the Duomo was pursued further, more energetically, through the simultaneous contracting with various masters for individual figures; and thus during the

Monte di Giovanni for the curtain painted with angels for the picture of the Virgin, Bernardino di Jacopo for the (1505) painted "Paliotto del Crocifisso" over the high altar; while various painted shields and pennants, including a series of eighty pieces with Passion emblems, were commissioned from Piero del Donzello. All the altars etc. mentioned were removed, partly in the seventeenth and partly in the nineteenth century. The relevant account notations may be found in Poggi, *Duomo*, passim and Vasari-Milanesi, 2:485-86.

next few years the statues of at least five of the twelve apostles came to completion. The remainder did so only in the middle of the century.[27]

In the years 1508 and 1509 two more sculptural accessions from other sources appear; a great wooden crucifix was bought from the legacy of Benedetto da Maiano and was set up in a polychrome mounting by Lorenzo di Credi over the high altar, in place of an older carved work, where it is still found today. In addition Baccio d'Agnolo provided the wooden angels with trumpets to crown the older organ, corresponding to their earlier counterparts on the organ case of 1448.

There was also a new upsurge of major sculptural activity for the Baptistery at the beginning of the Cinquecento. The occasion for the distribution of commissions was the desire to replace the Gothic figures crowning the portal with sculptures acceptable to modern taste.[28] Thus in 1502 Andrea Sansovino was immediately commissioned for the statuary representation of the Baptism of Christ for the main portal, which he nearly completed within the next five years, while the portal facing the house of the Opera received, above the old bronze doors of Ghiberti, the three-figure group of the preaching of John by Giovanni Francesco Rustici.[29]

A greater architectural work on the exterior of the Duomo was begun in 1508 by the Duomo construction manager at that time, Baccio d'Agnolo. The still-missing covering of the broad band under the base of the dome was begun following his model at one of the southeastern sides of the octagon. In the years from 1508 to 1515 work progressed on this arcaded gallery above a powerful cornice, until Michelangelo, returning to Florence at that time, gave a sarcastic critique that spoiled the building managers' as well as the architect's enthusiasm to continue— he called the arcades a cricket cage.

The result was that this part has remained a bare masonry shell up to the present day. The facade's fate was similar. It is true that for the reception of Leo X in 1515 it received an ephemeral show front in wood, stucco, and paint after a design of Sansovino's (supposedly based on the 1491 design by Lorenzo Magnifico). Yet this was a temporary measure,

[27] Executed at first by 1513 were only Andrew by Andrea Ferrucci, John by Rovezzano, St. James Major by Jacopo Sansovino; afterwards from 1515 to 1517, through the assistance of younger beginners, the Peter of Bandinelli and Tribolo's St. James Minor were completed. The painted apostle series by Bicci di Lorenzo was then removed.

[28] The medieval groups, criticized in the records as "figuracce goffissime," standing under a three-part Gothic tabernacle are probably those recognizable in a view of the exterior of the Baptistery on a cassone painting in the Bargello.

[29] It was completed only in about 1570, on account of disagreement between the artist and the Calimala, by Vincenzo Danti, who subsequently also made the beheading group over the Pisano portal. See Luca Landucci, *Diario Fiorentino (1450-1516)*, ed. Jodoco del Badia (Florence, 1883), pp. 306, 309.

which led to no more definitive solution than later attempts of the same nature before the neo-Gothic installation of the 1860s.

Then in the period from 1519 to 1521, the repeatedly planned renewal of the choir installation under the dome, which had gradually become untenable, finally ensued. It was executed by Nanni Unghero in fine, well-smoothed wood without rich decoration except for the choral book stand adorned with carving and intarsia by Domenico Bacelli.

The choral books themselves, the huge graduals for the singers of the high mass and the choir service, also form a constant entry in the accounts of the Opera during the whole period from the 1490s through about 1530, and they still represent an especially extensive and splendid group among the liturgical codices preserved today, partly in the Duomo itself and partly in the Laurenziana (Fondo Edili). The famous Attavante and the brothers Gherardo and Monte di Giovanni were primarily occupied at this time with the execution of the miniature decoration for the Duomo library. But San Giovanni also had a large, splendid missal prepared by Monte di Giovanni in 1509 and another in 1519.

As to costly new vestments, the Duomo had already received two dalmatics in gold embroidery on silk in 1499. The well-known embroiderer Galiena and his assistants were paid 150 florins for these. In 1514 two more noteworthy works of goldsmith art came into the Duomo treasury: a silver altar cross of very great dimensions, executed on the Opera's commission by Antonio di Salvi and Michelangelo Viviani, as well as a donation of the Parte Guelfa for its chapel in the south transept; a magnificent silver-gilt reliquary of St. Anthony in tabernacle form.[30]

The last contributions of the High Renaissance, on the whole not too productive for the Duomo, remain to be noted: the monument to Marsilio Ficino, which was executed in 1521 by Andrea Ferrucci in the same form as three monuments of earlier origin and set up in the left aisle; as well as a panel of the archangel Michael by Lorenzo di Credi, painted in 1523 and now hanging in the sacristy of the canons.[31]

Finally, looking back over the new objects produced for the Duomo and San Giovanni over the four decades just considered, we may ask about the general character of these enterprises and about the patrons' intentions expressed in them. On the one hand, we notice the echo of that decoratively rich ostentation that had developed so significantly in

[30] The work, over one meter high, provided with the arms of the patron, of the commune, and of the Arte della Lana, still exists; the cross, which had remained unfinished, was melted down at the time of the seige of 1529: See *RA*, 8, 1910, pp. 34-36 with illustrations; and Vasari-Milanesi, 3:290; 6:156n.

[31] Credi's altarpiece for the St. Joseph altar, which Cinelli (Bocchi-Cinelli, *Le bellezze della citta*, p. 59) still saw there, has vanished. On various small furnishings by Ridolfo Ghirlandaio from the years 1518-1519 see Vasari-Milanesi, 6:542n.

the time of Lorenzo de' Medici and persisted in many manifestations well into the second decade of the new century. We see this tendency in the various works manifesting a delight in ornament which were commissioned for the adornment of altars and chapels as well as in the most opulent and costly treatment of all liturgical utensils by cabinet-makers, painters, gilders, mosaicists, goldsmiths, and miniaturists.

Associated with this one older tendency, which lessened temporarily only during the 1490s of Savonarola due to external and internal causes, but reappeared after the turn of the century, is an almost opposite artistic sensibility. This is to be recognized in the works of large-scale monumental figure sculpture cited in the earlier discussion of the Duomo and Baptistery. It expressed itself also in the field of architecture with the covering of the dome drum that had begun as well as in the plain but solid renovation of the canons' choir under the dome.

Thus, in their creations for the Duomo and Baptistery, the early and high Renaissance once again contrast clearly with each other in their artistic sensibilities: after the activity of the middle and late Quattrocento, manifested and fragmented in so many small particular enterprises, there follows a type of commission aiming more at noble, large-scale unity in which, no less decisively than in the style of individual works, the new spirit of the High Classic becomes recognizable.

### The Church and Convent of Santa Maria Novella

The Dominican convent of Santa Maria Novella and its Franciscan counterpart Santa Croce were the first and most important foundations in Florence of the two mendicant orders. In Florence just as elsewhere, now just as in earlier days, these orders have understood how to maintain a particularly close relationship with the citizenry by virtue of their avowedly world-directed, pastoral-charitable activity. In the Renaissance these convents still did not lack for new recruits, even from the upper levels of the bourgeoisie. In addition there was the highly esteemed institution of the so-called Third Order, as well as the countless other lay confraternities that were connected by loose ties to the actual monastic communities of Santa Maria Novella and Santa Croce. Thus considerable civic subsidies and private donations were constantly accruing to these societies that, according to rule, were to own nothing. This also made possible the realization of their especially spacious and richly decorated church and convent complexes.

Santa Maria Novella in the fifteenth century, like Santa Croce, still lay on the outer edge of the city center, which we should keep in mind when trying to imagine the former appearance of these buildings.

No small quantity of architectural additions and enrichments in furnishings came to the church and convent of Santa Maria Novella during the Renaissance. This included many pieces of the highest value which still exist now in their old places, but a large part of the former inventory had to give way to the forcible Mannerist "sistemazione" that Vasari carried out, here as in Santa Croce and elsewhere, on the instructions of the Grand Duke Cosimo during the 1560s.[32]

At the beginning of the period here under consideration an architectural project was undertaken within the convent complex which was already quite extensive in the late fourteenth century: the construction of a distinguished guest wing to accommodate princely and other high-ranking visitors. This must have been desired more by city officials than by the monks themselves.

Thus in 1418 a spacious hall with adjoining living quarters and a chapel was erected over the outer wing of the large cloister; a lodging which, in the following year, could serve as a residence for Pope Martin, who had stopped for a long sojourn in Florence. For this Sala del Papa, as the whole apartment was henceforth called, the city spent a sum of 1500 florins and appointed two foremen from the Duomo workshop. Ghiberti and Giuliano Pesello furnished the design for the great exterior staircase that led up from the cloister along the new wing as in medieval palaces. On the lower stairposts Donatello in 1420 placed the stone *marzocco* that held the lily coat of arms of the commune in its paws, the same figure which much later in about 1810 was transferred to the front of the Palazzo Vecchio (see below).[33]

[32] Much was also lost during the nineteenth century by an impious sale of the old possessions.

Yet the same Vasari who carried out this measure as an artist and according to the views of his generation had, a short time earlier, considered and described with objective interest as a historian much of what he caused to be removed or destroyed. Thus he may stand—together with the documentary material of Milanesi's commentary—as the richest primary source for our reconstruction.

Another especially valuable contemporary source is the manuscript compiled in 1478 to 1480 by P. Johannes Caroli and preserved in the Laurenziana (Pluteus 89, infer. cod. 21), *Vitae nonnullorum fratrum domus beate Marie Novelle.* Extracts from it are in Robert Davidsohn, *Forschungen zur Geschichte von Florenz,* 4 vols. (Berlin, 1908), 4:470, 480. Here, in the *praefatio,* for example, is an enthusiastic overall description of the church and convent. See further the monograph by James Wood Brown, *The Dominican Church of Santa Maria Novella* (Edinburgh, 1902). Above all, there is the already cited inventory work by Walter Paatz and Elisabeth Paatz, Die Kirchen von Florenz (6 vols., Frankfurt am Main, 1940-1954), which the author was able to consult in manuscript form. I refer the reader to this for all source verification.

[33] The rooms were used by Eugene IV from 1434 to 1436, and again during the Florentine Council of Union from 1439 to 1443. In 1451 Emperor Frederick III took lodging there. See Giovanni Cambi, *Istorie* in *Delizie degli Eruditi toscani,* ed. Fra Ildefonso di San Luigi, 25 vols. (Florence, 1790), 21:278. The exterior staircase was removed during the renovation of the rooms for the papal visit of Leo X in 1515. More detailed information on the earlier furnishing of the rooms, wholly altered by frequent later reconstructions, is lacking.

The charming small-columned court in front of the refectory was the donation, as the inscription set up repeatedly over the wall consoles testifies, of the general of the order Leonardo Dati, who died in 1424. This court probably dates from the mid-1420s. Accordingly it is one of the first Florentine early Renaissance courts, still clinging somewhat to Trecento style in the leaf-work of the consoles and capitals. A similar style can be found in the broad wall fountains set up there as a necessary furnishing of the anteroom of a refectory for the monks to wash their hands before and after meals.

Next we look at the interior of the church, which was consecrated in 1420 by Pope Martin V.

First of all it must be recalled that before Vasari's above-mentioned intervention the interior of the nave showed a strongly marked organization by means of the stone choir enclosure, already built around 1300, which extended across the last two bays of the nave. This installation for the choir service of the monks, reaching almost up to the springing of the arcades, had the form of a double wall. It bore a small upper catwalk (*ponte*) on which stood two small organs and four private altars, while against the choir screen of the front side facing the nave, a stately altar was set up on each side of the central gateway. The aisles also had transverse partitions with grill gates aligned with the screen, so that the whole back part of the church space was separated from the four foremost nave bays, the preaching church, by a dividing wall—the *tramezzo*.

Within this spacial context, all sorts of new additions to the many furnishings provided in the Trecento were already arriving in the period from 1420 to 1450. Among these I cite first the various early works of the order member Fra Angelico, at that time living in the convent at Fiesole. His Annunciation panels painted as wings for the two small organs on the choir wall as well as the fine painted figural decoration of the carved wood Easter candlestick have either been destroyed or disappeared.[34] Only the four small wooden reliquaries, decorated by Fra Angelico and his assistants with ornate miniatures and donated by Fra Giovanni Masi, who died in 1430, have survived.[35] There were, in ad-

[34] The renovation of the organs and probably also the painting of the wings resulted from a donation of the order general Leonardo Dati (died 1424), according to a note of P. Caroli (Davidsohn, *Forschungen*, 4:480). Caroli mentioned the candlestick as a donation of the lay brother Fra Borghese and described it as "egregia scultoris arte et pictura insigni confectum." Ernst Förster allegedly still saw it in a half-destroyed condition in the convent. See *Leben und Werke der Fra Giovanni Angelico da Fiesole*, Regensburg, 1859.

Its approximate appearance may be imagined based on a slightly older wooden candlestick from Siena, likewise painted with figures, now in a Viennese private collection. (*Pantheon*, 17-18, 1936, p. 286).

[35] Of these, three are now in the San Marco museum, one in Boston. Their production was probably occasioned by a large gift of relics that a confrere of Masi, Fra Lorenzo

dition, frescoes by Fra Angelico depicting many Dominican saints in the
left aisle, near the door to the cloister, as well as some small legendary
scenes, according to Vasari, on the altar of the Coronation of the Virgin,
also in this aisle, behind the *tramezzo*. Close to this, an altarpiece by Fra
Angelico's pupil Zanobi Strozzi was set up. Finally, an altar of the Con-
fraternità di Gesù Pellegrino stood in the same aisle.

A picture structure in storage at the Uffizi is supposed to have come
from there (if not from the confraternity's assembly room). It represents
the Lamentation over Christ in a folk style of painting from about 1430.
Above this in an arched section is Christ between Dominican monks and
confraternity members, while in the piece attached at the base is a scene
of a funeral among the confraternity.[36]

After the loss of all the aforementioned, only one painting from that
time, admittedly of capital importance, can be found in Santa Maria
Novella today: Masaccio's fresco of the Trinity which formerly had its
place over the altar of the Trinity of the Cardoni—this is the name of
the pair of donors kneeling in the foreground—in the second bay of the
left aisle near the pulpit. It was rediscovered there about 1860 behind
an altarpiece by Vasari and was transferred to its present, fairly disad-
vantageous place.[37]

---

Cardoni who died in 1438 presented to his convent. Giuseppe Richa, S.J., who reports
this gift, mentions in addition a rich bronze cross decorated with enamels that came to
Santa Maria Novella as a donation from the city, probably at the time of the Council, but
it has been lost since then. See *Notizie istoriche delle chiese fiorentine*, 10 vols. (Florence,
1754-1762), 3:46.

[36] See Vasari-Milanesi, 2:520. See also the inventory of the confraternity, which around
the middle of the fifteenth century numbered close to three hundred members as reported
by Mesnil (*RA*, 1904, pp. 68ff.). Also in storage at the Uffizi (Magazine of the Archebusieri)
is a large Man of Sorrows, surrounded by instruments of the Passion, transferred from
Santa Maria Novella in 1867; the very beautiful head recalls somewhat Lorenzo Monaco
and the early works of Fra Angelico. This panel is also equipped with crowning and base
pieces.

[37] Anonimo Magliabecchiano, *Il Codice Magliabecchiano*, ed. K. Frey (Berlin, 1892), p.
81; Vasari-Milanesi, 2:291; James Wood Brown, *The Dominican Church of Santa Maria
Novella* (Edinburgh, 1902), p. 118. The altar patronage of the Cardoni and their donation
of a wall painting for this altar are related to the circumstance that around this time a Fra
Lorenzo Cardoni who died in 1438 belonged to the convent of Santa Maria Novella. On
the former Cardoni altar Vasari also saw the small wooden crucifix now preserved in the
sacristy, which Maso di Bartolommeo carved for it, probably about 1450.

An especially appreciative judge and perhaps even promotor of Masaccio's experiments
with the representation of perspective could be found in an inhabitant of the convent of
Santa Maria Novella at that time, Fra Ubertino Strozzi, who as a famous mathematician
was also concerned with the rules of linear perspective. This is according to Vincenzo
Marchese, O. P., *Memorie dei piu insigni pittori, scultori e architettori Domenicani*, 4th
ed. 2 vols. (Bologna, 1878-1879), 1:312. [*Translator's note*: Masaccio's *Trinity* fresco has
since been restored to its original position on the left nave wall. See the Translator's
Introduction, pp. xxiii-xxiv.]

Finally, a more important fresco cycle, also distinguished by perspectival and other advances falls into this period: the Old Testament murals by Uccello in the first cloister of the convent, which was called the Chiostro Verde after these scenes painted only in green earth. Beginning about the mid-1430s, Uccello painted the first scenes of the story of Creation here and, subsequently about ten years later, the more developed representations of the Flood as well as Noah's sacrifice and mocking in the same wing adjoining the church. The continuation of the pictorial narrative in the two other arms of the cloister is, in spite of their very retardataire and workmanlike painting technique, probably to be dated scarcely earlier than the beginning of the cycle judging by the subjects of Uccello's Creation scenes. Evidently the whole commission, for greater speed, was given contemporaneously to several workshops of unequal quality.

For sculptural work of the second quarter of the century, two famous tombs may be named at the outset: the iconic bronze tablet that Ghiberti executed for the order general Leonardo Dati, already mentioned repeatedly as a donor, around 1425 (it lay originally in the middle of the monks' choir before the crossing, but now is before the high altar). Then the wall tomb of the patriarch of Constantinople, who came to Florence as leader of the eastern delegation to the Council of Union, was set up in the right transept. In contrast to Ghiberti's tomb relief of fifteen years earlier, it exemplifies the transitional style that continued for a long time in ordinary workshops.[38]

Around the same time, however, an important work of sculpture found a place in the same church: the carved wood nude crucifix by Brunelleschi executed—according to Vasari's anecdote—as an idealistic reply to Donatello's cross for Santa Croce, but in reality probably completed thirty years later than that.[39]

As an architect, Brunelleschi in 1443 furnished the model for the stone pulpit on which his adoptive son Andrea Cavalcanti-Buggiano executed the four relief scenes up to 1448 (RA, 3, 1905, pp. 77ff.).

The erection of this pulpit structure occasioned an unusual controversy, fairly characteristic of an attitude of the time. The pulpit, donated by the Rucellai, had to be affixed to a pier which, together with the vaulted bay it was part of, had been erected with building funds from the Minerbetti.

[38] The standing portrait of the deceased, painted under the aedicule, was probably executed by a mediocre Byzantine painter who accompanied the delegation (RA, 1909, p. 117, with illustrations).

[39] It received its present place in the Gondi chapel only in the seventeenth century; up to Vasari's time and probably already from the beginning it hung between the two chapels of the right transept.

This family had since then claimed patronage over this section, which their arms painted there proclaimed publicly. The archbishop, whom the contending parties called in as arbiter, made the Solomonic judgment that the Minerbetti had either to donate a pulpit at least as beautiful for the pier in question or to renounce their rights. Naturally the Rucellai donation got the place that it still retains today and where it still serves its function after almost five hundred years.[40]

The construction and conclusion of the marble facade followed the erection of the pulpit as the most important architectural undertaking of the third quarter-century. This was a donation of Giovanni Rucellai, who thus impressively proclaimed, up to the present day, the more-than-century-old bond between his family, dwelling in the nearby Via della Vigna Nuova, and the Dominicans of Santa Maria Novella.

Since the mid-fourteenth century the Rucellai possessed the stately chapel, which still bears their name, at the east end of the transept of Santa Maria Novella. Its floor was raised to correspond to the old Strozzi chapel at the other end of the transept in 1464 at the instigation of a member of the convent at that time, Fra Andrea Rucellai. As his family's agent, he had already previously attended to the erection of the pulpit and afterwards to the restoration of the small All Saints chapel, likewise of the Rucellai, in the lower story of the Campanile and had had the small holy water basin, decorated with arms, set up before the entrance where it still exists.[41]

Giovanni Rucellai, however, who set his mind on the facade construction immediately after his family's pulpit donation, began first of all to make sure of the considerable amount of money necessary for it. This was done through the establishment of a building fund, into which the whole yield of his estate at Poggio a Caiano—which was later acquired by Lorenzo Magnifico and furnished with an imposing villa—was to flow from 1448 on under the notarial control of the money-changers' guild.

[40] See Raimondo Diaccini, *La Basilica di S. Maria Novella* (Florence, 1920) p. 46. The old-fashioned trecentesque leafwork on the front side of its steps suggests that before the Rucellai donation an older stone pulpit existed there, whose steps were reused.

[41] The old, patriarchal, familial relationship of the Rucellai to the Dominican convent is also clearly illustrated by the testamentary donation of a Bencivenni Rucellai that provided for an annual festive meal for the conventuals at a cost of fifteen *lire* on the day of St. Catherine, to whom the family chapel was dedicated, and by the splendid wedding feast for five members and relatives of the house that was held toward the end of the fourteenth century in the large cloister of the convent: "per modo che tutto il chiostro era apparecchiato intorno intorno con suoni balli e canti." This was reported, based on his grandmother's oral account, by Giovanni Rucellai in the *Zibaldone*, his family book compiled around 1460 to 1470 (in *Un mercante fiorentino e la sua famiglia nel secolo XV*, ed. Giovanni Marcotti, Florence, 1881, pp. 57-59).

So much money was thus already accumulated after eight years that construction work could begin in 1456 and reach its conclusion in 1470 after another fourteen years.

The facade design was provided by Leon Battista Alberti, who had already built the family palace. It retained the older revetment of the lower level and brought this section into harmony with the newly constructed pediment front. It must, however, appear more characteristic for the ambitious patronage of the late Quattrocento, asserting itself ever more forcefully, that this church facade was not only provided with the arms of the Rucellai; rather the full name of the donor in gigantic letters fills the frieze band under the pediment, as if this structure had been erected to honor not so much the Mother of God as the personal fame and memory of the builder.

Two years after the completion of the facade structure there occurred a strange miraculous event involving children playing in the outer cemetery along the side of the church. It occasioned the construction of a stately chapel building in a corner of this cemetery in front of the east arm of the transept to roof over an old image of Mary set up at a wall tomb there, which had asked the children in 1472 to purify it of dirt and spider webs. This subsequently named Madonna della Pura was surrounded within the chapel by a beautiful marble tabernacle which finally in the nineteenth century was widened into a continuous columned passage. All this happened around the middle of the 1470s at the instigation and expense of the Ricasoli whose arms appear on the exterior walls of the chapel as well as in various places in the interior.

Finally, for the history of the convent buildings in this period, mention should be made of the luxurious ball that the young Lorenzo de' Medici organized in 1465 with some friends in the papal apartment to honor the beautiful wife of Niccolò Ardinghelli.[42]

The proportions and formal details of the wide-spanned column arcades in the upper story of the large cloister point to their construction in the last quarter of the Quattrocento; building reports are lacking.

The church interior of Santa Maria Novella received all sorts of additions to its supply of monuments during this period. Specifically the tomb of Beata Villana, who died in 1370, was installed first of all from 1451 to 1452. It survives today only in somewhat reduced extent and in a place up front in the east aisle assigned to it only recently. The tomb had already been donated ten years earlier by a namesake of the Blessed, the widow of a Stoldo di Lorenzo, and was executed only now by Ber-

---

[42] A report on this is in the letters of Alessandra Strozzi to her son living in exile. See Alessandra Macinghi degli Strozzi, *Lettere di una gentildonna Fiorentina nel secolo XV*, ed. C. *Guasti* (Florence, 1877), p. 575.

nardo Rossellino.[43] The original position of the fine terra-cotta bust of another Florentine holy man from the Dominican order, as well as that of his grave, is uncertain. This was the Archbishop Antonino, already generally revered during his lifetime, whose tomb certainly received its place in the church soon after his death in 1459, not just after his canonization in 1522.[44]

Of altarpieces from this period, two works of middling quality from the Rucellai chapel of St. Catherine have recently been hung in the left aisle: a triptych of three saints by a follower of Castagno and an Annunciation by Neri di Bicci. On the other hand, Santa Maria Novella had another, much more valuable painting, Botticelli's *Adoration of the Kings* with portraits of the Medici and their circle, already lost around the end of the sixteenth century.* Painted around 1475-1476 (in any case before the Pazzi conspiracy) on commission for Gaspare del Lama, it was placed in a marble altar structure on the left near the central portal, where Masaccio's fresco of the Trinity is now. A lunette picture of the Nativity could be found in that place until 1867, however; it was subsequently moved to the interior tympanum of the main portal. This was a youthful work of Botticelli, according to Carlo Gamba, who asserts that it was already set up there before the arrival of Botticelli's panel of the Three Kings, perhaps to crown an earlier altar.[45]

A great new enterprise began in the 1480s with the Tornabuoni's commission to Ghirlandaio for the new decoration of the Capella Maggiore.

The Tornabuoni succeeded in acting as donors here in spite of the older conflicting patronage claims of two other houses. How this came about must be briefly noted as a characteristic example of patronage practices.

[43] As a crowning element, instead of the otherwise customary Madonna, a large old crucifix was set up—probably the noble carved work of about 1300, now installed in the Cappella della Pura—which Rossellino was to frame with a marble tabernacle. The inscription on the base names the two confraternities of Gesù Pellegrino and del Tempio that were especially concerned with the memory of the Blessed Villana and thus had also probably taken the chief action for the construction of her tomb (see Richa *Notizie*, 3:51; and *RA*, 1904, p. 70). The Compagnia di Gesù Pellegrino held an annual pilgrimage, by statute, to the burial place of the Blessed (Richa, *Notizie*, 3: 103-104).

[44] The church also possessed or received in 1466 a relic of a finger of another saint of the order from earlier times, St. Peter Martyr, patron of another confraternity associated with Santa Maria Novella. This confraternity, on an agreement with the prior of the convent, donated a wrought silver reliquary to display it appropriately.

* *Translator's note*: The Botticelli *Adoration of the Magi* in question is now in the Uffizi Gallery.

[45] Also designed by Botticelli, according to Vasari, were the many-figured scenes embroidered in silk on vellum, since lost, with which the processional cross of Santa Maria Novella was customarily draped.

During the Trecento a bipartite patronage had existed in the *cappella maggiore*. Since distant times the chapel space as a whole had belonged to the Ricci, who had earlier arranged for its painting with frescoes by Nardo di Cione. The Sassetti took over the high altar and had the large retable executed by Ugolino da Siena. This patronage right was expressly reaffirmed by Francesco Sassetti in 1469 when he determined not only to replace the high altarpiece with a new, more modern one, but also to have the dilapidated and unsightly wall paintings of the chapel renewed at his own expense. The project was thwarted, however, because Sassetti's intention to have painted the legend of his name patron St. Francis of Assisi instead of the previously existing picture cycle of the life of Mary and the Baptist was not acceptable to the Dominicans. The negotiations finally led to such a sharp dissension that in the mid-1470s Sassetti withdrew completely from Santa Maria Novella and erected the still-surviving family chapel in Santa Trinita and also retained the tomb monument of his father, already prepared for Santa Maria Novella, for use elsewhere. The Dominicans were left with only a set of costly gold brocade chapel vestments donated by Francesco for feast day masses at the high altar.[46]

In place of the Sassetti there now arrived, however, the house of the Tornabuoni-Tornaquinci, related by marriage to the Medici. Their chief, Giovanni Tornabuoni, also took upon himself the double project of Francesco Sassetti for a new high altar and a new wall painting, but without making special demands regarding the pictures' subject matter. He even soothed the envy of the old chapel owner the Ricci who lacked the means for the necessary renovation of the paintings (if the amusing anecdote reported by Vasari is founded on a genuine tradition) by pledging to have their Ricci arms set up "in a more honorable and important place" even in the new chapel decoration. How he subsequently fulfilled this clause, quite correctly according to the text, but in effect not at all as the other party to the contract had intended, may be read in Vasari.[47]

Thus in the years from 1485 to 1490 the great wall-painting cycle was produced, in whose execution, along with Domenico's independent assistants, his brother Davide, and others, the boy Michelangelo also participated as a beginning apprentice before his transition to sculpture.

For the general work program, a complete renewal of the old picture cycle with all previously existing scenes had evidently been desired. Only

[46] See Aby Warburg, *Gesammelte Schriften*, ed. Bing and Rougemont, 2 vols. (Leipzig, 1932), 1:136ff. On Sassetti see below.

[47] Cinelli in 1677 still saw the Ricci arms, placed in a tiny version on the sacrament tabernacle (Bocchi-Cinelli, *Le bellezze della citta*, p. 247). Vasari-Milanesi, 3:260ff. and Gaetano Milanesi, *Nuovi documenti per la storia dell' arte toscana . . .* (Florence, 1901), documents 134, 158.

thus is the rather archaic-looking arrangement of no less than four bands of pictures, one above the other with two scenes next to each other on each wall surface conceivable for this period.

Much more modern in the style and taste of the late Quattrocento was the composition of the individual pictures. In these the actual subject matter and meaning were completely overshadowed by the panoply of rich architectural or landscape scenery and by the patron's purely worldly, egotistical desire to introduce all possible portrait figures from his circle of friends and relations, whose broad deployment now often pushed the biblical proceedings completely into the background.[48]

With these peculiarities—which admittedly accord very well with Vasari's abovementioned anecdote—Ghirlandaio's fresco cycle appears as a thoroughly characteristic illustration of the change in manner of expression and form that prevailed in the second part of the early Renaissance, even in church painting. Yet how far removed already in precisely this direction was Botticelli's altarpiece of the Three Kings, with the portrait figures of the Medici and others in the foreground, from Masaccio's painting of the Trinity produced fifty years earlier! In the Masaccio, in spite of the very lively realism of the donor portraits and the painted architecture, a religious bearing and expression still completely dominated the overall effect. Ghirlandaio's murals, however, now represented, in their presentation of sacred stories, the emphatically secularized culture, the hedonistic, self-assured, and self-satisfied disposition of the Florentine patriciate in the last years of Lorenzo Magnifico, as they also received their classic formulation in the completion inscription by Poliziano for the fresco cycle (in the Zacharias picture).[49]

The execution of the great fresco work cost Tornabuoni 1000 florins, but completed only half of his total plan. There followed in 1491 the stained glass in the three great windows, also designed by Ghirlandaio, and executed by the glasspainter Alessandro Agolanti, otherwise active at the Duomo. At the same time Ghirlandaio also received the commission for the new high altarpiece, an imposing retable painted on both sides, which retained its place on the altar until 1804 when it was dismantled and sold off, its main sections reaching the state galleries of Munich and Berlin.[50]

[48] These portrait heads were named in 1561 in a record by Benedetto di Luca Landucci, at that time in his nineties, who in his youth allegedly knew most of those portrayed (Vasari-Milanesi, 3:266n.).

[49] "An. MCCCLXXX, quo pulcherrima civitas opibus victoriis artibus aedificiisque nobilis copia salubritate pace perfruebatur" (Vasari-Milanesi, 3:261n.). See also Landucci's *Diario* for the citation of the completion date of the paintings: 22 December 1490.

[50] Munich possesses the front side of the altar work with a Madonna in glory and several saints. Berlin has the former back side, with the ascension of Christ and individual saints on the wings (the formerly existing predella, with legend scenes by Granacci, has vanished).

Domenico Ghirlandaio died in 1494 during the execution of this great project and was buried in Santa Maria Novella, where he had primarily been active during the whole last decade of his life. His brothers and other workshop members who had already collaborated extensively in the painting of the chapel completed the altarpiece by 1496. The frame and altar tabernacle came from Baccio d'Agnolo, who in the period following 1490 had already executed the wall benches running around the choir with their intarsia and carved decoration.

The costly *spalliere* remained in place when a pew with two rows of folding seats was installed here during construction of the monks' choir in the chapel after 1570. The total impression of the chapel space was impaired, however, less by this installation than by the neo-Gothic marble structure of 1857 that so obtrusively blocks the view into the choir area.

The conclusion of the Tornabuoni patronage activity had extended beyond the general turning point following the collapse of Medici rule in the year of Ghirlandaio's death in 1494. Shortly before this juncture, however, another artistically significant chapel decoration was under way in Santa Maria Novella. This was in the first transept chapel adjoining the *cappella maggiore* on the right, which Filippo Strozzi had acquired for his family in 1486 from the impoverished former owners, the Boni, and which he thereupon also undertook to refurbish. Already in April 1487 he commissioned Filippino Lippi for the spendid painting of this space, which still exists. It was surely begun soon, but subsequently finished only after 1500, after long interruptions due to other demands on the artist.[51]

Filippo's tomb, on the rear wall of the chapel, was designed only just before his death on 18 May 1491; its execution by Benedetto da Maiano followed probably in the next two or three years.

The art history of Santa Maria Novella appears in its events up to now to be stimulated and determined by the patronage, increasingly directed toward worldly fame, of certain patrician and bourgeois families. As opposed to this, the solicitude of the city authorities and guilds, which played such a significant role at the Duomo, intervened only occasionally.

On the other hand, a few summarizing words should still be devoted to the existence, not art historically insignificant, of the various religious confraternities that were associated since distant times with the great monastic orders and whose patronage at Santa Maria Novella has already been mentioned here and there. No less than seventeen such congregations

[51] See the act of acquisition of patronage (3 July 1486) in Raimondo Diaccini, *La Basilica di S. Maria Novella* (Florence, 1920), p. 29. The considerable payments that Filippino already drew in 1489 and his letter to Strozzi of May 1489 suggest all sorts of work must already have been produced at that time. See Alfred Scharf, *Filippino Lippi* (Vienna, 1935), pp. 88, 90-91.

occasionally existed contemporaneously at Santa Maria Novella, of which eight still remained in Richa's time (around 1760; Richa, *Notizie*, 2:102ff.).

Among these, as the two most strongly developed already in the fourteenth and fifteenth centuries, were the Compagnia di Gesù Pellegrino and that of St. Peter Martyr. These confraternities had their individual assembly halls or oratories on land immediately adjacent to Santa Maria Novella, sometimes in complex installations with chapel, auxiliary rooms, and small arcaded courts. This was primarily behind the transept, still adjoined by the great convent garden until the construction of the old railroad station and the square in front of it. Two such oratories lay on the outer side of the nave, near the Pura chapel; certain smaller confraternities had obtained a lodging in various small rooms of the convent buildings themselves. It goes without saying that each of these oratories also possessed its religious art works donated by the brotherhood collectively for the decoration of their altar or by individual members due to a special occasion for devotion. Among these, along with modest pieces of popular style, were surely also many of high artistic value.[52]

The last section of the art history of Santa Maria Novella begins with the installation of the sovereign citizen regime in 1494 and ends with the collapse of the Florentine free state. Of architectural production from this period we can name only the arcaded court erected in 1505 behind the former gatehouse (now a fire station), as well as the interior decoration of the Gondi chapel in severe high classical forms executed in 1503 by Giuliano da Sangallo on commission from Giuliano Gondi as the new patron.

But the additions of sculptural works number only a few. Of these,

---

[52] A few older works from among these were mentioned in passing above; I have come across the following works formerly belonging to confraternities from the second half of the Renaissance period: for the Oratory of the Compagnia di San Lorenzo in Palco situated over the passage between the Chiostro Verde and the forecourt, Domenico Ghirlandaio painted a no longer traceable altarpiece. A panel painted by Davide Ghirlandaio in 1494 for the former altar of the St. Peter Martyr brothers, with St. Lucia and the donor Fra Domenico Cortese, is now found in the left aisle of the church; a panel that Antonio Fantozzi still saw on a pier in the transept, as a remnant of an altar of the Divine Pilgrim, has vanished. See *Nuova Guida di Firenze* (Florence, 1842), p. 515.

In the inventory of the Compagnia di Gesù Pellegrino we read of two no longer traceable Robbia works, a Madonna tabernacle by Luca and a relief of the Divine Pilgrim of 1475, probably by Andrea della Robbia. The great, colorfully glazed relief composition by Giovanni della Robbia, now displayed in the Chiostro de' Morti, presumably came from one of the confraternity oratorios since destroyed, if not from the former convent garden. See Richa, *Notizie*, 3:104; Vasari-Milanesi, 6:532; *MA*, 1903, p. 70; Vincenzio Fineschi, *Memorie sopra il cimiterio . . . di S. Maria Novella*, Florence, 1787, pp. 30, 95; and *Dedalo* 11, 1930-1931, p. 86.

the splendid sacristy fountain, which Giovanni della Robbia executed in
1497 as one of his first independent works, should be mentioned at the
outset.[53]

As for painting, the painted decoration of Filippo Strozzi's chapel
should again be recalled. This, together with the stained glass window
also executed according to Filippino's design, belongs indeed by commission and beginning of work to the much more active period around
1490, but was for the most part executed only around 1500 to 1502.

After the stylistically related sacristy fountain of Andrea della Robbia,
this work of Filippino's old age appears as a last, most extreme embodiment of late quattrocentesque taste. In refined realism of detail and
unbridled decorative splendor it goes far beyond the suppression of religious content already carried so far in Ghirlandaio's pictures. It is a
very characteristic manifestation of that spirit of the age against which
Savonarola had begun to declaim in the early 1490s and which finally
brought his own destruction shortly after this art work was begun in
Santa Maria Novella.* Yet his sermons helped to prepare the way for
a revolution in the whole manner of artistic expression. This revolution
made its immediate and decisive appearance right after the completion
of the Strozzi chapel, and also, first of all, again within the confines of
Santa Maria Novella, although without relation to this church. Scarcely
a year after Filippino's painting scaffolds were taken down, the necessary
arrangements were made in the great hall of the papal quarters for Leonardo da Vinci to work on the cartoon for the great mural on the battle
of Anghiari assigned to him in the Palazzo Vecchio.

Here, in the papal room at the large cloister of Santa Maria Novella,
where Leonardo also had a room assigned to him with his own access
broken through to the hall, the great working drawing was begun in the
winter of 1503-1504. It remained hanging there for a long period, much
sought out and studied by young artists as a model pointing the way to
the new style.[54]

For the visit of Pope Leo X in 1515 the hall was decorated (probably

---

[53] The richly decorated organ balustrade, executed perhaps around 1500 by Baccio
d'Agnolo, fell victim to the gothicizing restoration beginning in 1857 and afterwards came
to the South Kensington Museum in London.

Still extant, however, are the two mediocre marble tombs by Silvio Cosini, one for
Antonio Strozzi in 1523 and one for a Minerbetti in 1530, the latter formerly located near
the family altar against the choir enclosure as well as the antique sarcophagus, a reused
work of the thirteenth century, that Bernardo Rucellai had erected probably about 1510
as a tomb for his ancestor Paolo above the staircase of the family chapel.

* Translator's note: On Savonarola and Florentine art see the recent literature cited in
Translator's Introduction, p. xv.

[54] See the observations of October 1503 in Vasari-Milanesi, 4:43n; Albertini, in his brief
notes of 1510 on what was worth seeing at Santa Maria Novella also mentions the cartoon
hung in the Sala del Papa. See Francesco Albertini, Memoriale di molte statue e picture

only temporarily) according to designs by Bandinelli; the adjoining *ca-pella belissima*, as Albertini already calls it, was newly decorated just at that time with frescoes, still partially extant, by Ridolfo Ghirlandaio, Feltrini, and the young Pontormo.[55]

Of other painted work executed for Santa Maria Novella in this period, I can cite only an anonymous Madonna fresco in the forecourt of the Chiostro Verde, as well as a no longer surviving lunette picture that Franciabigio placed over the entrance to the convent library, and Bugiardini's great altarpiece, *The Martyrdom of St. Catherine*, donated by Palla Rucellai for the family chapel where it still has its place. With these, all artistic holdings that accrued to the church and convent buildings in general during the period from 1495 to 1530 have been named. We may assume that the contributions of the most recently past period still most readily found favor at the time of Vasari's *sistemazione* and that, in any case, in his records and those of his nearest predecessors, no works of the High Renaissance that were in any way noteworthy are omitted.

But in Santa Maria Novella, as opposed to the Duomo and San Giovanni, the curve of activity in this period sank almost to zero. This indicates that private zeal for patronage, to which this church owed so many and such significant monuments throughout the whole fifteenth century, had henceforth, so far as it still remained active in general, turned to other convent churches such as Annunziata and San Marco. It is indeed possible that the evident decline in monastic discipline in the convent of Santa Maria Novella, and its particularly agitated and vehement opposition, for precisely that reason, to Savonarola, were conducive to further and further withdrawal of the respect the convent had previously enjoyed and, with it, of the faithful's former willingness to donate.[56]

Be that as it may, in any case the period of the mature High Renaissance added virtually nothing to the total picture of this church interior, which accordingly remained preserved up to Vasari's time in the essential condition and appearance that it had acquired through the patron activity of the fifteenth century.

In conclusion we may attempt to evoke this total picture, as it may have appeared around the middle of the Cinquecento, in a summarizing overview:

What we find today since the reorganization carried out by Vasari as

---

*della citta di Firenze*, 1st ed., 1510, in J. A. Crowe and G. B. Cavalcaselle, *Geschichte der italienischen Malerei*, ed. M. Jordan, Leipzig, 1869, vol. 2., appendix. The same hall later served Piero di Cosimo for the secret work on his design for the "Triumph of Death" that he staged, probably for the carnival of 1510 (Vasari-Milanesi, 4:137).

[55] Vasari-Milanesi, 4:137ff.; 5:25 n. 3; 6:255; Heinrich Bodmer, in *Kunstchronik*, 1930, p. 11.

[56] Pope Leo X issued severe decrees against the degenerated discipline of the monks of Santa Maria Novella (see Schnitzer, *Savonarola*, 1:64).

well as the puristic neo-Gothic restoration around 1860 is a spacious,
clearly comprehensible interior organization with the most homogeneous
possible arrangement and development of all elements of the decoration.
This, however, is the complete opposite of the former condition, which
must probably have been regarded already in the High Renaissance as
no longer quite satisfying and in the Mannerist period as downright
intolerable.

First of all, as the most prominent feature, there was the massive
structure of the choir enclosure with all its paraphernalia of altars and
tombs cutting across the view down the nave. Altars and tombs also
appeared everywhere throughout the whole church space in planless as-
symmetrical distribution and variety of form. This was true primarily
along the outer walls of the aisles as well as against certain piers of the
central nave and in the transepts where finally the individual chapels
were grouped as particularly richly outfitted separate rooms. The church
was thus a remarkably richly branching, multipartite organism, whose
teeming abundance of forms was thoroughly entwined and interwoven
with no less rich a variety of colors. Above the fundamental harmony
of the already somewhat faded Gothic wall paintings, which probably
also covered the greater part of the aisle walls at that time, the fresh
melodic line of the altarpieces and individual frescoes of the Quattrocento, interspersed here and there, resounded brightly. To this were added
everywhere the coats of arms of donors and the banners or other memorial objects draped on many tombs. Finally the works of decorative
sculpture displayed a variety of polychrome embellishment and gilding.
What an effect this lavishly orchestrated polyphony must have produced,
especially in the homogeneous ensemble of the Tornabuoni *capella maggiore* and the adjoining Strozzi chapel in the time immediately after their
completion! The appearance of its present condition, fragmentary and
indistinct, gives only a dim suggestion of the original costly splendor of
this space. And the jumble of forms and colors in the total picture of the
church interior remains wholly inconceivable, as does the significance,
functional as it were and vitally active, that was once attached to all the
places of devotion and remembrance assembled in it, from the various
private masses and other family religious ceremonies often celebrated at
the different altars, the public pilgrimages, the offerings of candles and
the like from authorities and corporations at the tombs of particularly
honored saints, to the solemn final act of the Corpus Christi procession
in Santa Maria Novella which assembled the whole city.[57]

[57] The old custom of ending the procession here was confirmed by the Signoria for the
convent in 1425, rejecting opposing wishes of the Duomo chapter and expressly recognizing
the Signoria's duty to attend.

We also hear of annual religious spectacles in Santa Maria Novella, like in three other Florentine churches, on certain feast days. Specifically there was a play here in honor of the martyr bishop St. Ignatius of Antioch, for whose altar in the left aisle the above mentioned silver reliquary bust was created.

## THE PALAZZO VECCHIO

Most of the enterprises of the Duomo workshop, like those for the Opera of San Giovanni, stemmed from the initiative of the citizens and the organs they set in action for this purpose. Religious devotion and municipal pride in a unique interaction effected a continuing and sometimes very generous deployment of resources.

This civic character found a still more direct and exclusive expression. This was in the projects, a great part of which were actually carried out, for the renovation and expansion, furnishing and embellishment of the Palazzo della Signoria, the seat of the highest official bodies, during the last century of republican self-government.

It is true that little of this remains to be seen in the building's present aspect. The original structure of this lordly residence of the Signoria, a monumental expression of the character of the Florentine republic in the time of Dante, has survived in its core substance, even with its striking civic architectural preeminence. The ceremonial hall of the loggia, added in the Trecento, wide open to the piazza, has survived along with it. But even the exterior aspect of the medieval group of buildings underwent a marked change through the imposing new creations placed immediately next to it in the third quarter of the sixteenth century. These included Ammanati's large fountain with statues and the giant administrative building of the Uffizi, henceforth dominating the prospect between the palace and the loggia in place of the small Romanesque church of San Piero Scheraggio and a narrow cluster of simple bourgeois houses. Still more radical was the renovation, carried out at the same time, of the former palace of the Signoria for the purposes of Cosimo I's princely court. This renovation suppressed almost everything that previous centuries had created here, especially in the interior layout and decoration of the building.[58]

Accordingly, for the Palazzo Vecchio much more than for the church buildings discussed, we must depend on contemporary accounts, by all

---

[58] The last to go, only in 1810, was the broad stone platform in front of the palace, the so-called *ringhiera*, where the Signoria and its advisers took their places on great public occasions of state. Its balustrade bore the monumental art works of political symbolic significance, which now still stand on the low stepped platform and are visible in many old illustrations. See *RA*, 1910, plate on p. 42.

means fairly plentiful, in order to survey and imagine what was created during the Renaissance.[59]

The Renaissance artistic sense and treatment of form seem to have set in only relatively late for the central seat of the city government. At first, up to about the middle of the century, this involved only small furnishings for the completion of the old contents. Thus in 1416, as a first work of statuary, Donatello's marble *David* was requested from the Duomo workshop for the Palazzo della Signoria and set up there in the audience hall in front of a niche painted with lily patterns on a brightly colored mosaic base.[60]

Several painters, including Giuliano Pesello and Fra Filippo Lippi, were also entrusted with commissions for the palace in the second quarter of the fifteenth century. But only a lunette of the Annunciation by an anonymous artist of about 1430 can still be found there, above the upper exit of a staircase that is now walled up.[61]

Securely traceable, but also no longer in Florence, are the two *sopraporte* that Fra Filippo executed in 1447 for the chancellor's office: one of a St. Bernard before the Madonna in London at the National Gallery and the other of the Annunciation in an American private collection (*Dedalo*, 6, 1925-1926, pp. 553ff.).

As these pictures were set up in the palace, major architectural enterprises for the modernization of the old building were finally at least initiated, but hardly even begun. The courtyard in particular, disfigured by all sorts of amorphous additions, must now have appeared all too inappropriate to the outlook of the time. Thoroughgoing changes demanded far more funds than the current city budget could immediately provide. Thus in 1444, by decree of the Great Council, an extraordinary increment that had come into the city treasury from fines in the amount

[59] Two monographic works in particular, containing especially detailed documentary and other source material, offer a useful basis for this: Aurelio Gotti's voluminous quarto *Storia del Palazzo Vecchio* (Florence, 1889) and the more recent book prepared by the present city curator of monuments, Alfredo Lensi, *Palazzo Vecchio* (Milan, 1929), which also makes good use of the results of restorations directed by Lensi. See also Giulia Sinibaldi, *Palazzo Vecchio di Firenze* (Rome, 1934).

[60] A marble container was subsequently acquired for the golden rose bestowed by the pope on the palace chapel in 1419. See Richa, *Notizie*, 3:35.

[61] See the illustration in Lensi, *Palazzo Vecchio*, p. 21. Pesello's *Epiphany*, which hung halfway up the staircase (Vasari-Milanesi, 3:36), and probably be identified with a picture in the Uffizi (no. 26). Fra Filippo's *Nunziata*, which also had a place in the staircase, has vanished (Magliabecchiano-Frey, *Il codice*, p. 96).

On the other hand, the Madonna picture that Fra Filippo (according to Vasari-Milanesi, 2:65) was to paint for the meeting room of the eight-man college is identified by Mendelsohn in *Fra Filippo Lippi* (Berlin, 1909) with the picture in Palazzo Riccardi and by Raimond van Marle in *The Development of the Italian Schools of Painting*, 19 vols. (The Hague, 1923-1938), 10:420, with the Berlin Madonna.

of 6000 florins exacted from a group of Jewish usurers was released for construction work on the palace. At the same time, a special commission of five Operai, including Cosimo de' Medici, was set up for the administration and supervision of this work. Yet this commission does not appear to have gotten beyond preliminary consultations, and the building funds allotted to it were claimed in the meantime for other more pressing needs of the civic economy.[62]

A really thorough renovation in the palace, still recognizable and reliably attested to by the present condition of the structure, began only around the middle of the 1450s under the direction of Michelozzo. That architect, as a protégé of Cosimo and builder of his palace, must have seemed the worker with the best recommendation.[63] Renovations—which Vasari (Vasari-Milanesi, 2:434ff.) describes in some detail, based on intimate acquaintance with the building which he later renovated himself— were undertaken in 1454 and 1455, then slowly continued, and finally gave the inner courtyard a whole new appearance. Of this, the round-arch biforium windows of the upper story and its finely profiled cornice articulation have survived.[64]

The stucco encasement of the arcade pillars, executed on the ground floor in 1565 on the occasion of the marriage of the heir to the throne, added a strange note. And the outer staircase, which originally provided access to the first story as in the Bargello today and which was retained and renovated in the Renaissance form by Michelozzo, was removed by Vasari in 1561. But it was Michelozzo who opened up the arcade passage, which had been largely closed off by temporary dividing walls to provide quarters for the individual offices. In the process, Arnolfo's pillars, partially crumbling, had to be renewed and now received an alternating columnar and polygonal form with Renaissance capitals.[65]

The building committee newly installed in February 1454 was specifically assigned with the *reaptatio* of the lower part of the building. But only a meager sum from the tax revenues was initially allotted to fund this. No wonder that the work never got under way. In October of the same year the Great Council issued a new provision for the same goal: a special tax that withheld a small portion of the monthly allotment of all salaried employees of the communal government. The Operai, how-

[62] What Antonio Manetti in *Vita di Filippo Brunelleschi*, ed. Holtzinger (Stuttgart, 1887), p. 9 and Vasari indicate about Brunelleschi's construction work on the Palazzo Vecchio is very unclear and contradictory; contemporary reports on this are nonexistent.

[63] The bell that tolled the hours on the Palazzo della Signoria was also newly cast by him in 1448 (Lensi, *Palazzo Vecchio*, p. 58).

[64] Only the painted pattern of ornamental squares and heraldic lilies on the walls has disappeared since the French period (1809). See Lensi, *Palazzo Vecchio*, pp. 56-59.

[65] See Fabriczy in *JPK*, 25, suppl., pp. 58-59, 99-101.

ever, were at the same time obliged, through high penalties for breach of contract, to complete the removal of all the walling-up in the arcades within half a year "ut lodia (loggia) remaneat magis expedita et honorata pro magnificentia palatii."[66]

Contemporary reports are lacking on the work on the core structure of the palace, which probably developed only very slowly on account of the drop-by-drop financing. According to Vasari, after the restoration of the arcades the walls above them were rebuilt in a somewhat lighter structure and decorated with the aforementioned window articulation. The interior reorganization of this upper story went on at the same time with an arrangement of private rooms for the Signori instead of the previous common sleeping hall for these highest city officials and with the installation of the interior staircase, for whose entrance Michelozzo set up a beautiful portal with capitals he carved personally. Various ingenious provisions were also made for the water supply, etc.

Vasari relates this much about the renovation work that at first probably resulted in little more than temporary uses of the newly built rooms. Only in the recently uncovered mezzanine story, near remains of older decorations, can certain ceilings and wall decorations in Michelozzo's style be found.

In addition, a few particular pieces of work from this period are recorded: in 1453 the gilded wrought iron lion with the lily in its paws, first set up fifty years earlier above the tower, was replaced.

Its stone-sculptured counterpart below on the *ringhiera* in front of the palace seems also to have been erected or restored at that time. For the splendid marble base, which now bears Donatello's *marzocco* (transferred here in 1810 from the convent of Santa Maria Novella), can be assigned to the 1450s by its style. Together with this, however, comes another undertaking for the decoration of the *ringhiera* that can be specifically traced to the year 1453: the preparation of a costly wall hanging that was placed on the palace wall behind the benches of the high college on the platform for festive occasions. This was a masterpiece of Netherlandish tapestry weaving with figural representations whose striking truth to nature is stressed in a contemporary document. It was executed by Livino di Giglio of Bruges, living in Florence, from whom the Signoria also commissioned 1300 cubic feet of simple, that is, probably modestly ornamented, wall hangings for the interior rooms of the palace at that time.[67]

[66] The construction or renovation of an open loggia in one of the rear adjoining buildings toward the Via de' Leoni took place also in 1454. And in this case also the formula ran: "pro magnificentia et ornatu palatii Dominorum."

[67] Kauffmann, *Donatello*, p. 208; Lensi, *Palazzo Vecchio*, pp-59-60, Gaye, *Carteggio* 1: 563.

The design for that figured tapestry was assigned to Vittorio Ghiberti, who enlisted the

Also in 1454, a little cupboard in the form of a tabernacle was commissioned to preserve the revered codex of the *Pandects* that the state possessed, as well as the splendid manuscript edition of Leonardo Bruni's history of the city which his son had sold to the Signoria. Neri di Bicci decorated this cupboard with small ornamental figures in gilded architectural settings. It was set up in the audience hall.[68]

Finally, in this particularly productive period of the 1450s, the so-called *mazzieri*, the Signoria's ushers, were provided with silver scepters (*mazze*, hence the title of their bearers). It was also decided to obtain new, more imposing silver tableware for the common household of the Signori. A 1458 inventory gives a brief reckoning for this.[69]

These reports, together with other contemporary measures like the above-noted adornment of the *ringhiera* and the arrangement of private rooms for the Signori instead of their previous monastically unpretentious dormitory, make clear the determination to reinforce the respect and importance of the ruling officials—the Priores Libertatis, as the official title ran since 1459—even through a rise in the level of their living standard and appearance in public.

But it was reserved to the period of Lorenzo Magnifico to provide the new rooms on the second upper stories, constructed, of necessity, very slowly, with such interior furnishings as seemed appropriate to the representative function of these rooms and to the heightened love of splendor of that generation.

To secure the funds necessary for this, a high fine that the state had imposed on the Jew Isaac for serious moral offenses was initially appropriated in April 1469. But this time, too, the sum of more than two thousand florins was handed over for pressing fortification needs a few weeks later, except for a meager remainder for payment for furnishings that had already been delivered. In place of this, however, numerous small, steady sources of income were now established for the construction coffers of the Palazzo della Signoria: portions of expected revenues from fines for the next two years, shares of the yield from grain tariffs, of the returns of the city *mercanzia*, regular monthly remittances from the fortification fund; and in addition to these receipts, amounting to 400 florins

---

collaboration of Neri di Bicci. See the latter's note in his *Ricordi*, 24 January 1454 [1453 st. curr.]. Also see Vasari-Milanesi, 2:86 n. 1; *MA*, 1930, pp. 117-18.

[68] Luca della Robbia had already furnished a *spiritello*, that is, a small figure of an angel, as a *sopraporta* for the saletta of the chancery in 1449, and the sons of the late city chancellor Poggio were permitted to hang the latter's portrait in the same room in 1460. See Gaye, *Carteggio*, 1:559, 560, 565; Neri's *Ricordi* in *Il Vasari*, 1, p. 332; and Lensi, *Palazzo Vecchio*, pp. 58-59.

[69] The *mazze*, which the goldsmith Pier Paolo Tazzi produced in 1454, are probably essentially the ones that still exist today. See Gaye, *Carteggio*, 1:561; Cambi, *Delizie*, 21:321-22; Lensi, *Palazzo Vecchio*, pp. 49-50, 55; and Aurelio Gotti, *Storia del Palazzo Vecchio* (Florence, 1889), pp. 86-87.

per month in all, there came finally the yield of a newly decreed special tax on all foreign tradesmen setting in Florence. All this was done with the expressly stated purpose that the aspect of the new rooms should be appropriate "allo honore di questa citta" (Lensi, *Palazzo Vecchio*, p. 66).

From this time forth we are minutely informed on the progress of this work, the participating forces, and the expenditures by the Operai's account books which have survived in full for the period from 1469 to 1532. One of the first important measures came in 1472: the partitioning of the great hall in the upper story by a dividing wall that was erected on an ingeniously designed support constructed above the room below to create two separate rooms, the subsequent Udienza and the Sala dei Gigli. The director of this work, described in detail by Vasari, was Benedetto da Maiano. The richly ornamented coffered ceilings and the friezes with powerful relief decoration running beneath them in the two new rooms and in the Sala degli Otto (the eight-man college) on the first floor were designed and executed during the 1470s by him and his brother Giuliano, as well as various other masters like Francione, Giovanni da Gaiuole, and the del Tasso brothers. Subsequently, in 1471, and probably still according to Michelozzo's specifications, the lower hall of the Great Council, today called the Hall of the Two Hundred, received its frieze and ceiling decorations.[70]

In the year 1475 the marble portal in the dividing wall of the upper two rooms was also commissioned. It was completed by 1480 with its beautifully articulated frame, the crowning statuary figures of John and Justitia by Benedetto da Maiano and the costly intarsia doors executed by Giuliano and Francione.[71]

Finally, appropriate furniture and panelling had to be provided in the new rooms: payments were made in 1478 to Giovanni da Gaiuole and others for such work and in 1480 to Francesco la Cecca for wall benches in the council hall, whose high backs were to be decorated with intarsia in an architectural framework and a frieze of lilies.[72]

The unusually lively and diverse production that we must envision going on simultaneously throughout the 1470s in various rooms of the palace must of course have made many problems and annoyances for the responsible officials, the Operai. Certain settlements that appeared all

[70] See C. M. von Stegmann and H. A. von Geymüller, *Die Architektur der Renaissance in Toskana*, 11 vols. (Munich, 1885-1908), 2:23; Lensi, *Palazzo Vecchio*, p. 67; Gaye, *Carteggio*, 1:175; Vasari-Milanesi, 2:481; 3:341-42, 350; Fabriczy, *JPK*, 25, suppl., pp. 44, 58, 59.

[71] Vasari-Milanesi, 3:335-36. The complete documentary material on these works is in *RA*, 6, 1909, pp. 156-59.

[72] Further payment entries for the same artists continued into 1485 (Gaye, *Carteggio*, 1: 576; Vasari-Milanesi, 3:206, 211-12; and *JPK*, 24, pp. 142-43). A fragment of this work seems to have survived in the *spalliera* of a later chest-bench in the Sala dei Gigli.

too high for the masters working on the hall ceilings had to be examined and put right by nonpartisan experts in the summer of 1475, and the work foremen were not spared the accusation of insufficient care. The Signori and the Council of One Hundred subsequently issued new, more precise regulations on business dealings for the college of Operai and at the same time adjusted and somewhat increased the funding for the construction (Lensi, *Palazzo Vecchio*, p. 70).

Certain portable works of sculpture and painting that were installed in the Palazzo della Signoria in the last period remain to be cited. These include a bronze candelabrum by Verrocchio in 1468 for the audience tribune in the upper room, at that time still undivided.

The author and W. R. Valentiner, almost simultaneously but independently, rediscovered this bronze candlestick in a hitherto nameless piece in the Berlin Schlossmuseum, which bears the date inscription "Maggio e Giugno 1468" and in its decorative ornaments appears closely related to Verrocchio's Medici tomb in San Lorenzo.[73]

Then it was decided in 1476, in the midst of the intense building and decorative activity that was already occasioning so many continuing expenses, to provide a special grant of 150 florins for the purchase of Verrocchio's bronze statue of David from the Medici in order to install the image on the upper landing of the staircase in front of the so-called Porta della Catena on a marble pedestal decorated with the city arms. This second figure of the symbolic youthful hero was obtained for the palace of the Signoria in addition to Donatello's statue of David that had been there since 1416 (see above). Thus we may recognize in this acquisition a sort of collector's interest in art on the part of the Signoria and in any case a first manifestation of that patron's generosity that evinced itself further in the extensive mural commissions of the next years.

It is true that until then, throughout the 1460s and 1470s, no significant works of painting came into the Palace of the Signoria.[74]

However, in January 1478, a few months before the Pazzi conspiracy when the rooms of the Signoria's palace also witnessed some particularly

[73] See the illustrations in Hermann Lüer, *Kunstgeschichte der unedlen Muetalle*, vol. 1, *Geschichte der Metallkunst* (Stuttgart, 1904-1909), p. 397; and in Valentiner, *BM*, 62, May 1933, pp. 229-31. The inscription date corresponds to the first payment of eight florins in June 1468, which was followed by the remaining forty florins in the following year (Gaye *Carteggio*, 1:569-70, 575). In 1472 Antonio del Pollaiuolo completed a great silver bowl for the Signoria, probably for use at the table on festive occasions (Gaye, *Carteggio*, 1:571).

[74] Only a few small commissions to unimportant painters are named in documents: a Madonna above the door of the Saletta in 1468 by a certain Clemente di Giovanni, a crucifix by Piero di Francesco for twenty *lire* for no precisely determined location (Gaye, *Carteggio*, 1:569, 571, 575).

dramatic and gruesome scenes, we find the record of a painting commission to Leonardo da Vinci. This initially signifies only the introduction of a young talent, still none too prominent at this moment. Yet precisely for this reason it was a noteworthy sign of confidence in this beginner. For what was entrusted to him here was, after all, the altarpiece for the palace chapel, at that time still housed in the audience hall. It was to appear on this altar in place of the Trecento retable, which by now seemed all too old-fashioned.[75] Already in April 1478 Leonardo received a not inconsiderable advance payment for the altarpiece assigned to him; yet he seems never to have gotten beyond the earliest stages of this work.

A mural commission for the exterior wall of the Dogana, adjoining the rear of the palace, resulted from the Pazzi conspiracy: the full-length portraits of the conspirators that, according to old custom, were placed there for the terrifying perpetuation of their actual hanging. This was painted by Botticelli, who received the respectable fee of forty florins for it on 27 July 1478 (Vasari-Milanesi, 3:322, n. 2; Lensi, *Palazzo Vecchio*, p. 76).

Around 1480 and 1481 the construction work in the two new rooms of the uppermost story was completed along with their sculptural decoration. In 1482 commissions for the monumental painting of the vast wall surfaces of these rooms began to be awarded. Ghirlandaio, just back from his fresco work at the Sistine chapel, was the first to be assigned a major portion of the mural program; he was to cover the long wall opposite the marble portal in the Sala dei Gigli with fresco. For this purpose the windows of this room in what was at this time the exposed outer wall of the palace were walled up, some completely, some only in their upper portions. The city patron St. Zenobius, together with the Madonna and Sts. Stephen and Laurence, received the central place in the cohesive surface thus created. The secular historical elements in the side wall sections came next with triads of famous political and military heroes. All were in a festively splendid architectural setting of three great, richly decorated arcades on piers.[76]

In the meantime, another wall painting for the same room was assigned to Ghirlandaio and to Antonio Pollaiuolo, as well as Perugino, who was subsequently replaced by Filippino. But the execution of these paintings,

[75] The altar, which since 1404 had its own chaplain to attend to the daily mass, was dedicated to Saint Bernard of Clairvaux, and his feast was celebrated there with special pomp and the participation of the Duomo choir. On this day, as on only five other principal feasts of the church, the golden rose bestowed by the pope in 1419 and safeguarded since then in the chapel (see above), was displayed on the altar. Richa, citing an old manuscript (*Notizie*, 10: 220-23, 225-27) gives an inventory of the vestments and mass utensils of the chapel, pertaining to the years 1458-1476.

[76] The whole work was carried out in two sections during 1482 and 1483. Payment notices are given in Gaye, *Carteggio*, 1:577-80).

like so many others, was again abandoned or put off after the first decision, and the Signoria eventually settled for having the other wall surfaces painted with the pilaster articulation and lily patterns that still exist today (thus it is called the Sala dei Gigli). The adjoining audience hall was probably similarly decorated before its later painting by Salviati.

In 1483 Ghirlandaio was also entrusted with the execution of a new altarpiece for the altar of St. Bernard in this corner room as a substitute for Leonardo, who had received the commission earlier. But this time too, that commission remained without results. This was probably because another plan had gained precedence in the meantime: the erection of a new altar in the great Hall of the Council of Seventy (afterwards called the Hall of the Two Hundred) in the first upper story. And in this case the goal was achieved in the first campaign. Filippino Lippi, who received the commission, had already completed this altarpiece by 20 February 1486.[77]

Besides this, from 1483 on, the carved ceilings of both upper main rooms were polychromed and gilded by Clemente di Giovanni and other painting artisans. Many payment entries, some surprisingly high, continue over several years for this work (Gaye, *Carteggio*, 1:579ff.). In 1489-1490 the Aula Dominationum (that is, the Sala dei Gigli) had its windows glazed and was painted with the above mentioned lily pattern by Bernardo Rosselli.[78]

A review of the period considered up to this point reveals, first of all, a pattern similar to the one presented by the Duomo and Baptistery in the program and tempo of execution of the various enterprises carried on in succession or simultaneously. But the discrepancy between what

[77] This is the great panel with the enthroned Madonna under a baldachin and four standing saints to the sides, now hanging in the Uffizi; flower-strewing angels hover above and at the top are the arms of the Commune, the red cross in a white field. A considerable sum was spent even for the production of the richly carved frame—not surviving—by Clemente del Tasso (500 *lire*, while the painter received 1200). Finally the Operai also had a curtain of blue damask with red and white silk borders prepared, which (as with precious paintings in churches) was raised only for mass celebrations or other comparable occasions to reveal the painting. The document is now published by Poggi in *RA*, 1909, pp. 305ff. Cinelli still saw the panel around 1677, in its original place, but ascribed it erroneously to Ghirlandaio (Bocchi-Cinelli, *Le belleze della citta*, p. 92).

[78] Certain figural paintings, since lost, of declared or probable origin during the period in question remain to be mentioned: Vasari names a painting of John the Baptist by Antonio Pollaiuolo, probably a wall painting, near the Porta della Catena where one entered the halls in the upper stories from the steps. Likewise, in the staircase near the Catena was an Adoration of the Magi by Botticelli, who was also assigned to paint a tondo of an unnamed subject for the audience hall of the Massai della Camera. Horne identified the latter with the *Madonna della Melagrana*, while he sought to trace copies of the Magi painting whose original is lost. See Herbert Percy Horne, *Alessandro Filipepi, commonly called Sandro Botticelli, painter of Florence* (London, 1908), pp. 44-45, 154; see further Magliabecchiano-Frey, *Il codice*, p. 105; Vasari-Milanesi, 3:322.

was planned or initiated at any given time and what actually came to execution in the art history of the Palazzo Vecchio is considerably greater than in the case of those complexes of ecclesiastical commissions. This is probably because the planning and commissioning body here, in any case for all important projects, was the multimembered forum of the Council of Seventy (the college of Operai was responsible only for the details of execution) and also because the particularly complicated financing of all enterprises for the city palace was far more closely dependent on the political circumstances and temper of the moment than was the case for those major ecclesiastical buildings, whose care was a unanimously recognized duty and matter of honor for the two financially strongest guilds.

Thus the new desire for a more representative setting for the Signoria's public appearance is already noteworthy in the productions of the 1450s. And this truly Renaissance attitude, which also caused the catchword *magnificentia* to recur in many council provisions for work on the palace, finally led to the thorough renovation and embellishment of the interior courtyard and the contemporary restructuring of the whole core of the building in 1454 and 1455. It is self-evident, however, that painters and sculptors had little to do in the palace up to the end of the 1460s, during these costly (and thus only slowly developing) architectural projects. The basic structure of the rooms had to be completed before attention could be paid to their interior decoration.

In the meantime, however, the period of Lorenzo Magnifico had arrived with a delight in luxurious decoration that took effect and expressed itself very clearly even in the Signoria's palace in furnishings of the Great Council Hall undertaken since 1472, as well as in the newly created rooms of the second upper story. It is true that only a limited part of all that was planned for these areas actually came to realization and much was later removed. Other portions, like the splendidly shimmering gilding of the coffered ceiling and the decorative parts of the marble portal, appear today only in a few faded remnants. We can imagine in some measure the appearance and effect of the whole in earlier times only with reference to the general artistic and decorative behavior of the Laurentian era. But we must try to evoke the general character of what was produced and planned for the Signoria's palace at that time, so that the completely different attitude of the following period, to which we must turn now, contrasts all the more sharply with it.

But between the first enterprises of this new segment of the history of the Palazzo Vecchio and the last productions of the previous period there lies an almost totally unproductive vacuum lasting nearly ten years. During this time, probably on account of a shortage of funds, only temporary stopgap measures and a few minor special projects went on, instead of work on the still incomplete portions of the grandiose decorative program. The first immediate stimulus for new artistic activity in the context of the city palace came from political events of the years 1494 and 1495: the expulsion of the Medici on 9 November 1494 and the ensuing constitution of a radically democratic regime with a Great Council representing the sovereign popular will that was to include all citizens qualified according to certain standards and at least thirty years old. The first event, resulting in the confiscation of property left behind by the Medici, led first of all, by a decree of 9 October 1495, to the transfer of two Donatello statues of appropriate subjects from the Palazzo Medici into the Signoria's own palace: the bronze *David* and the Judith and Holofernes group. The David statue, which up to this time was set up in the Medici palace in the middle of the courtyard, now received a corresponding position in the courtyard of the Palazzo Vecchio.[79]

With this figure of David, so effectively placed, the Signoria palace received, in addition to the older marble *David* by Donatello and Verrocchio's bronze statue, its third monumental representation of the same heroic biblical figure who had long personified bold, victorious struggle in Florence.

But that other Old Testament figure, Donatello's bronze *Judith*, which the Medici had placed over a fountain basin in their palace garden, was meant to be understood in a still more specific and immediate sense. It was henceforth to stand as a monument to the recently enacted overthrow of a tyrant and the civic liberty that had thus been won back. Thus it was erected on 21 December 1495, immediately after its seizure, on the *ringhiera* in front of the main portal of the palace, facing the public and with the significant inscription: "Exemplum salutis publicae cives posuere."

A whole series of antique busts—twenty-four of marble and two of bronze—were also evidently desired for the decoration of the palace of the Signoria, as well as a few small bronze figures and those "*spalliera* pictures" not further described. However, as far as is known, only three great canvases of the deeds of Hercules, which Cosimo had had painted around 1460 by Antonio Pollaiuolo, were selected from the profusion of paintings in the Palazzo Medici. These were hung in the Hall of the Two Hundred on the first upper story.[80]

---

[79] Even the statue's particularly elegantly decorated pedestal, which Vasari (Vasari-Milanesi, 3:108) described as an early work of Desiderio da Settignano "with marble harpies and very pleasing tendril ornament in bronze" was taken along, but was provided with four Florentine coats of arms as a sign of its new ownership. Albertini, (*Memoriale*, p. 441) mentions this base as a slender column of bright-colored marble; while Cambi (*Delizie*, 21:257) also speaks of four leaves at the corners at the base of the column.

[80] Albertini's report of 1510 (*Memoriale*, p. 441) mentioned them there, in the "sala del

Of the other contents of the Medici palace, those of the household chapel were also appropriated. These included in particular the Filippo Lippi altarpiece, now in Berlin, that at last provided, without any expenditure, the replacement which had been sought unsuccessfully for years for the outmoded panel on the altar of the audience hall. The precious altarstone from the Medici chapel, decorated with mother of pearl and precious stones, was also added to this altar, which was also supplied with all the portable liturgical objects from there: the silver candlesticks, the great missal, and the mass bells as well as the whole stock of vestments that the Medici sacristy had contained (Magliabecchiano-Frey, *Il codice*, p. 97).

Finally, a great number of especially precious works were taken over from the Medici library. These were henceforth supposed to be preserved in the Signoria's palace as particularly honorable state property. But the book crates were never even unpacked there, for it must have been decided almost immediately to transfer their contents to the Dominicans of San Marco as a pledge for a loan of 3000 florins secured by the city authorities through their mediation.[81]

Far more significant, however, than these relatively modest enrichments that came to the Palazzo Vecchio from the confiscated possessions of the Medici is its contemporary architectural enlargement with a mighty hall to house the great citizens' council called for by the new regime. After consultations on the various competing designs, direction of the building project was assigned on 15 July 1495 to the architect Simone Cronaca and the carpenter Francesco Dominici. They were enjoined to carry on the execution of the project with the greatest possible speed. The new room was to be constructed behind the core structure of the old palace, above the one-story Dogana and the open court of the Capitano del Popolo, in such a manner that its length corresponded to the whole broad rear side of Arnolfo's palace building and its floor lay at the same height as the first upper story of the old palace. The work indeed advanced so energetically that toward the end of August of 1495 the whole substructure, vaulted on massive stone piers, was already executed and in December the wooden roofing of the hall could even begin (Gaye, *Carteggio*, 1:584-85; Landucci-Herzfeld, *Tagebuch*, pp. 159-61, 170).

The credit for raising the very considerable funds that this enterprise consumed is due chiefly to Savonarola. The institution of the great citi-

consiglio antiquo," albeit with an erroneous attribution to Verrocchio. See also van Marle, *Painting*, 11:37-39 and Eugène Müntz, *I Precursori e propugnatori del rinascimento* (Florence, 1902), pp. 217-20.

[81] See my essay "Die mediceischen Bibliotheken in Florenz" in the periodical *Italien*, 1, pp. 534ff. (November 1928); Lensi, *Palazzo Vecchio*, p. 85; Landucci-Herzfeld, *Tagebuch*, 1:109-110.

zens' council also proceeded from his advice and urging, among others'. For the construction fund he donated the money that had come to San Marco from five sons of patricians who had recently entered the convent. And the major loan that the city received at that time from San Marco for deposition of the Medici treasury of books was probably also earmarked for the hall construction. In February 1496, the Signoria inspected the completed masonry shell of the room. Subsequently the interior was well enough prepared so that already on May 1 the Great Council, numbering about 1750 members, could hold its first session here.[82]

In its essential dimensions, the hall is still recognizable in today's so-called Sala dei Cinquecento. But it was a good seven meters lower and considerably narrowed by the platform that ran around it, bearing at one end the Udienza of the Signori and, opposite this, an altar and the speaker's podium. Of these additional structures, already removed before Vasari's time, we know only that the balustrade and door frames were of reddish marble and that the seats of the Signori and the benches to the sides of the altar were enriched with partially gilded carving. A carved frieze ran around the uppermost level of the wall benches. The central decorative element of the coffered ceiling was a great heraldic composition of the various coats of arms of Florence.[83]

Beginning in 1497, the Capomaestro was Antonio da Sangallo who had been Cronaca's collaborator up to that time. Baccio d'Agnolo, who two years later received the superintendent's job himself, worked under him, as did a whole staff of carpenters and woodcarvers including Bernardo del Cecca, various members of the del Tasso family, and others.

The altar installation and the eastern platform, including the richly carved frame of the altar painting, were produced in 1498 as the last furnishings. Filippino himself was supposed to execute this painting, but remained in arrears regarding it until the end of his life. The aforementioned month of May 1498 was however also filled with highly exciting events in the political history of the Palazzo Vecchio. These included the trial and execution of Savonarola, who was dragged to the palace after his convent was stormed on the night of April 7 and imprisoned there in the dungeon cell of the so-called *alberghettino*, high up in the bell tower.

After fairly informal proceedings the judgment against the erstwhile spiritual leader of the bourgeois republic was finally handed down in

---

[82] The stone staircase planned by Cronaca was probably under way at this time, but completed only in 1510. Vasari, who erected the present double staircase in place of this one, represents Cronaca's structure as somewhat steep and narrow, but furnished with beautiful architectural decoration (Vasari-Milanesi, 4:541; Cambi, *Delizie*, 21:226, 276).

[83] See Gaye, *Carteggio*, 1:585ff.; Vasari-Milanesi, 4:449-51; Maria Lessing, *Die Anghiarischlacht* (Bonn dissertation, 1935), pp. 7-8; Lensi, *Palazzo Vecchio*, p. 80.

the hall constructed at his urging by the same Great Council whose selection Savonarola had instigated three years earlier. And on 23 May 1498 the death sentence was carried out in the piazza in front of the palace at a spot on a diagonal with the corner of the *ringhiera*. The spot was marked in 1898 with a bronze plaque (recently moved to the sacristy of San Marco) set into the pavement.

But to return to art historical matters; after the Savonarola affair the interior decoration of the hall continued under Baccio d'Agnolo's direction, with a few pauses, into the year 1502.[84] Along with this decoration, two figural artworks of the same subject are mentioned: Landucci cites the installation of "a very beautiful Christ in relief" on 14 April 1500 at the Porta dei Signori (thus at the entrance to the chambers of the Signori on the second upper story). The occasion for this was the arrival in Florence on that day of the news that the city's most dangerous enemy Lodovico Moro had been dethroned by the French and led away in captivity.

The choice of subject, however, followed the concept of the city's subordination to the kingship of Christ, once proclaimed by Savonarola. And this received still more emphatic expression in the marble statue of the Savior that was intended to be set up on the tribune of the Signoria in the Great Council Hall. Andrea Sansovino received the commission in 1502 and worked out the model for this figure; the marble block for it was even supplied to Sansovino's workshop in December 1503, but there is no further mention of the actual execution and installation of the figure.[85]

The idea of the kingship of Christ also probably had the additional, indirectly political meaning for the democratic city state of a fundamental wariness against any return of a human, medicean tyrant. And in view of this wariness it even seemed possible to hazard installing a standing constitutional head of state for the secure consolidation of the system of government. The office of *gonfaloniere*, hitherto changeable every two months, was at the end of September 1502 conferred for life on a personality who appeared particularly trustworthy, Piero Soderini.

This first and only *gonfaloniere a vita* in the history of the Florentine city government had now however to transfer his own household into the palace. His wife was the first woman to live in the palace in its two-hundred-year existence, and this also occasioned all sorts of architectural adjustments on which work was immediately begun.

Soderini received a spacious official residence in the first upper story. A wooden staircase was attached to the exterior of the building, in the

[84] See Lensi, *Palazzo Vecchio*, pp. 97-98 and documents cited there; also Vasari-Milanesi, 5:351, 353-54.

[85] See Lensi, *Palazzo Vecchio*, p. 96; *RA*, 1909, pp. 144-46.

style of the balconies and galleries in use at that time on many old private houses, as a direct connection from these quarters to the *gonfaloniere's* office above them. The account books of the Operai also record all sorts of work on furnishings in Soderini's apartment.[86]

Of far greater art historical significance, however, was the *gonfaloniere's* enterprise for the Great Council Hall in his second year of office: the painting of two mighty mural compositions with scenes from Florentine military history that, in the contemporary critical stage of the campaign against Pisa, were meant to stand before the eyes of the Senate and people of Florence during all proceedings in the council hall as a powerful exhortation to martial courage and energy.[*]

Thus first of all Leonardo da Vinci, whose experience as a military engineer had already been employed during the besiegement of Pisa in May 1503, received the commission in October of this year for the wall painting with the theme of the battle of Anghiari which had occurred in 1440. Work on the cartoon, in the papal hall at Santa Maria Novella, progressed so swiftly that, according to a note of 30 August 1504 in the account book, the painting was already begun by that time.[87]

But only one main section of the whole composition came to definitive execution, the equestrian battle for the standard; the rest was probably also sketched in working drawings and worked out in advance in individual figure studies. Then, from the beginning of 1506, Leonardo remained in Milan, in spite of severe warnings from Soderini who had granted him only two months leave. He could not make up his mind to take up the work again after certain unsuccessful experiments with the painting technique in it had ruined the whole thing.

The commission for the counterpart on the other long wall of the Great Council Hall, however, met with no greater success. Leonardo's most worthy competitor Michelangelo had been proposed to execute it, probably from the very start.

[86] Grotesque paintings by Morto da Feltre, highly praised by Vasari, had later to give place to the redecoration of the rooms for Duke Cosimo; one of two tondi with figures of saints, painted by Davide Ghirlandaio and his associate Domenico Domenici can now be traced to the Uffizi's storeroom (*Dedalo*, 11, 1931, p. 86, n. 10). Baccio d'Agnolo supplied cupboards with intarsia decoration and the goldsmith Simone Diotaiuti a table crucifix with rock crystal inlay. A small ornamental garden was finally planted on the terrace of the inner courtyard for Soderini's wife, Madonna Argentina. The master of works for the palace from 1503 on was again Cronaca (Vasari-Milanesi, 5:204; 6:533, n. 2).

[*] *Translator's note:* On the Hall of the Great Council and its decoration see the recent literature cited in Translator's Introduction, pp. xiii-xiv.

[87] Further entries in the same volume of documents of the Operai—outlays for all sorts of work materials, movable painting scaffolds, assistants' wages and the like—allow the continuing execution process to be traced through the end of 1505. See Gaye, *Carteggio*, 2:88-89; Vasari-Milanesi, 4:44n.; Maria Lessing, *Die Anghiarischlacht* (Bonn dissertation, 1935); Carl F. Suter, *Das Rätsel von Leonardos Schlachtenbild,* (Strasbourg, 1937).

In the beginning, in the winter of 1503-1504, when Leonardo had already begun his Anghiari cartoon, Michelangelo was still fully occupied with the completion of his great statue of David, which later in 1504 took its place in front of the Signoria's palace. A few words about this are in order first. The circumstances that resulted in this placement are well known: the conference of thirty artists and other interested parties was called on 25 January 1504. The opinion finally won out that the *David* should be set up neither on the Duomo nor under the Loggia dei Lanzi, but in front of the portal of the Signoria's palace where Donatello's *Judith* had stood for nearly ten years. The herald of the Signoria, the first to vote for this location, referred in particular to the highly shocking scene of the enemy slain by a woman. He declared that the political significance of an art work at the entrance portal of the city palace would be far better conveyed by the *David*.[88]

And the Signoria did indeed decide on this course. In the middle of May the gigantic figure was brought from the Duomo workshop to the palace in a laborious, four-day transportation process. In June the *Judith* was moved from its previous position into a niche in the palace courtyard, from which it was transferred to the Loggia dei Lanzi two years later (Albertini, *Memoriale*, p. 441); a pedestal for the *David* was erected, and the installation was completed at the beginning of September 1504.

In the meantime, however, on 4 August, Michelangelo had expressly taken on the commission for the second mural in the hall. The theme selected was an episode from the earlier Pisan campaign of 1346: the successfully repulsed ambush of the Florentine troops who were surprised while bathing at their encampment at Cascina.

Three thousand florins were allotted for the execution of this work, on which Michelangelo probably began preparatory work immediately. In any case a payment notice of 31 October 1504 for the immense sheets of paper for the working drawing suggests that the whole composition was by that time so far established that the full-sized design could be begun. Michelangelo was assigned a hall in the dyers' hospice near Sant'Onofrio for a workroom. In April 1505, when the artist followed the papal call to Rome after receipt of a large payment for the mural, the greater part of the cartoon design was probably completed. At least Michelangelo himself later once asserted, probably with some exaggeration, that the cartoon was "finished" in March 1505, and that thus the 3000 florins were "already half earned."[89]

[88] The protocol of the proceedings is in Gaye, *Carteggio* 2:455ff., 464 and Henry Thode, *Michelangelo und das Ende der Renaissance. Kritische Untersuchungen über seine Werke*, 6 vols. (Berlin, 1902-1913), 1:76-77.

[89] See his letter of 1504 to Fattucci in Michelangelo Buonarroti, *Le Lettere coi ricordi ed i contratti artistici*, ed. Gaetano Milanesi (Florence, 1875), p. 426; Henry Thode, *Mi-*

The cartoon probably also benefited somewhat from Michelangelo's brief visit to Florence in the summer of 1506. But the artist's subsequent absence of about ten years estranged him completely from the task. And since the process of transfer to the wall had not even been begun, the cartoon itself was hung up there, apparently already in the later summer of 1506, as a counterpart to the mural that Leonardo had begun; Albertini saw it there as late as 1510. But even this cartoon, like Leonardo's, was actually completed only in part.[90]

When Michelangelo spent a few weeks in Florence in March 1508, he probably did hardly any work on the battle picture; but the enterprising Soderini took advantage of his presence to discuss a new sculptural project with him: the erection of a counterpart to the *David*, a similarly over-life-size figure of Hercules with the vanquished Cacus beneath him, for which the *gonfaloniere* had already had a suitable block reserved in Carrara. The plan was taken up again only very much later and finally in 1534 realized by Bandinelli (see below). We return to the projects for the Great Council Hall. Soderini, after the collapse of the mural project, now turned his interest to another important item of furniture, the altar for one of the short walls. The carved frame for the painting had long been ready, but the painting, assigned to Filippino, remained unexecuted.[91]

The execution of this altarpiece was on 16 November 1510 assigned to Fra Bartolommeo, who at this time, after the departures of Michelangelo and Raphael, was the most important painting talent in Florence. He must have begun the honorable task with due enthusiasm and in two years had advanced the work so far that his convent received a fairly considerable installment of the payment in June 1513.[92] At that time the panel was probably in that state of execution, with an evenly applied sepia underpainting of all parts, beyond which it had not progressed in

*chelangelo und das Ende der Renaissance. Kritische Untersuchungen über seine Werke.* 6 vols., Berlin, 1902-1913, 1:99ff.

[90] See Gaye, *Carteggio*, 2:93; Albertini, *Memoriale*, p. 441, "li cavalli di Leonar. Vinci et li disegni di Michelangelo"; see also Michelangelo-Milanesi, *Lettere*, pp. 92, 95.

[91] In the meantime, Fra Filippo Lippi's Adoration painting, taken from the Palazzo Medici and forthwith used on the altar in the upper audience hall, appears to have been installed there for in 1510 Albertini (*Memoriale*, p. 441) mentions a "tavola di Fra Philippo" in the Great Council Hall.

[92] See Marchese, *Memorie*, 2:78, 179, 603; also Hans von der Gabelentz, *Fra Bartolommeo und die Florentiner Renaissance*, 2 vols. (Leipzig, 1922), 1:159-60.

The program for the painting, very significantly for its intended location, consisted of a Santa Conversazione of all Florentine local saints surrounding the Madonna and above her the heroic form of her mother St. Anne, who was honored as a special patroness of the city since the expulsion of the Duke of Athens and the restoration of Florentine liberty had occurred on her day (26 July 1347). (On this account the Signoria also held an annual pilgrimage to the altar it had erected to her at Or San Michele in 1349.)

the last years of the Frate's life and in which we find it in the Uffizi today. As though misfortune hung over this hall, which had been so shamefully dishonored by the Savonarola trial, this altarpiece intended for it came no nearer to completion than had the earlier Christ statue by Sansovino and the two great historical wall paintings.

In the year 1510 the palace's other furnishings had received a much-admired addition from the field of higher mathematics and astronomy, a great astronomical clock. This had already been completed in the early 1480s, probably on the commission or with the support of Lorenzo Magnifico, by Lorenzo della Volpaia. It now came to the Palazzo Vecchio as a donation from the Parte Guelfa and was set up in the Sala dei Gigli (since then also often called the Sala dell'Orologia).[93]

Finally, certain architectural works fall into this period. Thus the three-branched connecting section between the old palace and the hall building was now raised with a passage from the old to the new council hall on the first floor, and above this a new office for the chancery. The connecting section had previously existed, with its entrance to the Dogana, only at ground floor level. According to Cambi's *Istorie*, the stone staircase leading to the new room also appears to have been completed only at this time.

Last of all, in 1511, came the construction of a private chapel for the Signori near their audience hall, that is, the transfer of the altar that had hitherto been in that hall into a special room created by joining together two small spaces. The still extant painting of this chapel took place only in 1514, with wall and ceiling paintings by Ridolfo Ghirlandaio and an altarpiece by his pupil Mariano da Pescia. The whole is a characteristic monument of the eclectic aftermath of the High Classic.

But now a Medici again became a patron of painting: Lorenzo di Piero, the subsequent Duke of Urbino, a grandson of Lorenzo Magnifico. The latter's youngest son, Giuliano, already appears among the five Operai in January 1513. These two descendants of the formerly banished house, later immortalized by Michelangelo's tombs, could now, scarcely twenty years after the expulsion, participate in the artistic affairs of the city palace; this can be explained only by the revolution in the political situation that had occurred in the meantime, to which we must briefly refer.

After the coup d'état of 21 April 1512, which ousted Soderini, and with the support of the Spanish troops of the viceroy of Naples, which had assaulted and plundered Prato, Giuliano de' Medici appeared in the

---

[93] We must imagine this work, described by Angelo Poliziano in a letter of 1484 (*Opera*, vol. 1, *Epistolarum Libros XII*, Lyon, 1533, bk. 4, vol. 1, pp. 122ff.) in the taste of the period of its origin, as most richly decorated. The maps of the earth added to it according to Albertini (*Memoriale*, p. 442), were executed by the miniaturist Attavante (*RA*, 6, 1909, pp. 137ff.).

city and reclaimed possession of the old family palace as a private citizen; his brother Cardinal Giovanni followed him a short time later. But the latter ascended the papal throne in March 1513 after the death of Julius II. Thus, in place of Giuliano, who was called to Rome, came the young Lorenzo di Piero and the pope's cousin, Giulio, the latter as newly installed archbishop of Florence, in order to pursue more energetically the claims of their house. It is true that at first the old, free, civic regime remained superficially unchanged. The painting of the chapel of the Signori in 1514, initiated by Lorenzo Medici, probably at his own expense, was however the last artistic enterprise that came to realization in the palace before the end of the republican period. All other plans of the college of Operai, referred to on the occasion of its reestablishment at the end of 1513 (see Lensi, *Palazzo Vecchio*, p. 109) remained unexecuted. On the other hand, the interior decoration of the Signoria's palace even suffered some damage from the events of these stormy years. The chronicler Landucci laments in particular that during the temporary quartering of the Spanish garrison and Giuliano's guards in the Great Council Hall, there was no hesitation about breaking up much of the beautiful benches. Nevertheless, care was taken to protect Leonardo's Anghiari fresco with a wooden covering against damage by the soldiers lodged in the hall.

Later, however, after Leo X's death in 1521, the Signoria could experience more freedom of action and with it some degree of renewed self-confidence. The former zeal for decoration of the palace might have revived if these conditions had lasted long. Certain attempts in this direction do in fact appear around 1525 and 1526.

Thus at that time Soderini's old project for a Hercules group opposite Michelangelo's *David* was taken up again, and the marble block long prepared for this purpose in Carrara was brought to Florence. But no artist could be found to carry out this task, so that finally, after Michelangelo could no longer be tempted, the group to be seen standing in front of the palace today was produced by Bandinelli in 1534. In addition it was proposed to replace the wall hanging behind the benches of the *ringhiera*, woven in 1453, and Andrea del Sarto was commissioned to prepare working drawings for this tapestry.[94]

In contrast, around the same time in 1525 and 1526, a work of luxurious book miniature painting was commissioned and actually, if not completely, executed: the miniaturist Giovanni Boccardi produced a beautifully written three-volume parchment copy of the revered codex

[94] The cartoon, for which the artist received a partial payment in December 1525, appears actually to have been delivered; for Vasari (Vasari-Milanesi, 5:49, n. 3) describes its subject matter of guild arms with putti and personifications of rivers and mountains. But its woven execution never took place.

of the *Pandects* that the Signoria kept preserved in a special shrine in the audience hall (see above). The copy was supplied with lavish marginal and initial decorations (now in the Biblioteca Nazionale).

Toward the end of the 1520s, however, the political situation became so ominous for Florence that all thoughts and energy could henceforth turn only to the preservation of state independence. This atmosphere explains the sole work done for the palace at that time: the attachment of a large inscribed panel above the main portal with the text: "*Jesus Christus Rex Florentini Populi S.P. Decreto Electus.*"

This was an outspoken testimony to that theocratically oriented policy that Savonarola had first proclaimed and that Gonfaloniere Niccolò Capponi, and afterwards his successor Francesco Carducci, now solemnly established in the Great Council. A new, 1851 version of the inscription of 1528 still stands today above the portal of the Palazzo Vecchio, as does a second inscription of similar content that was placed upstairs in the palace above the entrance to the chapel in the old audience hall of the Signori.

In the year 1528 there were dealings once again with Michelangelo over the frequently mentioned Hercules block. Such a sculptural glorification of embattled heroism, next to that inscribed proclamation of Christ's kingship, must have appeared particularly appropriate to the city preparing to defend its freedom. But the time immediately following required Michelangelo to devote his powers to a more pressing requirement of the city, the direction of fortification work on the hill of San Miniato. The Palazzo Vecchio, in which the newly organized citizen militia had its quarters, was henceforth the scene of political and strategic deliberations only with regard to the encircling besiegement of the city by the imperial and papal forces in the spring of 1529. With the submission of the city completed on 20 June 1530 on the *ringhiera* of the palace before the assembled populace and the entry a short time later of the future Duke Alessandro de' Medici, the history of the Palazzo Vecchio ends, so far as it was to be traced here.

# CHAPTER 2

# SCULPTURAL COMMISSIONS

## SCULPTURE FOR CHURCH BUILDINGS

In conjunction with the reconstruction of the original decoration of certain churches and secular buildings, we shall now survey systematically the whole range and organization of the projects that continually called upon and activated the representational and decorative efforts of artists.

Only architecture may remain outside of consideration here; in this connection the reader is referred to Jacob Burckhardt's *Geschichte der Renaissance in Italien* where precisely this sort of survey of architectural works, systematically grouped by types of projects, was first presented in 1868 and largely completed in later editions. Only the province of architectural-sculptural decoration, also considered there, will appear in the following survey in a somewhat more detailed presentation, organized by subject.

First we shall deal with sculpture and its use in the decoration of buildings for public worship and convents as well as in secular public settings and private houses.

The exterior architecture of churches offered a principal and extensive field of activity for monumental statuary and reliefs in Romanesque-Gothic times. But the work of this type still available to masters of the early fifteenth century—the statue series on Or San Michele, on the old facade of the Duomo, and on the Campanile—was predetermined by the extant exterior architecture of the late Trecento that required sculpture to fill its still partially unoccupied niches and framing areas. This work was commissioned and carried out during the 1420s and 1430s with Luca della Robbia's Campanile reliefs even extending into the 1440s. Yet it is characteristic of the change in outlook already taking place at this time that the old decorative facade of the Duomo was not continued beyond the existing lower portion.[1]

The subordinated arrangement of figural sculpture in an architectural framework was in fact repugnant to the developed early Renaissance. The sole exception was clay reliefs, sometimes painted, more often glazed

[1] Even the original project to crown the corner piers of the tribunes with great statues was finally abandoned after several attempts by Donatello and Agostino di Duccio. A recently discovered fresco fragment by Starnina in the Carmine shows how such statuary decoration was pictured at the beginning of the Quattrocento (illustrated in *RA*, 1933, p. 161).

in many colors. These, however, could appear only as appropriately prominent accents on small facades designed to receive decoration. Examples include the *sopraporti* at Sant'Egidio, the Badia, and elsewhere, or the spandrels of the arcades at the Innocenti and San Paolo.[2] The only great church facade produced in the Quattrocento in Florence, Santa Maria Novella, is innocent of sculptural decoration. Only the architecture of the High Renaissance, with its sharper plastic articulation, could once again accord monumental figural sculpture a place in its exterior decoration.[3]

Relief sculpture also found a new task in the Quattrocento: the Madonna tabernacles on houses and street corners (see below), earlier executed exclusively, and still frequently in paint, now also began to appear often in marble, clay, or majolica reliefs. Even well-known sculptors such as Desiderio, Antonio Rossellino, the Robbia, and others were not infrequently called upon to produce such works. And along with many second-rate examples, we may still find some high quality works of this genre here and there in their original places in the Florentine cityscape mounted in simple stone frames and distinguished by little lamps hanging in front of them. Many others, however, belonging with private property that was frequently rebuilt in the course of time, ended up in museums. And there, while they are admittedly saved from the danger of further weathering, they have lost the direct effect of their everyday, public situation. In the context of an architecturally organized structure, however, relief sculptural fillers appear primarily in the interior architecture of ecclesiastical spaces.

Thus Brunelleschi—who probably had not in fact intended the relief decoration (applied only later) for his Innocenti hall—planned from the beginning to enrich the interiors of the old sacristy of San Lorenzo and the Pazzi chapel with various relief decorations in order to create a certain equivalent for the narrative painting that customarily covered the walls and vault surfaces in such places.[4]

A particularly expensive and accordingly rare type of figural sculptural project involved in ecclesiastical buildings is the splendid doors executed

[2] Characteristic of the rather provincial taste of Pistoia is the installation of a continuous relief band, full of figures, on the loggia of the Ceppo in contrast to the more sparing medallion decoration on the aforementioned Florentine arcades.

[3] Thus the old figures crowning the portals of the Baptistery were replaced at the beginning of the sixteenth century with new statuary groups. Similarly, on Or San Michele, an old stone figure of John the Evangelist was replaced in 1515 with the bronze by Baccio da Montelupo. And above all, statues and large reliefs were to play a prominent role in the structure of Michelangelo's model of 1516 for the facade of San Lorenzo.

[4] See also the colorfully glazed *sopraporta* reliefs above the sacristy portals in the Duomo and the figured friezes and majolica reliefs in later interiors like the tomb chapel of the Cardinal of Portugal, Santa Maria delle Carceri in Prato, etc.

in cast bronze. They appear, in resumption of a medieval practice, first and in particularly rich versions in the Baptistery doors and somewhat more simply in the Duomo for the entrances to the two sacristies; these last were already planned and commissioned in 1433, but were finally executed by Luca della Robbia only after the sacristy of San Lorenzo had received its two pairs of small doors by Donatello around 1440-1443.[5]

Finally, monumental statuary series are occasionally found in the context of an ecclesiastical interior. Such are the four evangelists that Donatello set up high on the crossing piers of San Lorenzo, first as temporary versions in stucco, probably on the occasion of the choir dedication in 1461.[6] Later, at the beginning of the new century, the life-size marble apostles were commissioned for the Duomo, first from Michelangelo. The commission was finally carried out gradually by Andrea Sansovino and others.

Far more numerous, however, were commissions for individual works of sculpture in the round that found places in church interiors as altar decorations or devotional figures set up for their own sake.[7] Thus, above all, crucifixes were constantly in demand as life-size devotional images of the most basic general significance, whether as a crowning element rising high above the main altar or as a private donation set up somewhere or other. The latter form admittedly appeared more often only after the beginning of the fifteenth century.[8] Besides the famous large wooden crucifixes of Donatello in Santa Croce and Brunelleschi in Santa Maria Novella, there are the anonymous examples, probably somewhat older, in the Martelli chapel of San Lorenzo and on the high altar of San Felice.[9]

After Donatello's completion of the bronze crucifix on the high altar of the Basilica del Santo at Padua in 1444, the preference for such large crucifixes seems to have reawakened in Florence, after a lapse of several decades, around the end of the century in connection with the general outlook of the time of Savonarola. Evidence includes the wooden cru-

---

[5] The bronze doors for the Siena Duomo, also commissioned from Donatello in 1457, were never executed.

[6] See Magliabecchiano-Frey, *Il codice*, p. 76; Albertini, *Memoriale*, p. 437; also Richa, *Notizie*, 5:35.

[7] On this see Fabriczy, "Kritisches Verzeichnis Toskanischer Holz-und Tonstatuen bis zum Beginn des Cinquecento," *JPK*, 1909, suppl.

[8] The large sculptured triumphal cross, which was in wide use in the North in Romanesque and Gothic times, has only a few counterparts in Italian sculpture in the round, along with the many painted wooden crosses of the Duecento and Trecento.

[9] Donatello's wooden cross originally had movable arms, so that during the season of the Passion it could be laid in a "Holy Sepulcher" (Kauffmann, *Donatello*, nn. 44, 47).

In the Chiostro degli Aranci is a work of sculpture of a simple, popular but powerfully expressive style, in a wooden casing whose interior wall probably originally already contained the painted attendant figures of Mary and John, renewed in the seventeenth century.

cifixes of Benedetto da Maiano and of Baccio da Montelupo in the Duomo and Santa Maria Novella, as well as the high altar crucifix in the Annunziata by Giuliano da Sangallo (1482-1483) and others.[10]

The seated figure of the Madonna and Child, so frequently encountered in Germany, is in general rather rare in Italian Renaissance sculpture. From the early Quattrocento we may cite only Quercia's Madonna in Ferrara of 1426, an approximately contemporary work attributed to the master of the Pellegrini chapel in the museum in Krefeld, and the bronze Madonna by Donatello in Padua, completed in the period from 1445 to 1450 and posed like a medieval miraculous image. Following these at the end of the Quattrocento are the large carved wood Madonna of Benedetto da Maiano in Prato and the incomplete figure that came into the Bigallo from Benedetto's estate, now in Berlin.[11] The individual standing figure of the Madonna only appears in the special theme of the Conception and in the frequently demanded pair of statues of the Annunciation, from which often only the figure of Mary has survived.[12] Complete Annunciation groups are the life-size wood statues of about 1425 from Santissima Trinita in Berlin, the somewhat smaller marble figures of Bernardo Rossellino's done in 1447 in Empoli, and Andrea della Robbia's clay statues in the Osservanza near Siena. Probably also by him, and not by Luca della Robbia, is the large white Visitation group in Pistoia. In any case, as has already been shown several times, large scale statuary only begins to appear in the early Quattrocento or else at the end of the fifteenth century and in the sixteenth.

Only in this later period is Tuscan sculpture and panel painting concerned with the theme of the Pietà, which had very frequently been represented by wandering German carvers and clay sculptors in the fourteenth and early fifteenth centuries for German patrons in Italy.[13] The subject and highly expressive execution of the Pietà images of Giovanni

[10] In a chapel of the cloister of the Annunziata is the Sangallesque crucifix from San Miniato fra le Torri. Of the various large crucifixes by Baccio da Montelupo that Vasari mentions, the one for the high altar of San Lorenzo, now on the altar of the old sacristy, has certifiably survived, as well as the one hanging in the chapter house of San Marco, from the winter choir of the monks (Albertini, *Memoriale*, p. 437; Vasari-Milanesi, 4: 541-44).

[11] Andrea Sansovino was to provide a marble Madonna for the Cathedral of Genoa in 1503, and even Michelangelo's "Bruges Madonna" was from the beginning not intended for Florence.

[12] Such are the two Madonnas of the Quercia school in the Sienese Duomo and in the Louvre (Adolfo Venturi, *Storia dell'Arte Italiana*, 25 vols., Milan, 1901-1940, 6:105-107) and the Madonna of the Brotherhood "della Concezione" in Empoli (Fabriczy, *JPK*, 1909, suppl., p. 29).

[13] Among the *Vesperbilder* of this type, cited by W. Körte, there are, however, none from Florence (*KJBH*, 1936, pp. 1ff.).

della Robbia and his school, so numerous since the end of the Quattro-cento, may probably be traced directly to the stimulus of Savonarola.[14]

Among individual statues of other saints the figure of John the Baptist occurs most frequently, sometimes in small format, sometimes nearly life-size. The figure was desirable in any Baptistery but in Florence was also repeatedly in demand as the image of the city's patron.[15] Hardly less popular was the figure of St. Mary Magdalen, an exhortation to penitence that we still occasionally encounter today as a large wood-sculptured standing figure in various Florentine churches.[16] Isolated standing figures of other saints, such as Sebastian, Francis of Assisi, and Anthony appear only occasionally and only toward the end of the Quattrocento, especially in the clay sculpture of the younger della Robbia school.[17] The erection of a statue of a saint in the piazza in front of a church is in evidence only for the terra-cotta statue of St. Peter Martyr, which was set up on a high column in front of the facade of Santa Felicita as a private donation in 1484.[18]

Finally there are the busts of individual saints that are set up here and there, as a likeness of the church's patron, in a sacristy, or even as

[14] Cinelli still saw a large Pietà group with attendant angels in a chapel in the garden of San Marco (Bocchi-Cinelli, *Le bellezze della citta*, p. 470). See Wilhelm Bode, *Florentiner Bildhauer der Renaisssance*, 4th ed. (Berlin, 1921), pp. 34, 382ff., where various examples still surviving in Florentine churches are also mentioned and illustrated.

[15] Donatello alone completed a whole series: bronze statues for the Baptisteries of Orvieto and Siena, a marble St. John for Palazzo Martelli, a carved wood one for the chapel of the Florentines in the church of the Frari in Venice; Michelozzo completed the large stone figure in the Annunziata; Antonio Rossellino, a statuette of the boy John for the Opera of San Giovanni (Bargello); and Benedetto da Maiano, the beautiful marble figure above the splendid portal in the upper story of the Palazzo Vecchio, etc.

[16] These include Donatello's statue in San Giovanni (of which there is a larger copy in the Collegiata at Empoli, dated 1455). Its counterpart in Santa Trinita, begun by Desiderio, was completed by Benedetto da Maiano. A figure of the penitent woman, carved by Bru-nelleschi before 1420 for the old church of Santo Spirito, according to Manetti, was destroyed in the church fire of 1471. Also lost is the over-life-size statue of the Magdalen by Simone Ferrucci, modelled in terra cotta, which Vasari and even Richa (1760) noted in the church of Santa Felicita. See Vasari-Milanesi, 2:332, 459; Manetti-Holtzinger, *Bru-nelleschi*, p. 9; Richa, *Notizie*, 9:308; and *RA*, 1931, p. 48.

[17] For example in Santa Croce, Castellani chapel, and in the Berlin Museum (Frida Schottmüller, *Die Bildwerke in Stein, Holz, Ton und Wachs. Die italienischen und spa-nischen Bildwerke der Renaissance und des Barock*, catalogue of the Berlin Museum, 2nd ed., Berlin, 1933, nr. 118, 219, 221). The St. Sebastian statue by Antonio Rossellino is the centerpiece of an altar in Empoli with painted side panels; similar is an altar by Leonardo del Tasso in Santa Maria Maddalena dei Pazzi and on his family altar in Sant' Ambrogio (Vasari-Milanesi, 4:523; *RA*, 7, pp. 45ff.).

[18] This devotional counterpart of Donatello's *Dovizia* (see below) fell down in 1722 and was never replaced (see Richa, *Notizie*, 9:323-33); see also M. Civitali's design drawing in London for a St. George group, also to be erected on a high column.

devotional offerings on a smaller scale in chapels and oratories, instead of paintings or statues.[19] Most of the works are executed in painted or natural colored clay sculpture or simply in stucco, a few also in della Robbia type glazing.[20] In the case of the aforementioned objects, and especially of the very numerous busts of the Mother of God, in marble, clay, or stucco, it must admittedly remain uncertain whether they were originally commissioned for a church setting or as household devotional images.[21] Carved wood busts of saints, a cheaper substitute for the costly reliquary busts in precious metals, were probably also produced as reliquaries, continuing a custom popular in the North as well as the South since Gothic times.[22] Only the bronze bust of San Lussore, made by Donatello in 1426-1427 for Ognissanti, is artistically important;[23] as well as the chased silver bust of the martyr-bishop Ignatius from Santa Maria Novella (now in the Bargello chapel), probably produced around 1500, with a moderately realistic head, and the cope and mitre set with rich relief and enamel decoration.[24]

To this should be added a special field of figural sculpture, produced in abundance but now traceable only in literary testimony, the execution of all those *ex-voto* images of individual parts of the body in silver[25] or

[19] By Donatello there is the clay bust of St. Laurence, vibrant with life, in the sacristy of San Lorenzo, the Giovannino in Berlin, and the female saint idealized in a more antique manner in the South Kensington Museum, London. A painted clay bust of St. Catherine by Benedetto da Maiano is in Berlin; also there is a St. Elizabeth by Antonio Rossellino (from the nuns' convent of Santa Maria Maddalena dei Pazzi). In Santissima Trinita is a bust of Christ from the Verrocchio school in painted terra cotta, etc.

[20] This includes Andrea's half-length figure of the Savior in the sacristy of Santa Croce, and two saints of the order in Giovanni's style in the novitiate chapel in the same place; a Giovannino by Andrea in Krefeld, a St. Catherine of Siena in Budapest, etc.

[21] One example, in a style close to Donatello's, with a putti relief on the base, is in the small church of the former hospital of Santo Stefano dei Bini, near San Felice. In the refectory of Ognissanti within a horizontal rectangular tabernacle embellished with angel figures is a bust of the Madonna attributed to Agostino di Duccio.

[22] Such is the early Quattrocento painted wood bust of a female saint in the sacristy of San Miniato, two others in San Giovanni de' Cavalieri, four busts from the early sixteenth century, of markedly antique character, in Santa Maria Novella.

[23] In 1592 it was transferred by the Grand Duke Cosimo into the Pisan church of his knightly order, Santo Stefano (see illustrations in *Pantheon*, 1936, p. 397).

[24] See in addition the silver bust of San Zanobi in the Duomo, already executed in the late Trecento, and the Beata Umiliana in the Canigiani chapel of Santa Croce.

[25] Small parts of the body executed in embossed silver (donated by invalids who were healed or seeking recovery) were stored in a wall cupboard behind the chapel of the Miraculous Image at Santissima Annunziata. Fra Angelico's workshop executed the famous series of small square panels (now in the San Marco Museum) for the doors of this cupboard (see *l'Arte*, 11, pp. 81ff.).

Such silver *ex-voti* were also produced, according to Vasari (Vasari-Milanesi, 3:254, 6:43) by Ghirlandaio's father Tommaso Bigordi, and later the goldsmith Girolamo dal Prato, among others.

complete life-sized portrait figures in wax, dressed in their own clothes, as they had been hung since Gothic times in various Florentine churches, but above all in the Annunziata where they gradually accumulated in distressing superabundance in the fifteenth and sixteenth centuries. A special firm, the Benintendi, comes into particular consideration with regard to these works, which they produced over several generations. Their prolific production of wax images enjoyed no less fame, even outside Florence, than the roughly contemporary majolica manufacture of the della Robbia. The last famous member of this family, Orsino Benintendi who died in 1497, modelled, among other things—allegedly with Verrocchio's help—the life-sized image of Lorenzo Magnifico that the latter had produced in three examples after the Pazzi conspiracy, two for Florentine churches, one for Assisi.[26]

The custom of making such figural donations to popular pilgrimage places, still continuing among us today, can be traced in Florence back to the late thirteenth century. It is associated in particular with certain especially venerated miraculous images; for this reason, the above mentioned Benintendi had their earliest workshop in the neighborhood of Or San Michele and later in the Via de' Servi near the Annunziata.

But in Santa Croce and elsewhere, it was customary in earlier times to deck the tombs of important families not only with clothes and armor, among other personal mementos, but also with wax sculptured heads and hands mounted on these (see Robert Davidsohn, *Geschichte von Florenz*, 4 vols., Berlin, 1896-1927, 4:1, p. 210, 4:2, p. 34). Such donations were still coming to the Annunziata toward the end of the High Renaissance; Montorsoli, for example, had commissions of this type (Vasari-Milanesi, 6:632-35). But Vasari notes a gradual dying out of this old custom during his own time. Only in the eighteenth century was it decided to remove the wax figures, which by this time had grown rather unsightly, from the Annunziata and store them in a small adjoining room, until they finally deteriorated completely.[27] The only surviving examples of wax busts, the head of a girl in Lille and the Leonardesque bust in Berlin, must have been produced not as *ex-voti*, but still depended technically on such works. We shall return below to the death masks once to be found frequently in Florentine middle-class homes.

The creation and decoration of the various principal pieces of mon-

[26] See the detailed description of these and similar works in Vasari-Milanesi, 3:373-75; in addition, in Strozzi-Guasti, *Lettere*, pp. 129, 134; in Angelo Fabroni, *Laurentii Medicis Magnifici vita*, 2 vols. (Pisa, 1784), p. 339; a summary in Aby Warburg, *Bildniskunst*, pp. 11, 29ff.; new documents in Masi, "La Ceroplastica in Firenze," *RA*, 9, pp. 124ff. and in Weigelt, *MKIF*, 3, pp. 546-48.

[27] A last description of the situation before the removal is in Richa, *Notizie*, 8:819, 12; and in 1:12 regarding Or San Michele.

umental church furniture, necessary everywhere, provided an especially broad field with various possibilities for sculpture. We begin by noting in passing the special genre of the *tempietti*, or free-standing tabernacle structures over particularly venerated images, in which the Quattrocento still followed the lavish precedent set in Or San Michele. These admittedly sometimes evidence only ornamental decoration, like the two sister structures in San Miniato and the Annunziata by Michelozzo and Pagno di Lapo done in 1447 and 1448; on the other hand, two *tempietti* of form similar to these in the pilgrimage church of the Impruneta, produced between 1452 and 1455, received a complex of relief decoration by Luca della Robbia with individual figures, groups of angels, and the like for the effective display of the devotional objects sheltered there: the Madonna image and a relic of the cross.[28]

The younger della Robbia school, under Andrea's leadership, took on a further development of this special genre as its chief and most requested project. This was the production of large altarpieces made completely in colored majolica sculpture, with decorated frames and predella (most containing a small receptacle for the Eucharist). These provided a cheap and yet very effective substitute for painted or marble sculptured altarpieces; it appears, however, that they found more customers in provincial locales than in the city of Florence.[29] Giovanni della Robbia carried on this genre until around 1530; but with an evidently decreasing market, since the more severe sense of form of the High Renaissance was turning further and further away from the overly coarse, folk-style decoration of such structures.[30] On the other hand, the sculptured altarpiece of stone or marble was always a rare exception in Florence.[31]

[28] See the reconstruction of the complete original installation by Paul Schubring, *Luca della Robbia und seine Familie* (Bielefeld and Leipzig, 1905), plate on p. 52.

[29] See the examples illustrated in Schubring's Robbia monograph (pp. 94 ff.) from Varramista (Berlin, Kaiser-Friedrich-Museum), from La Verna, from the Osservanza near Siena, etc. In Florence proper there are the beautiful Madonna altarpiece by Andrea from the oratorio of the Compagnia di Castel San Giovanni now in the novitiate chapel at Santa Croce and the altar, decorated with scenic reliefs by the same artist and a reliquary tabernacle in the middle, in the confraternity oratorio in the first cloister, now belonging to the Canigiari.

[30] Examples are: the large *Noli-me-tangere* altarpiece from the nun's convent of Santa Lucia, now in the Bargello, identified by de Nicola with the work named in Vasari-Milanesi, 6:606 (*BM*, p. 171); the large *Madonna of the Misericordia* with donor figures and inscriptions, dated 1528, etc.

[31] One may cite only Donatello's *Annunciation* in Santa Croce; this was originally located above the Cavalcanti altar and received a painted predella attached to its supporting consoles; and Mino's marble altars in Fiesole and in the Badia. The Neapolitan altars of Rossellino and Maiano, competing with painting in their illusionistic relief style, had their origins outside Florence; in Siena there was the large Piccolomini altar commissioned from Michelangelo, and in Lucca the carved wood altar of the Virgin by Matteo di Bartolo of about 1500.

We shall return later to the tomb altars of individual saints and the sacrament altars carved in stone.

Figural or ornamental relief decoration was occasionally applied to the front side of the altar table, instead of the painted or embroidered antependia otherwise used there. This was initially planned for the altars in the tribune chapels of the Duomo, as the reliefs begun by Luca della Robbia for the altar of St. Peter show. The marble altar of about 1440 in the old sacristy in San Lorenzo is articulated with small colonnettes, and also has little reliefs with prophet figures on the front and a Madonna in the center of the back wall.[32]

But it was tomb sculpture that offered the richest field of activity for sculptors in church interiors. Much of the former supply of works of this type has certainly been subsequently cleared out and destroyed. But if we compare Vasari—in whose time the first major encroachments on the contents of various churches took place—and the observations of reporters who preceded him with the material that has come down to us or is recorded in other ways, these reports do not appear to have omitted much. Based on these, however, it would seem that only a relatively small number of the historically prominent personalities of political, intellectual, and economic life were commemorated with noteworthy tomb monuments. For example, of the two greatest representatives of monumental patronage in the Quattrocento, Cosimo de' Medici received only an inscribed plaque in the pavement of San Lorenzo and an unadorned sarcophagus in the crypt and Lorenzo Magnifico, no tomb monument at all. Thus it should not seem astonishing that in spite of the very marked concern with fame—which admittedly led in certain cases to the commissioning of one's own tomb even during one's lifetime, or to the testamentary financing of one—the creation of an imposing, artistically significant tomb was by no means the rule.

In certain cases the city government attended to the erection of a worthy monument, as for the two state chancellors Leonardo Bruni and Marsuppini in Santa Croce; and in the Duomo—along with certain monuments only simulated in paint—the epitaphs of Brunelleschi and a few other deserving personalities were set up in a somewhat simpler, relief sculpted form.

Sculptural monuments were also created some time after the death of certain personalities of the past who were deserving of veneration chiefly on religious grounds. This was done in 1479-1480 by Mino for the half-

[32] The former altar of the chapel of the miraculous image in the Annunziata (1448, by Pagno di Lapo; now in the Museo Bardini) has the form of a curved sarcophagus with lion masks and a Trinity medallion (*Dedalo*, 6, p. 746). The high altar of 1475 in Santissima Trinita displays the three heads of this symbol as the central decoration with donor arms on the short sides.

mythical founder of the Badia, the Margrave of Anderburg, and in 1451 by Bernardo Rossellino for Beata Villana following a private donation. Similar were the combination tombs and altars for the local saints Fina and Bartolo in San Gimignano, completed in 1474 and 1494 respectively by Benedetto da Maiano, and for St. Giovanni Gualberto in Florence itself, executed from 1505 to 1515 by Benedetto da Rovezzano.[33] The last mentioned example already belongs, however, to a time when major impetus for the construction of monumental tombs is no longer greatly in evidence. Thus the grand scale plan for the Medici tomb chapel in San Lorenzo has all the more astonishing effect alongside the rather delicately articulated tomb of 1517 for the former *gonfaloniere* Soderini in the Carmine, the Altoviti tomb in Santi Apostoli, and a few other contemporary works. The Medici chapel, as the idea and enterprise of the patron, Cardinal Giulio de' Medici, achieved no less honor than the master who took on its execution and brought it to conclusion, if not actual completion, from 1524 to 1532.

The well-known special studies by Fritz Burger and Paul Schubring may be referred to with regard to the compositional arrangement of the tombs and the motifs appearing in them.[34]

Here we can further note only the special case of the completion of the sculptured nucleus of a tomb with painted sections, as with the Davanzati tomb in Santissima Trinita where the Madonna (now lost) with attendant angels was painted above the sarcophagus, and in the same place the Sassetti tombs, whose relief sculptured decoration was carried on in painted sections. Commissions of this last type were probably given out only in particular cases in which a generally existing desire found its fulfillment in a particular patron's readiness to carry it out.

On the other hand, the furnishing of a church interior for its liturgical functions presented some unavoidable tasks that depended on special circumstances only for the more or less lavish style and manner in which they were carried out. In addition to the decoration of the altar table with an image making more frequent claims on the painter than the sculptor as discussed above, these included the erection of an appropriate container for the Holy Eucharist or for any other relic the church owned. The general type of these small tabernacles is the aedicule form, usually

---

[33] The last was destroyed in 1530 and only scattered parts preserved in Santa Trinita.

[34] Fritz Burger, *Geschichte des Florentinischen Grabmals* . . . (Strasbourg, 1904); Paul Schubring, *Das italienische Grabmal der Frührenaissance* (Berlin, 1904); see also *MKIF*, 3, pp. 539, 552, regarding certain tombs of the early Quattrocento, still described by Richa but surviving only in fragmentary form; Abbot Vincenzo de' Trinci's tomb from San Pancrazio, for example, was built during his lifetime (1489). See the contract in Milanesi, *Documenti*, pp. 154-55. The main parts of the executed monument are preserved in the San Marco museum.

in marble, with angel figures in relief on both sides of the little door. The door was usually of bronze and decorated with gilded relief ornament. In the triangular pediment and in the socle field were the half-figure of God the Father, a Christ Child with the chalice, a Man of Sorrows, or another reference to the Passion of the Savior, whose Eucharistic body was concealed in the tabernacle. Frequently the eagle emblem of John the Evangelist appeared in the curved base section, recalling the text from St. John: "Et verbum caro factum est."[35] Luca della Robbia produced a tabernacle on a considerably more imposing scale for the hospital church of Sant' Egidio, 1441-1443. This is the one later moved to Peretola, in which brightly glazed majolica appears between sculptured marble parts for the first time. Complete small tabernacles in glazed terracotta were produced later.[36]

In certain cases the tabernacle installation was developed as a major sculptural structure on a special altar. Such, in its original condition, was Desiderio's tabernacle produced about 1461 for San Lorenzo.[37] Variants of this included Giovanni della Robbia's majolica tabernacle of about 1500 in Santi Apostoli, in which the attendant angels together with the tabernacle stand on a broad plinth above the altar, as was presumably true of Desiderio's structure in its original condition.[38] St. Ambrogio received an extensive tabernacle installation, or more properly speaking a sacrament altar, by Mino da Fiesole, with flanking side niches and appropriate decoration with small statuettes and reliefs, for an altar singled out on account of a miraculous event. A similar structure of 1489 by Andrea Sansovino is in Santo Spirito, and the Duomo of Fiesole has

---

[35] A particularly important example by Bernardo Rossellino, with relief figures of the church patron on the door done by Ghiberti in 1449 is in Sant'Egidio. In addition see Bernardo Rossellino's tabernacle for the *oleum infirmorum* in the choir of Sant' Ambrogio, with the base relief in Donatello's style, and many others (*ASA*, 1893, p. 5; *JPK*, 1900, p. 44). The tabernacle in the crypt of the Duomo at Fiesole has an especially elegantly decorated brass door with engraved decoration. Other examples of such tabernacle doors are in the Museo Bardini, etc.

[36] More examples from the early sixteenth century are in the Bargello, etc.

Benedetto da Maiano produced a wooden tabernacle for the relics of St. Sebastian in the Annunziata in 1479. A small sacrament tabernacle, carved by the younger Tasso and with three little Eucharistic paintings by Salviati, was produced later, around 1530. Both objects have come down to us only through Vasari (Vasari-Milanesi, 3:344; 7:10).

[37] Arbitrary alterations in 1677 had it built into the new Baroque wall organization (see *MKIF*, 4, p. 140); the crowning statuette of the Christ Child served temporarily in the sixteenth century as an object of adoration on the high altar on Christmas Eve. Contemporary terra-cotta copies of it may occasionally be found (for example, in the Berlin Museum, Schottmüller, *Bildwerke*, nr. 127).

[38] A smaller counterpart in Andrea's style is in the Duomo at Barga (Klassischer Skulpturenschatz T. 310).

one by Andrea Ferrucci.[39] The central section of the tomb altar of Santa Fina from 1474 and 1475 in San Gimignano is characterized as a sacrament tabernacle by adoring, candle-bearing angels and the chalice emblem in its base.

Along with these we find the genre of the free-standing tabernacle structure—the Italian counterpart of the tall tower-shaped tabernacles in German late Gothic churches—for example, in the Volterra Duomo, built by Mino in 1471 and shortly thereafter in San Domenico in Siena by Benedetto da Maiano.[40] In Florence, Desiderio had already executed such a free-standing, octagonal tabernacle for San Piero Maggiore. It was lost after the destruction of the church.[41] The new tabernacle planned for the Duomo in 1496 and 1504 was also envisioned in this style. Of the older tabernacle of the Duomo, only the two candle-bearing angels by Luca della Robbia have survived. Here, as in many other cases, these serve the liturgical need in the most beautiful, monumental form, with the Most Holy Sacrament taking its shelter only from the light of two candles.[42]

The necessary furniture of any parish church also included a pulpit. In most cases, it is true, this could have been provided in a simple, portable wooden form and thus perished easily later. Even documentary mentions of such wooden preaching lecterns are rarely found.[43] But wooden pulpits could serve only as modest or temporary expedients as long as a pulpit structure in stone or marble could not be obtained. Romanesque times in Tuscany had already produced a few examples offering the richest sculptural decoration. Thus in Santa Maria Novella around 1445 as well as in Santa Croce around 1474 we see the appearance of splendid stone pulpits with figural relief decoration, in each case at-

[39] In the South Kensington Museum is a high wall complex by Leonardo del Tasso, after 1495, once in the nun's church of Santa Chiara (with an older, classical tabernacle in the style of Desiderio in the center; see Richa, *Notizie*, 9:84-85). Dr. Middeldorf reports on a design drawing of a richly articulated wall tabernacle by Verrocchio in the Devonshire collection, no. 889.

[40] Both are crowned by statuettes of the Christ Child, in the latter case accompanied by two kneeling, candle-bearing angels. The bronze tabernacle by Vecchietta in the Duomo of Siena is similar, but still more richly decorated.

[41] See Vasari-Milanesi, 3:109; Bocchi-Cinelli, *Le bellezze della citta*, p. 356; Richa, *Notizie*, 1:144. In the Uffizi is a design drawing by Desiderio for a similar work (Alinari, photo 551).

See another, later tabernacle sketch in Munich, with a Last Supper relief in the predella, by Andrea Sansovino, according to Middeldorf (*MJ*, 1933).

[42] See also the two candle-bearing angels from a lost tabernacle in the Misericordia oratorio, two others in the Museo Bardini, etc.

[43] In 1469 Giuliano da Maiano supplied a *pergamo di legname* for the hospital church of Sant' Egidio. The low bill rules out rich decorative display. Benedetto da Maiano had many wooden pulpits to execute, some with intarsia decoration (*RA*, 3, 1905, p. 208).

tached to a pier in the front of the nave.[44] The long rectangular design preferred for Romanesque stone pulpits recurs in the pulpit from about 1430-1440 in Colle di Val d'Elsa with large, clumsy individual figures between decorated pilaster strips and also in the pair of pulpits surrounded with bronze reliefs that Donatello executed for San Lorenzo beginning in 1460.[45]

In 1473 the Pieve in Prato received a cylindrical marble pulpit with balustrade reliefs by Mino and Antonio Rossellino, set up on a rectangular base. Donatello had already been commissioned in the 1430s to execute an outdoor pulpit for the same church, chiefly for the display of the relic of the Virgin's girdle; this had a three-quarter cylindrical form, projecting from a corner of the facade, supported by a powerful bronze console and surrounded by a chorus of rough, joyous dancing putti.

The reading pulpits popular in refectories for the spiritual readings during the silent mealtime of the monks, customary in many orders, appear related to this basic form. So do the preaching pulpits in small, single-nave churches, as semicircular or polygonal shells standing out from the wall, generally with spare relief decoration. Such is the one in the refectory of the Badia of Fiesole completed in 1460 by Piero di Cecco and the somewhat later, simpler one in Sant' Ambrogio.[46]

The objects of fixed church furniture most closely related to the pulpits are the organ and choir tribunes in the form of balcony-like platforms projecting from the wall, with ornamental or figural reliefs on the balustrade. The first and most lavish examples of this kind were the marble creations of Luca della Robbia and Donatello, attached to the eastern crossing piers of the Duomo as a symmetrical pair during the 1430s; to these may be added the similar, Donatellesque singer tribune, datable after 1440, with ornamental decoration only, in a side aisle of San Lorenzo.[47]

Baptismal fonts also deserve mention, as do the greater or smaller

[44] In 1489 the abbot Vincenzo de' Trinci ordered a stone pulpit after the model in Santa Maria Novella for his church, San Pancrazio (see the contract for the work in Milanesi, *Documenti*, pp. 153-54).

[45] These pulpits were finished only after Donatello's death, probably not entirely according to the master's intentions and set up only much later, each on four columns (Kauffmann, *Donatello*, p. 177ff.).

[46] The Museo Bardini now owns the hexagonal pulpit, very elegantly decorated, from the Cestello convent (Santa Maria Maddalena dei Pazzi).

[47] Based on the style of its rich ornament, the stone-sculpture example of the Impruneta belongs at the end of the Quattrocento. The carved wood organ balustrade with gilded ornamental decoration on white in Santa Maria Maddalena dei Pazzi dates from the beginning of the sixteenth century.

The stone singers' balcony executed for Santa Maria Novella around 1500 ended up in the South Kensington Museum in London. See catalogue, J. C. Robinson, *Italian sculpture of the Middle Ages and Period of the Revival of Art* (London, 1862), illustration at p. 92.

lavabos in sacristies and refectories. Of the first type, in only a few churches with baptismal rights, besides cathedrals, nothing exists in Florence for the whole Renaissance period. On the other hand, Siena received the great octagonal baptismal font installation in the Baptistery under the choir of the Cathedral in the 1420s. Ghiberti and Donatello participated fruitfully in the reliefs and statuettes for this, along with Quercia, who was responsible for the whole project. In the same city, in the chapel of John the Baptist in the cathedral itself, is the small baptismal font with the reliefs of the story of Creation, produced after 1482 in Federighi's workshop.[48]

In addition, the need that existed in every church and convent for a small wall fountain in the sacristy and the anteroom of the refectory for handwashing before celebrating the mass and before mealtimes resulted in a whole series of charming versions. First of all, in the two sacristies of the Duomo are the fountain niches with the coarse putti by Buggiano sitting on the pipes (1440) and in the same place a second, somewhat simpler lavabo in Mino's style. The broad wall fountain in the Chiostro de' Dati, in front of the refectory of Santa Maria Novella, probably already dates from 1430. Then there is the very imposing, nobly articulated lavabo in Donatello's style from about 1450 in the former refectory of the canons of San Lorenzo (now the prior's residence).[49] Around 1465-1468 the Badia of Fiesole received its refectory fountain and the very handsome lavabo of the sacristy, by Francesco Ferrucci, with a transverse oval basin from which the water spout with two putti projects. The whole is set into a decorative wall installation.[50] Similar to this, and likewise a donation of Piero de' Medici (thus before 1469), but more brilliant and original in all its details and really the consummate example of the whole type, is Verrocchio's wall fountain in the room adjoining the old sacristy of San Lorenzo. A cheerful concluding example, rich in colors and forms, from the end of the early Renaissance, is the sacristy fountain of Santa Maria Novella, produced in 1497 as the first independent work of the young Giovanni della Robbia.[51]

[48] The baptismal font of the Duomo in Pienza, decorated with antiquarian forms, was probably made by Bernardo Rossellino before 1460. The relief-decorated baptismal basin in the Duomo of Pistoia was designed by Benedetto da Maiano and executed by Andrea Ferrucci in 1497 and 1498 with gilded ornament and a carved wood cover (RA, 1, pp. 271ff.). See also Peleo Bacci, Documenti toscani per la storia dell'arte, 2 vols. (Florence, 1910-1912), 2:136ff.

[49] In the sacristy of Santa Croce is a charming wall fountain with a marble setting and intarsiaed wooden doors (probably contemporary with the cupboards, around 1445).

[50] See ASA, 1892, pp. 376ff. and the illustration in Eduard Heyck, Die Mediceer (Bielefeld, 1897), p. 56.

[51] A somewhat clumsier version from the same workshop went to Sant' Anna (now San Niccolò) in Prato in 1520. The severe and simply decorated wall fountain in front of the sacristy of the Certosa is from about the same time.

Holy water basins in more or less decorative renditions can still be found in many Florentine churches. Thus, for example, in Santa Maria Novella alone—not including the simple stoup from the mid-Trecento set up in front on the right—there are no less than three examples from the early Renaissance: the little wall basin near the sacristy entrance donated by a Rucellai; its richer counterpart in the Pura chapel of about 1475; and the free-standing basin with a bowl in the form of a ship, in the right aisle.[52] Particularly lavish and splendid examples of this genre are found in certain neighboring Tuscan cities; in the Duomo of Siena (by Antonio Federighi, 1462-1463), in the Cathedrals of Lucca and Pisa (1518) and in San Sisto (also in Pisa). All take the form of a round basin on a candelabra stem, sometimes crowned with a Madonna statuette.[53]

All such decorative works in marble and stone sculpture—to which may be added, besides the aforementioned examples, many from the sphere of secular commissions—continually occupied a very great number of workshops especially adapted for such tasks. According to a statistic on trades of about 1478, there were in Florence at that time no less than fifty-four workshops for stone sculpture where such decorative works were carried out, sometimes exclusively, sometimes along with other, large-scale sculptural commissions.

In addition to these, eighty-four workshops for decorative wood sculpture, carving and intarsia were counted.[54] The products of this last type of decoration with figural and perspectival inlay work will be discussed in the sphere of painting projects as an essentially draftsmanly decoration of surfaces. Here we only refer briefly to the decorative carving of altarpiece frames and choir stalls.

A whole series of large altarpieces, with contemporary frames, from the late Quattrocento and early Cinquecento can still be found in their old places in Santo Spirito and Santa Maria Maddalena dei Pazzi, and occasional examples are in other churches. For Filippino's altarpiece for the Palazzo Vecchio, the original frame by Chimenti del Tasso cost almost

---

[52] Similar to this, but more richly worked out, is the basin for holy water below the Nori tomb in Santa Croce. The two acqua santiere at the entrance to San Marco, with stems in the form of candelabra with ornament in Michelozzo's style and Medici arms date from the 1440s (the basin was renewed later). From a little later is the pila at the front of San Felice. Two basins with richly decorated feet bearing the insignia of the Calimala and dating from 1465 to 1470 are at the main portal of San Miniato. The decorative wall basin near the cloister portal in the Innocenti church also comes from this stylistic phase. Others from the late Quattrocento are in the Badia, in Santa Maria Maddalena dei Pazzi, and elsewhere. A bronze statuette of the Baptist by Pagno di Lapo once crowned the holy water basin at the entrance to the Annunziata (Richa, Notizie, 8:59).

[53] Similar ones are also in the Madonna dell'Umiltà in Pistoia, in the Collegiata of Pietrasanta (by Stagio Stagi, 1521), etc.

[54] See Jacob Burckhardt, Geschichte der Renaissance in Italien, 4th ed. (Stuttgart, 1904), pp. 279, 324 (after Fabroni, Vita Laurentii, 2:338).

as much as the painting (see above). This Chimenti (Clemente) belonged to a whole family of carvers and intarsiators who played the leading role in this type of work in the late Quattrocento and afterwards. Preceding and contemporary with them were the two Maiano, Giuliano da Sangallo, Giovanni da Giuole, and Manno di Benincasa, etc.[55] On the other hand, in Sant' Ambrogio and Ognissanti we find a series of uniform stone altar frames, built at equal intervals along the side walls. This is an organization tending toward the more severe High Renaissance outlook and therefore probably originated only around 1500 as a forerunner of the uniform altar type that Vasari later introduced in Santa Croce and Santa Maria Novella.[56]

We come now to portable, utilitarian objects of small-scale sculpture executed and decorated in bronze or precious metal. As part of the inventory of sacristies, these underwent a broad development throughout the whole Middle Ages, often with major significance as art works or precious objects. Even during the Renaissance these still form a not inconsiderable branch of commissions for ecclesiastical, minor, and decorative arts. Yet the greater part of such works can still be traced only in reports and documentary citations. The few surviving examples from the Florentine artistic world can only provide a basis for a suggestive evocation of all the lost material.

The works of bronze sculpture include the large reliquaries in the form of caskets, reminiscent of the Romanesque type and at the same time of Etruscan cists, with low relief work on the sides; examples are the container that was commissioned from Ghiberti by Cosimo de' Medici in 1428 for Santa Maria degli Angeli or the larger, more richly worked version produced by him in the period from 1439 to 1446 for the bones of St. Zenobius in the Duomo.[57] Even the casing of church bells was sometimes decorated with small-scale relief bands; the classic example is the *Piagnona* in San Marco, on which putti and other Donatellesque

[55] See Jacob Burckhardt, *Geschichte, der Renaissance in Italien*, 4th ed. (Stuttgart, 1904), section 155; also Elfried Bock, *Florentinische und venezianische Bilderrahmen aus der Zeit der Gotik und Renaissance* (Munich, 1902); Vasari-Milanesi, 3:355; and Milanesi, *Documenti*, p. 71n.

[56] In the woodwork of sacristy cabinets, choir stalls, and the like, relief sculpture decreases so much in relation to intarsia work that little else may be said here about the former.

A center of the marble industry like Pietrasanta could indulge in the luxury of having wall pews in the apse of the collegiate church executed in richly decorated marble work by Lorenzo Stagi (1520-1524). Only the back parts of this have survived (see Vasari-Milanesi, 6:110-11).

[57] The aforementioned shrine is in the Bargello. On its original installation in a segmentally arched opening in the wall between the monks' choir and the church see *RA*, 5, pp. 120-21.

In 1466 Maso di Bartolommeo furnished the shrine in the form of a casket, decorated like Donatello's outdoor pulpit in the same place with dancing putti and freestanding colonnettes, for the relics of San Cingolo in Prato.

motifs appear along with a surrounding inscription from the donor Cosimo de' Medici.[58]

Other bronze work for church use included the large candelabra for the paschal candles or the seven-branched versions for other liturgical purposes, such as almost every church needed and may have possessed. The Easter candlesticks made for the Duomo during the period from 1445 to 1450, supposedly by Michelozzo, are still used there today at Easter and at other times are in the Museo dell' Opera. They may stand as an early and particularly valuable example of this genre (see above).[59] The bronze candelabra Verrocchio provided in 1468 for the chapel in the Palazzo Vecchio now belongs to the Berlin Schlossmuseum (see above).[60]

An occasional special project for decorative bronze sculpture was represented by the splendid grillworks that were provided, for example, on free-standing tabernacle structures above the much-visited miraculous images to protect them against the overly disorderly press of pilgrims. There was one dating from 1449 by Pagno di Lapo in the Annunziata and another dating from 1461 to 1465 by Filarete's assistant Pasquino around the Cingolo altar in Prato.[61]

Then there is the multiplicity of diverse small objects for use on the altar and in liturgical ceremonies, executed sometimes in cast bronze, more often in precious metal. Along with the candelabra as tall as a man, these include the smaller candlesticks, of which at least two were necessary for the service at any altar. These also, as often already happened in Romanesque times, were carried beyond the simplest functional types in lathed wood or simple cast metal to finer modelled bronze or wrought silver versions.[62]

[58] The original, pulled down after the fall of Savonarola and beaten through the streets in derision, was replaced in the campanile with a copy in 1908; the original now stands in the second cloister of San Marco. See the illustration in Giuseppe Benelli, *Firenze nei monumenti domenicani* (Florence, 1913), p. 224. We may probably imagine the bells donated by Cosimo to the novitiate of Santa Croce in 1445 as similar.

[59] From the same period come the two original bronze candelabra that Maso di Bartolommeo executed for Prato and Pistoia, with slender substructures in the form of vases above marble three-footed pedestals (like the Florentine Duomo candlesticks) and seven branches in somewhat naturalistic forms. See *RA*, 1934, pp. 190ff.; and Julius Baum, *Baukunst und dekorative Plastik der Frührenaissance in Italien*, Bauformenbibliothek, 11 (Stuttgart, 1920), p. 283.

[60] An Easter candlestick decorated with wood carving and paintings by Fra Angelico was once in Santa Maria Novella (see above).

In the Bargello is a large bronze candelabrum from about 1510 to 1515 with the insignia of the Parte Guelfa on its richly decorated base as a sign of its provenance. The Collegiata at Pietrasanta possesses two marble candelabra, probably carved by Stagio Stagi around 1510.

[61] See also Michelozzo's grate under his open table altar in the Duomo (see above).

[62] Thus in 1417 Or San Michele received a pair of candlesticks designed by Ghiberti and

Indispensable for any altar was a large or small crucifix. As a constantly recurring sculptural problem, the body of Christ on these probably usually appeared, as today, in stereotyped workmanship, but not infrequently also as an art work of high quality. It is indeed remarkable that such altar crosses, like the altar candlesticks, have so rarely survived.[63]

Frequently a small image of the Crucified can also be found at the bottom of painted altarpieces of the early Renaissance, worked into the image like a still-life object, evidently to eliminate the need for a sculptured crucifix.[64]

Among the surviving crucifixes in precious metal we may cite two processional crosses of the early Quattrocento in the Bargello. One has relief sculptured medallions on the ends of the cross, the other enamelled ones; in the same place is a cross reliquary with particularly rich enamel decoration. Several other crosses could be found in the 1933 exhibition, Mostra del Tesoro di Firenze Sacra; many of these were also enriched with attendant figures in low relief: half figures of God the Father at the head of the Crucified, Mary and John on the cross beam, another saint or an angel at the other end. Far surpassing all of this in size and splendor of execution is the silver cross that was commissioned from Pollaiuolo in the 1450s.[65]

The silver *portafuoco* for the Holy Saturday fireworks at San Giovanni deserves mention as a unique creation. It was probably executed after arrangements for this spectacle were transferred from the Pazzi to the Parte Guelfa in 1478. It can still be found today in the palace of the latter.[66]

---

worked by the goldsmith Guariento. Maso di Bartolommeo executed small bronze altar candlesticks on Piero de' Medici's commission for the altar of the miraculous image at the Annunziata; the workshop of Maso Finiguerra produced two splendid silver gilt candlesticks with enamel decoration for San Jacopo in Pistoia; they cost the considerable sum of 522 florins (Vasari-Milanesi, 2:259; 3:288-89, n. 4). None of the aforementioned objects have survived.

[63] The Berlin collection, for example, otherwise so rich in Italian sculpture, possesses not a single crucifix in bronze and only two carved wood ones of middling quality from the late Quattrocento (Schottmüller, *Bildwerke*, nr. 228-29).

[64] Antonio Pollaiuolo furnished a silver altar cross in 1473 for the Carmine church (Vasari-Milanesi, 3:288, n. 4, Richa, *Notizie*, 10:587); Maria Pandolfini donated the silver corpus, modelled by Antonio di Salvi, for a crucifix at the Badia in 1488 (Vasari-Milanesi, 2:290, n. 2).

[65] A few precious altar crosses were still produced in the beginning of the sixteenth century. Thus Antonio di Salvi furnished a silver gilt cross for the Annunziata in 1510 and a cross for the Duomo in 1514. This is probably identical with the one exhibited in the 1933 exhibit; see Museo di San Marco, *Mostra del Tesoro di Firenze Sacra*, exhibition catalogue (Florence, 1933), p. 57.

[66] It bears the eagle of the Parte sculptured in the round on a chased silver knob (*l'Arte*, 6, p. 289).

The pax, or small tablet for the clergy's ceremonial kiss of peace during the Agnus Dei of the Mass, was a liturgical utensil that often received a particularly painstaking execution. It was sometimes produced in cast bronze with a decorative architectonic frame and central figural relief of a Madonna or another subject—very frequently by Bertoldo (several examples are in the Berlin Museum). In other cases it had niello engraving or enamel with an elegant goldsmith's setting.[67]

Antonio Pollaiuolo made a decorative silver cover with figural reliefs for a volume of the Gospels in the Duomo; these probably made use of considerable material, since they were melted down in 1500 to use the metal for another work.

A few last general observations may be made on ecclesiastical goldsmith work of the Florentine Renaissance, of which almost all of the pertinent material from the sacristies of Florentine churches and the churches of the surrounding countryside was brought together and on view in the great Mostra del Tesoro di Firenze Sacra in the summer of 1933.[68]

The following sketch can provide no more than a summary survey of the types of projects, citing the most important preserved pieces and references to works of consequence that have survived only in reports.

Besides the altar crosses, candlesticks, and paxes already mentioned, the following objects were repeatedly produced in this field:

(1) Chalices and ciboria;
(2) Reliquaries in various forms, whether as cylindrical glass vessels with a metal base and top, or as containers in the form of coffers, or finally, as a special identifying sign of the particles preserved within, perhaps in the form of an arm with a hand, modelled in the round, or for fragments of a saint's skull, as life-size, wrought metal or carved wood busts (see above);
(3) Certain splendid examples of liturgical vestments and utensils—Bishops' croziers, mitres, morses for copes, etc.

Chalices and ciboria show a great similarity in design and decoration, with many echoes of older traditions, throughout most of the fifteenth century. Nevertheless, beginning about the second third of the Quattro-

---

[67] Such was the work of Maso Finiguerra mentioned by Vasari (Vasari-Milanesi, 3:289).

In 1472 Bernardo di Guccio produced a pax with a Deposition from the Cross, now in the Bargello, for Sant' Egidio; Vasari (Vasari-Milanesi, 9:280) cites a version with the same subject, created in 1453 for the Duomo by Giovanni Soldi. In the Impruneta are two paxes of 1515 (Museo di San Marco, Mostra del Tesoro di Firenze Sacra, Florence, 1933, p. 130).

[68] A scholarly study and publication of this treasure is in fact prepared, but has appeared only in part. The author has had occasion to study the individual objects closely only in certain cases (see RA, 1933-1934, passim; in addition see l'Arte, 6, pp. 215-216, the report on the small exhibition already mounted in 1911 of church goldsmith work from Florence).

cento the new taste in forms began to assert itself more and more in silhouette and proportions as well as in the use of purely Renaissance decorative elements.[69] Figural decoration, however, as a rule was added less in sculptural form than in niello engraving or enamelled medallions, thus in a decorative technique that may accordingly be discussed in the section on types of painting.

A few of the surviving examples of reliquaries and monstrances, none too numerous, may be mentioned. These include the costly setting for an arm bone of the Apostle Philip that Antonio del Vagliente produced for San Giovanni in 1425. It took the form of a tower-like structure, crowned with an admirable statuette of the saint, recalling the style of Donatello.[70] In the third quarter of the century we encounter several works surviving only in reports; Pollaiuolo's reliquary for the arm of San Pancrazio, and in 1476 his setting for the finger of St. John in the Baptistery treasury.[71] Many other similar examples must have been produced during this period, which delighted so greatly in ornament and was quite ready to spend money for church purposes, without even a reference to them having been found and published so far.

Nevertheless, certain works from the 1460s to the 1480s have survived. They include a reliquary of St. Reparata by Francesco Vanni in the Duomo treasury; a 1473 St. Andrew reliquary in San Salvatore al Vescovo. A rare curiosity of a nonreligious type from about 1460-1470 is the magnificent giant stalk of branching coral, mounted in monstrance style on a richly ornamented silver foot, with the donor inscription of Anichinus Corsi who dedicated this souvenir of a sea victory against the Moors to the Duomo. A reliquary of St. James was also dedicated to the Duomo by a Canon Mannelli. Dating from 1487, it has the form of a temple-like shrine on a high base, topped by the statuette of the saint, and flanked by two angels on symmetrically projecting side pieces.[72]

[69] Numerous examples of such chalices are in the Bargello—two particularly fine ones in the sacristy adjoining the chapel; the Carrand collection there includes a beautiful late Quattrocento ciborium base (no. 725). A ciborium of 1490, displayed in the 1933 exhibition is published in *RA*, 1933, p. 90. In 1494 the frequently mentioned Antonio di Salvi produced a chalice for the Badia with a relief of Christ on the base (Vasari-Milanesi, 3:290, n. 2).

[70] The casket for a piece of the chain of St. Peter, with two pairs of kneeling angels stationed upon it, was produced around 1430. See Arnaldo Cocchi, *Les anciens reliquaires de Santa Maria del Fiore et de San Giovanni de Florence* (Florence, 1903), pp. 25ff., 289.

[71] The reliquary, making use of an older foot-piece, exists now only in a gothicizing renovation of the late sixteenth century (Vasari-Milanesi, 3:298n; Arnaldo Cocchi, *Les anciens reliquaires de Santa Maria del Fiore et de San Giovanni de Florence,* Florence, 1903). See *MA*, 1903, p. 69, for the contract for a reliquary of the finger of St. Peter Martyr, commissioned in 1466 by the confraternity of the same name for Santa Maria Novella.

[72] Landucci even found the first exhibition of this object in the Duomo worthy of special mention in his diary (30 September 1487).

See Arnaldo Cocchi *Les anciens reliquaires de Santa Maria del Fiore et de San Giovanni*

A large number of ecclesiastical goldsmith works, sometimes very impressive, were produced in the late fifteenth and early sixteenth centuries. Many have survived, especially in the possession of the Duomo and Baptistery. These include the splendid case for a small French Gothic reliquary, the so-called Libretto in the form of a diptych. This came to San Giovanni from the Medici palace after it was seized in 1495, and the Calimala commissioned Paolo Sogliani to set it in a high-footed, tabernacle-style container with rich ornament and two large Calimala arms in enamel.

The same goldsmith produced the John Gualbertus reliquary for Vallombrosa in 1500. Two reliquaries of St. John the Baptist and St. Simeon Stylites in the Baptistery, likewise in the form of tall, slender polygonal vessels crowned with statuettes, also date from this period. So do the Verdiana reliquary in Castelfiorentino, dated 1506, and the particularly lavishly decorated monstrance for a relic of St. Anthony Abbot in the Duomo dating from 1514, a donation of the Parte Guelfa executed by Antonio di Salvi.[73]

Finally, let me make a brief reference to the decoration of objects of pontifical clothing with metal sculpture and enamel decoration. It is true that the various tiaras and morses that Ghiberti came to execute for the conciliar popes Martin V and Eugene IV have long since vanished. Only a mitre of a bishop of Fiesole has survived with silver gilt decorative borders in delicate relief and a wreath of enamelled half-figures of the Evangelists, all in the character of the early Quattrocento. It is now in the Duomo treasury there, set on a much later reliquary bust.

Several examples of bishops' crooks executed in artistic goldsmith work may be cited; these include two from the early Renaissance in the Bargello, and then the particularly magnificent pontifical ornaments from 1515 to

de Florence (Florence, 1903), p. 35 with illustration; and Landucci, Diario, pp. 51-52. The Badia at Settimo possesses two reliquaries in the form of tablets: one from the beginning of the fifteenth century, the other dated 1479, both with borders of decorative Gothic leaf ornament. The back of the more recent piece reveals ornamental engraving in contemporary style (RA, 1933, p. 218, with illustrations). Simpler counterparts to these are a pair of wooden altar decorations in the Carmine sacristy, framed with rich rinceaux work. One has an oval relic container, the other a Byzantine medallion as a centerpiece. In the Bargello are two monstrances very characteristic of late Quattrocento decorative arts, with relief rinceaux, enamelled medallions and lively curved knobs. A related object, in the Pitti Museo degli Argenti, was created around 1470 by using older parts with Renaissance ornament and a Medici coat of arms in enamel.

[73] Arnaldo Cocchi, Les anciens reliquaires de Santa Maria del Fiore et de San Giovanni de Florence (Florence, 1903), pp. 37ff.; Museo di San Marco, Mostra del Tesoro di Firenze Sacra (Florence, 1933), pp. 24-25; RA, 1933 pp. 90-91.

The canons of San Lorenzo had Antonio di Salvi produce a silver wash basin (for handwashing at the altar) and two altar cruets in 1508 in order to present them to the archbishop Cosimo de' Pazzi. The same workshops produced two silver basins, each with fifteen decorative enamels, for the Duomo of Pistoia (Vasari-Milanesi, 3:290, n. 2).

1516 donated by Leo X to the basilica of San Lorenzo. These consisted of a pearl-embroidered mitre, stola, and silver crozier whose curve, in the naturalistic style of northern late Gothic, was formed of interwoven knotty branches, surrounding a half-figure of St. Laurence sculptured in the round. This was a masterpiece of monumental effect, yet worked with the most loving detail (although probably north Italian).[74] Finally, Vasari (Vasari-Milanesi, 7:631) reports on the wooden walking sticks of the fathers of Camaldoli, whose knobs were adorned by Montorsoli's knife from about 1515 to 1520 with all sorts of fantastic heads and animal figures.

### SCULPTURE FOR DOMESTIC BUILDINGS

Much less extensive and diverse than the sphere of ecclesiastical commissions is the field of sculptural work for secular purposes. This is sculpture that was commissioned to decorate important dwellings and public secular buildings or took its place here and there on the exterior of buildings, somewhere along the streets. Yet it is remarkable enough, in contrast to all the countries north of the Alps, that in this context, besides the many devotional images, purely secular projects and subjects appear generally for the first time. And this meant not only statuettes, small-scale decorative pieces, splendid utilitarian objects, and the like—such as had long been produced already even in the North—but also monumental relief-sculpture and life-size busts and statues in the round. The portrait bust of a private person in clay or marble, executed on his own commission or on that of his family, already appears occasionally from the 1430s on and much more frequently soon thereafter. This is a type of sculptural project that at first was undertaken only in Italy and even here primarily and almost solely in Florence.

How then can we explain the emergence and swift rise to prominence of this type of image, previously just as unusual here as elsewhere?

Two preconditions in particular seem to have been decisive. One was the unusually lively interest, precisely in Florence, in the unique individuality of certain striking or otherwise prominent personalities. From such an interest arose the desire to seize and preserve for posterity the appearance of such personalities, not only in literary portrayals—see the early highly developed Florentine biographies—but also the physiognomic stamp of their features. The custom observed in many houses of preserving a tangible reminder of the facial features of a deceased family member through the production of death masks and of displaying such

[74] See also the bishop's staff of Donatello's St. Louis, ringed with figures of putti (RA, 1934).

masks in the house above doors or fireplaces arose from this and is repeatedly mentioned by Vasari (Vasari-Milanesi, 2:595; 3:372-73). Often the simple mask (*ritratto di gesso*) in some sort of casting material even seems to have been set up as a bust for more effective display in a room.[75]

Sometimes such heads were even cast in bronze, as the bust of an old woman (supposedly Annalena Malatesta) from the school of Donatello in the Bargello testifies. Cavalcanti based his 1447 memorial portrait of Brunelleschi on the original death mask of the Cathedral building master preserved in the Opera of the Duomo. Thus this represents a relatively early example of an artist's work based on a cast from nature (*RA*, 1930, pp. 535-37).[76]

A parallel to such casts of the facial features of the dead are the wax portrait heads of the *ex-voto* figures in the Annunziata and elsewhere, which were discussed above under church sculpture. According to an old report these were already being produced in considerable numbers in earlier times and were probably sometimes prepared by casting from the living model.

This, then, was one root of Florentine portrait sculpture. In addition, there was another impetus that pointed the way even more directly for artistic development. Ancient Roman portrait busts, prized from the awakening interest in collecting antiques, appeared in Florence along with other antiquities, sometime before the mid-Quattrocento.[77] The possession or examination of antique portrait busts must have prompted many connoisseurs and collectors to commission portrait sculpture themselves. In just the same way, the portrait bust and portrait statue had first been revived long before, in unmistakable connection with Roman prototypes, in the south Italian artistic circle of Frederick II with its similar antiquarian orientation. The new bond with the antique must have led the first sculptors of the Florentine early Renaissance, Nanni

[75] A certain Polo di Maestro Agnolo, who had his small bottega and residence on the Ponte Vecchio, had a reputation as a specialist in such brightly painted mask-busts (*RA*, 3, pp. 256ff.). Verrocchio supplied twenty different "maschere ritratte al naturale" to the Medici (*ASA*, 1, p. 163). In the Berlin Museum is a painted death mask with a head attached behind it (no. 239).

[76] In addition there is the death mask of St. Antoninus in San Marco, from which the various clay busts of the revered Dominican bishop are derived (in Santa Maria Novella, the Arch. Vescovile, etc.); the death mask of Lorenzo Magnifico in the Medici Museum, etc. The death mask of the prior Ambrogio Traversari, dating from 1439 and preserved in Camaldoli, was lent to the prior of the Angeli convent in 1491 (*RA*, 6, 1909, pp. 244-45).

[77] See Eugène Müntz (*Les Précurseurrs de la Renaissance*, Paris, 1882, pp. 110, 122) on antique busts in the collection of N. Niccoli, who died in 1437, of Poggio, and other humanists including Cosimo de' Medici.

and Donatello, to greet the realism and the decisive rendering of naturalistic details in Roman portrait sculpture as guides for their own striving
toward realism. Thus the first results of such studies (and this means an
additional direct training ground for portrait bust sculpture) appear in
their works of ecclesiastical statuary on the Duomo and Or San Michele.
Since about 1420, many of the heads there were so remarkably realistic
that certain of these prophets and apostles were recognized and designated by contemporary observers as actual likenesses of character types
known throughout the city (Donatello's *Zuccone*, etc.). Even in busts of
saints (for example, Donatello's *Laurence* and his *St. John* in Berlin) such
individualistic embodiment of ideal types appears with a highly immediate rendering of the expression, as a parallel to the contemporary secular portrait busts.[78] The same holds true for the portraits on tomb
monuments, which had already made considerable strides in realistic
portrait quality in the Trecento.[79]

Among all these preliminary stages and comparable objects, however,
the first commissions for individual busts stand out as something totally
new in conception and execution. In a survey of these works we are not
particularly preoccupied with the questions, so often pursued, of authorship and date. We ask less about the artistic authors than about the
initiators and subjects who created the preconditions for the emergence
and development of the portrait bust.

It is true that these questions can hardly be answered for what are
presumably the earliest busts that have come down to us, works of
Donatello and Michelozzo. Even the head of "Niccolò da Uzzano," so
strikingly realistic, does not unquestionably represent this important personality and can in no case be a realistic contemporary portrayal of the
man who died a septuagenarian in 1432.[80] The two bronze busts of

[78] Small heads that are clearly portraits of Ghiberti himself and his artistic contemporaries
can even be found in the series of medallions in high relief forming the corner decorations
in the borders of the Baptistery doors.

[79] Equestrian monuments are lacking in Florence—except for the wooden monument of
Piero Farnese dating from about 1370, which has not survived, and the painted equestrian
portraits of the Quattrocento, still extant in the Duomo. North Italy, on the other hand,
(Visconti in Milan, Scaliger tomb in Vernona) continues the Trecento beginnings with
various monuments cast in bronze by Florentine masters after antique models: Donatello's
*Gattamelata*, the contemporary, lost Este monument in Ferrara, Verrocchio's *Colleoni*, and
Leonardo's model for Milan that never reached the casting stage.

[80] This is true even if the bust was produced as early as 1427-1430, as Kauffmann
(*Donatello*, p. 49) believes. See the additional literature cited there. [*Translator's note*: The
"Niccolò da Uzzano" bust attributed to Donatello remains controversial with respect to
authorship as well as to the identification of the sitter. Accepted by Jane Schuyler in
*Florentine Busts: Sculpted Portraiture of the Fifteenth Century* (New York, 1976), pp.
114ff., it has nevertheless received other attributions as widely ranging as Desiderio da
Settignano (Ursula Schlegel, "Zu Donatello und Desiderio da Settignano. Beobachtungen

youths by Donatello in the Bargello, like the bust attributed to Michelozzo in a Roman private collection, are idealized in an antiquarian manner and also lack traditional identifications.[81]

Following these are the numerous busts of girls by Desiderio and Mino, commissioned, it may be assumed, by parents when one of their daughters was taken from the paternal household by marriage. Then there are the many busts of children that certainly in some cases are meant to represent the Christ Child or the young John the Baptist, but also are perhaps nothing other than likenesses of living or dead children of the patron; thus they are an intermediate stage between the family portrait and household devotional image.[82]

The male portrait busts are primarily likenesses of personalities who also played an active role in other aspects of Florentine art. It is true that among the Medici there is yet not one of Cosimo il Vecchio;[83] but his sons and grandsons are portrayed in busts by Verrocchio, Mino, and others. Then there is the stucco bust from the Palazzo Rucellai probably representing Giovanni Rucellai, builder of the palace, in Berlin and the marble bust of Pietro Mellini, donor of the marble pulpit in Santa Croce, by the same Benedetto da Maiano who later made the bust of Filippo Strozzi that has survived in two versions: a clay model in Berlin and a marble bust in the Louvre. Portrait heads of other prominent patrons may still occasionally be discovered among the none too numerous unidentified busts of the period. But the various commissions received by Mino and Antonio Rossellino indicate that the portrait bust's popularity was in no way limited to the merchant aristocracy.[84]

---

zur physiognomischen Gestaltung im Quattrocento," *Jahrbuch der Berliner Museen*, 1967, 9:135-55) and Pietro Torrigiano (M. G. Ciardi Dupré dal Poggetto, "Una nuova proposta per il 'Niccolo da Uzzano'," *Donatello e il suo tempo* [*Atti del VIII Convegno internazionale di studi sul Rinascimento, Firenze-Padova, 1966*], Florence, 1968, pp. 283-89). Rab Hatfield has suggested the subject is a member of the Capponi family, possibly Gino di Neri, the younger. See Rab C. Hatfield "Sherlock Holmes and the riddle of the 'Niccolò da Uzzano'," in *Studies Presented to Myron P. Gilmore*, ed. Sergio Bertelli and Gloria Ramakus, Florence, 1978, 2:219-83.]

[81] *Dedalo*, 12, p. 434.

[82] See Paul Schubring, *Die italienische Plastik des Quattrocento* (Berlin, 1915), pp. 93, 120, 126; and Wilhelm Bode, *Florentiner Bildhauer der Renaissance*, 4th ed. (Berlin, 1921), pp. 240ff. Two high relief heads in round medallions by Luca della Robbia (Bargello and Berlin), very individual in expression, represent a special type; both have slightly inclined heads and downward gazes and were thus intended to be placed in an upper wall zone, as is often noted of portrait heads in the Medici inventory.

[83] A bust from the Ergas collection was proposed as a portrait of Cosimo and a work of Donatello in *Pantheon*, 1932, pp. 117ff.

[84] These include the bust of the physician Giovanni da San Miniato in London, produced as early as 1456; that of the humanist Matteo Palmieri in the Bargello, dating from 1468; that of a monk, interpreted by Bode as the Florentine archbishop Orsino, formerly in the

Tombs and other honorific monuments sometimes also contain a bust or high relief profile portrait of the occupant as their main distinguishing feature.[85] There are also relief portraits in pure profile or three-quarter view on medium-sized plaques, as sculptural parallels to painted profile portraits. These may be executed either as simple, small format likenesses,[86] or in a decoratively enriched or otherwise idealized manner of portrayal.[87]

But after 1500 portrait sculpture comes almost to a complete stop while the painted portrait becomes cultivated to a particularly rich and significant extent in the High Renaissance.[88]

To go further, we may inquire about the first appearance of statuary sculpture in the round of a nonreligious subject, outside the ecclesiastical sphere. Until the late Quattrocento only one theme may be cited. Like the images of the months, the liberal arts, and other late medieval allegories, it stands on the border between the theological-ecclesiastical and the secular-bourgeois spheres: the statue of David.* This biblical figure had taken on a marked secular importance and application, not only

---

Hainauer collection, Berlin, and the head of an unknown Florentine from the Palazzo Guadagni, which came into the Berlin Museum. Mino did portraits of the Count della Luna (now in the Bargello), Dietisalvi Neroni, who also commissioned Mino to execute the marble altar of the Badia; of Niccolò Strozzi, who had settled in Rome; and also a Florentine apothecary, Antonio di Luca, who had himself portrayed in an unusual antiquarian costume (1485, Berlin).

[85] For the first case see: the Salutati tomb in Fiesole by Mino, that of Donato Medici in Pistoia by Antonio Rossellino, the honorific monuments to Brunelleschi, Giotto, and others in the Duomo. Examples of relief portraits are those on the Giugni tomb in the Badia by Mino and that of Lemmo Balducci dating from 1472 in Sant' Egidio.

[86] Examples are those of Cosimo de' Medici (Bargello and Berlin), Lorenzo Magnifico, Matthias Corvinus, and others. A marble relief portrait of Giovanni di Cosimo, who had died young, hung over a door in the Medici palace. See Eugène Müntz, *Les Collections des Médicis au XVe siècle* (Paris, 1888), p. 85.

[87] Examples are Mino's portrait of a richly costumed lady with the inscription, "et io da Mino o avuto el lume" (and I have received the light from Mino; Mino has given me life), in the Bargello, and above all, various antiquarian ideal heads sometimes identified as Roman emperors and generals: the "Caesar" by Desiderio in the Louvre, an "Aurelius Caesar" in the Bargello, and as a particularly splendid piece, the Scipio made by Verrocchio (if not by Leonardo) in the Louvre. There is a majolica variant in Berlin. Vasari (Vasari-Milanesi, 3:361) discusses bronze reliefs of Alexander and Darius, works of Verrocchio, sent to Hungary as gifts from Lorenzo Magnifico to King Matthias Corvinus (see also the antiquizing portrait relief in the Bardini museum). E. Möller in *Raccota vinciana*, 14, 1934.

[88] A few powerful busts from the 1520's in Berlin significantly represent not contemporaries, but personalities of the Quattrocento (Lorenzo Magnifico, Palla Ruccellai). Baccio da Montelupo was commissioned to execute a wax bust of the young Duke Giuliano as an *ex-voto* portrait for the Annunziata in 1513.

* *Translator's note*: For more recent literature on the David theme in Florentine art see Translator's Introduction, p. xiii.

through a realistic portrayal appropriate to the times, but especially through the special significance attached to him in Florence. For this youthful hero and victor of the Old Testament had in fact become a general symbol of military *virtus* for the Florentine consciousness somewhat in the same manner as the painted cycle of *Uomini famosi* (see below), the Neuf Preux, and figures from ancient history and the Old Testament had long been brought together and often displayed in secular contexts as universal representatives of all military, political, and spiritual virtues.

Therefore we see how already Donatello's first David statue, originally commissioned to crown a pinnacle above a buttress on the exterior architecture of the Duomo and therefore, naturally, as a biblical figure, was transferred a few years after its completion to the Palazzo Vecchio for a secular function. Thus the David theme could evidently have acquired that general meaning immediately. A little later Donatello was called on to execute a marble David statue (now in the museum in Philadelphia) for the family palace of his first patron, Martelli.* Donatello's third, bronze David figure, according to Kauffmann's convincing discussion, was produced only around 1455-1456, as a monumental central accent for the Medici palace, just completed at that time. From there it was transferred to the Palazzo Vecchio in 1495 to serve a corresponding purpose. In each place it had the same significance, to which its antique nudity also corresponded very well.[89]

But Verrocchio's bronze *David*, probably commissioned around 1465-1466 by Cosimo's son Piero, presumably for Careggi (now in the Bargello), embodies, instead of an antique heroic character, rather the richly adorned, aristocratic ideal type of the elegant victor in a tourney in the taste of the late Quattrocento. The circle closes at the beginning of the sixteenth century with Michelangelo's "Gigante," which once again, like Donatello's first *David*, was intended for use on the Duomo, in line with the theme's ecclesiastical-biblical significance. With its placement in front of the Palazzo della Signoria the political-military significance of the

---

* *Translator's note*: The "Martelli David," now in the National Gallery of Art in Washington, is particularly controversial as to attribution. John Pope-Hennessy has assigned it to Antonio Rossellino ("The Martelli David," *Burlington Magazine*, 101, 1959, pp. 134-39, reprinted in Pope-Hennessy's *Essays on Italian Sculpture* [London and New York, 1968], pp. 65-71). Frederick Hartt has suggested rather Bernardo Rossellino in "New Light on the Rossellino Family," *Burlington Magazine*, 103, 1961, pp. 387-92. Ursula Schlegel has proposed the statue is not by Donatello's hand but is based on his design, which she suggests survives in the bronze statuette of David in Berlin ("Problemi intorno al David Martelli," *Donatello e il suo tempo* [Atti del VIII Convegno internazionale di studi sul Rinascimento, Firenze-Padova, 1966], Florence, 1968, pp. 245-58.)

[89] See Kauffmann, *Donatello*, p. 143, with reference to the connection of this, as well as the Judith, with the contemporary plans for a crusade.

David theme, by this time much more obvious, asserted itself again with special emphasis.

In the meantime another figure from ancient Jewish history, the female counterpart to David, the tyrant-slayer Judith, also appeared in a very impressive statuary form as a general exemplary embodiment of heroic struggle for freedom. This was the work of Donatello's old age, originally planned and set up as the center of a fountain in one of the Medici villas (thus as an approximately contemporary counterpart to the two small paintings of the same subject by Botticelli). The original purpose of this group, still recognizable in the fountain opening at the foot, has nothing to do with the historical meaning of the form, and essentially it corresponds very little even to the paradigmatic significance attached to it. Yet this last meaning of the Judith theme received an unambiguous enough expression in the inscription placed on it at the time of its later installation on the *ringhiera* of the Palazzo della Signoria in 1495, as well as from this position itself (see above).

Donatello's and Verrocchio's Davids, as well as the Judith group, originated as monumental centerpieces for an architectural space, court, or garden parterre. The situation was similar for Benedetto da Maiano's *Justitia*, produced in 1475 to crown a decorated portal in the Palazzo Vecchio. From this very appropriate position it dominated the audience hall of the city's chief officials.

Donatello's *Dovizia* may be cited here as the sole recorded example of a statue erected in an open square. This over-life-sized stone figure, with a basket of fruit on its head, was set up on a high column in the center of the Mercato Vecchio toward the end of the 1420s.[90] A sort of counterpart to this was the bronze putto by Verrocchio, also lost, that served as a bell-ringer on the clock at the Mercato.[91]

Putto figures also appeared frequently as gracefully animated crowning or flanking elements in architectonic wall decorations above fountain columns, etc. They turn up singly or in pairs, often with garlands.[92] The genre character of Verrocchio's putto with the dolphin is echoed in var-

---

[90] It fell down and was shattered in 1721 (Bocchi-Cinelli, *Le bellezze della citta*, p. 215; Kauffmann, *Donatello*, p. 41, with a small illustration based on an old city view).

[91] See Vasari-Milanesi, 3:375; Bocchi-Cinelli, *Le bellezze della citta*, p. 217. His forerunner, in Siena, was a brass figure executed by Dello Delli for the clockwork of the town hall (Vasari-Milanesi, 3:147-48n.).

[92] Examples are in the wall decoration of one Duomo sacristy and on a wall fountain in the same place, then in a purely antiquarian rendition, once again by Donatello, in the unusual bronze figure of the cupid Atys in the Bargello and a small bronze putto with a water-spouting fish in the South Kensington Museum, probably from an indoor fountain. See Wihelm Bode, *Die italienische Bronzestatuetten der Renaissance, kleine neu bearbeitete Ausgabe* (Berlin, 1922), plate 5. In addition, there is Verrocchio's bronze putto with the dolphin, which came into the Palazzo Vecchio courtyard from the garden at Careggi.

ious individual figures of the Robbia workshop, like the urinating majolica putto from the garden of the Palazzo Pucci now in the Berlin Museum—a Florentine forerunner of the Brussels *Mannekin-Pis*.[93]

The putto, in his various decorative uses, is probably the first purely antique motif taken up in early Renaissance sculpture. Along with this came the nude ephebe that Donatello introduced as David. As such it is explainable only in the house of a patron who was also an antique collector. Thus here also, as in the beginnings of portrait sculpture, we see the interpenetration of the patron's admiration for the antique and the artist's formal interest in antique models. But in the second phase of the early Renaissance, secular statuary sculpture was cultivated as little as ecclesiastical statuary. This accords with the general tendency of this stage of development, leaning more toward delicate elegance and ornamental splendor than large-scale monumentality. New large-scale statuary commissions and creations, even in the sphere of secular projects, began to appear again only in connection with the stylistic change at the close of the fifteenth century. These include the lost statue of Hercules that the young Michelangelo undertook on his own initiative, according to Condivi, and his *Bacchus* of 1496-1497—the first figure fully antique even in subject—executed, it is true, for a Florentine living in Rome. Admittedly it took a form that was truly late quattrocentesque and from the range of antique models could make use only of the naturalism of the late period. Around 1515-1518 the young Jacopo Sansovino produced his spiritedly idealized *Bacchus* for the Bartolini garden casino in Gualfonda; it is now in the Bargello.[94]

In the problems they posed, these works of secular statuary, admittedly none too numerous, show a firmly established and pervasive bond with the rich stimulus of the antique. But beyond this, the steadily growing interest in the possession of original antique works, which stimulated increasingly frequent excavations, brought the artist himself into intimate contact with such examples through the completion, evidently demanded

[93] Several slightly earlier marble variants of the same motif are in Florence, Museo Bardini, the Louvre, etc. In addition there are all sorts of figures of playing putti, sometimes in pairs as in Vienna, Liechtenstein, and the Berlin Museum. See Wilhelm Bode, *Florentiner Bildhauer der Renaissance*, 4th ed. (Berlin, 1921), pp. 253ff.

[94] Vasari, however, mentions a colossal statue of King Porsena, already lost by his time, by Jacopo's teacher Andrea Sansovino in Montepulciano (Vasari-Milanesi, 4:522; 7:493).

Rustici's small bronze *Mercury*, poised on a sphere (like the subsequent famous work of Giambologna), is also lost. It was probably executed around 1525 on the commission of Cardinal Giulio de' Medici for a fountain in the Palazzo Medici. Finally there is the Orpheus statue by Bandinelli on a richly decorated pedestal by Benedetto da Rovezzano, executed for the same patron and place, as a central ornament for the courtyard (the pedestal is in the Bargello, the figure itself in a staircase of the Palazzo Vecchio; see *RA*, 9, pp. 59ff.).

rather often, of fragmentary finds and the production of copies of particularly popular pieces.[95] The eager demand for saleable antiques on the part of the first representatives of professional art dealership emerging at this time also gave rise to occasional efforts to pass off forgeries. The story of Michelangelo's sleeping cupid, palmed off on a Roman cardinal by an intermediary as an alleged discovery from an excavation, is a case in point.

A genre in recurring and wide demand in the High Renaissance may be mentioned only briefly in this connection. This is secular imagery of perishable material, created in the context of ephemeral festival decorations, triumphal arches, show facades, and the like, to be discussed later in another context (see below).

Only a little may be adduced here concerning relief sculpture with secular subjects and purposes, aside from the already mentioned portrait reliefs. And for these also antique models were the immediate point of departure and stimulus, with respect to type as well as form and content. The earliest examples are probably the marble medallions above the courtyard arcades of the Palazzo Medici, in which a sculptor of Donatello's school, Maso di Bartolommeo, made use of prototypes from the cameo collection of the old Cosimo in 1452. In addition there are two bacchic relief scenes in marble and clay from the 1460s now in Berlin.[96] Bertoldo's bronze equestrian battle from the Palazzo Medici was executed around 1475 as a fairly faithful copy of a damaged marble sarcophagus in Pisa. It indirectly influenced Michelangelo's youthful work of about 1493, the marble relief of the *Battle of Centaurs*.[97] From the High Renaissance we may cite only the terra-cotta reliefs from Villa Salviati, executed by Rustici shortly before their destruction in the *assedio*.[98]

But the sculptural inventory of domestic buildings also includes, besides works with secular subjects, the far broader area of religious household

[95] Records of such activities already exist for the late Quattrocento (Verrocchio's completion of a red marble Marsyas-torso for Lorenzo de Medici, now in the Uffizi) and later for Jacopo Sansovino (Vasari-Milanesi, 3:349, 367; 7:489-90; *Pantheon*, 1937, pp. 329ff.).

[96] Schottmüller, *Bildwerke*, 66, 195. The relief compositions of antique sacrifice scenes on Vittorio Ghiberti's base for the *Idolino* might also be mentioned here, as well as the frieze of figures by Giuliano da Sangallo on the portico of Poggio a Caiano (in brightly glazed majolica, around 1485). Finally there are the relief-sculptured frames around the Sassetti tombs in Santissima Trinita (see *l'Arte*, 13, pp. 385ff.).

[97] See Müntz, *Collections*, p. 84; Wilhelm Bode, *Bertoldo und Lorenzo de' Medici* (Freiburg im Breisgau, 1925), p. 53ff. Vasari (Vasari-Milanesi, 2:296-97) also mentions a bronze relief by Pollaiuolo, a "battaglia d'ignudi." Many plaster casts of it could be seen in Florence in his time, while the original was supposedly sold into Spain. Also by Bertoldo is a small bronze strip of relief, about fifty centimeters long (probably part of a frieze inlay) with a children's Bacchanal (Bargello). In the vestibule of Palazzo Guicciardini is a stucco relief of Hercules and Cacus.

[98] Vasari-Milanesi, 6:606.

art that we had best consider here in accordance with its location in private domestic settings.

On the one hand, there are all sorts of small works of sculpture in the round, like the previously mentioned busts of the Christ Child and John the Baptist, wooden crucifixes, and clay or bronze statuettes of particular saints, at first probably often originating as preparatory *bozzetti* for larger works in marble, but sometimes also specifically for such household use. Among these are above all the innumerable Madonna reliefs.

These works are distinguished from those intended for church settings by their relatively small dimensions and the more intimate, sometimes genre treatment of the theme, often also by the simpler material, such as painted plaster, stucco, or *cartapesta*, preferred here because of cheapness or the possibility of bright coloring. As to their shape and mounting, they were tondi, that is, round images, or *colmi*, that is, semicircular reliefs, often set in little painted or gilded tabernacles, sometimes of marble, more frequently of wood. These were sometimes provided with little doors painted with figural or ornamental decoration. Small niches could sometimes be found set into the walls of rooms, which could receive such half-length Madonna figures (as repeatedly, for example, in the Palazzo Davanzati, redecorated in its time).[99] The vast number of surviving examples of such images allows us to surmise the former enormous extent of this genre. Virtually every house must have possessed at least one example, if not several.[100] The series leads from Donatello and his contemporaries through Desiderio, Rossellino, Verrocchio, to the two monumental marble tondi of Michelangelo executed about 1504. Many of the especially numerous brightly glazed Madonna reliefs of the Robbia workshop were probably displayed in private interiors, but the great majority were intended for the exterior walls of houses and churches.

Narrative reliefs are found only rarely among household devotional images. It is uncertain whether Donatello's marble carvings belong in this category; on the other hand, according to the Medici palace inventory, Bertoldo's bronze Crucifixion panel hung there in the chamber of the future Cardinal and Pope Leo.[101]

[99] Regarding the tondo, verifiably in such use since about 1460, see the monograph by Moritz Hauptmann, *Der Tondo* (Frankfurt am Main, 1936), pp. 137ff. A variant uses a mandorla-shaped frame with a decorative border of cherubim and a broad base; an example is one in Berlin (Schottmüller, *Bildwerke*, p. 158). Earlier times generally still employed the pointed arch bordered with gothicizing decoration.

[100] In the Palazzo Medici alone, according to the inventory of 1492 (see Müntz, *Collections*), there were no less than nine sculptural images of the Madonna (and roughly as many painted household Madonnas).

[101] In the Bargello, besides the piece just cited and a Lamentation by Bertoldo, is an additional Crucifixion relief by Donatello. The ornate Forzori household altar, surviving only in an unfinished clay sketch (London, South Kensington Museum), was also completed

Besides these figural works, the furnishing of important interiors also called for much decorative sculpture in stone, wood, bronze, and wrought iron. At least a brief selection and survey of such work will be given below.

We may speak first of the stone-sculptured accents that stand out from the wood decoration between wall panelling and pieces of movable furniture: the frames of fireplaces, often provided with figural decoration, the lavabo niches, and all sorts of richly decorated interior portals.

For fireplaces, in the early Quattrocento and even later, the application of coats of arms or other sparingly distributed emblems seemed sufficient. The upper ledge of the mantelpiece was used for the display of family busts and other small works of sculpture.[102] The richer style that had developed since the middle of the century is illustrated by a marble fireplace attributed to Desiderio with putti sculptured in the round on the front of the side consoles, idealizing portrait medallions in the frieze, and other decorations. It is from a villa near San Miniato and now in the South Kensington Museum, London.[103] The exceptionally splendid marble chimneypiece by Giuliano da Sangallo in the Palazzo Gondi dating from after 1490 exhibits more extensive and diverse figural decoration. But the early sixteenth century developed the greatest display of splendor, together with an increase in size, in a chimneypiece from Palazzo Borgherini and now in the Bargello by Benedetto da Rovezzano, dating from around 1525. Its frieze relief is rich with figures, and it is crowned with putto figures and massive structures for the coats of arms.[104]

Among stone wall fountains from domestic interiors, the secular counterparts to sacristy and refectory fountains, I cite first of all the charming example in the Palazzo Vecchio with the lily arms in stone intarsia datable around 1460-1470. In addition, there is the wall fountain in the Bargello with the Medici-Federighi arms and decorative relief ornament on the pilaster; it is severely weathered and thus probably from the courtyard

by Donatello around 1460. The very elegant framed Entombment panel in Vienna is by a follower of his.

[102] See the examples in the Badia Fiesolana, the former Pitti Villa Rusciano, and in the upper story of the Fondazione Horne, etc.

[103] A fragment of a similarly decorated chimneypiece is in the Museo Bardini; in the same place is a mantelpiece, likewise in Desiderio's style, in pietra serena with an ideal female head as the central decoration, flanked by garlands, cherubim, and coats of arms. A richly decorated fireplace, probably part of the building's original furnishings, is in the Fondazione Horne, first upper story.

[104] See the fireplace design in Rovezzano's style among the drawings in the Uffizi (Alinari photo 549). See also the chimneypiece represented in Andrea del Sarto's birth of Mary dated 1514. Vasari mentions (Vasari-Milanesi, 4:310) two terra-cotta medallions with heads of Roman emperors by Andrea Sansovino for a wall chimneypiece, thus modelled as bozzetti for a definitive execution in stone.

of a villa. Finally, as a particularly splendid example of its kind, also from the late Quattrocento, there is the fountain niche attributed to Benedetto da Maiano in the South Kensington Museum, London.[105]

Examples of richly decorated interior portal frames are the elegant marble portal in the old meeting room of the Parte Guelfa, dating from around 1420-1425, still in the early transitional style; then the splendid double-sided portal with a decorative crown of statues, by Benedetto da Maiano, on the upper floor of the Palazzo Vecchio. Finally there is the severe, High Classical stone portal (thus dating from the early fifteenth century) from the Linaiuoli guild hall, now under the Bargello courtyard arcade.

The above mentioned indoor wall fountains suggest the existence of free-standing fountains set up here and there outdoors in courts and gardens, with sculptural decoration on the basin or central stem. Fountain statues by Donatello and Verrocchio that were once in Medici possession have already been discussed. Another lost fountain that was once in the rear garden court of the Palazzo Medici also bore putti with water-spouting dolphins executed by Antonio Rossellino, according to Vasari's description (Vasari-Milanesi, 3:93).[106] The richly decorated marble fountain basin from Villa Castello, probably by Francesco Ferrucci, now stands in the vestibule of the Pitti gallery.

In connection with this, reference should be made to the related form of certain decoratively enriched bases for statues. These include the base of Donatello's bronze *David* and four statue pedestals decorated similarly to each other from the second half of the Quattrocento, also in the Donatello room at the Bargello. The base of the *marzocco* in front of the Palazzo Vecchio from about 1450 is especially richly adorned with streamers and coats of arms. In addition there is the small marble socle of Verrocchio's *David*, produced and provided with the insignia of the commune for its installation in the Palazzo della Signoria, 1476. The richly decorated bronze pedestal that Lorenzo Magnifico had executed for the antique *Idolino* statue, probably by the younger Ghiberti, dates from about the same time (Museo Archeologico). This is a particularly

---

[105] Illustrations are in Lensi, *Palazzo Vecchio*, p. 217; and Attilio Schiaparelli, *La casa fiorentina ed i suoi arredi nei secoli XIV e XV* (Florence, 1908), p. 94, which includes a few additional simpler examples, pp. 83ff. A wooden intarsiaed *acquaio* is mentioned in the inventory of the Palazzo Medici.

[106] Its motif was thus closely related to Verrocchio's well-known bronze fountain putto with the dolphin from the Villa Castello. But Verrocchio also produced a marble garden fountain for King Matthias Corvinus in 1488, according to Vasari (Vasari-Milanesi, 3:361n.); see also *MA*, 1, p. 143. The clay model of a fountain sculpture, two putti with a dolphin, is in the South Kensington Museum. A charming majolica fountain, sculptured in the round, probably by Andrea della Robbia, is in the Dresden Albertinum. See also Bertha Wiles, *The Fountains of Florentine Sculptors* (Cambridge, Mass. 1933).

characteristic work for the Laurentian period's delight in splendor of detail. Finally, at the very end of our period, comes the powerful marble base by Benedetto da Rovezzano for Bandinelli's Hercules statue in the Bargello courtyard.

There were also certain tasks calling for functional sculpture attached to the exterior walls of palaces, in addition to the generally very sparing decoration of the architectural members. For one thing there were large coats of arms of the family dwelling there, usually affixed high up on the corners of the palace or above the central portal; then the wrought iron torch holders and the rings, originally for the tethering of horses; the corner lanterns (*lumiere*)—whose display was moreover a privilege granted only to certain families—and finally the bronze door-knockers.

Certain artistically noteworthy coats of arms may be cited to start with: the one made by the young Donatello for the Martelli, now in Casa Martelli on Via della Forca; also in Donatello's style is the large marble coat of arms of Niccolò da Uzzano accompanied by two putti, on the former Sapienza building, from around 1430; see below, and the especially ornate Rucellai arms by Bernardo Rossellino, surrounded by a fruit garland, with Fortune as a helmet crest, in the courtyard of their palace.[107] Finally there is the whole series of brightly glazed majolica arms that Luca and Andrea della Robbia produced, on Or San Michele and elsewhere.[108]

The torch holders and corner lanterns of the Strozzi and Guadagni palaces are especially noteworthy for their elegant workmanship. They are works of the artist-smith Caparra, also well known as an original personality (see below). He and other colleagues sometimes achieved remarkable results in executing wrought-iron andirons (called *alari*) and other utensils for household use.[109]

The field of projects in portable small-scale sculpture still remains to be discussed. This includes all small bronze statuettes as well as any kind of carefully and expensively executed objects for daily use: tableware, ornaments, decorated weapons, and the like. For the first field, the miniature world of statuettes, bronze medallions and plaquettes, the vast

[107] *RA*, 1933, p. 119. See also the conspicuous coat of arms still on the Becchi house opposite Or San Michele (by Donatello, according to Bocchi-Cinelli, *Le bellezze della citta*, p. 70). Nearby, on the palace of the Arte della Seta, is the shield with the guild's arms, surrounded by putti. The elegant Altoviti arms by Benedetto da Rovezzano, of about 1520, are on the *canonica* built by this family near Santi Apostoli, etc.

[108] Other examples are in the Bargello; there are also the brightly glazed arms of a *podesta* in the courtyard; a coat of arms of the Porta Rossa quarter by Andrea della Robbia, dated 1523, is in the Berlin Museum.

[109] See Schiaparelli, *Casa*, pp. 111-12, 255-57. Bode identifies the Donatellesque bronze figurine of a winged genius with a cornucopia in the Berlin Museum, around 1425, as a former sconce.

number of surviving monuments has been so extensively researched and publicized through special studies and comprehensive publications that we may confine ourselves here, in view of this special literature, to a brief summary. The other field, however, that of small works of applied arts in metal and precious metal, has understandably come down to us in only a few tangible examples. For certain types there is nothing at all but literary citations. The scholarly research on these things is also so far in arrears that here we may at best provide only a suggestive survey of the scope, the subject matter, and the formal character of this type of commission. In this field also, as is true in general, even famous artists were engaged to design and execute the objects, along with workers who were more strictly craftsmen.

We may view the production of bronze statuettes of secular subjects and the demand that gave rise to this production, like the emergence of large-scale secular sculpture, primarily as an outgrowth of the collector's interest in antique discoveries of a similar nature. Thus the models for these works, as far as subject matter goes, are taken almost exclusively from the sphere of antique images. The whole genre, except for certain statuettes of Donatello and his time which were first used as church or household utensils, appears fully developed only since about 1470, with Pollaiuolo's and Bertoldo's works. And an essential stimulus presumably came above all from the connoisseur's interest of Lorenzo Magnifico himself in the revival of this as well as other branches of small-scale antique art.[110]

Florentine production of portrait medals begins, after the earlier north Italian works of Pisanello and others, only around 1466-1468, with the commemorative medal for Cosimo de' Medici by an unknown artist and the portrait medals of his sons Piero and Giovanni.[111] Certain medals by Bertoldo, executed on commission from Lorenzo Magnifico, appear next. First of all there is the commemorative medal for the Pazzi conspiracy of 1478, which in an unusual manner displays a large portrait head of Lorenzo on one side and his murdered brother Giuliano on the other and under these the portrayal of a scene, usually contained on a medal's obverse, here the attack in front of the Duomo choir. Besides these there are numerous portrait medals of contemporary princely personages, also produced on Lorenzo's commission, not at the orders of the ones portrayed. These were probably cast in precious metal for his own great collection of medals, with bronze versions to be used as gifts.[112] These

[110] See Wilhelm Bode, *Die italienische Bronzestatuetten der Renaissance, kleine neu bearbeitete Ausgabe* (Berlin, 1922), and especially Bode, *Bertoldo*.

[111] These medals are copied as decorations in the title page border of a Plutarch manuscript in the Laurenziana, produced for Piero (illustrated in van Marle, *Painting*, 11:476).

[112] The Medici inventory of 1456, thus from Cosimo's time, listed only thirty-seven

portrait medals all exhibit richly symbolic allegorical compositions on the reverse, whose conceptual content was perhaps suggested to the artist by Lorenzo himself (Bode, *Bertoldo*, pp. 37-38).

The most active and prominent Florentine medalist was Niccolò Spinelli (1430-1514), who had first worked as a die cutter at the Burgundian court of Charles the Bold. Thanks to him in particular we possess a whole series of portrait medals from the intimate circle of Lorenzo Magnifico.[113] At least three other specialists, hardly less excellent and prolific, were active in Florence at the same time. For the present they can be designated only by their favorite reverse emblems: the Medailleur à l'Aigle to whom a portrait medal of Filippo Strozzi is due, among others; the Spes master, to whom a medal of Marsilio Ficino is attributed; and the Fortuna Master.

The whole genre consists, even more exclusively than for the bronze statuettes, of objects designed purely for collectors. Accordingly, they were geared at first only to the narrow upper class of the humanistically and aesthetically educated, the amateur and connoisseur. A series of commemorative medals of the most popular figure of the years after the overthrow of the Medici, Savonarola, shows how fully this most intimate form of portrait sculpture had become established as an impressive token of remembrance. These medal portraits, traceable in three different types, are attributed in some quarters to two members of the della Robbia family who lived as monks in Savonarola's convent, in others to the famous gem cutter Giovanni delle Corniole. Their public was surely an entirely different one from that of the medals cited up to this point.[114]

Finally there is the third species of small-scale relief sculpture, the plaquette, whose introduction and wide diffusion may be associated first of all with the late Quattrocento love of luxury and demand for ornaments and also with the period's inexhaustible craving for narrative images that is represented particularly in paintings, cassoni, and wainscoting panels, in a similar but more widespread and varied manner. Here it is a matter of bas-relief, mostly on a small scale, in a round, oval, or

---

bronze medals of his own period (thus probably primarily by Pisanello), along with about 350 antique gold and silver coins; while the inventory of 1492 numbers no less than 1844 bronze medals. See Cornelius von Fabriczy, *Medaillen der italienischen Renaissance* (Leipzig, 1902-1903), p. 10; in addition see Habicht, *Die Medailleure der italienischen Renaissance* (Stuttgart, 1923).

[113] The roughly twenty-five medals by him include, among others, Lorenzo himself and his brother Giuliano (with the figure of Nemesis, related to his murder, on the reverse); also their uncle, Giovanni Tornabuoni, the patron of the Ghirlandaio frescoes in Santa Maria Novella, and his son Lorenzo and daughter-in-law Giovanna degli Albizzi, to whom Botticelli's wedding paintings in the Villa Lemmi were dedicated; but also the two great humanists of the period, Pico della Mirandola and Poliziano.

[114] See Cornelius von Fabriczy, *Medaillen der italienischen Renaissance* (Leipzig, 1902-1903), pp. 55ff.; and Schnitzer, *Savonarola*, 2:817-18.

rectangular form. These were sometimes attached to or set into the exterior surfaces of small wood or metal caskets or the center of flat vessels, or worn as ornaments. It is true that only a few pieces have survived in the form of their original use that may be taken as the essential motivation and purpose of all these small reliefs. On the other hand, a very great number exist that have been removed from their settings or were even initially cast as separate copies in bronze and simple lead.[115]

Finally, certain diminutive household devotional images or small portable altarpieces cast in bronze, with Madonna reliefs in decorative frames, may be grouped with these. Among many others there are the little Madonna altar, attributed to Filarete, in the Louvre, a small relief plaque with a standing Madonna and putti by Bertoldo in the same place, and two fairly large round plaquettes of the Madonna from the school of Donatello and a similar small image in Verrocchio's style in the Berlin Museum.[116]

I pass over the most closely related branch of small-scale sculpture, the art of minute stone-carving on gems and cameos, with a reference to their appearance in the late Quattrocento, also called forth by a collector's interest in antique works of the same sort.[117] I also mention here the genre of die cutting for coinage and seals, only because large-scale sculptors like Ciuffagni since 1435 and, along with him, Michelozzo until 1447 were in the service of the Florentine mint.[118] Naturally much of the evidence for this branch has survived. On the other hand, almost all tangible evidence is lacking for applied small-scale decorative sculpture as it was repeatedly used in the creation and adornment of weapons and armor for tournaments and also in costly tableware and elegant fashionable ornaments for women and men.

We may imagine decorated helmets, for example, as particularly splendid objects of ornamental knightly armor. These were conferred on various occasions by the city government or the Parte Guelfa in its name as

[115] For example, the little round relief with scenes from the legend of Orpheus and other ancient mythology, attributed by Bode to Bertoldo. See Bode, *Bertoldo*, pp. 39ff., 50-51, the illustration of one side of a rectangular casket cast in lead with an inset relief, and a bronze inkwell with scenes from the story of Coriolanus.

[116] These are illustrated in Adolfo Venturi, *Storia dell' Arte Italiana*, 25 vols. (Milan, 1901-1940), 6:543; Bode, *Bertoldo*, p. 67; Hans Mackowsky, *Verrocchio* (Bielefeld, 1901), p. 5.

[117] Details are in Ernst Kris, *Meister und Meisterwerke der Steinschneidekunst in der italienischen Renaissance* (Vienna, 1929). The stone medallions in the courtyard of the Palazzo Medici show how antique gem images were sometimes used for larger stone reliefs (see above).

[118] Michelozzo, who received a fixed annual salary for this service, had, for example, to carve the seal of the *catasto* authorities, established in 1427. (See *JPK*, 1904, suppl., pp. 34-36; *Gallerie Nazionale Italiane*, 2, 171, pl. 31ff.).

prizes for the victor in a tournament (see below) or in the granting of knighthood, as was done for Florentine military leaders after particularly meritorious feats of arms. These *elmetti* were worked in silver and crowned with emblematic ornaments chased and sculptured in the round; sculptor-goldsmiths like Pollaiuolo and Verrocchio often handled the design and execution.[119]

The decorative form of such helmets may essentially be imagined by reference to that relief of a general, possibly by Leonardo da Vinci, but in any case stemming from Verrocchio's workshop. The finest version of it is in the Louvre collection in Paris (see above). The secure Leonardo drawing of an antique general also provides a point of reference. So does the ornate helmet with a splendid dragon figure of about 1470-1480, preserved in the Bargello, as well as another with an upraised snake's head in the Bardini collection.[120] Thus even that ideal image of a general in the relief just mentioned may not have gone too far beyond the level of splendor that was actually produced and in use.

The same holds true for breast-plates with relief decoration like the ones worn by Donatello's *Gattamelata* and especially the youthful warrior of a clay bust by Pollaiuolo in the Bargello and Verrocchio's portrait busts of the two Medici brothers in Paris, the André Collection, and Boston. The Palazzo Medici inventory of 1492 mentions several costly pieces of armor (see *l'Arte*, 17, 1914, p. 387). In Turin is an unusually splendid decorated sword, whose apocryphal Donatello signature admittedly also casts doubts on the genuineness of the object itself.[121] Such splendid swords were furthermore sometimes presented to the Signoria of Florence by Pope Eugene IV (1440), as well as by Leo X, to reward special service to the Curia.[122]

---

[119] Jacopo Salviati, for example, received such an honorific helmet with silver-gilt ornament, Florentine lilies, and emblems of the Parte Guelfa when he became a knight in 1404. After his death in 1412 this splendid object, which under other circumstances would surely have been preserved for generations as an honorable family heirloom, had to be melted down to defray the burial expenses for the knight, who had died in poverty (*RA*, 7, 1910, pp. 151-52).

Jacopo degli Alessandri had a silver helmet decoration with a griffon figure made by Maso di Bartolommeo around 1447, probably for a tournament. See Masi's *Ricordi*, trans. Hubert Janitschek, Quellenschriften für Kunstgeschichte, 11 (Vienna, 1877), appendix, p. 259.

Antonio del Pollaiuolo made the silver helmet that the city conferred on its military captain, the Duke of Urbino, after the subjugation of Volterra in 1472. In 1481 he furnished Bernardo Salutati's relief-sculptured equipment for a tournament (Gaye, *Carteggio*, 1:571; Vasari-Milanesi 3:298n.).

[120] *Dedalo*, 6:1, pp. 174ff. Compare also the rich small-figured relief decoration in the helmet of Goliath under Donatello's bronze *David*.

[121] Illustrated in Marcel Reymond, *La Sculpture Florentine* (Florence, 1897-1900), 2:123.

[122] Masi, Bartolommeo, *Ricordanze di Bartolommeo Masi, calderaio fiorentino, dal 1478 al 1526*, ed. G. Odoardo Corazzini (Florence, 1906), p. 185.

I can cite only a few other notices that concern small pendants produced by goldsmiths for festive wear. Yet I cannot name a single surviving example of this by no means inconsiderable field of Florentine goldsmith work.[123]

The tableware of precious metal, for which we find occasional literary mentions, has almost without exception been melted down in later periods. It must surely have been frequently provided with rich artistic decoration.[124] Numerous cups, bowls, and other tableware, sometimes decorated with great imagination, have survived only from the holdings of Piero and Lorenzo de' Medici. They are fortunately preserved, thanks to their subsequent use as reliquaries in the treasury of San Lorenzo, and will be discussed in greater detail below in the section on patrons.

[123] In 1462-1464 Maso Finiguerra produced all sorts of filigreed, nielloed silver ornaments for Cino di Filippo Rinucci, according to the latter's domestic chronicle in the Biblioteca Marucelliana; in the same place the chronicler mentions belt ornaments, two *tremolanti* (pendants) and small silver-gilt chains that he had Antonio Pollaiuolo make. See Michelangelo Gualandi, *Memorie Originali italiane risguardanti le belle arti,* 6 series (Bologna, 1840-1845) 4:140-41. According to Vasari, the silver garlands with which young girls bound their hair were first invented by Ghirlandaio's father, although they were in fact a type of decoration that had been in use much longer (Vasari-Milanesi, 3:254, n. 3).

[124] Vasari, for example, refers to two large silver-gilt *tazze* that Verrocchio had adorned with leaf decorations and a ring of putti as well as "animali ed altre bizzarrie" (Vasari-Milanesi, 3:358).

CHAPTER 3

# PAINTING COMMISSIONS

## WALL PAINTING AND STAINED GLASS IN THE INTERIOR OF CHURCHES AND CONVENT BUILDINGS

From the extensive field of commissions for painters we shall consider first the monumental genre of wall and ceiling paintings in churches or convents. Here in particular, in order to achieve some measure of completeness in a survey of the scope and nature of commissions as well as the employment of the major masters, it is necessary to include commissions that have survived only in the literature, that never or only partially came to completion, or that fell victim to subsequent destruction.

Toward the end of the fifteenth century Savonarola could still declare in a sermon: "The pictures in the churches are the books of children and women" (Schnitzer, *Savonarola*, 2:806). This means that even after the invention and wide diffusion of printing, church art could still be reminded of its primary task and functions, namely to teach the beholder through easily understood pictorial texts, to edify and admonish him. Such an attitude, expressed without hesitation by Savonarola, the preacher and pastor, stands in sharp contrast to the humanistic-aesthetic, intellectual orientation of the upper social level of his contemporaries; to the great majority, however, it must have seemed perfectly obvious. For only this would explain the inexhaustible delight in representation apparent in church decoration throughout the fifteenth century, which in this respect still hardly differs from the preceding medieval period.

Similarly, the whole style and manner of distribution of pictures in the architectural space points to a pronounced interest in the subject matter of the picture and to the desire to have the most numerous and exhaustively treated themes represented in the pictorial decoration of the church.

Accordingly, there was little concern at the beginning for systematic organization and overall decorative effect. A deliberate, well-disposed integration of pictures into a broad spatial context occurs only in new churches and chapels built in the Quattrocento, so far as wall painting in general appears at all. In the case of mural commissions in old Gothic churches, the often very extensive pictorial programs called for in the individual family chapels were arranged, now just as earlier, in the long-traditional series of scenes in bands along the high wall surface; and even an approximation of the scheme in the neighboring chapels seems only rarely to have been attempted. At most, the new feeling for architectonic forms had some expression in the painted framework.

In the High Renaissance, however, the desire for harmonious proportions and a large-scale overall impression in the interior space took an increasingly firm hold. And this demand subsequently established itself with such dictatorial exclusivity that in the second half of the sixteenth century the interiors of the older churchs were subjected to those remorseless *sistemazione* that were mentioned above in connection with Santa Maria Novella.

As regards Quattrocento church painting, we have just noted the different proceedings in the old and newly constructed churches. Where such old painting already existed, it must have seemed natural to continue in the traditional manner, as much in the addition of new works as in the replacement of older frescoes. It was, then, predominantly and most extensively in Gothic churches that the mural paintings of the early Renaissance were produced, sometimes as continuations, sometimes as renovations. In the new buildings, on the other hand, paintings as a rule consisted of altarpieces of similar type, and frescoes were introduced only occasionally. Painted decoration of the whole wall surface and vault of a chapel is generally found only in the older churches, whose chapels had for the most part belonged from the beginning to the patronage of one or another patrician family of the parish. If pictorial decoration here was in rather short supply or none too impressive, this often gave the patron family the stimulus to commission frescoes for these spaces in the fifteenth century.

We begin our survey of the pictorial programs and compositional arrangement of projects of this type with the painting by Masolino and Masaccio of the Brancacci chapel in the Carmine, dedicated to St. Peter, in the 1420s. This stands out as the first monumental manifestation of new life in Florentine painting.[1] What this work must have meant to the contemporary observer may be most readily imagined by comparing it with the frescoes of the life of Mary that Don Lorenzo Monaco produced a few years earlier in the Bartolini chapel of Santissima Trinita. A certain advance was already made here in the disposition and integration of the paintings in the chapel space. But the framing of the individual pictures by painted architectural elements is still lacking. Masaccio, ahead of all others, first introduced it immediately thereafter in the Carmine.[2]

---

[1] This chapel, attached to one transept of the Carmelite church, survived the devastating fire of 1771. But its vault was repainted around the middle of the eighteenth century (see the overall view in Jacques Mesnil, *Masaccio et les débuts de la Renaissance*, The Hague, 1927, pl. 29).

[2] Bicci di Lorenzo also produced two groups of murals, since lost, at the beginning of

We can compare a late Quattrocento counterpart in Santa Trinita to Don Lorenzo's chapel painting there: Ghirlandaio's Sassetti chapel, completed in 1485. The whole original interior appearance has survived virtually unchanged here also. This includes the black marble arcosolium tombs of the donor and his wife built into the side walls as well as the altarpiece of the *Adoration of the Shepherds*, also by Ghirlandaio, which has fortunately been returned from the Uffizi to its old place.[3] The chapel is probably one of the most complete and representative examples of its type and period. At the same time, in its great richness of detail it is a masterpiece of carefully considered, highly effective harmony of all decorative elements.

One other cycle of painted chapel decoration in the Trinita, produced a short time earlier, also deserves mention. It admittedly survives in only a few fragments, some of them dispersed, but may in some measure be visualized based on Vasari's description. This is the large choir chapel for which Baldovinetti first produced the altarpiece in 1470-1471 (now in the Accademia) with the Holy Trinity and saints of the order on the commission of the patron, Buongianni Gianfigliazzi. This was a replacement for the original high altarpiece, Cimabue's great Madonna panel, moved at that time into another chapel and subsequently into the Uffizi.

Of the fresco decoration of the tall chapel, also executed in the early 1470s, only the four patriarchs of the vault fields and a few scarcely recognizable traces in the lunettes below these have survived. All the rest, wall paintings with Old Testament scenes, were whitewashed in the eighteenth century.[4]

Also lost, and to be imagined only based on literary references, are the

---

the 1420s in Santa Lucia de' Magnoli: the legend of St. Laurence above the Bardi altar and the frescoes in the choir chapel patronized by Niccolò da Uzzano. The same Bicci later painted the Giovanni Gualberto legend and the altarpiece for the Compagni chapel in Santa Trinita between 1428 and 1431. Vasari-Milanesi, 2:54, 64-66; Richa, *Notizie*, 3:61; 10:289-95.

[3] The donor portraits absent from the altarpiece appear in large scale fresco versions on the wall sections to either side of the altar. Above, in zones one above the other on all three walls, are scenes from the life of St. Francis, in honor of the name patron of the donor Francesco Sassetti. Four sibyls in the vault and a decorative medallion with an inscription in the pavement below complete the decoration of the chapel interior. But a wall painting, *Augustus and the Sibyl*, also appears above the entrance arch, as in other chapels of the transept. Next to it, in the axis of the dividing pier, which bears the Virgin Annunciate on its front side, is a figure of David with the Sassetti arms, which also adorns the peak of the chapel entrance arch in a bright-colored majolica version.

[4] A description of one of the paintings, the Queen of Sheba's visit to King Solomon, and the identification of the portrait heads appearing in it is in Vasari-Milanesi (2:592-95); see also Bocchi-Cinelli (*Le bellezze della citta*, pp. 188-89), who saw the paintings still preserved in 1678 and even called special attention to the Cain and Abel scene. Richa, *Notizie*, 3:177-78) found the paintings already very dilapidated. Documents are in *MA*, 1903, pp. 50-52.

frescoes that Domenico Veneziano, Castagno, and finally Baldovinetti again painted in the choir chapel of Sant' Egidio in Santa Maria Nuova. Domenico had already begun his work on one of the side walls here in 1439-1440, assisted by Piero della Francesca and Bicci di Lorenzo, with scenes from the life of the Virgin in three bands, one above the other, in which Vasari again singled out various portraits of prominent contemporaries; Castagno continued the work on the other wall in 1450, but Baldovinetti finally completed it after another interruption of almost ten years.[5]

The most important monumental work of Florentine realism of the first generation after Masaccio probably perished with the choir chapel of Sant' Egidio. For this period, we shall be able to refer below only to a few individual paintings, and some from cloisters.

Next in the chronological sequence of complete painted chapels comes the cathedral in the neighboring subject city of Prato, where a follower of Domenico Veneziano painted scenes from the life of Mary on the walls of the Assunta chapel.[6] Fra Filippo Lippi's frescoes in the choir chapel of the same church, commissioned 1452 and executed from 1456-1466 with numerous interruptions, were painted afterwards. Stories of the city patron of Florence, San Giovanni, appear here on one side, in three zones one above the other. On the other side is the legend of St. Stephen, patron of the altar. In the vault are the four evangelists.

This extensive project—whose pictorial style, at least in the compositions of the lowest bands and because of the over life-size scale of the figures, appears decidedly monumental—was followed in Florence itself in the 1460s by a smaller but particularly ornate work: the decoration of the tomb chapel of the cardinal of Portugal in San Miniato. Here for the first time was a newly created space, built beginning in 1461, for whose projected decoration two well-known painters were hired along with the sculptor. And the architect of the interior, in the taste of the mature early Renaissance, had to deal with the disposition of all the elements, while the fresco painter was obligated only to fill certain sharply bounded compartments of the upper walls and vaults with figural compositions. At the same time the sculptor Andrea della Robbia installed five colorfully glazed medallions on the dome surfaces. Baldovinetti and Antonio Pollaiuolo did the painting in 1466-1468.[7]

---

[5] Vasari-Milanesi, 2:592, 673, 676ff., 687; Magliabecchiano-Frey, *Il codice*, pp. 98, 101; documents in *RA*, 1903, pp. 206ff.

[6] Pudelko in *MKIF*, 4, pp. 174ff.; Mario Salmi, *Paolo Uccello, Andrea del Castagno, Domenico Veneziano* (Rome, 1935), pp. 64-65.

[7] The former is responsible for the total of sixteen small individual figures of prophets, evangelists, and church fathers that are distributed over the spandrels, lunettes, and vault-surfaces and also for the large lunette painting of the Annunciation on the side wall opposite

The tomb chapel of Bishop Salutati in the Duomo of Fiesole was also decorated in the mid-1460s. In its homogeneous overall plan, along with the architectonic wall articulation and the main sculptural portions (tomb and Madonna altarpiece by Mino), the painter's contribution was limited to the pair of evangelists in the ceiling vaults, two individual saints on painted pedestals to either side of the central window, as well as some medallions and other purely ornamental dividing members. The painter was a pupil of Rosselli, close to Ghirlandaio.

Shortly before the painting of the tomb chapel in San Miniato, an extensive fresco cycle was carried out in the neighboring city of San Gimignano by Benozzo Gozzoli, one of the most prolific of Florentine fresco painters. It represented the legend of St. Augustine and was in the choir of his order's church. Gozzoli had to find places here for no less than seventeen separate scenes. He acquitted himself of this immense task, along with other works in the same place, with his customary promptness in the three-year period of 1463-1465. Ten years later in 1475, also in San Gimignano but in the Collegiata church, Ghirlandaio and his assistant Mainardi frescoed the tomb chapel of Santa Fina. Here, as in San Miniato in its time, there was a small, newly constructed sacellum built in 1468 by Giuliano da Maiano. The painting and figural sculpture had to be worked into its architectural context. The tomb altar of Santa Fina opposite the entrance, by Benedetto da Maiano, was surrounded by the three walls of the evenly-proportioned chapel, and the side walls each received a large fresco within a round blind arch: the death and funeral of the saint. Above, as in San Miniato, was a powerful cornice decorated with a sculptured frieze of cherubim, and two tiers of roundels in the corner fields, which here also were filled with painted individual figures of prophets and church fathers. In the vault were the Evangelists in glory with cherubim.

Next to its model, the chapel of the cardinal of Portugal, the ensemble of this chapel decoration is surely the most effective example of coordinated integration of architecture, sculpture, and painting from the height of the early Renaissance.[8] Nothing comparable in this respect was

---

the tomb. It fell to Pollaiuolo, as a mural painter, however, to execute only the two large angels hovering one to either side of a round window in the lunette of the middle wall. He also painted the altarpiece with the titular patron and two other saints. The original, long in the Uffizi, was recently replaced with a copy in the original setting in the chapel's decoration. Assistants from one workshop or the other painted the decorative architectonic frame around the entrance arch, with the great coat of arms of the entombed cardinal in the tympanum; also the long series of coats of arms of his lineage in the interior frieze (documents in RA, 1906, pp. 89ff.).

[8] Reference may be made here in passing to a roughly contemporary German counterpart: the Hardenrath chapel at Sankt Maria im Kapitol in Cologne. This is a rare example in our region of a private, patrician family chapel surviving in such completeness and stylistic

undertaken even in Florence in the period immediately following. The sacrament chapel in Sant' Ambrogio, which we encounter next, is only the last bay of a side aisle, set apart as a chapel. Besides Mino's beautiful tabernacle on its end wall, it received only vault painting and Cosimo Rosselli's major fresco on the exterior wall, with the graphic depiction of the legendary miracle that was supposed to have occurred here. The mural was executed in 1485, the same year of the completion of the Ghirlandaio paintings in Santissima Trinita discussed above.[9]

Shortly thereafter, Ghirlandaio received the great commission to paint new decoration in the main chapel of Santa Maria Novella, whose painting had been damaged by moisture. The distribution of the various scenes in four bands, one above the other within the tall wall-surfaces, was predetermined by the required association with the previously existing fresco cycle of the lives of Mary and John the Baptist. The tectonic sensibility of the early Renaissance contributed only the framing elements current since Masaccio. And above all, the spirit of the late Quattrocento achieved its freest expression in the conception and execution of the subject matter. Here also, just as in the small Sassetti chapel, the life-size full-length portraits of the donor couple were placed on the central wall to either side of the group of windows. The painting, commissioned by Giovanni Tornabuoni and executed 1485-1490, has already been discussed in detail above, along with other contents of the chapel (see above).

The family chapel of Filippo Strozzi is situated immediately next to this *cappella maggiore*. Its painted decoration, with murals and stained glass by Filippino Lippi, was undertaken even before 1490, but completed only after 1500. Apart from everything else, it is particularly significant here for the dissolution of the previously valid conventions of pictorial architecture that the painted pilasters, which in Ghirlandaio's work still enclose each scene like actual frames, are here actually worked into the pictorial stage setting and thus function henceforth as wings. The action of the figures surges in front of them to the outermost border of the image, which occasional figures even overstep.

After the completion of this work, which persists completely in the spirit and character of the departing Quattrocento on the very threshold of the new century, nothing of a similar nature was undertaken during the succeeding period of the High Renaissance.[10] Fresco painting of an

---

unity: it has a comparable splendor of execution in the architectural space as well as in the painting and decorative furnishings, with altarpieces, wall and ceiling paintings, carved pews, etc.

[9] The paintings by Ghirlandaio on the *facciata* of the main chapel in the Badia of Settimo may only be mentioned here (Vasari-Milanesi, 3:186, n. 1; 271; 4:466, n. 3).

[10] Only one project of the Duomo Opera, which in spite of three campaigns never went beyond fragmentary beginnings, may be mentioned here. This is the decoration of the

entire chapel appears again only much later, around the middle of the sixteenth century, with the murals of the story of Creation in the choir of San Lorenzo. The aged Pontormo spent the last ten years of his life on its execution (Vasari-Milanesi, 6:285).

A review of the material discussed up to this point indicates that along with such enterprises, the type of cyclical wall painting with narrative friezes of images on the nave wall taking a prominent place in Roman-esque and Gothic churches found no continuation in the Renaissance. Such a disposition of paintings appears only perhaps in the small rec-tangular rooms of confraternity oratorios.[11]

There were, however, small-scale fresco projects in almost all churches, whether above individual altars placed here and there along the outer walls of the nave, or for isolated donations of images, unassociated with any altar.

The series of such individual frescoes begins with Masaccio's *Trinity* in Santa Maria Novella, which was executed around 1426 above the Cardoni family altar in the left aisle. It was transferred to its present location only after 1860.[12] The suggestion of depth in the painted ar-chitectural setting alludes at least illusionistically to the chapel space that the altar in this case lacked. The sharp impression of depth in the per-spective construction and the large scale of the kneeling donor figures suggests that the fresco was placed rather high up on the wall and that the altar itself was already occupied by a small panel painting, possibly with the legend of the altar patron, St. Ignatius.

Paolo di Stefano's Madonna with two saints, in the right aisle of San Miniato, was produced in the same year of 1426. Three other separate murals from a slightly later period can also be found there: a Madonna with six saints in a painted architectural frame, a pair of saints, and a St. Jerome to the right and left of the choir platform.

The charming individual figure of a youthful saint, surrounded by an ornamental border, was recently rediscovered in San Niccolò, as the original pictorial adornment of an altar. It was first attributed to Gentile

chapel of St. Zenobius, first decreed as early as 1492. Appropriately to this period's love of splendor, there was a plan to employ the particularly costly medium of mosaic for this chapel (see above).

[11] As an example I cite the half-faded painted decoration of about 1440 in the chapel of the Compagnia di Santa Maria della Croce al Tempio in Via de' Malcontenti and the lunette paintings from the circle of Ghirlandaio's pupils, which take up all the lunettes under the vaults in the Oratorio of the Buonomini di San Martino; the latter represent the legend of St. Martin and works of charity. See *RA*, 1934, p. 147; Alessandro Chiappelli, *L'arte del rinascimento* (Florence, 1926), p. 237; *Dedalo*, 8, 1928, pp. 612ff.

[12] See above. The severely damaged Madonna with two saints in the Oratorio of Mon-temurciano near San Giovanni Valdarno is held, probably correctly, to be a youthful work of Masaccio (van Marle, *Painting*, 10:257).

da Fabriano, but others dated it around 1430 and assigned it to Bicci di Lorenzo, who was also supposed to have executed two more wall paintings, no longer surviving, between 1427 and 1432 above the sites of altars in San Marco.[13] Of far greater artistic importance is the pair of saints that Domenico Veneziano painted after 1455 in Santa Croce above the Cavalcanti altar against the exterior wall of the choir screen. It was moved from there to its present place in 1566.[14]

The figure of John the Baptist was evidently influenced by the St. Jerome in one of the three altar frescoes that Castagno painted from 1454 to 1456 in various aisle chapels of the Santissima Annunziata. Two of them survived under the late redecoration of these chapels, but only one has been permanently uncovered. A compositional arrangement that differs from that of most earlier altar frescoes appears here probably for the first time: the image does not appear on an unarticulated oversized wall-surface, but rather fills the entire surface between the altar-table and the framing arch of the chapel's back wall. In the late Quattrocento, corresponding to the more securely established tectonic outlook, only this arrangement is still in general use.

But a whole series of individual mural works from the second and third quarter of the century may still be mentioned. It is true that the majority are traceable only in more or less vague references. But even so, their number and variety testifies to the broad development of this type of commission. We note these examples below, with the reservation that the names of artists cited by early witnesses for all the objects that have not survived only repeat a tradition which cannot be verified.[15]

[13] See *ZBK*, 60, pp. 284ff.: Vasari-Milanesi, 2:64; Magliabecchiano-Frey, *Il codice*, p. 92. We also hear of a fresco of three saints by Fra Angelico in the left aisle of Santa Maria Novella, without further information on the date. Neri di Bicci was entrusted with the execution of images of the Apostles and other patron saints in the fifteen chapels of the Duomo tribune, which was done from 1439 to 1440.

[14] See Salmi, *Uccello, Castagno, Veneziano*, pp. 74, 128-29; *MKIF*, 4, pp. 183ff.

[15] Vasari names the saints Peter and Paul on the entrance piers of the Serragli chapel in the old Carmine church building as works of Masaccio and Masolino. A St. Ivo in an illusionistic perspectival niche, on the front of a nave pier in the Badia, passed for a Masaccio. Beneath it were several praying supplicants (Vasari-Milanesi, 2:290-91, 294-95, n. 2; Magliabecchiano-Frey, *Il codice*, pp. 81-82; see *RA*, 1932, pp. 196-98; in the same place, pp. 141ff., are all the other old reports on the decoration of the Carmine before the fire of 1771). Also in the Carmine was a St. Marziale painted on a pier by the young Fra Filippo, as well as an altar fresco of John the Baptist, flanked by scenes from his legend (Vasari-Milanesi, 2:613-14).

Individual frescoes by Uccello cited by Vasari include an Annunciation in a rich architectural perspective extending up to the vaulting in Santa Maria Maggiore (on an aisle pier, according to Richa); also three scenes from the legend of St. Francis above the left side portal in Santissima Trinita. In the same place he notes a figure of St. Andrew by Castagno, next to the chapel "di Maestro Luca." Another pier fresco of St. Bernard by Castagno was

Some surviving monuments by artists of note should be singled out: two large frescoes of St. Sebastian by Benozzo Gozzoli in Sant' Agostino and the Collegiata of San Gimignano (1463-1465), as well as an altar fresco of the Virgin giving her girdle to St. Thomas which fills a lunette in the stone-sculptured niche framing the altar site in the sacristy of San Niccolò and is attributed to Cosimo Rosselli. Next come certain large works of Ghirlandaio and his circle, especially the great image in the shallow niche above the Vespucci altar in Ognissanti, probably executed by 1473. Two pictures, one above the other, occupied the tall wall surface: below, the Pietà between individual saints in illusionistic niches; above, the Madonna of Mercy above a painted cornice.[16] A younger Vespucci had Ghirlandaio and Botticelli paint the church fathers Jerome and Augustine on the front wall of the choir screen on either side of the gateway in the same church. The pictures, moved to the side walls after the destruction of the choir screeen, each show, in symmetrically matching oblique perspectives, a view through a frame of painted piers into the study of the learned saint, furnished with still-life objects.[17]

in the Annunziata (Vasari-Milanesi, 2:206-207, 670; Richa, *Notizie*, 3:281; Magliabec-chiano-Frey, *Il codice*, p. 98; Albertini, *Memoriale*, p. 438).

Richa (*Notizie*, 7:36-37) mentions an Annunciation fresco with a donor figure, dated 1437, in the subsequently destroyed church of San Niccolò di Cafaggio, as well as two individual saints painted on a wall to either side of an old wooden crucifix in another chapel, with the donation inscription of 1440 beneath them.

Surviving works include a fragmented Martyrdom of St. Sebastian by Giovanni dal Ponte, from about 1434-1435, in the first transept chapel of Santa Trinita; fragments of a Nativity and individual figures of saints from about 1430 to 1440 in San Felice in Piazza, to the right of the entrance, between painted pilasters and cornices; a crucifix, probably by Giovanni di Francesco, in Santa Maria Maggiore in the arched field above the chapel to the left of the choir (*RA*, 1933, p. 255; 1934, p. 348); and in the same place, various unassigned frescoes of the early and mid-Quattrocento on certain nave piers. In the room adjoining the sacristy at San Miniato, the shallow niche above the lavabo—instead of the sculptural decoration preferred elsewhere for such locations—contains a frescoed half-length figure of a prophet from the Castagno circle (Salmi, *Uccello*, pl. 156). Similarly, a grisaille image is found above the lavabo in the corridor behind the sacristy of Santa Croce: Christ and the Samaritan woman, and above this the Medici arms; thus probably produced in connection with Cosimo's novitiate building of 1440-1445. The decorative painting of angels holding a curtain above Michelozzo's entrance portal to the corridor leading to the sacristy and novitiate belongs to the same enterprise.

Neri di Bicci painted some angels with a damask curtain to frame the sacrament tabernacle in San Pancrazio (1453); see his *Ricordi* in *Il Vasari*, 1, pp. 323-24). An altar fresco composed in what is clearly a retable form, representing St. Eustace in an illusionistic tabernacle niche with two scenes from his legend at the sides, by a Castagno pupil and dated 1462, was transferred to the museum in Sant' Apollonia (van Marle, *Painting*, 10:375).

[16] Heinrich Brockhaus, *Forschungen über florentiner Kunstwerke* (Leipzig, 1902), pp. 85ff.; Francovich, *Dedalo*, 11, pp. 68ff.

[17] Frescoes in Ghirlandaio's style have also survived in smaller churches in the neigh-

The Baroncelli chapel in Santa Croce received the fresco of the Assumption with St. Thomas receiving the Virgin's girdle, filling the whole back wall, by Mainardi, who painted the Annunciation of 1482 in a side chapel of the Collegiata at San Gimignano a short time later, as well as individual frescoes with figures of saints in Sant' Agostino.[18]

In addition to all these religious images, however, there are also certain wall paintings of monumental character that received places in the Duomo, where they still exist as honorific memorials to famous personalities, sometimes as their tomb monuments. These include the tomb frescoes of Corsini and Marsili, executed by Bicci di Lorenzo in 1423 and 1439, following the traditional type of stone wall tombs. Likewise, the monumental painted portraits of two military leaders by Uccello in 1436 and Castagno in 1456 appear instead of sculptured equestrian monuments.[19]

In conclusion, the few separate frescoes of devotional character produced during the High Renaissance have still to be mentioned. None of these survive, and they have acquired renown only through Vasari or Richa. They include a Holy Trinity with a pair of kneeling donors by Raffaellino del Garbo in San Pancrazio, above the tomb of the Federighi, and at the same church, two figures of saints on the entrance pier of the Rucellai chapel, mentioned by Vasari as youthful works of Franciabigio. In Or San Michele Lorenzo di Credi painted a St. Bartholomew and Andrea del Sarto the ascension of St. Mary Magdalen, each on the front of a central pier. In the Angeli convent church a Madonna with two angels, painted by Ridolfo Ghirlandaio, could be seen above a holy water basin.[20]

Before we turn to other scenes of ecclesiastical mural painting, a brief excursus is in order on a special type of monumental painting in churches. This is stained glass, whose figural portrayals often derived from design drawings by noted painters and sculptors; sometimes, it seems, even with

---

borhood: a large two-zone mural complex framed by painted pilasters and cornices, in Sant' Andrea in Brozzi; below, the enthroned Madonna with Sts. Sebastian and Julian on a balcony (similar to Pollaiuolo's image of three saints in San Miniato); above, in the lunette field, the Baptism of Christ. Then in Cercina on Monte Morello, the side apse of the old convent church was painted with three standing saints in an architectural frame (*Dedalo*, 10, p. 491, 11, pp. 73-74; van Marle, *Painting*, 13:10).

[18] In 1484-1485 Domenico and Davide Ghirlandaio executed the decoration surrounding the sacrament tabernacle in the choir chapel of Cestello (Santa Maria Maddalena dei Pazzi) of two flying angels with a baldachin, which perished in the Baroque period (Vasari-Milanesi, 3:280; 4:466, n. 3).

[19] In the old Carmine there was also such an epitaph portrait in fresco over the tomb of the Carmelite Fra Angiolo, probably from the time of his beatification around 1440-1445 (Richa, *Notizie*, 3:273).

[20] Vasari-Milanesi, 4:239; 5:190; 6:538; Richa, *Notizie*, 1:26.

their personal participation in the execution. Only a few brief observations on this whole medium may come into consideration here. We refer the reader to a special study that has appeared recently, dealing with all the relevant documentary and monumental material in great detail.[21] Some of the most important productions of this branch have already been mentioned above. This includes the stained glass in the Duomo, whose most essential portions were produced in the 1430s and 1440s.[22]

Shortly before the middle of the century Santa Croce received several valuable stained glass windows still existing there, in particular the great *Deposition from the Cross* in the round window of the facade. Its design was formerly tentatively attributed to Ghiberti, but recently assigned on more precise grounds to Giovanni di Marco.[23]

When a chapel space was to be newly painted, it is evident that the master of the wall paintings was as a rule also assigned to design the windows as an integral part of the painted decoration.[24] We encounter the creation of painted decoration for walls and glass for a single complete space by the same master in the late Quattrocento in Santa Maria Novella, for Ghirlandaio's great choir chapel and for the Strozzi chapel executed by Filippino.

Finally Santo Spirito and, on a more limited scale, San Francesco al Monte and Cestello (Santa Maria Maddalena dei Pazzi) offer remains of their stained glass decoration, once probably much more extensive. Particularly noteworthy in Santo Spirito are the St. Thomas window of the Antinori chapel, by Bartolommeo di Giovanni, and the beautiful Madonna of a chapel window in the choir ambulatory, suggesting Botticelli,

[21] Hildegard van Straelen-Conrad, *Studien zur Florentiner Glasmalerei des Trecento und Quattrocento* (Wattenscheid, 1938).

[22] Ghiberti, who had already provided designs for one large and two small round windows of the facade in 1403 and 1410-1412, later also took a major part in the extensive negotiations over three groups of ten lancet windows in the tribunes. In addition, of the eight oculi with scenes from the lives of Christ and Mary in the drum of the dome (of which seven still exist), two were executed based on his working drawings, the rest after designs by Uccello, Castagno, and Donatello. The work was carried out by glass technicians hired by the Duomo Operai. For certain important sections, the designing artists themselves evidently intervened (see van Straelen, *Glasmalerei*, pp. 53-90).

[23] See Toesca, *BA*, 1921, pp. 3ff.; van Straelen, *Glasmalerei*, pp. 91-92. At the same place are small windows with images of patron saints, in the altar spaces of the novitiate chapel and the chapter house (the so-called Pazzi chapel). The latter window was presumably designed by Baldovinetti around 1470, the former by a master of the Castagno school around 1445; the two foremost windows in the right aisle of the church are probably based on drawings by Gozzoli.

[24] Thus Baldovinetti, when working on the Santa Trinita choir chapel, also provided the working drawings for the stained glass (later destroyed) for this chapel. The same happened in Filippo Lippi's case in the Duomo of Prato, for the three windows of the main chapel he painted, as well as in the early 1460s for a window in the Inghirami family chapel, whose altarpiece was also Fra Filippo's work.

and the St. Peter figure in the left aisle. Finally, the great round window in the facade, depicting the Pentecost, appears to derive from a drawing by Perugino. The same is true of a window of God the Father above the side entrance of San Francesco al Monte.[25]

Cloisters and other spaces for common use in convents offered another richly cultivated field for mural painting commissions. For cloisters in particular, where the Trecento only rarely applied extensive paintings,[26] painting projects, surviving or cited in reports, became more numerous from the early fifteenth century on. Here, under the wide spans of the arcades, in the best light and adequate shelter from the weather, both the painter and observer could find the most favorable imaginable preconditions. A stimulus to undertake mural painting also came from the first cloister lying outside the area of strict closure in all the larger convents, and thus accessible to the public. Mural projects unfolded here either as continuous cycles of images running around the walls or else in individual images, sometimes over doors, sometimes as compositions extending lower down in the axial point of the entrance wing or elsewhere on the walls. Painted mural decoration occurs only occasionally in the interior corridors of the dormitory wings.

The oldest completely preserved example of cloister painting with continuous Old Testament scenes is the two pictures placed one above the other on each bay of the vaulting in the Chiostro Verde next to Santa Maria Novella, so-called on account of the technique of execution of these paintings: in green earth, renouncing the expensive profusion of colors that could probably never be dispensed with in murals in church interiors, but could be, if necessary, in cloisters or house facades. The picture cycle, executed by Uccello and a few more workmanlike contemporaries of less progressive tendencies between about 1433 through the end of the 1440s, has already been discussed above (see also *RA*, 1934, pp. 168ff.). Of other paintings in the cloister of the Carmelite convent, preceding these chronologically—by Masaccio and the young Filippo Lippi—only an approximate conception may be gained from old descriptions and surviving fragments.[27]

[25] We know only from literary testimony of various stained glass designs that Perugino provided for the Ingesuati monks, whose convent workshop, among other things, possessed particularly skillful stained-glass craftsmen who were greatly in demand (van Straelen, *Glasmalerei*, pp. 102ff.). Filippino also seems occasionally to have been entrusted with production of preparatory drawings for stained glass. His first design for the window (not surviving) in the Nerli chapel in Santo Spirito, which today still possesses an altarpiece by Filippino, is in the Uffizi collection.

[26] The painting of the Campo Santo in Pisa, like the whole complex, is a special case. In Florence, early cloister paintings may be found to my knowledge only in the cloister wing of Santa Croce running along the side of the church.

[27] Masaccio's portrayal of the consecration of the church in 1422, described by Vasari,

Around 1440, however, contemporaneous with the Chiostro Verde, twelve scenes of the legend of St. Benedict were produced in the upper passage of the small cloister, the Chiostro degli Aranci behind the Badia by an unknown second-rate master from the circle of Domenico Veneziano.[28]

Around this same time the Dominican convent of San Marco, just rebuilt, received a painted decoration of its foremost cloister by Fra Angelico, who lived in the convent. This, however, was limited to the placement of five *sopraporti* and a large Crucifixion with St. Dominic in a direct line of vision with the entrance door. Fra Angelico continued his work for the convent not only in such obvious places as the chapter room and refectory but even in the upper corridors between the cells of the dormitory. This included the great Annunciation fresco above the exit from the staircase, another Madonna composition in the center of one corridor, a Crucifixion at the end, and, above all, the whole series of individual images in the cells.[29]

Various larger and smaller fresco remains in the upper passage of the cloister of San Miniato have recently been freed from a subsequent coat of whitewash. Some of these suggest the style of Uccello and an origin in the middle of the century. This verifies the assertions of various early authors regarding extensive paintings that Uccello and also Castagno supposedly executed in this place.[30]

---

was destroyed in 1612; his *Last Judgment* in the second cloister of the Angeli convent was mentioned by Albertini (*Memoriale*, p. 439). In the Carmine cloister only fragments remain of monastic mural scenes that may probably be connected with Vasari's mention of a youthful work of Fra Filippo, who was living in that convent at the time. See Vasari-Milanesi, 2:295-97, 613; *Dedalo*, 12, 1932, pp. 587ff.; Mario Salmi, *Masaccio* (Rome, 1930), pp. 82, 104, pl. 199.

[28] Neumeyer, *JPK*, 48, 1928, pp. 25ff.; Salmi, *Uccello, Castagno, Veneziano*, p. 17, 105.

[29] A Crucifixion mural from the cloister of Fra Angelico's home convent, San Domenico, is in the Louvre. Vasari also attributed a *sopraporta* with St. Benedict in the cloister of the Florentine Badia to Fra Angelico. Milanesi found it, in a ruinous condition, as late as 1860, but it has vanished since then (Vasari-Milanesi, 2:513-14).

Extensive remains of the mural decoration in the cloister, chapter house, and corridor above the steps of a nuns' convent, now the Educatorio di Fuligno in Via Faenza, are attributed to Bicci di Lorenzo (*l'Arte*, 1903, p. 347).

In the first cloister of Santa Croce, Bicci di Lorenzo painted scenes from the history of the order and medallion heads of Franciscan saints. Several lunette frescoes from the 1440s can also be found in the novitiate, built around that time.

[30] Albertini specifically mentions twelve Uccello frescoes in the upper corridor of the first courtyard; the Anonimo Magliabecchiano, for his part, reports on paintings by Uccello in the lower passage of the cloister, which he did not esteem very highly. But Vasari mentions scenes from the lives of the fathers (that is, early saints of the order) in chiaroscuro technique; in addition he refers elsewhere to pictures from the life of St. Miniatus, which Castagno supposedly painted in this cloister. See Albertini in J. A. Crowe and G. B. Cavalcaselle, *Geschichte der italienischen Malerei*, ed. M. Jordan, vols. 2-4 (Leipzig, 1869-1871), 2:443. Magliabecchiano-Frey, *Il codice*, p. 100; Vasari-Milanesi, 2:207, 669.

I enumerate below the other cloister frescoes of Castagno and Uccello, certified only by old reports,[31] and mention here only the recently discovered, severely damaged fresco of a Nativity in the cloister of the former hospital of Santa Maria della Scala, recognized as a work of Uccello's not mentioned in the literature.[32] Then there are the two great Crucifixion frescoes that Castagno painted for the convent of Santa Maria degli Angeli in the space of about ten years. The earlier is still in situ in the rear court of the hospital of Santa Maria Nuova. The other has been transferred from a chapel of the former convent garden to the Castagno Museum of Sant' Apollonia, where yet a third cloister fresco by Castagno can be found: the lunette with the Man of Sorrows and two angels (probably from the cloister of this convent).[33]

In 1454, roughly contemporary with Castagno's late *Crucifixion*, Neri di Bicci, then still only at the beginning of his career, painted the fresco that far surpasses his whole later mass production, the St. John Gualbertus in the cloister of San Pancrazio, which is now a tobacco processing plant. The saint sits enthroned among other saints of his Vallombrosan order in front of a rich, shimmering golden architecture.[34]

In 1460 the painting of the newly built forecourt of the Annunziata was begun. It is true that at first, except for some medallion heads and other decorative motifs above the arcades, nothing was produced but Baldovinetti's mural of the Adoration of the Shepherds on the exterior wall of the chapel of the miraculous image. And only in 1476 did Cosimo Rosselli undertake the cycle of the life of St. Filippo Benizzi, founder of the Servite order, on the nearest adjoining wall section. Andrea del Sarto was finally to bring it to completion three decades later.

For the whole last quarter of the Quattrocento many records of other cloister paintings exist mentioning Ghirlandaio, Perugino, and Botticelli,

---

[31] By Uccello are scenes from the legend of St. Benedict in the long-vanished loggia behind Santa Maria Nuova (Vasari-Milanesi, 2:213; probably identical with the "molte figure di verde terra" which the Magliabecchianus mentions in that very place); in addition, individual pictures of the three patron saints of the sick, Anthony Abbot and Sts. Cosmas and Damian, in illusionistic niches in the Ospedale di Lemmo (Vasari-Milanesi, 2:206); finally several lunette frescoes in green earth, which Richa (*Notizie*, 9:216) saw in the cloister of the Badia di Settimo and attributed to Uccello.

By Castagno are "molte pitture" in the cloister and church of the convent of San Benedetto in front of Porta Pinti, destroyed in the 1529 *assedio* (Vasari-Milanesi, 2:669); a Saint Andrew as a *sopraporta* in the Chiostro dell' Ossa (cemetery) of Santa Maria Nuova (Magliabecchiano-Frey, *Il codice*, pp. 98-99) and the *Flagellation*, highly praised by Vasari, in the second cloister at Santa Croce.

[32] See *MKIF*, 4, p. 141; *RA*, 1934, pp. 112ff.

[33] Vasari-Milanesi, 2:669, 672-73; Richa, *Notizie*, 8:174; Salmi, *Uccello, Castagno, Veneziano*, pp. 44, 56.

[34] A crucifixion, also by Neri di Bicci, painted in 1469, was once in the cloister of Santa Croce (Vasari-Milanesi, 2:51, n. 3).

but only a few works of little importance have survived.[35] A Crucifixion with John, the two Marys, and two saints of the order was probably executed by Davide Ghirlandaio shortly before 1500 for the Angeli convent, which already possessed two older Crucifixion frescoes by Castagno. The fresco, now in the Sant' Apollonia museum, was surely far more effective in its original setting, placed on a wall of the great convent garden at the end of the prospect along its central path.[36]

We shall return below to the few other paintings produced in convent courtyards after the turn of the century. First, however, there is another kind of fresco project to consider, one occasioned by the great community rooms of the convent complex. In particular this meant the virtually indispensable mural decorations occupying the main walls in the refectory and chapter house and a short wall in rectangular dining halls. Probably the earliest surviving works of this type from our period are the solitary crucifix, still very old-fashioned, that Fra Angelico executed before 1430 in the chapter room of San Domenico di Fiesole, now half blocked up, and his large crucifixion fresco in the San Marco chapter house of about 1440 in which biblical attendant figures are associated with a great number of saints, especially from his own and other orders; there are, in addition, numerous portrait heads of canonized Dominicans in the lower frieze.[37] The same association of an image of the Crucifixion with one's

[35] Vasari praises Domenico Ghirlandaio's St. Michael above a portal in the cemetery of Santa Maria Nuova and several paintings by him in the cloister of the Badia of Settimo, 1487 (Vasari-Milanesi, 3:272; 4:406-407).

Perugino, however, painted a whole series of murals in the early 1490s in various courts of the Gesuati convent of San Giusto, destroyed in 1529 but described in detail by Vasari. These included the theme from the history of the order that we have already encountered in other convents—the establishment of the rule by the pope; besides this there was a frieze with medallion portraits of saints, as well as individual scenes from the life of Mary, running above the arcades of a cloister (Vasari-Milanesi, 3:574-75).

Two documentary reports relate to wall paintings, now lost, which were once in the upper corridors in the cloistered areas of nuns' convents. Cosimo Rosselli painted eight "quadri in muro" in the dormitory of Sant' Ambrogio in 1486; the nuns of Santa Maria di Monticelli had Botticelli execute a St. Francis in 1496 (Vasari-Milanesi, 3:186, n. 1; Horne, Botticelli, pp. 275-76).

[36] Vasari-Milanesi, 6:533, n. 1; Dedalo, 11:1, pp. 82-83. An Annunciation lunette by the same artist is also in the corridor of the Santa Croce novitiate. Finally there are the ruins of a Pietà by Perugino, originally on the exterior staircase of the convent of San Piero Maggiore, now in Palazzo Alessandri. See Vasari-Milanesi, 3:576; Walter Bombe, Perugino (Stuttgart, 1914, p. 26).

[37] A small Madonna fresco with two Dominican saints in Petersburg at the Hermitage also comes from San Domenico. The Crucifixion in the former chapter room of the nuns of Fuligno on the Via Faenza is attributed to Bicci di Lorenzo (l'Arte, 1904, p. 347). Two murals from the former lecture hall of the convent school of San Marco show the two principal figures of Dominican scholarship, Albert and Thomas, each at his lectern in the midst of a circle of pupils. These were executed by an assistant of Fra Angelico on large

own order can be found, moreover, with portrait figures of contemporary inhabitants of the convent, in a mural probably coming from the chapter room at Sant' Apollonia in the museum there (signature and date 1440 by Paolo di Stefano; van Marle, *Painting*, 9:39).

Fra Angelico, according to the convent chronicle, supposedly painted a mural in the refectory of San Marco, for which only the theme of the Crucified with Mary and John is actually mentioned. But it is likely that, as in the later repainting of this wall, the lower zone also contained an image of the Last Supper or some other scene appropriate to a refectory. This hypothetical composition by Fra Angelico would thus have been comparable to a small, earlier forerunner in the convent of Dominican nuns, San Niccolò in Prato. There, portrayed under the *Crucifixion*, with five saints in the decorative frame, is a scene with appropriate subject matter from the legend of the founder of the order, a meal in the convent with the miraculous distribution of food by angels.[38]

The first *cenacolo* mural of a clearly Renaissance appearance is the Castagno fresco in the refectory of the former nuns' convent of Sant' Apollonia, now serving as a museum. It is equally distinguished for its powerful perspective and plastic illusionism and its solid, steadfast gravity. It was painted around 1445-1450, thus only a little later than the Crucifixion fresco just mentioned from the chapter house of the same convent. Even here, among all the other progressive features, we still find the traditional two-zone division of the wall surface, probably imposed on the artist, with the three Passion scenes rising in a landscape prospect above the roof of the Last Supper room.[39]

We encounter some further examples of this type of commission at a fairly distant time in the last quarter of the Quattrocento. There are, to begin with, no less than five Last Supper frescoes by Ghirlandaio and his assistants: the *cenacolo* of Ognissanti (dated 1480) and its variant in the small dining hall of San Marco. A third picture of the same subject

---

semicircular panels, which we should regard as adapted lunette paintings (van Marle, *Painting*, 10:194). Remains of frescoes, probably by Dello Delli around 1446, are in a great hall (formerly the hospice) of Santa Maria Novella (*RA*, 1934, pp. 183ff.). A large image of the Trinity with supplicants, probably done by Bartolommeo Caporali in 1487 is in a room (probably once a confraternity oratorio) of the former convent of San Giorgio alla Costa (*RA*, 1933, p. 260).

[38] Dated 1423 and signed Piero di Miniato (Alinari, photo 30794).

[39] According to W. R. Deusch (Königsberg dissertation [1928], 1937), the Last Supper was already painted before 1440, the upper scenes only after 1450.

Castagno offered a later version of the same theme, executed in 1457, in the Cenacolo of the lay brothers of Santa Maria Nuova. This, however, was destroyed in a renovation of the hospital (Vasari-Milanesi, 2:673, n. 3.; *RA*, 4, p. 24; Richa, *Notizie*, 8:301, 309) On the anonymous fresco of the Last Supper, produced around 1450 in the refectory of the former convent of San Matteo (now Academy) see *BA*, 1907, p. 25.

perished in the destruction of the nuns' convent of San Donato in Polverosa during the 1529 *assedio*. A somewhat earlier Last Supper image by the Ghirlandaio brothers has survived at the Vallombrosan abbey of Passignano, as well as one of about 1488 in the former convent of San Giorgio alla Costa (now a barracks).[40] Ghirlandaio still maintains a certain dignified solemnity in the atmosphere of the proceedings; only the colorfully dappled profusion of still-life and other incidental elements and the blooming serenity of the view into the garden suggest that the proper inner seriousness is beginning to vanish from the conception of the theme. Finally, in the Cenacolo di Fuligno in the nuns' convent of Sant' Onofrio, probably executed only at the end of the 1490s by Perugino and his assistants, a tone of banal pleasantness governs everything, and superabundant decorative trimmings run wild around the row of frail figures gathered at the table, contained in a rather small space. The prayer on the Mount of Olives appears above their heads as a diminutive detail in the background. One may consider that in roughly the same year as this insipid composition, Leonardo's *Last Supper* was completed in Milan! Perugino, however, seems in another case to have risen to the occasion for his thematic task: in the mural produced a few years earlier between 1493 and 1496 in the former chapter house of the Cistercians near their church Santa Maria Maddalena dei Pazzi, in the secularized convent complex on Via della Colonna.[41]

Fra Bartolommeo also painted a fresco contemporary with the Cenacolo di Fuligno, at the hospital of Santa Maria Nuova in the little courtyard in front of the charnel house, the Chiostro dell'Ossa. This work, the donation of one Gerozzo Dini, had the theme of the Last Judgment, most appropriate to the setting. Drawing spiritual stimulus from the sermons of Savonarola, its interpretation and mode of portrayal displays, much more emphatically than Perugino's Crucifixion, the characteristics of the maturing High Renaissance style.[42]

[40] Vasari-Milanesi, 3:272, n. 2; *JPK*, 1906, p. 61; *RA*, 1933, p. 266, n. 1. Particularly noteworthy in Ognissanti is the organic relationship of the painted architecture to the actual space, which seems to be extended for an additional bay by the illusionistic framing of the Last Supper scene.

[41] For the Crucifixion scene called for here also, the artist has dispensed with the numerous attendant figures preferred elsewhere. He has distributed the available wall space so that within a painted architecture bound to the existing sculptured corbels of the vaults, only the Crucified with Mary Magdalen occupies the prospect under the central arcade. Mary and John appear under the side arches, each accompanied by a kneeling saint of the order (thus here also order members are associated with a biblical scene). The sentimental mood of these figures is echoed in the wide, peaceful hill landscape in the background.

[42] The fresco was completed by Albertinelli after Fra Bartolommeo entered the monastery. The cemetery allowed it to be transferred elsewhere, and it is now in the Museo of San Marco. Portrait figures of the donor and his wife, who was buried beneath the painting, were on the framing wall piers in the original location. These have perished (*RA*, 1909, pp. 64-65; Vasari-Milanesi, 4:177-78, n. 1, 100-101; Richa, *Notizie*, 8:195).

In his own convent Fra Bartolommeo found no opportunities for mural painting activity, since Fra Angelico and his contemporaries had already given such full attention to this matter.[43] On the other hand, he executed several murals in his order's rural hospice in Pian di Mugnone during frequent periods of retreat there. Thus as early as 1506-1507, as his first painting after a work cessation of several years, he executed the *sopraporte* with Christ and the pilgrims to Emmaus (now in San Marco) as well as two half-length Madonnas and several individual heads of saints, painted on large tiles set into the wall; he seems also occasionally to have executed such small individual heads for San Marco (all now assembled in the Academy).[44]

A few wall painting cycles were also produced in convent courtyards in the first and second decades of the Cinquecento.[45] In particular there are cloister frescoes executed chiefly by Andrea del Sarto in a confraternity building of the Compagnia dello Scalzo near San Marco. He also carried out the greater part of the painting of the Annunziata forecourt about the same time. The *Legend of Filippo Benizzi*, founder of the order, had been begun about 1476 by Cosimo Rosselli but not carried beyond a few scenes. Andrea del Sarto completed it with five additional scenes around 1509-1510, when he was still only at the beginning of his career. Thus the individual wall sections of the whole left half of the square court were decorated, and the decoration of the right half of the arcade walls with five scenes from the life of Mary followed in 1513-1515. A scene each was entrusted to two young beginners, Pontormo and Rosso, as well as to Franciabigio. Andrea del Sarto completed the cycle with a classic composition of the Birth of the Virgin and an Adoration of the Magi. The Servites also obtained two more frescoes from him, two rep-

[43] A compositional sketch by Fra Bartolommeo, discovered in an English private collection, represents the burial of St. Antoninus—for whose beatification the Dominicans were energetically campaigning around 1515-1516. It suggests that a mural with this theme was planned for the first cloister of San Marco around that time. See Fritz Knapp, *Fra Bartolommeo della Porta und die Schule von San Marco* (Halle, 1903), p. 263.

[44] Remaining at Pian di Mugnone are a beautiful Annunciation lunette of 1515 in the church and a few other wall paintings by the Frate, a Pietà, a Christ bearing the Cross, a lunette with Dominic and Francis as well as the larger composition, Christ as gardener (*Noli me tangere*), in the chapel situated in the hospice garden, executed around 1517 during Fra Bartolommeo's last visit there before his death.

Finally, a fresco of the Deposition from the Cross and two heads of Christ, again painted on individual tiles, still existed in 1943 in Lecceto near Gangalandi, according to an eyewitness report. Fra Bartolommeo left them in the small hermitage-convent, which also belonged to the Dominicans in his time (Knapp, *Fra Bartolommeo*, pp. 256, 258; and Marchese, *Memorie*, pp. 144, 152-53).

[45] To mention the earliest first, five Passion scenes were executed in 1504 in sepia by Angelo Donnini in the forecourt of the contraternity chapel of the Compagnia di Gesù Pellegrino. This was behind Santa Maria Novella and perished when the train station was built.

resentations of the parable of the workers in the vineyard, highly praised by Vasari. These were appropriately placed on two end walls of the convent garden. There was also a Pietà on the upper landing of the novitiate staircase, and finally, the sole one of these individual frescoes surviving in its original place, the so-called *Madonna del Sacco* (1525) in the first cloister above the door to the church transept.[46]

Andrea's work in the small, ornate arcaded courtyard of the Compagnia dello Scalzo began contemporaneously with the last Mary scenes in the Annunziata forecourt (1514-1515). The cycle, totalling twelve scenes from the life of the Baptist and four separate figures of cardinal virtues, was continued by Franciabigio during Andrea's stay in France. Andrea completed it in 1520-1527.[47]

Final examples of cloister frescoes are Pontormo's five impressive Passion scenes in the great cell-cloister of the Certosa, each at one end of an arcaded passage. They were executed from 1522 to 1525 in a unique style mixing Dürer studies and early Mannerism. In addition, an Albertinelli Crucifixion fresco in a stone frame above the altar could be found in the Certosa chapter room, already painted by 1505.[48]

The task of refectory wall painting was still frequently assigned and undertaken in this period; and indeed, sometimes with a theme other than the customary one. Thus Raffaellino del Garbo painted the miraculous multiplication of loaves and fishes in the Cistercians' dining hall at Santa Maria Maddalena dei Pazzi; the badly damaged painting is now in the totally rebuilt setting of a school on Via della Colonna. In addition, in 1534 Sogliani dealt with the corresponding theme from the history of the Dominican order, particularly appropriate for a Dominican refectory, on a wall of the great dining hall of San Marco, presumably completing the earlier decoration of this wall by Fra Angelico (see above).

On the other hand, Franciabio's two *cenacolo* compositions in the refectory of San Giovanni della Calza and in the former convent of Santa Maria di Candeli (now a Carabinieri barracks on Via de' Pilastri) again

---

[46] See Vasari-Milanesi, 5:34; Bocchi-Cinelli, *Le bellezze della citta*, pp. 466-68. On the vineyard frescoes (of which a fragment is in the *cenacolo* room at Ognissanti) see *RA*, 1929, p. 293. The Pietà is preserved in the Academia store-room, temporarily inaccessible. A small, almost genre-like fresco of female saints caring for the sick in a women's hospital, from the former hospice of San Matteo, is now in the Academy as an "Andrea del Sarto." Berenson, however, considered it an early work of Pontormo.

[47] On the Scalzo confraternity and its oratorio, see Richa, *Notizie*, 7:196ff. Two *sopraporte* (of St. Thomas Aquinas), by Franciabigio above the entrance to the library of Santa Maria Novella and by Ridolfo Ghirlandaio in the first cloister of the Angeli convent, have not survived. The latter artist completed Uccello's chiaroscuro scenes from the St. Benedict legend in the loggia of the Angeli with one final picture (Vasari-Milanesi, 5:196; 6:537-38, 558).

[48] Vasari-Milanesi, 6:266-69; Hermann Voss, *Die Malerei der Spätrenaissance in Rom und Florenz* (Berlin, 1920), 1:188-89.

take up the customary Last Supper theme. And Andrea del Sarto, in the major work of his maturity, did the same in his spacious *Last Supper* fresco of San Salvi, dating from 1526-1527. This elegant development of Leonardo's example, with servant figures appearing in its upper architectural prospect, almost seems to foreshadow Paolo Veronese.[49]

## Panel Paintings in Sacred Settings

We encounter the surviving works of wall painting and stained glass almost without exception in their original spacial contexts, even if rarely undisturbed by later changes, renovations, or additions. The case of church panel painting is different. An extensive legacy of the original, incredibly vast development survives, but the great majority of pieces are no longer found in their original settings but in completely different surroundings and types of exhibition. Almost all the important altarpieces from Florentine churches have survived solely in museums. And this fact has so deeply affected our habitual outlook and consciousness that we almost have to force ourselves to remember how little this fundamentally corresponds to the original destination of the work, which also in many ways affected its form. We can nevertheless gain a certain conception of their original purpose and effect through those pieces that have remained in their original settings and today still stand before us in the original structure, context, and light of the altar setting for which they were ordered and produced. It is true that even for these examples the whole ensemble has survived only rarely with its original accessories, predella, and antependium, as perhaps in some altars in Santo Spirito.

The number of altars in Florentine churches, as in northern ones, was moreover far greater throughout the fifteenth century than later periods, concerned with a less dense and more systematically organized distribution, would retain or permit. The plan type of the churches newly built or remodeled in the Quattrocento, surrounded by uniform separate chapels, immediately called for a similarly regular arrangement and a correspondingly limited number of altar places. Such a harmonious overall effect was achieved in other cases by framing the altar spaces on the side walls of single-nave churches with tabernacles of similar design (see Sant' Ambrogio, Ognissanti, and others).[50]

Until about the middle of the Quattrocento, however, the type of plan

[49] See also Maria Baciocchi del Turco, *I cenacoli fiorentini*, with eight plates (Florence, 1904).

[50] See Richa, *Notizie*, 9:20-26, 33, for a survey of the many altarpieces by famous Renaissance masters that were still in Santo Spirito in the eighteenth century; records of the forty-four separate altars in the Carmine before the 1771 fire are in *RA*, 1932, pp. 141ff; see also James Wood Brown, *The Dominican Church of Santa Maria Novella* (Edinburgh, 1902) and Filippo Moisè, *Santa Croce di Firenze* (Florence, 1845), passim.

and contours of altarpieces for the most part followed long-traditional patterns. The old-fashioned division into several vertical sections, each crowned by a late Gothic arched gable with finials sprouting up between them, disappeared only gradually in progressive works of the second quarter of the century. Similarly, the long-traditional gold ground in many paintings by Neri di Bicci and his associates, corresponding to the old-fashioned tendency of the taste of the petty bourgeois clientele of such workshops, occasionally lasted even into the third quarter of the fifteenth century and was taken up again at the end of the Quattrocento in connection with certain archaizing aspirations of the period.[51]

Many altarpieces of Fra Angelico, for example, show the long adherence to Gothic traditions in the form of frames. This is most striking in the *Descent from the Cross* dating from 1440 to 1445, his mature period, at the Museum of San Marco. For this, however, it appears that an available older, richly ornamented frame structure was used.[52] But even the altarpiece of the Virgin from the nuns' convent of San Pietro Martire, now in Museo San Marco, executed from the beginning in Fra Angelico's workshop, adheres to the old three-part blind arcade organization with rich late Gothic decoration; and only the insertion of the whole into a rectangular outer frame shows, except for its cornice profile and console frieze, an approach to the frame type of the early Renaissance.[53]

But notwithstanding all the numerous stragglers of the old altar type, the new retable form already appearing sporadically in the 1430s became the rule after the mid-century. This type, an undivided horizontal rectangular panel with pilaster and cornice frame, predominated until it was gradually superceded around the end of the century by the tall, vertical rectangular type, sometimes semicircular at the top. And this form, probably appearing for the first time with Botticelli's *Coronation of the Virgin* and Filippino's altar for the Palazzo Vecchio of 1485, became generally customary for all large altarpieces after about 1500.

[51] See, for example, Filippino's *Crucifixion* in Berlin and an anonymous Antoninus in the same place; on this and the following see also Jacob Burckhardt, *Beiträge zur Kunstgeschichte von Italien: Das Altarbild* (Basel, 1898).

[52] The painter only removed the dividing colonnettes from the central section in order to gain space for his broad composition. The small paintings in the pinnacles show the hand of Don Lorenzo Monaco, who thus probably received the commission first, but only began these portions. For an opposing view see Siren, p. 114. [*Translator's note*: this probably refers to O. Siren, *Don Lorenzo Monaco*, Strasbourg, 1905; the page reference does not match, however.]

[53] Several altarpieces by Neri di Bicci and other mid-century contemporaries in the Academy, in San Giovannino dei Cavalieri and elsewhere present similar cases, as does a Madonna altarpiece dating from about 1450-1455 in the Carrand collection by "Carrand Master" Giovanni di Francesco and also in the Last Judgment by Domenico di Michelino, dated 1456, in Berlin. See also the later rectangular reshaping of Lorenzo Monaco's *Adoration of the Magi* (Uffizi), carried out around 1470.

The little altarpiece of the Madonna in the Academy (nr. 8508), datable about 1440-

The subject of the great majority of altarpieces is the enthroned Madonna with saints, that is, the Santa Conversazione theme. Thus, for example, of the altarpieces still in Santo Spirito or traceable to there between about 1480 and 1520, more than half repeat this theme. The Annunciation, Nativity, and Adoration of the Kings also appear frequently. Beginning in the late Quattrocento the more pathetic or otherwise strongly emotional moments of the Assumption and Coronation of the Virgin appear more often.[54] The theme of the Pietà and Descent from the Cross, handled previously only by Fra Angelico and in a picture from the Castagno school in the Sant' Apollonia museum, begins to recur frequently in painting and sculpture only in the late Quattrocento, presumably as a result of Savonarolan stimulus. The Crucifixion and Baptism of Christ were less frequent. Quite unique is Fra Bartolommeo's 1516 image at the Pitti of Christ the Savior raised like a statue on a high pedestal with four evangelists, similar to a Marian Santa Conversazione.[55] The Last Judgment, frequently depicted by Fra Angelico and his school in small altarpieces, also recurs only toward the end of the century and only in wall painting principally by Fra Bartolommeo. Thus here also, in altarpiece iconography as already noted in other connections, we find a return at the end of the Quattrocento to long-neglected pictorial fashions of the early fifteenth century.

Less frequently we encounter paintings with subjects related to the particular patronage of the church or altar such as the Holy Trinity

---

1445, also has the medieval division of the retable into several small rectangular pictures above and beside one another. There are three scenes respectively in two superimposed rows, crowned by triangular gables with finials between them.

In San Felice in Piazza is a triptych by Neri di Bicci with a sacrament tabernacle inserted into the central blind arcade, flanked and crowned by adoring angels, with a small Christ figure painted on its door. In the lunette field of the arcade, still with a Gothic profile, is a Man of Sorrows and two angels. The same church also has an early Cinquecento altar by Raffaellino del Garbo that revives the early partition into three blind arcades.

[54] The Assunta first appears in Castagno's work of 1449 in Berlin; then, with a notably archaic figure organization, in Cosimo Rosselli's large tabernacle in Fiesole, Museo Bandini; also by Botticelli (Uffizi) and particularly in two highly animated versions by Andrea del Sarto; by Fra Bartolommeo are the *Madonna della Gloria* hovering on the clouds (now at Besançon) and the *Immaculate Conception* of 1515 (now in the Louvre); the latter, however, was represented somewhat earlier by Piero di Cosimo (Uffizi). Mariotto Albertinelli contributed the God the Father hovering in the clouds for an altar of the Annunciation (1510, Academy). The monumental two-figure scene of the Visitation was represented once by Ghirlandaio (1491, Louvre), then in a solemn high classical treatment on the altarpiece for a congregation of priests with this title by Mariotto Albertinelli (Uffizi). The Madonna of Mercy, widespread in Italy only in Umbria, appears in the altarpiece of the Fra Filippo school in Berlin.

[55] This panel, together with the two detached prophet pictures now in the Uffizi, originally formed a three-part chapel decoration in the Annunziata (chapel of Salvatore Billi), held together by a rich marble frame; see Bocchi-Cinelli, *Le bellezze della citta*.

images by Pesellino now in London and by Baldovinetti for the Santa Trinita high altar, the martyrdom of St. Sebastian by Pollaiuolo, and sometimes also groupings of three to five individual saints.[56]

If a small separate picture of the Crucified is occasionally inserted in the lower central area of many Quattrocento altarpieces, sometimes painted with the illusion of being raised from the surface of the large panel or leaning against it, then the Crucifix that was liturgically necessary for any altar where mass was to be celebrated was already provided.

A rare special form, the panel painted on both sides, should also be mentioned. This was designed for a setting in which it was freestanding and equally visible from front and back; such were the original high altars of Santa Maria Novella (see above) and that of the Annunziata by Filippino and Perugino. The three-part combination of a statuary centerpiece with painted side sections occurs, for example, in the St. Sebastian altar at Santa Maria Maddalena dei Pazzi and in Empoli.

A necessary base for the altarpiece structure was the socle platform called a predella. Small rectangular picture fields with scenes from the legends of particular saints in the altar panel generally appeared, now as well as earlier, on its frieze-like front, sometimes only in the looser organization of separate painted medallions containing half-length figures. The donor's arms usually appeared at the end of this step. The execution of these predella panels was in no sense considered a mere secondary chore to complete the commission. Rather, these narrative paintings in small format offered the head of the workshop himself an opportunity, apparently eagerly seized, to exercise his descriptive and staging abilities, which could not have free reign in the usual, very simple treatment or arrangement of figures in the main panel, with all sorts of whims and new combinations. These small, intimate pictures, then, more than monumental painting, offered a particularly fruitful area for experiment with new means of representation and expression in the period just preceding the style change and then particularly beginning in the 1420s and 30s. It is true that the great majority of churchgoers might notice scarcely any of the surprises and the sometimes extremely delicate refinements of detail execution introduced there. What new and exquisite things the artist could offer in the choice delicacies of these predella panels were accessible only to a connoisseur's close observation and presupposed just such an interest from a qualified intimate observer.[57]

[56] Examples are the St. Laurence altar of Fra Filippo Lippi, work by Pollaiuolo in the chapel of the Cardinal of Portugal, by Ghirlandaio in San Lorenzo, etc., and the group of five saints by Andrea del Sarto in the Uffizi.

[57] The Kupferstichkabinett in Berlin preserves as a curiosity a predella from the late Quattrocento whose frieze band is set with thirteen hand-colored Florentine engravings of the Life of Mary and the Passion.

A third, customary part of the painted decoration of an altar is the *paliotto* or antependium, which was hung on the otherwise unadorned front of the altar table, whose substructure consisted of walls or four corner supports. We know of the early and high medieval custom, perfectly natural considering the celebrant's former position behind the altar, of covering the front of the altar structure on high feast days with an antependium of precious metal chased with relief decoration. Such heightened liturgical splendor survived in the Florentine artistic milieu well into the late middle ages; for example, in the silver antependium of San Giovanni, begun in the fourteenth century and brought to completion in the middle of the fifteenth, and its counterpart in the Duomo of Pistoia. The old custom of creating festive altar hangings in silken figured embroidery or in costly brocade with figural decoration in the upper border survived into the Renaissance; details on this will be presented later.

Here, however, in connection with painted altarpieces and predellas, we may mention the cheaper replacement of embroidered cloth hangings with painted imitations of such cloths on simple wooden front panels attached to the altar table. Many of the various surviving examples of such antependia on the altars of Santo Spirito date from the time of the first altarpieces of about 1480-1500, some also from later periods. These make it clear that for these purely decorative portions of the whole altar complex, only assistants or painters of a more artisan level were ordinarily called upon.[58]

A last occasional appendix to the altar equipment was the covering or veil, provided to close off the altar panel, in the form of a painted or embroidered curtain (*cortina*), or occasionally even of wooden closing wings with painted decoration such as appear almost as a general rule on our German altars. It is true that not a single traceable example of such a work has survived, but many are cited in the literature. It is, moreover, evident that these were by no means appraised and produced merely as artisan's decorative pieces. Thus, for example, Fra Filippo, who completed Pesellino's altarpiece in Pistoia, also made a *cortina* for it.[59]

---

[58] Neri di Bicci, according to his book of *Ricordi* in 1456, undertook the execution of a palio for the high altar of San Pancrazio in a damask pattern, partly in white, partly in bright colors, with a painted fringe border on the upper frieze (Vasari-Milanesi, 4:193). Certain painted *paliotti* from the rural churches of the environs of Florence appeared in the Mostra del Tesoro di Firenze Sacra, 1933.

[59] The same altar also received wooden closing wings (*sportelli*), admittedly executed only by a humble local painter (*RA*, 1904, pp. 172-73). Filippino's altar of St. Bernard at Campora, now in the Badia, also had a *cortina*, according to Vasari (Vasari-Milanesi, 3:464, n. 1).

In 1510 Andrea Feltrini painted a curtain with figural decoration for the high altar of the Annunziata. Vasari (Vasari-Milanesi, 5:8) mentioned it as a youthful work of Andrea del Sarto.

Such temporary veiling of the altarpiece was necessary whenever the altar was placed in an otherwise secular setting and needed to be made visible only for occasional religious celebrations. As a rule in such cases it was admittedly only a colorfully patterned curtain (as, for example, in the great council chamber, the Hall of the Two Hundred, of the Palazzo Vecchio; see above). The *cortina* or *sportelli* painted with figural decoration, on the other hand, functioned like the exteriors of our German polyptychs, as a sort of simple everyday dress auxiliary to the appearance of the actual altarpiece as it was displayed without any veiling on solemn occasions.

Finally, painted organ wings deserve mention. These served as permanent decorative covering for the organ works. Such were the *sportelli* for the two small organs on the choir screen of Santa Maria Novella, with paintings on canvas of the Annunciation by Fra Angelico.[60] The organ wings for Or San Michele, painted by Francesco d'Antonio in 1429, are probably identical with two panels painted on both sides in the Collezione Toscanelli. The Evangelists are on the outside, singing angels on the inside.[61] The former organ wings from San Michele in Orto with individual saints by Lorenzo di Credi and Sellaio appeared in the exhibition of Firenze Sacra. All organs presumably had such painted wings. These disappeared in the later renovations of the instrument and received no mention in the literature when the artistic quality was not especially noteworthy.

In the church interior, along with altarpieces, there were, as we have already noted with respect to wall paintings, numerous separate pictures that appeared here and there on exposed sections of wall, probably also frequently on the front side of nave piers without association with an altar; these were special donations occasioned by various devotional or *ex-voto* purposes. Such separate pictures, which in the first half of the Quattrocento usually took the traditional form of a vertical rectangular or pointed arched panel, generally represented an especially venerated saint or a patron preferred for personal reasons or in association with some special matter. This was readily made evident by the representation of the donor along with the saint.[62]

[60] Such was the silk hanging of the Camaldoli organ, by Neri di Bicci in 1453, painted with ornamental borders and medallions with coats of arms. See also *Il Vasari*, 1, p. 320 and Vasari-Milanesi, 3:275-76 regarding organ wings by Bastiano Mainardi for the Pisa Cathedral.

[61] *RA*, 1929, pp. 18ff.

[62] See the two early paintings in the Duomo museum (Bischeri votive painting and St. Ivo, as patron of notaries, with a pair of donors, evidently depicting the conclusion of a marriage contract). See also the panels with Sts. Bernardino and Vincent Ferrer in the Accademia: the latter with a predella on which are two legendary scenes and a group of supplicants before the sarcophagus hung with *ex-voti*. In the same place is a panel in a

St. Sebastian, invoked everywhere as a protector in time of plague, was represented, for example, by Pollaiuolo not only in the large *Martyrdom of St. Sebastian* in the Servite church and now in London but also in a smaller separate panel now in Dresden; Botticelli also depicted him in the picture now in Berlin, from Santa Maria Maggiore, where it was probably attached to a nave pier.

Particularly frequent in Florence was the image of the archangel Raphael as a guide on a journey and protector of the little Tobias, hence the traditional patron saint of young travellers. These were primarily the sons of Florentine merchant families who left the parental home to go somewhere abroad, perhaps to gain further training in the foreign bureau of a local firm. Many of these paintings of the guardian angel with the little Tobias must have been commissioned on just such occasions and hung up in the commissioner's parish church, if not in his own household chapel.

Many of the surviving pieces of this type from the late Quattrocento, and probably also many which are only mentioned in the literature, derive from the prototype of the well-known altarpiece in the Uffizi that was painted probably about 1465 for the Confraternity of the Archangel, called Compagnia Il Raffa for short, in Santo Spirito by an artist of Verrocchio's circle, still not securely identified (perhaps even the young Botticelli). The two other archangels are also represented in the horizontal altarpiece. Such, for example, is the Tobias painting by Botticini from the Badia in the Academy, with the small portrait of the donor's son in travelling costume kneeling at the lower left, and the parents' coats of arms. Other free copies of the main group are in Munich, Turin, and elsewhere.[63] Pollaiuolo's archangel painting in Turin (possibly identical with the panel that originally hung on a pier at Or San Michele) and that of a Verrocchio pupil in London show no dependence on the large altarpiece from Santo Spirito.[64]

Individual donated paintings of various types and sizes were also often attached to the choir enclosures of the churches of the orders. Along with larger paintings, these included many *tavolette* that had probably orig-

style close to Botticini's with the same Dominican saint and small donor figures in tertiary cowls at his feet.

Of later date is the St. Lucia in Santa Maria Novella, with the donor portrait of Fra Tommaso Cortese, painted in 1494 by Davide Ghirlandaio (van Marle, *Painting*, 13:140), as well as the large St. Michael by Lorenzo di Credi in the new sacristy of the Duomo.

[63] Botticini painted several Tobias pictures, and Neri di Bicci no less than nine (see above all Mesnil in *RA*, 3, pp. 38ff.; 4, pp. 19ff; and Gronau in *MKIF*, 3, pp. 430ff.).

[64] Vasari-Milanesi, 3:292, n. 1; van Marle, *Painting*, 11:325, 541. Sometimes the Tobias group is only inserted or appended in the background landscape of a larger altarpiece, such as Botticini's crucifix altarpiece, as well as Piero di Cosimo's large Adoration in Berlin and Ghirlandaio's Madonna in the same place.

inally served as household devotional images and had perhaps come into the church as a bequest; this may also hold true for occasional tondi appearing in such settings, for the religious painting in a round format occurs otherwise only in private domestic contexts.[65]

As with many household Madonnas (see below), the frames of small devotional paintings for churches were sometimes painted with decorative attendant figures. One example of 1483 is the twelve small angel figures in Botticelli's style on the frame of a small, long-venerated crucifix painting in the Carmine (illustrated in *RA*, 1932, p. 177). Also related to household painting commissions are certain portrayals of legends for church settings, which seem to be substitutes for large wall painting compositions, in the style of cassone or wainscoting panels.[66]

Triumphal crosses, however, generally customary in earlier times, were now produced only rarely; such is the painstakingly executed wooden crucifix in Brozzi with half-figure medallions on the ends of the bars by Giovanni di Francesco dating from about 1450. Small painted wood crosses for use on altars or in processions were much more frequently produced, supplanting the sculptural versions preferred elsewhere.[67]

Even small pax plaques, which include numerous fine pieces among the ecclesiastical goldsmith's work noted above, received simple makeshift decorations with small paintings on wood.[68]

## BANNERS AND VESTMENTS

The large processional banners painted with figures, the so-called *gonfaloni* or *stendardi*, form an artistic genre closely related in format and content to the stationary individual paintings in churches. A few examples have survived, although now, it is true, they are preserved in museums in fixed frames so that their original purpose is scarcely recognizable. Many other examples are at least mentioned in the literature.

Even well-known artists were often secured for such commissions. This shows what high value patrons—chiefly religious confraternities—placed

[65] A Botticelli tondo, installed in a square frame, was in San Francesco al Monte. See Vasari-Milanesi, 3:258, 318; 4:141 with regard to certain small Piero di Cosimo panels on the *tramezzo* of San Francesco in Fiesole.

[66] See the horizontal rectangular panel from Uccello's early period, with scenes from the legends of the Hermits (Accademia) and a painting from the Fiesole Duomo (now Museo Bandini in the same place) with small-figured episodes from the life of St. Romulus.

[67] Many examples of the type were in the *Mostra di Firenze Sacra*. A processional cross painted on both sides in the style of Neri di Bicci is in the Museum in Fiesole. Zanobi Strozzi painted a wooden crucifix "per morti" for San Marco in 1448. The payment of three florins suggests an especially painstakingly executed work (*l'Arte*, 11, p. 91).

[68] An example with a Man of Sorrows, allegedly a youthful work of Fra Filippo, is in the Fondazione Horne (room 3, no. 64).

on giving the highest possible artistic worth and impressive form to these procession insignia with which they appeared in public. It is certain in any case that the more famous of the numerous Florentine confraternities possessed at least one such procession banner and had the right to display it publicly in the numerous parades and processions which were part of the public life of the city and that such banners or standards were also carried by all the other state and civic corporations.[69]

The whole genre of such painting must have been much more extensive than is evident in the surviving monuments and literary references. The great majority of the ordinary pieces would naturally have become so worn and unsightly through use in the course of time that they would have been thrown out without a thought as soon as a replacement was obtained. Understandably, only the examples executed by famous masters, and therefore carefully conserved, were recorded in the literature or even preserved in concreto. The following notices should shed some light on the former importance, at least quantitative, of the type of commission as a whole, and indicate its place in the whole complex of painting commissions.

Two types of such processional images belong together here. The banners or standards painted on canvas are distinguished by material and size from the small wooden panel paintings raised on poles (segni di processione) that were already in use in the Duecento as shown by an example preserved in the Museo dell'Opera.[70] For the Quattrocento this type is represented by a pair of panels from the mid-century in Santa Maria Primerana in Fiesole, in the form of shields with the Madonna della Cintola on one side and the arms of Fiesole on the other. A small segno from the late Quattrocento, painted on both sides, is in the Museo Communale in Pistoia. It was carried ahead of criminals as they were led to execution and accordingly was painted with scenes of the martyrdom of saints (it was still used for this purpose as late as the eighteenth century). We may also refer, for illustrative evidence of the custom, to the painted panels carried on poles in many triumph scenes on cassone panels and in Mantegna's Triumph of Caesar, as well as to Vasari's description of lost triumph pictures by Pontormo in which bearers of such panels are referred to as tavolaccini.[71]

[69] In contemporary literary sources these "Compagnie di stendardo" were explicitly distinguished from the smaller associations, which did not have the right to a banner (see, for example, Masi, Ricordanze, p. 80 and passim.).

[70] This is the panel, newly cleaned and restored in the fifteenth century, which represents a half-figure of St. Agatha on each side, by a master of the Berlinghieri style. See Osvald Siren, Toskanische Maler im XIII Jahrhundert (Berlin, 1922) p. 109, pl. 33.

[71] Vasari-Milanesi, 6:273. Many small panel paintings now stored in museums might on closer examination prove to have originated as segni da processione.

More frequent and more continuously traceable in reports and surviving examples is another type, the *gonfaloni* executed as pictures on
canvas. These are pictorial counterparts to the large banners of patterned
brocade such as were carried in particular in processions for the feast of
St. John.[72] The subdivisions of the urban quarters of Florence were also
called simply *gonfaloni* and distinguished by the devices under which
they gathered.[73] Of all this, nothing is preserved or traceable. Most painful
of all is the loss of some works of this type by Botticelli, of which once
again only Vasari has left us a report; he speaks in particular about a
baldachin for processions with the host, existing in Or San Michele,
which was trimmed with small Madonna figures sewn-on in the new
*commesso* technique introduced by Botticelli; he was also familiar with
a hanging for the processional cross of the monks of Santa Maria Novella
with figural embroidery based on Botticelli's design.

The use of such processional banners survived among the confraternities at least until the end of the republic; and Andrea del Sarto was
hired as late as 1528 to paint a *gonfalone* for the Compagnia di San
Jacopo. The painting, showing the titular patron of the confraternity

---

[72] Two former processional banners painted on canvas from Fra Angelico's workshop
and school still exist; one in the Pisa Museo Civico shows Christ with the chalice on a
damask ground; the other, much smaller, which Savonarola used in his penitential processions, according to an inscription, has a painted crucifix on plain canvas. It is now in
Savonarola's cell in San Marco.

In 1424 the Calimala guild had a new figured *gonfalone* painted by Arrigo Pesello (Vasari-
Milanesi, 3:42).

A *gonfalone* for the Compagnia del Vangelista, thus probably with the image of John,
was painted by Castagno, according to a record quoted by Milanesi (Vasari-Milanesi,
2:670-71). In 1454 the Florentine painter Mariotto di Stefano undertook the execution of
a medium-sized Madonna standard for a penitential confraternity in San Gimignano following the example of a small image of the Mother of God in the convent of Santa Maria
degli Angeli (Milanesi, *Documenti*, pp. 96-97).

Vasari (Vasari-Milanesi, 3:295) attributes a *gonfalone* in the possession of the Compagnia
di Sant' Angelo in Arezzo to Antonio Pollaiuolo; on one side was a crucifix painted in oil
on canvas, on the back the patron of the confraternity, St. Michael. Richa (*Notizie*, 10:355)
also cited as a work of Pollaiuolo's a procession banner with St. Sebastian, still preserved
in San Jacopo sopr'Arno in his time. Vasari was acquainted with a processional standard
(whether a wooden panel or canvas banner) for the children's division of the Compagnia
di San Bernardino, and that of the confraternity of San Giorgio with an image of the
Annunziata (Vasari-Milanesi, 3:185), both by Cosimo Rosselli. Benozzo Gozzoli also
painted many *gonfaloni* during his late period in Pisa (two banners for the Opera del
Duomo in 1488 and several other standards in 1494; van Marle, *Painting*, 11:116).

[73] One Bernardino di Jacopo painted a banner with a serpent for the Gonfalone della
Vipera in the quarter of Santa Maria Novella in 1500. It was "painted in gold, with
embroidered outline and shading" (Jodoco del Badia, *Miscellanea fiorentina*, 2 vols., 1902,
2:174 [periodical]).

attended by two acolytes, has survived; but it now hangs in a room in the Uffizi, set like an altarpiece in a heavy frame.[74]

The funeral ceremonies for distinguished personalities also provided painters with occasions to prepare certain necessary decorations, such as the bier-cover, sometimes painted with figures.[75] Painted pennants or *drapelloni* were also frequently used in funeral ceremonies to adorn the *castrum doloris*, often hung in a row on the baldachin. This is recorded in particular for the obsequies for the young Medici dukes Lorenzo and Giuliano (1516, 1519), when *drapelloni* were painted by Franciabigio. See also the extensive count of all the *drapelloni* that were provided by the bushel, "*in filze,*" by the state authorities and great guilds for the funeral processions of both dukes, and subsequently hung in San Lorenzo.[76]

One may see how such *drapelloni* looked and were hung in the large image of a sacramental procession in the *Diurno domenicale* of Boccardino Vecchio (Biblioteca Laurenziana, Cor. no. 4), in which seven *drapelloni* (executed in paint or embroidery) hang together on each side of the baldachin, each decorated with a standing figure of a saint on a gold ground; the top of the baldachin was red with gold ornaments.

Only in a very few cases was the costly embroidery technique employed instead of the customary painted cloth in the type of works surveyed above. Yet this "needle painting" with colorful silk and gold threads is the sole decorative medium for the liturgical vestments essential for use

[74] Bocchi-Cinelli (*Le bellezze della citta*, p. 480) still saw the banner in the confraternity oratorio, near the Innocenti hospital.

[75] Lorenzo Monaco painted such a one in 1417 for the Compagnia di Gesù Pellegrino with the figures of Christ and a pilgrim (Vasari-Milanesi, 2:32).

[76] A total of eighteen filze of *drapelloni* as well as eighteen large taffeta *bandiere*, some all black, some painted with coats of arms or guild insignia, were all carried by individual riders at the mourning ceremonies for Duke Lorenzo (Masi, *Ricordanze*, pp. 198-99, 241).

Vasari gives a similarly detailed account of the mourning banners furnished by the young Pontormo for the funeral procession of Bartolommeo Ginori; there was a series of twenty-four *drapelloni* of the unusually imposing length of two braccia, of which the two hanging in the middle bore the image of Ginori's name patron as well as small Madonna figures with the family arms below them. For the funeral ceremonies of a Rucellai (presumably Bernardo, who died in 1514) Bugiardini painted something exceptional: instead of a set of pennants, a single great banner with the family arms and four figures of saints.

Around the same time Ridolfo Ghirlandaio took on many similar occasional commissions, such as, on the one hand, the preparation of painted insignia of the *potenze*, social clubs with fantastic ceremonies, for their annual tournament and on the other hand, the macabre images of 1519 on two great black curtains that were hung over the high altar in the Duomo on All Souls Day (Vasari-Milanesi, 5:208; 6:202-203, 260, 542). At the wedding festivities of Lorenzo de' Medici, Duke of Urbino, who died a short time later on 9 November 1518, these *potenze* all appeared with new painted banners whose insignia were enriched with gilding (Masi, *Ricordanze*, p. 237).

in church services. And even for altar antependia, the above-mentioned execution in decorative painting on wood or canvas was only a surrogate, frequently chosen to save money, for the nobler type it imitated: brocaded cloth with an upper decorative border and a central decoration in figural embroidery.

The rich material of the Mostra del Tesoro di Firenze Sacra held in the summer of 1933 offered the first fairly clear and comprehensive presentation of the whole field of vestments that we shall discuss below as well as of the ecclesiastical goldsmith work to be discussed later. It is true that even the assembly here, the most complete possible, of all surviving pieces, could still amount to only a fraction of the former incredibly rich and splendidly developed province of ecclesiastical decorative art. What we still possess is only a remainder of what once existed in all the churches of the city and its environs—a remainder that, moreover, has almost all come down to us only in an extremely worn, often mutilated condition, sometimes subjected in later times to arbitrary, makeshift repairs.

Particularly noteworthy is a *paliotto* in gold brocade in Santa Maria Novella, whose upper band was decorated during the mid-fifteenth century with a broad frieze of fourteen embroidered scenes from the life of Mary. From a little later is the upper frieze of an altar hanging in the Duomo, restored besides, in which are the half-length figure of the Madonna and eleven saints in relief-like embroidery.

The Duomo also possesses a sixteenth-century *paliotto* of mottled red velvet with a frieze of the Madonna and several Florentine saints, partly embroidered, partly painted on silk. The Annunziata has an altar hanging of the same type, also of red velvet, enriched with doves and figures of the Madonna and of St. Filippo Benizzi (founder of the Servite order), cut out of silver cloth and sewn on.[77] The altar cloth that Pope Sixtus IV donated to San Francesco at Assisi in 1472 has survived. It is evidently Florentine work, perhaps based on Pollaiuolo's design.[78]

---

[77] Museo di San Marco, *Mostra del Tesoro di Firenze Sacra* (Florence, 1933), pp. 32-33, 76, 80-81.

Other works of the type are known at least through literary citations: they include an embroidered altar hanging of 1480 for the Badia and another of 1487 for the Convent alla Campora with a frieze of leafy garlands containing five medallions with half figures of saints (see the agreement on the commission with the embroiderers Paolo di Bartolommeo and Galiena di Michele in *RA*, 1903, pp. 2, 144).

The inventory of Palazzo Medici of 1492 mentions an *arazzo* with religious subjects, fashioned as an altar frontal (Müntz, *Collections*, p. 84).

[78] A large scene of the pope kneeling before St. Francis adorns its central field; above this is the usual frieze band with fifteen small half-length figures of the Madonna and other saints. The cloth of the antependium is velvet with an ornament of Rovere oak leaves worked in, ornamental decorative medallions, and donor inscription. See Vasari-Milanesi,

The most beautiful work of this type, however, probably deriving from a design by Leonardo da Vinci, belonged to Santa Maria delle Grazie and is now in the Museo Poldi Pezzoli in Milan; it was the gift of Duke Lodovico Moro in 1497; one side, in a festive tone, has a pelican in the central field surrounded by blooming vine rinceaux with putti; the back, for masses for the dead, is of dark velvet with Christ standing in the sarcophagus in the center and with the initials of the Duchess Beatrice who died around that time.[79]

As mentioned above, people admittedly settled in many cases for the cheaper and yet more durable substitute of wood or canvas painted *paliotti*; yet it may be assumed that the few embroidered altar hangings surviving or mentioned in the literature represent only a fraction of the number that once existed.

Works in this most delicate medium, figural needlework, must often have perished when they became worn out through use on the altar and were finally discarded. This is most evident in the case of mass vestments, of which only occasional remnants have been preserved; yet surely once nearly every church must have possessed, along with countless simpler examples, at least one complete set of accessories trimmed with embroidery for the high feast days, and many must have acquired several during the course of the Renaissance.

The data to be discussed later concerning the decoration of secular festival costumes, frequently so rich in figural decoration and material splendor, necessitates the conclusion that liturgical vestments must, for self-evident reasons, have received at least equally luxurious treatment.[80] Certain representations of magnificent mass vestments worn by priest-saints in altarpieces should also be noted: for example, in the *Madonna of Mercy* by Giovanni di Paolo in the Servite church in Siena dating from 1437, and in Botticelli's *Madonna with Six Saints* in the Uffizi dating from about 1475. Here the somewhat old-fashioned figures in the decorative stripe on the chasuble suggest the painter was copying old vestments available to him. The same is true in Ghirlandaio's two Madonna altarpieces in the Uffizi.

3:299, n. 2; *l'Arte*, 1906, pp. 215ff.; *Rass. A.*, 1920, pp. 202ff.; Otto von Falke, *Kunstgeschichte der Seidenweberei* (Berlin, 1913), 2, ill. 435ff., in which closely related objects of ornamental silkwork, in particular the former throne back for Matthias Corvinus, are also published.

[79] Adolfo Venturi, *Storia dell' Arte Italiana*, 25 vols. (Milan and Rome, 1901-1940), 9:167-75; *l'Arte*, 1925, pp. 141ff.

[80] Vasari knew of many designs for *paramenti* by Raffaellino del Garbo, who produced these for a living (Vasari-Milanesi, 4:239f.); Vasari (Vasari-Milanesi, 2:59) refers to the frequent execution of vestment embroidery in nuns' convents. Production of particularly costly works, however, was entrusted to professional male embroiderers (see below the *paramenti* for San Giovanni).

Several surviving mass vestments or portions of them may be cited here:

(1) The uneven figural embroidery in the frieze of a *paliotto* in the Oratory of the Vanchettoni evidently stems from a mass vestment of about 1460-1480, which was later taken out of use.

(2) The red velvet cope in Santa Margherita a Montici with a shield with rich figural decoration, dates probably from about 1460-1480 (Museo di San Marco, *Mostra del Tesoro*, pl. 29).

(3) The figural decoration of a whole set of chapel vestments of white damask was executed probably on Pollaiuolo's design between about 1466 and 1480. Provided for San Giovanni by the Calimala, this was separated from the threadbare vestments in 1730 and is now in the Museo dell'Opera, displayed in a frame under glass.[81]

(4) No less consummate in the artistic quality of its design and execution was the shield of a cope of about 1470 with the Coronation of the Virgin, kneeling portrait figures of the donors, and hovering angels in the Poldi-Pezzoli museum, Milan. The arms represented with them appear to be those of the Cardinal of Portugal who died in 1459; accordingly the vestment would belong to his tomb chapel at San Miniato which was decorated during the 1460s. The attribution of the design to Botticelli or his circle is more convincing than van Marles's reference (*Painting*, 11:272) to Baldovinetti.[82]

The Bambino of the Madonna image of Impruneta repeatedly received gifts of precious little cloaks; for instance, on the occasion of a solemn procession through Florence with this image in 1522, arranged by the Signoria, the Signoria itself and four other civic bodies donated such splendid little cloaks of gold brocade.[83]

Various examples of a less costly type of work have survived in the Berlin Decorative Arts (Kunstgewerbe) Museum and elsewhere. This is

[81] Twenty-seven scenes still exist. Schwabacher has attempted to reconstruct the original distribution on three mass vestments and a cope. All are scenes from the life of the Baptist, executed by nine different embroiderers, with precise accounts surviving on their wages and expenses for materials. The total expenditure of 3179 florins plus 7646 *lire* would correspond, according to Schwabacher, to a total of 45,000 marks.

Cinelli (Bocchi-Cinelli, *Le bellezze della citta*, p. 34) who still saw the vestments in use in 1677 writes: "Stories can be seen at the bottom and in the middle." Details are in Sascha Schwabacher, *Die Stickereien nach Entwürfen des Antonio Pollaiuolo . . .* (Strasbourg, 1911).

[82] Compare with the embroidered roundel with the Coronation of the Virgin from the convent of Santa Verdiana in Florence in a private collection in Venice (illustrated as "Florentine, c. 1460," *Pantheon*, 1936, p. 285).

[83] One of these seems to have survived; it was displayed in the Mostra del Tesoro di Firenze Sacra, 1933 (Masi, *Ricordanze*, p. 260).

not embroidery, but designs woven in brocaded velvet (*brocatello sto-riato*) with broad borders that served as vertical and horizontal strips of trimming in mass vestments. In their delicate but assured play of line they correspond most closely with contemporary Florentine woodcuts of about 1470.[84]

It is relevant to refer here, at least in a few words, to still another branch of minor ecclesiastical arts—the miniature decoration of luxury liturgical manuscripts. A few famous examples have already been mentioned above in the history of the Duomo and Baptistery.[85] In the field of book painting for churches, which adhered for a particularly long time to the traditional late Trecento style, the first effects of the new formal outlook set in only after the middle of the Quattrocento. This has not yet occurred in the works that Fra Angelico's pupil Zanobi Strozzi executed from about 1445 to 1450 on the commissions of Cosimo de' Medici for San Marco and the Badia. But it does appear in his later miniatures, which he executed from 1463 to 1470 in collaboration with the somewhat younger Francesco d'Antonio del Chierico for the Duomo sacristy.

Above all, however, it is the brothers Gherardo and Monte di Giovanni who most emphatically personify the delight in luxurious decoration of the Laurentian period for instance in their large altar missal for Santa Maria Novella executed from 1474 to 1476 and now in the Bargello and again in their splendid later works for the Duomo, San Giovanni, and San Lorenzo. These last churches still provided them with commissions through 1528. The case of their contemporary Attavante, quite famous in his time, is similar. His commissions included certain unusually costly books for foreign patrons of high rank (see below). The fact that no less than forty-five miniature painters are recorded in Florence for the period 1450-1520 testifies to the rich efflorescence of this whole branch of the

[84] In the Loevi collection, Venice, are many examples, including an Assunta, a Madonna della Cintola, and a Resurrection executed in similar style on a cope of about 1510-1520. On the whole genre see Otto von Falke, *Kunstgeschichte der Seidenweberei* (Berlin, 1913), 2:112, ill. 533ff.

Festival mitres of bishops also occasionally received figural decoration, as may be seen for instance in images of bishop saints in altarpieces; a mitre of the early Quattrocento in the Duomo treasury of Fiesole, on the other hand, is decorated with small enamel images in silver settings.

Finally there is the *infula* of the prior of San Lorenzo, adorned with rich pearl embroidery, a gift of Pople Leo X dating from about 1515-1516 whose arms appear in an enamel shield on the bands of this mitre. Pope Leo gave another mitre, probably of similar magnificence, to the archbishop of Florence; it was sold in 1531 and has since disappeared (Masi, *Ricordanze*, pp. 186-87).

[85] The whole field of religious and secular book painting is thoroughly treated in the voluminous comprehensive work of Paolo d'Ancona, the best connoisseur in this field, *La miniatura Fiorentina (secoli xi-xvi)*, 2 vols. (Florence, 1914).

arts. See Paolo d'Ancona, *La miniatura Fiorentina (secoli xi-xvi)*, 2 vols. (Florence, 1914), 1:71-76. It is true, however, that we can connect only about ten to twelve names with secure works.

## PAINTINGS IN DOMESTIC INTERIORS

In this context we shall speak first of the genre that grew out of the architectural structure of the interior, wall and ceiling painting. This is the only type of domestic painted decoration whose prehistory goes back to the early Trecento, if not earlier, and in which, in Florence and elsewhere, elements of secular subject matter first appeared. In ceiling decoration, which in rare cases was articulated with sculpture, painting at first concerned itself only with the ornamental and decorative. This was true for the traditional ceiling organization of narrow cross beams with board panels nailed over them, so that only motifs arranged in bands were possible; but also even for the *soffitti* often hung beneath these true ceilings, whose coffered articulation was decorated with carved or even simple painted filling ornaments and framing elements.[86] A striking special case is the vaulted ceiling of the small study (*scrittoio*) of Piero de' Medici, covered with painted majolica tiles, already admired by the contemporary Filarete. Piero de' Medici had Luca della Robbia execute it in the family palace, and Vasari was still able to mention it with praise.[87]

Many vestiges survive even from the Trecento, as noted, of the spread

[86] Examples of such painted ceiling decoration may be found, for example, in the recently reopened rooms of the mezzanine between the first and second upper story in the Palazzo Vecchio, and here also in the beam ceilings of certain small rooms, probably even from the Trecento, as well as in a large hall covered by a noble coffered ceiling from Michelozzo's time; the latter itself is executed only in paint, but the narrow molding with egg and dart and other motifs is carved.

Other examples and records of this kind of work are in Schiaparelli (*Casa*, pp. 137ff.), in which in particular various monuments that came to light during the demolition work on the old city center are mentioned.

In Casa Peruzzi in Vasari's time there was still a painted vault, thus probably in a ground floor room, allegedly by Uccello with a perspectival ceiling showpiece: interlocking illusionistically recessed triangles, and between them figural decoration representing the four elements and animals (Vasari-Milanesi, 2:215).

[87] The room, which also had a corresponding tile pavement, was sacrificed during renovations of the palace by the Riccardi in the seventeenth century. The twelve slightly curved majolica disks with images of the months, from the school of Domenico Veneziano, can probably be regarded as having been part of this ceiling. These came from a Riccardi villa, and are now in the South Kensington Museum in London. See Antonio Filarete, *Traktat über die Baukunst*, ed. W. von Oetingen, Quellenschriften für Kunstgeschichte, N.F. 3 (Vienna, 1896) p. 678; Vasari-Milanesi, 2:174; *BM*, 9, pp. 404-407, 10, p. 191, 292; Salmi, *Uccello, Castagno, Veneziano*, p. 75, pl. 94-99. From the early sixteenth century Vasari (Vasari-Milanesi, 5:209) mentions ornamental ceiling painting by Andrea Feltrini in a hall in the Palazzo Strozzi and Palazzo Benintendi.

of wall painting in private domestic interiors. They show either a purely ornamental, carpet-like patterned covering of the wall, which sometimes even attempted to simulate hanging tapestries, or else figural representations of small and medium-sized format, worked in a regular series into the articulation, also painted, of the upper wall.[88] It is above all the Palazzo Davanzati that offers an extensive selection of partially preserved examples in various rooms. These include all the favorite kinds of ornamental, vegetable, heraldic, and even narrative figural types from shortly before and after 1400.[89] The richest of these motifs is the suggestion of a break in the wall at various points in the upper wall zone with a view of regularly organized decorative tree tops, inhabited by birds and other animals, often also framed with pointed arcades. Finally, however, one of the most interesting types, and most important for further development, is the cycle of large-figured narrative paintings from the *novella* of the Chatelaine of Vergy, presumably executed in 1395.[90]

Elsewhere we encounter fresco cycles with portrait figures of important personalities from the distant and more recent past. Even this theme of the *Uomini famosi* is already recorded for the early Trecento in a version attributed by Vasari to Giotto in the Anjou castle in Naples. The first deserving mention for our period is the cycle of roughly 1420 that Bicci di Lorenzo allegedly painted in the house of Giovanni de' Medici, Cosimo's father.[91] Only from about 1450 do we have a surviving painted decoration with such monumental figures, and these are incomplete. They are the nine figures by Castagno from the former Villa Pandolfini Carducci in Legnaia near Florence.[92] The series, complete in itself, of three

---

[88] Many examples are preserved in the Museo di Firenze Antica in the rear cloister of San Marco since the destruction of the old city center; others are at least published in *Il Centro di Firenze*, 1900.

[89] Another interesting example is in the former Casa Machiavelli, now Bardini, in Piazza de'Mozzi (Schiaparelli, *Casa*, ill. 105, 107, 110, 113, pp. 141ff.).

[90] The recently discovered monumental frescoes in the former bedroom of the *podesta* in the San Gimignano town hall, with particularly lively and realistic scenes from the life of a young married couple, dates from as early as 1360 (see *Belvedere*, 7, 1925, p. 11; *MK*, 9, pp. 366ff.).

[91] Vasari-Milanesi, 2:50; see Schubring, "Uomini famosi," *Rep.*, 1900, p. 424-25.

The next figure cycle of this type, likewise known only through literary tradition, was by Domenico Veneziano (1438) in the Baglione palace in Perugia; there were no less than twenty-five figures of famous military heroes, statesmen and poets, with accompanying texts by Maranzio (Vasari-Milanesi, 2:674n). The Anonimo Morelliano saw a chiaroscuro fresco of *giganti* by Uccello in the Vitaliani palace in Padua (Salmi, *Uccello, Castagno, Veneziano*, p. 25); on presumed copies in drawings by Tiusto see *RA*, 1935, pp. 385ff.

[92] Vasari-Milanesi, 2:670-71; Schaeffer in *Rep.*, 25, pp. 170ff. Poggi in *RA*, 1929, p. 58; Salmi, *Uccello, Castagno, Veneziano*, pp. 50-52.

Of the frescoes that Milanesi still saw in the old room, only the nine figures from one of the long walls measuring about fifteen meters survived to be transferred to Florence in

Italian military heroes, three poets, and three heroic women in the middle, was brought to Florence and hung on a long wall in its original order according to an old drawn copy. The painted framing architecture with pilasters and cornices is topped by garland-bearing putti.[93]

The earliest example of mural decoration of a private household chapel we possess is Castagno's altar fresco (2 by 2.83 meters) of about 1443 from the Pazzi castle of Trebbio with the enthroned Madonna, two saints, hovering foreshortened angels, and two worshipping children of the house owner's family.[94] Most large palaces and villas probably possessed household chapels with the requisite wall or panel paintings.[95] But only a few altar paintings from household chapels are verifiably preserved (see below); nor are there any more numerous traces of mural decoration of such rooms besides the altar fresco of the Pazzi castle just cited.

In this, too, the Medici palace must have far surpassed everything customary at the time in the completeness and figural richness of the fresco decoration of its chapel. The project, executed around 1460, is a perfectly integrated ensemble, with the conception of Gozzoli's mural composition luxuriously developed. Thus it provides us with a highly significant example for the attitude of the late Quattrocento, which emerged here in the last years of Cosimo's life and under the auspices of his son Piero. One of the few examples of an interior decoration surviving almost in its original state, it was somewhat altered in the eighteenth century during the Riccardi renovation of the palace, but restored as far as possible in 1929.

Upon the brightly patterned marble pavement of the originally square

---

sad condition. Along with them went one more almost completely faded figure with its frame and a few decorative fragments from the other walls. The latter were cut off in many places, probably by windows.

[93] See the Hercules fresco in the court of the Palazzo Bardi Serzelli, probably the sole survivor of a cycle by a follower of Uccello, from about 1460 (Salmi, *Uccello, Castagno, Veneziano*, p. 106, pl. 28b). Two pairs of *Uomini famosi* appear in the depiction of an interior on a cassone panel in Hannover (illustrated in Frida Schotmüller, *Wohnungskultur und Möbel der italienischen Renaissance*, 2nd ed., Stuttgart, 1928, pl. 10), as something evidently not unusual in patrician residences.

Reference should also be made here to the series, related in subject, of portraits of famous juridical scholars, in the guild hall of the Giudici e Notai, the Palazzo del Proconsolo. The series, begun in the early Quattrocento, then continued with portraits of recently dead jurists (Leonardo Bruni in 1444, Poggio, and Giannozzo Manetti) by Castagno and Piero Pollaiuolo, has vanished without a trace (Vasari-Milanesi, 3:292; Poggi in *RA*, 1929, pp. 54-55).

[94] The fresco was recently transferred to the private Florentine Contini collection (*RA*, 1930, p. 37; Salmi, *Uccello, Castagno, Veneziano*, pl. 101-105, p. 115).

[95] The Sassetti even had two of them (Warburg, *Gesammelte Schriften*, 1:139). In the Medici palace there was also, besides the chapel to be discussed immediately below, a second small chapel room in the uppermost story (Müntz, *Collections*, p. 85).

main room of the chapel are the splendidly carved and inlaid wall pews of the household congregation, and above these the multicolored shimmering tapestry of Gozzoli's murals spreads out around the whole wall surface. The upper zone is completed as a counterpart to the pavement and furniture, with a powerfully carved coffered ceiling enriched with gilding and colors. The sanctuary, one step up, contains the recently restored altar with a substructure severely articulated in red marble and at least an old copy in the place of its original altarpiece by Fra Filippo which is in Berlin.[96]

This image of the adoration of the newborn Savior represents, thematically as well as compositionally, the central goal, first for the group of worshipping and singing angels on the side walls of the altar space and the shepherds on the short wall sections in front of it, and then for the great, magnificent cavalcade of the Three Kings and their retinue. Thus the internal contrast between the archaizing tender piety of Fra Filippo's work and the essential mood of the Gozzoli frescoes is all the more remarkable. For here the religious biblical theme is used quite openly, as it frequently was in church wall painting of the second half of the century, for the illustration and glorification of purely worldly, personal meanings and interests. In this case it is above all a freely varied reminiscence of festivities and important visitors to the Medici house. Throughout the picture, and surely to an even greater extent than the tradition has preserved, there are portraits of the whole Medici circle and its princely guests with their splendid modish costumes, substituted for the figures of the Three Kings' procession.[97]

The densely spun web of the composition and the unusually old-fashioned landscape prospect into which the figure groups are woven seems to strive for a reminiscence of Netherlandish pictorial tapestries—the costly type of wall-hanging to be discussed below—which the Medici themselves also acquired in the course of time and used to hang up on special occasions. In the chapel, where the hanging of such tapestries was inadvisable on account of the candle smoke and incense, the richly colorful effect could at least in some measure be simulated in the frescoes. Since the chapel, then (as again now) virtually windowless, was illumi-

---

[96] According to Pudelko's discussion (*RA*, 1936, p. 48) it would not be a youthful work, but executed for the new palace chapel only around 1458.

[97] The Epiphany theme, particularly well suited to such a treatment, may however have been important to the Medici for other reasons: the cell in San Marco kept ready for Cosimo's occasional periods of retreat there contains a mural of the same subject. It appears again in a tondo below the pictorial decoration of Lorenzo's *camera terrena* in the palace (see below). But Lorenzo was evidently president of the Compagnia dei Tre Magi, affiliated with San Marco, as were presumably also his father and grandfather. See Giuseppe Benelli, *Firenze nei monumenti domenicani* (Florence, 1913), pp. 218-19.

nated only by the solemnly dim candlelight, this illusion must once have been even more effective.[98]

Only brief mention may be made of various randomly surviving references to small mural works, once certainly not rare, by Neri di Bicci and others in various middle-class houses of the city.[99] One generally accessible and significant monument of this type, also the only state commission, should be mentioned here. This is the powerful mural composition executed by Ghirlandaio in 1482-1483 in a newly created upper hall in the Palazzo Vecchio. Here, in the framework of a magnificent illustionistic architecture, the three city patron saints appear and along with them the theme of the *Uomini famosi* with three hero figures from the antique on either side.[100]

Otherwise, however, secular wall painting in the late Quattrocento occurred only in certain important country houses in the environs of Florence. Castagno's figure cycle had already been commissioned for the hall of one villa; it was similar to the few other secular frescoes that can be mentioned for the succeeding period. These include the remains of figural wall painting in a ground-floor room of the Villa la Gallina in Arcetri, rediscovered only fifty years ago, which belonged to the Lanfredini in the fifteenth century, later to the Galletti counts, and which belongs now, like the immediately adjacent Torre del Gallo, to the antiquarian Bardini. The theme of these paintings, surviving only in large fragments, is highly unusual and very individually handled: nude dancers are executed in half life-size in a frieze under the consoles that supported the vaulting and were probably intended as bacchants in the spirit and taste of the humanistic antiquarian cult of the time. Only the immediately proposed name of Antonio Pollaiuolo can be considered as the artist, with a date of about 1460-1465.[101]

[98] Above the small anteroom, evidently a former gallery of the chapel (now the telegraph bureau of the prefecture) there are fragments of earlier wall paintings exposed under a later coat of plaster: gold and tapestry patterns with Piero's device ("Semper") and fluttering ribbons.

[99] Neri di Bicci notes in his *Ricordi* book that in 1456 he painted an illusionistic interior doorway with ornamental frame in the house of Piero Benini on Via de' Maggi, "drento all 'uscio," that is, probably inside the main door of the house. It was crowned with a phoenix figure. He also did other door frames upstairs in the house. A later entry mentions decorative work for Giovanni Rucellai in his palace; again door frames in imitation cut stone, a coat of arms decorated with a helmet crest and a half-length figure group of a young couple (see *Il Vasari*, 4, pp. 191-92).

Alessandro Chiappelli discusses two surviving individual religious frescoes in other houses, including that of Baldovinetti behind San Lorenzo, in *L'arte del rinascimento*, pp. 203-204; unfortunately with such imprecise information on the location that the author could not find the cited pictures.

[100] On this and on the other mural commissions (never executed) for this hall, which went to Botticelli, Pollaiuolo, and others, see above.

[101] This would be a monumental version of the theme of male nudes in lively action,

There follows, after a period of about twenty years, the fresco commission of Giovanni Tornabuoni for his villa, the subsequent Villa Lemmi on the Chiasso Maceregli near Careggi. The first of these, still surviving in faint traces in situ, was probably the portrait of the house owner wearing the official *gonfaloniere* regalia (thus dating from about 1482) and accompanied by his daughter. Next, in the same long rectangular hall, on the occasion of the wedding of Giovanni's son Lorenzo with an Albizzi in 1486, came the two mural compostions by Botticelli that went into the Louvre shortly after their rediscovery. The pictures, framed by architectural members and painted on either side of a central window on one long wall, are in their themes also homages to the spiritual world of the antique. The presumed portrait figures of the newlyweds are each solemnly received into a gathering of classical personifications: she by Venus and the Graces, he by the liberal arts.[102]

The last great secular paintings in a country house in the late Quattrocento were commissioned by Lorenzo Magnifico. These were above all a series of frescoes in the Medici villa of Spedaletto in the vicinity of Arezzo, for whose execution Botticelli, Ghirlandaio, Perugino, and Filippino Lippi were called on in succession and together around 1485-1490.* The destruction almost without a trace of this whole picture cycle, which stood out as a competitive collaborative work of the best Florentine talents of that period, certainly represents an especially painful loss. We know all too little about these pictures even from old literature, probably because of their remote location. They must have been images from Greek mythology, since the only one mentioned by Vasari represented the Forge of Vulcan.[103] Still surviving, though only partially realized, is the fresco of an antique sacrifice scene that Filippino, the youngest of the four collaborators at Spedaletto, was commissioned to paint in the loggia of Lorenzo's Poggio a Caiano villa, probably before 1489-1490.[104]

---

repeatedly handled by Pollaiuolo at that time in drawings and engravings, as well as in the painted Hercules panels of the Medici palace (*ZBK*, N.F. 11, pp. 260ff.; Guido Carocci, *I dintorni di Firenze*, 2 vols., Florence, 1906-1907, 2:232).

[102] The whole seems to depend on Martianus Capella's description of the marriage of Mercury with Philosophy. See Franz Wickhoff, *Die Schriften Franz Wickhoff*, ed. M. Dvorak (Berlin, 1912-1913), 2:424ff.; and Carocci, *I dintorni di Firenze*, 1:224-25. Tornabuoni had Ghirlandaio, whom he employed in the late 1480s primarily on the choir of Santa Maria Novella, paint pictures for a chapel on the grounds of the same villa. Vasari could still see them in the half-ruined chapel (Vasari-Milanesi, 3:269).

* *Translator's note:* The Spedaletto villa was actually located in the Volterra region. See André Chastel, *Art et humanisme à Florence au temps de Laurent le Magnifique* (Paris, 1961), p. 171, nn. 4, 5.

[103] Milanesi also could still see faint traces only of this fresco by Ghirlandaio in the 1870s; some of these still allegedly exist today (Vasari-Milanesi, 3:258; *l'Arte*, 1900, pp. 146ff.; Horne, *Botticelli*, p. 109).

[104] Vasari-Milanesi, 3:473-74; *MKIF*, 3, pp. 393ff., 530-32.

A few other works of this type were produced from about 1489 to 1530. First of all, there are individual paintings of religious subjects for the two city palaces: for example, two murals of a penitent Jerome and a Madonna painted by Bastiano Mainardi on the commission of high civic officials in 1490 in the chapel of the Bargello, below the great old Paradise fresco.[105]

In 1503, however, preparations began for a highly significant fresco project, unprecedented in type, for the Hall of the Great Council in the Palazzo Vecchio: the mighty murals with scenes from Florentine military history, of which one was assigned to Leonardo, the other a short time later to Michelangelo. These paintings and their fate have already been discussed above.

Their initiator, Gonfaloniere Soderini, had besides this had his office in the Palazzo Vecchio decorated (probably soon after taking office at the end of 1502) with grotesque ornament, a type of decoration newly fashionable at that time, cultivated in particular by Morto da Feltre. But neither these works nor other examples of the same type mentioned by Vasari (Vasari-Milanesi, 5:201-202, 204) have survived.

Finally, also in Palazzo Vecchio, the new chapel received wall and ceiling decoration by Ridolfo del Ghirlandaio in 1514. Here also the decorative element of heavy rinceaux filling in the painted wall pilasters and individual compartments of the densely woven framework of the ceiling played a major role. Between these were individual figures of the Evangelists and pairs of putti. In the central field of the ceiling was the Trinity and in the short wall opposite the altar niche, the lunette painting of the Annunciation. This is the sole painting of a sacred room completely carried out in the Florentine High Renaissance.[106]

These paintings have an extensive secular counterpart in the salon of the Medici villa at Poggio a Caiano where two large murals were commissioned by Pope Leo for each long side of the high vaulted hall, with a program by Paolo Giovio: scenes from the antique, which each seem to be related to a particular moment in Medici history. Andrea del Sarto painted the bringing of tribute to Caesar in front of massive architectural scenery, whereas Franciabigio painted the return of Cicero from exile and *Flaminius in the Council of the Achaeans* on the opposite wall. In the lunettes of the short walls the young Pontormo dealt with the theme of Vertumnus and Pomona. But neither he nor his fellow artists com-

---

[105] In addition, there were pictures, no longer surviving, in the halls of the new Consiglio di Giustizia in the same building, executed by painters of little consequence in 1503 (Vasari-Milanesi, 3:191n.).

[106] For the paintings of the chapel in the papal suite of Santa Maria Novella, produced in 1515, also by Ridolfo Ghirlandaio and Pontormo, exist only in poorly preserved fragments in a barely accessible room (Vasari-Milanesi, 6:255-56).

pleted their task, since the death of the pope brought the works to a halt in 1521.[107]

## HOUSEHOLD PAINTINGS ON WOOD AND CANVAS

Commissions and works of monumental wall and ceiling painting are far outnumbered by portable works, surely because of the variety of special types of such works and of the relevant formats and painting techniques. If we group the whole great mass of such pictorial decoration according to manner of display and function in an interior, three main branches become immediately apparent:

(1) Large or medium-sized panel or canvas paintings sometimes fixed into the wall articulation, singly or in a cyclical series in the upper zones of wall, surely as a substitute for mural painting;
(2) Certain small pictures that were also worked into the wall covering but in the lower zones, in wall panelling or even on large pieces of furniture (bedsteads, chests);
(3) All those paintings that, without such spacially determined positions, might still find an appropriate place somewhere.

We begin with the first named genre and must at the outset explain that in the principal living rooms the upper wall zones, assuming they had no actual mural decoration, were readily hung with large panel paintings or canvas pictures in a regular order, sometimes in a series. We must imagine almost all large secular pictures as once making up part of such displays. They are known to us now only as museum pieces, that is, in completely different frames, organization, and general appearance. It must also be considered that probably only a relatively small part of precisely this kind of painting has survived physically in museums, though this admittedly includes in particular the especially valuable pieces. A

---

[107] They were completed only around 1580-1582 by Allori, who also added the fourth picture, which had still been lacking. Also deserving mention are the Nativity fresco of about 1510, a youthful work of Franciabigio, which was in the private chapel of the Quaratesi-Baroncelli villa and is now in the refectory of San Marco. Vasari also mentions a modest odd job by him, the mural of *Noli me tangere* on the terrace of a cloth weaver's house (Carocci, *I Dintorni, di Firenze,* 2:192-93; *RA,* 1929, p. 213; Vasari-Milanesi, 5:198).

Finally there is the lost chiaroscuro image of St. George fighting the dragon painted by Fra Bartolommeo in a niche above the steps of the house of Piero del Pugliese (Vasari-Milanesi, 4:194, n. 2). Bocchi-Cinelli (*Le bellezze della citta,* p. 173) still mention this painting; and in addition (see above) a small Andrea del Sarto fresco in the same house, on the Sdrucciolo near Or San Michele, whose facade displayed an Annunciation fresco by Andrea. Finally, Vasari cites a political mural, a satire on Pope Clement VII that Vittorio Ghiberti the Younger painted in 1529 in the principal room of a house on Via Larga (Vasari-Milanesi, 2:244, n. 2).

more or less sufficient conception of the scope and variety of this type of commission can once again be gained only by adducing the numerous pieces of recorded evidence.

In contrast to most altarpieces, the cheaper support of stretched canvas was often used here instead of wooden panel. This is true also for many pertinent works of the chief masters, such as Uccello, Pollaiuolo, Botticelli, and others. It was true above all for the great mass of unknown and often only average works whose former existence we encounter almost exclusively in old inventory records, among other sources under the term *panni dipinti alla franzese* or *panni di Fiandra*. To what extent such canvas paintings actually came from France or the Netherlands or were acquired in domestic imitation of such models still remains to be researched. The still-life and emblematic designs that are named for many of these *panni* do by all means recall the interest in such motifs which had become prominent particularly in Flanders since the early fifteenth century. Nor is direct evidence lacking for the occasional acquisition of such works from Netherlandish production centers.[108]

Among traceable works of well-known masters, the series of three great equestrian battles by Paolo Uccello must be mentioned first. These are episodes from a victorious Florentine encounter with the Sienese ("La rotta di S. Romano") that are mentioned in the inventory of the Palazzo Medici for the large ground floor room, along with three other pictures "each 3½ *braccia* high": a Judgment of Paris and fighting beasts by Uccello and a hunting scene by Pesellino. Of the three battle scenes, one is still in Florence in the Uffizi; the other two are in London and Paris.[109]

The three frequently mentioned large canvases of deeds of Hercules by Antonio Pollaiuolo, painted around 1460, each measured about 3.5 meters square. These were taken from the main upper room of the Medici palace in 1495, and have since been lost. Another considerably smaller

---

[108] Thus Alessandra Strozzi had her sons acquire three *panni dipinti* from Bruges for resale in 1460; and the same letter states that no more than three florins should be spent for each of these. The works in question were religious subjects and a peacock image with leafwork (see Strozzi-Guasti, *Lettere*, pp. 230-31). See also Schiaparelli, *Casa*, pp. 168-75.

[109] The identification of these pictures with those of the Palazzo Medici results from the height measurement (1.82 meters), corresponding with the inventory citation, as well as from the ensign of the Florentine general Niccolò da Tolentino. These are dated (according to Salmi, *Castagno, Uccello, Veneziano*, pp. 30-33, 109) around 1456-1457, in association with the honorific monument to the general in question in the Duomo. See also Horne's information on the original arrangement (*Rep.*, 1902, pp. 318-19). Uccello also painted four other lost battle scenes, apparently frescoes in chiaroscuro technique, which Vasari still saw in their original place in a loggia of the Bartolini Villa in Gualfonda, where they had been clumsily restored by Bugiardini (Vasari-Milanesi, 2: 213-14; Salmi, *Uccello, Castagno, Veneziano*, p. 86).

Hercules scene with Nessus and Deianira by Pollaiuolo has, however, survived in the gallery of Yale University in New Haven. There is, in addition, the cycle of seven virtues commissioned for the meeting room of the College of the Mercanzia, painted in 1469-1470 by Pollaiuolo and Botticelli. These great individual enthroned figures were originally installed in the wall panelling above the wooden back of the wall bench. Arranged in a series next to each other, they must have presented an effect of solemnity totally different from their present appearance on the wall of a bare room in the Uffizi.[110]

Botticelli's two great Venus scenes, the *Primavera* and the *Anadyomene*, now united in the Uffizi, belong to this category. Over and above the stylistic difference of perhaps fifteen to twenty years between them, their present setting makes particularly evident the totally different treatment of the carefully detailed costly panel painting of the early work and the summary broad execution of the *Birth of Venus*, painted on canvas. There were also several compositions by Botticelli in vertical rectangular format, such as the large canvas of Pallas with the centaur and a counterpart of similar size, now lost—the Pallas with a shield and arrow (*lancia d'archo*) that was once in the Medici palace.[111]

The theme of the standing Venus was often chosen for this format, which may have been favored especially for the decoration of small wall strips, for instance between two windows. We find no less than three variants of Botticelli's, which also confirm a reference by Vasari to several "femmine ignude" by Botticelli, and in the Uffizi the *Venus* by Lorenzo di Credi.[112] Counterparts to Botticelli's great horizontal compositions are Signorelli's *Festival of Pan* in Berlin on canvas, also once in Medici possession, and the slightly smaller early work by Piero di Cosimo, *Hylas and the Nymphs*.[113]

The subjects of these pictures come sometimes from antique mythology and poetry, sometimes from medieval allegories or even Florentine military history. Only the two animal scenes by Uccello in the Medici in-

---

[110] Castagno had already received a similar commission in 1447 for the audience hall of the judicial body: the figures (since lost) of the three chief virtues, which were also set into the wall panelling behind the seats of the *priori*.

[111] Müntz, *Collections*, p. 86; *l'Arte*, 1902, pp. 71ff. (Poggi). The *Pallas with the Centaur*, now in the Uffizi, measures 1.47 by 2.39 meters, the *Primavera* about 3 by 2 meters.

[112] Vasari-Milanesi, 3:312; Wilhelm Bode, *Botticelli* (Stuttgart, 1926), pp. 36-37; the *Venus* in the Gualino collection in Turin, cited in Horne, *Botticelli*. See also the school picture of an allegory of spring in Chantilly (Bode, *Botticelli*, p. 133).

[113] The dimensions are 175 by 180 centimeters, and it is from the Benson Collection, now at Duveen's, New York. Vasari mentions a Botticelli Bacchus raising a little cask to his lips, which is probably identical with a canvas of the same theme, about 1.5 meters square, recorded in the Grandducal collection in 1637 (Vasari-Milanesi, 3:313, 322; Horne, *Botticelli*, p. 365).

ventory are of less significant content. These, however, according to their type of material, can be associated with numerous nameless *panni dipinti* cited in the same inventory. For among these, along with various biblical or allegorical representations, are found simple themes of a completely nonliterary type. They include a group of bacchic figures (above the lavabo niche), a feast by a fountain, two apparently grotesque pictures with fat-bellied singers, further landscape and architectural scenery (a view of the Palazzo della Signoria), and a still-life motif (a cupboard with books). These were all among the contents of the family palace on Via Larga, mixed in with the works of the best Florentine painters, some already named, some to be mentioned below. The inventory of the Villa Careggi, however, cites almost exclusively such *panni dipinti*, without the names of masters, sixteen items in all; in the great hall alone were five *panni* overdoors whose subjects were listed as birds, bathing women, a group of singers, a dance scene, and an unusual counterpart, the penitent St. Jerome; in the same place, painted in terra verde (thus imitating a fresco) was a large architectural scene with accessory figures.

The above excerpt from the inventory gives at least a general idea of this whole category of generally acceptable pictorial wall decoration, evidently very widespread. Naturally these must once also have appeared prominently in all the other palaces and villas, but today survive in only a few concrete examples.[114]

We turn now to the category, also very widespread, of those pictures hung at the beholder's eye level, thus planned for close observation and therefore executed most carefully and ornately, generally in small format. This was particularly true for certain *quadri da camera*, that is, cabinet pictures, literally and figuratively, which were either hung individually somewhere, usually filling a place in the wall panelling (the *spalliera*), or even appearing in the back wall of a bed headboard. This kind of outspokenly luxurious and almost excessive enrichment of the lower wall covering made its appearance for the most part only somewhat later than picture hanging or fresco painting on the upper walls. Its significance is self-evident and corresponds, like so much else, to the exaggerated, profligate magnificence and costliness that so sharply distinguishes the later Quattrocento from the first half of the century.

We shall speak separately of painting on chests, but stress here that assuredly many small pictures in horizontal rectangular format that are now removed from their former setting and are usually summarily identified as chest paintings actually belong rather to the class of wainscoting

---

[114] Even the linen window panes of simple houses were occasionally painted. See Schiaparelli, *Casa*, pp. 120ff. and n. 1; excerpts from various private inventories, including an *impannata* with a picture of the Annunciation, 1417.

panelling. We consider this type much less frequently because, in contrast to the many surviving cassoni, not a single example has come down to us in its old setting.[115] One of the most famous and charming examples of the type, the great wedding procession, allegedly of an Adimari from about 1440-1445, can indeed be understood, on account of its size, only as a *spalliera*.[116]

The subjects of these small decorative paintings are once again, as in the more elevated pieces of the *cornicioni* in the upper wall, primarily motifs from antique mythology, ancient Roman history and poetry, the Old Testament, and from allegories and *novelle* of the late middle ages. There are also scenes from the life of the patron himself, like the wedding picture just cited and the multifigured stag hunt in the forest by Uccello (in Oxford; 1.65 by 65 centimeters, Schubring, *Cassoni*, nr. 101), or even the portrayal of Lorenzo Magnifico's *Giostra* of 1469, surviving only in inventory citations, on a *spalliera* 5 meters long in Palazzo Medici.[117]

A few examples of the innumerable wainscoting panel paintings of the late Quattrocento may be cited for a closer characterization of the whole class: two Orpheus scenes by Sellaio now in private collections in Vienna and Petersburg; the allegorical triumphs in the Museo Bandini in Fiesole, now also attributed to Sellaio; three horizontal rectangular pictures from the story of Esther, likewise by Sellaio, in the Uffizi (Schubring, *Cassoni*, nr. 357-59, 369 A). There are also some works of Botticelli or his workshop, like the pictures of the *novelle* of Nastagio degli Onesti, already singled out by Vasari, who saw them in Casa Pucci.[118] Vasari also saw a room decorated with four small pictures by Botticelli, set in carved frames, in the Vespucci house on Via de' Servi. The three Botticelli pictures

[115] Two *spalliera* paintings dating from 1465 with the story of the Sabine women have survived in a London private collection with at least the most pertinent parts of their original installation; they are installed as wall decorations, each above a small bench on whose front side are the allied arms of the Davanzati and Redditi. See Paul Schubring, *Cassoni. Truhen und Truhenbilder der italienischen Frührenaissance*, 2 vols. (Leipzig, 1915), nr. 298-99, pl. 72; and *BM*, 1913.

[116] Without its brightly colored patterned frame it measures about 280 by 65 centimeters; according to an old reference the panel was still "collocata nel mezzo d'un antica grandiosa spalliera" around 1750 (cited by Schubring, *Cassoni*, pp. 84, 103).

[117] There is also the chivalric legend of Saint George's fight with the dragon on two small panel paintings perhaps by Uccello in Vienna, Lanckoronski Collection, and Paris, Jacquemart-André Collection, they measure 90 by 52 and 73 by 57 centimeters respectively (Salmi, *Uccello, Castagno, Veneziano*, pl. 24-25).

[118] From there they were sold off to England in 1868. They are now in private possession in London and America; according to Horne they were painted in 1483 for the Pucci-Bini wedding (see *BM*, 1, pp. 6ff.; and Vasari-Milanesi, 3:313). The four panels of the St. Zenobius legend, now in New York and Dresden, were executed partially by Botticelli himself. Originally they were probably set into the panelling of the household chapel of the Arcivescovado (Schubring, *Cassoni*, nr. 306-309).

with scenes from the stories of Lucretia and of Virginia probably come from there.[119]

Two wainscoting panels from Ghirlandaio's workshop with the legend of Jason bear the date 1487. The arms on them give evidence that they were painted for the same young bridal couple Tornabuoni-Albizzi whom Botticelli immortalized in the frescoes of the subsequent Villa Lemmi.[120] Piero di Cosimo painted "several bacchic scenes which decorate a room all the way around," also for the Vespucci, probably somewhat later. This is according to Vasari, whose description is most closely matched by five pictures, now widely scattered, which are for the most part attributed to Piero's pupil Bartolommeo di Giovanni.[121] Various pictures with small figures by Piero di Cosimo could be found, according to Vasari, in the wall panelling of a room in Francesco del Pugliese's house with "fable scenes executed in the most fantastic manner."[122]

Figural painting on individual pieces of furniture, particularly on chests and bedsteads, forms a class by itself.

Evidence of painted decoration of bedsteads already exists for the early Trecento in the form of a single surviving concrete example, a bed donated to the Hospital of Pistoia (Schubring, *Cassoni*, pl. 7). And it may probably be assumed, even though tangible examples in their old contexts or published references are almost totally lacking, that this custom gained ground and developed only more richly with the growing demand for decoration during the Renaissance.

Only various *lettiere* with intarsia and gilded carving are occasionally mentioned in the Medici inventory. Yet several pictures in broad but relatively low format on which the reclining lovers Mars and Venus appear (such as Botticelli's in London and Piero di Cosimo's in Berlin, both about 70 by 172 centimeters), may probably be regarded, as Bode suggests, as originally pictorial decoration for the headboard of a broad double bed. The same may be true of the reclining Venus with putti, a

[119] In Bergamo, Boston, and the Pitti (Schubring, *Cassoni*, nr. 304-305; Horne, *Botticelli*, p. 275.

[120] This is in a private collection in London; in addition, a third piece from the Jason cycle, probably to be explained as a *spalliera* behind the bed, is in the Paris Museé des arts décoratifs (Schubring, *Cassoni*, nr. 349, 389-90).

[121] Vasari-Milanesi, 4:141; Schubring, *Cassoni*, nr. 383-86; suppl. nr. 932; van Marle, *Painting*, 13:249, 347.

[122] Vasari-Milanesi, 4:139. A picture now in Strasbourg and one in the former Kauffmann collection are from Piero's *spalliera* cycle of the Prometheus Legend dating from about 1495 (Schubring, *Cassoni*, nr. 412-13). Two small pictures of bacchic motifs (each 40 by 48 centimeters) in English collections were attributed by Knapp to Piero di Cosimo. Two pictures in Amsterdam private collections are also assigned to that artist: pairs of half-length figures in drastic caricature (an aged drinker with a woman and two people arguing: van Marle, *Painting*, 13:363).

picture by Sellaio in the Louvre, and the painting by Piero di Cosimo of Procris unwittingly shot by her lover now in London, admittedly a very tragic subject for a bedchamber.

Then there is the pictorial decoration of chests, the cassoni or *forzieri*. This piece of furniture, a forerunner of the later tall vertical cupboard, was, after the bed, among the most indispensable requisites of every household. And every newly married woman brought her dowry of linen and clothing with her into wedlock in precisely this container, prepared ad hoc, more often in two chests created and decorated as pendants.

At least an approximate conception of the numerical extent and significance of this category of secular applied painting is possible, according to Schubring. First of all there is the work statistic, passed down from documents of one of about ten special workshops for chest painting and the like which were active in Florence during the fifteenth century. This is the account book of the *forzinari* firm of Marco del Buono and Apollonio di Giovanni, located by Warburg and published by Schubring.*It records over one hundred seventy cassoni decorated with paintings from this workshop during the seventeen-year period of 1446-1463, making an average annual turnover of nine to ten chests. This number should be multiplied at least by six to determine the total production of chests on the Florentine art market.[123]

The numerous commissions for chests naturally also included many with only modest decoration of a simple, popular sort. Yet, as might be expected from their nature, only a few examples of this unimposing but certainly very widespread type have survived, such as the so-called nun's chests from Santa Maria Nuova.[124]

A middle level, of higher stature than this, consisted of chests with

---

*Translator's note:* It was actually Heinrich Brockhaus who discovered this workshop book in the Carte Strozziane and called it to Warburg's attention. See E. H. Gombrich, "Apollonio di Giovanni . . ." in *Norm and Form* (London, 1966), p. 11.

[123] On the other hand, Schubring's by no means complete list of the Florentine chests known to him for the period from about 1370 through 1470 contains over three hundred examples, which perhaps represents a surviving one-eighth or one-tenth of the objects actually produced during this period.

See Schubring, *Cassoni*, pp. 88-89, 117-18; and appendix 2, pp. 430-37, for the publication of the cited workshop book. Schubring assumes that his list for 1370-1479 includes about a third to a fifth of all the painted chests that once existed, but this does not accord with his other calculation of about ten chest-painting botteghe of probably no less productivity than that of Marco del Buono. This estimate also probably calculates the quota of normal loss or destruction at too low a rate.

[124] Schubring, *Cassoni*, pp. 18, 92-93, pl. IV. Furthermore, even a master like Alesso Baldovinetti occasionally furnished such unpretentious paintings; these included four travel chests with arms and devices in round fields for the *podesta* preparing for a trip to Arezzo in 1478. See his *Ricordi* in *Alesso Baldovinetti, pittore fiorentino, con l'aggiunto dei suoi "Ricordi,"* Florence, 1907.

narrative paintings on the front, provided by artisan *forzerinai* at an average price of about thirty florins. Finally there was the aristocratic, sporadically distributed higher level of chest paintings for which, as for many *spalliera* pictures and *cornicioni*, wealthy customers frequently employed well-known artists. These, according to documentary evidence or convincing attributions, included Uccello, Domenico Veneziano, Pesellino, and Sellaio.[125]

The united coats of arms or *imprese* of the bridal couple for whose household the chest or pair of chests was intended appear on the frames of certain chests or inside the painted architectural scenery. These often make it possible to determine both the patron and the date of origin by means of the date of a marriage in two known families that can be determined elsewhere. For example, two chest paintings in the Simon collection, Berlin, can be associated with the marriage of Piero de' Medici and Lucrezia Tornabuoni in 1448 on the basis of such clues.[126]

With regard to the form and in particular the organization of the pictorial decoration of chests, it appears that the decorative system previously customary, with several separate pictures within an ornamented framing field, was largely replaced by a unified horizontal rectangular pictorial field that ran across the entire front side of the chest beginning in the second quarter of the fifteenth century; in addition there were small vertical rectangular images on the short sides. The corners as a rule were decorated with sculptural, profiled frames or small pilasters, often with the arms of the bridal couple attached.

From the late Quattrocento on the framing members frequently received a stronger grade of relief and sometimes corner elements had contours curved in the form of consoles. At the same time, the formerly flat bench-like cover was often raised and decorated with rich moldings in several tiers. Sculptured feet appear under the corners of the cassoni, which now evidently often served not merely as functional furnishings for the bedroom, but rather, in such enriched form, as impressive showpieces in the main hall of the palace.[127] To be considered with these are

[125] Two bridal chests for Caterina Strozzi were ordered from Domenico Veneziano in 1447 for a total price of fifty florins. (Strozzi-Guasti, *Lettere*, 21).

[126] *MKIF*, 1917, pp. 149ff. Schubring, *Cassoni*, suppl. pl. 911, with color pl. 7-9. Werner Weisbach (*Trionfi*, Berlin, 1919, p. 28n.) relates a chest painting of the Triumph of Scipio (in Paris, Musée des arts decoratifs; Schubring, *Cassoni*, nr. 111) to a wedding of 1466 on account of the *imprese* of the Medici and Rucellai it contains.

[127] See the examples of entire chests illustrated in Schubring, *Cassoni*: for the still Gothic early period around 1400, plates 2, 3, and supplementary plate 1; for around 1430, plate 5, with powerful architectonic articulation and relief-sculptured putti with coats of arms and for around 1440-1450, plate 68, with a somewhat more simply organized frame structure. See also van Marle, *Painting*, 10:561 for discussion of cassoni with sculptural corner decoration and arms from around 1450. Further enrichment of the framing elements

also the series of chests with figural relief-sculpture decoration modelled in gilded stucco or even with inserted terra-cotta reliefs. These are much less numerous, and were probably also more frequently destroyed over the years.[128]

The chest brightly painted with narrative decoration represents a characteristic specialty of Italian household furnishings, one which was also cultivated in Florence to an unusually rich extent. And indeed, the coloring of these cassoni pictures in the middle and late Quattrocento takes on an outspoken multicolored gaiety, with varied bright tones interwoven almost as densely as in mosaic and interspersed with all sorts of gold ornaments. Yet this appearance of the pictures, so naively original and yet, even in mediocre works, enviably refined corresponds perfectly to the contents and whole narrative tone of their portrayals. The subjects are more than three quarters secular and indeed derived primarily from the antique, especially from Ovid and his mediators Boccaccio and Petrarch. These chest decorations provide a surprising proof of the lively interest in humanistic ideas and the evidently very extensive familiarity of the broad Florentine public with representations of this subject matter. Thus even Savonarola, and from his standpoint justly, had to fume that the pictures on wedding chests with their "heathen stories" made newly married women more familiar "with the deceit of Mars and the tricks of Vulcan than with the deeds of holy women" from bible stories.[129]

Only occasionally do illustrations of festive spectacles of the period also appear on chests. See, for example, early chest paintings with the *palio* for the feast of John the Baptist in the Bargello and the tournament in Piazza Santa Croce, 1439 (Schubring, *Cassoni*, pl. 4, 27, suppl. pl. 5). An especially intimate type of painting project would sometimes be

and livelier contours in the chests of Serristori and Strozzi in the Bardini collection from about 1460-1465 can be seen in plates 62, 65, 66, and in the Lee collection in Richmond (illustrated in van Marle, *Painting*, 10:561). Finally, plates 167-69 depict the splendid and majestic Medici-Strozzi chest now in Berlin, from 1512, with a painting of about 1480 set into it. Other contemporary chests show only colorless, carved wood decoration and empty inner panels. See also the various examples in Mario Tinti, *Il mobilio fiorentino* (Milan, 1928), pl. 89-103.

[128] Examples from the first half of the Quattrocento are in Schubring, *Cassoni*, nr. 44ff., 77, pl. 8-11; see also pp. 93, 99ff. A particularly splendid example from about 1460-1470 with antique ideal figures, centaurs, etc., between candelabra and trophies, female arms-bearing genii on the corners, all of a character between Pollaiuolo and Verrocchio, is in the Museo Bardini.

A unicum in its form is the tall rectangular cupboard-like piece of furniture in the Fondazione Horne museum, painted with four triumphal pictures (Schubring, *Cassoni*, pl. 48).

[129] Savonarola's sermon on the Book of Ruth is quoted from Schäffer by Schubring (*Cassoni*, p. 19). See pp. 16, 20, for general comments on the subject matter of chest paintings.

found on the inside of the covers of chests installed as a pair in a bedroom with the half-idealized nude reclining figures of the sleeping spouses.[130] When medieval allegories of the virtues or liberal arts adorn a chest, as they occasionally still do in the Quattrocento, this probably denotes an original destination of the piece of furniture for a convent.[131]

Intarsia decoration appearing in panelling and pieces of furniture should be considered in association with the paintings in similar settings. This decoration, however, appears only rarely to have gone beyond frugal border designs. Occasionally intarsia fillings of ornamental or emblematic types, sometimes also combined with some carved decoration, may be found on a chest or chest-bench (*cassapanca*). The inventory of Palazzo Medici, for example, mentions a bedstead with intarsia with perspectival showpieces as well as gilded figural reliefs in Lorenzo's room.[132] Examples of figural intarsia survive only in the doors of the marble portal of 1475 in the Palazzo Vecchio by Giuliano da Maiano. These are figures of Dante and Petrarch, with perspectival still lifes filling the lower panels.[133]

The panelled woodwork predominating in the lower wall zones, with benches and other furniture in front of it, creates in some measure the basic harmony to the treble voice of the inset paintings in the polyphonic symphony of prominent interior decoration. At least an intimation of this overall harmony can be gained from one room in the Palazzo Medici:

[130] Such was a pair of chests of about 1450 from Casa Frescobaldi, in an English private collection; also two chests in Somerset, Eastnor Castle, and in a pair of chests divided between the Uffizi storeroom and the South Kensington Museum in London, in which only the wife appears nude, while her spouse appears in fashionable dress, reclining in a meadow (Schubring, *Cassoni*, pl. 30, 38, 69).

[131] So, for example, for the chest panel from the convent of Santa Croce in the former Spiridon collection in Paris, with the liberal arts and their representatives seated below them (Schubring, *Cassoni*, pl. 81, as well as a somewhat earlier counterpart, p. 63). There is also a chest (or perhaps a *spalliera*) picture by Filippino with female allegories in the Corsini gallery, Florence (52 by 155 centimeters). See Alfred Scharf, *Filippino Lippi* (Vienna, 1935), cat. 61.

[132] Müntz, *Collections*, p. 63. In the same place there were also several other pieces of furniture with intarsia decoration in vegetation patterns (Schiaparelli, *Casa*, p. 251-52). See also the contract between Piero degli Alberti and Giuliano da Maiano in 1463 concerning a bedstead for whose intarsia decoration of "una figura con cavalli" Baldovinetti drew the design (Baldovinetti-Londi, *Ricordi*, p. 92; Schiaparelli, *Casa*, p. 253n.). See Schiaparelli also for two other Pistoiese contracts for beds with rich intarsia decoration of allied arms between putti and fruit garlands from 1468 and 1488.

Ornamental intarsia decoration appears in the birth chamber of Mary as painted by Ghirlandaio in Santa Maria Novella and in that of Fra Filippo's *Annunciation* in the Galleria Doria, Rome.

[133] The intarsia of the door of the treasurer's room in the Bigallo is somewhat earlier and simpler. Very splendid wall benches with intarsia and carved ornament of about 1515 still exist in the *salone* of the Palazzo communale in Pistoia (Alinari, photos 10227ff.). The wall panelling and furniture of the rooms in Palazzi Benintendi and Borgherini, decorated with rich spalliera pictures, were designed by Baccio d'Agnolo (Vasari-Milanesi, 5:392).

the household chapel that survives almost in its original condition. Yet here it is a matter of a relatively simple composition, made up only of the pews and fresco tapestry of the upper wall, with the polychrome coffered ceiling and the multicolored pavement echoing them (see above).

The compositional texture was surely interwoven and developed in much greater richness and variety in the interiors of the main residential and ceremonial rooms of the Medici and also probably in other palaces. The wall panelling some two meters high and the larger pieces of furniture were not decorated only with carving and intarsia decoration like the chapel benches. Here, in addition, all those multicolored, ornate, figurally rich inset pictures discussed above were installed in tasteful arrangements, and these pictures, known to us today only as isolated pieces, except for certain completely preserved chests, had particularly effective foils in those darked-colored substructures and frames, enriched here and there with discreet gilding.

We must strive to imagine, in its total arrangement and effect, the original harmony of all these elements of an interior decoration, with the addition of large paintings and frescoes or uniformly framed *cornicioni* on the upper walls, as well as some freely distributed separate pictures and sculpture. At least some basis for such graphic documentation of the highly refined life style of that period is provided by representations of interiors in contemporary painting. Yet these, for the most part, provide only a fragment or perhaps an exaggerated fantasy image: such, for example, is the splendid interior in Ghirlandaio's fresco of the Birth of the Virgin (Santa Maria Novella).

Nevertheless, with the help of the Medici inventory, so inestimably precious even in all its terseness, and of the scattered surviving fragments of the former furnishings, an attempt will be made below to arrive at a conception of what was assembled toward the end of the Quattrocento in the main rooms of the Medici palace, in rich and yet well-ordered, carefully planned abundance and opulence.[134]

Based on the record of the contents of 1492, we shall first reconstruct the furnishings of the large ground floor room to the left of the entryway that Tarchiani has identified with the so-called "camera terrena di Lorenzo" in the inventory.[135] This room, together with the adjoining rooms of the left wing, has been returned at least architecturally to its original

[134] Along with the fragmentary publication of this inventory in Müntz, *Collections*, the complete copy of the text prepared by Warburg has been used (typescript in the Warburg Library, London, and in the Florentine Institute).

[135] See Nello Tarchiani, *Il Palazzo Medici-Riccardi e il Museo Mediceo* (Florence, 1930), pp. 32ff. Geymüller and Stegmann in their work on Tuscany seek this *camera terrena* in the right wing of the palace, in the position of the large new staircase. This, however, is supported by no evidence and even seems very improbable on account of the poor lighting conditions of that side of the building, which is not free-standing.

condition during the recent restorations. Thus this interior space stands immediately before our eyes in its original dimensions, proportions, and lighting conditions, as a first and extremely valuable point of departure for the attempted reconstruction.[136] It is no more than a point of departure, though. The present contents of this spatial shell, for purposes of the newly created Museo Mediceo, certainly reflect many documentary references, among other things even to the original furnishings of this room: its present interior aspect, however, constitutes the greatest possible contrast to its former appearance.

First we must imagine panelling articulated with nutwood frames finely profiled and interspersed with small bands of intarsia and smooth cypress wood panels running all the way around the walls, instead of the simple display cases of the museum. Three stone door frames and a stately chimneypiece equipped with wrought iron andirons interrupted the wooden wall covers. Various pieces of furniture, moreover, were set against and into it. First a double-doored cupboard, rather low but very broad, and a magnificent chest against the other wall in front of the *spalliera*; then a bed (*lettiera*) with a low step around it and a smaller *lettuccio* of cypress wood, each with a low cabinet at each end. In addition, there were two small chest-like cases or coffers (*forzeretti*) with the Medici arms painted on them, while the aforementioned beds were provided with all sorts of intarsia decoration on their nutwood frames. Finally a large table on heavy carved feet stood in the middle of the room. The only seats cited by the inventory are two chairs upholstered in leather and an arm chair "alla cardinalesca."

So much for the furnishings of the lower wall zones.

Above, however, we now find in particular, distributed along the wall, the aforementioned six large paintings in gold frames, each about two meters high, with a total length of about 25 meters, specifically the three episodes from the battle of San Romano (see above), a judgment of Paris, a battle between lions and dragons by Uccello, and a hunting scene by Pesellino; in addition, several smaller pictures whose positions are not described more precisely: an Epiphany tondo by Fra Angelico—probably the round painting completed by Fra Filippo and existing under his name in the Cook Collection, Richmond (*RA*, 1936, pp. 68ff.),* a head of St.

---

[136] The interior area is 7.85 by 9.87 meters, with a vault on consoles; the height to crown of vault is 7.5 meters. The lighting conditions must by all means have been somewhat better at that time on account of the much lower height of the houses originally lying opposite the palace.

* *Translator's note*: The Cook tondo, now in the National Gallery of Art in Washington, has recently been discussed as the work of Fra Filippo and a follower of Fra Angelico. See Jeffrey Ruda, "The National Gallery Tondo of the Adoration of the Magi and the Early Style of Fra Filippo Lippi," *Studies in the History of Art*, 7, 1975, pp. 7-39.

Sebastian by Squarcione, and also a Last Communion of St. Jerome in a *quadro* with six small paintings (probably on the frame molding). Finally, there were the portrait of Galeazzo Maria Sforza now in the Uffizi, by Pollaiuolo, and perhaps, as a counterpart to it, the portrait of a Duke of Urbino referred to without the artist's name. We pass over the further information of the inventory concerning separate objects in various places and the whole contents of the various cupboards (weapons, dishes, and a few small works of sculpture). Rather we shall attempt to depict two important rooms on the upper story, these being the actual "camera di Lorenzo," accessible only to the most intimate circle of visitors, and the large hall in front of it, extending across the middle of the front wing.

Lorenzo Magnifico's private chamber, a rectangular room in the corner above the former loggia, has dimensions of about 9 by 10.5 meters and is 6.5 meters high, roofed with the surviving, powerfully articulated coffered ceiling of the first building period.

This room was also fairly extensively supplied with sturdy furniture, at once comfortable and luxurious. The inventory names first a *lettiera* of considerable size (5½ *braccia*, or about 3.2 meters long), with a chest built in below. This contained a woven bed curtain with plant patterns and a bedspread with figural decoration. The exterior was decorated with perspective intarsia panelling and carved gilded heads and figures.[137] There were also a *lettucio* (probably meaning a simple, light bedstead) and a cassone, decorated in a manner similar to the first piece of furniture mentioned, as well as a pair of chests gilded and painted with scenes from Petrarch's *Trionfi*. These *forzieri* and the aforementioned cassone served as containers for Lorenzo's wardrobe which the inventory enumerates piece by piece. The first thing on the wall above the pair of chests was a *spalliera* painted with falcons and golden coats of arms on a blue ground; farther up on the wall hung a velvet tapestry about seven meters wide. Beyond the chests was a long bench with arms (*cassapanca*) of cypress wood with intarsia decoration. In the middle of the room stood a large table with a valuable cover spread over it; the only movable piece of sitting furniture cited in the inventory was a large armchair with colonnette balusters and intarsia decoration.

The decoration of the upper wall zones is mentioned next. We shall consider the pictures installed there in the order of their enumeration in the list of contents, since this presumably repeats the distribution of the original objects, proceeding along the walls and on the wall sections

---

[137] Müntz, *Collections*, p. 63; or Warburg's inventory copy, Warburg Library, London, p. 34; Müntz erroneously included this *lettiera*, as well as the *colmo* with a Madonna relief following it on the list, under the preceding rubric "sala grande."

adjoining one another. The inventory writer begins with a marble Madonna relief in a carved gilt wood frame, hung probably near the entrance to the room from the hall.

Next he names two objects also framed as *colmi*, with allegorical (or perhaps cartographic) depictions of the Terra Santa and Spain; between these a round picture (a *desco da parto*, see below) with the Triumph of Fame. There follows, probably in the corner near the door to the adjoining room, a small cupboard, ornately painted with images of a lady and two other figures (the former probably on the back wall inside, the latter on the doors). A marble bust of Lorenzo's father Piero was set up above the cited door, and the bust of his mother, Lucrezia Tornabuoni, set up as a counterpart to it above the other door of the room. Another small decorative item follows: a rectangular alabaster relief in a little frame decorated with bone inlay.

Thereupon the inventory refers one after the other to a whole series of mosaics, mostly small: two heads of Christ of various sizes, three heads of individual saints (Peter, Paul, and Lorenzo's name patron St. Laurence) as well as two small secular pictures, also in mosaic, the head of a young girl and the *impresa* of Lorenzo's brother Giuliano in a round frame. Finally, three works of marble sculpture, specifically two nude figures, one standing, one seated, in high relief (*di tutto rilievo*), presumably antique sculpture; then a relief of the Ascension of Christ by Donatello. Last came a large horizontal rectangular "*panno di Fiandra*" (2.25 by 2.90 meters) with figures in front of the landscape and architectural scenery ("*archi e paesi e fighure*"). In addition, the inventory cites the following objects (not included in Müntz's transcription): a costly clockwork in gilded copper, four copper sconces decorated with leafwork, a gilded copper lily—a *palio* prize from the feast of John the Baptist—and as a rare curiosity, an ostrich egg and a mirror-glass sphere (*palla di specchio*) hung on a silken string.

What distinguishes the furnishing of Lorenzo's room as a whole is that, along with the rich and costly furniture, the portable wall decorations assembled here are predominantly examples of rare artistic types with a connoisseur's refinement: the mosaics, the alabaster relief and the two small antique marble works, the little painted decorative cabinet, the upright clock, and the *panno di Fiandra*, evidently of especially high quality considering the uncommonly high estimate of its value.[138]

Art objects of a type frequently encountered in domestic rooms elsewhere were the *colmo* with the Madonna relief and the small ascension

[138] This canvas picture is appraised at twenty-five florins, that is, as high as the Madonna relief in the gilded *colmo* frame and the *lettiera*, whereas the somewhat larger Hercules *panni* by Pollaiuolo in the hall (see below) were valued only at twenty florins, and the Donatello relief at fifteen.

relief by Donatello (this, besides, the only piece with a master's name), as well as the portrait busts of the parents.

I believe this room should be recognized, from its contents alone, as Lorenzo's private living room, even if the inventory does not say so. For its whole decoration displays a decidedly personal stamp, which also corresponds closely to the nature, known to us from other sources, of the master of the house.

The character of this living room is also very clearly perceptible in comparison with the solemnly severe style of the great hall lying before it. Here, naturally, there was no such multiplicity of elegant furnishings, choice art objects, and rarities such as was found in Lorenzo's room. Instead, there were relatively frugal, loosely arranged furnishings, mostly large scale, designed for an overall harmonious effect, certainly appropriate for the spacious room used for festive occasions.

First there were small wall benches of pine with profiled nutwood frames, bands of intarsia, and carved feet all the way around the approximately 45 meter perimeter and two large tables. On the upper wall were only the three Hercules pictures by Pollaiuolo, already mentioned above, with gilded frames, and two small pictures in similar settings over the doors: the *Lions in a Cage* by Pesello (or Pesellino) and a St. John by Castagno. The inventory also names several painted shields with arms of the city and the Medici as well as twelve sconces of wrought iron and a wooden wash stand. Not mentioned are the three antique "Hercules figures," which were taken from this room in 1495 along with other antique art works and two bronze statues by Donatello and transferred to the Palazzo Vecchio (Müntz, *Collections*, p. 103).

The preceding survey and reconstruction indicates that the art works of secular subjects produced for important domestic rooms were to a very great extent commissioned or created for specific places in the wall articulation and covering, and that they were set into the panels of the wainscoting and the larger pieces of furniture, or distributed along the upper wall zones. Yet among the paintings that survive or are described in the literature we also encounter many separate pieces that, considering their form and content, must have found places as special thematic projects and artistic creations here and there outside of fixed contexts. We must imagine just such an arrangement for the greater part of the art works in the *camera di Lorenzo* in the Medici palace. Such, for example, were the two city views, *Piazza di San Giovanni* and *Piazza della Signoria*, to which Vasari alludes as perspectival bravura pieces by Brunelleschi.[139] Or, from a later period, the *Calumny of Apelles* now in the Uffizi painted

---

[139] These may perhaps be identified with the two panels mentioned in the Medici inventory "dipintovi una prospettiva" (Vasari-Milanesi, 2:332; Müntz, *Collections*, p. 62).

by Botticelli for a man of letters he had befriended as well as Filippino's *Allegory of Music* now in Berlin, and the small contemporary history painting of 1495 by Granacci representing the entry of Charles VIII through Via Larga.[140]

On the other hand, certain ornate cabinet pieces were probably used, based on their minimal dimensions, as decorative insets in small coffers; for instance, perhaps, the two diminutive pictures with deeds of Hercules by Pollaiuolo in the Uffizi.[141] In addition there are the *Apollo* and *Daphne* in London and the small victorious *David* in Berlin by the same artist, as well as the two small Judith paintings, early works of Botticelli in the Uffizi, and Ghirlandaio's *Judith* in Berlin. Thus the themes for such images appear almost always to be those personifications of strength and courage that we have already frequently encountered in Florentine statuary. Finally, a special project of very personal stamp is the small allegorical scene by Filippino in the Uffizi (22 by 29.6 centimeters) with the inscriptions apparently alluding to a family quarrel.

Secular paintings were also occasionally set into small tabernacles, the so-called *colmi*, like the majority of household *Madonnas* (see below), as various references in the Medici inventory indicate.[142]

The separate portable pictures in all of the better bourgeois houses also included round or polygonal platters decorated with figural painting, which were offered customarily to the new mother in celebration of the birth of a child, probably in general only the firstborn. These birth salvers (*deschi da parto*) thus represented familial commemorative objects, like the marriage chests of newlyweds, which were often probably handed down through several generations as part of the household inventory. Therefore, a painstaking decoration of high artistic quality was preferred for these small round pictures, and well-known masters were often entrusted with their execution. Thus the Palazzo Medici inventory mentions a *desco* with the depiction of a battle scene (*schermaglia*) under Masaccio's name (Müntz, *Collections*, p. 86). And the well-known birth salver in the Berlin museum was long considered a work of Masaccio; its lovingly executed representation of an interior with skillful handling of perspective does honor to the newly proposed artist, Bartolo di Giovanni (with a date around 1430), as well as to the whole genre.[143] Other

---

[140] 122 by 76 centimeters; now in the Medici Museum of the Palazzo Riccardi.

[141] The minute detail of their execution makes it difficult to consider them as preliminary studies, as is often suggested, for the large lost canvases of the same themes.

[142] Müntz, *Collections*, pp. 84, 85 (nudes by Domenico Veneziano and Filippino; a "poesia" without a master's name); p. 63, the *colmi* with "Terra Santa" and "Spagna."

[143] The new attribution is by Cesare Brandi in *JPK*, 1934, pp. 154ff.; see also there the illustrations of putti with small animals on the back of the painting.

The scene represented here of the woman in childbed congratulated by a deputation of the Signoria heralded by a trumpeter with the state banner appears in similar form on four

birth salvers deal with genre or amorous themes: Civetta games, the Judgment of Paris, the Garden of Love, the abduction of Helen (Gozzoli, London); also often an allegorical triumph.[144]

Closely related to birth salvers in form and type of decoration are the wooden cake boxes in which sweets were presented to the bride on the wedding day. Examples, understandably extremely rare, show a Venus with a putto on the round cover, like the one in the Louvre dated 1421. The one in the Figdor collection in Vienna from about 1430 displays the Garden of Love theme (Schubring, Cassoni, nr. 47-48, pl. 8).

Next to consider is the whole, vast genre of painted portraits that made their first appearance in Florence roughly contemporaneously with portrait busts (in about 1425-1430). It is presumed that the individual painted portraits that seem to be the oldest are in fact the work of Massaccio; on the other hand, Donatello's Uzzano bust is dated before 1430. But only around 1440 does the surviving inventory of such pictures, in some measure datable, become more extensive: even more numerous than the roughly contemporary portrait busts.

It must be particularly stressed that the painted individual portrait appeared early and often in the world of Florentine art, since of the earliest surviving examples of this genre not a single one can still be found in Florence itself. All have migrated into foreign, particularly American collections, and have only recently been traced and published.[145] It is furthermore noteworthy that, in any case among the surviving examples, portraits of women decidedly predominate. We know of seven male and twelve female portraits from the period up to about 1460.[146]

---

other surviving birth salvers of the period from 1430-1440 (Schubring, Cassoni, nr. 78ff., pl. 11).

[144] See Schubring, Cassoni, p. 13-14; van Marle, Painting, 10:199; 11:117. In Schubring's supplement volume plate 7 shows a desco with the magnanimity of Trajan and another with David and Goliath. The salver with the Triumph of Fame and the allied arms of the Medici and Tornabuoni is related by Warburg to the birth of Lorenzo Magnifico in 1449 and identified with a desco named in the Medici inventory (Schubring, Cassoni, pl. 43-44; van Marle, Painting, 10:566-67).

In the Fondazione Horne there is a twelve-sided salver with the Last Judgment and on the reverse a Cupid with a bagpipe and two coats of arms (Schubring, Cassoni, nr. 217, p. 206).

[145] Even Emil Schäffer (Das Florentiner Bildnis, Munich, 1904) knows of only two examples from the early period. For illustrations of the pieces that have come to light since then (frequently with divergent attributions) see especially van Marle, Painting, 10:235ff., 270, 326ff.; further in l'Arte, 1930, p. 53ff.; Salmi, Uccello, pl. 29, 36b, 121, 160ff.; BM, 1935, pp. 92ff.

[146] Portraits of men include first of all the Masaccio just mentioned, in Boston, and the one probably by Uccello in Chambéry, as well as the panel representing members of the Olivieri family in New York, whose authorship, either by Uccello or Domenico Veneziano,

All these portrait heads appear in nearly life-size, sharp profile and, except for the ones attributed to Fra Filippo, against a neutral blue ground that only in a few of the later works (the portraits of women in Berlin and Milan) is distinguished as a lightly shaded atmosphere enlivened by bright little clouds. The people represented appear with severely formal, almost abstract stylization of their features, enriched in the female portraits by decorative, splendidly colorful treatment of clothes and coiffure.[147]

A special case is the horizontal rectangular panel in the Louvre (210 by 42 centimeters) with a row of five bust portraits of famous personalities of Florentine art, presumably intended as an overdoor (*Rep.*, 1931, pp. 52, 145ff.).[148] In this painting of five men by Uccello several heads appear in three-quarter view. The same is true in Castagno's frescoes from Villa Pandolfini. This type of separate portrait had already appeared in early Netherlandish painting in the late 1420s; but Florence at first only rarely hazarded such deviations from the customary profile view. The oldest example of a separate portrait of this type, in half length with one hand included, is the portrait of a young man by a Masaccio follower from around 1440 in Munich. Somewhat later and higher in quality are the two of Piero and Giovanni de' Medici in Zurich and the portrait of a youth from Palazzo Torrigiani from 1450-1455, attributed to Castagno, in the Pierpont Morgan Library, New York.

A thoroughgoing change in the direction of the greatest possible diversity of viewpoint, arrangement, and conception together with a much more animated reproduction of nature occurred only after about 1470. Pollaiuolo's portrait of the Duke Galeazzo Maria Sforza from 1473, now in the Uffizi, may serve as one of the earliest examples.[149] Then an almost

---

is contested. This is also true of four portraits of women in American collections in Boston, Philadelphia, and New York, the Bache and Lehmann collections. Other portraits of women are those in the National Gallery in London (Domenico Veneziano or Antonio Pollaiuolo) and a small picture in Richmond. In addition, there are the particularly charming portraits perhaps by Pollaiuolo in Berlin and Milan (Poldi-Pezzoli) as well as the severely overpainted one in the Uffizi; and two portraits in Berlin and New York that may be considered early works of Fra Filippo (see also ZKG, 1933, p. 270).

[147] An exceptional portrait of a woman by Fra Filippo (New York, Metropolitan Museum) also shows the profile head of her husband Lorenzo Scolari looking in through a window on the left, and his coat of arms; 1441-1442 (RA, 1936, p. 67).

[148] It has a forerunner in the small picture in the Uffizi, painted around 1400, that unites three painters of the Gaddi family. Thematically it belongs with the fresco cycle of the *Uomini famosi* mentioned above and with the portraits of jurists from the Palazzo del Proconsolo. The lost panel by Zanobi Strozzi, with Giovanni Bicci de' Medici and Filippo Valori (Vasari-Milanesi, 2:521) belongs in this category as a posthumous double portrait of famous men.

[149] In addition there is the portrait of a youth in the Galleria Corsini in Rome, attributed to the same master and showing a marked influence by Netherlandish art.

unlimited abundance of new possibilities was developed in particular by Botticelli in his numerous individual portraits and along with him by the young Leonardi da Vinci, as well as by Ghirlandaio and Piero di Cosimo. It is striking that Botticelli as well as Ghirlandaio and his pupil Mainardi frequently return to the pure profile view, while with other artists the three-quarter view far predominates; the frontal presentation also appears only occasionally in Botticelli's work. Ghirlandaio twice grouped together the figures of an older man and a child: in the Sassetti double portrait now in the Bache collection in New York, and in the Louvre picture of the old man with a warty nose, distinguished by its unsparing naturalism and inspired by Netherlandish models.[150]

Occasionally the personality portrayed will now also be raised into a higher sphere by the addition of a saint's attribute or antiquarian regalia. See Piero di Cosimo's portrait of a woman as Mary Magdalene in the Galleria Corsini, Rome, and his portrait of Simonetta Vespucci as Cleopatra in the Chantilly Collection.[151] Botticelli's "Simonetta" in the Staedel introduces an increase in size to an over-life-sized format, combined with fantastically rich ornamental finery and coiffure.

A thematic innovation was the artist portrait. It probably already appears in the head of a man, attributed to Botticelli, in the Uffizi, who holds in front of him as an attribute a gilded gesso impression of the medal of Cosimo de' Medici. The person portrayed is accordingly probably the still-disputed author of this medal, perhaps Niccolò Spinelli. Compare this with the later "goldsmith" by Ridolfo Ghirlandaio in the Pitti. The portraits of the musician Giamberti and the architect Giuliano da Sangallo by Piero di Cosimo in the Hague are also distinguished by professional attributes in the foreground. The same is true of the portrait of a viola da gamba virtuoso probably by Filippino in Dublin. On the other hand, there is the portrait in the Uffizi assigned by an old tradition to Lorenzo di Credi as a portrait of Verrocchio, which has recently been proposed as a portrait of Perugino by the young Raphael.[152]

The enrichment of the portrait tradition through various scenic properties, which occurs only sporadically before the middle of the century, belongs from about 1470 on among the most indispensable aspects of portraiture everywhere. The section of space that is sometimes suggested also frequently includes still life details or a landscape view. The open

---

[150] See Jean Alazard, *Le Portrait Florentin de Botticelli à Bronzino* (Paris, 1924); Hans Timotheus Kroeber, *Die Einzel-porträts des Sandro Botticelli* (Leipzig, 1911); and Jacob Burckhardt, *Beiträge: Das Porträt.*

[151] There is also a Simonetta as Caritas, pressing milk from her breast, in Richmond, Cook collection from the Botticelli school. Antiquarian costume also appears repeatedly in contemporary portrait sculpture by Mino da Fiesole.

[152] Van Marle, *Painting*, 12:297; *BM*, 1934, pp. 65, 245ff.

landscape probably appears for the first time in Leonardo's portrait of Ginevra de' Benci (Vienna, Liechtenstein).[153]

In conclusion, let us take a brief glance at portraits of the early Cinquecento. Leonardo stands at the summit here with the Mona Lisa, of about 1503-1505. The subject of the portrait is no longer a young girl or a new bride, as in most portraits of women of the preceding century, but mature beauty in full bloom, in a pose and attitude that exercised its effect on many other Florentine portraits of women of the period: for example, Raphael's Florentine portraits. The tectonic impulse of the High Classic period now frequently results in placement of a portrait figure between powerful, symmetrically ordered architectural elements, as, for example, with the Uffizi "Monaca" or the portrait of a general in armor possibly by Piero di Cosimo and now in London.

Of particular interest for their subjects are finally Andrea del Sarto's self-portrait with the head, almost frontal, painted in fresco on a tile in the Uffizi and the portrait of Michelangelo by Bugiardini from about 1522 (exemplars in Casa Buonarroti and the Louvre).

Finally, by Bachiacca, there is the pair of allegorical portraits of a youth with a lute and an old man with a death's head in his hand: both have small triumphal chariots in the background landscapes.[154]

By far the greatest contingent of individual paintings was composed of religious images, of which we have already encountered several examples among the *panni dipinti* and in frames in the rooms of the Palazzo Medici described above. Overdoors of religious subjects also belong thematically to this group, like the ones commissioned from Fra Filippo for the Palazzo Medici and in 1447 for the Palazzo Vecchio. Such also were the altar paintings for household chapels, like that of the Palazzo Medici by Fra Filippo now in Berlin and paintings by Baldovinetti and Signorelli coming from the villas of Cafaggiolo and Castello and now in the Uffizi.

Above all, however, the actual household images intended purely for devotional purposes should be mentioned here. These belonged, even in the later Quattrocento, to the indispensable furnishings of a household and thus might not be absent even where other pictorial decoration had still not been obtained or planned.[155] These devotional images, found everywhere more or less as a matter of duty, may well have included many pieces of scant artistic value. And such works still exist among the

---

[153] A portrait of a woman by Lorenzo di Credi in New York is based on it (van Marle, *Painting*, 13:272).

[154] Illustrated in Weisbach, *Trionfi*, pp. 124-25.

[155] Thus the Medici inventory of 1492 for the villa of Poggio a Caiano could mention, along with the other household furnishings, only a few works of art or applied arts; yet in each of the eight bedrooms was a small Madonna or image of a saint, sometimes painted on wood, sometimes "di que' panni franzesi" (Warburg inventory copy, pp. 270ff.).

uncommonly numerous examples of this type of picture that survive. On the other hand, this very type of commission often gave well-known masters the occasion for a particularly loving and delicate execution in which the special nature of the task worked its effect in the most careful refinement of detail treatment and in a conception of pronounced intimacy.[156]

Former household devotional images may be recognized as such by their form and format: they appear predominantly in the form of the *colmo* or tondo, which we have already encountered in household sculpture. The first of these forms in particular resulted in the greatest diversity in the types of frames. The *colmi* ranged from medium-sized full- or half-length Madonnas, often with very richly designed carved and gilded or painted tabernacle frames, sometimes altogether a match in size and splendor for the pictures they contained, to diminutive panels in vertical rectangular format, sometimes hardly bigger than a hand and executed with a miniaturist's fine and costly care, whose charm and value could be appreciated only under the very closest observation. In between there were elegant little folding altarpieces, diptychs or triptychs, which were easily portable objects of private devotion sometimes taken along on journeys. Painted wings were also not infrequently added to the larger *colmi* belonging to the fixed contents of a room's furnishings, in particular when such a *colmo* was placed in a small wall niche prepared for it or was set up as a deep wooden tabernacle and filled with a piece of sculpture in the middle.[157]

The continuing demand for such domestic images naturally clung to the old familiar compositional types of Trecento household devotional images, often still available in the hereditary possessions of a family and in continued use. The new form of the tondo, the round picture in a carved frame, emerges in the early Quattrocento and is taken up by sculpture at the same time. These ranged in size, according to desire and ability to pay, from daintily small to medium-sized dimensions.

Below are a few particularly interesting or high quality examples of the different types and forms of household devotional image from the immense quantity of pertinent material. Monuments from the early and middle decades of the Quattrocento may be grouped as follows, according to theme and form:

[156] Such a painting was often given as a wedding gift from parents, along with the marriage chests, as a "quadro da sposa" for the new household. For example, Benedetto Aldobrandini gave his son a wedding present of a *colmo* picture that he had commissioned from Zanobi Strozzi (van Marle, *Painting*, 10:164).

[157] The outside of such wings usually show no decoration or else purely ornamental imagery, arms, emblems, etc.

(1) Madonnas in the smallest format are found in rectangular, sometimes also octagonal panels, whose dimensions vary between perhaps 15 and 35 centimeters; in these the Madonna, sometimes almost on a miniature scale, appears as a whole enthroned figure surrounded by angels or saints.[158]

(2) Medium-sized Madonnas, full length, are found on a scale of about 50-60 by 70-100 centimeters, in which the principal figure, in order to make her appearance as broad and dominating as possible, is assigned a low seat on a flat bench or a cushion directly on the ground and provided with a gold-patterned tapestry as a foil closing off the space; accompanying figures are at most a pair of angels, holding back curtains or kneeling in the foreground playing music.

This type, which is derived from the trecentesque prototype of the Madonna dell' Umiltà, also appears in particular in the works of Fra Angelico and his circle, and in the Masaccio Madonna in New York (in the Duveen collection).[159] Some of these pictures already had frames, painted with attendant figures or the like, in tabernacle form, with a socle below and a pediment at the top. Such a frame may in any case be presumed for all panels with semicircular or pointed-arch forms at the top.[160]

(3) The third type presents a half-length Madonna in a vertical rectangular or tabernacle-framed picture field of medium size, sometimes attended by an angel or the child John the Baptist. The earliest examples are probably the Madonna by Domenico Veneziano in the Berenson collection at Settignano and two pictures by Fra Filippo in Berlin and in the Palazzo Riccardi. New types appearing after the middle of the century are the Madonnas in front of a spreading, freely growing rose hedge by Pier Francesco Fiorentino in Berlin and elsewhere and the Madonnas in

[158] This group includes, among others, several early works of Fra Angelico in Boston, in the Vatican (17 by 22 centimeters), in the Staedel and two little pictures by Pesellino of Sacra Conversazioni with numerous figures (New York, Knoedler Collection, 24 by 26 centimeters, and Chantilly).

[159] Fra Angelico paintings of this type can be found, for example, in the Museums of Berlin and Turin. One by Domenico di Michelino is in the Oppenheim collection, Berlin (*Dedalo*, 12, p. 525). Masaccio's panel (*Dedalo*, 1929, p. 331) could also have been a church painting, considering its size and monumentality. On the other hand, Gozzoli's picture in Berlin is unmistakably a household Madonna.

[160] One has survived on Fra Angelico's painting in Parma (56 by 100 centimeters without the frame) in which the groove of the frame molding is painted with cherubim; in the gable field is the dove of the Holy Spirit. In addition, there is the charming little household altar by Andrea di Giusto from around 1430-1440 in the Academy, in which the pediment field has a medallion with the Man of Sorrows, while a human skeleton appears on the socle with the inscription evoking sober meditations: "Respice Frater, qualis eris, fui sicut tu es."

front of an open landscape by Fra Filippo in the Uffizi and by Baldovinetti in the Louvre. Along with these, particularly with Botticelli, came the half-open architectural framing of the Madonna figure in a happy harmony with the elegantly structured polychromed carving of the tabernacle frame.

Household devotional images with narrative subjects are considerably rarer. An example is the Crucifixion in a sensitive early work by Fra Angelico in Cambridge (U.S.A.) with kneeling Dominicans and at the top the Pelican symbol.[161] Then there is the Annunciation, sometimes on a small separate panel (for example, by Domenico di Michelino in Philadelphia), more often on the wings of a small triptych (see the little folding altarpiece from the Fra Angelico school in the Cathedral treasury at Hildesheim and the small wing panels by Filippo Lippi in the Frick Collection, New York). There are in addition the Adoration of the Child perhaps by Giovanni di Francesco in Karlsruhe with three kneeling saints in front of a landscape background and the little St. Jerome panel by Pesellino from Palazzo Medici (Müntz, Collections, p. 64), now in Altenburg, and others.

The household devotional image in the tondo form first appears only with the portrayal of the Epiphany. Examples are the early work of Fra Filippo in Richmond, Cook Collection and the controversial tondo by Domenico Veneziano in Berlin. But the magnificent late work of Fra Filippo in the Pitti (1452) contains, along with the Madonna who has already grown very charmingly more worldly, a view into the chamber of her birth and farther back the scene at the Golden Gate.[162]

For the late Quattrocento we have in particular the great Madonna tondi of Botticelli: the Madonna of the Magnificat and Madonna of the Pomegranate in the Uffizi as well as the Berlin picture, among others. All show only the half-length figure of the Madonna amid a crowd of attending angels, without a view into the distance; thus the monumental power together with lavish splendor of detail has been increased, following the taste of the period. On the other hand, the smaller, later round painting in the Ambrosiana shows the dainty full-length figure of the Madonna with loosely distributed child angels in front of landscape scenery, as in the graceful garden of the Madonna by Botticini in the

[161] See also the small crucifix with two monastic saints against a gold ground (l'Arte, 1924, p. 95) and the diminutive triptych from the Castagno school in the Acton collection, Florence (van Marle, Painting, 10:381). Neri di Bicci supplied a tabernacolo with wings painted with "4 storie" to a goldsmith for four florins in 1461 (Vasari-Milanesi, 2:74).

[162] These are both subjects that perhaps earlier were sometimes chosen for birth salvers and taken over from these into the large round paintings; see Hauptmann, Der Tondo (Frankfurt am Main, 1936), pp. 179-80, 187. See Hauptmann, Der Tondo, p. 175 for an exhaustive, systematically organized survey of the whole vast field of the tondo in Florentine painting.

Pitti.[163] Ghirlandaio again treats the theme of the Adoration of the Kings in two large tondi now in the Uffizi and the National Gallery in London. One of these pictures is probably the one executed for the Tornabuoni palace (Vasari-Milanesi, 3; 258)[164]. A last example from the end of the Quattrocento is Filippino's tondo with the standing Madonna and angels in front of rich architecture (Palazzo Corsini, Florence) and the rectangular Strozzi Madonna, clearly for family use, precisely identified by the coat of arms in the painted architecture (60 by 80 centimeters, now in the Bache Collection, New York). There also are numerous tondi surviving by Lorenzo di Credi, Botticini, and Raffaellino del Garbo.

A sort of counterpart to the half-length Madonnas is Botticelli's *Man of Sorrows* in Detroit. Several other small pictures with particularly fine execution by Botticelli exist: images of the Annunciation in small separate panels and diptychs, a triptych with the Transfiguration and two church fathers, an Augustine in his cell, and the *Communion of St. Jerome*, all in the Uffizi or New York. [165]

In the early Cinquecento the delight in detail and delicate painting, now essentially suppressed in all larger works, remains active in household devotional images of the smaller and smallest formats. A particularly characteristic example is the triptych by Albertinelli in Milan, dated 1500.[166]

Finally there are the larger household Madonnas of the sixteenth century, sometimes in tondo form, sometimes on rectangular panels, often with the motif of the entire Holy Family or the Adoration of the Child. Many examples exist from Raphael's Florentine period, by Fra Bartolommeo, Piero di Cosimo, Bugiardini, Andrea del Sarto, and virtually all other contemporaries. A markedly personal version is Michelangelo's tondo of the Holy Family from about 1504 in the Uffizi, in a particularly rich, relief-sculptured frame. Devotional images of the Madonna and

---

[163] There are also two full-length Madonnas by Botticelli in medium-sized tabernacle frames in the Uffizi, etc.

[164] The same theme also appears in the small, almost frieze-like panel by Botticelli in London, which in view of its format should probably be considered a household devotional image.

[165] The last was painted around 1500 for the Savonarola admirer Francesco del Pugliese. The remarkable small Crucifixion allegory in Cambridge is more closely related to Savonarola's martyrdom; and the "Derelitta" in Rome is perhaps also to be understood as a religious allegory of contemporary significance (42 by 64 centimeters); see below.

[166] Piero del Pugliese had two shutters, now in the Uffizi, painted by the young Fra Bartolommeo for a Madonna-relief by Donatello, with the Annunciation on the exterior and other scenes from the life of Mary on the insides. An old source twice mentions a small diptych by Fra Bartolommeo ("a uso d'un libretto") with the Crucifixion and Nativity (see the list of works drawn up in 1516 in Marchese, *Memorie*, 2:180-81). There are two small panels by Bachiacca with Tobias and the Angel in the Uffizi and an American private collection; *l'Arte*, 1904, p. 77.

other subjects for private domestic rooms were evidently commissioned in undiminished numbers even in the High Renaissance, and sometimes from the best masters.

It is, however, striking that religious subject matter, hitherto almost totally excluded from small figured paintings to be set into wall panelling, cassoni, and other pieces of furniture, now also comes into frequent and extensive use in these types. Many examples of the type survive scattered in various museums. These include in particular the multipartite picture cycle of the story of Joseph, which was formerly in the house of Pier Francesco Borgherini on Borgo Santi Apostoli, installed in the wall panelling and the bedstead of the master bedroom.[167] A counterpart, also from around 1520, could be found in the house of Giovanni M. Benintendi. The *Adoration of the Kings* by Pontormo in the Pitti, *David and Bathsheba* by Franciabigio, the *King's Sons Shooting at the Corpse* (after *Gesta Romanorum*) by Bachiacca, and the *Baptism of Christ* by the same artist in Berlin can be traced to there.[168] Even the birth salver category, scarcely traceable any longer after 1500, appears in an example executed by Pontormo in 1526 for the Tornaquinci with the biblical theme of the birth of John.

In addition, we can naturally still find in cassone and wainscoting panel painting the secular themes from the antique or medieval *novelle* that were almost exclusively preferred in earlier times.[169] There are also still late representatives of the picture type of the large reclining figure (see above), like the three panels by Bugiardini dealing with the old theme of the sleeping Venus and the Leda motif.[170]

Among these contemporary household devotional images, provided on order, we occasionally come across older works of art here and there in

[167] The two pictures in the Pitti, painted in 1521 by Andrea del Sarto (97 by 134 centimeters), come from this cycle, as do two pictures by Granacci in the Uffizi and three pictures of different sizes by Pontormo in London at the National Gallery; see Panshanger); finally six small panels on the same theme by Bachiacca are in Rome at the Galleria Borghese.

[168] Vasari-Milanesi, 5:26, 196-97, 342-43, 353; 6:262, 455; Schubring, *Cassoni*, p. 174, cat. 810-19.

Two *spalliera* panels with stories of Moses from Filippino's last period belong to this group, for example; they are now in the National Gallery, London (*Pantheon*, 1938, p. 199). Then there are the two Tobias scenes with the Medici arms, from about 1500, and the *Presentation in the Temple*, attributed to Franciabigio (Strasbourg Museum). The generic relationship with the rich intarsia compositions for similar function is apparent in the symmetrically organized architectural perspectives of these pictures.

[169] Piero di Cosimo supplied many examples even in his last years, in particular three paintings from an Andromeda cycle in the Uffizi; See Schubring, *Cassoni*, nr. 406-408, pl. 97. Then there are the *Temple of Hercules* by Franciabigio in the Uffizi and Bachiacca's *Apollo and Daphne* in Florence at the Galleria Corsini.

[170] Florentine and Milanese private possession (illustrated in *Dedalo*, 6, pp. 777, 779).

places where a collector's interest in art had awakened. And this means not only pictures that had been reverently left in their places as legacies from a father or grandfather, but works that had been acquired by purchase based on historically conscious, knowledgeable appreciation. The sources name many such works: old Byzantine panels, by which we may understand not only Italian Duecento works but also Greek icons, and also small mosaics of Byzantine craftsmanship and certain small paintings which on account of their old-fashioned character were summarily baptized with the venerable names of Giotto and Cimabue. In the possession of the Medici and other cultivated art connoisseurs there were also individual examples of Netherlandish painting of the fifteenth century, easily acquired through the continual trade relations of various Florentine firms. More details on this will be provided in the second main section.

In conclusion it remains to consider the pictorial wall hanging as a special category related to painting. These appear sometimes in the simple and probably fairly widespread type of a tapestry with a repeating pattern of stylized plant motifs as a kind of wallpaper made of woven woolen cloth. Their character and appearance in the absence of surviving pieces may be imagined based on their frequent occurrence in depictions of interiors of the period. Here we see these dark-colored cloths, woven with multicolored, large, flowering plant patterns or else with regularly repeating animal images, sometimes as a covering for a whole wall surface, sometimes as a *spalliera*, and sometimes as a substitute for wooden panelling or even spread out as a *pancale* above wall benches and their backs.[171] They also occur, as evidenced primarily by the Medici inventory, as bed covers or *portiere* (*usciali*) in front of doorways, and sometimes several are made into a whole bed canopy, as for example the "cortinaggio di Piero," made of seven pieces on which figures from tournaments and hunts could be seen, along with individual bird figures and devices.[172]

These works, however, no longer belong to the most marketable class—the tapestry patterns turned out in what amounts to a mass produced manner to cover vast areas. They are the elements of transition to the costly and therefore rare type of the *arazzi*, originally produced in Flanders and thus named after the city of Arras, a principal center of their manufacture there.

---

[171] See, for example, certain paintings by Fra Angelico and Baldovinetti from the Annunziata cupboard paintings in the Museo San Marco, in Castagno's Last Supper fresco, etc.

[172] In addition there was in "Piero's antechamber" a bed canopy (painted or embroidered) with a *Fortuna* by Botticelli. A pictorially decorated hanging appears draped over the bench in the foreground in the so-called Adimari wedding in the Accademia with the heads of individual figures and the inscriptions "Venatio," "Orticultura" etc. recognizable on it (see Müntz, *Collections*, pp. 60-61, Warburg inventory copy, fol. 48r).

Since the middle of the century when this most important category of pictorial tapestries appeared more frequently in Florence, certain Netherlandish tapestry weavers even set up their workshops in Florence itself.[173] But for the most valuable pictorial textiles, Netherlandish even in design, later customers also turned when possible to the long-famous Flemish production centers.[174]

Concerning the use of the costly pieces, it should be noted that they were apparently brought forth from the chests only on special occasions, to be hung up as wall decorations or *portiere* in the principal rooms of the palace, or even in the street loggia, as well as under the palace windows against the grey walls of the house for public display and enhancement of the festive mood.[175] The chronicler Bartolommeo Masi (*Ricordanze*, pp. 235-36) reports a most unusually extensive use of decorative wall hangings for the year 1518. For the wedding of the young Medici duke Lorenzo, the whole palace along the Via Larga as well as the larger interior rooms and especially the garden where the wedding feast took place were hung with about three hundred pictorial and decorative tapestries. These included many acquired as gifts from Leo X, while others were old family possessions that had been recovered; a few were also probably contributed from other palaces as loans, as was customary on similar occasions earlier.

The Medici and other inventories also provide some information on the pictorial motifs occurring in these works. Preferred themes for the simpler decorative pieces of *spalliere*, *portiere*, and bed curtains seem to come from the world of courtly, chivalric culture of the late middle ages, also of Netherlandish inspiration. Individual figures and whole scenes form the main amusements of this caste: hunts, tournaments, and courtship among these, heraldic and emblematic motifs, and more rarely narrative scenes from antique and contemporary *novella*-literature, *trionfi*, etc.[176]

---

[173] Such were Lievin of Bruges and Giovanni d'Alemagna, whom we have encountered in the history of the Palazzo Vecchio and the Cathedral. See Eugène Müntz, Hist. de la Tapiss., p. 62. [*Translator's note*: This reference may refer either to Eugène Müntz et al., *Histoire générale de la tapisserie*, 25 vols., Paris, 1878-1885, or to Müntz's *La Tapisserie*, Paris, 1882f.]

[174] See the exchange of letters between Cosimo's son Giovanni de' Medici and his agent Tommaso Portinari concerning the commission and purchase of a great tapestry series from Antwerp (Gaye, *Carteggio*, 1:158; Eugène Müntz, *I Precursori e propugnatori del rinascimento*, Florence, 1902, pp. 122-23).

[175] The Signoria also had figural hangings executed by the aforementioned Lievin to be draped against the palace wall behind their *ringhiera*. Their replacement was considered in 1524 (see above).

[176] Thus Piero de' Medici's inventories of 1456 and 1463 already name, among numerous covers and wall hangings with figures, three wall tapestries with depictions of hunts, hawking, and fishing. There are also many pieces with vegetable motifs and a bed cover

Only the Medici inventory of 1492 cites a large number of particularly costly *arazzi* as the contents of two large chests in one of the ground floor rooms of the palace. Prominent among these in one chest are an especially large wall hanging (11.60 meters long, 3.50 meters high) with a "hunt of the Duke of Burgundy" as well as three somewhat smaller *arazzi* with tournament scenes, mounted hunters and hounds; in addition, a *spalliera* with antique figures and Medici arms, and two others with leaf-work and landscapes. As the most interesting contents of the second chest I cite two *spalliere* (each about 7.5 meters long) with the story of Narcissus between candelabra and arms of the house, four *spalliere* of the same size with triumphal scenes, together with wall coverings belonging to them on which were the arms and emblems of the master of the house. There were also several *portiere* with the Triumph of Fame, a pair of lovers, and other things. The Medici also owned a few *arazzi* with religious subjects, including one specifically described as an altar frontal (*dossale*).[177]

Nothing is now preserved or traceable of all these splendors. And even a *portiere* with Adam and Eve, allegedly after a design by the young Leonardo da Vinci, which Vasari saw in the possession of Ottaviano de' Medici, is known to us solely through this citation (Vasari-Milanesi, 4: 23). Of surviving pieces I can cite only a Pallas tapestry executed after a cartoon in Botticelli's style: its emblematic accessories suggest it belonged to Lorenzo Magnifico.[178]

## PAINTING ON THE EXTERIOR OF BUILDINGS AND THROUGHOUT THE CITYSCAPE

In spite of considerable destruction of what once existed, so much still survives of painting in the interior of churches, convents, and secular buildings that we can arrive at an approximate conception of the original total character of painted interior decoration. However, if we wish to evoke the former development and effect of mural painting on the exteriors of churches and secular buildings, we must rely almost solely on literary evidence and on our own reconstructive imagination. Only oc-

---

with the family arms and *impresa* of Piero. Similar items were in the Careggi and Cafaggiolo villas. Furthermore, there is occasional reference to figural decoration embroidered in silk (Müntz, *Collections*, pp. 20-22, 27-29, 59-60; Jacob Burckhardt, *Beiträge: Die Sammler*, pp. 456-57).

[177] Particularly noteworthy was a small square embroidered image of the Duke of Burgundy before the Madonna, valued at sixty florins on account of its fine quality and costly technique of silk and golden threads; while the tax assessor considered an Annunciation of considerably larger dimensions worth only seven florins (Müntz, *Collections*, p. 84).

[178] Formerly this was in the Comte de Baudreuil collection: see Poggi in *l'Arte*, 1902, pp. 71f. A preparatory drawing for it is in the Uffizi; see Horne, *Botticelli*, pp. 161-62.

casional examples have survived, and even the works mentioned in the literature probably represent a relatively small part of the former whole. Above all, however, the entire appearance of the city has completely changed in the course of time, in the architectural context as well as, in particular, in the ubiquitous advance of modern advertising displays and the like. Thus it has become almost impossible to imagine even approximately the effect of facade painting along the streets and squares as it appeared in the fifteenth and sixteenth centuries and as Vasari and even some eighteenth-century reporters still saw it.

First it must be considered that rich architectural articulation of house facades appeared only sporadically in the late fifteenth and the first quarter of the sixteenth century among the multitude of undecorated house fronts. The latter were in part small, medievally rough, ashlar buildings, sometimes with towers, but more often simple brick houses of the bourgeoisie whose exteriors were besides often crossed by attached wooden galleries, eaves, etc. These can be recognized in street views in old paintings and miniatures, and their former existence is confirmed by many extant beam holes in the old masonry. Fragments of this uniform, neutral, grey-brown architectural ground can still be found today at certain points in the old city. And it received an interruption and enrichment, which must have been doubly effective against just such a foil, from the painting scattered everywhere in large and small murals, painted tabernacles, brightly glazed terra-cotta reliefs and the like, which were also joined temporarily on the numerous festive occasions by woven rugs hung from the windows.

This was more than the assertion of that southern delight in color that still survives today. In all this imagery, and in a long-dead manner scarcely conceivable to us now, the fundamental need of a whole culture for visualization and illustration expressed itself. This was a culture in which the image and its representational content were not yet overpowered in their public effect by the written text and the beholder's eye was not yet deadened to the reception of an image by the constantly changing spectacle of mechanically reproduced posters, mutually striving to drown each other out by the most drastic means. Only by keeping in mind these circumstances, so thoroughly and detrimentally changed, shall we be able in some measure to appreciate the original significance and function of the remains of outdoor painting that still exist here and there today.

Below we shall attempt a survey of the different types of these images that an observer wandering through the city might have encountered anywhere in free public view.

First of all, murals appeared particularly often on the front walls of churches and convents, above or near the portals, and these were most frequently figures of the titular patron who was placed here before the

eyes of passersby for his or her demonstrative identification and veneration. Some other figures of saints might also be here, according to the
wishes and commission of a donor. Thus on the facade of Santa Croce
one could see not only the Jesus monogram of St. Bernardino of Siena,
in a high position, but also the fresco representing the Ascension of the
Virgin above the central portal, painted in the same year 1430 by the
same artist Bicci di Lorenzo. Its general outlines are indicated in a view
of the piazza in a cassone panel of 1439.[179]

Tommaso Spinelli, a zealous patron elsewhere too, had his name patron, the doubting Thomas, painted near the outer portal of the convent
of Santa Croce, as well as the giant figure of St. Christopher 12½ *braccia*
high, once again by Bicci di Lorenzo. Richa in 1760 still knew of no less
than four such over-life-sized images of the patron of travellers, namely
the aforementioned one and the Christophers of the facades of San Matteo (today destroyed or surrounded by construction), San Miniato fra le
Torri, and San Piero Maggiore.[180]

The vertical rectangular Madonna, framed by rich bands of ornament,
above the portal of Santi Apostoli, has also survived from this early
period, in ruinous condition, but recently well-restored. It is probably by
Paolo di Stefano, around 1445. Above the now walled-up portal of a
former oratory on Via della Costa San Giorgio is a Crucifixion with
Francis and Jerome before a craggy landscape; on the broad borders of
the surrounding niche are two worshipping angels, one above the other.[181]

Several outdoor frescoes by Fra Filippo, Castagno, and Uccello were
also produced around the middle of the century, but are known only
through literary references.[182] Surviving works of this type are a charming

[179] Moisé, *Santa Croce*, p. 85; Schubring, *Cassoni*, pl. 28.

[180] Richa, *Notizie*, 7:263-64. Faint remains of all the exterior painting on Santa Croce
still existed in the eighteenth century; see the engraved view in Richa *Notizie*, 3; Vasari
(Vasari-Milanesi, 2:51, 53) attributes to Lorenzo di Bicci (actually Bicci di Lorenzo) a
fresco, since lost, above the convent door of Santo Spirito, the confirmation of the order's
rule by St. Augustine. [*Tranlator's note*: Milanesi in Vasari-Milanesi, *Le Vite* 2:63 explains
how Vasari actually wrote a life of Bicci di Lorenzo under the name of that artist's father
Lorenzo di Bicci.]

[181] By Arrigo Pesello, c. 1430, according to Karl F. Suter in *Allgemeine Lexikon der bildenden künstler*, ed. Ulrich Thieme and Felix Becker, 37 vols. (Leipzig, 1907-1950), 26:464.
Richard Offner, *Italian Primimitives at Yale University* (New Haven, 1927), pl. 14 G.

[182] An Annunciation by Fra Filippo Lippi was above the outer portal of the Carmine
convent, according to Magliabecchiano-Frey (*Il codice*, p. 97); a doubting Thomas by
Uccello at the portal of San Tommaso al Mercato and two figures, not further identified,
next to the entrance of the Annalena convent (Richa, *Notizie*, 7:232; Magliabecchiano-
Frey, *Il codice*, p. 100). A Castagno crucifix with four saints was over the church door
of the *monache* of San Giuliano. Crowe-Cavalcaselle (J. A. Crowe and C. B. Cavalcaselle,
*Geschichte der italienischen Malerei*, ed. M. Jordan, Leipzig, 1864-1871) saw a fresco of
similar subject there, but in sixteenth-century style.

lunette fresco, the Madonna with two angels in the tympanum of the pointed-arched door of the property formerly serving as a hospice at Via Romana 25; in addition, the large tympanum picture above the Innocenti church entrance, with God the Father surrounded by putti and two groups of heads of the holy Innocents (the victims of the Bethlehem slaughter) to whom the church is dedicated.[183] A third is the large St. Christopher from the facade of the destroyed church of San Miniato fra le Torri, which was deported to the Metropolitan Museum in New York; Vasari and his predecessors correctly attributed it to Pollaiuolo.[184] The Botticelli *Annunciation* from the portico of the former Ospedale, later the nuns' convent of San Martino on Via dell Scala, survives from the late Quattrocento. Rescued in two large pieces, it is dated 1481 by documents.[185] The well-preserved *Annunciation* by Ghirlandaio above the church door of the Ospizio dell'Orbatello is dated 1485.[186] Finally, a most beautiful and costly piece in this category is the Annunication lunette executed in 1492 by Ghirlandaio in the unusual technique of mosaic above the Porta della Mandorla of the Cathedral (see above).

Quattrocento outdoor frescoes also appear on public secular buildings. Such were the large images of the Madonna placed on the inside of the city gates, sometimes above the portal. First executed soon after the construction of these gates around the middle of the Trecento, some underwent a first or a repeated necessary restoration already a hundred years later and some in the early sixteenth century.[187] Two separate pictures, no longer surviving, were of semisecular format: a fresco on the palace of the Parte Guelfa was commissioned by the Signoria in commemoration of the day of the occupation of Pisa, 9 October 1406. It represented the saint of that day, St. Dionysus, with two angels, and

---

[183] Toesca established that this was painted in 1458-1459 by Giovanni di Francesco, formerly known as the Carrand master (*Rass. A.*, 1917, pp. 1ff; van Marle, *Painting*, 10:384). Baldovinetti painted an Annunciation, since lost, above another portal of the Innocenti building, also in 1458 (Baldovinetti-Londi, *Ricordi*, p. 31; BM, 1905, p. 189).

[184] See Vasari-Milanesi, 3:293; Richa, *Notizie*, 4:71; c. 1465-1470, according to van Marle, *Painting*, 11:391.

[185] Now in storage in the Accademia (*BM*, 28, pp. 129ff.).

[186] Via della Pergola 28, in the courtyard. Richa ascribes to Ghirlandaio a Madonna fresco above the portal of the little church of Santa Maria Ughi, now destroyed, which had been recently touched up in his time (Richa, *Notizie*, 1:297; 3:183; Vasari-Milanesi, 3:259). A Perugino Pietà was formerly to be found above the side portal of San Piero Maggiore (Bocchi-Cinelli, *Le bellezze della citta*, pp. 358-59).

[187] The most beautiful, and also relatively well preserved, is the enthroned Madonna with Sts. George and Laurence on the Porta San Giorgio dating from 1430-1440 (*l'Arte*, 1904, p. 347). See the corresponding paintings on the Siena city gates, where Simone Martini himself allegedly collaborated on the Porta Romana (Lorenzo Ghiberti, *Lorenzo Ghibertis Denkwürdigkeiten*, ed. J. von Schlosser, 2 vols., Berlin, 1912, 1:42; 2:148).

beneath them a faithful view of the city of Pisa; this work, attributed to Gherardo Starnina, was still in good condition when Vasari saw it.[188]

Besides this there were several narrative paintings on hospitals and the like as a monumental declaration of the function of these buildings or in commemoration of important episodes in the history of the institutions they housed. One of the earlier examples has survived in a very conspicuous, central location: the two frescoes on the exterior of the Bigallo hospice executed in 1445-1446, by Rossello Franchi and Ventura del Moro. Their large-scale breadth lends the rather small buildings an impressive accentuation above the rest of the old piazza. They represent the founder of the confraternity, St. Peter Martyr, distributing banners to the members and a miracle scene from the legend of that saint.[189]

Two other still more attractive paintings may be seen on the facade of the church of Sant' Egidio, belonging to the hospital of Santa Maria Nuova. Now somewhat overshadowed under the later portico hall and difficult to see through the protective but always dusty glass, they must once have stood out very effectively against the small, simple church front. The historical content of the two images was of direct interest to contemporary observers. On one side was the consecration of the church by Pope Martin V, which had taken place a few years earlier, painted by Bicci di Lorenzo about 1429-1430; it is represented as a well-attended ceremony against a background of realistically portrayed scenery of the building in its condition at that time. A counterpart, probably planned from the beginning, was painted only in 1474 by Gherardo di Giovanni, the solemn investiture of a master of the hospital.[190]

Other such hospital frescoes are mentioned in the literature but no longer preserved: on the one hand, the exterior loggia of the former Spedale di Bonifazio (on Via San Gallo) where, according to Vasari, the Cosimo Rosselli associate Angelo Donnini painted a large mural with "a group of beggars and the *Spedaliere* who receives them." Thus it was a scene of markedly realistic character. In contrast, the early Cinquecento for a similar occasion represented a biblical devotional theme, Christ as a pilgrim, in a chiaroscuro by the young Pontormo above the entrance to the former women's hospital near San Marco. Fra Bartolommeo had

[188] Vasari-Milanesi, 2:9. A nude ideal figure of Charity was painted by Castagno on the vicar's palace of Scarperia in Mugello (Magliabecchiano-Frey, *Il codice*, p. 99).

[189] See the documents in *RA*, October, 1901, and Luigi Passerini in *Curiosità storico-artistiche fiorentine* (Florence, 1866), 1:97.

[190] See Vasari-Milanesi, 3:238-39, 251; 4:55, 56; Fiocco (in *RA*, 1929, pp. 25ff.) associates Bicci's fresco with Masaccio's dedication procession for the church of the Carmine. He also refers to Bicci's painting of the portal tympanum and other reliefs by Dello Delli in Santa Maria Nuova.

treated the same subject a short time earlier in the Dominican hospice of Pian di Mugnone.[191]

Only a few more outdoor paintings on churches and convents from the beginning of the sixteenth century may be mentioned: the Annunciation fresco of 1510 on the Santissima Annunziata by Tommaso di Stefano and the lunette mosaic of the same period by Davide Ghirlandaio above the outer door of the atrium, as well as a fresco, almost completely destroyed today, by the young Pontormo above the central arch, the only one that existed at the time. This represented female allegorical figures and angels framing the sculptured arms of Pope Leo X (1514). Finally, two lunette paintings by Raffaellino del Garbo of the Madonna and the Pietà, dated 1503, were on the church of San Giorgio which was torn down in 1705.[192]

The renovation of the large fresco inside Porta Romana, the Madonna with three Florentine city saints, was carried out during this period by Franciabigio.

But the streets were also adorned with religious pictorial decoration of various types and subjects on the exteriors of private dwellings.

These took the form primarily of painted tabernacles representing by far the largest contingent of outdoor religious painting and appearing throughout all the districts of the city and beyond. Rather numerous examples may be seen today, most of them admittedly in damaged, barely visible or over-painted condition, particularly in quarters of the city which have not been too heavily modernized. Thus the survival of this type, at least, when so little or nothing at all is preserved of the others, makes it possible in some measure to envision the former wide diffusion and effect of mural showpieces in the Renaissance cityscape. We find many of these pious installations still serving their old devotional purpose and, as the little burning lamps or occasionally renewed bunches of flowers in front of them show, cared for today just as earlier by the folk piety of the neighborhood residents.

The sermons of St. Peter Martyr seem to have provided the first impetus to erect such street tabernacles. They appeared more frequently during times of plague in the mid-fourteenth century. And many examples have survived even for this period, thanks to the long-standing protective regulation of clerical and secular authorities.

The new interest in these simple monuments awakened by several local writers about thirty years ago resulted in the most valuable examples being protected by glass, which also made them much harder to see. The inventory it stimulated never got beyond occasional forays. Thus only approximate conclusions are possible concerning the number of tabernacles that once existed, even for those which were set up or renewed during the Renaissance century.[193]

The fifteenth and sixteenth centuries, in any case, found occasion and opportunity to add many new tabernacles to the already numerous ones from earlier times. And to these we may add the relief sculpture tabernacles, not customary before the fifteenth century, of which many survive today (see above).

Street corners were generally chosen as appropriate places for these small devotional images, preferably where streets opened out into a square. But outside the city walls, in the nearer and more distant environs of the city, many such tabernacles were set up at the entrance to estates or convents or at crossroads, sometimes even in the form of small field-chapels. City tabernacles usually took the form of a recessed or projecting niche, with sloping sides and pointed-arched, later semicircular tops. Inside, the Madonna usually appeared enthroned with saints or angels, often with a small portrait figure of the donor or donors.

In the following enumeration we present a selection of the reasonably well-preserved tabernacles or those recorded with the names of important artists in approximately chronological order, beginning with the early and mid-Quattrocento:

(1) A large tabernacle is on the corner of Piazza Santa Maria Novella and Via della Scala with a Madonna on a high throne attended by many figures, allegedly painted by Francesco Fiorentino around 1420 (see Salmi in RA, 1929, pp. 12ff.).

(2) A Madonna with two saints and a donor figure, ascribed by Vasari to Lorenzo di Bicci, is on the Canto della Cuculia at the corner of Via Serragli and Via Santa Monaca. The traditional date of 1427 is supported by slight Renaissance elements in the frame ornament more than by the painting itself (Vasari-Milanesi, 2:53; van Marle, Painting, 9:14).

(3) Not far from the one named above, behind Piazza del Carmine on the corner of Via de' Leoni, is a Madonna with two archangels of

---

[193] See Arnaldo Cocchi, Notizie storiche intorno antiche immagini di Nostra Donna . . . (Florence, 1894), pp. 109-46; Carocci in Arte e Storia, 1904, pp. 147ff.; Gerspach in Rassegna Nazionale, December 1904; Alessandro Chiappelli, Arte del rinascimento (Florence, 1926), p. 7f. Gerspach estimates the total number of surviving or otherwise traceable painted tabernacles of the thirteenth to eighteenth centuries at about five hundred. Chiappelli's survey in the oltr' Arno section cites around twenty examples of reasonably discernible and therefore datable works of the fifteenth century, plus a good half-dozen from the early Cinquecento. The distribution in other parts of the city at the same times may be imagined as similar.

around the mid-Quattrocento in a rich frame structure. It is in ruinous condition, but a rather high quality painting.

(4) A large chapel-type tabernacle attributed to Paolo di Stefano who was active about 1430-1450 is in Castello near Florence, with the Annunciation and two individual saints in a broad gabled field above a niche (Richard Offner, *Italian Primitives at Yale University*, New Haven, 1927, pl. 14H).

(5) A tabernacle Madonna seated on an elegant throne, with Sts. John the Baptist and Anthony Abbot, very well preserved and recently carefully cleaned, is in the narrow Via della Morte near the Campanile of the Duomo.

(6) A Madonna of similar character, thus also of about 1450, is in the "tabernacolo delle 5 lampade" on Via Ricasoli (near a half covered up older picture, allegedly by Buffalmacco).

(7) Vasari mentions several tabernacles by Neri di Bicci in and around the city (Vasari-Milanesi, 2:50, 53, 55). Only the one executed in 1453, at Campanuccia near Lastra a Signa, survives (van Marle, *Painting*, 10: 527-28). Another such field shrine that Vasari (Vasari-Milanesi, 2:680, n. 1) mentions as Castagno's work in l'Anchetta before the Porta alla Croce can no longer be found.

(8) On the other hand, a single work by an important master on this type of commission still exists, although alienated from Florentine possession. This is Domenico Veneziano's tabernacle Madonna with the Trinity appearing above in precipitous foreshortening, as well as two saints on the inner frame moldings, of about 1455. Once on the Canto de' Carnesecchi near Santa Maria Novella, it is now in the National Gallery in London (Vasari-Milanesi, 2:675; van Marle, *Painting*, 10: 319-21 with illustration; Pudelko in *MKIF*, 4, pp. 179-80).

Further examples from the late Quattrocento are the following:

(1) The most impressive and best preserved example is the niche tabernacle by the miniaturist Gherardo di Giovanni set up on the house at the corner of Via Cavour and Piazza San Marco which once belonged to his family. It contains a charming Madonna before a rich throne with two standing and two kneeling saints on each inner side of the niche frame (*AS*, 1904, p. 3); Vasari (Vasari-Milanesi, 3:238, 251) mentions yet another tabernacle, since almost completely destroyed, in front of Porta alla Croce, that was commissioned from the same painter in 1487 by the Compagnia del Bigallo.

(2) A still well-preserved tabernacle of the "Madonna della Tosse" by Benozzo Gozzoli from soon after 1484 is near Castelfiorentino (van Marle, *Painting*, 11:166, illustrated on p. 213).

(3) The large fresco of a Pietà recently attributed to Davide Ghirlandaio can be found in the chapel-like tabernacle of the Madonna del Cantone on the city wall (Torrione della Rosa) near Porta San Frediano. It survives from a small destroyed convent church (see, *Richa, Notizie*, 9: 136ff.; illustrated *JPK*, 1917, p. 47).

(4) The very badly preserved tabernacle on Via de' Preti, at the corner of Via Caldaie, is somewhat reminiscent of Filippino's style.

(5) Prato possesses a secure, well-preserved and important work of Filippino of 1498 in the magnificent tabernacle on the corner of Strada Santa Margherita: it contains the standing figure of the Madonna and two saints in each sloping side of the niche (for good illustration see van Marle, *Painting*, 12:333-35).

The employment of well-known masters on such commissions, among a multitude of mediocre colleagues, can be traced and recognized only in sporadic cases in the Quattrocento. But as the following list should indicate, almost all the important masters of the High Renaissance were also active in this province, at least according to literary evidence.

(1) Vasari names two tabernacle paintings by Franciabigio, one in Rovezzano, the other on the building of the congregation of San Giobbe behind the Annunziata (Vasari-Milanesi, 5:191, 193).

(2) The tabernacle at the entrance to Via de' Serragli on the far side of the bridge seemed especially praiseworthy to Vasari as an attractive and carefully executed composition by Raffaellino del Garbo. It was completely repainted in the eighteenth century (Vasari-Milanesi, 4:236).

(3) There were also at least two pertinent works by Andrea del Sarto. One was an Annunciation which Milanesi still could find, though it was half-faded, in the little street between Or San Michele and Mercato Nuovo.

(4) The other by Andrea del Sarto was a Madonna with the child John the Baptist on a street-corner before Porta Pinti. It was protected during the clearing of the glacis in 1529 on account of its beauty and still survived in Milanesi's time, about 1875; since then it has disappeared, though there is a partial copy in the Uffizi corridor. The Anonimo Magliabecchiano mentions, instead of this, another Madonna tabernacle by Andrea, not far from Porta San Gallo (perhaps identical with the one just cited). See Vasari-Milanesi, 5:14, 33; Fritz Knapp, *Andrea del Sarto* (Bielefeld, 1907), p. 49; Magliabecchiano-Frey, *Il codice*, p. 108; Bocchi-Cinelli, *Le bellezze della citta*, p. 482.

(5) Carocci attributes a tabernacle on Via dell' Agnolo to Andrea's school.

(6) Ridolfo del Ghirlandaio painted the tabernacle of the Madonna delle Rose on the corner of the Via Senese near the Certosa in 1519 and somewhat later a Madonna with two saints and the portraits of the house-owner's two small sons on the corner of a house near Santa Maria Novella (Vasari-Milanesi, 6:538-39, 541).

(7) The imposing and tolerably well-preserved tabernacle of 1526 with the Marriage of St. Catherine and the arms of the Compagnia del Bigallo that had commissioned it from Domenico Puligo is on the corner of Via San Zanobi and Via delle Ruote. It is related in subject to the nearby convent of Santa Caterina.

(8) According to Vasari, the young Pontormo also painted many crucifixes and other tabernacles in the environs of the city (Vasari-Milanesi, 4:467; 6:272).

Besides the numerous tabernacle paintings on residential buildings, the open family loggie sometimes afforded space and occasion for the application of publicly visible painting, though it admittedly merged only indirectly with the visual impression of the street. These loggie, whose construction was permitted at all only to a certain number of old patricians as a special prerogative, probably always received some sort of painted decoration. This becomes clear from a passage in the treatise *Del Governo della Famiglia*, now generally attributed to Alberti, in which the decoration of the loggia is recognized as an expenditure which if certainly not indispensable was nevertheless reasonable ("Agnolo Pandolfini," *Trattato del governo della famiglia*, Milan, 1802, p. 124). In the sole family loggia still extant today, that of the Rucellai, such wall paintings survived up to recent times; Crowe and Cavalcaselle still saw and described briefly scenes from the life of St. Benedict and Joseph in Egypt, in the chapter on the Peselli.[194]

In contrast to the abundance of outdoor painting of religious subjects and the variety of possible commissions for such work outlined above, secular wall painting in public squares and streets is almost astonishingly insignificant. It appeared only on occasions of public honor or defamation of particular personalities. The worthiest place for pictorial honorific monuments was considered not the exterior facade of any civic building, but rather the interior of the Cathedral, as shown above. There such monuments, occasionally tomb monuments executed in sculpture as well as wall paintings or large panel paintings, were continually erected or renewed by the state from the late Trecento through the beginning of the sixteenth century.

[194] J. A. Crowe and G. B. Cavalcaselle, *Geschichte der italienischen Malerei*, ed. M. Jordan, vols. 2-4 (Leipzig, 1869-1871), 3:96; the new Italian edition, 1894, 6:13, confirms the loss of the painting under modern whitewash. The interior of the portico-hall has since been completely blocked up.

The above mentioned fresco on the exterior of the Parte Guelfa palace was indeed occasioned by a secular-political event: the acquisition of Pisa. However, besides the portrait of the newly subjected city it did not show the *gonfaloniere* responsible for this state action, but rather the calendar saint for the appropriate date, St. Dionysus, suggesting that the acquisition was owed to his assistance.

On the other hand, we also have information on two secular wall paintings relevant here that were set up in subjugated cities on state commission: in Prato the memory of the deserving Podesta Pandolfo Petrucci was honored by the placement of his portrait by Fra Diamante, in a decorative frame and with a Latin inscription, under the loggia of the Palazzo Publico in 1470. In Pisa, however, in memory of the military expedition of Charles VIII of France, a true-to-life portrait of the King "quando raccomanda Pisa" was painted on the facade of the Duomo Opera, allegedly by Domenico Ghirlandaio, but in reality probably by one of his younger brothers.[195]

But in Florence itself, as a counterpart to the painted honorific monuments in the Duomo, there were only the derisive and ignominious pictures on the exterior of the hall of justice, the Bargello. Such pillorying in effigy was carried out here since early times and documented in individual cases since the beginning of the Trecento; in the beginning it was by no means limited to the Bargello wall. In 1415 an express prohibition was even placed on arbitrary application of such insulting pictures to private houses or even, for the most extreme disparagement, to bordellos.[196] The Signoria evidently wanted to reserve this particularly effective and enduring form of punishment to itself alone, as expiation for political crimes, high treason, or other offenses against the commonwealth.[197]

Skimming over earlier works, we cite only two examples from the early Renaissance and refer in particular to the occasions on which, after a coup d'état, a whole series of such defamatory portraits appeared on the exterior wall of the Bargello. The first in 1440, after the battle of Anghiari,

[195] Vasari-Milanesi, 3:628, 271 (Milanesi found the Pisan work, obliterated today, still in the specified place, admittedly in poor condition).

[196] Robert Davidsohn, *Geschichte von Florenz*, 4 vols. (Berlin, 1896-1927), 4:327f.; *Forschungen*, 4;3: 218, 221-22; Gino Masi, "La pittura infamante nella legislatura e nella vita," in *Studi di diritto commerciale in onore di Cesare Vivante*, ed. Alfredo Rocco et al., Rome, 1931; Luigi Passerini, *Curiosità storico-artistiche fiorentine*, Florence, 1866, 1:28f.

[197] In 1424, the portraits of the Condottiere N. Piccinino and other mercenaries were painted hanging by their feet on the Palazzo di Condotta, for disloyalty and embezzlement of state funds (Masi, "La pittura infamante . . . ," in *Studi di diritto commerciale . . .* , ed. Rocco et al., Rome, 1931, p. 22). In 1425 the dilatory debtor Ranuccio Farnese was stigmatized by such an ignominious portrait, which was later removed only after pressing complaints from the Pope (Gaye, *Carteggio*, 1:550).

were the portraits of the Albizzi and other heads of the group expelled by Cosimo de' Medici. The task was carried out, evidently very successfully, by Castagno, only eighteen years old at the time, and earned him the nickname "degli impiccati."[198] The next similar commission did not arise until forty years later, after the Pazzi conspiracy of 1478. At this time men who had in fact already been executed were still painted as a chilling example on the walls, this time not of the Bargello, but in the immediate neighborhood of their actual execution, on the Dogana behind the Palazzo Vecchio. And once again the task was assigned to a famous artist, already known for other works, who in our opinion was not particularly well suited to the assignment: Botticelli.[199]

At the very end of the republican period in 1529, there was a third project of the same type, the defamatory portrait of a personality pronounced a traitor to Florence, depicted hanging by his feet. The commission went to Andrea del Sarto, who did not disdain to execute at least the surviving, very realistic preliminary studies with his own hand, though he did by all means entrust a pupil with its execution on the wall.[200]

Lastly, the sgraffito facade decorations, almost exclusively or predominantly ornamental, remain to be mentioned. These were probably found rather often on the exteriors of places with simple plastered walls, as well as in the courtyards of important houses, as a substitute for sculptural-architectural articulation that was either lacking or all too meagre. A few fragmentary examples of the type have survived here and there.[201]

Many citizens demonstrated their joy at the election of the Medici pope, Leo X, in 1513 by the application of Medici arms to their houses: this was done in particularly splendid form, as already noted above, by Pontormo on the exterior portico of the Annunziata (Vasari-Milanesi,

[198] Vasari-Milanesi, 2:680, 864; Poggi in *RA*, 1929, pp. 49ff., in which the date of 1435, accepted earlier, is reported.

[199] He received forty florins "pro labore in pingendo proditores" (Horne, *Botticelli*, p. 350; Magliabecchiano-Frey, *Il codice*, pp. 105 and 359).

[200] Magliabecchiano-Frey, *Il codice*, p. 367; Vasari-Milanesi, 5:53-54, n. 1; Fritz Knapp, *Andrea del Sarto* (Bielefeld, 1907).

[201] Such are the faint remains in the court of the Palazzo Medici, by Maso di Bartolommeo in 1452, which have been recently somewhat touched up and the ones in the courtyard of Palazzo Vecchio (*JPK*, 25, suppl., p. 31). In addition, the spandrels in the arcades of the Renaissance cloister at Santa Croce were filled with putti and coats of arms around 1455.

Somewhat more interesting on account of the introduction of figural motifs of an antique character with scenes of Hercules and Cupid are the sgraffiti in the court of Palazzo Spinelli (Borgo Santa Croce no. 10) and its facade (Alinari photo 4572). Vasari names many facade decorations of this type from the early Cinquecento, which he atributes chiefly to Andrea Feltrini. One of the examples he mentions, the very rich facade decoration of Palazzo Sertini-Corsi on Via Corsi at the Pescioni corner is still partially preserved (Vasari-Milanesi, 5:206-207, 209; around 1520; details on the technique, Vasari-Milanesi, 1:192ff.; the Palazzo Corsi is published in a drawing in *ZBK*, 1881, pp. 369ff.).

6:247-48). Along with this there were the more popular, workman-like emblematic designs of painted signs for inns and the like; these were evidently occasional works in frequent demand from run-of-the-mill painting workshops, since the statute of the Siena painters' guild in 1367 gave the guild *camerlengo* control over assignment of commissions for them, with a fixed maximum rate (Gaye, *Carteggio*, 2:25).

# CHAPTER 4

# ARTISTIC PARTICIPATION
# IN THE STAGING OF
# PUBLIC FESTIVITIES
# AND SPECTACLES

A special section must be devoted here to the activity of artists in the arrangement and staging of all sorts of spectacles, festive processions, tournaments, dramatic performances, and the like. In this type of project the functions of all branches of art, architecture, decoration, painting, and sculpture are interwoven more closely and variously than elsewhere. These projects also were not confined to a fixed context such as the interior of churches or private houses or the free public space of squares and streets. They developed in all these places, although primarily in the last named.

Jacob Burckhardt took up the productions, whose Florentine circumstances will be considered more closely here, in the last chapter of his *Geschichte der Renaissance in Italien*. And there is also a special chapter in his *Kultur der Renaissance* on festivals, one of the few in this book in which art and artists are discussed in a more than cursory manner. "The Italian festival in its highest form is the true transition from life into art," he says here at the very beginning. We learn also that the Florentines already were famous and sought after since the fourteenth century as the best *festaiuoli* for the staging of any kind of public production. The secular stage presentations of the Renaissance developed out of and alongside the old religious mysteries, as is well known. Festive processions, too, with representations of antique or medieval allegorical subjects, may be regarded as a secular, Renaissance offshoot from church processions, but they had their origins in carnival festivities precisely in the context of the religious year, with an eye to the approaching period of Lent. Thus here also we find the same intimate correlation between the elements of secular and spiritual life that we have already repeatedly noticed in other connections.

Various occasions for such productions arose in the course of a year. In the first place came the feast day of the city patron and patron of the Baptistery, Saint John, celebrated on June 24 and the preceding day with totally extraordinary pageantry.

In his biography of the architect and decorator Cecca (1447-1488) Vasari describes the unusual apparatus for the festive procession on the eve of San Giovanni from his own recollections and those of older informants. The extremely lavish production probably diminished greatly in the postrepublican period, yet the old ceremonies continued to take place at a circumscribed level until their complete abolition in 1807.[1] Thus we read in Vasari how the whole square of the Baptistery was covered over with a gigantic blue canvas awning decorated with sewn-on coats of arms and pennants with guild emblems and the like hanging all around it. The report called special attention to the so-called *nuvoli* in the procession, that is, the large decoratively painted wooden structures set up by the various confraternities, each carried by a troop of strong men hidden underneath. On these structures, in the midst of hemp cloud balls, the patron of each confraternity would appear, represented by live costumed men as well as a few child angels who were attached to revolving iron poles, sometimes in rows one above the other. Other groups showed the martyrdom of a saint, also represented by a living performer or, since the secular, fantastic element was not lacking here either, individual male and female *gigantic* played by people walking on stilts with giant masks and curious draperies. Finally there was the consecration of candle wax for use on the altar in the form of colossal candles decorated with primitive ornamental painting.

Decorative painting and carving tasks of a higher order were provided in particular by the decorated carts that came into use more and more in the late Quattrocento instead of the carried platforms that were difficult to move. The number of such carts had allegedly already risen to twenty-two before Lorenzo Magnifico's time, but was then limited to ten at most. They carried with them the so-called *edifizi*, that is, sculptured and painted models of the subject cities and small castles of the Florentine dominion. Thus these places expressed their obligatory homage on these principal feast days of the city and at the same time made their imposed contribution of candle wax for the titular church of San Giovanni.

The wax thus offered in kind for altar candles might admittedly be used only partially for divine services there. Most of it was converted back into money and entered the construction funds of the Baptistery, representing a fixed item of annual income in its budget. But it is characteristic of the contemporary concept of the value of currency as well as the manner of sculptural symbolic expression of the period that these annual tributes to the Baptistery should be offered not in cash but in

[1] Vasari-Milanesi, 3:199-203; Cesare Guasti, *Le Feste di S. Giovanni Battista in Firenze* ... (Florence, 1884); Pietro Gori, *Le Feste Fiorentine* ... (Florence, 1925), vol. 1; Alessandro d'Ancona, *Origini del Teatro in Italia*, 2nd ed. (Turin, 1891), 1:230ff.

kind, and solemnly and festively, in the visible form of such gigantic decorative candles.[2]

The Cinquecento, with its more refined taste, seems more and more to have given up the realism, probably somewhat coarse, of the "living pictures" of religious subjects.[3] Therefore the processional carts themselves received extensive pictorial decoration in chiaroscuro painting. Andrea del Sarto and Franciabigio were hired to execute some of these in 1516. Vasari names the Carro della Moneta, arranged by the board of the city mint, as an especially splendid example of this type. It was originally produced by the above mentioned Cecca together with Marco del Tasso, and enriched in its later remodelling with inset paintings by the young Pontormo. Only these four large and fourteen small decorative paintings were saved when the old wagon was destroyed in 1810, and they still exist in the possession of the city government.[4]

A single survivor of those rolling showpieces of the St. John's procession still persists in the custom, going back at least to the early Quattrocento, of the firework cart set up in front of the Cathedral on Holy Saturday. With the famous spectacle of the *scoppio del carro*, it intervenes in the liturgy of the festival high mass, making dramatically visible the joy of Easter that arrives with the moment of consecration. The preparation of the cart was until the Pazzi conspiracy an old privilege of that family, passing subsequently to the Parte Guelfa. The elegant fuse-holder

---

[2] A contemporary depiction of these brightly painted *ceri*, the immense brocade *palie* or *gonfaloni* carried by riders, and the linen tent with colorful coats of arms spread above it appears in a cassone painting of about 1430 in the Bargello. Other showpieces of the St. John's day procession can be imagined based on *trionfi* depictions on other chests. See also the later representation in a fresco by Vasari (*RA*, 1910, plate at p. 42).

See Weisbach, *Trionfi*, p. 15; for further comparison see the illustration of Goro Dati's festival (1428), Matteo Palmieri (1454) and others in Guasti, *Le Feste Fiorentine . . .* (Florence, 1925). See also *RA*, 1905, pp. 128-29, relevant collaboration of Neri di Bicci on the *edifizi* set up by Giuliano da Maiano for 1461; a very detailed illustration of 1475 is published in *RA*, 1909, p. 194. In Masi's *Ricordanze*, p. 141, is an eyewitness account of 1514, which also mentions the dues levelled on all the tradesmen to defray the costs of the festival. Various of the first-hand reports cited are translated in Landucci-Herzfeld, *Tagebuch*, p. 38-39, n. 1, 74-75, n. 3.

[3] Disturbing incidents that could sometimes occur during such presentations must also have encouraged their abolition. According to Giovanni Cambi (*Delizie*, 21:164), the person portraying Judith in the procession of 1500 had the misfortune to stumble and wound the city herald with his sword when he bowed to the Signoria assembled in front of the Palazzo Vecchio, which was generally seen as an evil portent.

[4] Vasari-Milanesi, 5:21, 195; 6:257, n. 1. As a German counterpart from the same period we have the *Triumphal Procession of Maximilian*, although this appeared only on paper, in the woodcuts of Burckmair and his associates; here also the richly adorned wagons with their crew occupy considerable space; the models in concept and form were the real and pictorial *trionfi* of Italy, for Germany certainly still had nothing of the kind.

of the *carro*, probably newly produced at that time, is still kept in their palace (see above).

The feast of John the Baptist was an occasion that had its origins in concerns of the church. Nevertheless, as the principal feast of the city patron, it developed more and more into a civic and political day of honor to the Republic of Florence. The homage of subject cities in the procession was directed at least as much to the ruling city as to the saint of the day. It could also happen that in the context of the festive procession, along with the representation of the principal scenes from the sacred teachings and along with the patron saints of the confraternities, the bizarre "giants" might also appear and also, at the high point of humanistic enthusiasm for the antique, the idea of the Roman triumph which had already come forward on other occasions gained admittance to the St. John's day procession. In Lorenzo Magnifico's time four triumphal groups of ancient Roman emperors marched among the portrayals of biblical and local political figures.[5]

Above all, however, it was the carnival festivities, with their markedly secular, sensually joyful mood, that offered artists fruitful occasions to devise and arrange the most diverse productions, sometimes highly fanciful and ostentatiously magnificent.

Much of this sort was already undertaken in the early and mid-Quattrocento. The carnival procession achieved its most colorful development, however, in the time of Lorenzo Magnifico. And it is known that Lorenzo himself contributed poems for the songs performed by roving bands of Mardi Gras singers, the Canti Carnascialeschi. The often cited "Quant'e bella giovinezza" is the refrain of one such song whose further content concerned the love of Bacchus and Ariadne and thus must have been composed for a carnival group that was representing this theme. Motifs from antique mythology and *trionfi* from ancient Roman history probably also provided the most popular material for Mardi Gras costumes. Lorenzo Magnifico had a Triumph of Aemilius Paullus produced in 1491. It was perhaps for this occasion, as well as for many others, that Filippino Lippi, according to Vasari's very credible report (Vasari-Milanesi, 3:476), exercised his ingenuity.

The costumes of his figures, often so particolored and unusual, like those in the Strozzi chapel frescoes, suggest even without Vasari's reference that Filippino was an artist with a particular talent for such tasks. We might in general most readily imagine all the customs of carnival staging of this period with the help of Filippino's artistic style or that of Piero di Cosimo. Vasari also testifies to the latter's frequent collaboration

[5] Granacci staged a Triumph of Camillus for the feast of St. John in 1514. (See Weisbach, *Trionfi*, p. 15; Vasari-Milanesi, 5:341, n. 2.)

on such performances, which is easy to imagine from his artistic behavior, especially in small secular paintings.[6]

One can perhaps best visualize the appearance of the carnival show-pieces of the High Renaissance with the help of the antique scenes in the frescoes of Sarto, Franciabigio, and Pontormo at Poggio a Caiano.

Between these annually recurring presentations, originally of eccle-siastical significance, street spectacles of a purely worldly character also took place on special occasions, for example, the celebrations to greet princes and popes on their arrival. It is true that in such cases the Flor-entines themselves only had to arrange for the retinue paying homage to the entering potentate; but instead of diverse and fantastic costumes, both sides arranged rather for uniform, sometimes colorful and costly festive costumes for each individual group of marchers. The chief task calling on the imagination of artists, however, was to carry out the most impressive possible decoration of the streets and squares through which the procession was to pass. And this especially meant the construction of magnificent showpieces and surprises throughout the city, namely large wooden triumphal gateways and other decorative illusionistic architec-ture. Even painters and sculptors of stature were called on to prepare these.

Much of this sort was already undertaken in the late Quattrocento: for the visit of Pope Pius II in 1460, for the festive reception of Galeazzo M. Sforza, Duke of Milan, in 1471, and even on the visit, so little wel-come, of the conqueror Charles VIII of France in 1494.[7]

But all the foregoing was far surpassed by the decorations Florence produced for the entry of the Medici Pope Leo X in November, 1515. The Pope's first visit to his maternal city after the ten-year proscription of his family was certainly sufficient occasion for an extraordinarily lavish production. Vasari, Landucci's diary, and other sources provide detailed information on this and on the participation of major artists in the work.[8]

---

[6] See Vasari-Milanesi, 4:134-37, for the detailed description of the Triumph of Death prepared by Piero di Cosimo for the carnival of 1511, with a large entourage on foot and horseback in outfits conveying appropriate significance. Besides Granacci's work on the Triumph of Camillus (see above), Vasari reports on Pontormo's and Andrea del Sarto's arrangement of a carnival wagon dispatched by two social companies of young aristocrats in 1513-1515, bearing allegorical representations and triumphal groups of antique heroes (see Vasari-Milanesi, 6:250-55).

[7] On the decoration of the Palazzo Medici by Verrocchio and others in 1471 see *ASA*, 1895, pp. 167, 176 (see also *RA*, 1909, p. 74). Landucci-Herzfeld (*Tagebuch*, pp. 114-15) describes the street decorations and festivities of 1494; ibid., Italian edition, p. 337: the festivities occasioned by Pope Leo X's election, which included among other things such demonstrative ceremonies as the burning of War, Dissension, and Fear.

[8] Vasari-Milanesi, 5:24-25, 595; 6:255; 7:494-95; Landucci, *Diario*, pp. 352-59; Masi, *Ricordanze*, pp. 162-76, 181-82.

No less than twelve triumphal arches and several other decorative structures of antique character were erected along the extensive parade route
from Porta Romana to the Cathedral, and from there to the papal quarters
at Santa Maria Novella. While it is true that everything was only dummies
made of wood and other surrogate material, the best talents among
Florentine artists were employed to design this architecture, as well as
for its rich adornment with decorative painting, reliefs simulated in paint,
and even some real sculpture in clay or stucco. The governing idea was
a sort of reconstruction of ancient imperial Rome that Florence, according
to the taste of the period, wanted to offer the Pope as a splendid setting
for his Via Triumphalis. The most grandiose showpiece, however, was
the facade constructed in wood, stucco, and paint across the whole front
of the Duomo that was furnished with decorative sculpture by Jacopo
Sansovino and with large, painted imitation reliefs by Andrea del Sarto.
It followed a design which according to Vasari went back to the model
Lorenzo Magnifico had submitted to the contest in 1491. Besides this,
Sansovino had set up a full-size, free copy of the Roman statue of Marcus
Aurelius in the square in front of Santa Maria Novella. The "Trajan's
Column" in the mercato was the work of Baccio Bandinelli, as was the
whole, particularly splendid decoration of Via della Scala near the papal
residence and a colossal statue of Hercules positioned as a temporary
counterpart to Michelangelo's *David* opposite in the Loggia dei Lanzi.
Granacci, Perino del Vaga, Rosso, and Pontormo worked along with
other, less famous people on the painted decoration of the various triumphal arches. Extensive decorations were also set up in the interiors of a
few churches, where their construction necessitated a temporary removal
of services.[9] Yet the cost to the state for conjuring up all this ephemeral
splendor amounted, since only cheap surrogate materials were used, to
no more than 5000 florins.[10]

[9] Something similar had already been undertaken during an earlier papal visit (Pius II,
1460); see the contemporary illustration of arrangements for this after a manuscript in the
Biblioteca Magliabecchiana in Script. Rer. Ital. II:719-52. [*Translator's note:* It has proved
impossible to trace this publication under a title corresponding to the author's abbreviation.
The reference could be to one of the numerous volumes of *Rerum Italicarum Scriptores*
edited by Lodovico Antonio Muratori.]

[10] As a reward, the pope granted the Signoria the long-sought privilege of providing their
most important state acts with the lead seal, like Vatican briefs, and also a sword of honor
and a biretta for the *gonfaloniere* (Del Badia, MF, 1, p. 50).

Many paintings of evident value from the triumphal decoration of the city, soon removed,
were probably saved for a while. Vasari, for instance, singles out for special praise a
decorative piece of Pallas with the lyre of Apollo by Pontormo from the triumphal arch
in front of the Badia. The only presumed remnants of the festive decoration of 1515 still
existing today are a few large chiaroscuro paintings of secular subjects on canvas, in the
style of Sarto and the young Pontormo, in the print room of the Uffizi (published by Giglioli,
*l'Arte*, 29, pp. 261-66).

Along with such monumental decorative works, here as in other festive processions, the provision of costumes for the participants provided a wide scope for developing fantasies in visual form. For all special cases, as has already been noted several times, designs were sought from artists; in addition, the professional skills of the tailor and embroiderer and not least the personal taste in color and ornament of individual clients might exercise their effect on a festival costume. On the whole, we must take into consideration, as the foundation for artistic invention, the general taste in forms and colors of the contemporary population and the delight in color and elegant, rich ornament that so strongly and peculiarly marked the Quattrocento in particular.[11] Much of this also appears already in the diverse habits of the orders and the varied regalia of rank and office, whose style and selection of colors must have enlivened the everyday appearance of the streets in so eloquent and distinctive a manner. The most impressive of these included the red velvet and violet official robes in whose solemn splendor the *gonfaloniere* and signori appeared in public.[12]

The finery worn for display by individual contenders and their entourage in the tournaments even surpassed these everyday costumes. It was enriched with all sorts of heraldic and other emblems, often with truly fantastic ostentation.[13]

We can form an approximate idea of them from a chest painting of about 1440-1450 in the New Haven Museum. Most striking here is a large standard with figural decoration, while further display remained somewhat restrained.[14]

But the heightened and finally exaggerated ostentation that gained ascendancy in all fields in the second half of the Quattrocento probably asserted itself prominently for the first time in this field in the tournament of 1469. It is true that there is no pictorial record of this *giostra*, in which Piero de' Medici gave his nineteen-year-old son Lorenzo, later the Mag-

---

[11] One example among many are the festival costumes in the cassone picture of the so-called Adimari wedding (Academy, see above), and approximately contemporary with it, the statement and settlement concerning the preparation of a splendid jacket for Lena Castellani around 1448-1450, with all sorts of gold and pearl embroidery in the form of flowering branches and other ornaments, executed by the embroiderer-artist Giovanni Gilberti (*RA*, 1906, pp. 148-54).

[12] See del Badia in *Miscellanea fiorentina*, 1, p. 44.

[13] Sometimes the city government staged these battle-games, perhaps on the occasion of a princely visit, such as Pius II's presence in 1460, but also annually to commemorate the acquisition of Pisa (1406). For this the Parte Guelfa, entrusted with the arrangements, could claim a subsidy from communal funds (del Badia, *Miscellanea fiorentina*, 1, pp. 119-20; 2, pp. 137-38). Yet such tournaments could also result from the private initiative of individual members of the patriciate. As a rule they were held in Piazza Santa Croce.

[14] Offner, *Italian Primitives at Yale University* (New Haven, 1927).

nifico, a splendid debut. But an eyewitness left a very thorough report which noted the costumes and equipment with special interest. A few examples from these *ricordi* will be given here.[15]

The young Lorenzo himself, as the official organizer of the chivalric encounter in which twelve other members of prominent families took part, appeared with a suite comprised of a whole troop of trumpeters, pages, and allied comrades-in-arms, in a beret embroidered with precious pearls and a half-cuirass with a sash also embroidered with pearls, on which the device *"le temps revient"* was embroidered in a frame of blooming and faded roses. Rich pearls also adorned the red and white caparison of his horse and his shield-cover which, slipped off before the battle, revealed the shield itself painted with the French lilies. Of greater artistic interest, however, was the large standard with emblematic figural decoration, carried by a page: a lady in costly garments standing under a laurel tree with partly dry, partly green branches, from which she was weaving boughs into a garland; individual laurel leaves fluttered over the whole surface of the picture, on whose borders the sun and rainbow appeared.

The other warriors naturally also displayed such allegorizing images, permeated with devices and imprese, on their standards, pages' costumes, horse livery, etc. Thus, for example, the son of Luca Pitti had on his banner a standing woman in red damask garments, plucking the wing feathers from a child cupid, and above them a great golden sun spreading its rays over the whole picture field. The records note that Jacopo Bracciolini, son of the chancellor Poggio, had a black velvet horse-caparison with five hydra figures in pearl embroidery. A Milanese guest from the house of Borromei held his own among the Florentines well enough with the long, flowing cover of his horse whose crimson velvet was richly embroidered with a densely entwined garland of pearls enlivened with birds (a total of twelve pounds of ordinary pearls, not including certain larger examples) and, in between, orange blossoms and fruits of chased silver foil, seventeen hundred in number.

The goldsmiths thus also had to provide all sorts of ornamental furnishings for these knightly games; in particular the ornamental and honorific silver helmets, on which the emblems of individual combatants, represented so extensively on the banner images, must reappear in sculpture in the round. Then there was the relief decoration for their horse harnesses, which was designed not only to protect the animals, but equally

---

[15] Manuscript in the Magliabecchiana, published by Tanfani in the journal *Il Borghini*, 1864, pp. 475ff., 530ff.; a subsequent description is in Reumont, *Lorenzo de' Medici*, 1:267-68.

for the costly and splendid adornment of the riders.[16] Of these pieces of armor, not one has survived; but possibly a few tournament shields with sculptured and painted decoration have; in particular the large wooden shield painted with a David by Castagno in Philadelphia. A few simpler ones are in the Bardini Museum (*Dedalo*, 4, pp. 174ff.). Many designs for standards came from artists like Verrocchio and Botticelli. The preparatory sketch for one such, a reclining Venus with Cupid in a triangular field, by Verrocchio or the young Leonardo, can be found among the drawings in the Uffizi collection.[17]

We shall not go any further here into other matters such as the *armeggerie*, that is, the serenades and processions to pay homage, arranged at great expense by prominent cavaliers in front of the houses of their ladies, or the semipublic wedding festivities celebrated among the merchant aristocracy.[18]

Only a few references from other sources may be given here concerning artists' collaboration on the furnishings for dramatic productions of spiritual or secular character.

In particular it is a matter of certain ecclesiastical *rappresentazioni*, that is, scenic performances of mysteries from sacred history which were presented in certain churches according to old custom, at least since the

[16] The young Lorenzo's helmet ornament in 1469 was a silver figure of Mars; Verrocchio devised a decorated helmet for Giuliano de' Medici for the tourney of 1475, crowned with the elegant statuette of a lady (Fabroni, *Vita Laurentii*, 2:40-41; *ASA*, 8, 1895, p. 167). See also the honorific helmets of meritorious generals, above.

The harness of Giuliano's horse in 1475 had a golden lion mask on the breast, dragon figures on the throat guards and sidepieces; Bernardo Salutati, however, had a horse harness made by Antonio Pollaiuolo, also with a lion head, and besides this, ten small pictures in relief, and enamel ornaments. Documentation on this is in *Rass. A.*, 1918, pp. 213-14; *ASA*, 8, 1895, pp. 167, 172.

[17] Illustrated in Adolfo Venturi, *Storia dell' Arte Italiana*, 20 vols. (Milan and Rome, 1901-1940), 9:1, p. 51. Documents testify that Verrocchio designed a standard for Lorenzo as well as for Giuliano de Medici; the same is true of Botticelli's design for a Pallas standard for Lorenzo, 1475 (*ASA*, 8, 1895, pp. 171ff.; Poggi in *l'Arte*, 5, pp. 71ff.; Aby Warburg, *Sandro Botticellis "Geburt der Venus" und "Frühling,"* Hamburg, 1893, pp. 18-21; Horne, *Botticelli*, pp. 156-57, 354).

[18] See the detailed contemporary description of the *armeggeria* that a Benci arranged in honor of his lady friend, the beautiful Marietta Strozzi (1464), published in *Il Borghini*, 2, pp. 542ff.; in a brief extract in Reumont, *Lorenzo de' Medici*, 2:436-37. Several Florentine patricians offered another *armeggeria di notte* to Pope Pius II during his visit to Florence, 1460 (see P. Gori, *Firenze Magnifica*, 82ff. [*Translator's note*: This work has proved impossible to trace under the title given here]). The detailed description of the wedding festivities for Bernardo Rucellai and a daughter of Piero de' Medici in 1466 is in Giovanni Marcotti, *Un mercante fiorentino e la sua famiglia nel secolo XV* (Florence, 1881, pp. 82-92). On the extravagant luxury for other brides see various references in Strozzi-Guasti, *Lettere*, pp. 5-6, 15, 19-20, 548-49, 575; also Landucci, *Diario*, pp. 6-7.

Trecento, each on the appropriate feast day. And these were the Ascension of Christ in the Carmine, the Pentecost in Santo Spirito, the Annunciation in San Felice in Piazza, the legend of St. Bartholomew in Santa Croce, and that of St. Ignatius of Antioch in Santa Maria Novella. For these, the determined sense of realism of the early Renaissance evidently demanded the most concrete possible realization of the mystery play. Both the engineering technique of the architects—for the construction of movable machinery—and the newly won illusionistic art of the painters were called into service.

Thus Brunelleschi is supposed to have first invented and built the ingenious mechanism in San Felice that made possible a representation of the vault of heaven with live child angels revolving in it and the angel of the Annunciation hovering suspended from it. It was described in detail by a chronicler of the period of the Florentine council in 1438 and by Vasari according to old accounts; while Masolino (according to documentary evidence) produced the cloud scenery for the Ascension in the Carmine in 1425. For the same church, and probably also for the play of St. Ignatius in Santa Maria Novella, the engineer Cecca later, about 1480, produced a scenic apparatus surpassing even Brunelleschi's stage machinery.[19]

Secular dramas with supposedly antique content seem to have been produced in Florence, where the cited religious plays had drawn since early times on the efforts of all talents and interests, only at the beginning of the sixteenth century. We know, without details, of one stage set that Franciabigio furnished for a performance at the wedding feast of the young duke Lorenzo de' Medici and of works by Granacci and Ridolfo Ghirlandaio for similar occasions.[20]

The whole general category of problems posed and the various categories of projects that we have traversed in the preceding chapter find a significant culmination and synthesis in the projects for festivals. For

[19] See Davidsohn, Forschungen, 4:3, pp. 298-99; ZBK, 1919, pp. 11ff., in which Fischel (without information on his source) publishes in translation the detailed eyewitness report of an oriental bishop and conciliar visitor on the spectacle of the Annunciation mystery, and alludes to the closely corresponding painted decoration of Michelozzo's Portinari chapel in Milan as a supposed free copy of that theatrical production; Vasari-Milanesi, 2:375-78; 3:197-98; Jacques Mesnil, Masaccio et les débuts de la Renaissance, The Hague, 1927, p. 60, n. 2; Landucci-Herzfeld, Tagebuch, p. 120; Vasari-Milanesi, 3:197; Richa, Notizie, 3:41-42.

Certain of the religious confraternities probably also staged smaller productions of religious mystery plays. Thus the Compagnia dei Tre Magi produced an Epiphany play, for which Michelozzo was called on to make arrangements in the year 1446 (JPK, 25, suppl., pp. 39, 52, 93-94).

[20] Aristotile da Sangallo, together with Andrea del Sarto, painted decorations for Machiavelli's Mandragola and another comedy that was staged by one of the social clubs of young patricians (Vasari-Milanesi, 5:195, 341; 6:437-38, 541-42).

almost all the observations of a general character that arose here and there in the earlier chapters can be found here somehow confirmed in a more concentrated form or more sharply emphasized. These included the peculiar interplay of the religious and worldly spheres of life in the feast of John the Baptist and the carnival processions, in which Christian-Catholic and pagan-antique representations mingle without the slightest constraint on the level of a fundamental, insatiable craving for display arising from the general demand for the most visually striking, colorful, and formally rich portrayal of intellectual concepts, both religious and secular.

Furthermore, it is precisely here that the mingling of late medieval traditions with elements of the young civilization of the Renaissance becomes particularly evident. On the one hand, a new kind of realism became desirable and possible in the apparatus for mystery plays and their traditional biblical or legendary subject matter, as well as for the spectacles of particular groups in the St. John's day procession. The new demand for actuality, characteristic of the Renaissance, brought to these a previously unknown vigorous realism and tangibility. Consider, for example, the directness, so naive and crude for our taste, of the movable theater machinery for the productions in San Felice and the Carmine, and the special effects, as in the *nuvoli* of the St. John's procession, of the living figures of saints and angels installed in these!

Along with this, the tournaments brought forth that whole panoply of strange emblems in which the world of courtly ideas of the Franco-Burgundian culture of the fourteenth century, a model far distant by that time, had its last flowering. At the same time, classical antique imagery intervened everywhere even in this context.

Finally there is the boundless luxury that was unfurled in particular in the tourney parades, that splendor of pearl embroidery, costly cloth, and wrought silver ornaments. It is true that such material lavishness was counterbalanced and ennobled here, on the one hand, by the no less high standard of artistic fantasy and formal selectivity—thanks to the collaboration of some famous artists—and, on the other hand, by the addition of well-contrived intellectual seasoning and significance to the general allegorical, emblematic, or even antique-humanistic elements that were interwoven everywhere.

Yet along with this, the works invented and erected for San Giovanni and carnival and the sham buildings for the entrances of princely guests were no less lavish, in particular considering the purely ephemeral lifespan of these things.

All this would seem to establish that here, both in tournament finery and in the other displays described in this chapter, there is a perfectly obvious initiative, desire, and ability to spend on the part of the organizers, the veritable *primum agens*, be they individuals or societies or the city government itself.

From this, and more generally from the passionate desire for spectacle in the whole contemporary society, the ideas and more precise conceptions for these presentations first grew. Here also the readiness to realize a plan in one form or another must have been a given factor in order for the whole undertaking even to be considered and actually staged.

In any case, the fact that artistic skills were thereupon called on to develop and carry out the plans for a representation justifies the inclusion of these works, even if they have perished almost without exception, in a total overview of the character of Florentine art at the time. But in their planning and general arrangement, a major share, just now stressed, falls first of all to the organizers and supporters of these festivities, before the intervention of the artist; this circumstance, also apparent in almost all other fields of artistic activity, even if not always to such a far-reaching extent, may thus in conclusion suggest the necessity of turning our attention in the second main section of our presentation to this fundamental and primary component of the whole genesis of artistic activity, the patrons and customers, as the first and essential stimuli for artistic production.

# PART II
## *The Patrons*

CHAPTER 5

# THE CITY GOVERNMENT
# AND THE GUILDS

The tasks, occasions, and possibilities for artistic activity considered in the preceding section actually became effective, in each individual case, only through the intervention of that agent who commissioned an artist to work on such a task and was in a position to finance its execution. Thus the impetus for the creation of the art work and the material means for its realization came almost without exception from the patron, the donor, or commissioner. Accordingly, following an apt analogy of Georg Lills', in the biology of artistic events, the service of generative paternity falls to the patron. The "maternal" operation of the artist in the conception, internal maturation, and delivery of the work, can only subsequently go into action on the basis of this.[1]

This indubitable primary component of artistic life will be brought under closer scrutiny in this section. We shall survey the whole group of patrons in its extent and classification from the great public-state bodies and the secular or spiritual corporations down to the petty bourgeois individual customers who, alongside the aristocratic, exacting upper class, made up the broad substratum of private demand for art. Thus the special interests, motives, and needs, the tendencies of sentiment and taste of the different circles, their attitude toward the artists, etc., will also be examined. The final result of this should be an appreciation of the general artistic sense of the epoch, which in its gradual variations, its positive and negative characteristics, represents an accompanying phenomenon parallel to the formal change in style.

The commissioners of the ecclesiastical projects and enterprises still greatly predominating throughout the fifteenth century were by no means, as today, the church officials themselves or the members of the orders or some other official representatives of the religious community. The initiative, the financial backing for such plans, the selection and super-

[1] Not without reason do we find the artist's name lacking in inscriptions on many monuments of architecture, sculpture, painting, and the minor arts; or else with it, as a rule, also the "father's name," the *fieri fecit* of the first, essential, if only indirect author, the initiator and donor of the artistic creation.

In Fra Filippo Lippi's great *Coronation of the Virgin*, the portrait figure with the inscription band "is perfect opus" represents by no means, as is most often assumed, the artist, but rather the donor of the altarpiece (see *l'Arte*, 1912, p. 497).

vision of the executing artist, and all the rest rather lay fully and securely in the hands of citizen solicitors.

These are, on one hand, the great, rich guilds, as for the Duomo and other principal churches, and along with them various smaller societies, religious confraternities, and the like. Above all, however, they are the many private donors of individual pictures, altars, chapels, and large sections of the buildings of churches and convents. What thus came into being was produced first of all with intentions involving religious devotional merit; also, however, with thought to the personal reputation augmented by such donations, to the prestige of a family or corporation, as well as to the honor and adornment of the whole city of Florence.

We begin our survey of the individual categories of patrons with the civic authorities and the great guilds that indeed, through their delegations, made up an essential component of the general republican organization and city regime of Florence.

Much information about artistic commissions at the highest point of the city hierarchy, the Signori and their *gonfaloniere*, could be found precisely in the history of their own residence, the Palazzo Vecchio. The active interest of these organs is perceptible also for the Duomo and Baptistery and in a smaller measure for the other famous churches of the city. The attitude that architectural and other embellishment of public buildings will contribute "ad honorem et magnificentiam" of the whole city can be found repeatedly stressed in many relevant decrees of the city government from the thirteenth century on.

This attitude worked to the benefit of the monastic foundations, for example, in repeated and sometimes continuous city architectural subsidies. It is true that the government also obtained the right to control the planning and execution of such buildings and to place on them its arms as donor.[2]

The Operai of the two great guilds also cared for the Duomo building and Baptistery, dealing indirectly in the name of the Signoria and the Commune, hence that small share from all inheritances for the Duomo construction fund legally required in Florence (see above). The coat of arms of the city and the commune—a lily and a red cross—on conspicuous parts of the Duomo, besides the Lamb of God seal of the Arte della Lana, really means more than a decorative emblem; they are essentially a symbol of sovereignty and an honorable reminder of the donor role of the bearer of the arms. The monumental furnishing of the exterior of Or San Michele with the fourteen statues of guild patron saints (see below) occurred only

[2] Note the imposition of a special tax for four years for the reconstruction of Santo Spirito after the fire of 1471 (*RA*, 1931, p. 484). Considerable donations were made for the extension of the Santa Croce convent, still before 1420, and later for the restoration of the Annalena convent in 1511 (Richa, *Notizie*, 10:162), etc.

as a result of an express demand, several times repeated, from the city government, which moreover created a collegiate foundation at this church, in order to make sure of a regular and solemnly celebrated religious service at that place (Richa, *Notizie*, 1:24-25). With an eye to the civic duty of representation, however, the great annex of the Sala del Papa at Santa Maria Novella was erected, with its own chapel and access by an outside staircase, over which the Florentine heraldic animal, the *marzocco*, kept watch (see above).

It is true that money for fixed construction plans of the commune was frequently forfeited to some more pressing necessity and even that the city government as trustee of privately donated capital decided to expend the money illegally for military purposes.[3]

It was shown above how the highest city authorities concerned themselves over the artistic enrichment and equipment of their own residential palace. Noteworthy also is the diplomatic use made of certain art works already in the city's possession or produced ad hoc as gifts to the French king or his plenipotentiaries.[4]

Unless the Signoria alone or the directors of works of the Palazzo Vecchio were responsible, the decision on all important artistic matters resulted from the deliberation and decree of the Great Council. Sometimes the opinions of all citizens with any kind of interest or else the vote of a commission of experts were also sought.[5] Occasionally we also come across state protection of certain artists through safe-conduct letters or

[3] This is what happened, for example, in the case of the centralized building of the Angeli, founded by Pippo Spanno and begun according to Brunelleschi's design, and with Niccolò da Uzzano's Sapienza building (Vasari-Milanesi, 2:54-55, 372). Also in the case of the erection of the domed rotunda of the Annunziata (1451-1477), paid for by the Marquess of Mantua on the credit of a debt owed him by the Signoria, there often occurred pauses of several years as a result of the city treasury's difficulty in paying (Gaye, *Carteggio*, 1:225; more details below).

[4] In 1499 the Signoria sent to the Maréchal Pierre de Rohan nine antique busts formerly in Medici possession, which Leonardo del Tasso still had to fix up a little. On the express wish of the same demanding courtier they commissioned a bronze David statue from Michelangelo in 1502, which was sent to France in 1508 where it vanished (Vasari-Milanesi, 2:349; Henry Thode, *Michelangelo und das Ende der Renaissance. Kritische Untersuchungen über seine Werke,* 6 vols., Berlin, 1902-1913, 1:84ff.). A later envoy of the French crown, Jacques Hurault, Bishop of Autun, received in 1512, besides other presentations, the great recently-made altarpiece by Fra Bartolommeo (*Marriage of St. Catherine*) in San Marco, which the Signoria had to buy from the monks for 200 florins. The painting later found its way from the Cathedral of Autun to the Louvre (Vasari-Milanesi, 4:184, n. 2; Landucci, *Diario*, p. 315).

[5] In the contest for the Forteguerri tomb monument in Pistoia of 1476 the local great council made a decision first, but then afterwards still requested the advice of Lorenzo Magnifico. (See the document in E. Wilder Weismann, P. Bacci, and C. Kennedy, *The unfinished monument by Andrea del Verrochio to the Cardinal Niccolò Forteguerri at Pistoia,* Florence, 1932, pp. 76-79; see also above.)

recommendations to external governing authorities.[6] Frequently artists invoked the help of their Signoria, whose secretariat then had appropriate letters sent off, in disputes over payment with employers in other cities.[7]

Finally there also even occurred in Florence an occasional case of state relief to a needy artist, such as an old age pension, tax exemption or the like, as happened, for example, in Siena in 1455 for the impoverished old woodcarver Domenico di Niccolò, to whom the city granted two florins a month on his petition (Gaye, *Carteggio*, 1:155-57). Such cultural interest manifested itself on a greater scale, however, in later times in the effort to induce the old Michelangelo to return to his native city (Gaye, *Carteggio*, 2:352).

Between the civic governing bodies and the great guilds, of which we will be speaking shortly, stood the Parte Guelfa, a special organization of unique form not to be discussed in more detail here, and at one time of very prominent political significance, which, however, occupied no correspondingly prominent place in the circle of patrons of Florentine artistic life.

What we know about artistic commissions of the Parte Guelfa is by all means rather considerable in quality, but much less so in extent. This includes first of all the powerful addition to the old quarters of the Parte, built according to Brunelleschi's design. The exterior of this building remained incomplete and the internal organization of its stately hall was also only completed in recent times. The building was preceded in about 1420 by the addition, still within the context of the older structures, of the richly decorated marble portal with relief-carved wings, in the style of the transition to the first early Renaissance. From this palace comes also the marble wall fountain with the red Florentine lily on its wall surface that was transferred to the Palazzo Vecchio in 1846. The marble medallion in the lunette of the aforementioned portal, a representation of the Trinity (or Prudentia) in the form of three heads with haloes, appears again in 1426 as emblem of the building supervisors of the tabernacle by Donatello which the Parte erected on the central pier of the Calzaiuoli front of Or San Michele and filled with the bronze statue, also by Donatello, of its patron, St. Louis of Toulouse.[8]

[6] For example, in 1459 for Filarete; later repeatedly for Michelangelo, after his conflict with Pope Julius; likewise for Antonio da Sangallo, for Serlio and others (see Gaye, *Carteggio*, 2:85, 91-93, 160, 170). The city's chancery also had often to take care of importing a marble supply and other material provisions for the exterior of the Duomo.

[7] So for Agostino di Duccio in 1461 to Perugia; in 1487 an admonition to the cathedral authorities in Pistoia regarding a second, fairer assessment for a marble tabernacle furnished to them by Andrea Ferrucci (Gaye, *Carteggio*, 1:196-97; Milanesi, *Documenti*, pp. 93, 143-44).

[8] The Parte later in 1463 gave up its patronage right to this pier, because it did not seem fitting to it to appear here on the same footing with tradesmen. The tabernacle passed to

In the Cathedral the Parte had secured patronage of the middle chapel of the south tribune, in which the sacrament tabernacle was also supposed to be installed. The usual dispute over the placement of arms, however, in which the exacting Parte behaved with particular obstinacy, frustrated this plan of the Duomo authorities, honorable as it would have been for the whole chapel and its patron. For its part the Parte concerned itself repeatedly with the rich furnishing of the chapel. In 1463 they authorized Piero de' Medici to arrange for such work. And even in 1514 they commissioned, at a cost of 900 florins, the splendid reliquary, still preserved, of St. Anthony Abbot, to whom the chapel was dedicated (RA, 1910, pp. 31-34; here also much about the general behavior of the Parte Guelfa).

The sacristy chapel of the Annunziata was further protected by the solicitude of the Parte Guelfa. In 1447 and in years following it was newly constructed by Michelozzo on the Parte's commission and in 1459 enriched by the magnificent portal crowned by the eagle of the Parte.[9]

Verifiable individual artistic commissions of the Parte include the Madonna lunette, probably set up over a door in their palace, supposedly by Piero del Pollaiuolo, which Vasari mentions (Vasari-Milanesi, 3:291); then the ornamental wrought silver *portafuoco* for the Holy Saturday fireworks in front of San Giovanni, sponsored by the Parte since the Pazzi conspiracy (see above). In the *udienza* of the palace, according to Vasari (Vasari-Milanesi, 3:689) hung Signorelli's tondo of the Holy Family, which is now in the Uffizi. Finally there is the bronze candelabra now in the Bargello, tall as a man and marked with the coat of arms, whose fine, rich decoration of about 1500 once more illustrates the artistic behavior, always particularly lavish and selective, of important patrons.

Now, however, we turn to the great guilds. Of these, only the following will now be somewhat more closely examined by virtue of their special economic significance, as well as their extraordinary prominence in public artistic life: the guild of the woolworkers, the Arte della Lana, and that of the merchants, the Mercanti or Mercatanti, more commonly called simply Calimala after the street of the same name where their warehouses and offices were situated (just as the Arte della Seta is also frequently called Arte di Por San Maria). These two guilds comprised the most important industrial branches of Florence and its export business. We

---

the Mercanzia, which subsequently provided it with the Christ-Thomas group by Verrocchio, while the Parte Guelfa turned its Saint Louis over to Santa Croce (see Kauffmann, *Donatello*, pp. 203, 229, n. 77, 316). For the interpretation of the three-headed emblem as Prudence see Erwin Panofsky, *Hercules am Scheidewege und andere antike Bildstoffe in der neueren Kunst,* Studien der Bibliothek Warburg, 18 (Leipzig, 1930), p. 4.

[9] The archives of the Parte Guelfa were also stored here (*JPK,* 25, suppl., pp. 39, 52-53; Richa, *Notizie,* 1:279). For a beautiful early Renaissance table, also from the palace of the Parte Guelfa, see Augusto Pedrini, *L'Ambiente, il mobilio e le decorazione del Rinascimento in Italia* (Turin, 1925), pl. 103.

have already made their acquaintance in their constant and at times very free-spending activity as patrons and custodians of the workshops of the Duomo and Baptistery.

Here, first of all, some supplementary and summarizing material on activities and accomplishments of the Calimala as a patron, which it also sometimes was for projects other than at San Giovanni.

Above all, the church and convent of San Miniato were objects of solicitude, cared for with great zeal and ambition since as early as the twelfth century and still during the Renaissance.[10] The Calimala heraldic sign of the eagle above a bale of goods not only was placed in a sculptured bronze version on the pediment of the Romanesque facade in 1401, but also in the interior of the church on various furnishings newly installed by the guild in the course of the Quattrocento: on the marble holy water font near the main portal, over the door leading from the choir to the cloister, in the intarsias of the choir stalls and on the magnificent *leggio*, now in the Bargello chapel, which was once here; again also on the marble tabernacle structure over the altar of the Cross, whose actual donor Piero de' Medici was only permitted to apply his own arms and *impresa* on the back and was forced to pledge to let the sign of the Calimala appear "nel luogo piu eminente" of the object he had contributed.[11]

The merchants' guild was also entrusted in 1441 by the Franciscan general and the Signoria with authority over the workshop of Santa Croce. In 1361 the city government had already earlier recommended protection of this convent to the guild, and the guild had accordingly carried out construction of a library wing between the two cloisters through the bequest of Michele Guardini. The Calimala had also marked this building tract with its arms, in addition to those of the testator (Moisè, *Santa Croce*, pp. 491-98; Vasari-Frey, 1: 382-83, Richa, *Notizie*, 1:111). On the other hand, another private donation intended for Santa Croce—that of Castello Quaratesi for the facade of the church—appears to have been frustrated by the Calimala itself through its stubbornness in the dispute over the placement of arms. This, however, did not deter the same Quaratesi, who henceforth bestowed his zealous patronage on the convent of San Francesco al Monte, from assigning the Calimala yet

[10] For the documentary evidence see Vasari-Frey, 1:320ff.; also, Robert Davidsohn, *Geschichte von Florenz* (Berlin, 1896-1927), 4:35ff.

[11] All designs for the funeral chapel of the Cardinal of Portugal also had to be submitted to the *Operai* of the Calimala for approval.

The records mention in 1463 an official breakfast at which the consuls of the guild appeared in the refectory of San Miniato, as a mutual testimony to the protectorate (*a recognizione del dominio*) of the Calimala over this convent (Robert Davidsohn, *Geschichte von Florenz*, 4 vols., Berlin, 1896-1927, 4:107-108).

again with trusteeship over the considerable capital designated in his last will and testament for the church and adjoining convent, and expressly appointing it as *procuratrix* and *protectrix* of San Francesco (Vasari-Frey, 1:325). Visible testimony to this is the great Calimala seal over the triumphal arch and in other places in the church that attained definitive construction only in the late Quattrocento.

Large legacies for purposes of church construction appeared in fact generally most safely assured of being spent as designated when their administration was consigned to such legally established nonpartisan bodies and when these at the same time had an interest in the conscientious execution of the donation plans through certain duties assigned to them as a matter of honor.[12] The obligations that the Calimala had to assume for a favorite concern of Piero de' Medici, the chapel built by him in 1467-1468 for the miraculous image in the Annunziata, appear especially complicated; from the annual rent, fixed at fifty florins, of a spacious house on Borgo San Lorenzo transferred to the guild by the Medici, their consuls pledged to provide the necessary oil for the thirty silver lamps hung around that tabernacle, as well as to furnish candles and consecrated wine for celebration at the altar of the same and also to carry out a pilgrimage to the altar of the miraculous image annually on the morning of the feast of the Annunciation with the whole guild *in corpore*, with the customary candle donation.[13]

[12] Michele Guardini entrusted the Calimala in his will not only with the library building for Santa Croce just mentioned, but also with the execution of smaller building works at San Niccolò, where the Guardini owned a family chapel. The Calimala was further entrusted in the will of a younger member of the Quaratesi family dated 1481 with the ownership of three houses, whose rent yield was to pay for the maintenance of his family chapel in the same church and the enlargement of its high altar, whose patronage also belonged to the Quaratesi. Likewise the guild received a share in the choice of a chaplain for San Niccolò, whose benefice was probably also to be taken from the three houses mentioned (Vasari-Frey, 1:385; Richa, *Notizie*, 10:266, 271, 269-70). These arrangements adequately explain the appearance of the Calimala seal also over the portal of San Niccolò.

[13] In addition, the indices published in Vasari-Frey (1:380-85) contain a whole series of smaller works that were to be ordered and supervised by the Calimala in pursuance of certain bequests and endowments committed to its administration. The guild attended to the construction and furnishings of the funeral chapel of Niccolò Acciaiuoli in 1405 to 1426 near the great cloister of Santa Maria Novella. In 1418 it assumed responsibility for the completion of the church and convent of San Domenico of Fiesole, being carried on through the legacy of Barnaba degli Agli (*Nuovo Osservatore Fiorentino*, 1885, pp. 118, 126ff.; Richa, *Notizie*, 7:119). As executor of the will of Filippo de' Scolari known as "Pippo Spano," who died in 1427, the Calimala began, on Brunelleschi's design, the peculiar centralized building at the Angeli convent. It is true that this soon came to a halt because the donated funds entrusted to the city were expended for the war against Lucca in 1437. See Cornelius von Fabriczy, *Filippo Brunelleschi* (Stuttgart, 1892), pp. 236-38.

In 1436-1439 the guild had a Madonna altar in Santa Lucia painted by Andrea di Giusto from the donation of one Lapa Benozzi; in 1439-1440 it provided for stained glass for a

Thus we see what a diverse range of obligations representatives of the guild had responsibility to carry out; how valuable and welcome to private testators also was this opportunity to guarantee the fulfillment of their donations for all time to come through the involvement of such a body; and how significant and far-reaching was the Calimala guild's position among patrons in Florentine artistic life. Above all this, however, the protection of San Giovanni, which was discussed in detail above, took precedence among the patronal obligations of the Calimala as its most particular and distinguished duty.[14]

The administration building of the Opera of San Giovanni, mentioned several times in reference to that place, also received various artistic and applied art enrichments during the Quattrocento. The exterior of this house on the piazza, opposite the older Ghiberti doors, is fairly well preserved; it is recognizable by its charming early Renaissance portal, crowned with the Calimala eagle, with the small statue of the boy John the Baptist by Rossellino in the lunette.[15]

Finally it remains to mention those commissions that resulted from the most immediate interest of the guild itself. The tabernacle at Or San Michele with the bronze statue of the Baptist, the acknowledged patron of the guild responsible for the city's baptismal church, was executed by the same Ghiberti whom the Calimala had already taken into its service for the bronze portals of that baptismal church. In 1416 this figure, which is, incidentally, the first monumental work of statuary cast in bronze in the early Renaissance, was set up in the niche adorned with ornamental mosaic, which for its part occupied one of the most imposing positions in the whole series of tabernacles, on the corner toward the Piazza della Signoria. The guild also had a small Madonna tabernacle, probably painted, set up on Via degli Spadai in 1437. Finally, however, came a variety of works for the furnishing of its own guild house and for the Calimala's use for special events; in 1405 they had a new painted *gonfalone* prepared by Pesello; it was probably of fairly high quality, based on the considerable sum of fifteen florins expended for it.[16] New pews

facade window of Santi Apostoli, belonging to the chapel of Stoldo Altoviti; and in 1468-1470 for the setting up of Mariano di Stefano Nese's chapel in San Piero Scheraggio, with an altarpiece by Cosimo Rosselli.

[14] In 1466 the guild had this protectorate and its right, in the face of other pretensions of the Bishop, reaffirmed through a papal brief.

[15] Various capital consoles, some decorated with the heraldic animal of the Calimala and otherwise richly sculptured, now in the first hall of the Museum of the Opera, probably come from a vaulted room of this workshop building.

[16] In 1444 a painted and gilded frame by Bicci di Lorenzo was provided for a marble Madonna relief, donated by a guild member, in the meeting hall. To this work, mounted over the outside door of the meeting room, another Madonna relief was added ten years later, which found a place in the audience hall of the consuls.

and wall panelling with intarsia decoration by Monciatto were installed in two rooms of the guild building in 1473-1475. They were evidently a very elegant job, since the bill was no less than 1200 florins.

The Calimala was in a position to spend (and always deliver promptly) enormous sums for its undertaking at San Giovanni in the fifteenth century from the income of the Baptistery's holdings placed under its administration, but certainly also in part from its own treasury. Thus it could evidently proceed with corresponding generosity in the artistic tasks necessary for its own residence.[17]

So much for the effect and behavior of the Calimala as a patron, to which the other great guilds, with the exception of the Arte della Lana, which administered the Duomo building, remain pretty much in the background as initiators of artistic enterprises. Following are yet a few reports, supplementing the example of the Calimala, from the sparse available recorded material.

The silk-weaver's guild had a prominent place as attorney for one of the great public institutions of religious character; this is the foundling home, the Ospizio degli Innocenti, for whose construction the guild took the first step by acquiring a site for the building as early as 1419 at the city government's instigation. Considerable private donations and a city subsidy came to their aid in this. The building, begun according to Brunelleschi's plan in 1421, was completed and went into use in 1444. The final settlement records a total cost of 30,000 florins. But the further architectural and other equipment of the hospital and its church, as well as the administration of the whole institution, remained the responsibility of the Arte della Seta, which appointed the Spedalingo and other officials.[18]

The guild made various other provisions for the fine arts furnishing of the buildings as the Quattrocento went on; Baldovinetti and Giovanni di Francesco painted the lunettes over the portals in the portico in 1457-1459, and somewhat later the door leading from the cloister into the church received the beautiful Annunciation tympanum by Andrea della Robbia and a small marble holy water font. Ghirlandaio's painted high

---

[17] It is true that later, in the sixteenth century, explicit complaints occurred over the stinginess and untrustworthy payment practices of the Calimala Operai. One was from Giovanni Francesco Rustici, who found himself greatly disadvantaged in the evaluation and payment for the statue group over one of the Ghiberti portals in 1511, according to Vasari's extensive account (Vasari-Milanesi, 6:605).

[18] We know from one of the Operai who was a guild member, Francesco della Luna, that as a dilettante at architecture and a student and friend of Brunelleschi's, he occasionally had a part in the technical construction management (see Gaye, Carteggio, 1:549-50; Richa, Notizie, 8:114ff.; Vasari-Milanesi, 2:366, 392ff.; Fabriczy, Brunelleschi, pp. 246ff.; the building accounts are published in ASA, 4, 1891, pp. 291ff.).

altarpiece of the Epiphany executed in 1488 is now in the Museum of the Hospital.[19]

From 1427 on the Arte della Seta also held the protectorate, in accordance with a city decree, over the convent of San Marco, still at that time occupied by the Silvestrines. Their subguild, the goldsmiths, had a particular altar in San Marco, for which the guild donated a new altarpiece at the end of the 1480s, the great *Coronation of the Virgin* by Botticelli now in the Uffizi. In this altarpiece the patrons of the whole guild and of the goldsmiths—St. John the Evangelist and St. Eligius—are noticeable below, along with the church fathers Jerome and Augustine.[20]

The hospital on Piazza San Marco which is now the Accademia di Belle Arti was founded by Lemmo di Balducci, a member of the Arte del Cambio, and placed under the guild's protection in 1389 through his testamentary order. The small church attached to it, originally San Niccolò, was subsequently given a new dedication to the guild patron St. Matthew, and, like the other hospital buildings, marked in various places with the guild arms.[21]

Along with these and other individual commissions, the installation of statues in the piers at Or San Michele went on as a general duty of a whole series of guilds. The idea for this enterprise went back to the middle of the Trecento with the Signoria decree of 1340, and the first three figures were set up at the end of the century.[22] In 1406, the year of the acquisition of Pisa, in an energetic new order, the Signoria pressed

[19] Besides this, the Madonna with saints attributed to Cosimo Rosselli, now in the Wallraf-Richartz Museum in Cologne, probably comes from one of the subsidiary altars of the Innocenti church; in its foreground, similarly to the Ghirlandaio altarpiece and the *sopraporta* fresco, appear a series of Innocenti-children with bloody wounds.

[20] In addition to scenes from the legends of these saints, preserved as small individual pictures, the predella contained the donor seals of the guilds. The altar was set up under a structure in the form of a baldachin, erected in front of the entrance wall of the church. See Horne, *Botticelli*, pp. 168-70, 356; and Walter Paatz and Elisabeth Paatz, *Die Kirchen von Florenz*, 6 vols. (Frankfurt am Main, 1940-1954).

The very beautiful relief of the guild arms surrounded by angels can still be found today in the former guild hall of the silk weavers on Via del Capaccio, behind the Mercato Nuovo; similarly, in a majolica version, probably by Andrea della Robbia, above the guild's pier at Or San Michele.

The marble tondo by Giovanni Francesco Rustici (Vasari-Milanesi, 4:603) now in the Berlin museum, comes from the magistrates' hall of the guild where Baldinucci still found it in its old place (1:571). [*Translator's note:* Filippo Baldinucci lived from 1624-1696; his *Notizie de' Professori del disegno da Cimabue in qua* was published in 6 volumes in Florence, 1681-1728. Wackernagel does not indicate a specific edition here.]

[21] Richa, *Notizie*, 7:82; a St. Matthew fresco of the early Quattrocento was disclosed during the recent reopening of the loggia of this hospital.

[22] On this and on the following see Gaye, *Carteggio*, 1:542; August Schmarsow in *Festschrift zu Ehren des Kunsthistorischen Institutes in Florenz* (Florence, 1897), pp. 36ff.; and Paul Schubring, *Die italienische Plastik des Quattrocento* (Berlin, 1915), pp. 30ff.

for the pier statues that were still lacking to be provided within ten years at the latest. Within the period between 1410 and 1416, seven guilds did in fact fulfill their obligations: the Maestri di Pietra e Legname with the group of four, the Quattro Coronati, by Nanni di Banco, and the stocking makers, Calzolai, with the Apostle Philip by the same artist, who also furnished the St. Eligius for the smiths. Donatello executed the St. Peter for the butchers' guild, the St. Mark for the linen weavers, and finally in 1416 the knight George for the armorers.

In the same year of 1416 there also appeared, as a costly piece and a technical innovation, the bronze statue of the Baptist, patron of the Calimala, by Ghiberti. Then it took a full decade before the remaining guilds filled their piers. Besides the furriers whose St. James was provided by a mediocre master who cannot be more precisely identified, these were the important Parte Guelfa with St. Louis by Donatello, the Arte del Cambio with Ghiberti's Matthew, and as a last straggler, the Arte della Lana, which took on no pier at first, probably on account of its obligations to the Duomo, and only now in 1425-1426, in place of the bakers who couldn't pay, completed the series of fourteen pier figures with Ghiberti's statue of St. Stephen.

One who walks along beside these figures today little thinks what deliberation and effort by the individual patrons, often over several years, had to be summoned up for each individual piece in the series before these donated figures, together with their settings, came to realization. At least for one of the statues, the St. Matthew of the money changers' guild, the whole voluminous account of the committee of Operai is preserved and accessible in a careful publication with extensive commentaries.[23]

In this "libro del pilastro" the three Operai delegated by the guild for this purpose—among them Cosimo de' Medici—had recorded all their deliberations and decisions and the countless individual notations over the ensuing installment payments for the material, assistants' labor, and work of the artist himself from 1 May 1419, to 8 March 1423. It gives us a clear and sometimes most surprising picture not only of the whole course and progress of the work, of the various stages and shares in which the total expenditure was distributed, and of how the necessary funds were obtained at any given time, but also (and we shall return to this later) of the attitude and behavior of such a work supervisory commission toward an artist and his assistants.[24]

[23] The account book for Ghiberti's statue of St. Matthew at Or San Michele, published by Dr. Alfred Doren, in *Italienische Forschungen*, issued by the Kunsthistorisches Institut, Florence, 1906, 1:1-58.

[24] To this can also be added, as an admittedly less detailed counterpart from the late art history of Or San Michele, the account material on the new Christ-St. Thomas group by

One of the oldest statues, the marble John the Evangelist of the silk-weavers, was finally replaced in 1515 by a bronze statue by Baccio da Montelupo; probably because the Arte della Seta, with its by this time all too old-fashioned patron figure, must have felt itself inadmissably retrograde with respect to the other guilds.

The multitude of smaller guilds received an occasion for public prominence as patrons only through participation in this statue series for Or San Michele. At the same time, however, the more or less imposing decoration and furnishing of its own house or assembly room was almost unavoidable for each individual corporation.

It is true that only a few monuments and pieces of information are extant that can be related with certainty or probability to this context. The great Madonna tabernacle painted by Fra Angelico for the linen-weavers' guild in 1433 belongs to the first rank of these. The very imposing dimensions and high quality of the execution of this Madonna panel, with painted wings on either side and a predella, in the beautiful stone frame designed by Ghiberti surely represent no unique instance, but still an unusually lavish version of the requisite household Madonna, probably not as a rule lacking in any guild quarters.[25]

As a rule a small *colmo* in paint or relief sculpture was considered sufficient here; the Madonna relief by Andrea della Robbia with the guild insignia of the Maestri di Pietra e Legname, which the guild commissioned in 1475 to replace an older, no longer satisfactory Madonna, can serve as an example of this.[26] The stately series of allegories of the virtues commissioned by the college of the Mercanzia for their meeting room can be grouped in the same special category. The former arrangement and effect created by this series has already been discussed above.[27] We

Verrocchio, reported by Fabriczy, which the magistrate of the Mercanzia (the six-headed merchants' court) provided for the tabernacle vacated by the Parte Guelfa (1475-1483). See *JPK*, 21, 1900, pp. 256ff.; Vasari-Milanesi, 3:363, n. 1).

[25] The tabernacle, now, with its frame, in the San Marco Museum, cost the guild about 175 florins, of which the stone frame alone came to 70 florins, the woodwork for the panel to fifteen (Gualandi, *Memorie*, 4:109ff.).

The similarly large *Coronation of the Virgin* by Cosimo Rosselli in Fiesole at the Museo Bandini, likewise surrounded with a frame painted with figures, probably was also once the centerpiece of such a wall tabernacle from a guild or confraternity room.

[26] The documents on this in *MA*, 1903, pp. 208-209. It is now in the Bargello, arbitrarily joined with a richly sculptured stone console (c. 1460), which originally probably also supported a guild Madonna, in whose frieze appear the arms of the Arte della Seta along with the two city seals of Florence (illustrated in Julius Baum, *Baukunst und dekorative Plastik der Frührenaissance in Italien*, Bauformenbibliothek, 11, Stuttgart, 1920, p. 215).

The Linaiuoli, however, also had Ghirlandaio paint a little "tabernacolino" to supplement the great Fra Angelico tabernacle (Vasari-Milanesi, 3:259).

[27] See the documents in *MA*, 1903, pp. 43-46, on the precise circumstances of the distribution of the commissions. According to this, first of all, up to December, 1469, only

know that the guild of judges and notaries had already had wall panel pictures of the three cardinal virtues executed by Castagno for their *proconsolo*'s meeting room in 1447; and that fresco portraits of famous jurists (by Castagno, Pollaiuolo and other painters) were set up in one of the rooms of the same building (see above).

How widespread similar decoration with images of devotional, allegorical or purely secular nature might have been in the residences of other guilds must be determined from the still unpublished archives of these guilds. The same holds true for the countless confraternities that were partly narrower professional associations with religious connotations (like the St. Eligius confraternity of the goldsmiths and the painters' confraternity of St. Luke) and partly mixed societies from all classes on a religious or Christian-charitable basis, mostly in connection with one of the great monastic orders.

All, however, possessed a fixed meeting place, which sometimes consisted of a little oratory with adjoining rooms and a small forecourt. The existence, along with this, of a more or less impressive array of movable and fixed art works as well as various pieces of artistically decorated furniture and utensils for liturgical and processional purposes can immediately be posited and in individual cases can also be proved through documentary evidence.[28]

---

Pollaiuolo's Caritas was executed as a replacement for an older picture of the same subject. Verrocchio, among others, tried for the commissions for the six other figures. He was paid eight *lire* for a submitted trial piece, but not awarded a commission. They stuck with Pollaiuolo and besides him brought in only the young, at that time still almost unknown Botticelli for one of the pictures ("Fortitudo," executed 1470). Pollaiuolo was obligated to the fastest possible completion of the series, to finish two pictures each quarter year, for which—provided they matched the quality of the previously furnished *Caritas*—he would be paid twenty florins each.

[28] See above on the various confraternity oratories at Santa Maria Novella. For the rest the reader is referred to a special study, now in preparation, by W. Isermeyer.

# CHAPTER 6

# PRIVATE PATRONAGE IN
# THE EARLY AND
# MID-QUATTROCENTO

Some mention of the art commissions and donations of individual personalities or families has already been made in the first main section. Here, however, the scope and significance of individual patron initiatives in general within the world of Florentine art will now be examined in context, along with the attitudes, convictions, and customs expressed in this circle. In order also to make clear the changes in the historical development of the tendencies of patron interest and behavior during the course of the Renaissance century, we begin our survey first with the patronage of the early and mid-Quattrocento, in order subsequently to take up the period of Lorenzo Magnifico and finally the epoch of the High Renaissance.

## REPRESENTATIVES OF THE FIRST STAGE OF
## THE EARLY RENAISSANCE

The first glance at the factual material under discussion here already shows that private patronage activity developed, at first almost exclusively and later still predominantly, in donor activity for the equipment of church and convent complexes. And along with this, beginning about the middle of the Quattrocento, art works and decorative implements of a wordly character began to take a more prominent place in expenditures for one's own house.[1]

Among the famous patrons of the first stage of the early Renaissance, the first to be named is that Niccolò da Uzzano (died 1433) whose features are supposedly preserved in the well-known terracotta bust by Donatello,

---

[1] Thus, to single out only one illustrious and especially significant example, Cosimo de' Medici during the first ten years devoted all available energy only to donor activities for church and convent sites (San Lorenzo, San Marco, novitiate of Santa Croce, etc.); only afterwards, in the mid-1440s, did he turn his attention to the new construction of his own family palace; on the other hand, the megalomania of his younger rival Luca Pitti proves itself only in the immediate exaltation of his personal existence through his own giant palace (built about 1456 to 1466).

but expressly certified in a medal of Niccolò Spinelli's from about 1445.* The family palace on Via de' Bardi where the bust used to be, now Palazzo Capponi, was built by Niccolò and his older brother Angelo, probably at the beginning of the 1420s. Behind the great simple surface of its exterior, this palace contains a beautifully formed columned court heralding the coming early Renaissance.[2] In the church of Santa Lucia next to the palace, where the Uzzano held patronage over the main chapel and a family crypt lying before it, Niccolò had scenes from the legend of St. Lucy painted by Bicci di Lorenzo in 1425. These have disappeared since then. Only the great escutcheon reliefs on the exterior wall of the choir still recall Uzzano patronage.

It testifies to his reputation as an art connoisseur that Niccolò, as one of the most important members of the merchants' guild, had to preside over its special commission for the decoration of the Baptistery (the *Offiziali del musaico*). At his instigation Leonardo Bruni drew up the detailed program for Ghiberti's second bronze doors in 1425. At the time of the construction of the tomb monument for Pope John we also find Niccolò among the testament executors involved in negotiations with Donatello (Vasari-Milanesi, 2:54, 64; Richa, *Notizie*, 10:289, 295; Vasari-Frey, 1:341, 357). Finally, however, as a testator himself, he had the intention to provide the necessary capital for a great university building. The building, begun between the Annunziata and San Marco, never got past its beginning because the city spent the building funds, which had been entrusted to it, for pressing military purposes. Here also, as at Santa Lucia, only a stone coat of arms fixed on the present structure near the Annunziata still testifies to Niccolò's personality and intended donation, which took at least indirect effect, much later, however, through the present housing of the Florentine university in the part of its property adjoining San Marco.

---

* *Translator's note*: The Niccolò Spinelli (Niccolò Fiorentino) portrait medal of Niccolò da Uzzano should be dated rather around 1480. See Jane Schuyler, *Florentine Busts: Sculpted Portraiture of the Fifteenth Century* (New York, 1976), pp. 125-26.

[2] The inventory of Angelo's estate in 1425 (published by Walter Bombe in vol. 36 of Walter Goetz's *Beiträge zur Kulturgeschichte des Mittelalters und der Renaissance*, Leipzig, 1928) shows a very modest interior decoration. The only elegant object among honest, undecorated, simple furniture and utensils was a silver parade helmet with a unicorn for the crest, which was later hung up in the Uzzano chapel in Santa Croce with other family trophies (Richa, *Notizie*). There was no pictorial wall decoration but a couple of painted coats of arms and some Madonna pictures in the bedrooms. On the whole there is an atmosphere of marked patriarchal severity. In the following year, though, when Niccolò was master of the house, it must have changed greatly to make the commission and installation of his portrait bust conceivable in such an ambient. See also Franz Studniczka in *Festschrift Heinrich Wölfflin* (Munich, 1924), pp. 135ff.

The sphere of Niccolò da Uzzano's enterprises already encompasses all the points that characterize the Renaissance patron type: palace building, a family chapel and its decoration, an honorary office among the civic cultivators of art, and finally a large bequest for the public interest.

The situation appears similar for his slightly younger contemporary Palla Strozzi, born in 1372. He was likewise delegated by the Calimala to the Offiziali del musaico of the Baptistery and stood out among Florentine merchants for his wealth, as the largest taxpayer. But in the 1420s and until his banishment in 1434 he played a role similar, through his uncommon humanistic education and interests, to the subsequent one of his victorious adversary Cosimo de' Medici.

We are concerned here less with Palla's importance for the nature of Florentine culture, for his love of books, and especially for the beginning of Greek studies in Florence, than with his expenditures as a patron for the church of Santa Trinita, long closely associated with his family. Here the uniquely beautiful structure of the family chapel, serving simultaneously as a sacristy, was executed and furnished in 1418-1424 as a testamentary foundation of his father Onofrio. It received an elegant marble portal in mixed gothicizing style leading in from the transept, and wall pews (since lost) by the intarsiator Arduino from Modena, and above all the costly, magnificent Epiphany altarpiece of 1423, now in the Uffizi, by Gentile da Fabriano, who was in demand all over Italy and stayed for a while in Florence primarily on account of this commission. The tomb of Palla's father, in its pronounced Renaissance form in a section of the wall between the chapel and sacristy, was probably installed only last of all, in 1425.[3]

Palla Strozzi also appears elsewhere as a generous patron of the monks of Santa Trinita, for whom he had choir stalls (likewise lost) carved in 1421 by Manno di Benincasa, and in whose convent—long before Cosimo's library of San Marco—he first had the idea of establishing a public library. The banishment of the sixty-two year old man, which Cosimo de' Medici, at a heavy cost to his own moral account, deemed politically necessary in 1434, brought this project—and probably many others—to naught. His former bookdealer, Vespasiano da Bisticci, tells in one of his most absorbing biographies how the exile in Padua coped with his hard fate; it is further relevant for our context only that it was primarily through Palla's mediation that Donatello was called to Padua and his important activity there took place.[4]

[3] Giovanni Poggi (La cappella e la tomba di Onofrio Strozzi . . . , Florence, 1903) dates the tomb to 1418 and attributes it to Piero di Niccolò Lamberti. Here also are all surviving construction documents. See further Milanesi, Documenti, pp. 75-76.

[4] Vespasiano da Bisticci, Vite di uomini illustri del secolo XV, ed. Angelo Mai (Florence, 1859), pp. 271ff.; l'Arte, 10, p. 436.

The exiles of 1434 also included Felice Brancacci, the donor of the most important fresco undertaking of the early Renaissance, the chapel in the Carmine, which today is still honorably associated with his name.[5]

And yet a Medici, Cosimo's father Giovanni di Averardo, called Bicci (1360-1429), played no insignificant part in the artistic events of those years, peacefully dominated by Niccolò da Uzzano and the Albizzi, which Vespasiano da Bisticci extolled as the happiest period of the recent past. He could claim above all the merit of having instigated and begun work on the first clearly Renaissance building. As contributor to the new construction of San Lorenzo, he brought about the acceptance of Brunelleschi's building plan in 1421. And the section he founded, the so-called old sacristy along with the adjoining family chapel, completed at least in brickwork by 1429, was the first and initially the only completed part of the church building, setting the determining standard for its subsequent continuation. Admittedly it may be supposed that the old Giovanni de' Medici followed in this the advice and stimulation of his son Cosimo, who already in 1419, at that time in his thirties, was chosen for the four-man commission of Operai for an important artistic task of his Cambio guild, the St. Matthew statue at Or San Michele. We hear of only one other artistic commission of the father, Giovanni Bicci, and that admittedly only through an uncertain tradition: wall paintings of the "famous heroes," which Vasari (Vasari-Milanesi, 2:50) still apparently found surviving in the hall of the old Medici house, afterwards passed down through a collateral line, and considered as works of his Lorenzo di Bicci (actually Bicci di Lorenzo).

We shall further discuss Cosimo's later artistic commissions below in their context and here give only a few more characteristic examples of other private patronage from the middle years of the Quattrocento.

Various gifts by individual donors to the convent of Santa Croce should be mentioned first of all. The legacy of Michele di Guardino who died in 1426, from which the Calimala had the library wing built, has already been cited above. This Michele, a rich merchant, was allegedly a slaughterer, hence the springing ox in his donor's coat of arms. He had been twice elected to the Signoria and had in addition provided substantial

---

[5] The patron's banishment, however, according to Brockhaus' discussion, would furnish an obvious explanation for the completion only much later by Filippino of this chapel painting, which Brancacci had probably assigned to Masolino and Masaccio already in 1423 after his return from an important diplomatic journey.

The gaps in the lower row of the picture, filled in by Filippino, would be, according to this, not parts of the Masaccio composition left unexecuted, but rather would have resulted from the striking out in 1434 of portrait figures of the politically outlawed chapel patron and his closest associates. Thus Cosimo de' Medici would have on his conscience not only the prevention of Palla Strozzi's valuable cultural plans, but also the mutilation of the most important monument of early Florentine painting (Brockhaus, *MKIF*, 3, pp. 160ff.).

funds for construction costs for the church of San Niccolò oltr' Arno, where his family chapel and tombs were located. Subsequently in his will he assigned various duties for San Niccolò to the Calimala, appointed as his universal heir (see above).

The construction of the new chapter room, simultaneously a Pazzi family chapel, also began at Santa Croce around 1430 through Andrea de' Pazzi's donation. Construction, according to Brunelleschi's design, went on slowly by means of the annual interest from the donated capital. The interior was also decorated in a very distinctive style. Above all, however, from about 1440 on, Tommaso Spinelli repeatedly acquired merit through various contributions and embellishments for the church and convent of Santa Croce. At his instigation several wall paintings were executed on the exterior of the gate house; then the cupboards and panelling of the sacristy, decorated with fine intarsia; and in addition the whole decoration of his family chapel, for which he furnished a golden chalice and several mass vestments, all provided with the representation of the doubting Thomas, whom the donor venerated as his name patron and to whom he also dedicated one of the frescoes just mentioned. Finally came the greatest object, the construction of the second cloister with its beautiful two-story arcades, behind Michele Guardini's library wing. The total expenditure for all these productions came, according to Spinelli's own reckoning, to around 6800 florins, of which close to 3000 went just for the construction of the cloister and the tract of buildings surrounding it. To all these sums paid out during his lifetime, Thomas added in his will (died 1471) still a larger amount for the construction of a new *infermeria*. Until recent times there was still a Latin memorial inscription in the cloister that ceremoniously enumerated all these contributions of Spinelli's.[6]

Another contemporary of Spinelli, Castello di Piero Quaratesi, appears no less generous and enterprising; although it is true that in his intentions for donations he sometimes could not quite come to an agreement with the responsible authorities. At Santa Croce, where he thought to provide the still-missing marble covering for the facade in the mid-1440s, he fell out with the Calimala, which had charge of construction, over the application of his arms as donor (see above). And in the case of the Franciscans of San Francesco al Monte, whose church and convent he was ready to rebuild after 1449, misgivings arose among the prospective recipients over the magnificence of Castello's construction plans, all too contradictory of their order's principle of poverty. Nevertheless, in this case, the construction of the convent was partially begun at the outset.

[6] See Richa, *Notizie*, 1:111; 10:266-71 and Spinelli's *Ricordi* in Moisè, *Santa Croce*, pp. 298ff., 480-84, 501-502. The old Spinelli family palace with its rich sgraffito decoration of about 1480 stands on Borgo Santa Croce; see above.

And in his testament Castello (died 1465) assigned to the Calimala, as was customary, the administration of a large bequest of capital, with the obligation to provide for the continuation of the "operibus principiatis et designatis" at San Salvatore.[7]

In addition, the Quaratesi held patronage of the choir chapel in their parish church of San Niccolò since distant times; and Castello presumably also made some sort of donations for this. In any case, we know that his ancestor Bernardo di Castello was regarded in San Niccolò as "Restaurator et Innovator Ecclesiae" and that this Bernardo in 1425 had the costly altarpiece of the Madonna with four individual saints painted by Gentile da Fabriano. It remained preserved there for four hundred years, but then was dismantled and sold off piece by piece.[8]

Next we shall consider other individual patronage enterprises of the mid-Quattrocento and shall begin with two by female donors.

The erection of the tomb of the Blessed Villana, who died in 1370, in the church of Santa Maria Novella was arranged by a Donna Villana of the parish to honor her namesake. This was done through the income from two houses designated for this purpose in 1441. Bernardo Rossellino executed the tomb, whose central section still exists in Santa Maria Novella, in 1451-1452.

More important is the foundation of a whole convent of Dominican nuns by the Countess Annalena, widow of the Condottiere Baldaccio d'Anghiari, who was executed in 1441 for political reasons. She established it soon thereafter on a piece of property she owned in the neighborhood of Santo Spirito, in order to retire from the world there herself. The convent, built around 1445 and later even nicknamed Annalena after its founder, subsequently achieved a very significant development and in Richa's time (Notizie, 10:119ff) was one of the most respected institutions of its kind.[9]

[7] Initially 6000 florins were set aside for construction of the convent and 8000 for the church building. The latter, however, appears to have begun in earnest only in 1475. After the completion of all work in 1494, the final account of the whole expenditure in principle and interest came to a sum of 25,000 florins (Vasari-Frey, 1:325-26; Richa, Notizie, 5:316 [taking 1475 as the year of Castello's death]; Giovanni Felice Berti, Cenni storico-artistiche per . . . S. Miniato, Florence, 1850, pp. 125-26; Rassegna del Commune di Firenze, 2, 9 September 1933).

[8] The sole wing section preserved in San Niccolò after this came into the Uffizi in 1880 through the head of the old patron clan at that time, Marchese Quaratesi. On the Madonna sold off to London and the lost predella pictures of the legend of the church patron, St. Nicholas, see Horne in BM, 1905, pp. 470ff.; Richa, Notizie, 10:269-70. For a later Quaratesi's legacy of 1481 for San Niccolò see above.

[9] Giovanni di Amerigo Benci donated the altarpiece of the Annunciation by Fra Filippo Lippi in 1443 when he took over patronage of the main chapel of the convent church of the Murate (the painting is now in Munich; RA, 1936, p. 64). Mariotto di Benozzo Lippi subsequently had the beautiful facade, still extant, of the church of San Felice in Piazza

Of the various family chapels whose construction gradually brought San Lorenzo to completion, I cite the one donated by Niccolò Martelli, who died in 1425, and built by his sons around 1447 in the left transept. Of its old interior decoration there can still be found the various Martelli arms, the sarcophagus of the donor by Donatello, and the Annunciation picture by Fra Filippo, which was transferred from the altar of the Annunziata in the older church into the new chapel, and at that time provided with the predella of St. Nicholas in honor of the donor's name patron. Next came the chapel in the left aisle, acquired by Dietisalvi Neroni at the time of his political ascendancy in 1457, for which Dietisalvi had ordered the marble altar by Mino, later removed to the Badia, as well as the clay bust of the altar patron St. Leonard by Donatello, which is now exhibited in the sacristy and erroneously called St. Laurence.[10]

## GIOVANNI RUCELLAI AND COSIMO DE' MEDICI

Up to this point, more or less fragmentary allusions have been made to the activity and mentality of individual personalities as patrons. Besides Cosimo de' Medici, only one of his contemporaries, Giovanni Rucellai, presents a somewhat fuller picture. And indeed it is his own autobiographical notes that allow us to discern with all desirable clarity not only the very imposing scope of artistic undertakings and commissions, but also the man's mode of thought underlying these commissions. Giovanni Rucellai (1403-1481), who came of an old patrician family grown wealthy as wool-dyers, was son-in-law and business partner to the above-mentioned Palla Strozzi; however, he managed to become reconciled with the Medici and even to enter into a family relationship (Cosimo in 1448 was godfather to Giovanni's son Bernardo, to whom he later married his granddaughter). Giovanni Rucellai, who was elected a prior in 1463 and in 1475 was gonfaloniere, although advanced in years, ventured in the retrospective old age notes of his Zibaldone to acknowledge his gratitude to God that he had been granted an unusually happy life, blessed with wealth and honors. With due pride he cited also in this connection the architectural and other artistic enterprises that he had commissioned and carried out during the last decade. Some of these, such as the facade of Santa Maria Novella, have already been discussed above.

The primary enterprise cited in the passage mentioned in his book of reminiscences, however, is the new construction of the family palace that Giovanni probably began shortly after his father's death, but still before

---

near the Annalena convent erected in 1457. In addition he donated the holy water font, provided with his donor inscription, at the entrance to the church, where he himself was buried in 1460 (Richa, Notizie, 10:200-201).

[10] See Pudelko in RA, 1936, pp. 60-61; Paatz in MKIF, 4, p. 140.

1450, and evidently brought close to completion fairly quickly. This no less innovative architectural creation came into being approximately at the same time as the palace of Cosimo de' Medici, begun slightly earlier. It was on a plot of land cleared by means of the acquisition of eight small individual houses ("di otto case n'ho fatto una"). The loggia built onto the small piazza diagonally across from it was added around the end of the 1450s. The account of his own buildings in the *Zibaldone* names this loggia in the fourth place, but first mentions the Villa Lo Specchio in Quarracchi (now belonging to the Franciscan order), surviving today only in fragmentary form.[11]

In the last place, after the facade of Santa Maria Novella and the "loggia dirimpetto alla casa mia," the *Zibaldone* names the chapel of the Holy Sepulchre in the church of San Pancrazio, near the family palace, where the Rucellai also already possessed another private chapel. Only that chapel of the Holy Sepulchre, adjoining an aisle of that otherwise secularized church, has survived. It has indeed lost its former interior articulation, designed by Alberti, to which the column arrangement with cornice now applied to the exterior also belongs; but the strange imitation of the Holy Sepulcher still stands in the center of the rectangular space, with elegant pilaster articulation and marble intarsia and a dedicatory inscription that states the date of construction and the religious motivation of the builder: ". . . ut inde salutem suam precaretur onde omnium cum Christo facta est resurrectio." Giovanni also provided carefully for continuing religious services here supplied with indulgence privileges by the pope. In his testament of 1470 he assigned the money changers' guild, which had already been entrusted with the financial security of the facade of Santa Maria Novella, the right to use several pieces of land, with the obligation to go annually in solemn procession to the chapel of the Holy Sepulchre with the whole Rucellai family on the first Sunday after San Pancrazio's day, to hear mass there and afterwards to invite the donor family for a breakfast in their guild hall.

The *Zibaldone* notes another donation for San Pancrazio: the provision of an extensive set of wall hangings in red and gold brocade for the festive draping of the whole church interior on high feast days. Two thousand florins were spent for this, that is, as much as Rucellai set out as a dowry for each of his daughters.

---

[11] Rucellai gives a detailed description of it in another context, telling specifically of the decorative arrangement of the garden surroundings that once existed, in which the boxwoods trimmed into every possible ornamental and figural form betoken the formally rich character of the period, manifesting itself even here. See Giovanni Marcotti, *Un mercante fiorentino e la sua famiglia nel secolo XV* (Florence, 1881), pp. 72-80; Bernhard Patzak, *Palast und Villa in Toscana*, 2 vols. (*Die Renaissance und Barockvilla in Italien*, Leipzig, 1908-1913), 2:105-106.

The author of the *Zibaldone* adds a few more observations on the accounting of his activity as a patron, of which the most characteristic sentences may be cited here: "All these things have given me and give me the greatest satisfaction and the greatest pleasure (grandissimo contentamento e grandissima dolcezza); for they contribute to the honor of God as well as to the honor of the city and to my own memory." And furthermore there follows the naive explanation: "I have done nothing for fifty years now but earn money and spend money; and it has become clear to me that spending money brings much more pleasure than earning it" (ed accorgomi che ancora sia maggior dolcezza lo spendere che il guadagnare).[12]

Only one side still remains to be touched on to complete the picture of this patron personality's multi-faceted activity: Giovanni's artistic holdings in his own house. At least a concise allusion to this is also given at one point in the *Zibaldone* in the account of a series of works of famous Florentine masters existing in the house, in which almost all the important names of contemporary sculptors and painters come up.[13]

Here, however, in general, the names of the artists are cited and only the names, but not the subjects represented by their work. This shows that the author of the notes was inclined to value the art works in his possession primarily as works of certain well-known masters. What must have been drawn up was not an inventory of the certainly very extensive stock of art works that existed in the Palazzo Rucellai in general, but rather a survey of the most important masters represented within these total holdings.

Along with this, however, in the autobiographical description of Giovanni Rucellai, besides the signs of the donor and patron and the cultivated builder, the amateur-connoisseur interests of the collector are also prominent. And only this third characteristic, in combination with the two others, which already appeared frequently in the Trecento, makes the builder of the Palazzo Rucellai a complete representative of the new artistic sense according to Renaissance standards. For this reason, as long

[12] See Giovanni Marcotti, *Un mercante fiorentino e la sua famiglia nel secolo XV* (Florence, 1881), p. 66; Richa, *Notizie*, 3:315; and John (Giovanni) Temple-Leader, *Autografo tolto dal Zibaldone di Giovanni Rucellai* (Florence, 1871), pp. 3, 5. The declarations of due self-esteem over the success achieved during his life, wealth, and respect, as well as proof of gratitude to God ring out in a long, earnest prayer of thanks reported by Marcotti (pp. 44-50).

[13] Painters include Castagno, Uccello, Domenico Veneziano, Antonio Pollaiuolo and sculptors are Verrocchio, Giuliano da Maiano (designated an intarsia master, thus probably only represented by work in this medium), and Maso Finiguerra (as a goldsmith); in addition are mentioned Desiderio da Settignano and Vittorio Ghiberti, along with Giovanni Bertini, who had also been active on the facade construction and portal decoration of Santa Maria Novella.

as we know of no such clear evidence of similar attitudes among other contemporaries, he alone in Florentine artistic life since the mid-Quattrocento appears in some measure comparable, in the variety of his enterprises and directions of interest, to his one-time political opponent and subsequent relative Cosimo de' Medici.

Certain artistic commissions have already been mentioned above which came from Cosimo's father Giovanni (called Bicci) and from Cosimo himself during his father's lifetime.* Cosimo came into his rich paternal inheritance in 1429 only at the age of forty. From then on, but especially after his return from his brief banishment in 1434, Cosimo's extraordinary, all-surpassing activity as a patron begins. It was to go on for a full thirty years afterward, until his death, with a clearly emerging culmination period in the 1440s and 1450s, during the sixth and seventh decades of his own life.

As early as the late 1420s Cosimo initiated a relatively simple church and convent building far from Florence for the Franciscan-Zoccolanti of San Francesco al Bosco in upper Mugello. The architect of the modest Franciscan complex was the same Michelozzo whom Cosimo later had with him during the years of his banishment, and kept busy with architectural commissions in Venice, and who was afterwards chiefly entrusted with Cosimo's much greater subsequent enterprises. These included first of all Cosimo's first great act of patronage in Florence itself, the comprehensive enlargement of the church and convent of San Marco.

The occasion for this enterprise was, on the one hand, the transfer of the convent, previously owned by Silvestrine monks, to the Dominicans of San Domenico, and, on the other, according to Vespasiano da Bisticci's clear declaration, the burden of conscience that Cosimo felt on account of many political acts of violence. It was to remove this burden that he had received from Pope Eugene the confessional penance that he might "build" 10,000 florins as expiation money for the renovation of San Marco (che si murasse fiorini dieci mila). In fact, Cosimo finally allowed the matter of San Marco to cost him more than 40,000 florins. For the reconstruction and expansion of the choir chapel and the bell tower, undertaken at the outset, were immediately followed by a nearly complete reconstruction of the whole convent complex, of which only the chapter hall and refectory were retained in their previous state.

All the new construction admittedly took severely restrained forms, according to the principles of the order, with cautious decorative elements only in the capitals of the two cloisters. In addition, in the upper story, between the markedly unassuming cells and corridors of the dormitory

---

* *Translator's note*: On Medici patronage in general see especially the recent studies cited in the Translator's Introduction, pp. xv-xvi.

with the open roof-beams over them, the only space of an outstanding character was the library. This indeed was also to be accessible not only to the convent's inhabitants, but to all citizens with scholarly interests, such as had already been planned by Palla Strozzi in his own time for the Santa Trinita convent.

The nucleus of the book collection at San Marco was formed by the book holdings of the humanist Niccolò Niccoli, who died in 1437; they were extraordinarily vast for a private citizen. Cosimo acquired them from the heavily debt-ridden estate and, in accordance with the last wish of the deceased, transferred the greater part to San Marco. Cosimo took additional care for the projected further expansion of this institution, which lay very close to his heart, through the purchase and production of copies of particularly desirable works. The prior of San Marco had full authority to charge all outlays for the library directly to the Medici bank.[14] The library room was already ready for use in 1444, while the other construction work on the convent continued into the 1450s.

In the same wing of the dormitory with the entrance to the library, the rear-most double cell, distinguished by its immediate proximity to the church, was reserved for Cosimo himself. He desired it so as to be able to retire there on certain days for religious contemplation. This cell, like all the others, some with their original vaulting, contained in its rear main room a mural by Fra Angelico. It did indeed stand out from the pictures in the monastic cells for its joyfully triumphant theme, the Adoration of the Kings, as well as for its more expansive format and an execution especially rich in figures.

Cosimo certainly also provided the material support for the very extensive mural decoration of the passageways and cells of the convent of San Marco. His personal commission appears directly manifest in the large Madonna composition in the south cell corridor through the presence of the Medici patron saints Cosmas and Damian as well as St. Laurence. The same saints can also be found with special prominence in the high altarpiece of the church which was donated by Cosimo around 1440 and likewise executed by Fra Angelico and which is now in the museum of San Marco. Cosimo's solicitude extended beyond this as far as the campanile, whose mournfully ringing bronze bell, later in Savonarola's time becoming so famous as the *Piagnona* (now displayed in the second cloister), shows his donor inscription and a decorative band with a group of putti lovingly executed in relief.

San Marco was, however, only one of Cosimo's large scale enterprises as a patron. In addition, two more monastic foundations in Florence were endowed with new buildings and decorations, also fairly imposing,

[14] See my essay, "Die mediceischen Bibliotheken," in the journal *Italien*, 1928, pp. 536-38.

by the same munificent hand at about the same time and indeed already from the early 1440s on.

On the one hand, the construction of the novitiate buildings at Santa Croce falls in the period from about 1440-1445, along with the chapel and entrance corridor, into which a stately portal with beautifully decorated doors opens from the transept. In addition, the expansion of San Lorenzo above all made continuous heavy demands on Cosimo's coffers, exactly in these years (1440s) and on until the end of the tireless patron's life. The highly energetic assistance already provided by his father for the new building begun around 1421 (see above) presented a special stimulus to Cosimo's continuing commitment of forces to this ancient canons' convent and its church in the immediate neighborhood of the Medici house. It is true that in the first years after old Giovanni de' Medici's death, his son does not seem to have undertaken anything essential for the portion founded by his father, the sacristy and family chapel, finished only in rough masonry. Only after his return from his brief banishment did he find occasion through the death of his mother in the same year of 1434 to set up the tomb of his parents in the form of the marble sarcophagus placed in the center of the old sacristy under the great stone platform of the vestment table (probably by Buggiano).

And this was followed, probably in the very next few years up to shortly after 1440, by the commission for the decoration and equipment of the sacristy and its altar chapel: the marble altar, the railing in front of it, the wooden intarsia cupboards, wall pews, and, above all, the works of figural sculpture by Donatello. These consisted of the originally polychromed reliefs in the lunettes and spandrels, the costly bronze doors, each with ten scenes of dialogues between pairs of saints, and the heavily articulated frames around these two small doors to the rooms adjoining the altar chapel.[15]

In the meantime, however, the remaining parts of the new church building, the choir chapel and the other chapels around the transept, begun even before 1420, had come to a standstill more or less at the beginning. And thus Cosimo decided to intervene here also. In 1442 he pledged himself, although already heavily committed to San Marco and Santa Croce at precisely that time, to erect at his expense the main chapel, executed only to half its height, as well as the crossing with its dome and the adjoining section of the nave up to the high altar of the old basilica, still standing and in use; for this, he and his heirs were to have the sole right of patronage over these most important sections.

This far-reaching project, for which Cosimo had providently set aside

[15] The relief images of the upper wall relate to the name patrons of the donor family: John, Cosmas, and Laurence (Kauffmann, *Donatello*, pp. 85-86). Brunelleschi had his competition relief for the Baptistery doors installed on the altar mensa.

a construction capital of 40,000 florins, was also subsequently carried out, although over a rather long drawn-out period. It was finally brought to a conclusion, fifteen years after Brunelleschi's death, with the completion of the dome over the crossing and the subsequent consecration of the high altar in 1461.[16]

But Cosimo had also already taken over the new construction of the canonry adjoining the church and gotten it under way in 1457. He wanted for his part to attend to the "casa dei preti," he allegedly told Vespasiano, since the completion of the church building as an honorable thing would more easily find other helpers. And thus the beautiful cloister court with its surrounding two-story columned passage and the canonry wing came to be built, at such a quick tempo that certain parts were already usable in 1461. In the same year, after the completion and liturgical consecration of the transept section, the nave of the old church, still then in use, could be razed and the building ground thus cleared for the erection of the new nave. Even the last section of the building was so promptly and energetically carried forward that already for Piero de' Medici's funeral in 1469 the whole church could be used at least provisionally.

But even a few sculptural furnishings were also commissioned and begun in the last years of Cosimo's life. Donatello, although in the meantime he had passed the age of seventy, was once again entrusted with their execution.[17] The marble choir tribune in the left aisle, similar to Donatello's earlier cantoria in the Duomo, is still in place; but without its figural decoration, probably also intended here. In addition, there are the two bronze pulpits whose side reliefs were in part modelled by Donatello himself in the passionate style of his old age. These were only much later assembled into the pulpit structure that exists today.

This was the last enterprise that Cosimo de' Medici arranged for San Lorenzo, and for which he had seen at least the model before his death in 1464. What his son and grandson found to do later on for this, their family church, will be discussed below. All the essentials, however, had come into being through the action of Cosimo himself. Above all, he had for his own part clearly completed the ascent from the role of a pacesetting donor—who, as his father did before him, contributed some of his means for the creation of a new building—to the more princely than private citizen's munificence of sole responsibility for a whole great

[16] See Fabriczy, *Brunelleschi*, pp. 62-63, 187 for the description in verse of the interior aspect of San Lorenzo by an anonymous writer from the year 1459. In Richa, *Notizie*, 5:54-57 is a record of 1444 concerning the removal of relics from the high altar, according to an agreement with Cosimo as builder and patron of the new sections of the building and excerpts from a speech extolling the Medici by a canon of San Lorenzo around 1465.

[17] The first of these were the four life-size evangelist statues in stucco, which were attached high up on the crossing piers and remained there into the mid-eighteenth century (see Richa, *Notizie*, 5:35; Kauffmann, *Donatello*, n. 614).

church. In San Lorenzo only the secondary chapels were erected and patronized by individual families in the customary manner. All main parts, however, including the whole stock of furnishings, were the result of donations solely from the house of Medici. In the context of other private patronage of the time this represented a completely unique accomplishment that can be explained only through the no less unique development of Cosimo's position in the commercial and political life of the city republic and that may stand as the most evident monumental demonstration of this.

It seems most astonishing, however, that along with such an extraordinary readiness and capacity to spend as was manifested for San Lorenzo, Cosimo was in addition continually making almost as important an investment of resources in certain other convents and churches from the 1440s, through the last decade of his life. Thus during the first building period at San Lorenzo came the novitiate of Santa Croce and the still greater enterprise of San Marco. Besides these, there was the lesser burden of construction subsidies for the convent of San Girolamo in Fiesole, above the Medici villa, where Cosimo had already begun a new building in 1430, for which his son Giovanni took responsibility from 1451 on and continued to support until his death in 1463. In the late 1450s, however, Cosimo himself, contemporary with the canonry of San Lorenzo begun at that time, took upon himself a further most imposing convent reconstruction as the fourth establishment of a type that immortalizes his name as a patron: the Badia located on the hillside of Fiesole near San Domenico.

This was an old, formerly Benedictine abbey occupied since 1440 by Augustinian canons, with whose prior and subsequent general of the order Cosimo cultivated friendly relations. This personal connection and the condition of the convent buildings, which had by this time become practically uninhabitable, moved Cosimo in September 1456 to initiate work on a complete reconstruction of the complex. Thus began this truly ideal convent complex, essentially completed with all its furnishings already by 1482, built around a central arcaded court; it included a costly library also contributed by the generous builder. Vespasiano da Bisticci, Cosimo's book supplier and biographer, reports, as a record-setting performance of his scriptorium, how at Cosimo's instigation he managed to provide no less than two hundred codices in twenty-two months for the creation of this library. Finally, the reconstruction of the church was also begun during Cosimo's lifetime, but brought to completion as we know it today only by Piero de' Medici.[18]

Still other smaller undertakings for more distant places, some even

[18] See Vespasiano, *Vite*, p. 255; Fabriczy, *Brunelleschi*, pp. 266ff., 584ff., in which are also the building accounts and other literature.

located outside Italy, may be added to this series of great building donations.[19] Of these, it is true, little or nothing is still extant. Yet it appears noteworthy and very characteristic that Cosimo was generally regarded as capable of such interests for non-Florentine matters also, and that his aid could be successfully requested for such things.

Vespasiano da Bisticci gives a general overview of the enormous sums that Cosimo spent in his Florentine building enterprises. We find more details in the original accounts which have been preserved and published for the main building periods for San Lorenzo and for the Badia.[20] According to these, the total expenditure for the four principal and most expensive projects comes to an even 180,000 florins, that is exactly as much as the whole liquid capital that Cosimo and his brother Lorenzo had inherited from their father. This expenditure, in addition to 60,000 more for the new family palace and its furnishing and 15,000 for the villa in Careggi, was admittedly distributed over three decades and was matched by the enormous business income that had already brought Cosimo's capital to 235,000 in 1440 at the death of his brother, and afterwards further increased it in an equal measure.[21]

An anecdote of Vespasiano's, already mentioned above, testifies to Cosimo's religious feeling directly underlying all these donations, intentions of penitence and atonement, in particular with thought to his political acts of violence and none-too-praiseworthy methods of making money. In addition, there is Cosimo's statement, handed down by Machiavelli, that in spite of all his donations to churches he must still acknowledge himself in his books as God's debtor. The same witnesses,

---

[19] These include the library building for the convent of San Giorgio in Venice of 1435, building subsidies for San Girolamo in Volterra in 1447, restoration of Santa Maria degli Angeli near Assisi, the new building for the Florentine student hostel in Paris, and a pilgrims' hospice in Paris (see Vespasiano, Vite, p. 253; Müntz, Précurseurs, p. 137; and JPK, 1904, pp. 25, 39, 53).

[20] The conto book for San Lorenzo of 1441 and the years following was published by Ozzola in Rassegna Nazionale di Firenze, 1903; concerning the Badia see Fabriczy, Brunelleschi, pp. 585ff.

Vespasiano's list mentions over 40,000 florins for San Marco; over 8,000 florins for Santa Croce; more than 60,000 florins for San Lorenzo; according to other sources 80,000 (probably including the completion work after Cosimo's death); and for the Badia 70,000 florins.

[21] See Otto Meltzing, Das Bankhaus der Medici und seine Vorläufer (Jena, 1906). Cosimo's own judgment of the annual expenditure figures for buildings is in an anecdote from Vespasiano da Bisticci's biography (Vite, p. 254): His bookkeeper indicated at the end of the year, with the idea of frightening him, that 5,000 florins had been spent in the past year for San Lorenzo alone, and for the Badia another 7,000. Cosimo gave him "one of his worthy answers": he observed from this that the building managers of the Badia deserved special praise for skillful performance of their work, while those of San Lorenzo might be criticized because they had completed less.

however, also point to the stimulus of ambition for fame, no less powerful for Cosimo than for other contemporaries. In Vespasiano's work is a statement of Cosimo's about building as the only assurance of lasting fame after death; still stronger, however, is the version of the same idea that Vasari places on Brunelleschi's lips in a conversation with Giovanni Bicci on the occasion of the beginning of construction at San Lorenzo: "No other memorial of us endures but buildings (*le muraglie*) which bear witness to their author through hundreds and thousands of years."[22]

Thus can be explained the concentration of Cosimo's activity as a patron almost exclusively on architectural enterprises and the commissions to sculptors and painters only for the most essential items of figural decoration for these buildings.[23]

If, however, all this patronage activity for churches may also have served personal fame and fame after death only as a secondary aim, the most direct embodiment and perpetuation of the *magnificenza* of his personality and his family resulted for Cosimo from the construction of a new residential palace. This building, through its innovativeness and highly distinguished architectural form, but also through the towering stateliness of its dimensions among the other palaces in the contemporary cityscape, took on the same special position that its builder occupied in the political life of Florence.[24]

---

[22] Machiavelli, however, gave it the classic formulation when he said of Cosimo: "Apparve la sua magnificenza nella copia degli edifici da lui edificati." See Vespasiano, *Vite*, pp. 257-58; Vasari-Milanesi, 2:369; and Machiavelli, *Historie fiorentine* (Florence, 1556), bk. 7, chap. 6.

[23] Along with all his generosity, the merchants's thriftiness occasionally also came into play. It is characteristic of this that Cosimo and his brother used the old altarpiece that had become superfluous through the donation of a new high altar in San Marco as a new donation for the Dominican nuns' convent in Cortona and provided it with an extensive donor's inscription (Vasari-Milanesi, 2:533-34; Gaye, *Carteggio*, 1:140-41). Before 1449 Cosimo also allegedly sent an altarpiece to the Franciscans of the Bosco ai Frati in Mugello, which probably erroneously became identified with the Lazarus altar of Nicolas Froment, dated 1461, which reached the Uffizi from there. See Ulrich Thieme and Felix Becker, eds., *Allgemeine Lexikon der bildenden Künstler . . .* , 37 vols. (Leipzig, 1907-1950), 12:520; Galleria degli Uffizi, *Catalogo dei dipinti* (Florence, 1926), p. 147.

[24] Cosimo even seems, corresponding perfectly to his political tact in other matters, to have paid careful attention to exceed the usual measure in this palace building only so far as he believed might be expected by the republican sensitivities of his fellow citizens. On this account he is supposed to have rejected an overly grandiose project that Brunelleschi wanted to execute for him and had already worked out in a model. In this also he stood in sharp contrast to his later temporary and evidently victorious rival Luca Pitti. The latter, during the years of his transitory preeminence, from about 1456-1457, perhaps as *gonfaloniere* in 1458, had his palace designed and begun in such a manner that, as he himself may have boasted, even the windows of his Palazzo Pitti were bigger than the portals on Cosimo's older palace. See Ferdinando Leopoldo del Migliore, *Firenze città nobilissima illustrata* (Florence, 1684), p. 464.

Cosimo had by no means already begun this palace around 1430 or 1435, as was assumed earlier; during the first ten years of his political ascendancy he continued to reside in the old house of his father. As for the older Villa Careggi, already in his possession in 1417, he modernized it around 1435 only with two small, charming wings and an open loggia and certain changes in the interior.[25] Meanwhile, in Florence itself, he was indulging his passion for building in the great campaigns at San Marco, Santa Croce and San Lorenzo.

The two first mentioned enterprises were nearly concluded and the construction of the crossing section of San Lorenzo in full swing when Cosimo, at the age of fifty-five in 1444, set about commissioning the new palace for himself and his family from his favorite architect, Michelozzo. The execution of the mighty edifice was carried forward at the leisurely but steady pace that can be observed in all his undertakings. Thus in the course of about six or seven years the building was finished at least in rough masonry and in 1452 the sgraffito decoration could be applied to the courtyard walls.[26]

Between these graceful black and white ornaments, executed by Maso di Bartolommeo, the marble relief medallions with enlarged copies of scenes from antique cameos, supplied by Donatello's workshop around 1455, are set into the spandrels of the court arcades. Thus yet a third favorite branch of Cosimo's interests as a collector was accentuated, the delight in works of small-scale antique sculpture, in carved stones, coins, medallions, and the like. His own unlimited means and the far-ranging connections of his business firm enabled Cosimo, first as a pupil, then as a competitor and later chief purchaser of their estates, to far outstrip and overshadow the older Florentine humanists and collectors: Niccolò Niccoli who died in 1437, Leonardo Bruni who died in 1443, and Poggio who died in 1459). But works of ancient Roman monumental sculpture also evidently appeared early in Cosimo's collection; and Donatello's bronze David, represented in ideal antique nudity, commissioned by Cosimo for the central point in his courtyard, may stand as the first and for a long time the most important example of the power of such models to stimulate imitation (see above).[27]

[25] See Hans Willich, *Die Baukunst der Renaissance in Italien* . . . (Berlin, 1921), pp. 48-49; and Julius Baum, *Baukunst und dekorative Plastik der Frührenaissance in Italien*, Bauformenbibliothek, 11 (Stuttgart, 1920), p. 105. In Vespasiano da Bisticci's *Vite* (p. 257), is the anecdote about the construction manager's miscalculations, which Cosimo for his part foresaw and readily took upon himself.

[26] *JPK*, 25, 1904, suppl., pp. 38, 41-42, 50; *Monatshefte*, 5, pp. 216ff. On the subject matter and meaning of the relief images in the courtyard see Kauffmann, *Donatello*, pp. 172ff.

[27] Kauffmann's dating of the figure in the mid-1450s (see above) must appear all the

With the help of later inventories we can surmise approximately, as already attempted above, what other works of antique and contemporary sculpture and painting may have been displayed even in Cosimo's time in the palace court, the back garden, and the principal residential rooms of the Palazzo Medici. For by far the greater part of the later stock of paintings and sculpture acknowledged to have originated before the beginning of the 1460s may stand as purchases or commissions of Cosimo's.

It must be self-evident that as soon as the palace was ready for habitation, attention was given not only to the most necessary furniture, but also to the no less indispensible artistic furnishing of the main rooms; for the objects brought over from the old family house could by no means suffice for the spacious new residence. Yet Cosimo himself, who finally moved into this new building in the seventh decade of his life, seems to have left provision for its furnishing almost completely up to his sons Piero and Giovanni.

Cosimo himself in his old age evidently felt only half at home in the still somewhat unfamiliar rooms. Machiavelli (*Historie fiorentine*, Florence, 1556, bk.7, chap. 6) depicts him as he wandered about the palace in deep depression after the death of his younger son Giovanni in 1463 and lamented: "Questa è troppo gran casa a si poca famiglia!"

## COSIMO'S SONS, PIERO AND GIOVANNI DE' MEDICI

Cosimo's sons, Piero and Giovanni de' Medici, were well into manhood around the middle of the Quattrocento (Piero was born in 1416, Giovanni in 1421). They had both begun early to compete with their father's artistic and collecting interests; but with an especially marked preference for small-scale works of art, gems, and other precious objects, Flemish pictorial tapestries, and the like. Cosimo's great and principal passion, on the other hand, was and remained building. This they had to leave to him, and could accordingly make all the more extensive use of the means at their personal disposal for their particular collecting desires, as well as for commissions to painters and sculptors.[28]

---

more illuminating, from the point of view of the statue's monumental function, than the origin around 1435 generally accepted up to now. According to him the *David* closely preceded the Judith group, created for a fountain in the palace garden; on its significance see Kauffmann, *Donatello*, pp. 170-72. On Cosimo's collecting efforts, focused on antique sculpture, and their traceable results, see, for example, Müntz, *Collections*, pp. 3ff. and, *Précurseurs*, pp. 135ff. [*Translator's note*: It is in fact by no means certain that Cosimo de' Medici commissioned Donatello's bronze *David*. See recently H. W. Janson, "La signification politique du 'David' de Donatello," *Revue de l'Art*, 89, 1978, pp. 33-38, for the suggestion that the statue was commissioned by the city government of Florence.]

[28] Only one architectural matter was carried forward in the late 1450s directly by Gio-

Very characteristic of the position that Piero in particular assumed in Florentine artistic life in the late 1430s and 1440s are the various petitions and applications for commissions addressed to him by Florentine and other artists, for example, Domenico Veneziano, Fra Filippo Lippi, Filarete, and Matteo de' Pasti. In such matters it was to him that they turned, not to his father, who was known to have too many demands on him already from his political tasks and the great building enterprises. It was also Piero himself who gave the commission for the execution of Benozzo's murals in the house chapel of the palace and personally supervised it even in detail. He would presumably also have provided for the furnishing of the living rooms of the palace with movable pictures.

In addition, his own collection at that time included the most comprehensive, varied, and costly contents. We can obtain a detailed overview of these from an inventory of his possessions in small art objects, gems, silver vessels, books, decorative weapons, and wardrobe that he drew up in 1456 and had completed in 1463 based on the state at that time.[29]

The entire holdings of painting and sculpture in the palace, which at that time were certainly fairly extensive, unfortunately remain out of consideration in these lists. We shall encounter them only in the 1492 inventory to be discussed below. Only the bedcovers, curtains and *arazzi*, often decorated with figural and ornamental images, are enumerated in a long series in Piero's inventory. Of these, some particularly costly pieces must have come from commissions of Piero's brother Giovanni. Certain letters from the correspondence with business agents of the Medici in Bruges relating to these have survived and been published (Müntz, *Précurseurs*, p. 161; see above).

The direction of Piero's personal taste, his delight in precious objects, in the luxurious, and the splendidly ornate can be recognized clearly enough in a survey of the treasures that spill forth in the long columns of his inventory. Of all the holdings in this collection, almost nothing has survived but the books, and these chiefly in Florence in the Laurenziana. Here indeed this taste is very clearly perceptible in the title borders and the initial ornaments. In the densely woven forms, rich in motifs, certain particularly prized pieces from Piero's collections of cameos or

---

vanni, and not by his father: the construction of the Medici villa on the slope of Fiesole (built by Michelozzo in 1448-1461). The same Giovanni thus also took personal charge of the expansion of the small convent of San Girolamo, situated in front of the villa.

The silver reliquary of St. Verdiana, for the church of the same name, was a donation of Giovanni's of 1451. Richa (*Notizie*, 2:231) describes it as a supposed work of Donatello.

[29] It is an official document of seventy-six pages, of which Müntz has published the most essential parts. In addition, a supplement to the 1456 inventory was drawn up in Janaury 1465, thus a few months after the father's death; this, it is true was limited to precious objects and books, but also added their estimated value (Müntz, *Collections*, pp. 11ff., and *Précurseurs*, pp. 147ff.).

portrait medals often appear copied and worked in as decorative objects (see above).[30]

But what about the other great artistic commissions that are acknowledged to stem from Piero's initiative? Two small, richly decorated sacred buildings may be cited first of all; the two chapel tabernacles in San Miniato and in the Annunziata. Both were constructed according to Michelozzo's designs at approximately the same time, 1447-1448, to provide worthy surroundings and coverings for venerated miraculous images.[31] In addition Piero had the sacellum above the Annunciation fresco (allegedly completed by the hand of an angel) effectively decorated, corresponding to its importance, with the splendid bronze grate and the thirty silver lamps hung from the cornice (see above). But the whole decoration, particularly in the pilaster ornaments of the small adjoining room constructed after 1460 clearly illustrates the already noted tendency of the patron's taste toward a delight in ornament. It expressed itself further in the furnishing of one of the rooms designated for Piero's personal use in the palace, the *scrittoio*. The original and certainly very charming effect of this private workroom of Piero's, with walls and ceiling vaults covered with colored majolica by Luca della Robbia, can only be imagined now through the laudatory descriptions of Filarete and Vasari (see above).

This cabinet section of the interior decoration was presumably fitted up even during Cosimo's lifetime. But for the bare five years that Piero survived his father (Piero died in 1469), the only other results of his patronage we can cite are the completion of the great projects inherited from Cosimo, at San Lorenzo and especially at the Badia of Fiesole. At San Lorenzo this involved the final completion of the nave and the addition of a small decorative piece very characteristic of Piero's period, the costly lavabo, probably by Verrocchio, in the auxiliary room of the old sacristy, presumably as well as the sacristy doors, decorated with particularly rich intarsia; at the Badia, however, almost the entire church building may probably be ascribed to Piero's efforts.[32]

[30] The decorative style of the manuscripts executed for Piero may be compared with the much drier and more sparing decoration of the Laurenziana codices which came from Cosimo. The change in taste that set in with his sons even in Cosimo's lifetime, from about 1450 on, can be particularly clearly observed in the costliness of their private book collections, so directly personally determined. See Guido Biagi, *Reproductions from Illuminated Manuscripts . . . in the R. Medicean Laurentian Library* (Florence, 1914), pl. 33ff.

[31] In San Miniato the donor had to submit to certain confining strictures of the Calimala (see above); in the Annunziata, on the contrary, he had a free hand, even to announce expressly and immortalize his own merit as a donor through an inscription in the frieze that bore his name and that of the executing artist Pagno di Lapo along with the otherwise unusual statement of the cost: "Costo fior. 4 mila el marmo solo."

[32] The keystone of the vault indeed shows the family arms with the addition of the Anjou

Finally a work of figural sculpture was commissioned by Piero around 1465-1466, probably for Careggi: Verrocchio's bronze David, whose stylish, courtly elegance belongs most obviously to the whole essential character recognizable in Piero's other commissions.

As Machiavelli has it, Piero finally sought to divert the citizenry from political unrest through the production of public spectacles: a Three Kings play and the magnificent tournament of his young son Lorenzo in the troubled year 1465. This detail completes the picture of his personality very well. With his cultivated and epicurean, but not forcefully creative behavior—a passion for collecting and refined delight in ornament instead of monumental building inclinations—Piero stands out in character as well as in generational position as the transitional link between the old Cosimo and his grandson Lorenzo Magnifico.

## ATTITUDES AND FORMS OF PATRONAGE

The personal, family, or corporate ambition that played an essential role in church donations as well as in the shaping of palace buildings already manifests itself as a new Renaissance sentiment in the patronage of the early fifteenth century.[33]

The first Renaissance palaces, around 1420-1440, remained then as before undecorated on the exterior; only their facades became somewhat broader, more regularly proportioned, and thus they also gained a somewhat more spacious form in their interior courts and the surrounding arcades of these. A rich organization of the facade appears for the first time in the Medici and Rucellai palaces. But the Trecento palace facade, almost fortress-like in its closed aspect, was already becoming enriched in many cases with an open arcaded hall, the family loggia, on the ground floor of the building or erected adjacent to it. This structure, intended for festive occasions, served essentially for the distinguished representation of the proprietary clan—just as was the case with the great official loggia of the Signoria adjacent to the palace.[34]

---

lily, granted by the king of France, in one ball; in addition, the completion inscription, already framed, with Piero's name and the date 1466, is in the choir chapel. Piero also had the newly enriched *stemma* set up in the courtyard of the family palace (Kauffmann, *Donatello*).

[33] With regard to palaces, the self-esteem of important clans had already found its particular means of expression in the late Trecento in the tall exterior forms of these buildings, recalling early medieval towers. These, by virtue of their execution in stone masonry, maintained an appearance of relatively unusual prominence amid the rest of the cityscape.

[34] The right to erect such a private loggia accordingly remained reserved to a limited number of families of ancient eminence as a sign of their nobility, just as the wrought iron *lumiere* could be set up on the corners of palaces only on the basis of an assigned privilege. Even in the later Cinquecento, when according to Vasari some twenty-five such loggie

Most of the new palaces built in the Quattrocento were probably also supplied with such loggie. That of the Palazzo Medici was located in the left corner of the palace, and subsequently, in ducal times—when it had lost its original significance—was renovated into a closed room. That of the Palazzo Rucellai, diagonally across from it, still exists, but it is walled up and its interior partitioned by a dividing floor.[35]

The secondary goal of personal or family honor and fame in donations of sacred buildings or art works may be particularly clearly traced in the application, sometimes recurring several times, of the donor's arms or his name in an inscription. This occurs very frequently in altarpieces and occasionally also on buildings, particularly in monumental form on the facade of Santa Maria Novella. Finally, the desire for fame shows in the addition of portraits of the donor and his closest relatives in altarpieces and other donated images. At Santo Spirito, even on the outside of the building, the family seals of the private chapels surrounding the whole church create a testimony, visible from a distance, to the variety of individual patronage that dominates the interior of the church. And the same seals appear again and again inside the chapels, on the predellas or frames of the altarpieces, in the stained glass windows, etc.[36]

Not rarely, however, all manner of differences over the placement of arms arose between the donor and the administrators of a building project, who were naturally jealous for the prestige of their own emblem. Conflicts also occurred between various donor families, of which the story of Santa Maria Novella provides a particularly telling example (see above).

A primary and frequent type of donation was the erection or acquisition and furnishing of a private altar, if not a whole chapel, inside or in the near vicinity of a church that was in some way close to the patron. But

---

of the thirteenth to fifteenth centuries were known, it was a matter of special pride for old clans to be a "famiglia di loggia" or "famiglia di torre," that is, in hereditary possession of a medieval tower. See Antonio Franceso Gori, *La Toscana illustrata nella sua storia* . . . (Livorno, 1755), 1:74-75; *Osservatore Fiorentino*, 3:203ff.; Benedetto Varchi, *Storia Fiorentina*, ed. Settimani (Cologne, 1721), bx. IX, chap. 40; and Ferdinando Leopoldo del Migliore, *Firenze citta nobilissima illustrata* (Florence, 1684), pp. 453, 466, 488.

[35] In Granacci's small historical painting of the entry of Charles VIII (1494; Museo Mediceo in Palazzo Riccardi) the Medici corner loggia is clearly noticeable, as well, however, as the singular mightiness of the whole palace, towering over all neighboring houses.

[36] In the entrance portico of the Badia, donated by the Pandolfini, there appears, besides the whole seal of the family, also the special device, the dolphin, repeatedly worked into the decoration of the capitals and the outer frieze. Similarly, the Calimala seal appears on certain wall consoles (now in the Duomo museum), and there are numerous other examples. The Alberti, who had once provided rich choir stalls for the monks' choir built in the nave of Santa Croce, were anxious that when the choir was removed in 1570, its former extent should be represented by a strip of white marble containing numerous Alberti arms set into the pavement, to the lasting memory of their ancestors' generosity.

in the new churches of the Quattrocento this time-honored custom had such an effect in the very building plans that these came to include as many altar niches and chapels as could be arranged in an architecturally homogeneous, unified, coherent grouping. Thus the building project came to realization largely through the lining up of a succession of such altar niches and chapel donations.[37]

We see, then, in general a systematically ordered mobilization of private willingness to donate in the service of a harmoniously organized architectural whole. And the artistic desire of the planner for such a multipartite, rhythmical articulation of the spacial structure, in the spirit of the new Renaissance ideal, coincides most happily with the existence of a multitude of contributors who were prepared to enter into the common realization of a building project in virtual parade formation, without special wishes, and to contribute to the whole their uniform portion— the altar site along with the bounding wall and sector of space immediately nearest it. For the construction and roofing of the central nave that remained to be done after this, yet another generous individual donor was often found (like Cosimo de' Medici for San Lorenzo) or that tract was provided for from a general building fund, which supplied the necessary income through collection money, private bequests, subsidies from the commune, etc. Once the church interior was finally finished and usable, the enthusiasm of the builders and donors did tend to flag. The external adornment of the building, which for its effect on the general aspect of the city was certainly very desirable and necessary, appeared nevertheless quite dispensable for the moment to the use of the church for public worship. Thus the facade, planned from the beginning and occasionally even partly begun, in most cases remained a fragment. Sometimes it was not even begun, in spite of frequent campaigns and competitions, as was the case for the Duomo, Santa Croce, Santo Spirito, and for the facade of San Lorenzo, prepared according to Michelangelo's design but never executed.[38]

The possession of a private chapel in a public church—even simple private altars are called chapels in contemporary usage—gave the proprietor occasion to provide an altarpiece, which made its special private associations recognizable through the patron saints of the commissioner

[37] The first church of the early Renaissance, San Lorenzo, was made possible precisely because seven other wealthy neighborhood families besides the Medici each promised to build a chapel in the transept area. And even the nave, built somewhat later, has outer aisles composed purely of individual chapels with deep altar niches. The same holds true for the plan disposition of Santo Spirito and in simplified form for the single-nave churches of the time, like Cestello, San Francesco al Monte, San Domenico di Fiesole, etc.

[38] For the Badia of Fiesole they made do with the charming but much too small facade of the little Romanesque church that had existed previously. A bare brick wall, like the whole front of San Lorenzo, still sticks up over it today.

represented in it and sometimes also through donor portraits, inscriptions, and family arms. Family burial plots also found a place under the floor of the chapel and were sometimes effectively represented in the chapel space itself by great sepulchral monuments.[39]

The private altar was accordingly the traditional place for celebration of the regularly recurring masses for the souls of dead family members and other religious ceremonies of a family nature, such as marriages and the like. The donor family held patronage over this altar position and the space immediately around it as a sort of right of their house. They had the sole right of disposal of it, and with this the duty to provide for the proper maintenance of the place of worship. Such rights of patronage naturally often changed hands through sale, reversion of heritage, or friendly agreement. In many cases, however, the patron family's ancient responsibility was continuously passed down as a legacy to descendants even into the present day. In the process it could of course happen that later owners of the old hereditary possession removed and sold articles of artistic furnishing from their chapels, whether from a well-meaning desire to renovate or because they wanted money.

In the precinct of his family altar, his chapel, the proprietor in any case considered himself so completely at home that all manner of trophies and personal memorabilia of famous ancestors were freely hung there on the family tombs: armor and other military apparatus, festive clothes, coats of arms, banners and the like. Although this custom gradually died out in the course of the Quattrocento, its effects were not removed from the church interiors until much later.[40]

Such practices—like the whole construction and care of family chapels in general—make it abundantly clear how even in the early Renaissance, in accordance with a consummately medieval mode of thought, the ecclesiastical and lay world on the one hand, but also private and public life could freely mingle and interpenetrate as a matter of course. This situation and attitude also explains the occurrence of patronage for churches and convents to benefit the common and public interest of the convent's inhabitants, the needs of all church visitors, and the honorable increase of the whole city's wealth of monuments.

So we have the donations of particular furnishings for the church

[39] The most completely preserved examples of chapel furnishing of the early Renaissance, with altarpiece, wall and ceiling painting, tomb and heraldic decoration, are the Sassetti chapel in Santa Trinita, the chapel of Filippo Strozzi in Santa Maria Novella, and the tomb chapel of the Cardinal of Portugal in San Miniato.

[40] In Santa Croce, where a particularly large quantity of such memorial objects had evidently accumulated, these were set up in 1439 in a judicious selection and orderly arrangement in the upper gallery, from which they later had to be removed again; see Moisè, *Santa Croce*, p. 73. Richa, (*Notizie*, 1:68ff) gives an inventory of family trophies existing in the church in 1440.

interior, like marble holy water fonts—many of which can still be found, with donor inscriptions—stone pulpits decorated with relief sculpture (especially in Santa Croce, Santa Maria Novella), reliquaries of bronze or precious metal, carved choir stalls or sacristy furniture and other single, fixed and portable objects of a church inventory such as individual works of sculpture and painting independent of altars, as well as the whole profusion of outdoor street tabernacles in the city and its environs. And along with these medium-sized and small donations came admittedly rare undertakings on a grand scale: reconstruction of whole convent complexes or extensive sections of church and convents. The most important examples of these have already been considered above with individual patron personalities.

In all these donations within a church-convent framework, the devotional, transcendental purpose is inseparably bound together with the worldly, fame-seeking intention. This accords with the above mentioned outlook, the thoroughly spontaneous mingling of worldly bourgeois and ecclesiastical elements, secular and religious life. Only with the further advance and spread of pronouncedly Renaissance modes of thought does the accent shift ever more strongly in the direction of a sense of fame and personal representation.[41]

As an obligation of devotional character, there appears in the will of Jacopo Villani in 1454 the provision that the annual bequest assigned to his chapel in the Annunziata would lapse if a certain ancient, time-honored crucifix hanging in this chapel should be removed. Accordingly, Richa could still find this cross around 1750 in the midst of the otherwise wholly renovated chapel furnishings.

Individual donations frequently appear with certain obligations of a purely human and familial nature attached that illuminate charmingly and vividly the close relationship between worldly and ecclesiastical life, already frequently accentuated from another angle. For instance, the Servites of the Annunziata, as a result of various donations of the Pucci including the oratory of St. Sebastian in the atrium of the church with the famous Pollaiuolo altarpiece, now in London, had, in addition to the duty of fixed yearly soul-masses, the responsibility to invite the two oldest

---

[41] The religious formulas in door inscriptions: "pro remedio animae suae et suorum" and the like, still frequently recurring up to about 1450, are rare after this date. Examples occurred in 1418 on a holy water basin in Santa Croce, in 1428 on a bronze reliquary in the Angeli cloister donated by Cosimo and Lorenzo de' Medici, in 1440 on an altarpiece donated to Cortona by the same two, and in about 1450 with the altar inscription of the Pazzi chapel; still later in 1467 the religious text was inscribed on the Rucellai Holy Sepulcher chapel at San Pancrazio (see above). Lorenzo Valla does say somewhat flippantly: "ne deo quidem sine spe remunerationis servire fas est" (cited by Alfred von Martin, *Soziologie der Renaissance. Zur Physiognomik und Rhythmik bürgerlicher Kultur*, Stuttgart, 1932, p. 23).

members of the patron family to a meal in their refectory every St. Sebastian's day. This apparently still held good in Richa's time.[42]

One particular circumstance that played no insignificant role in great, costly patronage enterprises must still be taken into consideration; the financing. In the conditions of economics and the money market at that time, it was indeed possible only for the owners of a large-scale banking house like that of the Medici to have more or less constant and immediate access to important capital. The uniqueness of Cosimo's total activity as a donor and builder lies not only in the great number and enormous expense of the buildings he founded, but also in the virtually uninterrupted and thus, by contemporary standards, amazingly short period of execution in which most of his great enterprises came to completion. For all other donors the execution of a major project often had to be spread over a considerable number of years because they could not, like Cosimo, simply take the necessary funds out of a full coffer. A certain quota *pro anno* was available to them only from the annual yield of their land holdings or commercial business, so far as the affairs of these in general allowed a greater or lesser amount in any year.[43]

Donors and testators often entrusted the great guilds or certain religious and charitable organizations, as dependable executors, with the administration and appropriate use of income from property, capital, or debtor's bonds assigned for a certain patronage project. Sometimes this took the form of naming the guild in question universal heir, but charging it with a series of patronage commissions and continuing duties; a method which in other cases was also used in relation to natural heirs.[44]

Even the execution of smaller individual works of sculpture and painting was frequently accomplished in sections through the annual income

[42] Richa, *Notizie*, 8:57. The money-changers' guild had a similar obligation to the Rucellai (see above). Here also belongs the particularly Florentine custom for the administrators of certain churches to present a little bunch of flowers to the participants in legally established devotional visits.

[43] According to this system, moreover, for better or for worse, the city government itself handled the execution of the major renovation of the Palazzo Vecchio; and the civic grants of subsidies for certain churches and convents were thus based on percentages of fixed revenue figures in the annual budget. Likewise, then, private donors also could save up the necessary funds for their undertakings in advance only slowly, year by year, or else provide for the step-by-step advancement of the execution process in separate annual installments. This probably also accounts in great part for the exceedingly slow, halting progress of certain not always particularly large donated buildings, often extending over several years (Pazzi chapel, facade of Santa Maria Novella, etc.).

[44] See above. Besides the Calimala and the Cambio guilds, the Compagnia del Bigallo or the Capitani of Or San Michele was frequently engaged for such purposes. On the many individual donations to small hospices and hospitals entrusted to the Compagnia del Bigallo see Richa, *Notizie*, 7:257ff. The unusually detailed donor inscription on Botticini's Tobiolo altar in the Berlin Museum, for example, most probably refers to such a connection.

from rent on property or agricultural land, so that even here the term
between the commissioning and completion of a work often had to extend
over an excessively long period.[45]

Finally, however the complicated case could arise that, because of the
unforeseen ruin of a patron, the funds were lacking for a donation work
that he had commissioned but had not yet fully paid for. Then the artist
had to make the best arrangement he could with the other creditors of
the bankrupt patron. Mino da Fiesole had this experience with Dietisalvi
Neroni concerning an altar of the Virgin ordered for his chapel in San
Lorenzo. After Neroni's banishment in 1468 this was put up for sale as
bankrupt's property, but was acquired by the Badia and still stands there
today.[46]

Now, however, a few remarks are pertinent concerning the membership
of the patron group and its various levels and categories, as well as the
patterns of thought and behavior relevant here.

For larger works of architecture, sculpture, and painting the principal
patrons or donors are the heads of the famous Florentine merchant families and trading firms, as well as the great guilds and the city government
itself. Florentines living elsewhere occasionally competed with their acts
of patronage, already discussed in detail above. These included the condottiere Filippo de' Scolari (Pippo Spano) who achieved honor and wealth
serving in Hungary. He died in 1427 and in his will provided for the
construction of an oratory at the Angeli convent. This is the central plan
building begun by Brunelleschi in 1434, but afterwards left unfinished
(see above).[47]

[45] Thus, for example, the tomb of the Beata Villana in Santa Maria Novella, for whose
construction the patroness assigned the rent of two houses in her will in 1441, only came
to execution ten years later (see above). Likewise the altar of the Coronation of the Virgin
by Fra Filippo Lippi, although already begun in 1441 at the donor's death, was completed
only in 1447. The nuns of Sant' Ambrogio paid the artist from the yield of a piece of land
assigned to them for this purpose. See Igino Benvenuto Supino, *Fra Filippo Lippi* (Florence,
1902), p. 68; and Henriette Mendelsohn, *Fra Filippo Lippi* (Berlin, 1909), pp. 230-31.

The *Adoration of the Magi* painting for San Donato a Scopeto (Uffizi), begun in 1480
by Leonardo da Vinci and executed later by Filippino Lippi, was financed by a large piece
of land bequeathed to this convent in a will. The stipulation was attached that the revenue
or sale of these *poderi* should pay both for the dowry of a niece of the testator and for the
cited altarpiece; see the documents on the whole proceeding in *RA*, 1910, pp. 93-101.

Documents of 1475 published in *RA*, 1906, p. 183, concerning the altar of St. Lucia in
the church of the same name, show how two donors could share the cost of an altarpiece.

[46] The remaining payment to the artist was calculated based on the next rent payment
he owed on a house he was renting from the Badia (Vasari-Milanesi, 3:120, n. 2; Paatz
in *MKIF*, 4, p. 140).

[47] Previously, however, even a Florentine aristocrat banished from the city, Gherardo
degli Alberti (1394), had set aside 800 florins in his will for the construction and furnishing
of a chapel, also near the Angeli church. This was finished in 1411 and received an altarpiece
by Lorenzo Monaco.

Finally, even a foreign prince and general, who as such had admittedly been of special service to the city of Florence, the Mantuan marquess Lodovico Gonzaga, made a major architectural donation to Florence in 1451. He had the great rotunda, the subsequent choir of Santissima Annunziata, built according to Alberti's designs. It is true that he foresaw quite accurately that the large debt of wages, about 5000 florins, which Florence owed him could be most easily realized if he assigned it, through a donor's contract with the city, to serve the needs of one of the most venerated sacred places in Florence. To be sure, it was still difficult enough for his agent to effect the fulfillment of the contract by the city and a full twenty-five years passed before the structure was actually begun and finally brought to full completion in 1476-1477.[48]

No less important than these individual manifestations of the donor and patron on a grand scale was the existence and intervention, astonishingly varied if less extensive in its particulars, of the middle class of citizens in the artistic life and art market of Florence. Even the petty-bourgeois artisan lower class occasionally participated in this with modest commissions and purchases.[49] Individual commissions, even to famous artists, of works that are sometimes still traceable also came not infrequently from members of the educated middle class, merchants, municipal officials, clerics, etc.[50] Representatives of this class are also found among identifiable portrait busts from about 1450 on (see above).

Particularly noticeable and noteworthy, however, from about the mid-fifteenth century on and contemporary with the change in style setting

---

[48] See the lengthy correspondence on this matter in Gaye, *Carteggio*, 1:225-42; also *MKIF*, 3, pp. 268ff. In 1454 the marquis had already had a separate painting of the Inferno made by Castagno and Baldovinetti. See Baldovinetti-Landi, *Ricordi*, p. 92.

[49] We can learn especially clearly about this broad lower class through many of its representatives recorded among the clientele in Neri di Bicci's workshop journal.

There, to cite only two particularly characteristic cases, we find a smith, Antonio of Lastra, who commissioned a little Madonna panel (*tavoletta da camera*) from Neri for the price of five *lire* (about one florin). The finished painting was severely damaged by a mule's kick during transportation to the patron, but was quickly repaired by Neri. In the same year, 1454, Neri painted a tabernacle with wing panels for the ropemaker Lorenzo of Ponte Rubaconte for his *podere* near Porta San Miniato. It featured a Madonna with four saints on a gold ground, and good ultramarine was used. The price was set by two experts (see the publication of the *Ricordi* in *Il Vasari*, 1, pp. 328, 330-31).

[50] Thus in 1435 the chancellor Carlo Marsuppini (who later received the beautiful tomb by Desiderio in Santa Croce) had the great *Coronation of the Virgin* by Filippo Lippi (now in the Vatican Pinacoteca) painted for a church in his home town of Arezzo. He himself and his father appear as portrait figures on the wing panels. The somewhat later *Coronation of the Virgin* by the same master from Sant' Ambrogio (Louvre), is a donation of the chaplain of this church, Francesco de' Maringhi, who was also a canon at San Lorenzo. He also had a donor portrait with the demonstrative inscription "Is perfecit opus" added to this picture. The Baldovinetti altarpiece in Sant' Ambrogio was a donation of Prior Domenico Maringhi (1469ff.; the documents are in *RA*, 1909, pp. 86ff.).

in around this time is a sharp ascendancy and increase of artistic commissions for the furnishing and enrichment of private homes. This, indeed, does not occur at the expense of donor activity elewhere, yet it presents a newly accentuated competition, compared with earlier times, with patronage activity for churches and other public places.[51]

These manifestations apparently represented a general change in artistic taste, in the particular interests and needs of the patrons, as we have already observed above in the comparison of Cosimo's behavior with that of his sons. And this observation also goes together very well with the general change in modes of thought that von Martin has observed and set forth in a sociological-economic relationship within this section of the history of early capitalism: after the heroically monumental builder generation of Palla Strozzi and Cosimo de' Medici comes the generation of their immediate successors, more consumers than producers, accustomed to enjoyment—"a spirit of men of private means rather than men of enterprise."[52]

Expenditures for artistically enriched furnishings for distinguished homes seem to have become more common and important only during the second quarter of the century, as may be concluded from inventory statements and a few surviving works. From the 1450s on it also becomes apparent that the patron, along with his activity as a donor on the outside, was increasingly concerned with the most artistically splendid and costliest possible furnishing of his private ambient, accessible only to himself and his guests. And thus he was finally going beyond the inventory of directly functional objects into a manifest collector's delight in possessions, gathering objects of artistic value into his house for their own sake.

We must try to imagine this gradual emergence of the collector type in the sphere of late Quattrocento patronage as a significant new phenomenon. The client and donor bestow their commissions with respect

[51] The survey of painting and sculpture in a house (see above) illuminates this in detail. It is especially clear in the sharp increase in surviving or otherwise traceable pictures of secular figures for living rooms (cassoni, panelling pictures and the like), as well as in the province of sculpture through the new cultivation and development of various types of secular sculpture, on a large and small scale, setting in around the middle of the century. See Wilhelm Bode, *Die italienische Bronzestatuetten der Renaissance, kleine neu bearbeitete Ausgabe* (Berlin, 1922), p. 9.

[52] See Alfred von Martin, *Soziologie der Renaissance, zur Physiognomik, und Rhythmik bürgerlicher Kultur* (Stuttgart, 1932), pp. 66-70. In 1424, in the palace of as generous a donor as Niccolò da Uzzano, no other works of painting or sculpture were yet to be found besides the most indispensable household devotional images, and there was only completely undecorated furniture (see above). This may be taken as characteristic of the austere lifestyle of that whole generation, for which wall paintings in living rooms (as, for example, in the case of Giovanni Bicci de' Medici and in the Palazzo Davanzati) or chests with figural painting could still represent only a none-too-frequent exception.

to a particular function and destination, for a given task determined by a prospective location and objective. This means that they order a painting, a piece of sculpture, or a decorative object that appears desirable and necessary for a particular place in a church space or in their own house and represents an object appropriate to the situation in which it is displayed. The collector, however, is interested in the art work for itself on account of its creator, its particular artistic qualities, or other noteworthy characteristics. As a collector he also endeavors to bring together as many possessions as possible of a particular, or even every favorite type.

Cosimo, like the older humanists along with him, already had such collecting interests, but probably only for antiquities, especially small-scale sculpture, and for books. But even Cosimo was a collector only in the second place, alongside his predominant interest and concentration of forces in architectural patronage. On the other hand, with his sons the passion for collecting predominates. Even in works they commissioned themselves, the preference for the costly and decorative, corresponding to their special collectors' interests, holds sway.[53]

Roberto Martelli (born 1408) seems to have manifested what might be called a connoisseur's appreciation of the works of a particular artist, Donatello. Evidence for this is the various works of sculpture that he himself (or already his father) commissioned from Donatello for their palace: the marble statues of a John and a David of around 1430, the splendid coat of arms of the house, and a small bronze relief which Vasari mentions. Furthermore, assuming Vasari was reliably informed, there is the circumstance that the young Donatello allegedly found a guest's welcome and furtherance of his talent in the Martelli house and that Roberto Martelli later in his testament charged his successors with the obligation never to part with Donatello's statue of John, as a valuable talisman of the house.[54]

The respect for the superior artistic personality and his creations to which this testifies could be compared in the mid-Quattrocento only with the forebearance with which Cosimo de' Medici indulged his Fra Filippo Lippi's occasional avoidance of work: a forebearance that he is supposed to have explained with the platonically tinged sentence: "The extraor-

---

[53] Of the rest of the circle of patrons of the period, the only pertinent data I can cite is the list of works by famous masters that Giovanni Rucellai added to his *Zibaldone* with a marked collector's satisfaction. Otherwise, however, even Rucellai was active primarily as a builder and donor.

[54] Vasari-Milanesi, 2:396, 408. These last instructions of their ancestor were constantly respected by his descendants into recent times, but then finally broken. Only the great escutcheon relief by Donatello is still found today in the family's possession in the palace on Via da Forca (the Saint John statue went into the Uffizi, the David to Philadelphia).

dinary gifts of a rare talent are heavenly forms, and not pack mules."[55]

But even within the old attitudes, first overturned probably only by Cosimo, it must have appeared necessary for a patron who wanted to be well served to have some understanding of art himself. Thus it is no accident that in the commissions for the administration of important building and artistic enterprises, for the Palazzo dei Signori, among the "Offiziali del musaico," among the four Operai for the St. Matthew statue for Or San Michele, etc., we find again the same personalities who play a leading role as patrons and donors in their own right: Niccolò da Uzzano, Palla Strozzi and Cosimo de' Medici.

[55] "Che l'eccellenze degli ingegni rari sono forme celeste e non asini vettorini" (Vasari-Milanesi, 2:617).

# CHAPTER 7

# LORENZO MAGNIFICO,
# PIERO DI LORENZO, AND
# LORENZO DI PIERFRANCESCO
# DE' MEDICI

Lorenzo, though barely twenty-one years old at the death of his father Piero in December 1469, had already previously given evidence of his political astuteness in the repulse of the Pitti-Neroni conspiracy and on other occasions. In June 1469 he was married to a member of the high Roman aristocracy, Clarice Orsini. On the offer of the Signoria, and supported by the counsel of old friends of his house, he now took command of the business of governing the city state. Opposing currents, aroused by a certain youthful roughness in his political proceedings, did indeed seek to overthrow Medici rule a few years later in the Pazzi conspiracy. Lorenzo's younger brother Giuliano fell victim to the murderous attack in the Duomo; he himself, however, escaped, and popular rage turned against the assailants and their adherents. The most gruesomely violent retribution, which was enacted with Lorenzo's knowledge and consent, involved Florence in a sharp conflict with the Pope. But Lorenzo's position and authority, far beyond Florence, were from then on decisively established. And only then did the now thirty-year-old man begin to enter openly in important measure into the field that particularly interests us, as a commissioner and patron. It is true that there are no architectural enterprises of Lorenzo's from the first decade of his political leadership, and his commissions in the figurative and applied arts, in significant contrast to the behavior of his grandfather, proceeded not from a donor's intention, but solely from personal or family motives.

Thus, first of all, came the tombs that the young Medici brothers had built for their father and for their uncle Giovanni in San Lorenzo. It was probably commissioned soon after Piero's death and quickly completed. In 1472 both the deceased could be laid to rest in it.

This monument, built into an arched opening in the wall between the sacristy and family chapel, renounced all figural decoration, but instead surpassed all precedent in the splendid costliness of its material and the greatest possible richness of ornamental furnishings. This is surely as characteristic of the direction of taste of the patron and his generation as of the artist who created it himself, Verrocchio, who since Donatello's death had become the Medici's favorite sculptor.[1]

For Lorenzo, probably in the late 1470s, Verrocchio provided a small bronze work, the putto with the dolphin for a fountain in the park of Careggi. The clay relief of the Resurrection, recently discovered in that villa and now belonging to the Bargello, also went there. Since in theme and composition it agrees so closely with the large terra-cotta relief by Luca della Robbia above the bronze doors in the Duomo which saved Lorenzo's life during the Pazzi attack, its origin is probably correctly associated with that event. In addition, the style of Verrocchio's work points to the period around 1478-1479.

On the occasion of his escape, in accordance with tradition, Lorenzo also had a life-sized ex-voto figure of himself, with head and hands modelled in wax, executed in three copies. One of these sculptures, dressed in his own clothes that he had been wearing during the attack in the Duomo, was for a convent church on Via San Gallo, another for the Annunziata. He donated the third to the Angeli church in Assisi. It is very probable that, as Vasari reports, Verrocchio participated in the execution of the portrait heads of these votive offerings, for he had already executed the still-extant clay busts of Lorenzo and his brother before 1478. These were both half-length portraits in richly decorated dress armor, perhaps commissioned for the occasion of Giuliano's joust of 1475.[2] At this joust Lorenzo wore a decorative silver helmet crowned with the figure of a doe, which he also had made by Verrocchio. Here also may be added the relief of an ideal portrait of "Scipio," with splendidly ornamented armor and helmet, as well as its lost counterparts, the two bronze reliefs of generals of antiquity, which Verrocchio produced on Lorenzo's commission for the Hungarian king Matthias Corvinus. Verrocchio's assistant at that time, Leonardo da Vinci, probably had a share in the execution of the Scipio relief.[3]

An earlier painted work of Verrocchio's also appears in the list prepared by Verrocchio's heirs (see note 3): the portrait of the beloved of Lorenzo's

[1] Verrocchio had already designed the tomb plaque for Cosimo de' Medici, which lies embedded in the floor before the high altar of San Lorenzo, as large-scale, severe memorial to the Pater Patriae in 1464-1465. The sacristy fountain in the same place was produced afterward (see above), as well as his first statuary work, probably also on Piero's commission, the bronze David.

[2] The first (not securely autograph) is in Boston; Giuliano's is in the Dreyfus collection in Paris, (Vasari-Milanesi, 3:374). On various portraits of Lorenzo see BA, 25, pp. 179ff.).

[3] See Vasari-Milanesi, 3:361; Emil Möller, "Leonardo e Verrocchio" in Raccolta Vinciana, 14, 1934. A list drawn up by Verrocchio's heirs in 1496 brings together for the first time all the works executed for him by Verrocchio. It is published by Fabriczy, ASA, 1895, pp. 166ff.

youth, Lucrezia Donati, whom he celebrated in sonnets and in whose honor he organized his first joust in 1469. Through Vasari we also learn of a Madonna relief of Verrocchio's for Palazzo Medici (probably the one in the Bargello). In the same place, however, near the garden exit, can be found an antique porphyry torso of Marsyas that Lorenzo had received from Rome and had completed by Verrocchio. It was a counterpart to an antique Marsyas allegedly completed by Donatello on Cosimo's commission (see *Pantheon*, 1937, pp. 329ff.).[4]

After Verrocchio, Donatello's pupil Bertoldo was particularly esteemed and frequently employed by Lorenzo. Already from the 1460s on he executed several bronze reliefs for Palazzo Medici: the *Crucifixion* and the *Lamentation* as well as the joyful children's bacchanal, to be explained as a fireplace frieze (now all in the Bargello). The larger high relief of a battle of horsemen was produced somewhat later as a free copy of an ancient Roman sarcophagus at the Campo Santo in Pisa, in marked pursuance of Lorenzo's antiquarian artistic aspirations. The lovingly worked image received a place above the fireplace in a small room near the main hall of the palace and there later gave the young Michelangelo the stimulus for one of his first works: the Battle with the Centaurs. Bertoldo later also received a commission related to the Pazzi conspiracy: the production of the commemorative medal with the very lively depiction of the attack in front of the choir screen in the Duomo and the large profile heads of the murdered and saved brothers above it. It was not the first or the last commission of this sort, which he owed directly or indirectly to Lorenzo's strong interest in such display and commemorative coins. And the same holds true for the other branch of small-scale sculpture cultivated no less prolifically and successfully by Bertoldo: plaquettes, bronze statuettes and the like. Countless excellent examples, mostly antique subjects, have been attributed to him through recent research.

Bertoldo was from the start Lorenzo's actual household artist and almost constantly a live-in guest in the palace and villas of the Medici. His jocular letter to the all-powerful master of the house in July 1479 shows how familiar and unconstrained the tone of their relations must have been.[5]

Almost all of the above-mentioned purchases or commissions of Lorenzo's occur in antique motifs and small format. This admittedly cor-

---

[4] See Vasari-Milanesi, 3:361, 366-69; the two Marsyas figures, which Fichard also found in 1536 in the positions cited by Vasari, are now in the Uffizi.

[5] Bode, *Bertoldo,* pp. 11-12 and passim; Müntz, *Collections,* p. 88; in addition, Lorenzo also acquired or commissioned a bronze statuette from Antonio Pollaiuolo. One of his best pieces of the kind, the Hercules-Antaeus group, is supposed to have come from the Palazzo Medici.

responds completely to his other collecting preferences, which, like his father's, inclined in particular to works of small-scale antique sculpture.[6]

A principal portion of holdings in the Medici collections consisted of medals, among which the works of fifteenth-century *medailleurs* certainly by far predominated. The estate inventory of 1492 cites no less than 284 silver and 1844 bronze medals, in addition to 200 coins "of various sorts." The antique coins, however, were surely counted among these.[7]

But the numerous plaquettes by Bertoldo and others, surviving almost solely in carelessly chased bronze or in simple lead casts, are to be understood in their original raison d'etre as decorative inserts in costly household utensils, coffers, table settings, show weapons and the like. These small reliefs naturally must have appeared in such positions only in precious metal versions with the most meticulous treatment of details. Very few complete examples of objects of this sort have come down to us. One of these, an inkwell with plaquettes with the story of Coriolanus, is in silver, certain others in bronze. All the rest, however, evidently on account of the value of their metal, perished partly already in Lorenzo's lifetime, partly later in the melting pots (Bode, *Bertoldo*, pp. 46ff.).

Thus here also we may surmise yet another entire vast province of applied art for the luxurious conduct of daily life. Its original extent and appearance has come down to us only indirectly and in fragments and as a whole may be conceived of in some measure only in the imagination.

A pronounced luxuriousness and lavish splendor of detail is manifest in the time of Lorenzo Magnifico in many other areas of artistic problems and activity. This general trend of the period found a particularly characteristic and direct embodiment in the precious small-scale world of such ornamental sculpture for the decoration of utilitarian objects, similar to elegant book illustration.

There is only one group of such highly refined tableware, demonstrably from Lorenzo's own possession and use, of which relatively many pieces have come down to us; in the Museo degli Argenti of the Pitti palace, in a display case in the next to the last room, are assembled no less than

---

[6] The Medici since Cosimo's time had by all means also endeavored frequently and successfully to acquire large antique figural works. Lorenzo, for example, brought two marble busts of emperors, besides various costly pieces of antique carved stonework back from his embassy to Rome in 1472. And his agents in Rome and Naples later also managed to procure many more important objects of statuary for him from excavations. But these things, none too easy to acquire, naturally remained in the minority compared with the mass of small sculptural acquisitions.

[7] Yet in Lorenzo's estate, of the hundred gold medals which Piero's last inventory lists, only a single one, that of the old Cosimo, was still present; and only the greater half of the 500 silver medals from Piero's collection. These sharp decreases may probably be explained only through Lorenzo's occasional extremely pressing need for precious metal that could be turned into cash in his last years.

eighteen nobly formed bowls, tankards, and other table vessels of crystal and semiprecious stone. All are distinguished by the engraved initials "LAUR. MED." as a mark of provenance. Most have feet and crown elements in studded or otherwise ornamented gold plate, sometimes enriched with enamel. The knobs sometimes appear as spheres marked with the emblematic diamond rings and provided with inset Medici arms in enamel.[8]

To these we may now add thirty-two similar but often still more magnificently equipped vessels from Lorenzo's household treasury, which came down to the later Pope Clement VII with the Medici legacy. They were later in 1532 adapted by him as reliquaries and consigned to the old Medici patronage church of San Lorenzo. They are still in its possession today, but are not accessible to visitors, and were on public display for the first time in the exhibition *Firenze Sacra* in 1933.[9]

Confronted with these show-pieces from the table of Lorenzo and his father, the visitor to the 1933 exhibition could gain a fairly clear conception of the life style in the house of Medici, reflected equally in material richness and tasteful elegance of ornament. Here, in an almost fairy tale splendor, it suddenly came to light out of the past, only to disappear again after a few months into the inaccessible keeps of San Lorenzo.[10]

The following excerpt from the endless enumerations of the inventories may provide at least an overview of the range and the objects of Lorenzo's collecting interests. Thus here, along with certain precious stones of various sorts, are found above all the countless cameos, carnelians, and other antique carved stone work, most of them set off by some sort of gold mounting. There are also many gems set in precious rings and the like.

---

[8] These mountings, still heavily interspersed with late Gothic decorative elements, belong to Lorenzo's time; the vessels themselves are of antique, Roman, or oriental provenance (see Walter Holzhausen, "Zum Schatz des Lorenzo Magnificos," *MKIF*, 3, p. 104).

[9] Particularly impressive among this series are certain drinking cups and tankards, whose handles and spouts are modelled in the forms of lively dragons; among these also a wonderful goblet, probably going back to the time of Piero de' Medici, whose crowning knob is formed by Piero's diamond emblem, with the three feathers belonging to it and the device "Semper"; the lid is covered with multicolored ornamental carpet patterns in enamel. At the neck is a broad frieze, also executed in the most elegant enamel work, in which little Bacchus heads and bacchic panther figures appear interwoven with fine rinceaux motifs.

[10] A whole group of such vessels was listed in the great inventory of 1492 as stored in a room adjoining Lorenzo's, and even in the *scrittoio*. We must surely imagine this *scrittoio*, however, as a sort of treasury of built-in cupboards with many compartments and shutters. An antique relief hung over its door, according to a notice preceding the inventory (Müntz, *Collections*, p. 64). This *scrittoio* housed, in addition, a hoard of other small collector's items, precious objects and curios, whose enumerations fills many pages of the inventory manuscript (Müntz, *Collections*, pp. 66-80). An essentially briefer list of similar objects follows, under the heading "gioie sono nello scrittoio di Piero." These were stored in a coffer handed down from Lorenzo's father.

Then come other gold ornaments, every possible decorative and utilitarian object in costly versions: belt buckles, Agnus-Dei salvers, hoards of rosaries, plus certain ink wells in elegant cast bronze, crystal drinking cups, silver salt cellars, decorated knives, show weapons, various small table clocks (oriuoli), etc. In any case, they are all exclusively objects which, through their material value or refined elegance of execution, could stimulate the collector's pride of possession and please the accustomed taste of the master of the house.[11]

The same abundant treasure chests also hid many works of small-scale painting and sculpture and related genres of the more refined crafts. Thus there were a number of small images of religious subjects, sometimes in enamel or mosaic—and then probably of Byzantine origin, as is expressly noted in certain cases—sometimes in reliefs of ivory, alabaster, or gilded sheet silver, and among these certain reliquaries of the most ornate form with enamel decoration and sculptural ornament. There were a few small antique bronzes and, above all, the whole collection, containing about 2300 items, of portrait medals in bronze and silver, which was already discussed above. Finally, as particularly interesting pieces, there were many small paintings by known early Netherlandish masters; a Jerome in his cell by Jan van Eyck, a portrait of a woman by Petrus Christus, a small Deposition by Giotto and a little Judith picture by Squarcione.

The sheer quantity of all these precious objects and rarities is enormous, and the same utilitarian and devotional objects sometimes occur in multiple versions. Thus it is clear that for their acquisition and retention it was hardly their actual function that was most decisive, but rather the insatiable passion for collecting. To possess such things in the greatest possible number and diversity and selection, to take them out occasionally for the pleasure of contemplating them or to be able to show them to specially favored guests of the house, surely in this lay the meaning and value of the collection for Lorenzo. It was not the only one of its kind in the period, but stood beyond all comparison in the range and quality of the individual pieces.[12]

Certain types of objects from this diverse collection, such as the mag-

[11] A comparison with the corresponding rubrics in Piero's inventory of 1466 (Müntz, Collections, pp. 35-36, 70ff.) results in the conclusion that Lorenzo had in the meantime liquidated the majority of the most materially valuable of these things, probably for the same reasons as in the case of the most valuable pieces of his father's medal collection (see above). On the other hand, Lorenzo seems to have made considerable acquisitions of antique cameos. Thus for Lorenzo, artistic and antiquarian value must have taken absolute precedence over material splendor among the objects in the collection.

[12] On this see the rather detailed information in Jacob Burckhardt, Beiträge: Die Sammler, pp. 340-45. A somewhat earlier counterpart, the collection of Pope Paul II, may be surveyed through the inventory of 1457 in Ludwig von Pastor, Geschichte der Päpste seit dem Ausgang des Mittelalters (Freiburg im Breisgau, 1866-1938, 2:349-50)

nificent bowls, pots, and drinking vessels as well as the great hoard of valuable *arazzi* that the inventory cites as the contents of various chests, surely did come into practical use on special occasions. They must have appeared in the festive banquet hall, on the table and the splendidly bedecked sideboard behind it—"in conviviis lautioribus," as Valori expresses it in his Lorenzo biography.

But the permanent interior decoration of Lorenzo's personal living rooms in the palace, which we sought above to reconstruct according to their contents and general character, already shows the same orientation of personal artistic taste that is recognizable in the assemblage of collectors' items in the *scrittoio*: a connoisseur's specialized preference for products of foreign and historic cultures—ancient, Byzantine, Netherlandish (of which much admittedly was probably already acquired by the father and grandfather). In addition, we may observe the desire for decorative costliness of detail execution and for luxurious, tastefully attuned splendor in the collecting of objects of the smallest possible format or elements, which could be properly appreciated and enjoyed only in a connoisseur's close observation.

Here as there we are surrounded to the same degree by this peculiar atmosphere of the most artful, already almost somewhat decadent refinement of spirit and consciousness. And from this atmosphere, as from the concrete spatial setting of Lorenzo's domestic world, we also gain an almost palpable image of the personality itself which shaped these rooms with their whole contents and decoration as the direct emanation of its own nature. This is the type of the true collector and epicure, for whose eyes and the touch of whose fingertips it was necessary to be surrounded only with things of the most artistically ennobled and costly splendor of form, even in objects of daily use.

We encounter this need finally in a characteristic form even in Lorenzo's dying hour, in the detailed description of it in a letter that we possess from an eyewitness, Poliziano. The letter dwells at length first of all on all the demonstrations of religious feeling that the dying man gave in confession, his reception of communion and the peacefully composed leave-taking from his relatives. Then, however, it also expressly mentions a detail that in the preceding context rings rather strangely: the silver crucifix, set with costly pearls and precious stones, that Lorenzo had extended to him as a last comfort to his soul and kissed fervently.[13]

---

[13] "Sigillum crucifixi argenteum, gemmis margaritisque magnifice adornatus." (Fabroni, *Vita Laurentii*, 1:206ff., in which the whole letter is printed).

The lavish costliness of the collection and household furnishings stand furthermore in contrast to a lifestyle whose frugal simplicity may have appeared almost blameworthy to certain contemporaries (see the statement of Filippo Rinuccini in Müntz, *Précurseurs*, p. 177, n. 2, as well as Reumont, *Lorenzo de Medici*, 2:477).

In the preceding we have noted almost exclusively works of sculpture, particularly small-scale and decorative sculpture, as characteristic of Lorenzo's activity as a patron and collector. Painting first appears in the midst of this only in various small *cimelia*, strictly old and foreign art, which lay secure in the drawers of the great *scrittoio*. And even as colored wall decorations in Lorenzo's private rooms we found only special types, such as painted furniture, small mosaic images, and a Flemish *panno dipinto* (see above). After this, even before the mention of other painting commissions of Lorenzo's, a particular branch of intimate small-scale painting should be considered: the miniature decoration of manuscripts. In this art form, the humanistic cultural interest in the possession of valuable works of literature, which had thrived in the house of Medici for three generations, was bound up with the purely bibliophile desire for the artistically refined decoration of these codices. This was already true for Cosimo's son Piero (see above), but now in a much stronger degree for Lorenzo, in whose time book illustration in general experienced an exalted, sometimes even exaggeratedly lavish display of decoration and color.[14]

As to panel paintings and canvases cited in the inventory of 1492, they appear, for the most part, to come from an older stock, acquired by Cosimo or Piero, since the frequently given names of masters are predominantly from the generation active in the second and third quarter of the century. Occasional acquisitions of Lorenzo himself were surely also assigned the names of masters by the compiler of his estate inventory, and not registered among the great mass of anonymous works. Lorenzo, at his father's death, presumably found the rooms in the city palace, as well as in his favorite villa Careggi, already provided with such abundant and high quality painted decoration that he scarcely had the impetus to increase or renew this stock of pictures in important measure. His personal collecting interests in any case did not tend in this direction. Only a few panel paintings may be demonstrably traced back to Lorenzo's own commission.[15]

[14] For the increase of the Medici household library in individual pieces with rich miniature decoration, I refer to Enea Piccolomini, "Intorno alle vicende della libreria Medicea" (*Archivio Storico Italiano*, ser. 3, 1874-1875, vols. 19-21), and note here only the special case of the acquisition of a whole group of manuscripts with the costliest decoration. This came to Lorenzo in his last years, when he took over the luxurious codices commissioned by the Hungarian king Matthias Corvinus from the Florentine miniators Gherardo and Attavante after the king's death in 1490 (Vasari-Milanesi, 3:240).

[15] Such was Pollaiuolo's portrait of the Duke Galeazzo Maria, which must have been produced on the occasion of his visit to Florence in 1471, a large canvas of Pallas with a shield and arrow (*lancia d'arco*) by Botticelli, as well as a small painting by Filippino (likewise lost) with a sleeping *ignuda* and accompanying figures in front of architectural scenery, and the charming round Madonna painting by the same artist in the Galleria

Lorenzo conferred only two major secular painting commissions in the late 1480s. One was for the villa Lo Spedaletto near Arezzo, where the four most important masters of Florentine art at that time, Ghirlandaio, Botticelli, Filippino, and Perugino executed a whole fresco cycle of antique subjects, since destroyed (see above).

The other commission was produced in the entrance hall of the new villa in Poggio a Caiano, where the two small side walls were supposed to receive fresco decoration first of all. Only one of these pictures was actually begun and executed, at least in its upper half, and that was by Filippino Lippi. The theme, recognizable only from two design drawings of the whole composition, since the severely weathered executed parts show only the rich upper architectural scenery, was Laocoon's sacrifice and downfall. This subject had been brought to Lorenzo's attention already in 1488 through a Roman antique discovery, even before the famous marble group was unearthed in 1506.[16]

The villa construction at Poggio a Caiano, however, also shows Lorenzo at last in the role of a builder; here, on a country seat acquired from the Rucellai by 1479, he had a new mansion erected by Giuliano da Sangallo in 1485-1486. With this building, vast as a palace, the Tuscan villa type went beyond the closest previous version at the Medici villa in Fiesole of 1460 to receive a new, pronouncedly princely form. The unique character that the architect gave to this villa—in particular the fine decorative organization of the portico, permeated with antiquarian elements, in the midst of the otherwise almost undecorated broad mass of the building in general—surely did not originate without Lorenzo's personal participation. We have several testimonies to a strong interest in architectural matters, even besides the specific reference in Valori's biography and in Redditi's panegyric.[17]

We also encounter various instances of Lorenzo's efforts as head of the city for the increase of private construction activity and of public

---

Corsini which, like a tondo of the Botticelli school now in the same place, comes from Careggi (Müntz, Collections, pp. 60, 84, 86; Poggi, "La giostra del 1475 e la Pallade di Botticelli," l'Arte, 1902, pp. 71ff.).

[16] This is assuming the extremely confused description of the find in a letter to Lorenzo (Gaye, Carteggio, 1:285) is correctly interpreted as a representation of Laocoon (Vasari-Milanesi, 3:473-74; Alfred Scharf and Peter Halm in MKIF, 3, pp. 393ff., 530ff.). The wall painting was probably begun around 1488-1489 and remained incomplete following Filippino's departure for Rome. For who would have urged the artist to finish the work, and paid for it, after Lorenzo's death and especially after the expulsion of the Medici?

[17] In 1481 he requested and received from Pontelli a drawing of the latter's famous palace for the Duke of Urbino; later we see Lorenzo take a lively part in the debate over the facade form of Santo Spirito, as well as in the design and execution of the sacristy of the same church, for which his personal architect Giuliano da Sangallo supplied the plans. The same was true for the construction of the Carceri church in Prato.

construction in Florence. His behavior toward Filippo Strozzi in connection with the latter's great palace project also appears very characteristic. In this case the apparently hesitant builder, with skillful diplomacy, allowed himself to be incited to his extravagantly massive project by Lorenzo himself. Lorenzo also instigated the great competition in 1491 for a new decorative facade of the Duomo, for which the Magnifico himself composed and submitted a design entry (see above).[18]

Only in the last place can we finally speak, in Lorenzo's case, of what for his grandfather Cosimo was the first, vastest, and most expensive of his patronage activities; donations for architectural and figural decoration for ecclesiastical purposes. A passage of his *ricordi* shows what he himself thought about his ancestors' generous patronage and unceasing expenditures for buildings, welfare purposes, and other needs of the commune. He probably wrote it down only in his later years, after perusing an old account book of his house. He ascertains here that in the period from 1434 through the end of 1471, the total sum of 663,755 florins was doled out only for charity, construction, and tax payments (*elemosine, muraglie, e gravezze*), excluding all other expenditures. And he notes in addition "Indeed an incredible sum of money, over which, however, I shall not complain; for if many others would much prefer to have even a part of this money in their pockets, I find these expenditures are most honorable for the reputation of our house, and well-spent money, and I am quite well satisfied about it." (Giudico esser grand'onore allo stato nostro e paionmi ben collocati e sonne molto ben contento).[19]

Yet Lorenzo was in no particular hurry to add to the house of Medici's ancient fame as patrons, which he himself duly appreciated, through activities of his own. A single great undertaking of this sort may above all be cited, and even this falls in the last years of Lorenzo's life. It was the construction of a great convent building with its church outside the Porta San Gallo for the Augustinian order, which up to then had been rather badly housed in old dilapidated buildings on the same site. A member of the order from this convent, Fra Mariano, who had come into Lorenzo's special favor and respect through his brilliant preaching, now managed to reawaken the old Medici patronage tradition in Cosimo's grandson. Consequently the reconstruction of the church and convent began in 1487-1488. It was not totally finished by Lorenzo's death, but was essentially complete and already occupied. After scarcely

[18] The wooden facade set up in front of the Duomo for the entry of Leo X in 1515 was supposedly based on this design (Gaye, *Carteggio*, 1:274; Reumont, *Lorenzo de Medici*, 2:183ff., 198ff.; Fabroni, *Vita Laurentii*, p. 183; JPK, 1902, suppl., pp. 5, 30-31; Müntz, *Précurseurs*, p. 171; ZKG, 1936, p. 347).

[19] See A. F. Gori, *La Toscana illustrata*. (Livorno, 1755), 1:194; Fabroni, *Vita Laurentii* 2:47, n. 25; 217, Lorenzo's own formulation of his three principles in life was "Patriae decus, familiae amplitudo, incrementum artium."

forty years, however, it was destroyed when the city was beseiged in 1529.[20]

Besides this by all means imposing enterprise, we find among Lorenzo's other activity as a donor only the subsidy that allowed Gozzoli's great mural cycle in the Campo Santo of Pisa to be completed (1483-1485); and further, that Lorenzo gave two Ghirlandaio altarpieces to the abbey of San Giusto near Volterra of which his son Giovanni, the subsequent pope Leo X, had become commendatory abbot (Vasari-Milanesi, 3:273n.). Thus in this respect Lorenzo lags far behind his father and grandfather; nor did he do a great deal for the enrichment of his own palace and the villas.

Lorenzo's importance in the artistic life of his time in general lay not so much in the category of the donor and patron, but rather in a direction and form of activity scarcely known before: for one thing, in the commonly acknowledged authority of his artistic judgment. Especially in his later years this was often called on by other, even foreign patrons, be it for expert opinions in the decisions on competitions, or for the recommendation of an especially appropriate artist for a particular commission.[21]

Also the fact that even non-Florentine artists sometimes approached Lorenzo in the most unaffected faith in search of some sort of assistance shows how closely the concept of the true Maecenas, the benefactor ever ready to help the artist, had become associated with his name far beyond Florence.[22] Lorenzo, however, had earned this reputation, which may have been somewhat naively exaggerated far from Florence, both for

[20] The design came once again from Giuliano da Sangallo, who according to a later assumption is supposed to have received his surname from this work of architecture. Of the whole complex we know only that it was of considerable size since it encompassed four interior courtyards, that it must have been very complete, and that its destruction was felt to be a particularly painful sacrifice even at that time. An old record published by Richa (Notizie, 1:265-66), refers only very tersely to the individual buildings with their measurements and construction costs, in the sum of 23,000 florins (see also JPK, 1902, suppl., p. 16).

[21] Thus in 1480 he recommended Giuliano da Maiano as court architect to the king of Naples, at the king's request, and after Giuliano's death in 1490 endeavored to provide him with a substitute; he procured Andrea Sansovino for the king of Portugal (Gaye, Carteggio, 2:300; Reumont, Lorenzo de' Medici, 2:186-87, 192-93; Müntz, Précurseurs, pp. 171ff.). In Pistoia he gave the final decision in the contest over the execution of the Forteguerri monument (see above). Filippino Lippi also received the commission for the Carafa chapel in Rome due to Lorenzo's recommendation; and the Cardinal wrote afterwards, somewhat overexuberantly, that on account of this recommendation he would not have exchanged the Florentine painter even for one of the famous ancient Greeks (Vasari-Milanesi, 3:269n.).

[22] See Mantegna's letter begging for a subsidy for the construction of his house in Mantua in 1484, and that of the goldsmith Lorenzo da Foligno in Ferrara for a gift for the dowry of his daughter (Gaetano Milanesi, "Lettere di artisti dei secoli XIV e XV" in Il Buonarroti, April 1869, no. VI, VIII).

several measures taken at his instigation for the honored memory of famous Florentine artists of the immediate and distant past and for his concern for the rising artistic generation in Florence.[23]

A completely new idea of Lorenzo's, and one which for long afterwards had no successor, was the creation of a training center for young artists, which opened in the casino and garden near San Marco under the direction of the sculptor Bertoldo in 1489.*

Here, not far from the great family palace, but in an area on the outskirts of the city, at that time not heavily built up, Lorenzo had erected a sort of country house for his wife Clarice within the city walls. In its interior rooms, loggia, and garden most of the pieces of his rich antique collection were set up, along with large working drawings and study sheets of old Florentine masters, in some sort of decorative grouping. When this dependency of his house lost its original purpose with Clarice's death in 1488, it must have seemed a particularly happy solution to Lorenzo to realize the idea of such a school for artists here, where even the already existing private museum placed such beneficial study material right before the eyes of the young students.

Thus in this first academy known to the history of art, almost all Florentine artists who became prominent in the immediately succeeding period found acceptance and initial training; specifically (according to Vasari's list) the painters Lorenzo di Credi, Granacci, Bugiardini, the sculptors Rustici, Torrigiano, Baccio da Montelupo, and above all the young Michelangelo (Vasari-Milanesi, 4:256ff., 7:141ff.; Burkhardt, *Beiträge: Die Sammler*, pp. 352-54).

Lorenzo, however, seems to have soon noted and duly appreciated the singular talent of this last. Condivi recounts a few anecdotes about this in his life of Michelangelo (chapters 7-10). The most important, however, and a sign of particular favor, was that Lorenzo took the boy, at that time fifteen years old, into his house, where the latter had his room and his place at Lorenzo's table as a member of the family, and like Poliziano, the literary counselor of the master of the house, received all manner of encouragement in intellectual as well as artistic respects. Before Lorenzo's death and under his eyes, as it were, the young Michelangelo produced

---

[23] Thus he begged the city of Spoleto for the remains of Fra Filippo Lippi, who had died there in 1469 and rested in an unadorned tomb, for honorable burial in the cathedral of his native city. And since the Spoletans would not cooperate, he saw to the construction of the beautiful tomb monument in the Cathedral there, according to Filippino Lippi's design (1488-1489), and with a sonorous inscription in Latin distiches composed by Poliziano (Vasari-Milanesi, 2:630; 6:468; illustrated in Müntz, *Précurseurs*, p. 175). In the Florentine Duomo he had the memorial tablets for Giotto and the musician Squarcialupi set up.

* *Translator's note*: On the garden of San Marco, whose nature and very existence are more controversial today, see the literature cited in the Translator's Introduction, p. xvi.

his first two works of marble sculpture, the Madonna relief and the *Battle of Centaurs*; convincing evidence for the Magnifico that he had rightly recognized an extraordinary talent.

It is this particular merit that we must above all regard as the high point of Lorenzo's patronage: the establishment of that school for artists in the museum near San Marco, and the personal education that Lorenzo afforded beyond this to the greatest Florentine artist of the subsequent period, in his house and private association.

With Lorenzo's death Michelangelo still did not lose his previous membership in the Medici household. The young Piero knew well how highly his father had esteemed the young sculptor. He himself, however, was evidently capable of appreciating this genius only for his manual dexterity and as an admittedly very remarkable member of his staff, in whose possession he took as much pride as in his well-built and incomparably fleet-footed Spanish runner. Thus the first artistic commission for which it occurred to him to employ Michelangelo was only an ephemeral odd job: at the time of the snowfall in the winter of 1492-1493 he had him model a snow statue in the courtyard of his palace.[24]

When Michelangelo, troubled by another person's threatening dreams, later abruptly left the house of his protector and his native city a few weeks before the revolution of 1494, Piero de' Medici was barely twenty-four years old. After the influence of the atmosphere of his father's house and the unusually careful education that he had received, one might indeed have expected some cultural activity from him in spite of his youth. Yet we encounter almost nothing of this nature.[25]

The artistic sensibilities and patronage of his father lived on not in Piero, but in his younger brother Giovanni, the later Pope Leo X; this, as far as it touched Florence, will be discussed below.

Among the contemporaries of Lorenzo Magnifico who stood out as patrons and collectors, however, another Lorenzo de' Medici should be cited above all: Lorenzo di Pierfrancesco (1463-1503), of a collateral line

[24] Ascanio Condivi, *Vita di Michelangelo Buonarrotti* (Rome, 1553), chaps. 11, 12; Vasari-Milanesi, 7:145. Michelangelo, then not yet twenty years old, was surely not vexed by this assignment. When there were heavy snowfalls, such snowmen—as Landucci tells of 1511 (*Diario*, p. 306)—were often built by artists here and there in the city for amusement, in the character of antique statues.

[25] There was perhaps some evidence of antiquarian collecting interests: in 1490, during his father's lifetime, he acquired a small ancient picture that passed for a Cimabue from the holdings of the convent of San Benedetto (outside Porta Pinti). Further, Piero functioned as expert adviser on the construction plans for the sacristy of Santo Spirito and during his exile in 1497 commissioned a marble figure from Michelangelo, who was present in Rome at that time. This, however, was never executed because the patron, as Michelangelo reported to his father, did not keep his pledge (*RA*, 1905, p. 153; *RA*, 1932, p. 36; Milanesi, "Lettere" [*Translator's note:* or Michelangelo-Milanesi, *Lettere*], p. 4).

descending from the old Cosimo's brother that stood in political opposition to Piero and was not affected by his expulsion. Three important works of painting from the young Lorenzo's collection were formerly assigned to his homonymous relation, the Magnifico. These are the two great mythological paintings by Botticelli, the *Primavera* and the somewhat later painting on canvas of the birth of Venus, both of which came from the Villa Castello, which formerly belonged to Lorenzo di Pierfrancesco. *Pallas with the Centaur* now in the Uffizi figured in the inventory after division of the estate among Lorenzo's sons in 1516. Lorenzo di Pierfrancesco also initiated the great cycle of Dante drawings by Botticelli, begun around 1492 and continued, though not to final completion, in Botticelli's last years. Besides this he had Botticelli paint some murals in Castello in 1497, which have not survived.[26]

Michelangelo, however, returning from Bologna to his native city, found a new patron in Lorenzo di Pierfrancesco. The latter immediately had him execute a youthful John the Baptist statue, now lost, and, according to Condivi (Chapter 18), next incited him to handle the theme of a sleeping Cupid in such a fashion that this figure could be sold in Rome for a high price as a supposed antique. Finally, he provided Michelangelo with some letters of recommendation for Rome, on whose use the latter reported to him in a frequently published letter (of 2 July 1496) in care of Botticelli (Milanesi, *Lettere* [*translator's note*: or Michelangelo-Milanesi, *Lettere*], pp. 375-76).

[26] Signorelli's *Court of Pan* now in Berlin and the Madonna tondo with the nude youths in the background also come from the Castello villa and supposedly resulted from commissions of Lorenzo's (see Magliabecchiano-Frey, *Il codice*, pp. 105, 359ff.; Aby Warburg, *Sandro Botticellis "Geburt der Venus" und "Frühling,"* Hamburg, 1893; Horne, *Botticelli*, pp. 50-51, 59, 158, 184, 189, 278).

CHAPTER 8

# PATRONS FROM THE
# MEDICI CIRCLE IN FLORENCE
# AND THE NETHERLANDS:
# THE SASSETTI, PORTINARI,
# TORNABUONI, FILIPPO STROZZI,
# AND OTHERS

Francesco Sassetti (1421-1490) was already active as a younger contemporary of Piero de' Medici in the 1440s and 1450s, even under the old Cosimo, in the French branches of the Medici banking house in Avignon and Lyon. So he himself became a rich man and independent partner of the Medici. From 1450 on, however, he was again resident in Florence, where later, after Piero's death, the task fell to him to support the young chief of the house with his experienced counsel. We are fairly well informed on his personality and his artistic enterprises, principally through his autobiography that, although lost itself, was used in its essential points, together with other contemporary documents in the family historical *Notizie* that his great-grandson of the same name compiled around the year 1600.[1]

From these documents we also learn much about the architectural enterprises, of private as well as charitable nature, that Francesco had initiated since the beginning of the 1460s. First of all there is the palace, constructed near Santa Trinita on a buiding site enlarged by the purchase of several adjoining properties on the small street bearing the name Sassetti even today when the palace no longer exists. In addition, from 1468 on, there was the stately villa on the hillside of Montughi on Via Bolognese, which the contemporary poet Verino proclaimed a "kingly work." Sassetti himself also referred to this "Palagio di Montughi" with partic-

[1] We know more through the last instructions of the old Sassetti written down in 1488 not long before his death and discovered by Warburg and published along with the aforementioned information (see Warburg, *Gesammelte Schriften*, 1:129ff., 353). This was not a testament in notarial form, but a general expression of convictions and admonitions for his sons as to how he wished them to administer their legacy of capital in mobile and immobile possessions, as well as old family rights and associated obligations of honor.

ular satisfaction in his records as a building that "has brought great honor and reputation to his name and house through all Italy."[2]

The great-grandson Francesco cites only the general estimated values of certain items from the old list of the contents of the city palace (which, according to a letter of Marsilio Ficino, contained the uncommon number of two household chapels, both with particularly magnificent furnishings; Warburg, *Gesammelte Schriften*, 1:139) and the villa. With these impressive figures he meant to illustrate in some measure the lifestyle of his ancestor. The most culturally significant part of the private holdings, the only one of which considerable remnants are still traceable today, was the library. A number of codices from it eventually ended up in the Laurenziana; these are sometimes distinguished by beautifully painted *ex libris* with Francesco's emblems of the centaur and the sling, as well as the devices "*Sors placida mihi*" or a "*mon pouvoir*."[3]

All that has been cited so far was intended to set off, enrich, and accentuate Sassetti's personal existence. Along with this came the patronage enterprises for public religious purposes.[4]

In Florence Francesco's patronage begins in 1466 with the acquisition of a family chapel in the Badia of Fiesole, finished around that time, that he had decorated with "figure bellisime in terretta," thus in monochrome earth-colored fresco (vanished today).

After this, however, Francesco was chiefly preoccupied with his family's old right of patronage over the high altar of Santa Maria Novella, which he had reaffirmed in 1469, in order to demonstrate it as effectively as possible. It was discussed above how this intention was nevertheless thwarted, on account of particularly sharp disagreements between Francesco and the Dominicans, to the point of abrogation of Sassetti patronage.

Yet in his last instructions of 1488 Francesco returns specifically to this matter, which was particularly painful to him. He admonished his sons not to be resigned to the removal of their coat of arms from the high altar of the Dominican church, for these arms in such a position testified to the honor and ancient reputation of the family ("l'onore di casa nostra

---

[2] See Warburg, "Francesco Sassettis letzwilliges Vermächtnis," in *Gesammelte Schriften*, 1:143; the villa, today Martini Bernardi, still bears the nickname Il Sassetto, but is greatly changed by new construction (see Carocci, *I dintorni di Firenze*, 1:183).

[3] Warburg, *Gesammelte Schriften*, 1:133, 353-54, ill. 37; Paolo D'Ancona, *La miniatura fiorentina (secoli xi-xvi)*, 2 vols., (Florence, 1914), 1:41. For a particularly beautiful French Vitruvius manuscript from Francesco's estate see *RA*, 1933, p. 321.

[4] Among these, from the activity of Francesco's younger years north of the Alps (according to its location and probably also its time) was a chapel that he had built on the Pont du Rhône in Geneva, with an expenditure of between 500 and 600 florins. Accordingly Francesco must have had to attend to commercial and probably other weighty matters there from Lyon.

et il segnio della nostra antichità"). Perhaps it might still be possible later, at some good opportunity, to establish the old right of patronage in that very place.

In the meantime, however, he had for his part already acquired a Sassetti chapel in the church of Santa Trinita near the palace and had it newly decorated. Here the glorification of his patron saint, Francis of Assisi, which had been denied him at Santa Maria Novella, could be realized. This decorative work has already been discussed above; only the aspects of it most closely related to the particular tendencies of the patron's taste and interests are to be added here.[5]

In certain of the murals, portrait figures—which demonstrate well Sassetti's close association with the ruler of the city and his literary court— have a particularly prominent place. This might appear strange in the case in question, since the essential content of the legendary text represented lay so close to the patron's heart that he had even yielded up his patronage in Santa Maria Novella on its account. Such proceedings can be explained, however, through the desire to forge a sort of magical, blessing-bearing bond with the superterrestrial world through the insertion of his own likeness and those of friends into a religious composition and to make this bond as visible as possible. The wax sculptured *ex-voto* figures in the Annunziata and elsewhere served a similar purpose in a still more direct manner (see above and Warburg, *Bildniskunst*, pp. 138-39). And this is probably also the deeper religious significance, along with the worldly personal one, of all donor portraits and donor arms on ecclesiastical buildings and art works.[6]

Then, in the subsidiary figural and decorative work in the Sassetti chapel, the humanistically trained enthusiasm for antiquity is frequently recognizable: on one level in the antique Roman architectural fragments in the Adoration scene of the altarpiece, in the Augustus-sibyl fresco above the chapel entrance, and in the painted and relief-sculptured small figures around both sarcophagi. In addition, there is that insatiable joy in emblematic allegorical figures (centaur and sling in the relief frames of the tomb niches and David with the sling above the entrance arch to the chapel). Finally, however, we find again in Ghirlandaio's altarpiece, in the shepherd group right next to the copy of a Roman sarcophagus serving as a manger the familiar, obvious influence of a masterpiece of

[5] See especially Warburg, *Bildniskunst*. The Santa Trinita chapel is still under the patronage of Francesco's descendants; it was last restored in 1896 by the head of the family at that time, a count Sassetti.

[6] There are in addition two separate portraits of Francesco Sassetti commissioned for living rooms in the palace: a marble bust by Antonio Rossellino in the Bargello and the Ghirlandaio double portrait of about 1487 representing Francesco frontally with his little son Teodoro (Duveen Collection, New York).

early Netherlandish painting that had arrived in Florence shortly beforehand; the van der Goes Portinari altar.

By this, however, we are at least indirectly reminded of the group of early Netherlandish paintings, to be discussed below, that came to Florence through Florentine merchants in Bruges, agents of the Medici and other houses. We recall first in this connection certain earlier picture commissions and acquisitions in which the Florentine-Netherlandish trade relations brought about this sort of art historical effect.[7] Of early Netherlandish paintings of known Florentine commission, two works by Rogier in particular have survived: the small Madonna altar with the arms of Florence and two Medici saints now in the Städelsches Kunstinstitut, Frankfurt and the *Entombment* in the Uffizi, which in composition and other aspects so closely matches a Munich painting of the Fra Angelico school and is supposedly identical with the former altarpiece from the house chapel at Careggi. Both paintings were thus probably commissioned by Cosimo during or shortly after Rogier's Italian journey of 1450.[8]

Now we turn to commissions of Netherlandish paintings by the Medici agents in Bruges. The head of the Florentine merchant colony there during the 1460s and 1470s was Tommaso Portinari, who in 1459 and 1462 had already advised Giovanni di Cosimo de' Medici on an order for a Flemish tapestry.[9] Tommaso Portinari also personally distinguished himself most impressively as a patron of Netherlandish masters, above all through the altarpiece by Hugo van der Goes. About 1476-1477 Portinari sent it to the hospital of Santa Maria Nuova which had been founded by his ancestor, the father of Dante's Beatrice.* This mighty retable, with the Adoration of the Shepherds in the central panel and on the wings the

---

[7] The earliest traceable record of this, the van Eyck double-portrait of Arnolfini of 1434, admittedly involves a Lucchese, not a Florentine merchant. But various other small early Netherlandish pictures, sometimes going under the names of Jan van Eyck and Petrus Christus, came into Medici possession, at unknown times by equally unknown routes. And there is frequent evidence for the early interest of Florentine collectors in Netherlandish panel paintings as well as Flemish or French canvases and *arazzi*. Many pieces of these genres were also cited in the Medici inventories (see above).

[8] See Warburg's essay "Flandrische Kunst und Florentinische Frührenaissance," as well as "Flandrische und Florentinische Kunst im Kreise des Lorenzo Magnifico," in *Gesammelte Schriften*, 1:185ff.; and Berthold Haendcke, *Der Französisch-Deutsch-Niederländische Einfluss auf die Italienische Kunst von etwa 1200 bis 1600* (Strasbourg, 1925), pp. 40ff.

[9] Warburg, *Gesammelte Schriften*, pp. 371-72. He was a relative of that Pigello Portinari, the Medici agent in Milan, who had the chapel that still bears his name today built there by Michelozzo behind Sant' Eustorgio; he was later buried in it in 1469.

* *Translator's note*: The arrival date of the Hugo van der Goes Portinari altarpiece in Florence has been pinpointed by a recently discovered document as May 28, 1483. See Bianca Hatfield Strens, "L'arrivo del trittico Portinari a Firenze," *Commentari*, 20, 1968, pp. 315-19.

great portrait figures of the donor with his wife and children, accompanied by their patron saints, was transferred from the still existing hospital into the Uffizi's possession only in the recent past. The altar for Santa Maria Nuova was not, however, Portinari's first and only commission in Bruges.

Warburg also found him and his young wife again in the donor portraits of a Memling painting with various Passion scenes now in Turin. Its dimensions and highly decorative execution suggest this was a household devotional image; it was done around 1472-1473.[10]

But a second very famous altarpiece donation besides that of the Portinari, one which failed to reach its destination in a Florentine church only through a mischance, should also be mentioned here. This is Memling's Last Judgment altarpiece, which was produced on the commission of the Medici agent in Bruges, Angelo Tani. In 1473 it was dispatched for Florence, by way of England, on a ship loaded chiefly with Portinari merchandise that was raided en route by the Hanseatic captain Benecke. Through his mediation the painting ended up in Danzig in the Marienkirche, where it remains today in spite of decade-long efforts of the injured parties. The aforementioned Angelo Tani is established as commissioner and donor of this altarpiece again on the basis of the alliance arms represented on it. He was head of the Medici office in Bruges already before Tommaso Portinari, and subsequently along with him. He had probably already commissioned this altarpiece from Memling in 1467.[11]

We now return to internal Florentine matters and note first of all, in connection with the Sassetti paintings in Santa Trinita, the far larger fresco cycle that another patron commissioned from the same Ghirlandaio, shortly before he completed that work. This is the decoration of the *cappella maggiore* in Santa Maria Novella, whose patronage Sassetti had lost on account of the aforementioned dissension over the subject matter. Lorenzo Magnifico's uncle Giovanni Tornabuoni now took his place. Giovanni was quite willing to satisfy the requirements of the monks

[10] In addition there are two portrait panel paintings, which again represent Tommaso and his wife, also by Memling and now in New York. In the Uffizi are three other portraits, partly also from Santa Maria Nuova, which Warburg, on the basis of arms or other points of reference, was able to identify as specific personalities, agents of the Medici and the Pazzi in Bruges (*Gesammelte Schriften*, p. 202).

[11] Warburg, *Gesammelte Schriften*, pp. 190ff., 373ff. In connection with these Florentine artistic commissions from Netherlandish painters, the admittedly rare evidence of a cultural exchange in the opposite direction should not go unmentioned. The same Angelo Tani in 1469 commissioned a terracotta sculptured tomb monument from Andrea della Robbia for the Benedictine abbot and Bishop Guillaume Fillastre in St. Omer. Fillastre had become acquainted with this master's work in Florence in 1463. Tani and Tommaso Portinari saw to the transportation of the work from Florence to its destined place, where it still exists today (Warburg, *Gesammelte Schriften*, pp. 373-74, note to p. 193).

regarding subject matter, as he had managed to displace the old claims of the earlier patron family, the Ricci, by a sly manoeuvre. The amusing anecdote that Vasari tells concerning this is admittedly not confirmed elsewhere. But the particularly firm assertion of the new patronage right to the chapel, which Tornabuoni even thought worth inserting in his contract with Ghirlandaio, suggests previous differences concerning this matter had been successfully overcome.[12]

The total result of this donation, including wall and vault painting, stained glass of the three-part window, the high altarpiece painted on both sides, and the wall pews with fine intarsia decoration, has already been discussed in detail above. Its execution made more or less important claims on the donor's resources for a full ten years. But the whole, after its completion around 1496, must have appeared as a uniquely splendid manifestation of private patronage expenditure; this can be adequately recognized even today, with the chapel decoration only a shadow of its former state and partially mutilated by later measures.

Two other Tornabuoni enterprises have come down to us only in fragmentary form. The family's urban palace, on the street still bearing their name today, was probably built already around 1450 by Michelozzo; it is entirely modernized, even the courtyard. Only a few individual pieces of its former furnishings, surely not inferior to those of the chapel in Santa Maria Novella, are traceable, and these are of insecure provenance.[13]

Of the former Tornabuoni villa—later Villa Lemmi, situated near Careggi—at least a few notices have survived, as well as various portions of the former mural decoration. Vasari informs us of frescoes by Ghirlandaio, since lost, in a chapel on the grounds of the villa. A severely damaged fresco is located in a rectangular hall of the upper story of the main house of the estate representing the master of the house in the official regalia

---

[12] "Ad presens ut asseritur patronus et iura indubitati patronatus tenens capelle." From the contract of 15 September 1485 (Milanesi, *Documenti*, p. 158ff.) we also excerpt the phrases that refer so emphatically to the donor's intentions: "intuita pietatis et amore Dei . . . in exaltationem sue domus et familie et ornationem . . . dicte ecclesie et capelle." In addition, the painter was promised a fee of 1100 florins and was allowed a period of four years for execution. See also Enrico Ridolfi, "Giovanna Tornabuoni e Ginevra dei Benci . . . ," *Archivio storico Italiano* (Florence, 1890), pp. 426-56.

[13] These include the Ghirlandaio tondo of the Epiphany, which Vasari cites from the Palazzo Tornabuoni (probably identical with a picture in the Uffizi) and perhaps also the beautiful Verrocchio marble relief with the death of Francesca Tornabuoni now in the Bargello, which in any case cannot have belonged to her tomb in Rome, as was formerly generally accepted (see Hermann Egger, *Römische Forschungen des Kunsthistorischen Institutes, Graz*, 1934). The portrait medals of himself and several of his relatives that Giovanni had executed by Niccolò Fiorentino also served private purposes; see the example dated 1493 (George Francis Hill, *A Corpus of Italian Medals of the Renaissance before Cellini*, London, 1930, pp. 267-68).

of the *gonfaloniere*; thus dating from the year 1482, in which Giovanni held this highest office of the city republic. The much more precious paintings of Botticelli, which went into the Louvre after their rediscovery (see above), formerly decorated a long wall of the same room. They are evidently related to the marriage in 1486 of Giovanni's son Lorenzo Tornabuoni, who appears here, together with his young wife, in the company of female allegorical figures (Horne, *Botticelli*, 142ff.).[14]

The same Lorenzo Tornabuoni (whose patron saint is worked into the intarsia of the wall panelling in Santa Maria Novella as a counterpart to the St. John of his father) also had Ghirlandaio paint the altarpiece of the Visitation (now in the Louvre) for his chapel in the Cestello church (Santa Maria Maddalena dei Pazzi) in 1490-1491.[15]

In the immediate vicinity of the former Palazzo Tornabuoni there also stands that palace building of the Laurentian period whose completely extraordinary imposing appearance has kept the builder's fame alive up to the present day, the Palazzo Strozzi. Such an enduring effect was, however, precisely what the builder, Filippo Strozzi, was striving for. "Desirous of fame more than riches" (cupido piu di fama che di roba), he wanted, as his son and biographer expressed it, "to erect a building which would bear witness to him and his family throughout all Italy and beyond" (Gaye, *Carteggio*, 1:354).

It was not granted him to see the ambitious project realized beyond the initial stage. But even the planning and beginning of construction of this palace was a truly triumphal ending for Filippo's life, which had begun in such straitened and difficult circumstances. A brief backward look at the course of his life will allow us to appraise fairly what such an undertaking meant for him and for his contemporaries.

As son of a man banished by Cosimo de' Medici in 1434, subsequently banished from Florence for decades himself, Filippo Strozzi (born 1428) had been able to build a solid businessman's life in Naples, to acquire wealth and respect, and finally even, thanks to the intercession of King Ferrante, to effect the lifting of his banishment in 1466. It is true that he still maintained his residence in Naples until the end of the 1470s, on account of his banking business. His mother, however, lived in Florence, in modest circumstances. To him and his brother, who was active in France, over a period of several decades she sent the "Lettere di una

[14] The three cassoni or wainscoting pictures with scenes from the Jason and Medea legend, whose origin is recognizable through the alliance arms and the date 1486, once decorated the bedchamber of this young couple (Schubring, *Cassoni*, pp. 349, 389, pl. 83, 92).

[15] A few years later, in 1497, the patron, suspected of a conspiracy in behalf of the expelled Medici, was hanged in the court of the Bargello (Vasari-Milanesi, 3:269, n. 2, 281; *l'Arte*, 1906, p. 259).

gentildonna fiorentina" that have become so famous since Guasti's publication in 1877. These documents are equally precious in a cultural-historical and general human sense, full of direct insights into the life and social world of the writer.

Filippo's personal situation—of which much is indicated by his mother's letters and the other documents provided in Guasti's commentary—must concern us closely only from the time when he himself again took up permanent residence in Florence. At that time, after the Pazzi conspiracy that had been successfully suppressed shortly before Filippo's homecoming, Lorenzo Magnifico stood at the height of his power and renown.

But how did Filippo Strozzi now fit into this period? His son's biography reports that already in his Neopolitan household he had spent considerable sums for rich table silver and choice furnishings for the rooms. And the costly stock he brought back to Florence with him must have lent a sharply different aspect to the old Strozzi house, in which his mother had previously led her spare existence. Of patronage activity we know initially only that Filippo as son-in-law of a Gianfigliazzi had for his part completed the great enterprise of this family, the painting of the choir chapel in Santissima Trinita.[16]

But a more direct interest bound Filippo to the church of Santa Maria Novella, in which the Strozzi had already owned the great chapel, painted by Orcagna and Nardo, since the fourteenth century. Filippo now acquired for himself and his branch of the family the patronage of one of the transept chapels, which had become free through the impoverishment of the previous owner. The magnificent new decoration of the adjoining *cappella maggiore* by the Tornabuoni probably gave Filippo the impetus to set something similar in motion for his Strozzi chapel. It is true that the painted decoration, commissioned from Filippino in April 1487, came to completion only long after Filippo's death (see above). And the patron's tomb, set in a shallow niche of the window wall, was probably only begun when Filippo died on 18 May 1491.

The completion, however, came soon thereafter. This was by Benedetto da Maiano, who had already earlier created the fine portrait bust of Filippo, and as architect had also designed and begun his great building enterprise, the new family palace (cornerstone laid on 6 August 1489). At that time Filippi Strozzi himself was already in his sixties. When he died three years later, even the outer walls of the giant block of a building had risen only a few meters above the street level (Landucci, *Diario*,

---

[16] He is also supposed to have toyed with the idea of replacing the excessively small Romanesque facade, reproduced in a fresco by Ghirlandaio in the Sassetti chapel, with a new decorative facade. See Lorenzo di Filippo Strozzi, *Vita di Filippo Strozzi il vecchio*, ed. G. Bini and P. Bigazzi (Florence, 1851), pp. 15, 28; Gaye, *Carteggio*, 1:357.

passim). Even before the actual beginning of construction Filippo must have spent important sums to lay free the building ground for his project, which reached far beyond the old Strozzi property, and to found the planned massive structure sufficiently deeply and securely.[17]

In his will, however, the builder left binding instructions to his wife and his sons, then still minors, for the continuation and completion of the palace. And that was with the compelling clause that in the case of any failure by his heirs to observe these provisions, the city head Lorenzo Magnifico himself or the consuls of the Calimala guild were empowered and obliged to collect the money from the Strozzi estate for uninterrupted execution of the building through the continuous occupation of fifty workers and transfer it to the building fund (Gaye, *Carteggio*, 1:362-64). Such a guarantee of testamentary provisions admittedly is quite consistent with the generally customary proceedings that we have encountered earlier in donations in wills for religious purposes. Yet here it is a matter of the execution of a purely private building project that was to benefit only the posterity of the testator as a dwelling, and to bring honor and fame to them and him for all time to come.

If Filippo felt he could entrust Lorenzo Magnifico himself with the obligations of executor, he knew of the latter's personal interest in the creation of his mighty building. We learn in his biography how Filippo, with skillful diplomacy, brought the Medici expressly to urge him to execute the whole exterior architecture in heavy rustication, although Filippo felt obliged to tell him that such a manner of building did not correspond to his status as a citizen ("non esser cosa civile") and that in general the whole undertaking would greatly overtax his financial resources.

In fact, Filippo had charged his widow with a severe and long-lasting burden in the two enterprises begun shortly before his death—the chapel in Santa Maria Novella and the palace. And this also probably explains the greatly belated execution of Filippino's paintings in the chapel, as well as the slow if also steady progress of the construction of the palace, which only about twelve years after Filippo's death was nearly completed in brick and ready for use.[18]

[17] No less than fifteen small separate buildings were originally located on the site of the subsequent Strozzi palace. They included the tower of the counts of Poppi and the simple house in which Filippo's parents and even he himself had first lived (compare the catasto declarations in Guido Carocci in *Illustratore Fiorentino*, Florence, 1907, pp. 74-75; and Strozzi-Bini-Bigazzi, *Vita*, pp. 73-74). According to Luitpold Dussler (*Benedetto da Maiano: ein florentiner Bildhauer des späten Quattrocento*, Munich, 1924, pp. 63-64), Giuliano da Maiano, who received payments for a wood model of the palace building, may also have been its designer.

[18] In order to bolster her finances in some measure, Filippo's widow had subsequently to decide in 1508 to marry her only son to a daughter of Piero de' Medici, although this

Filippo's funeral, as a member of the confraternity of San Benedetto, dressed in its habit, corresponds to the generally customary forms of private religiosity. It appears more extraordinary that the entire staff of workmen from the palace project joined his long funeral procession, from the leading architect down to the *plebaglia* of masons' assistants and handymen, all dressed in dark clothing at the expense of the mourning household. For these obsequies in Florence, as well as for the mourning feasts at Filippo's branch offices in Naples and Rome, probably also including the erection of the tomb in Santa Maria Novella, the expenditure came to over 3000 florins. The truly princely lifestyle that Filippo's palace embodied was accordingly also quite effectively manifested in his funeral solemnities.[19]

With this prominent figure we conclude the individual descriptions of representatives of the group of patrons and donors from the period of Lorenzo Magnifico. The total picture of this period may be completed by a few more pertinent notes and references. First of all it must be remembered that in the course of the last two or three decades of the Quattrocento, no less than four new church buildings received their completion with their decoration of more or less numerous private altars and chapels: above all Santo Spirito, then San Francesco al Monte, in addition the Cistercian church Cestello, later called Santa Maria Maddalena dei Pazzi, as well as San Domenico di Fiesole.

This list, however, includes only churches that have survived along with a considerable part of their former contents. Foundations destroyed during the *assedio* of 1529 also belong to this period: Lorenzo Magnifico's Augustinian church outside the Porta San Gallo and the church of the Gesuati convent, decorated primarily by Perugino. In the aforementioned churches, however, particularly in Santo Spirito and Cestello, the competing efforts of a whole series of individual donors in the 1480s and 1490s may still be traced today from chapel to chapel. If even here many valuable altarpieces have passed into museums and been replaced by later substitutes, the former general character of these church spaces is still in large measure imaginable through the surviving altars and much reported evidence. Thus each of these churches functions as a museum of Florentine altar painting and altar decoration of this period—an organically

---

union still appeared politically very risky. But Clarice de' Medici was the niece of Cardinal Giovanni, the subsequent Leo X, and brought more than twice the normal dowry to the marriage. See Lorenzo di Filippo Strozzi, *Le vite degli uomini illustri della Casa Strozzi*, ed. F. Zeffi (Florence, 1892), pp. 87ff. [*Translator's note:* The reference may also be to P. Stromboli's edition, *Vite di alcuni della famiglia Strozzi*, Florence, 1890].

[19] Lorenzo Strozzi, *Le vite degli uomini illustri della Casa Strozzi*, ed. F. Zeffi (Florence, 1892), pp. 66, 75. [*Translator's note:* The reference may also be to P. Stromboli's edition, *Vite di alcuni della famiglia Strozzi*, Florence, 1890.] See also "Ricordi di San Benedetto," (*RA*, 6, p. 244).

grown, not artificially created museum—and as a hall of honor for the patrician families of the neighborhoods to which they belonged.[20]

In certain cases we encounter multiple altar foundations by one and the same man or family. Thus Tanai de' Nerli had Filippino Lippi paint the altarpiece still in its place in the transept of Santo Spirito, as well as an altar panel for San Francesco al Monte. The Frescobaldi, that is, probably various branches of this house, possessed four different chapels in Santo Spirito (Vasari-Milanesi, 3:464-72).

The redecoration of the choir chapel in Santa Trinita came into being as a large-scale donation of Bongianni Gianfigliazzi, who met his death in 1485 as commissioner of the Signoria at the siege of Pietrasanta. It included stained glass (destroyed in 1616) designed by Baldovinetti in 1465-1466, a Baldovinetti altarpiece, and the painting of the whole chapel by the same artist, of which only the vault decoration survives. The Vespucci secured their honorable memory through several donations of images to the Franciscan church of Ognissanti, through the multipartite mural composition by Ghirlandaio in the altar niche of their chapel, and through two individual frescoes executed in 1480 of the two church doctors Augustine and Jerome on the choir screen, later moved to the side walls. In these, Ghirlandaio and Botticelli engaged in a dialogue side by side.[21]

For the family palace (now Palazzo Incontri on Via dei Servi), which Guidantonio Vespucci acquired in 1498 when he was *gonfaloniere*, Botticelli decorated a room with a panel painting in a richly carved framework; in another room of the same palace, Piero di Cosimo added a *spalliera* cycle with representation of bacchic scenes.[22] The incidental information we have on the artistic contents of the Palazzo Vespucci only further establishes what was observed above in the section on household painting: the general sharp increase in the demand for elegance and high artistic value in domestic furnishings in the late Quattrocento.

Yet it must again be emphasized that such luxury in private houses finds a constant counterpart in the public sphere in the no less lavish art commissions for churches which served in particular, now as earlier, to enrich the chapels of private patrons.

A last example of this is the behavior of Piero del Pugliese. Filippino, for example, painted for his house a "picture with small figures," espe-

[20] On the altars in the Cestello church see *l'Arte*, 9, 1906, pp. 255ff; 262; 10, pp. 225-26; as well as Horne, *Botticelli*, p. 355. On Santo Spirito see *RA*, 1906, p. 117. On San Domenico see *Nuovo Osservatore Fiorentino*, 1885, pp. 127-28.

[21] In the floor is the tomb plaque of Amerigo Vespucci of 1471. See *l'Arte*, 15, 1912, pp. 287-89. On the Vespucci donations and the portraits of the patron family surviving in them, see Heinrich Brockhaus, *Forschungen über florentiner Kunstwerke* (Leipzig, 1902), pp. 85ff. and Horne, *Botticelli*, pp. 70ff.

[22] Vasari-Milanesi, 3:312; 4:141. Certain surviving pieces are believed to be traceable to each cycle (see above). Horne, *Botticelli*, p. 282.

cially praised by Vasari (Vasari-Milanesi, 3:467) who was probably referring to the Lucretia panel now in the Pitti. In 1498-1499 Fra Bartolommeo provided the two little painted wings of a household altar that contained a Madonna relief by Donatello. Piero Pugliese, however, was also the founder, as early as 1479, of a family chapel in the convent church alle Campora outside Porta Romana, belonging to the Badia. For this, around 1485-1486, he had the young Filippino Lippi paint the altarpiece of the Madonna with St. Bernard (in the Badia since 1529), in which he himself appears as a portrait figure. In addition, he endowed the chapel with a chalice and beautiful vestments and sent it a precious illuminated manuscript with the sermons of St. Bernard.

Besides this, Piero owned an altar in the Innocenti church, for which Piero di Cosimo painted the marriage of St. Catherine now in Berlin with the donor's patron saint at the side.[23]

[23] Vasari-Milanesi, 4:140-41; *RA*, 1903, pp. 1ff.; and Raffaello Borghini, *Il Riposo*, (1st ed., Florence, 1584), 2:168. [*Translator's note*: Wackernagel does not indicate which edition of *Il Riposo* he used.] On the Lucretia and Virginia *spalliere* by the young Filippino see Scharf, *Filippino Lippi*, p. 17. [*Translator's note*: The *Marriage of Saint Catherine* altarpiece by Piero di Cosimo is in fact in the museum of the Spedale degli Innocenti in Florence, not in Berlin.]

CHAPTER 9

# PATRONS OF THE
# HIGH RENAISSANCE AND
# EXTRA-FLORENTINE
# COMMISSIONERS
# AND COLLECTORS

In the period still to be surveyed, from about 1498 to 1530, the pertinent factual material lags decidedly behind that of the preceding period in scope, variety, and brilliance of examples. To begin with, the former leading spirit that for three generations of the house of Medici had spurred the Florentine patriciate to competing efforts is palpably absent. A new era of Medici supremacy in Florentine artistic life begins only after the election of Leo X to the papacy in 1513.

We begin by tracing the transition from late Quattrocento to High Renaissance patronage from father to son within one family, from the above-mentioned Piero del Pugliese to Francesco di Piero.* Differing from what we observed of Piero, still active predominantly as a donor, the young Francesco appears more as a personally interested connoisseur. An avowed member of Savonarola's following, he had Fra Bartolommeo paint a fresco of St. George on the staircase of his palace, probably in the last years of the artist's life. From the Frate's estate he received the gift of a small crucifix painted by him. On the other hand, however, he commissioned a cycle of secular wainscoting panel pictures from Piero di Cosimo, from which the three panels of the Andromeda legend in the Uffizi executed about 1512-1515 supposedly come. Finally, he made an effort to acquire from the nuns of Santa Chiara the Perugino Pietà, now in the Uffizi and offered three times the original price for it. This already shows in him the emergence of that collector's appetite, ready to sacrifice

---

*Translator's note:* The important patron Francesco del Pugliese was actually Piero's nephew and ward, not his son, and was called Francesco di *Filippo*. See Alison Luchs, *Cestello: A Cistercian Church of the Florentine Renaissance* (New York, 1976), pp. 50, 164, n. 26. See also the dissertation by Stephanie Craven, *Aspects of Patronage in Florence 1494-1512* (Courtland Institute of Art, London, 1973).

anything for a precious old work, for which we can cite further evidence from other quarters.[1]

Besides this, the names we encounter among the patrons of the High Renaissance are almost entirely new; one is Francesco del Giocondo, for whom the sought-after Leonardo painted the portrait of his wife, Mona Lisa.[2] Then there is the rich wooldealer Agnolo Doni (1476-1539) who had himself and his wife painted by the young Raphael in 1506, and shortly before that, on the occasion of his wedding, commissioned the great tondo of the Holy Family from Michelangelo. The Strozzi arms of his wife are worked into its richly carved frame. Vasari recounts that as a patron he was constantly determined to pay the lowest possible price. He probably got away with it in the case of the Urbinate, at that time still unknown; with Michelangelo, however, according to Vasari's anecdote, he seems to have miscalculated. From the look of his prosperous, prosaic face, one would certainly not attribute to him too much understanding for the powerful originality of Michelangelo's painting. In addition, ten years later he had Fra Bartolommeo paint him another Holy Family (now in the Galleria Corsini, Rome, and dated 1516), which must surely have suited him perfectly. Cinelli still saw the cited paintings in his house on the Corso dei Tintori, along with a beautiful *spalliera* with grotesque ornament by Morto da Feltre and carved pilasters in 1678. The Donatello bronze putto (*Amor Atys*, in the Bargello) was also in his sons' possession, probably inherited from their father. Cinelli described it also, but as an antique.[3]

The commission of another work by Fra Bartolommeo is known to us thanks to the continuing account books of the San Marco convent administration: To begin with, Bernardo del Bianco, with the support of the prior of the order at that time, Dietrich von Schönberg, induced the Frate to take up painting again after a lapse of several years. This was to execute an altarpiece, now in the Accademia, of the appearance of the Madonna to his patron saint, St. Bernard, for his chapel in the Badia, as well as the fresco image above the entrance arch of the chapel

[1] Vasari-Milanesi, 3:569-70; 4:139; Fritz Knapp, *Piero di Cosimo* (Halle, 1878), 273; Schnitzer, *Savonarola*, pp. 497, 529, 554, 563.

[2] Francesco di Giocondo, born 1460, married Lisa di Antonio Gherardini, of Neapolitan origin, in 1495; he himself appears among the Buonomini di San Martino in 1499, among the Priors in 1512 (Woldermar von Seidlitz, *Leonardo da Vinci, der Wendepunkt der Renaissance*, Berlin, 1909, 2:48).

[3] Vasari-Milanesi, 4:325; Bocchi-Cinelli, *Le bellezze della citta*, pp. 275-76, 565. Davidsohn (*Rep.*, 1900, pp. 211ff., 451) established Maddalena Doni-Strozzi's birth year as 1489 in connection with Raphael's double portrait; the woman portrayed must thus have been considerably younger than Raphael represents her. The old identification must nevertheless be correct, since the two paintings came into the Pitti from the Doni estate.

in 1504-1506. Benedetto da Rovezzano provided the rich architectural and marble sculptural decoration.[4] Then there is Piero Cambi, to whom San Marco owes the one altarpiece of Fra Bartolommeo that is still there in the original; the standing Madonna of 1509 with six saints, including the donor's patron, St. Peter Martyr.

Finally we cite the merchant Salvatore Billi, the donor of Fra Bartolommeo's classical masterpiece, *Christ the Savior* (Christus Salvator) with the four Evangelists, now in the Pitti, which originally had the two large prophet paintings now in the Uffizi as wings. The former Billi chapel in the Annunziata still exists today under the organ on the right hand side, with the richly sculptured marble structure, probably by Benedetto da Rovezzano, from about 1520, in whose tabernacle-style altar niche the three great paintings were installed. One must evoke these conditions and the total effect that can thus be imagined, in order to appreciate what was dismantled and destroyed here by the egotistical collector's greed of later times.[5]

Important architectural donations also still occurred, like the Pandolfini entrance structure for the Badia with the exterior portal, columned portico, and adjoining family chapel, built in 1503-1510 by Benedetto da Rovezzano.

Besides this, the overriding desire for the most splendid possible decoration of private houses, which could already be noted frequently in the late Quattrocento, now manifested itself with particular strength.

Thus the Altoviti, as patrons of the church of Santi Apostoli near their palace, enriched the rough ancient facade with Benedetto da Rovezzano's marble portal and erected a beautiful tomb inside. The same sculptor also came to their palace, according to Vasari (Vasari-Milanesi, 4:530-31), to erect a splendid marble fireplace and a wall fountain, as well as other "cose sottilmente lavorate." Such fireplaces, magnificent, richly-sculptured structures, were produced at that time also for the Palazzo Gondi by Giuliano da Sangallo, as well as for Giovanni Gaddi at Palazzo

---

[4] The payment for Fra Bartolommeo's work, however, became the subject of lengthy negotiations between the painter, his convent which at that time was sorely in need of money, and the patron, for Bernardo wanted to pay only half the sum that the convent demanded. An agreement was finally reached on the sum of 100 florins by calling in two appraisers (there were more long disputes on the choice of these). The chapel decoration perished during the later renovation of the church; the altarpiece is now in the Academy (Marchese, *Memorie*, 2:594ff.; Vasari-Milanesi, 4:183; Raffaelo Borghini, *Il Riposo* (1st ed., Florence, 1584), 2:170 [*Translator's note:* Wackernagel does not indicate which edition of *Il Riposo* he used]).

[5] The beautiful *Visitation* by Mariotto Albertinelli of 1503, now in the Uffizi, resulted from the commission of the congregation of priests "Della Visitazione" as an altarpiece for its oratory (Richa, *Notizie*, 8:265ff.).

della Madonna by Jacopo Sansovino and in the house of Pier Francesco Borgherini, afterwards the Palazzo Rosselli del Turco, by Benedetto da Rovezzano; the latter work is now in the Bargello.[6]

In the palace of the aforementioned Borgherini, who was Michelangelo's banker in Rome and Florence, there was above all the precious painted and carved panelling of the 1520s. Numerous parts of this ensemble, described by Vasari but later destroyed, have survived scattered in various museums (see above). A similar cycle of panelling paintings was produced around 1520 for the house of Giovanni Maria Benintendi, who in addition owned the half-length figure of the youthful John by Andrea del Sarto now in the Pitti. It should be well noted that almost exclusively religious themes from the Old and New Testaments are treated in these panelling pictures. Ancient *historie*, however, which occur only occasionally in such a context, appear in monumental treatment and in more significant typological associations with certain moments in Medici family history in the painting of the grand salone of Poggio a Caiano, undertaken at Leo X's commission in 1516 but still incomplete at his death (see above).

With this, in the second phase of the Florentine High Renaissance, Medici patronage begins to emerge again after a twenty year pause in a heightened, grand-scale style of enterprise corresponding to the political as well as the stylistic juncture. It begins with the lavish decoration set up in the city on the occasion of Pope Leo's first official visit to his native city in 1515 (see above). This was followed, along with the paintings in Lorenzo Magnifico's villa just cited, by the important architectural-sculptural enrichment that was planned and partially carried out for the old patronage complex of the Medici line, the church and convent of San Lorenzo.

The commission for the church facade, which Pope Leo assigned to Michelangelo immediately after his visit to Florence, admittedly came to an early halt. On the other hand, Leo's nephew, Cardinal Giulio, already in the 1520s and then again as Pope Clement VII, had two other building sections within the province of San Lorenzo designed, again by Michelangelo, on the grandest scale. These were the "new sacristy," with the Medici tombs, and the great library with its vestibule, for the worthy installation of the old Medici treasury of books which had come back into the family's possession after various vicissitudes. Pope Clement now gave these over to the canonry of San Lorenzo, along with countless

---

[6] Vasari-Milanesi, 4:530-31; 6:58. Two splendid marble niches, probably by the same Rovezzano, came into the Bargello from the same palace. But it is hard to believe they were originally commissioned for this palace. They perhaps belonged to the tomb of San Giovanni Gualberto, never completely finished, of which similar parts were used in Santa Trinita.

precious vessels, made into reliquaries, from the possession of Lorenzo Magnifico (see above).

These assignments to Florentine artists by the two Medici popes, thus by nonresident patrons, lead us on finally to the activity of external and foreign customers in the Florentine art market.

Prominent among these is the king of Hungary, Matthias Corvinus, who showed particularly zealous interest already during the time of Lorenzo Magnifico. The Magnifico sent him a gift of Verrocchio bronze reliefs with ideal portraits of ancient generals (see above). On the king's commission, however, the same Verrocchio was assigned to execute a marble decorative fountain in 1468. Of this, only the distich inscription provided by Poliziano has survived. Florentine intarsiators also worked frequently for the Hungarian royal court, among others Benedetto da Maiano, who personally delivered a pair of costly chests. The king also had a tapestry decorated with figural and emblematic motifs executed as a worthy decoration for his throne room, apparently according to Pollaiuolo's design; fragments of this still survive.

Filippino Lippi declined a personal invitation to Hungary. But he provided two panel paintings of religious subjects. The Hungarian king also turned to Florentine miniaturists, specifically to Attavante, to replenish his important stock of books. Lorenzo Magnifico took over a major commission for these, which was still incomplete at the king's death, as already discussed.[7]

The same Attavante also executed another miniature work of equally unusual magnificence in 1494-1497: a seven-volume bible, for King Emanuele of Portugal. This is the *Bibbia dos Hieronymos*, still extant in Lisbon.[8] For sculptural work, the king of Portugal had Andrea Sansovino recommended to him by Lorenzo Magnifico.

Of Florentine Quattrocento sculptors, Verrocchio, in addition to the aforementioned Hungarian commissions, received the great commission from the Venetian signoria for the equestrian monument of their condottiere Colleoni, also in the 1480s. The architect Giuliano da Sangallo and the sculptor Benedetto da Maiano worked in Naples for King Ferrante and other highly placed patrons; Agostino di Duccio was active in Urbino, along with other Florentine decorators. In Milan, however, where Michelozzo and Filarete had already worked for some time, Leonardo

[7] See Milanesi, *Documenti*, p. 148; Vasari-Milanesi; 3:334-35; Scharf, *Filippino Lippi*; Schaffran in *RA*, 1932, pp. 445ff., 33, 191ff.; and André de Hevésy, *La Bibliothèque du Roi Matthias Corvin* (Paris, 1923).

[8] A Florentine merchant, Chimenti di Ciriaco, drew up the contract with the miniaturist on the king's commission; he continually supervised the progress of the work and paid out the salary installments according to it (Milanesi, *Documenti*, p. 164; *Bibliofilia*, 15, pp. 205ff.).

da Vinci entered for nearly two decades from 1482 to 1499 into the service of the city ruler. Even the Certosa of Pavia commissioned several altarpieces from the Florentine painters Filippino, Perugino, and Fra Bartolommeo.[9]

Above all, however, the Roman Curia drew the best Florentine painters into its service, since the time of Sixtus IV as well as earlier, and afterwards with ever increasing frequency.

The various papal and prelates' tombs by Pollaiuolo, Mino da Fiesole, and Sansovino testify to this, as does the painting of the Sistine Chapel, that even in its first stage with the murals of the 1480s was carried out chiefly by Florentine masters. Michelangelo, however, was throughout his life active primarily in Rome and for the Roman popes, although a few highly-placed patrons from lands north of the Alps also asked and received works from his hand (the bronze David for the Marshall of Rohan and the Bruges Madonna).

Likewise, an altarpiece by Fra Bartolommeo went to the Bishop of Autun as a gift of the Florentine city government in 1506 and soon thereafter the same master painted the high altarpiece for the Cathedral of Besançon for Chancellor Carondelet, Maximilian's representative at the Curia.

All these desires for works of Florentine artists, forthcoming from so many directions, and all their external activity also mean an appreciable stimulus for Florence itself, in terms of a respectable, expansive development of its art market and general artistic life.

Florentine export of art and artists to France since the beginning of the sixteenth century was a principal manifestation of this. Since Charles VIII's Italian campaign (leaving aside earlier matters), progressive diplomatic and cultural relations existed between the French royal court and the Florentine republic. In this connection, valuable objects of art were frequently used by the Florentine government for the advancement of political goals (see above). Finally, however, the French king himself began to invite Florentine artists of well-known importance to France. First and foremost was Leonardo da Vinci, who then remained close to the French court from 1516 until his death. Fra Bartolommeo also received an invitation from the king, which he declined, in 1514-1515; on the other hand, Andrea del Sarto followed the call to Paris in 1518, admittedly to come home again after only a year. His *Caritas* in the Louvre is the only work of his Parisian sojourn still remaining there.

The mediating role of Florentine merchants active in France and elsewhere took on increasing importance in these foreign relations of Flor-

[9] Along with this, the varied earlier activity of Florentine sculptors, traceable particularly since the early fifteenth century, should be recalled, as well as certain painters in Venice, Padua, and other north Italian cities (on this see for example *RA*, 1931, pp. 45ff.).

entine artists. Their extensive personal connections, in the artistic world of Florence as well as among Frenchmen interested in Italian artworks, must have made them especially well suited for such a function. Thus it happened that repeatedly, since the end of the fifteenth century and especially in the beginning of the sixteenth, Florentine artists were brought to France, Spain, and England by agents of home trading firms and recommended to patrons there (see below for details). In this manner these mediators probably also brought themselves into good standing with their important clients, thus benefiting at least indirectly. They would have been poor merchants, however, if they had not soon also sought to do direct trading in artistic works of their homeland, just as they did with other Florentine products. At first only a few opportunities arose for this, since the artists indeed worked almost without exception on fixed commissions, so that objects for free offer on the outside were only occasionally available.

In the early sixteenth century, however, it happened more often that a merchant commissioned a painting from a well-known artist at his own risk in order to pass it on, naturally not without good recompense, to a French amateur.[10]

A Florentine patrician, Giovanni Battista della Palla, finally developed into an art dealer in the fullest and truest sense, that is, a systematic purchaser of contemporary as well as antique art works. As a young man he had distinguished himself among the *jeunesse dorée* of Florence by his lavish standard of living. But in 1521, as accessory to a conspiracy, he was banished to France, where he gained the king's favor. Then, after the second expulsion of the Medici in 1527, he reappeared in Florence, with the specific assignment from the king to acquire or commission valuable art works for him.

Vasari, who must have known Palla personally, speaks of him several times; he represents the exceedingly energetic activity of this agent, who gave out numerous commissions to painters and sculptors, also kept an eye out for older works of famous masters and antiques, and—this probably expressed with some exaggeration—"every day had something to pack up and send off." Certain of his commissions and acquisitions were specifically mentioned by Vasari.[11]

[10] Thus a certain Domenico Perini had the *Noli me tangere* painted by Fra Bartolommeo "per in Francia" (see Knapp, *Fra Bartolommeo*, p. 59). Bernardino de' Rossi commissioned a painting of St. Sebastian from Perugino, likewise "per mandarlo in Francia," for which he paid the artist 100 florins, but sold to the French king for 400 (!). The sale of certain pictures by Andrea del Sarto, negotiated by Florentine merchants, preceded his invitation to France (Vasari-Milanesi, 3:577; 5:23-24, 26, 37).

[11] He had a fountain figure for the park of Fontainebleau executed by Tribolo, ordered from Ridolfo Ghirlandaio a copy of Pollaiuolo's Hercules painting, which at that time hung in the Palazzo Vecchio; in San Marco he managed through special circumstances to purchase

Palla may occasionally have sought to acquire some fine object or other from private possession. In the process he may admittedly sometimes have come to the wrong address, and once received as sharp a rebuff as Vasari describes for a certain case, with the complete immediacy of an eyewitness report. This concerned the magnificent room decoration in the house of Pier Francesco Borgherini, cited above, who at that time had to leave Florence on account of the political situation. This appeared a favorable situation to Palla. And even the city Signoria, which was eager to please the French king, supported his plan with an emphatic message of recommendation to Borgherini's wife, who had remained in Florence. The latter, however, a Florentine patrician of old lineage (the distinguished Acciaiuoli family) sent Palla and the city's emmissary an answer whose unprecedented sharpness made such an impression that it was even passed down more or less verbatim to Vasari, who later added it to the *vita* of Pontormo in full detail, in direct quotation.[12]

Vasari finally concludes with special praise for the plucky noblewoman, that thanks to her determination the house of Borgherini could still call that precious room decoration its own. Battista della Palla, however, came to an unexpectedly tragic end soon after this episode; after the conquest of the city in 1530 he was thrown into prison as an enemy of the Medici and an agent of France and put to death there two years later.[13]

We have lingered over this first representative of the pronounced art-dealer type because his whole activity and behavior carried a symptomatic

---

a painting of St. Sebastian by Fra Bartolommeo (now in Pèzenas); he engaged Andrea del Sarto to execute two paintings: the *Sacrifice of Isaac* now in Dresden and a Pietà. But his unfortunate fate befell him before these last pictures came into his hands (Vasari-Milanesi, 4:188).

[12] Vasari-Milanesi, 6:252-53.

Approximately the following is heard:

"Do you, Giovannia Battista, miserable ragmonger and worthless fourpenny huckster, dare to strip the ornaments from the chambers of *gentilhuomini* and rob our city of its noblest and most precious possessions to decorate foreign parts and the houses of our enemies? I am not astonished at you, who are a plebeian and enemy of our country, but rather at the rulers of our city who are willing to aid you in this disgusting and infamous business! This bed, which you in your commercial interest and lust for profit are so anxious to obtain, was my wedding bed, for whose honor my father-in-law had all this splendid and costly decoration brought. For the sake of his memory and the love of my husband this bed is sacred to me, and I am ready to defend it with my own blood and life."

Some similar pleasantries follow in Vasari's report, addressed to the city officials, who "should trot out their own beds and other household ornaments, if they need so desperately to pay court to the king of France."

[13] Vasari-Milanesi, 5:27, 50-51; 6:61, 540; Agostino Ademollo, *Marietta de' Ricci*, ed. Passerini (Florence, 1845), p. 180; Giovanni Battista Busini, *Lettere di Giovambattista Busini a Benedetto Varchi sopra l'assedio di Firenze*, ed. Milanesi (Florence, 1860), p. 94; see also my essay, "Giovanni della Palla, der erste Kunsthändler," in *Die Kunst*, 37, June, 1936, pp. 270ff.

importance for the general change in artistic circumstances in these last years, the 1520s. This is the stylistic watershed in which the transition to Mannerism and later Baroque is preparing its way. At the same time it reveals the function of the professional middleman on the art market, embodied for the first time by Palla, a function previously unknown to the famous artist and the art work itself.

The collector's demand for valuable art works of the recent and distant past, with the quest for and the buying up of works with highly prized masters' names—works which in their own time had originated through other commissions and had already been displayed and admired elsewhere—was a phenomenon that appeared only occasionally and sporadically in the late Quattrocento. It occurs more frequently since the beginning of the sixteenth century; now, however, when external customers and patrons turned their interest to the Florentine supply of monuments and art market, it was only natural that the intermediary figure of the expert negotiator of contracts and purchaser should begin to develop and take his place, along with or instead of the merchants or political emissaries of an artistically interested princely court who had hitherto occasionally been employed for such services.

This means a perceptible increase in trade and value on the Florentine art market, in any case for all products of well-known origin and quality. But it also represents an equally perceptible loosening of the former direct personal relationships between patron and artist that sustained and determined the whole artistic production of the preceding period. Countless direct orders and commissions naturally continued to occur as before, and the art market in Florence as elsewhere still remained for a long time attuned to the traditional client production, not market production. But with the more frequent intervention of princely art connoisseurs from other lands, who were in a position to pay record prices for particularly desired names, there resulted a previously almost unknown price scale even in the market price of contemporary Florentine art. The old-fashioned, sound, artisan price-fixing for artistic work survived in general only for the middle and lower levels of local everyday production.[14] On the other hand, the few great masters became ever more estranged from the local circles of patronage as their international reputation grew, with foreign potentates striving to keep them in their service with star salaries.

In the next section we shall trace the manner in which these factors, admittedly generally pervasive only after 1530, but beginning to set in since the early sixteenth century, began to affect the economic and social class relationships of Florentine artists.

[14] Here we refer also to the printing house of Alessandro Rosselli, a nephew of the painter Cosimo Rosselli. For his estate inventory of 1525, see *JPK*, 1914, pp. 90ff., also Brockhaus in *MKIF*, 1, pp. 98, 151ff.

CHAPTER 10

# THE GENERAL ATTITUDE

# TOWARD ART:

# THE PUBLIC AND

# THE ARTIST

With respect to what has been shown so far, the question immediately at hand concerns the direction and level of the general artistic sensitivity and taste within the various strata of the Florentine population; we must also consider how the artistic attitudes, desires, and needs of the public—the patrons, commissioners, and purchasers of art works—adapted to the changes in artistic style, and perhaps even encouraged these changes.

There are admittedly only a few hints in Vasari and other sources that can be cited at the outset to answer these questions. More precise and comprehensive information on these tendencies might perhaps be gained only through systematic investigation of the whole of contemporary literature, including writings on aesthetics and the very extensive correspondence.

Jacob Burckhardt ("*Beitrage: Die Sammler*," p. 382) speaks of the "rise to power of private taste" and its influence on the art of the period. This is with reference to the individual, personal character of many works of art, thoroughly adapted to a connoisseur's taste. We first encounter such objects in the circle of Lorenzo Magnifico (here, it is true, mostly by hearsay), later at various Italian princely courts, and above all in Venice.

The outspokenly luxurious character of important secular art of the Laurentian era, with its great delight in ornament, and the spillover of this small-scale, densely woven ornamentation even into monumental sculpture and painting of this period has been repeatedly noted above. This is certainly an obvious effect of "the private taste," as it must have taken form in the circle of cultivated, demanding, hedonistic collectors and connoisseurs.

But even outside this circle, a lively interest in art seems to have been a thoroughly widespread and self-evident fact already in the late fifteenth century.[1] It is pertinent that contest designs or models for ecclesiastical

[1] Even a popular preacher like Savonarola could refer to this, in order to emphasize the comparatively all too feeble interest of the public in religious matters.

and other public buildings and art works were subjected to the opinion and comments of all—"utrum placeat populo" (see above). Even active participation in such competitions was open to all, which presupposes a broad distribution of specialized architectural knowledge in dilettante circles.[2] Only further contemporary testimony, however, can specifically establish the extent to which dilettantish artistic practice in one field or another generally occurred at that time in the middle or upper strata of the Florentine public.

From Vasari and other authors we gain some positive as well as negative data on the general understanding of art and the particular appreciation of the artist as such, as well as of certain prominent artistic personalities. Particularly informative in this direction are the comprehensive notes on artists and art works in the biographical and theoretical art literature of the time. It is true that only the few such writings composed by nonartists can come into consideration here. These include observations on earlier artists by Filippo Villani in 1404 and Antonio Manetti's series of biographies, to which the detailed vita of Brunelleschi presumably also belongs. In the 1480s there are the concise characterizations of famous Florentine artists of the recent and earlier past in Cristoforo Landino's Dante commentary. To this may be added, as a solitary, particularly remarkable document, the evaluation of the four most famous monumental painters active in Florence around 1495, as an instructive appraisal for Duke Lodovico Moro, probably furnished by an informant close to his court.[3]

At the beginning of the sixteenth century comes Ugolino Verino's *Illustratio urbis Florentiae* in verse. The most important architectural monuments and artists' names figure in it. A Florentine cleric, Francesco Albertini, a canon of San Lorenzo, composed a small *Memoriale di molte*

---

Savonarola says (1492): "The people are often so enthralled by a good painting that sometimes they are quite carried away and almost forget themselves in contemplating it." (Schnitzer, *Savonarola*, 2:812). On the public interest in Leonardo's St. Anne cartoon see Vasari-Milanesi, 4:38.

[2] Thus even Lorenzo Magnifico and others took part in the 1491 competition for a new cathedral facade. More noteworthy are the general interest in the debate over the facade project for Santo Spirito concerning whether there should be three or four portals (*RA*, 1931, pp. 505-507) and the great public excitement over the unfamiliar innovation of pedimented windows on Baccio d'Agnolo's new Palazzo Bartolini of 1517, which expressed itself in mocking sonnets and ironic garlanding of these windows (Vasari-Milanesi, 5:351).

Even a small tradesman like the spice dealer Luca Landucci, who admittedly appears in his well-known diary as an observer of his time with varied interests, ventured to work out a whole church project around 1505-1507 for the new building he initiated for San Giovanni Evangelista near Palazzo Medici. He then submitted his design to the judgment of the architect Cronaca (Landucci, *Diario*, pp. 272, 296).

[3] This characterization of Botticelli, Ghirlandaio, Filippino Lippi, and Perugino, probably based on their work alongside one another at the Villa Spedaletto, was discovered and first published by Müller-Walde, *JPK*, 18, pp. 113, 165).

*statue et picture* . . . , a sort of art historical city guide to Florence published in 1510. This work, unfortunately all too terse and somewhat careless, was the first and for long thereafter the only undertaking of its kind and still represents an important testimony to local art historical interests in the early Cinquecento. It is followed over the next three decades by the compilations of artistic-biographical material, never completed, of the *Libro di Antonio Billi*, of the Anonimo Magliabecchiano, and of Giovanni Battista Gelli, which, based largely on older, lost forerunners, form the last preparation for the great biographical work of Vasari, begun in the 1540s with the first edition in 1550.[4]

What becomes perceptible in these records of artistic biographical information appearing long before Vasari, and what in general gave impetus to such records, is the conviction of the historical and cultural significance of certain preeminent artists. This conviction was setting in more and more securely at least since the mid-Quattrocento. It held that the memory of artists whose names, personalities, and most important creations impressed themselves on the consciousness of contemporaries ought to be preserved for posterity.

This cultivated interest in individual artistic personalities, moreover, found its focus and a particular stimulus in all sorts of anecdotes and outlandish remarks by artists that were seized on from oral tradition and passed on by the ever fruitful line of Florentine *novelle* and delight in storytelling.[5]

Beyond this, however, in Vasari there are innumerable totally individual sketches, all details of the personal lives of many artists of earlier times. They can have come down to him only out of that broad stream of oral tradition—certainly not passed on solely in the workshops—from which earlier contemporary literature had picked up and made use of only a few. In the next section we shall come back to what concerns the artists themselves in these anecdotes. Here, however, we had first of all to establish the emergence and repetition of a whole vast stock of tales about artists, elaborated by fact or legend, as a fact illuminating the

---

[4] See Karl Frey, "Abriss der Florentinischen Kunsthistoriographie" in his edition of the Magliabecchiano's *Codice* as well as Julius von Schlosser, *Die Kunstliteratur. Handbuch zur Quellenkunde* (Vienna, 1924), pp. 92ff., 168ff.; Krautheimer, "Die Anfänge der Kunstgeschichtsschreibung in Italien," *Rep.* 1929, pp. 50ff.

[5] This is evident even since the Trecento, in certain witty comments attributed to Giotto and in the various jokes that his follower Buffalmacco is supposed to have played in a whole series of Sacchetti *novelle* where artists play some prominent role. In the early Quattrocento the malicious joke that Brunelleschi and his friends played on the "grasso legnaiuolo," the fat intarsia master Manetto Adamantini, was on every tongue.

Evidence of Donatello's popularity, for instance, is that not long after his death he appeared as a speaking character in a religious folk drama (Hans Semper, *Donatello, Seine Zeit und Schule*, Quellenschriften zur Kunstgeschichte, 9, Vienna, 1875, pp. 321-22).

interest of the public. This means that evidently even the peculiarities of artists, their deviations from normal bourgeois behavior, were noticeable to contemporaries and appeared remarkable and that the unusual aspects of the artist's personal behavior, if not of his productions, made an impression even on the simple bourgeois and kept alive the names of the heroes of such anecdotes.

Thus it is no longer astonishing, although without parallel elsewhere, that a tomb monument was erected to Brunelleschi in the Duomo by order of the state; or that in the same place, in 1490, as a counterpart to the painted memorial to Dante that was already there, the memory of his contemporary Giotto was also immortalized with a relief sculptural monument similar to Brunelleschi's and in the style that was also used later for the musician Squarcialupi and the philosopher Marsilio Ficino. It has already been mentioned above how Lorenzo Magnifico, who was chiefly responsible for the erection of these monuments, concerned himself with a similar purpose over the remains of Fra Filippo Lippi, who had died in Spoleto, and had his tomb there marked with a beautifully decorated epitaph.

Lorenzo's emphatically Maecenas-like and at the same time friendly behavior toward artists like Bertoldo and Michelangelo may be recalled once again here. In this Lorenzo was admittedly only following an inclination manifested already repeatedly by his father and grandfather (see above). Something completely new, though, is the creation of that remarkable training ground for the coming Florentine artistic generation in the statue garden near San Marco, a creation that long thereafter remained without a successor, just as it came to life without any predecessor to its idea.

If, however, after his departure from the Medici house, we see the young Michelangelo likewise finding other patrons and protectors such as Ulisse Aldovrandi in Bologna, who received the restless fugitive so warmly, "primarily because he understood that he was a sculptor," and then Lorenzo di Pierfrancesco Medici in Florence, who paved his way to Rome, this is certainly no mere act of providence. We find nothing similar for other artists of his time, because on none of them are such detailed and direct reports available, even from the youthful years, as on Michelangelo.[6]

The conscious and rightful appreciation of artistic talent is, however, by no means self-evident and general even in the beginning of the sixteenth

---

[6] Condivi, Michelangelo, chaps. 15-17; Vasari-Milanesi, 7:146-147. Raphael, in his first Florentine period, enjoyed the hospitality of Taddeo Taddei and repaid with the gift of a painting, probably the *Madonna of the Meadow* (Vienna), which is traceable to Taddei's possession. Vasari relates similar things for Perino del Vaga from the 1520s (Vasari-Milanesi, 4:321; 5:352, 607-608).

century. For many patrons, even from the upper clergy, the artist still remained no more than another manual employee with whom one did not need to concern himself much.

Very characteristic of this are certain anecdotes that again are reported only from Michelangelo's unusually closely recorded life, but are probably valid as examples of a widespread attitude at the time. We find that his father, whose family pride was sorely irritated by his son's artistic aspirations, could be convinced only by Lorenzo Magnifico's assurance that a sculptor and a *scarpellino* were not the same thing. And even in 1506 there occurred that highly dramatic episode of the reconciliation between Michelangelo and Pople Julius, when the Florentine cardinal and archbishop Soderini sought to calm the enraged pontiff with the remark that artists were ignorant of all save their art and without proper manners; whereupon the pope's full wrath exploded against the clumsy intercessor: "Lo ignorante sei tu" ("that you insult this man as I would never have done"—see Condivi, *Michelangelo* chap. 32).

But even in the late Quattrocento artists themselves began to defend their rights and reputation. Vasari, who in general had a particularly important concern for the class standing of the artists, has some especially charming tales to tell about this, to which we shall return in the next section.

The personal and class position of prominent masters, however, also sprang from the understanding of contemporaries for the special worth of a high artistic mastery. And such appreciation of a new confrontation and solution of problems beyond the average level and the familiar, conventional stylistic range is clearly and notably enough evinced, even without express testimony, by the frequent appearance of bold new formal solutions, even within the province of ecclesiastical commissions. For it is precisely here that such innovations were permitted and appeared only when at least the respective patron or donor gave his imprimatur.

Thus we must call to mind the extraordinary nature of Masaccio's art in comparison with all other Florentine painting of the 1420s or later, in the context of the generally customary artistic practice of the midcentury, the problems boldly posed and the highly unique performance by an Uccello or a Castagno. Only then can we measure and appreciate what it meant for the patron to allow these revolutionaries, who so recklessly threw all previously valid artistic conceptions to the winds, to express themselves in publicly displayed altarpieces or church murals. But that such things could happen at all, in spite of all the consternation and the anger, which certainly often became very loud, of the majority of contemporary observers, is surely a testimony not only to the progressive insight, the resolute cooperation, and the genuine artistic understanding of those who commissioned these works and had them placed in churches; it also sheds light on the far-reaching freedom in the choice of artist and artistic style that the church authorities concerned allowed to the patrons. If, instead of this, the judgment and approval of the designs had been left to the decision of a church board or a committee of laymen, as today, many highly valuable pieces of ecclesiastical art might not have been produced at all, or only with considerable stifling of their originality. For in spite of everything, we must not imagine the artistic taste of the broad majority of the Florentine bourgeoisie and clergy as overly cultivated and of unconditionally progressive tendencies. Otherwise, how could a workshop like that of Neri di Bicci have developed such a broad and unremitting productivity? And along with him, throughout the Renaissance, come still many more fellow workers of similar stamp, of whom we cannot survey the scope of their work and circle of customers so completely as is possible with Neri di Bicci, thanks to his surviving workshop journal.* The whole dense lower layer of Florentine painting, which is represented by many works of third and fourth rank and by countless names of more or less obscure artists in the guild registers, surely reflects the primitive taste of a correspondingly extensive lower stratum of the public, in the negative as well as the by no means absent positive qualities of their work.

A certain staunch, workmanlike solidity of execution, seasoned and made appealing by bright folk-style colors and all sorts of decorative gold-glittering trimmings and the like, are the qualities that the average commissioner and consumer of this sort of painting probably prized and desired above all; along with them also that soft, ingratiating charm and accentuated sentimentality in the choice of types and attitudes, such as in a somewhat elevated form determined Perugino's great public success.[7]

In artistic circles, moreover, the unrefined and often misguided taste of the great majority was a known, often explicitly confirmed fact.

If, for example, as Vasari reports, in the beginning of the sixteenth century many young artists reproached Perugino for the schematic repetition of his usual types, these criticisms probably also concealed anger

---

* *Translator's note*: Neri di Bicci's workshop journal is now available in a new, more complete edition. See Translator's Bibliography, section ID.

[7] Especially characteristic of this, for example, is the Last Supper fresco of Sant' Onofrio (the Cenacolo di Fuligno) stemming from his workshop, in which even toward the end of the fifteenth century all the aforementioned traits of mediocre art of that time are assembled in such a marked degree that this work surely represented the fulfillment of the fondest wishes of the nuns of Via Faenza, whose refectory it was intended to decorate. It is in fact typical "nunnish" painting as we still often encounter it even in the style customary in our present church art, with wholly similar characteristics. It is in any case doubly astonishing, if we glance briefly back to an older object for comparison, that it was also a nuns' convent, Sant' Apollonia, which could receive and tolerate the emphatic, masculine harshness and progressive boldness of Castagno's *cenacolo* image in its dining room.

that so many patrons so readily accepted these overworked stereotypes.[8] Malicious tongues said even of a papal patron on a grand scale, like Sixtus IV, that in judging the murals in the Sistine chapel he had preferred above all the mediocre Cosimo Rosselli because his paintings had the brightest colors and the most gold highlights.[9]

Even in the dialogues on painting which Francisco de Hollanda is supposed to have carried on in 1538 with Michelangelo and some nobles in Rome, that is, in the literary result of these conversations (J. de Vasconcellas, ed. and trans. *Vier Gespräche über die Malerei geführt zu Rom 1538*, Vienna, 1899, pp. 107, 139), the talk frequently concerns the uncomprehending artistic judgments that supposed connoisseurs from important cities sometimes expressed.

It remains uncertain, however, how frequently such comprehending or uncomprehending critiques and reasoning conversations on artistic questions may generally have occurred in Florence among educated nonartists and whether it was perhaps the stimulus of such utterances, or even the critical observations of other Florentine artists, that Donatello missed during his long stay in Padua (Vasari-Milanesi, 2:413).

Only one more point should be touched on in this connection: a certain discord may finally have resulted between the aspirations and interests of the artists on the one hand and the patron's and observer's desires on the other when the aesthetic-artistic goals and the intended purpose according to the commission no longer harmonized perfectly.

During the fifteenth century, though, the purely artistic striving for truth to reality in the manner of portrayal developed so sharply and masterfully that the didactic or edifying subject matter was often unduly overshadowed, particularly in church painting. The thematic tasks assigned to artists in the context of church spaces and their meaningful decoration appear in many cases almost solely as occasions for the pursuit and innovative solution of certain purely formal artistic problems. The profusion of scenic surroundings and realistically portrayed accessories, the many portrait figures of known personalities, often wholly unconcerned with the matter represented, all this, in many church murals of

---

[8] Leonardo da Vinci, however, in a letter to the city authorities of Cremona, admonished them to choose for a certain commission only such an artist as was recognized as skillful not by the judgment of the crowd, but by the appraisal of experts. In his book on painting, moreover, he criticizes those artists who obtained cheap success with the crowd through extreme color effects. See Leonardo da Vinci, *Das Buch von der Malerei*, ed. and trans. H. Ludwig, 3 vols. Quellenschriften für Kunstgeschichte, 15-17 (Vienna, 1882), sections 71, 120.

[9] Vasari-Milanesi, 3:386-87, 188-89; Vasari (Vasari-Milanesi, 5:43-44) also mentions the anecdote on the patron in Prato who preferred Niccolò Soggi to Andrea del Sarto; Condivi, *Michelangelo*, chap. 47, tells of the uncomprehending judgment of Michelangelo's Leda by a courtier of the Duke of Ferrara, etc.

Gozzoli and Ghirlandaio, for example, almost completely overran the actual subject of the picture. Even in the Madonna type of the altarpiece, above all in the household devotional image, from Fra Filippo Lippi on, the individual, immediately contemporary character with decidedly modish, mundane stamp became predominant. Even Botticelli, in all his Gothic idealism, did not remain wholly untouched by it.

It has already been shown, however, how much the tendencies of taste and interests of many commissioners of works for church donations furthered this development. Finally, however, the increasing discrepancy between the artistic aims and the actual meaning and purpose of religious art must have been noted and protested, precisely from the side of the commissioner, recipient, and observer of the art work. This opposition found a decisive, clearly based expression only from about 1490 on, in the name of ecclesiastical-religious as well as moral demands, in the sermons of Savonarola.

In the context of his passionate efforts for the purification and deepening of the religious-moral standard of living and for the restoration of the old, sternly believing piety, Savonarola could not overlook how far the religious art of his time had changed in its whole nature and expression. In the paintings of Fra Angelico that he encountered daily in all the rooms of his convent of San Marco, he may well have recognized the last complete embodiment of an artistic ideal corresponding to his own religious outlook. This standard of comparison immediately clarified what he found to reproach in contemporary painting.[10]

The truly demagogically rousing fire of his speeches from the pulpit must, however, at least for a time have inflamed a very large part of the Florentine population to enthusiastic support, which even led to the frequently repeated "burnings of the vanities" in the Piazza della Signoria.

We do not know how many art works of high value actually perished on those pyres, as in certain iconoclastic attacks of the German Reformation thirty years later. The genres of applied household art of worldly and especially of erotic tint were surely decimated in them. It has already been noted that in the province of chest and wainscoting panel painting, the gallant motifs of antique and medieval novelry almost disappear from about 1500 on, giving way to biblical and sternly ethical themes from

---

[10] Savonarola criticized the all too naturalistic figures of saints with the features of personalities known throughout the city and the frivolously fashionable finery of many Madonna pictures: "I tell you, the mother of God dressed like a poor woman, simply and modestly; you, however, represent the most holy Virgin like a harlot!" He criticized the wasteful luxury of many tomb monuments, the many immodest pictures in homes, and the fact that people would decide against getting rid of such pictures only because of their artistic value. See Schnitzer, *Savonarola*, 2:807-808 and compare to his volume 1, pp. 392-95, where there are also references to similar performances from earlier preachers of penitence.

the antique. This in particular can probably be traced back to the change in attitude presaged by Savonarola that by no means ended with the penitence preacher's martyrdom. A good part of the stylistic change beginning to set in around the turn of the century, however, might be at least indirectly related, as a positive artistic result, to Savonarola's affecting lessons. What appears, according to Wölfflin, as a "new conviction" in the spiritually intensified treatment of religious and other themes in any case harmonizes very closely, in its decisive change from the artistic behavior of Lorenzo Magnifico's time, with Savonarola's severe judgment of the spirit of that time. We know, furthermore, that certain of the most important artists of the turn of the century and the early Cinquecento were known as avowed adherents of the prior of San Marco, even and especially after his tragic end: Botticelli above all, Lorenzo di Credi, Fra Bartolommeo, Andrea and Giovanni della Robbia, but also Michelangelo, Baccio da Montelupo, and others (Schnitzer, *Savonarola*, 2:819ff.).* The heightened sensitivity and severity in moral and dogmatic respects even took offense at certain works of the aforementioned admirers of Savonarola. In a Botticellian altarpiece that the philosopher Matteo Palmieri had painted according to his instructions, heretical characteristics were supposedly discovered, so that the panel in Sant' Ambrogio had to remain covered for several years.[11]

If, however, all manner of extraartistic viewpoints could influence the criticism and treatment of publicly displayed religious art works, how much more might such viewpoints have often affected the artist's resolution in a limiting or form-changing manner in the first stage of the design and assignment of a commission? More noteworthy, however, is the contrary fact, already emphasized above, of the tolerance and the emergence of so many boldly progressive solutions in the context of

---

* *Translator's note*: On the question of artists' personal involvement with Savonarola see the literature cited in the Translator's Introduction, p. xv.

[11] [*Translator's note:* The altarpiece in question, now attributed to Botticini, is in the National Gallery in London. See Martin Davies, *National Gallery Catalogues: The Earlier Italian Schools* (2nd rev. ed., London, 1961), pp. 122-27.] Even a work of the pious painter-monk, Fra Bartolommeo, a large St. Sebastian in San Marco, aroused scandal a few years after the Frate's death, so that it was decided to transfer this painting to the convent's chapter house and later, toward the end of the 1520s, to sell it off to Giovanni della Palla. This was because some women had blamed themselves in the confessional for sinful thoughts that the sight of the beautiful naked youth's body had aroused in them (Vasari-Milanesi, 4:188). A punitive decree issued in 1470 by the Cremonese painters' guild against the makers of immodest pictures probably relates to outright obscenities (cited by Hubert Janitschek, *Die Gesellschaft der Renaissance in Italien und die Kunst*, Stuttgart, 1879, p. 78, after Federico Sacchi, *Notizie pittoriche cremonesi*, Cremona, 1873). On the other hand, it was due rather to an outbreak of primitive folk piety that in Castagno's Flagellation fresco in the second cloister of Santa Croce (since destroyed), the figures of the tormentors, as Vasari related, were scratched up by "persone semplici."

church patronage assignments as well as secular, domestic artistic commissions.

Finally, however, we should once more call to mind certain points in reviewing this whole section. First to consider is the extraordinarily large extent and stratification of the patron group in official bodies, corporations, and individuals, and the decisive initial factor of their inexhaustible delight in projects and readiness to spend.

Then there is the cooperation and interpenetration, so often with fortunate results, of the two principal stimuli of patronage and donations—religious devotion and the zealous Renaissance quest for fame—which must often have worked as a competitive stimulus among various families and associations to raise as high as possible the extent and splendor of the buildings and art works they commissioned.

Along with these donors' commissions for public purposes, however, the personal requirement and interest in artistically enriched furnishing of private residences, as well as the sites for public secular functions, emerged as a further important stimulus to artistic activity. This type of commission developed more fully and is accordingly more fully recorded only in the second third of the fifteenth century, after beginnings which go farther back but can only be sketchily traced. Primarily in the context of this kind of commission there arose also a connoisseur's appraisal and appreciation of the intrinsic artistic value of a work of art, that is, of the formal, representational qualities that were emphasized in it for the first time, or in particular perfection and originality. This artistic point of view is focussed on the one hand in a connoisseur's interest in art and on the other in a collector's passion. It leads at the same time to a conscious and accentuated appreciation of certain particularly outstanding artistic personalities. Nevertheless, it must be established that such an attitude toward art and artists, which comes very close to the outlook predominating today, remained limited to a rather small circle of patrons and amateurs of art throughout the Renaissance and into the sixteenth century. For the vast majority, even of the cultured middle class, artistic creation counted then as earlier only as a branch, at best somewhat elevated and especially esteemed, of the artisan trades. The executing hand of the artist, of which only a few presaged an unusual creative genius, was for the general public the welcome and necessary tool for the fulfillment of all the countless and varied tasks for which they saw it employed day after day by patrons, customers, and donors of all classes.

PART III

# The Artist's Workshop and the Art Market

One does not learn to know works of art when they are finished; one must catch them at their origin in order to understand them in some measure.

GOETHE TO ZELTER, 1803

# CHAPTER 11

# THE ARTIST CLASS:

## ITS NUMERICAL STRENGTH,

## PROFESSIONAL ORGANIZATION AND

## OCCUPATIONAL DIVISIONS

The indispensable although only indirect preconditions of artistic activity were surveyed and sketched in the preceding sections. The general substructure and nourishing soil, the cultural and material atmosphere, have thus been represented, in which the whole existence and activity of the artist developed. We enter now into his more intimate, immediately personal world. The artist group itself must be illustrated, with all the institutions and regulations of its class and guild organization and also the private living and working circle of the artist, the workshop, in which he carried out the commissions he received, often supported by apprentices and assistants. Also bound up with this is the question, already touched on from the patron's side, of the material valuation and compensation of artistic labor and the economic position of the artist class in general. Finally, however, our task is to recognize the specific nature and essence of the artist's personality as it more or less clearly manifested itself and varied in the course of the Renaissance centuries, based on all sorts of contemporary reports and recorded personal comments of individual representatives of the species.

We shall attempt, first of all, to establish a general conception of the numerical strength of the artistic professions and of how the status of the arts might perhaps have related to that of other trades within the same period.

The points of reference available for answering the first question—the surviving membership lists of professional societies of artists for particular periods and other documentary references to individual names of artists—are admittedly very fragmentary. Yet they are enough to show that the number of artist workshops simultaneously active in Florence was much greater than the number of personalities known through verified works.

Thus, for example, the guild list of Florentine painters in the period from 1409 to 1444 mentions no less than forty-one names, a sum that

resulted from the addition of eight or nine newly matriculated masters
for any given five-year period during the span of time cited. And in the
later Quattrocento the painters' guild still shows about the same numerical strength. A membership list of the company of St. Luke in 1472—
for the control of the legally prescribed votive candles to be offered by
each member to the Virgin on Candlemas—lists forty-two names, in
which, it is true, certain artisan specialists and representatives of side
branches of peculiar artistic practices (like the "battiloro" who produced
gold leaf for the decorative trim of altarpieces) are also counted. Among
about thirty who are specifically figure painters on this register, however,
we encounter only eight masters known in any other context.[1]

Even in other surveys of artistic professional activity we find again
about the same proportion of a quarter to a third of traceable names,
that is, those represented by secure works, in the midst of a great majority
of guild members of whom nothing more has survived than their names,
without any kind of report about the possible quality and significance
of their work.[2]

Beginning from this evidence, much of whose documentary verification
has long been available in published form, recent research has finally
been moved, in its attributions of unassigned works, to consider one
name or another from this broad circle of followers and in any case to
exercise somewhat more caution in the whole attribution practice in
general. This is in opposition to the earlier tendency that all too unhes-
itatingly sought to file as many anonymous pieces as possible into the
life-work of one of the famous masters, or at least his workshop production, and thus sent the great majority of contemporaries known only
by name away with nothing to show.

Particularly informative for the question of the extent and significance
of particular branches of the arts within the general professional statistics
of Florence is a survey from the annals of Benedetto Dei, drawn up
toward the end of the 1470s, in which unfortunately only the painters
and masters of figural sculpture are not considered.[3] According to this
there were at that time, along with 270 workshops of the Arte della Lana
and 83 silk-weaving firms, almost as many, namely 84 ateliers for wood-

[1] In the decade from 1492 to 1502 there were fourteen new entries in the guild register;
in the year 1519 alone nine matriculations, among which the only well-known name is
Giovanni Battista il Rosso. See R. Ciasca, *l'Arte dei Medici e Speziali* . . . , Florence, 1927,
pp. 696, 699; Karl Frey, *Die Loggia dei Lanzi zu Florenz* (Berlin, 1885), pp. 313ff., 344;
Horne, *Botticelli*, pp. 347-48.

[2] A statistically noteworthy indication results from Milanesi's establishment of the fact
that in the first quarter of the sixteenth century no less than sixteen painters with the first
name Raffaello were active in Florence, a seventeenth being Raffaello Santi (Vasari-Milanesi,
4:244).

[3] Cited by Fabroni, *Vita Laurentii*, adnot. 200, pp. 377ff.

carving and intarsia decoration. Furthermore, there were 54 workshops for decoration in marble and stone and 44 master gold and silversmiths; thus about the same number as the painters in the cited list of 1472.

If one now compares with these figures the frequency, only a little greater and sometimes even smaller, of trades serving daily material needs (70 slaughterers and butchers, 66 *speziali*, that is spice-merchants and the like), it becomes evident that there is proportionately a truly astoundingly broad development of the artistic professions, a development which indicates a correspondingly great and constant demand for decorative works to enrich the life-style of the bourgeois-patrician population. The need for decoration and ornament in a population in which the number of woodcarvers was greater than the number of meat merchants (84:70), was evidently still far livelier, more widespread, and extravagant than the remnant of surviving works representing it today. For even in the artistic and artisan branches of production the supply holds itself in economically rational, healthy approximation to the demand at any given time. There was obviously an extensive and varied range of tasks for artistic activity, as well as a delight in projects and a readiness to spend on the part of donors and other kinds of patrons in virtually all classes, described in the preceding section. Thus the relatively great number of workers and production workshops in the different branches of the fine and applied arts should not surprise us too much.

Given the living and working habits of most of the artists, however, still predominantly those of artisans, their class-corporate organization and their integration into the Florentine economy seems equally self-evident.

In the guild composition of Florence, which indeed essentially determined the whole political structure of the city-state, the artists collectively did not exactly represent a guild in themselves; they appeared rather divided according to their type of work, and sometimes grouped together with other trades related to them only superficially, that is in the handling of the same raw materials, as branches of various greater guilds.

Thus the painters were in the guild of Medici e Speziali, the physicians, apothecaries, and spice-dealers, which last in fact also sold the raw material of painting, the pigments. The goldsmiths were a member of the Arte della Seta, in which the gold beaters and spinners of gold thread (for costly vestment cloth) also found themselves together as a connecting link between the goldsmiths' art and silk-weaving. Only, as we just saw, the especially numerous masters and workshops for wood, stone, and marble work formed a guild in themselves, the Arte dei maestri di pietra e legname that was also responsible for figural sculptors and carpenters. The architects, whose planning and construction-supervisory function did not count as a separate trade, were probably also recruited mostly from the last-named guild, to which they already belonged originally through their training as sculptors or carpenters.[4] Artists who were active in succession or cooperation with each other in different artistic media accordingly could or had to be members of more than one guild.[5] The documents published to date give only a fragmentary conception of the professional regulations and institutions that applied to the artistic guilds and branch guilds.

We hear the most about the painters. But even with them, and it was probably similar in other branches of the arts, a notable relaxation of fixed guild obligations as they had been administered earlier, at least according to detailed testimony from the late Trecento, shows up in the middle of the Quattrocento.[6] The fact, incomprehensible in itself, that Botticelli and Perugino did not matriculate in the Medici e Speziali until 1499 can be explained by the fact that at that time, after a long decline, the guild reorganized itself and began again to enforce membership obligations even with regard to masters who had long been accredited.[7] Among the later new enrollments we find, for example, in 1508 Andrea del Sarto and Franciabigio, who both made their debut at that time and in 1522 Francesco Granacci etc. (see Karl Frey, *Die Loggia dei Lanzi zu Florenz*, Berlin, 1885, pp. 349ff.).

In the guild regulations of the painters we find among others the rather high rate of enrollment dues of six florins for natives and twelve for non-Florentines which, however, was gradually lowered in the course of several years. A small amount of data on the organization of the guild appears in the regulations of 1470 and 1516 published by Jacques Mesnil.[8]

[4] Accordingly the Maestri di pietra e legname could also claim the building-master of the Duomo, Brunelleschi, and in 1434, two years before the completion of the Duomo cupola, they even went so far as to have him imprisoned for debt because he refused to pay his guild dues. The Duomo building authorities, however, arranged for his speedy liberation and the arrest and punishment of the responsible guild officials (Vasari-Milanesi, 2:362, n. 1).

[5] Thus Ghiberti was enrolled in 1408 in the goldsmiths and in 1427 in the Maestri di pietra e legname (Vasari-Milanesi, 2:259-60).

[6] The statutes and rolls of the painters' guilds of Florence, Siena, and Perugia are published by Luigi Manzoni, *Statuti e matricoli dell'arte dei pittori* . . . Rome, 1904); see also the excerpts in Karl Frey, *Die Loggia dei Lanzi zu Florenz* (Berlin, 1885), pp. 311ff., 334-35, 344ff. and Giuseppe Gonetta, *Bibliografia statutaria delle corporazioni d'arti e mestieri d'Italia con saggio di bibliografia estera* (Rome, 1891).

[7] Horne, *Botticelli*, p. 281. Ten years earlier in 1488 a painters' guild had besides been formed in the neighboring city of Pistoia, with twelve members, of which only two names appear to be traceable otherwise. For the protocol on the first assembly in a chapel of the Duomo and the ordinances concluded there, see Milanesi, *Documenti*, pp. 145-46.

[8] *RA*, 4, pp. 133-36. These almost solely concern the proceedings over expert appraisal of works of art in differences between artists and customers, in which, besides, the assessment fee falls not to the assessor appointed by the guild, but to the guild treasury.

The leadership of the guilds belonged to individual officials. Thus Luca della Robbia in

Along with these constitutionally obligatory guilds of the different branches of the arts there was also, already since the Trecento, the voluntary, more informal and friendly association of painters in the religious confraternity of the Compagnia di San Luca. Founded in 1339, with its own chapel in Santa Maria Nuova for whose altar Jacopo di Casentino provided the patron image of St. Luke painting the Madonna, it accepted also, besides the painters, other artists and members of related professions. Thus Ghiberti from 1423 on and Luca della Robbia belonged; Andrea della Robbia was invested here with the office of *camarlengo* in 1472.[9]

As for the regulation of artistic operation by the concerned guilds, its function and purpose involved, among other things, the union-style protection of native labor against foreign competition on the art market. This included, for example, the admission of non-Florentine artists only through double matriculation fees for purposes of guild enrichment, at least as a fundamental precept which admittedly was not strictly enforced.

The frequent infiltration of foreign, primarily German art, is noteworthy, for example. Thus repeated evidence can also be found for the temporary or longer activity of German and Netherlandish artists in Florence, not to mention the early and frequent introduction of early Netherlandish pictures already discussed above. As stonemasons and construction workers we find them among the personnel of the Duomo workshop from the late Trecento on; in isolated cases certain skillful woodcarvers, glasspainters, and tapestry weavers from the North were called in or readily accepted.[10] There must have been in general a very small colony of artists from the German lands toward the middle of the fifteenth century. They possessed their own chapel in the Annunziata, for which a wooden crucifix was provided later, in 1516, by Veit Stoss.[11]

his extreme old age still held the honorary office of *consigliere* and later that of *sindaco* of the Maestri di pietra e legname (*l'Arte*, 22, p. 242).

[9] Vasari-Milanesi, 1:675; 2:259-60; *l'Arte*, 22, p. 249. For the founding statutes of the St. Luke brotherhood, with addenda from 1406, 1444, and an evidently very incomplete membership list continued up to 1525, see Gaye, *Carteggio*, 2:32ff. under the erroneous title "Statuti dell'Arte dei Pittori." After long stagnation the confraternity was finally reorganized by Montorsoli in 1561 and transferred to the Annunziata, where its chapel still exists in the first cloister, with the artistic furnishings provided at that time.

[10] In 1457 the woodcarver Johannes Enrici de Alemania was recommended by the Signoria to Rome as "scultor egregius praesertim in crucifixis effingendis" (Gaye, *Carteggio*, 1:174). German sculptors probably also worked occasionally in Florence, as often elsewhere in Italy, for their countrymen who were active as artisans or otherwise (see Körte, "Deutsche Vesperbilder in Italien," *KJBH*, 1, 1936). On the Netherlandish tapestry worker Livino di Giglio in the 1450s and on Giovanni de Alemagna, active after 1475 in Florence, see above. An "Aloysius Tommasi Uterussi de Alemania" was still registered as a painter with the Medici and Speziali in 1492 (Karl Frey, *Die Loggia dei Lanzi zu Florenz*, Berlin, 1885, p. 344).

[11] Voss in *JPK*, 1918, p. 20. On the whole extent and influence of transalpine artistic

In addition, however, the guild regulations, and this is probably their most meritorious endeavor, were also supposed to offer a guarantee to the buyers on the art market that in any case only "guild-approved" products, that is, at least up to high standards of craftsmanship, would be supplied. This accounts for the provisions concerning an adequate fundamental process of education for future masters, the prescriptions on the use of genuine, durable painting materials, on conscientious work methods, etc. There were also certain general guidelines on fixing of prices, on which more details below, and appointment of nonpartisan assessors to settle arguments over price, whose names, like those of other guild officials, were determined every four months by drawing lots among the members (RA, 4, p. 133).

The continuation of traditions of good craftsmanship in the individual workshops was also further secured—exclusive of the technical pupil training in the workshops of individual masters—through the transmission of the same artistic calling in certain families. Sometimes through many generations, one or more representatives carried on the ancestral trade at any given time, such as the Robbia from old Luca through Andrea's son Giovanni and the Lippi from Fra Filippo through Filippino's son, who first entered the painters' guild in 1525, almost a hundred years after his grandfather began work. Neri di Bicci was also the son and grandson of a painter. In the Ghiberti family activity as goldsmiths and sculptors continued through five generations from Bartolo, the father of the great Lorenzo, up to the great-grandson Vittore II, who was still living in Vasari's time. Among the Rossellini, three more brothers were active as stone sculptors besides Bernardo and Antonio, partly in workshop association with Bernardo. Mention should also be given to less extended family connections in the same artistic medium, such as the great goldsmith family of the Dei, the many-membered woodcarver dynasty of the del Tasso, and the wax image firm of the Benintendi, famous far beyond Florence, that can be traced from an early representative of the name in the late Trecento up to Giulio Benintendi about 1530-1540.[12]

Next let us consider a few more details on the external limitation and interior organization of the artist class within the rest of the Florentine bourgeoisie. First the specialization of certain workshops in a particular medium should again be noted, especially in the applied arts. Competition was prevented partly through monopolistic maintenance and passing on

---

activity in Italy see Berthold Haendcke, *Der französisch-deutsch-niederländische Einfluss auf die italienische Kunst von etwa 1200 bis 1650* (Strasbourg, 1925), pp. 17, 34ff.

[12] Guild dues were fully waived for artist sons whose father already belonged to the guild; brothers of guild members paid a half rate. See Gaye, *Carteggio*, 1:107-110, 188-89; see also the genealogies in the appendices to the relevant biographies in Milanesi's Vasari edition (Vasari-Milanesi, 3:348-55; and RA, 1904, pp. 881ff.; 9, p. 126.

of a particular technical procedure, which as a special workshop secret could not be easily copied by others, and partly through the inherited, generally acknowledged, and constantly increased mastery of their operation.

Such was the case with the glazed terracotta sculpture of the Robbia workshop whose production method was only betrayed in the sixteenth century, supposedly by a woman of Andrea's household, to Benedetto Buglione, who then for his part made skillful use of it, and with the realistic wax sculpture of *ex-voto* busts, in which the specialist workshop of the Benintendi, just named, enjoyed the reputation of greatest excellence for more than a century and half. It was similar with certain side branches of the arts, such as glass painting, miniature painting, figural embroidery for vestments and costly secular festival costumes, branches of the arts which demanded special technical training, a particular talent, and skill and in which one could thus achieve true mastery only through specialization and limitation.[13]

Along with such voluntary limitation to a personally discovered or perfected specialty there existed also, however, the necessary renunciation of varied activity in all workshops which, for the sake of simple management, geared themselves to certain types of applied arts for everyone's daily needs; artisans who, perhaps, concerned themselves with painting chests, or the decorative painting of cloth hangings, equestrian trappings, pennants, and the like.[14]

This applied to the whole substratum, in those days much broader, more colorful and lively, of the essentially representational arts, which we know today simply as handicrafts, "decorative arts." More noteworthy than such specialization, however, is the opposite phenomenon: multifaceted, universal competence and activity of individual artists in different, even materially different branches of the arts. This was doubly remarkable because thereby the generally prevalent guild separation of artistic media was in some measure broken down, so that under lawful regulation—assuming it was observed—changes of guilds or multiple guild membership must have become necessary.

The transition in later life from goldsmith to monumental sculptor, with occasional further activity perhaps in silver figural relief, occurred repeatedly, as with Antonio Pollaiuolo and Verrocchio.[15] Ghiberti, ac-

---

[13] Vasari-Milanesi, 3:375-76; 2:184-85n. *RA*, 1904, pp. 48ff., 139ff.

[14] These include forzerinai, "pictores cofanorum, pictores sargiarum, Pittori di barde," or whatever else they are called in a limiting sense in the documents of the time (Karl Frey, *Die Loggia dei Lanzi zu Florenz*, Berlin, 1885, pp. 342ff.; pp. 346-47, a *pictor cartarum* and a *pictor schatularum*, 1501). "Pittori di mazzonerie," who specialized in decorative painting of architecture, are discussed in Vasari-Milanesi, 6:217, n.1.

[15] But even Ghiberti had guild membership rights from 1409 on with the Orefici and

cording to his own assertion, had also been active in earlier years as a painter, while other sculptors, like Pollaiuolo and Verrocchio, still later on achieved distinction with a fairly large production of painted works, some of which have survived. Michelangelo, however, felt and declared himself all through his life, and with reason, primarily a marble sculptor, not a painter.

On the other hand, we see some painters occasionally engaging in sculpture. Dello Delli, for example, modelled the brightly painted terra-cotta relief over the portal of Santa Maria Nuova, as well as a whole series of statues of saints in the interior of this church. Leonardo da Vinci, trained in Verrocchio's workshop as a painter as well as a sculptor, is probably to be considered, according to Emil Möller, as the actual author or finisher of the finest sculptural work of Verrocchio from the 1470s; in Milan he ventured upon the most difficult task of monumental sculpture, the bronze equestrian statue (*Raccolta Vinciana*, 14, 1934). Indeed, the crossing of boundaries between one art and another was already nothing unusual in the Trecento.[16]

It remains finally to mention the connection of the artistic vocation with some other subsidiary occupation or with the clergy.

The woodcarver and intarsiator Baccio Cellini, who was Benvenuto's uncle, was also employed as municipal piper (*piffero della signoria*); likewise his pupil Girolamo della Cecca (Vasari-Milanesi, 3:345, n. 1).

In the Quattrocento, however, there was also a whole series of painters who belonged to monastic orders. These included first of all, in contin-uation of a markedly medieval convent artistic practice, certain excellent miniaturists in the Camaldolese convent of Santa Maria degli Angeli, whose names and works, still preserved at the time, are cited in Vasari; likewise several Dominican fathers in San Marco, Fra Benedetto di Mu-gello among others (Marchese, *Memorie*, 1: 209ff., 216ff.).[17] From the

---

would be enrolled in the Maestri di pietra e legname only in 1437. His whole activity as a bronze sculptor thus fell, as may probably be supposed for bronze sculpture in general, under the competence of the goldsmiths' guild (Vasari-Milanesi, 2:259-60).

[16] Giotto reportedly modelled the first reliefs for his Campanile. Maso, the pupil of Giotto, according to Ghiberti's commentary was held as "molto dotto nell'una arte e nell'altra." Cennini's book on painting also contains many instructions for sculptural and casting work. See Lorenzo Ghiberti, *Commentarii*, ed. Julius von Schlosser, *Lorenzo Ghibertis Denkwürdigkeiten*, 2 vols. (Berlin, 1912), 2:166, 38; and Cennino Cennini, *Das Buch von der Kunst* or *Traktat der Malerei*, ed. and trans. A. Ilg in Quellenschriften für Kunstgeschichte, 1 (Vienna, 1871), chaps. 125, 127, 169, 182ff.

[17] Furthermore, a center for glass painting and glazing techniques had long existed in a Florentine convent, that of the Gesuati (San Giusto alle mura) in front of Porta Pinti (Vasari-Milanesi, 3:272ff.). In the Angeli convent some monks also engaged in embroidery of costly mass vestments, of which Vasari could also still see evidence surviving in his own time (Vasari-Milanesi, 2:23-25).

miniature schools at the Angeli and San Marco came two monk painters on a large scale: the Camaldolese Don Lorenzo Monaco and the Dominican, later pronounced blessed, Fra Giovanni Angelico da Fiesole.

His slightly younger contemporary and opposite is Fra Filippo Lippi, who admittedly entered the Carmelite order without his own decision or a true vocation, and subsequently turned out rather badly as a member of the order. Also Carmelite, and later Vallombrosan, was Fra Filippo's pupil and occasional assistant Fra Diamante. Savonarola's preaching and martyrdom at the end of the Quattrocento led an artist of already proven talent, Fra Bartolommeo della Porta, to the Dominican order, which since the time of Thomas Aquinas had devoted a special, finely cultivated interest to sacred art as well as learning. Only subsequently, after many years of exclusive concentration on the spiritual heritage of his model Savonarola, did he return in a new, more powerful development to his natural predisposition to paint. Along with and after him there were still more painters, glass painters, and miniaturists in San Marco. Also in the Dominican convent of Santa Caterina near San Marco, Savonarola's explicit instruction to "foster the fine arts for the honor of God" was observed. Of the women painters of this convent, admittedly only Suor Plautilla Nelli achieved any reputation.[18]

However, while the Dominican men and women painters pursued their art within the context of monastic life, were excused only from their choir prayers, and let the business administrators of their convents negotiate and settle accounts for their works produced for outside commissions, both Don Lorenzo and Fra Filippo were allowed to leave the cloister and live as secular clergy on the income from their work.[19]

But purely secular clergy also appear in the late Quattrocento who were active as a sideline, and probably only mediocre, as painters of ecclesiastical images.[20]

[18] Schnitzer, *Savonarola*, 1:371; 2:823; see especially the comprehensive work by Padre Marchese, *Memorie*, 2:327. A daughter of Uccello, who lived in the Carmelite order, was also active as a painter (Vasari-Milanesi, 2:217).

[19] Don Lorenzo, nevertheless, maintained a close connection with his order, and in the last years of his life even acquired a house belonging to and near the Angeli convent. Fra Filippo, on the other hand, with the rectorate of San Quirico consigned to him, came to enjoy a benefice, whose yield admittedly could not protect him from occasional financial difficulties.

[20] Such were the parish priest Jacopo di Bartolo, whose signed fresco of 1454 Richa (*Notizie*, 3:320) mentions in San Pancrazio; the Prete Matteo Sordo in Pistoia, with works of 1465-1475 cited in documents; and the "Presbyter" Pier Francesco Fiorentino, an imitator of Fra Filippo, some of whose altarpieces from the late Quattrocento are preserved (*RA*, 3, p. 167; *Dedalo*, 7, p. 86ff.). For several secular clergy, as well as monks of the Gesuati convent, who were active as glass painters in the Duomo, the Pazzi chapel, and elsewhere see van Straelen, *Glasmalerei*, pp. 63-64, 66, 98n. etc.

CHAPTER 12

# STUDIOS AND THEIR WORKING

# PROCEDURES

LIVING AND WORKING PLACES AND THE ORGANIZATION OF WORK:
MASTER, ASSISTANTS, AND APPRENTICES

We turn our attention now to the artist's environment in its strictest and most immediate sense, his workshop.

We know in what street or even on what building lot many Florentine artists of the Renaissance period lived and where they had their workshops, often housed elsewhere. For in their own declarations for the official catasto (which was first instituted in 1427, then repeated at various intervals), the possible ownership of land or else, on the debit side, the rent price for living and working space is as a rule recorded.[1]

Following are only such data as can convey a fairly clear conception.

Thus Masaccio in his last years worked in a cramped ground-floor shop ("parte di una bottega" ) near the Badia, opposite the Bargello palace, while Michelozzo at that time could live in the house in Via Larga inherited from his father and along with Donatello rented a workshop near Santo Spirito. For his Duomo sculptures the Opera assigned him one of the choir chapels, already in 1413 and again 1433, as working space.[2]

Ghiberti had his workshop beginning in 1450 opposite Santa Maria Nuova. Vasari in his youth (Vasari-Milanesi, 2:228) still allegedly saw its giant casting furnance there. According to a declaration in a later *denuncia*, this was a courtyard surrounded by porticos; it was rented to Perugino toward the end of the fifteenth century by Lorenzo's grandson, Buonaccorso Ghiberti.[3]

---

[1] Gaye published many such tax declarations; various statements pertaining to this are also found in Milanesi's Vasari commentary; likewise in Chiappelli (*RA*, 1906, pp. 46ff., 48ff.; repeated in his *L'arte del rinascimento*, pp. 202-209) and in Bombe (in *Cicerone*, 1911, pp. 172-74).

[2] Poggi, *Duomo*, pp. 38, 257. On Donatello's frequently changing lodgings see Hans Semper, *Donatello, seine zeit und seine Schule* (Vienna, 1875), pp. 235-37. In Via Sant' Egidio stood the house where Luca della Robbia was born and where he first worked; he later moved to a house in Via Guelfa near San Barnaba, which in Vasari's time (Vasari-Milanesi, 2:167n.) still belonged to his heirs. On Desiderio's purchase of a dwelling (1458, on Via Santa Maria) and rental of a workshop near Santa Trinita, see *RA*, 1930, pp. 250, 267.

[3] Similarly, the dwelling and workshop that Donatello occupied in 1443, in a Bischeri

Benedetto da Maiano had no less than three different workrooms in use at the same time. One was in his home on Via San Gallo and a second was set up especially for marble work in Via dei Servi, which after the master's death in 1497 was leased to Lorenzo del Tasso and later to Giovanni Francesco Rustici. Benedetto rented a third bottega for wood work from the convent of the nuns of Monticelli. See Lorenzo Cendali, *Giuliano e Benedetto da Maiano* (San Casciano, 1926), pp. 185-86.

All the buildings named have since been either destroyed or completely remodelled. Only the house on Via Pietra Piana (No. 7), which Mino da Fiesole acquired in 1464, but used as a dwelling only from 1480 on, has survived at least partially in its original condition. It was not suitable for the workshop operation of his art; in 1470 he still had his atelier near San Firenze.[4]

We find Andrea del Sarto's house, which he acquired in 1520, in a completely altered form, marked by a memorial tablet behind the Annunziata in Via Gino Capponi. His former studio installation in the courtyard of this property was replaced by a fantastically decorated building by a later owner, Federico Zuccari. The famous Casa Buonarroti, however, in Via Ghibellina, which contains the small Michelangelo museum, was built by his nephew on a lot acquired by the master; its present form dates from the mid-seventeenth century, and Michelangelo himself never saw the house. During his earlier stays in Florence he lived in the old paternal house and often changed his working quarters.[5]

So much for the locations of individual artists' workshops. As regards their interior appearance and arrangement, it must first of all be said— before we go into concrete details, equipment, and the like below—that in these places the master did not pursue his creative task all alone, as in artist's studios of recent and present times. This is true even if intellectually aspiring theory in the late Quattrocento occasionally put forward the necessity of solitude and quiet contemplation for the artist, and Michelangelo later, as the first and only one, even in practice kept assistants out of his studio as much as possible.[6]

---

house (now Palazzo Guadagni) behind the Duomo, passed in 1480 into the possession of Verrocchio and subsequently Lorenzo di Credi (del Badia, *MF*, 1, pp. 60-62).

[4] But in the second upper story of the home, drawings of unusually large format were discovered on certain sections of wall, ornamental designs with candelabra and the like in the character of the late Quattrocento. Each wall once thus belonged to a living or sleeping room, perhaps of the master's assistants, who in their leisure hours apparently sketched on the wall those ornamental studies, which are still visible today, having been done in soft coal (Chiappelli, *L'arte del rinascimento*, p. 207).

[5] The cartoon of the bathing soldiers was produced in a room of the dyers' hospital at Sant' Onofrio, just as Leonardo worked out his Anghiari cartoon at the same time in the papal room at Santa Maria Novella; for the sculptures of the Medici chapel, however, Michelangelo used a studio set up ad hoc on Via Mozza near San Lorenzo (See Michelangelo-Milanesi, *Lettere*, pp. 393, 397-98).

[6] But Uccello already mentions his private workroom, near the common workshop, in

The rule for artistic practice in the Renaissance—and for the most part still in the Baroque—was a workshop organization corresponding to the artist's general position in the social and economic sphere of the artisan class. It appears most closely comparable to production procedure, work allocation, and work organization as we still meet with them today in any small artisan's workshop. The master, directing and producing the main work, is at the head, with two, three, or more apprentices and assistants who help him out and thus for their part undergo their gradually progressing training.

It can be illustrated by a few examples how this system of a working group with apportioned, differently graded roles functioned in the artist's studio. Frequently, for example, we come upon the temporary partnership of two beginners of about the same age, who thus commonly take over and share the cost of setting up a new workshop and its profits for as long as it takes for each to be in a position to continue alone in his own workshop.[7] A similar relationship, and then often of long duration, resulted from a more natural impetus in artist families in which several brothers or even father and son ran the business together; thus with Antonio and Piero Pollaiuolo, with the Robbia, Rossellini and others (see above).

An actual large-scale operation, however, with numerous personnel, was developed especially in certain sculpture workshops during the execution of an important commission. This was true of Ghiberti for his bronze doors and the projects going on simultaneously. The contract for the first bronze doors, still surviving, thus also concerns the large staff of the atelier and the wage allotments for all collaborators; in the first version of 1403 it refers to eleven assistants, in the second contract of 1407 to as many as twenty. Among these, along with various young helpers and handymen, a few skilled assistants could also be found who already or soon thereafter would make themselves known for their own independent production.[8]

---

the *denunzia* of 1458 (*ZKG*, 1933, p. 252). On Leonardo's opinion on this see sections 48, 55, and 58a of his book on painting; on Michelangelo's need for solitude see Vasari-Milanesi, 7:270 and Condivi, *Michelangelo*, chap. 66.

[7] Thus Donatello and Michelozzo in the 1420s and 1430s. Giovanni dal Ponte had a certain Smeraldo with him around 1425-1430 as a partner who received thirty-five percent of the profits (*RA*, 4, p. 169). Pesellino assumed a half share of the Trinity altar for Pistoia with Pierlorenzo Pratese, which gave rise to all sorts of business complications after the former's untimely death (Chiappelli, *L'arte del rinascimento*, p. 211). Later Fra Bartolommeo and Albertinelli worked together, until the former took holy orders; then Andrea del Sarto worked with Franciabigio from 1508 to 1510. See the separation contract after Fra Bartolommeo's withdrawal in Knapp, *Fra Bartolommeo*.

[8] Donatello occasionally used eighteen to twenty assistants in Padua; there were four of them for the San Lorenzo pulpits in Florence, including Bertoldo and Bellano (see Kauffmann,

Among painters, it was probably only those who were working on important fresco projects who attracted and employed, at least for a time, a large circle of assistants of different grades. There is specific evidence for this for Ghirlandaio, as well as for Benozzo, for Pinturicchio for the Sienese cathedral library, etc. (Hermann Egger, *Codex Escurialensis. Ein Skizzenbuch aus der Werkstatt Domenico Ghirlandaios*, 2 vols., Sonderschriften des Osterreichen Archäologischen Institutes in Wien, no. 4. Vienna, 1906, pp. 47ff.). The extent to which certain skillful assistants collaborated and worked independently on such projects is sometimes established by documents and often even possible to ascertain through stylistic comparisons.[9]

Sometimes it happened that an assistant outgrew his master artistically even during the period of his apprenticeship; thus with Piero di Cosimo and the old Cosimo Rosselli, who let him execute many important parts of the frescoes in the Sistine chapel (Vasari-Milanesi, 4:132); thus the young Leonardo da Vinci in his notorious participation in Verrocchio's *Baptism of Christ* and—if Emil Möller is right—even in the execution of many sculptural works that go under Verrocchio's name. Small specific commissions were probably often assigned by the shop master to a trust-worthy assistant for completion.[10]

If a master died after beginning a work, the independent members of his workshop immediately took over the completion.[11]

A form of division of labor in which design and execution fell to two different masters also occurred repeatedly: Michelangelo in the 1520s and later several times gave designs to younger followers, Sebastiano del Piombo and others, which they then worked up into their own paintings. Conversely Bandinelli, who drew good cartoons but could not handle colors, took on a painter to help with the execution of his pictures (Vasari-

---

*Donatello*, pp. 131, 256, n. 649; Vasari-Milanesi, 2:421n.). A whole series of such independent assistants, along with helpers of lesser rank, could be found working for Jacopo Sansovino at the beginning of the sixteenth century, as well as for Andrea Sansovino on the Santa Casa in Loreto and with Montorsoli on the monumental fountain at Messina, etc. (Vasari-Milanesi, 6:58, 302, 647).

[9] Benozzo's assistant Andrea di Giusto tells in detail in his *Ricordi* the parts of the frescoes of San Gimignano he personally painted (Gaye, *Carteggio*, 1:21-22).

[10] For example Castagno gave a picture of hell commissioned from him by the Duke of Mantua to the young Baldovinetti to execute in 1494, and Squarcione let his partner Pizzolo design a picture assigned to him, and had a third person execute it. See Baldovinetti-Londi, *Ricordi*, p. 92; or Paul O. Kristeller, *Andrea Mantegna*, London, 1901 or Berlin, 1902 [*Translator's note*: edition not indicated].

[11] Thus Ghirlandaio's brothers and assistants took over the execution of the high altar for Santa Maria Novella, and Lorenzo di Credi that of Verrocchio's Pistoia altar; to complete the Colleoni, however, which Credi himself could not carry out, he hired, as Verrocchio's rightful successor, a Florentine sculptor Giovanni d'Andrea (Milanesi, *Documenti*, pp. 150-52).

Milanesi, 6:152; 7:272). On the other hand, however, Michelangelo's procedure in his own undertakings is above all, as already noted, particularly remarkable and unusual. To paint the Sistine ceiling he probably initially hired some helpers, like any other in a similar situation, even Raphael, who was beginning the Stanze around the same time; within a short time, however, he sent them all away, retaining only a purely technical amanuensis to grind colors etc., and devoted nearly four years of intense personal energy to the whole gigantic work of the vault painting, executing it alone and with his own hand down to the last brushstroke.

When we trace below the work procedures of the time in wall and panel painting as they were otherwise customary in their various stages, it will become clear that the collaboration of assistants of various grades, certainly very useful and necessary, was entirely out of the question with respect to Michelangelo's procedure, wholly different and peculiar to him alone. For with him a painted work did not come into being as a transfer into colors of a drawing worked out in detail in advance and at last fixed in a final form. For Michelangelo all preparatory drawing was like a first attempt without binding force, even if this preparatory work—as in the first mural commission in Florence, preceding the Sistina, of the attack on the bathing soldiers—had been advanced as far as a great cartoon (and even this probably executed only in part). His delight in formal invention continued to work even during the final execution, and often certain decisive details in Michelangelo's work appear to have been created and developed only in the final exertion of the completion stages of a work, from the inspiration of the moment. "Si dipinge col cervello, non con le mani," he himself once said. The same holds true for his chiseling work on marble, in which it was precisely the confrontation with the enticingly resistant working material that was so exciting and essential for his own form-creating imagination.[12]

The procedure of other masters of the same period on corresponding projects should now be compared to this. As a counterpart to the Julius tomb we might take the execution of the figure complex, no less extensive, of the Santa Casa at Loreto. This was completely finished in a little more than fifteen years from 1513 to 1530 by Andrea Sansovino in cooperation

---

[12] The primary evidence for this is the long history of the Julius tomb, which, after the joyful beginning and after the extravagant grandeur of the project, finally came to a conclusion so disappointingly inadequate for the master himself and his patrons. This was chiefly because Michelangelo even here insisted on the longest possible time, to execute virtually every blow of the chisel with his own hand and even to direct personally the procurement of marble in Carrara. The same course of events in the later great commission for San Lorenzo, however, had the result that Michelangelo himself at last lost all joy and spirit and, as at the end with the Julius tomb, finally allowed whole figures to be executed by assistants.

with a huge number of other sculptors and stonemasons. Or we should consider what Raphael accomplished with his workshop staff during the last six years of his short life, in the Vatican, the Farnesina, and elsewhere.[13] This is not to speak of the downright entrepreneurial organization of work procedure which became generally customary in the succeeding Mannerist period, with an army of collaborators and specialists for particular branches of the work for the speediest possible execution of extensive wall-painting cycles.

For the production of most great art works and artistic complexes, it was thus largely a question of a multimembered working collective. The head of the workshop might at best give it his stamp by force of his personal supervision and efficiency of execution, without—even for small panel paintings—keeping every detail of the execution in his own hands. Such division of labor was occasioned and made almost indispensable by the particularly laborious execution procedures for painting as well as sculpture at that time, with the many, in part purely technical preparatory and subsidiary tasks they involved.

## THE PROCESS OF SCULPTURE

The sculptural process begins, if we except drawn preliminary sketches, with the execution of a model molded in soft material, usually in the form of a small scale bozzetto in wax or clay.

This procedure is admittedly attested to only for Michelangelo; it can be assumed, though, that such three-dimensional sketches of a subject were already in use in the Quattrocento. At that time, however, neither the artist himself nor anyone else held such preliminary conceptions to be worth preserving.[14] Only the more sharply developed collector's interest of the late sixteenth century valued even such preparatory studies, earlier carelessly destroyed, when they came from a master of renown, so that in certain cases they have survived until today.[15]

---

[13] See Hermann Dollmayr, "Raffaels Werkstätte," in *Jahrbuch der Kunsthistorischen Sammlungen des Allerhöchsten Kaiserhauses*, no. 16 (Vienna, 1895); Wackernagel, *MK*, 2, 1909, pp. 23f.; on the painting of the Vatican Loggie see Vasari-Milanesi, 5:593.

[14] Vasari (Vasari-Milanesi, 7:154) speaks of a small wax model of the *David* and of similar ones for the saints Cosmas and Damian for the Medici chapel. These have not survived; but other small figures have, which can be considered as preparatory studies for certain forms for these tombs (*MK*, 6, pp. 309ff.). On sculptors' drawings of the early Renaissance see *JfK*, 1930, pp. 43ff.

[15] Of the above-mentioned bozzetti of Cosmas and Damian, one came into Vasari's possession, while the other was acquired by Pietro Aretino, who expresses himself on the subject in an enthusiastic letter of 1530 (*MK*, 2, p. 399); Vasari-Milanesi, 6:146-49, 150-51 mentions small wax models of Bandinelli's for the Hercules-Cacus group and other works.

We note in passing that certain contemporary painters occasionally used such small figures represented in motion as models, and even had such figures prepared by sculptors specifically for that purpose.[16]

After sculptural sketches in bozzetto form, which we may also suppose were the first stage in the production process of major sculptural work in the Quattrocento, the preparation of a full-size clay model followed as a second stage. In bronze work this model is indeed the technically indispensable point of departure for the execution of a cast. But also for statuary and relief sculpture in stone and marble, such carefully considered preparations could hardly have been less necessary at that time than was, for instance, the production of a full size working drawing for the execution of a mural or a panel painting.

Even in the sculptural ateliers of the Renaissance it was doubtless generally true, just as today, that a major part of the laborious chiselwork was done by assistants and pupils after the master's model, and the latter reserved for himself only certain essential details, as well as the final completion. Only for Michelangelo did his own direct work on the block represent the ultimately decisive phase in the formation of the work. This phase was certainly preceded even in his case with drawings and small sculptural sketches of his ideas; not, however, by a full-sized clay model worked out in detail. Therefore he could use assistants almost solely for the first, coarse technical work of cutting the block properly for its transport from the quarry and in the first stage of its workshop preparation. And even in the work in the marble quarries, Michelangelo himself was present whenever possible. The sight and the direct, palpable contact with the unquarried, still unformed raw material in Carrara and Seravezza evidently awakened his formal inspiration and gave him the liveliest stimulus to conceptions of images.[17] There are also many informative statements from Michelangelo himself and from his immediate circle of pupils on the creative process, the bringing forth from the amorphous stone of a form prepared in the conception and through small model sketches.[18]

[16] Jacopo Sansovino modelled such bozzetti for the young Andrea del Sarto and for Perugino; similar cases are reported of Bugiardini and Pontormo (Vasari-Milanesi, 6:208, 287; 8:488-90). See also the altar design by the painter Utili in Chatsworth, RA, 1932, p. 24. From the late Trecento, however, we hear several times of figure sketches that Agnolo Gaddi, Spinello, and others were to furnish to the sculptors of the Duomo workshop (Poggi, Duomo, pp. xxvii, xxxiii, doc. pp. 53, 112).

[17] On this see the remarks by Carl Justi (Michelangelo. Beiträge zur Erklärung der werke und des Menschen, Leipzig, 1900, pp. 381ff.). The preliminary cutting of the blocks in Carrara under the sculptor's supervision is also attested elsewhere, for example, around 1400 for certain statues of the Duomo workshop and in 1525 for Tribolo (Poggi, Duomo, pp. xxxiii, xxxv-vi; Vasari-Milanesi, 6:61, 85).

[18] See, for example, Vasari-Milanesi, 7:158 and also the detailed discussion of Michel-

But as has been said, Michelangelo's marble work, exclusively by his own hand and virtually improvisatory, must be seen only as a purely personal, exceptional case alongside the generally customary studio practice. In the latter, on the one hand, the carefully considered formulation of the whole and all details in a definitive clay model was viewed as indispensable preparation; on the other hand, however, the decorative character of early Renaissance artistic style, delighting in detail, affected even monumental statue sculpture. The frequent polychromy and gilding of the ornamental parts of sculptural monuments, still perceptible here and there in faint traces, also reflect this characteristic.[19]

However, collaboration of a designing and modelling sculptor with other professionally specializing coworkers was above all, and almost always, necessary for the execution of bronze sculpture; for only a few sculptors were also able to master the difficulties of the casting technique. First to be in a position to do so were those who were originally goldsmiths: Ghiberti, Pollaiuolo, Verrocchio, Bertoldo. Michelozzo was also a good bronze caster. Donatello let him handle the rough casting of his bronze work during the period of their partnership, which he himself then only finished with chasing etc.[20]

## The Painter's Working Procedure: Drawing

Hardly less varied than in the field of sculpture are the techniques of the various branches of painting; and the production processes for canvas and panel paintings, wall painting, glass painting, and miniature sometimes appear still more intricate, composed of more separate divisions than is the case for sculpture.

We gain a general conception of the usual work management in painter's workshops of the early Quattrocento first of all from the prac-

---

angelo's chisel technique in Alois Grünwald, *Florentiner Studien* (Prague, 1914); and further in Leonardo's book on painting (Section 512 on transfer of the clay model into marble).

[19] On the small statues on the Duomo facade that were once painted and gilded see Poggi, *Duomo*, p. xxvii, doc. 70, 72, 77; see further the watercolor reproduction of various great tomb monuments in Buonaccorso Ghiberti's *Zibaldone* of 1480 (*MKIF*, 1, pp. 168ff.). A few notes on coloristic treatment of small sculptures are in Neri di Bicci's workshop book.

[20] In Padua, however, he used the help of a bellcaster; Michelozzo, on account of his technical experience, was occasionally also hired to cast bells and cannons. We find details on the casting procedure of the Renaissance and the metal alloys selected for it, since Leon Battista Alberti's treatise *De arte aeraria* is lost, in Pomponius Gauricus's *De sculptura* (Florence, 1504) and the later statements and reports of Benvenuto Cellini and Vasari (Gauricus, *De sculptura*, ed. Brockhaus, Leipzig, 1886, pp. 59ff., 223ff.). Some relevant information is also in *Della Pirotechnia*, a manual of a Sienese cannon and bellcaster Vannoccio Biringuccio compiled in 1535-1538 (new Italian edition by Aldo Mieli, Bari, 1914, German edition by Otto Johannsen, Braunschweig, 1925).

tical manual written down around the turn of the century by Cennino Cennini. The author of this record, who for his part passed through a twelve-year period of apprenticeship and association with Agnolo Gaddi, testifies accordingly to the viewpoint and working methods of the late Trecento, which, however, still remained prevalent for almost the whole first half of the fifteenth century. Thus most painting of this first early Renaissance period, its whole production and manner of expression, had its origins in a workshop practice such as Cennini describes and teaches in great detail.

The content and tenor of these instructions reflect a solid, meticulously careful artistic practice, still thoroughly couched in artisan tradition. The preparation of the colors, carried out in the workshop itself, as well as all the other painting and binding agents, the production of the various types of brushes, and the laborious preparation of the panel and its gesso coating are presupposed as the first preparatory stage and foundation of any painted work. The sketching of the picture composition, the application of the gold ground and other underpainting, the execution in colors, first of all the clothing parts, then the uncovered parts of the body and the heads, are the further steps in the creation of the painting. All these procedures are expounded by Cennini as knowledge to be learned gradually in a long series of greater or smaller chapters, almost as recipes.

If Cennini thus provides us with a fairly clear picture of the working procedure of the painter in the early Quattrocento, any kind of similar illustration from the immediately following stage of development and from the High Renaissance is sorely lacking. For neither Alberti nor even Leonardo gives more than particular passing remarks about the technical usages for painting in his time and the details of execution of his pictures. Accordingly their *trattati*, and especially Leonardo's, elaborate on the essentially artistic training of the painter. To this belongs in the first place the methodical sharpening of the powers of perception—the enriching and deepening of the imaginative faculties through drawing studies. Their instruction books thus deal above all with drawings in preparation for painting, which have also survived in a boundless profusion of original examples. These painters' drawings were produced on the one hand as nature studies undertaken incidentally or for a particular motif and on the other hand as sketched designs of a picture composition or as more precise final bases for the execution of a painting.

In the following pages we shall briefly survey the process of preparatory drawing as it relates directly or indirectly to a projected painting.[21]

On what most closely concerns the extent of drawing efforts, the occasion for them and their object, only so much may be said here:

[21] See Joseph Meder, *Die Handzeichnung; ihre Technik und Entwicklung* (Vienna, 1919); Heinrich Leporini, *Die Stilentwicklung der Handzeichnung, XIV bis XVIII Jahrhundert*

In Trecento practice, the naturalistic execution of details on the basis of specific observation studies still hardly came into consideration. By contrast, such drawn preparation for painting appears certain beginning in the second quarter of the Quattrocento and occurs clearly and plentifully after the middle of the century. For only at that time had the general stylistic aspirations and also the demands of the patrons and public taken an orientation that made the execution of a picture of high quality impossible without basic draughtsmanly observation of nature in any given case.

The scarcity of preserved or recorded drawings by the older masters, including the first generation of the early Renaissance, surely also corresponds strongly to the rarity of preparatory drawing work in the customary process of painting at that time. In general what survives consists only of preparatory sketches of individual figures and groups, decorative arrangements of draped parts, or the first sketch of a narrative composition.

It is true that Masaccio's astonishing nudes in various pictures in the Brancacci chapel, and the donor portraits as well as other realistic and perspective details of his Trinity fresco, are inconceivable without previous drawn nature studies. And of Uccello Vasari still knew that he left whole chests full of drawings to his heirs. Nothing securely by Masaccio has survived, and by Uccello probably only the sketch for the equestrian portrait of 1436 in the Duomo, recognizable by the superimposed grid of lines as the last preparatory stage for the cartoon.[22]

Meanwhile Leon Battista Alberti had already proclaimed diligent nature study as an indispensable requirement in his treatise on painting in 1435 and at the same time had recommended, at least in fundamental training and overcoming of errors, to make the largest possible drawings, if not actually full scale, after nature. He spoke also, as though of an already established procedure, of the necessity to sketch clothed figures in motion first as nudes and only afterwards in their clothing (Leon Battista Alberti, *Della pittura e della statua,* ed. and trans. Hubert Jan-

---

(Vienna, 1925); Bernard Berenson, *The Drawings of the Florentine Painters*, 2 vols. (London, 1903), and Carlo Gamba, Carlo Loesser, P. N. Ferri and others, *I Disegni della R. Galleria degli Uffizi in Firenze*, 5 vols. in 20 (Florence, 1912-1921).

Drawings by famous masters were used quite early by young artists for their own inspiration, but were also saved by art lovers out of an interest in collecting. Vasari, for example, assembled a fairly broad collection, going back to Giotto's time, to which he repeatedly refers and from which many pieces in their original mountings are still preserved.

[22] Heinrich Leporini, *Die Stilentwicklung der Handzeichnung, XIV bis XVIII Jahrhundert* (Vienna, 1925), ill. 25; Vasari-Milanesi, 2:215. The drawings of these first realists have perished, perhaps due to overly diligent study use by younger followers. From Fra Angelico and from Fra Filippo Lippi, for example, only three or four drawing sheets are preserved as secure works.

itschek, Quellenschriften für Kunstgeschichte, II, Vienna, 1877, pp. 110, 120, 152).

Yet such teachings of the theoreticians could become firmly established in general practice only considerably later, in part not before the High Renaissance. The development stages of drawing at any given time naturally also correspond to the materials and technical procedures used for them.

Until about the middle of the Quattrocento the draughtsman still frequently used small panels impregnated with bone meal or covered with parchment as a foundation and practice field, according to an old tradition—an intermediate step between antique writing slates coated with wax and the later sketchbook. Loose parchment sheets might also be employed, although their small proportions and relative costliness must have called for the most sparing possible use (see Cennino Cennini, *Das Buch von der Kunst* or *Traktat der Malerei*, ed. and trans. A. Ilg in Quellenschriften für Kunstgeschichte, 1, Vienna, 1871, chaps. 5-10).

A more profuse drawing practice, a freer drawing method, and one which could also appear in larger formats only became possible—at the same time as the desire for really extensive and penetrating drawn preparation for a painting—when useful and cheap types of paper came on the market (Joseph Meder, *Die Handzeichnung, ihre Technik und Entwicklung*, Vienna, 1919).

Actual sketchbooks for the collection of pattern types, from models handed down or even from occasional nature studies, probably came into sporadic use from the early Quattrocento on.

With the requirement, widespread since the middle of the century, for a draughtsman's observation and other preparation for each important image to be planned, we shall have to imagine the use of such *taccuini* in greater or smaller format as the general practice.[23]

[23] Leonardo recommended that the painter constantly carry a little notebook with him in order to note down in passing particular observations of movements, gestures, character heads, as the occasion presented itself. At another point he speaks of sketchbooks with colored grounded paper, thus for carefully executed study drawings modelled with white highlights. The varicolored profusion of drawn subjects in the so-called sketchbook of Verrocchio (which more likely belonged to his pupil Francesco di Simone) can be taken as a generally valid cross section of a sculptor's range of interest in drawing in the 1480s. About twenty-five sheets from this, covered with all sorts of pen drawings, are preserved in Paris and elsewhere (Mackowsky, *Verrocchio*, Bielefeld, 1901, pp. 91-92). For a volume of collected drawing studies from the circle of Benozzo's pupils, see *RA*, 1930, pp. 87ff.

Condivi in his history of the youth of Michelangelo (*Michelangelo*, chap. 5) reports on a drawing book by Ghirlandaio with nature studies as well as drawings after Roman ruins and ornamental motifs, which also served as a pattern book for the students of his workshop.

In the estate of Fra Bartolommeo who died in 1517 were found no less than twelve books with drawings, probably essentially preparatory figures and composition sketches, which might surely appear to demonstrate the broad extent and intensity of the practice of drawing in the early Cinquecento in general.

In the draughtsmanly preparation for painting, three successive steps in the creative process can be distinguished, at least from the second third of the Quattrocento on. The first step is the sketching of the picture arrangement and composition idea, often based on special instructions of the commissioner. The latter might also require the presentation of a binding compositional sketch at the conclusion of the contract.

By this time such summary establishment of the design was naturally always the first step, even for large-scale sculpture. After this, however, introduced only now as an intermediate stage, came nature studies for all possible details of the projected image, and finally, as the last stage, the final, more or less precisely detailed sketch of the whole composition. Based on this, then, either through tracing from a full-size sketch in the case of panel paintings, or through enlargement with the help of a grid network in frescoes, the working drawing, the cartoon, and with it the final picture went into execution.[24]

At the same time, one of the general stylistic developments corresponding to changes in the draughtsman's manner of observation and representation becomes noticeable after the middle of the Quattrocento. This appears, on the one hand, in the sense of minute precision in the character of textile surfaces, in detail studies after the living or inanimate object and, on the other hand, in the gradually freer, lighter, more sketchy execution of composition designs.[25]

Along with this, the corresponding change in drawing material, hand in hand with the general stylistic change in the type of stroke and the whole conception of form, is once again noticeable. Silverpoint, the preferred instrument for the careful and delicate drawing style of the early and mid-Quattrocento, is found to yield its predominance more and more around the end of the century. It is succeeded both by the quill pen, whose brisk, bold, sharply tapering stroke combines easily with broader

[24] See in Bernard Berenson, *The Drawings of the Florentine painters*, 2 vols., (London, 1903), vol. 1, pl. 32-33, the rough altar sketch enclosed in a letter by Fra Filippo Lippi and the neat *disegno* of a retable by Lorenzo di Credi.

[25] It is true that the transition from a traditional to a progressive new drawing style was first accomplished with bold determination only by the marked naturalists. For illustration of the gradual transformation of draughtsmanly expression see the examples offered by Leporini (Heinrich Leporini, *Die Stilentwicklung der Handzeichnung, XIV bis XVIII Jahrhundert*, Vienna, 1925, pp. 25, 27, 29) and Vasari-Milanesi, 2:595 (on a particularly naturalistic animal study by Baldovinetti).

Only the later Quattrocento, from about 1470 on, subsequently develops from the free, loose, and painterly manner of execution already frequently adopted by Fra Filippo to the delicately opalescent or bubblingly animated style that distinguishes many sheets by Botticelli and Filippino, and which is not a total mystery even to the prosaic Ghirlandaio. On the other hand, especially with sculptor-painters, in certain larger preliminary drawings we encounter the broad-faceted, shaded surface modelling that characterizes the sculptor (Heinrich Leporini, *Die Stilentwicklung der Handzeichnung, XIV bis XVIII Jahrhundert*, Vienna, 1925, ill. 30-34, 36-37, 41).

brush washes, in watercolor or brown bistre or with soft colored chalk, and by the broad, hasty chalk technique and the red chalk drawing that came into fashion around 1500.[26] And these also became the accepted drawing media for the large scale style of the Cinquecento, which begins to stand out clearly in drawing practice from the turn of the century on.[27]

The exclusive use of chalk or red ochre also brought an end to the tinting of drawing paper, customary up to then and occasionally still practiced in the early Cinquecento. For the complicated structure and rich scale of modelling thus obtained with the basic reddish tone (produced by ground cinnabar powder or pigment of another color), the dark line or brush drawing and shadow hatching, and finally white highlights had, like so much other elegance of the older artistic taste, to yield to the new boldly simplified manner of representation.[28]

In association with the new artistic aims, the earlier interest in carefully modelled, elegant drapery, for which Lorenzo di Credi still made a practice of setting up clay models with cloth stiffened by soaking in wax as models for drawing, also gradually disappeared. Instead of this, the striving for the clearest possible structure and organic quality of the total appearance came to the forefront; so also did the concern, now particularly lively, for the study of the nude, and the anatomical interest and knowledge so useful for this.[29]

[26] Leonardo appears to be one of the first to use red chalk, first occasionally around 1480, then predominantly during the Milanese period. Charcoal was used, on account of the somewhat rough structure of its strokes, only for large-scale cartoons or for preparatory sketching (to be wiped away after the definitive establishment of the design in pen or chalk).

[27] Compare as one of the first decisive examples of the new drawing style the study of a woman's head by the young Fra Bartolommeo, to be dated already before 1500, with the head of a man by Lorenzo di Credi originating scarcely fifteen years earlier (Heinrich Leporini, Die Stilentwicklung der Handzeichnung, XIV bis XVIII Jahrhundert, Vienna, 1925, ill. 36, 124). See also the coarse, completely summary, and broadly handled composition sketch by Mariotto Albertinelli for his Visitation of 1503 (Heinrich Leporini, Die Stilentwicklung der Handzeichnung, XIV bis XVIII Jahrhundert, Vienna, 1925, ill. 127).

[28] But a transitional master like Raffaellino del Garbo still used color-grounded paper and a correspondingly traditional drawing medium: silver-point, feather, or brush heightened with white (Vasari-Milanesi, 4:235).

[29] In the early Quattrocento even the determined realists, Masaccio, Uccello, or Donatello would probably have turned to the living model only for certain specific cases of necessity. Somewhat later it became customary to study young assistants available in the studio for certain standing or action motifs, in that one had them assume the necessary pose after taking off their outer garments. Numerous study sheets of youthful figures in close-fitting undergarments attest to this procedure. See Joseph Meder, Die Handzeichnung, ihre Technik und Entwicklung (Vienna, 1919), pp. 379ff., with illustrations.

Subsequently, however, for Pollaiuolo, the naked male body in the most various, often exaggeratedly lively motifs of movement, for Botticelli more often the female nude, became a frequent object of draftsmanly observation, as must be concluded from many of their paintings, even without the lost studies for them.

A systematically pursued drawing after the nude, now utilized in a wholly different sense, was instituted only with the masters who began in the late Quattrocento to envision the artistic goals of the High Renaissance. Thus in composition sketches for the *Adoration of the Magi* of 1480, Leonardo probably already followed for the first time the method advocated by Alberti in his time (see above) of initially sketching figures in motion unclothed, a procedure that quickly achieved general acceptance in the Cinquecento. His practical anatomical studies were, however, probably carried on as much from natural scientific as from artistic interest.

For Michelangelo, on the contrary, who through the intercession of the prior of Santo Spirito took the opportunity to dissect cadavers as early as 1493 and later still at times pursued such studies so zealously that he got sick to his stomach from it, only the artistic use of anatomical insights could be in question (Condivi, *Michelangelo*, chaps. 13, 60; Vasari-Milanesi, 7:268-69).

The young Fra Bartolommeo had produced and collected drawings from the nude, including the female model, in great numbers; he destroyed them subsequently out of moral considerations under the influence of Savonarola's sermons.

Franciabigio, for the constant enrichment of his sense of form, later drew a nude study daily in summer. That he used paid models ("uomini salariati") for this—that thus as a result of general demand, modelling could already have become practiced as a trade—is proved by the custom of drawing from the nude, at that time evidently generally established. In addition, the same Franciabigio also pursued anatomical studies together with a physician.[30]

On the basis of such observations of the living model or anatomical preparation, there finally developed the practice of sketching the standing and sitting poses of all the main figures of a picture. In the process one studied not only the normally unclothed limbs, specifically hands and feet, often in numerous variations and stages of execution. It also became customary, as Leonardo had already done, to establish more or less precisely the parts of the body covered in the completed painting, at least their principal joints, first of all in their uncovered appearance.[31]

[30] Vasari-Milanesi, 5:196; 6:8. As a boy, Bandinelli already made nude studies from peasants who were working half naked in the fields (Vasari-Milanesi, 6:136).

[31] Fra Bartolommeo's red chalk studies for the Bartholomew of his St. Catherine painting (in the Albertina; Joseph Meder, *Albertina*, pl. 15, 86 [*Translator's note*: This probably refers to Meder's *Handzeichnungen alter Meister aus der Albertina und anderen Sammlungen*, 12 vols., Vienna, 1896-1908]) illustrate very clearly the draughtsmanly preparation for an individual figure, with action sketches for the poses, a precise model study and larger individual representations of the head, feet, and a hand.

## EXECUTION OF PANEL AND WALL PAINTINGS

Concerning the execution of the painting itself following the draughts-manly preparatory stages, only a little and incomplete information can be reported here. It is based on suggestions that can be found in the Quattrocento theorists or Vasari, or which even occasionally find expression in work contracts where certain obligations of the artist are set down.

The traditional work practice, as Cennino Cennini represented it and as it still remained valid in many ways long after the author's generation, has already been discussed. With the progressive breakthroughs in the new attitudes toward art, however, the procedure of picture execution necessarily also had to change. The most important innovation, the adoption and combination of the oil painting technique with that of egg tempera, still in predominant use in the early Cinquecento, already appears to have been employed somehow in Florence from the 1440s on by Domenico Veneziano and subsequently by Baldovinetti.[32]

Vasari in his *Introduzione*, Chapters 20-21, gives a few terse but fairly graphic indications about the work procedure of the earlier painters, drawn from the surviving Florentine workshop tradition as it was in fact still generally practiced with some modifications around the middle of the sixteenth century and from recollections of earlier customs. Based on all these statements and the clues to be read from the paintings themselves, we shall have to imagine the execution process of a panel painting of the early Renaissance and in the beginning of the sixteenth century approximately as follows.

First of all, the painter had to provide a ground for the picture panel, which was not infrequently ordered in advance by the patron from a carpenter, and for smaller paintings, often even already furnished with the carved frame. The ground was provided by coating the panel with carefully smoothed plaster or gypsum, either directly on the wooden substratum or, when this consisted of several boards in larger pictures, on a canvas glued over the whole picture surface. Immediately thereafter, the parts set off with gold leaf, halos, and so forth were applied to the ground thus prepared.[33]

---

[32] Precise contemporary accounts on this are lacking, however, and even the numerous investigations by specialists in the field such as Ernst Berger, Frimmel, and others have still yielded no unanimous definitive results concerning the particular methods and progress of the new painting technique. See Ernst Berger, *Beiträge zur Entwicklungsgeschichte der Maltechnik* (Munich, 1897-1905), vol. 3; Theodor von Frimmel, *Handbuch der Gemäldekunde*, 3rd ed. (Leipzig, 1920), pp. 36ff.

[33] See, for example, the express reference to this preliminary work in a contract with Benozzo Gozzoli, 1461 (*RA*, 1904, p. 10) and in addition the documents concerning Ghirlandaio's altar of the Magi for the Innocenti in Paul Küppers, *Die Tafelbilder des Domenico Ghirlandaio* (Strasbourg, 1916), pp. 87-89.

Only then did the actual execution of the picture begin with a sketch of the whole composition, for which a secure basis was provided by the working drawings for all large or in any way complicated figures, previously worked out on paper and transferred onto the painting ground. Thereupon the modelled shadow areas had to be executed with a brush in brownish colors as a fundamental layer of underpainting. These were done in hatched strokes, sometimes with cross hatching, or even in shading blended into the surface as well as fine, greyish tonal modulations of light and shadow. Finally the transparent coat of local colors was applied over this to complete the painting.

A few well-known paintings that have come down to us in an incomplete state show the structure of the underpainting in various stages of execution.[34]

Only with the consequent adoption and domination of the oil technique, which after the Venetian precedent, and specifically since the second decade of the Cinquecento, generally established itself in Florence too, was the stylistic change to the High Renaissance provided with an appropriate technical means of representation.

On the whole, in view of the preceding exposition, it must be expressly pointed out how closely all the technical conditions of the creation of paintings were bound up with the actual nature of artistic invention and formation. From the final result, the completed work, the uniqueness of a master and his relationship to the art historical conditions surrounding him can be only incompletely understood. More direct information can, however, be gained where we can achieve some sort of insight into the different preparatory and execution stages of a work of art on the basis of surviving preliminary stages.

As fragmentary and almost accidental as the preserved selection of study sheets appears, the information to be gathered from written reports is equally scarce. The same is true of what we can learn about the execution process from particular paintings that have survived incomplete or with their structure partially exposed because the uppermost layer of paint has been worn away; when we bring all these pieces of evidence and references together, we do gain at least an overall picture of the working process in a painter's studio, comprehensible enough at least in

[34] Thus on the back of one of the Pollaiuolo Virtues now in the Uffizi is found a first, evidently rejected brush sketch of the planned figure; carried somewhat further, however, and remaining in this condition, is the underpainting of Leonardo's *Adoration of the Magi* and his *St. Jerome* in the Vatican as well as the Fra Bartolommeo altarpiece for the Palazzo Vecchio in the Pitti (compare to Fra Bartolommeo's underpainting procedure in Vasari-Milanesi, 6:203). On the especially painstaking and fussy painting methods of Lorenzo di Credi, who even used different brushes for the many intermediary tones of his palette, see the description corresponding closely to the whole character of Lorenzo's art in Vasari-Milanesi 4:571.

its general outlines. And thus the idea of the artist himself who labored and created in his workshop together with his apprentices, whether he was one of the great leading masters or any of their guild colleagues who were merely average craftsmen, becomes truly comprehensible.

True creativity, as we think of it primarily in connection with the great artists, manifested itself in decisive measure only in these relatively rare leading personalities. But even for them it was still always somehow bound up with and influenced by the methods of the work procedure, the concrete conditions of the raw material and the "craftsmanly" details of the preparation and execution of an image which were customary at any given time. This was true also of the stipulations regarding form and subject matter, in most cases dictated by the patron and function, which were discussed in the first and second part of this book.

From this point of view even the great and famous master was still at the same time a craftsman, like all the more or less inferior colleagues who participated along with him as well as they could in the same artistic field. Sometimes, as already noted above, many parts of the picture execution in addition to certain purely manual necessities were also taken over from the master by the staff of pupils and assistants present in almost every workshop. Thus his personal achievement was confined to the truly essential and centered in the design process, the allocation and supervision of the assistants' share in the work, the final retouching, and the finishing of the whole. Yet even so, the master had still at the same time to be in constant touch with conditions and requisites of the technique and practice customary at that time.

It is all the more necessary to call this to mind, however, because our modern conception of the artist and his work rests on assumptions and circumstances that are in many essential points so very different from those of the Renaissance as we have just pointed them out.

The preceding is concerned essentially with the execution method for panel painting; whereas the technique of mural painting, as far as it is still used today in the old classic fresco method, differs only a little from the Renaissance working procedures and on this only a brief comment is necessary. The completion, section by section, of each individual part of a wall painting in a day's work at any given time, on the plaster freshly applied in the early morning (hence "al fresco") for this purpose, naturally demanded a somewhat different manner of work distribution than was customary for panel painting. Yet here also the master could entrust any less important parts of the composition, in whose personal execution he was not directly interested or expressly obligated by the work contract, to a well-trained assistant.

In many wall-painting cycles the portions by different hands have been ascertained and large parts assigned to certain traceable collaborators. The fact that Michelangelo, however, even on the giant surface of the

Sistine vault, engaged in no sharing out of work, is founded in his own singular manner of creation. The hardships and unpleasantness of such months of work, stretched out on his back* under the smooth shell of the vault on the hard, shaking board of the scaffolding, annoyed by paint dripping into his face and beard—all these bodily miseries he himself represented vividly and drastically enough in some letters and an often-cited poem.[35]

Only in the second half of the Quattrocento did the cartoon gain general acceptance, in consequence of the increasing desire for realistically defined execution of all details; and even Masaccio, as recently demonstrated, evidently preestablished his Carmine frescos only in the manner customary up to his time, with scratched-in or pounced vertical axes and hastily presketched brownish outlines on the rough plaster underlayer, based on these loose linear frameworks. Yet Masaccio was the first to abandon the traditional working procedure of supplementary secco overpainting of particular details, which Masolino still used in the 1430s, much to the detriment of durability then as now. In the paintings of the Brancacci chapel there are no peeled-off places such as can be found everywhere else where the combination with the none-too-stable secco technique was used. All is homogeneous, exclusively "buon fresco," as it was called in the High Renaissance and only then was again demanded and practiced as a matter of principle.[36] For the intervening period, the middle and late Quattrocento, with its different stylistic attitude, did not want to bind itself to that exclusively fresco technique, since the finesse of detail and decorative splendor of particulars striven for then could not be achieved with the pure fresco procedure.[37]

* *Translator's note*: Contrary to the popular legend, Michelangelo probably worked on the Sistine ceiling standing up. See Charles Seymour, Jr., ed., *Michelangelo: The Sistine Chapel Ceiling* (New York, 1972), p. 93, fig. 140.

[35] See the translation in Karl Frey, ed. and trans. *Die Briefe des Michelangelo Buonarroti* (Berlin, 1907), p. 272. In the otherwise current work practice of a shop, however, the assistants already had a good deal to do even with the sketching of the cartoon as a proportional enlargement of the master's *disegno* by means of a grid work. They also participated in the tracing of the cartoon parts with a metal stylus, furrowing into the still soft plaster of each day's section. Such scratched-in summary outlines can still be recognized today from close up on the Sistine ceiling, here executed by Michelangelo himself.

[36] Compare to the preceding the very informative study, based on detailed observations, by Robert Oertel, in the *JPK*, 1934, 55, pp. 229ff.

[37] Thus the desire occasionally arose to bring the coloristic charm of oil painting into play for wall painting also in the very risky combination of fresco technique and oil overpainting. This was furthermore already in use in the thirteenth and fourteenth centuries (see Berger, *Beiträge zur Entwicklungsgeschichte der Maltechnik*, Munich, 1897-1905, 3:206). In the late Quattrocento such attempts are specifically recorded for Baldovinetti and for Leonardo. The experiments of both, however, achieved only unsatisfactory results with respect to durability (see also Vasari-Milanesi, 6:20 concerning similar, equally ill-fated attempts by Niccolò Soggi).

Scaffolding, most necessary for the execution of wall painting, occasionally already comes into use even for the sketching of the cartoon. For Leonardo at least this is attested for his work on the original working drawing for the *Battle of Anghiari*. According to his own acccount, the scaffold he used was a mobile and adjustable vehicle set up in the papal room at Santa Maria Novella as he needed it for his special working procedure.[38]

Here a few observations might be made on the customary contents of the atelier, tools, etc., as well as on installation and equipment of the artist's studio in general.

Leonardo had already prescribed, at least theoretically, that the painter's workroom ought to have its window on the north side—long before the north-lighted studios always in demand today. Besides this he recommended, in the interest of the most delicate possible modulation of the light supply, that the customary linen window panes be provided with dark-tinted borders.[39] Thus we learn, again partly from his and Alberti's treatises and still more specifically through the estate inventories of other artists, of certain movable utensils that were probably in frequent use, particularly as resources for drawing studies: a veiling with a woven net of perpendicular threads for easier grasp of perspective foreshortening; a mirror for the self-critical examination of executed work (Alberti-Janitschek, *Pittura*, pp. 100-101, 134; Leonardo-Ludwig, *Das Buch von der Malerei*, sections 407-408). The use of jointed dolls for the selection and draughtsmanly study of certain attitudes of the body with drapery hung over them is attested first by Filarete and then in Fra Bartolommeo's studio inventory.[40]

---

[38] His cartoon thus did not originate, in the manner otherwise customary, as a mechanical enlargement of a smaller, definitively worked out model drawing. The individual parts of his composition were finally established for Leonardo, as also for Michelangelo, only by means of spreading out a full-size drawing surface against a wall, (Gaye, *Carteggio*, 2:88). The painting scaffold for the Sistine Chapel was arranged for by Michelangelo himself since he found Bramante's arrangement for it unsuitable (Vasari-Milanesi, 2:174; Condivi, *Michelangelo*, chap. 61). The monumental painter finally also used a *turata*, that is a screen for the working area, consisting of a canvas with lattice supports, in order to be shielded during the execution of his wall painting from the eyes of uninvited spectators and critics. Vasari also mentions such a device several times (for example, Vasari-Milanesi, 2:216; 6:271).

[39] In another place in his book on painting he appears to envision the ideal open-air studio in the form of an open courtyard, covered with a linen tent when necessary; the surrounding walls would be painted dark and furnished with a small projecting roof to provide shadow (Leonardo-Ludwig, *Das Buch von der Malerei*, sections 85, 95, 138, 431). That he himself had been able to set up such a workshop is not very likely.

[40] See Vasari-Milanesi, 4:195; and Marchese, *Memorie*, 2:167. According to these, two such dolls still existed in the late sixteenth century, both from the estate of the Frate. In the same place, however, even already in Verrocchio's estate (Milanesi, *Documenti*, p. 152),

Among the material factors of painting we note last what really represents one of the first and most elementary provisions: the color materials and the other substances which were used for the execution of paintings.

The spice dealers (*speziali*), already named above as purveyors of these working materials, were united with the painters in the same guild, probably precisely on account of these articles. What these shops generally sold, however, were only the most usual pigments obtained from indigenous raw materials; while the gold leaf, for example, still much in use in the early Quattrocento, had to be bought either directly from the goldbeaters or from occasional middlemen. The fine ultramarine or azure blue which was produced in the best quality only in Germany and the Netherlands, *azzurro della magna*, came into consideration only for the most exacting patrons, on account of its costliness. It was as a rule exported from outside, chiefly from Venice, where many German merchants in their own offices carried on barter business with products from home.[41] Since, however, the use of this material weighed heavily in the total cost of a painting and had considerable bearing on its market price according to quality and convenience of procurement, many patrons preferred to obtain it themselves for the artist or to require a separate accounting for it from him. In contracts and correspondence between artists and patrons this question is almost always discussed.[42]

The preparation of the painting medium, however, took place subsequently in the painter's workshop, carried out by pupils or other helpers.[43] In the mixing and combination of the individual pigments and the binding

---

various plaster casts, some after antique sculptures, as well as wax molds of human limbs and heads are cited as study materials and studio equipment (Knapp, *Fra Bartolommeo*, pp. 269ff.). In addition there were evidently all sorts of graphic master sheets of German or Netherlandish origin, whose use will be discussed below.

[41] In 1518 Raphael sent an assistant from Rome to Venice to buy colors (Giuseppe Campori, *Notizie inedite da Raffaello da Urbino tratte da documenti dell' Archivio Palatino di Modena*, Modena, 1863. p. 12). In Florence only the Gesuati monks of San Giusto appear to have engaged in the production and trade in ultramarine.

[42] See, for example, the letters that Benozzo Gozzoli wrote to Piero de' Medici in September, 1459, during the painting of the palace chapel; once he reminded his employer of the necessity to procure ultramarine from Venice; in the following letter, however, a favorable offer of gold leaf from a Genoese dealer is mentioned and the purchase reckoned up of two ounces of ultramarine, which Benozzo had acquired from the Gesuati (Gaye, *Carteggio*, 1:175, 192-93, 583, etc.).

[43] Such a color-grinder is for example the only assistant that Michelangelo retained for his work in the Sistina. Also for the execution of Leonardo's *Battle of Anghiari* in the Palazzo Vecchio, besides the collaborating assistant Fernando, one more young color-grinder was paid (Gaye, *Carteggio*, 2:89-90).

As a ground for color-grinding one needed the hardest possible smooth polished stone plate. Three such pieces of porphyry were cited, for example, in the estate inventory of Fra Bartolommeo (Marchese, *Memorie*, 2:185).

media for tempera or oil technique, certain artists who were especially interested in this certainly attempted, be it according to their own ideas or on the basis of suggestions and recipes received from others, to produce somehow more perfect effects. Details pertaining to this can be ascertained more or less by observation of the works themselves; written reports on such peculiarities in the painting procedure are almost completely lacking.[44]

## THE NEW GENERATION OF ARTISTS: TRAINING FOR APPRENTICES AND ASSISTANTS

The new generation of artists was recruited on the one hand, as would be expected, in fairly many cases through the hereditary continuation of a trade that the father and perhaps the grandfather had already practiced. This has already been discussed in the passage on artist families (see above). The ascent from other artisan origins into the field of the figurative arts, at that time not distinguished generically but only by degree, was also not rare. The painters Cosimo Rosselli, Piero di Cosimo, and Lorenzo di Credi among others were sons of goldsmiths, Mariotto Albertinelli the son of a gold-beater. Francesco Botticini's father was a painter of playing cards, while the architect Giuliano da Maiano and his sculptor brother Benedetto were descendants of a stonemason.

Noteworthy, yet at the same time by no means rare, was the adoption of the artistic profession by descendants of craftsmen or tradesmen in fields remote from art.[45] It is easier to understand that certain strongly original talents should have arisen from the upper bourgeoisie and class of officials: Masaccio was the son of a notary; Baldovinetti came from a well-off merchant family; Ghirlandaio's father in later years was a

[44] Vasari knew of Fra Bartolommeo that he, following Leonardo's precedent, used printer's ink and burnt ivory black for shadowed areas (Vasari-Milanesi, 4:185). From a voluminous Bolognese manuscript of the fifteenth century with the title *Segreti pei colori* Gualandi (*Memorie*, ser. 3, pp. 110-111) reports at least the titles of the individual paragraphs.

[45] Uccello was the son of a barber, Castagno of a small farmer from the Mugello, Verrocchio of a brickmaker (*fornaciaio*); the Pollaiuolo brothers got their surname as sons of a poultry dealer who had his bottega at the Mercato Vecchio; Botticelli's father achieved some prosperity as a tanner; of that man's sons, the oldest became a bank agent and it was he who primarily took care of his brother Sandro (whence his own nickname "Botticello," little barrel, stuck also to the painter "Sandro del Botticello"). In Fra Filippo one would not easily have recognized, in view of his finely cultivated, sensitive art, the son of a butcher; just as little in Fra Bartolommeo the paternal calling of a muledriver (*vetturale*). On the other hand, it is not too incomprehensible that Andrea del Sarto, as his surname suggests, in fact grew up in a tailor's shop. The preceding personal particulars come chiefly from the tax declarations of artists' fathers published by Gaye; for Pollaiuolo see *l'Arte*, 1905, pp. 381ff.

broker (previously a silk goods dealer, and, as Vasari had it, the inventor of a new kind of hair ornament for young girls, wrought gold *ghirlandi*, which was supposed to explain his surname); above all, however, the two greatest of the period were the (illegitimate) son of a notary, Leonardo da Vinci and Michelangelo, whose father was a civic government official.[46]

Why it happened that exactly this class of bourgeoisie and civil servants would initially consent most unwillingly to artistic careers for their sons, will be discussed below in the section on social status of the artist. Here, however, the upward striving from the small craftsmanly lower class as well as the unhesitating "descent" from a socially superior caste into the artistic career must be recognized as evidence and consequence of an immanent drive of artistic talent. Not by accident, then, do we also find the innovative personalities more frequently in the group of those who came to art from other classes and professional groups than among the artists' sons.[47]

Vasari has many anecdotes to recount about the innate, initially purely autodidactic drive of an artistic predisposition which, even if impossible to check out, may lay claim to a certain general ring of truth.[48]

The resolution to enter the artistic profession had, of course, to be taken in the early years of boyhood; for already at the age of twelve to fourteen, in which today the general obligation to go to school still takes precedence over any other professional training, the training period of the budding artist usually began.[49]

For Florence, Vasari's occasional information on beginning training

[46] Michelangelo, probably half jokingly, attributed his particular bent toward marble sculpture to the milk of his nurse, a stonecutter's wife of Settignano; it appeared seriously important to him, however, that in the astrological constellation of his birth records artistic talents were augurred (Condivi, *Michelangelo*, Chapter 4; Vasari-Milanesi, 7:137).

[47] This holds true also for the sons of masters newly entered into the artist class who became active in the art of their fathers: compare Fra Filippo and Filippino and Domenico and his son Ridolfo Ghirlandaio. Just so, at the beginning of the Renaissance, it was not the goldsmith's son Ghiberti who became the decisive trailblazer, but Donatello, born farther from the artist's workshop as the son of a woolcarder.

[48] See, for example, the youthful histories of Castagno, Andrea Sansovino, Girolama Genga, Beccafumi, and Pierino da Vinci (Vasari-Milanesi, 2:668-69; 4:500; 5:633; 6:120, 315). Of Michelangelo, however, Condivi reports (*Michelangelo*, chap. 5) very graphically, after the master's own account, how as a boy in grammar school he was repeatedly caught drawing or even, in spite of all the reproaches and punishments of his father, ran away from school to watch sculptors and painters at their work (see also Vasari-Milanesi, 7:137).

[49] The guild statutes issued for Venice prescribe an age of twelve years (cited from Sagredo by Hubert Janitschek, *Die Gesellschaft der Renaissance in Italien und die Kunst*, Stuttgart, 1879, pp. 47-48). Elsewhere sometimes even younger boy apprentices were admitted. Thus Mantegna already at the age of ten (1441) is found inscribed in the Padua guild register as a "fiuolo" of his master Squarcione. See Paul O. Kristeller, *Andrea Mantegna*, London 1901 [*translator's note*: or Berlin and Leipzig, 1902], p. 504.

for individual artists of the early sixteenth century—Giovanni Lappoli and Pierino da Vinci began at twelve, Perino del Vaga in his eleventh year, Girolamo Genga went in with Signorelli at fifteen—is verified by documents such as the training contract that old Buonarroto concluded with Ghirlandaio in April 1488 for the then fourteen-year-old Michelangelo, after he had first for a long time opposed his son's artistic inclination.

From this transaction, which Vasari (Vasari-Milanesi, 7: 139) reported verbatim based on a *ricordo* of Michelangelo's father and various information from other sources, we learn a little about the bilateral relationship of obligations between the master and his pupil and about the general manner in which the young trainee found his schooling regulated.

The training period, which for Cennino Cennini at the end of the Trecento, admittedly with allowance for later activity as an assistant, encompassed a full twelve years, was arranged for the young Michelangelo according to the three years customary at that time. During this period the pupil was taken into his master's house and in addition received, for the various services for which he could be employed in the workshop, a cash compensation of six florins in the first year of training which was supposed to be raised to ten florins in the third year.

These handyman's services of the apprentice involving preparation of the painting materials and other assistance in the workshop actually already formed the first, elementary foundation of artistic education. Alongside this, however, came the drawing practice work for the training of the eye and hand, to which Michelangelo's biographers in particular allude frequently.

Drawing models included sheets of studies by the master himself, or else his completed works. After this, however, came famous works of older and contemporary artists, which were on display in all the churches of Florence as well as in as many public art collections.[50] Study drawings after completed paintings are certified for various young artists, partly by reports, partly by surviving drawing sheets. And it would indeed be interesting, although hardly completely feasible, to establish which masters received preference as objects of study at any given time in the successive development stages of the Renaissance.

---

[50] In Ghirlandaio's workshop, for example, at least one *libro di disegni* of the chief was in circulation, from which student copy drawings have been preserved in the *Codex Escurialensis* as well as in the Barberini drawing book of Giuliano da Sangallo. (Here it is chiefly a matter of sketches after Roman monuments, decorative motifs, reliefs, etc.)

Even Michelangelo later mentioned that pattern book to Condivi; he asserted, however, that he was denied use of it on account of the jealous disfavor of the master. His biographers also report on deceptive facsimile copies after drawings of older masters that Michelangelo prepared during his training period (see Condivi, *Michelangelo*, chaps. 5, 6; Vasari-Milanesi, 7:141-45).

Among the youthful drawings of Michelangelo are found unmistakable studies after Giotto's figures in the chapels of Santa Croce. Above
all, however, Michelangelo and other aspiring artists of his age group
were trained in the observation and copying of Masaccio's frescoes. To
that extent the Carmine chapel may stand as one of the decisive points
of departure for the formal development of the High Renaissance, just
as twenty years later Michelangelo's battle cartoon became the advanced
school of the succeeding generation of artists.[51]

It was chiefly the young sculptors, primarily those admitted to the
casino at San Marco (see below), who studied antique art works, of
which there were many to be seen even in Florence in Medicean and
other possession; also, however, certain already mature painters of the
incipient High Renaissance studied these works, such as Mariotto Albertinelli, for the refinement of his formal repertory (Vasari-Milanesi,
4:218, 7:488-89).

Occasionally, even in the waning Quattrocento, engravings of Schongauer appear to have been copied by skillful youths; just as at the same
time Dürer, but certainly also Italian art students, was using Mantegna
sheets as models.[52]

Leonardo above all advised nature drawing at that time in the countless
detailed instructions of his treatise on painting (Leonardo-Ludwig, *Das
Buch von der Malerei*, 2, sections 45, 50, 79, 82); yet even he required,
as a prior foundation for the beginner, that the latter should first of all
train himself in copying drawings of good masters under the guidance
of his teacher, in order only afterwards, after similar training in perspective, to approach the drawn reproduction of three dimensional natural objects. Even then, however, exemplary works of skillful artists were
still to be constantly observed and compared.

[51] On this see especially Vasari-Milanesi, 7:161; 6:137-38; further 5:590; 7:156-590;
6:533, 534. Compare also Georg Gronau, *Aus Raphael's Florentiner Tagen* (Berlin, 1902).
Finally, Vasari also tells of his own boyhood efforts in drawing after art works from his
paternal city of Arezzo before arriving in Florence at the age of thirteen in 1524 when he
enjoyed the instruction of Michelangelo and Andrea del Sarto (Vasari-Milanesi, 7:651; see
Vasari-Milanesi, 7:6 for the data reported on the early career of Vasari's friend of his
student days, Salviati).

[52] Paul O. Kristeller (*Andrea Mantegna*, London, 1901 [*translator's note*: or Berlin and
Leipzig, 1902], pp. 427-28) indeed supposes that Mantegna's prints first originated as study
materials for young artists. Michelangelo, who in his first study period copied Schongauer's
St. Anthony sheet in a pen and ink drawing, enriched this drawing still more, according
to Condivi and Vasari, through nature studies after all sorts of sea creatures that he got
from the fish market. That Michelangelo in those years frequently ventured quite instinc-
tively to draw directly from nature is strikingly illustrated by that other Vasari anecdote,
if it is true, according to which Ghirlandaio's pupil tried one day to commit to paper in
a sketch the scaffolding in Santa Maria Novella with all its paraphernalia and the crew
working upon it (Vasari-Milanesi, 7:140; Condivi, *Michelangelo*, Chapter 5).

Neither Leonardo nor anyone else, however, discussed nude studies from the living model as a first training stage. Such studies apparently belonged, so far as they were already generally practiced with any intensity in the Quattrocento, only in the circle of advanced students and already approved masters.[53]

The training process for the sculpture apprentices passed no differently than for the young painters, with the addition only of special education in their working materials and tools. For them also the copying of exemplary work was in question, now however not only by drawing but by modelling, especially after the antique as the most beneficial means of study.[54]

Finally it should be recalled in this connection that many masters who later became prominent as painters, sculptors, or architects gained access, sooner or later, to their subsequent "liberal" artistic trade only by the roundabout route of a training period as an artisan. Thus certain stonemasons and decorative sculptors advanced to figural sculpture.[55] Primarily, however, it was to the goldsmiths' art, as an apparently especially promising, lucrative, and respectable trade, that many fathers first introduced their sons who aspired to become artists.[56]

[53] On the other hand, it was probably a duty of young apprentices as well as older assistants that they occasionally should be at their master's disposal as nude models, wholly unclothed or in light undergarments. Jacopo Sansovino, for example, had his *garzone* Pippo del Fabro stand the whole day as a model during the execution of the marble statue of Bacchus; from which, however, the poor boy, according to Vasari's strange account (Vasari-Milanesi, 7:493), seems somehow to have lost his mind.

[54] That Medicean sculptor's seminar in the garden at San Marco (see above), where besides ancient sculpture, drawings and cartoons of old masters were also available as pattern material, was thus equipped as well as could be imagined for such training of the sense of form. And the anecdote, believable at least in essence, about the sculptured copy of an antique faun mask by the boy Michelangelo who had been admitted there, illustrates this clearly enough. Even the student goldsmith Baccio Bandinelli trained himself for his later trade as a sculptor through drawing and modelling after examples in Florentine churches and ventured afterwards to try marble copies after the antique (Condivi, *Michelangelo*, Chapter 7; Vasari-Milanesi, 4:257-58; 6:135-37).

[55] For example, Montorsoli worked first in the quarries of Fiesole and then in the stonemasonry workshop at St. Peter's in Rome; Tribolo studied with Nanni Unghero as an ornamental carver and only afterwards became Jacopo Sansovino's pupil. The Sangallo brothers also began as intarsiators, etc. (Vasari-Milanesi, 4:268; 6:56-58, 629; 7:516, 527).

[56] Brunelleschi, Donatello, and Luca della Robbia began their careers in a goldsmith's workshop. The same appears also to have been the case for Botticelli and later Andrea del Sarto and Bandinelli. Ghiberti, Pollaiuolo, and Verrocchio in later life still carried on the first-learned art of working precious metal alongside their other, more important activities. Vasari worked during the *assedio* in 1529 for a goldsmith until the possibilities of other kinds of work were once again available. And according to his autobiographical account, even a famous sculptor like Baccio da Montelupo gave his son Raffaello first of all, in 1526, to a goldsmith for training on account of the better prospects; this son admittedly ran away

A few other old accounts are still available to us concerning the beginning of artistic training. How the trail proceeded further, how the youthful beginners and schoolboys advanced into the ranks of journeyman and assistant and finally became the almost independent colleague of the head of the shop, on this our sources report in narrative form next to nothing; and only particular notices of payment, employment contracts, and the like suggest certain conditions that were perhaps generally valid.

Even a beginning pupil probably did not pay tuition to the master; rather, from the first year of his education on, he received a small, annually increasing remuneration in cash from the master (as in the training contract of the young Michelangelo cited above). This testifies that even the working energy of the still untrained pupil could somehow be profitably harnessed in the activity of the studio and thus really "pay its way." The pupil in his third year in Ghirlandaio's workshop already had the prospect of a salary of ten florins. A note from 1458 from the workshop book of Neri di Bicci shows that seventeen-year-old Giusto d'Andrea, in this case already taken on as an assistant, allegedly received in the first year twelve and in the second eighteen florins cash compensation, and in addition, every year a new pair of stockings (Gaye, *Carteggio*, 1:211-12).

Even considering the chronological distance and the difference in rank between the two workshops, the concordance of items on both sides indicates that advancement from pupil to assistant ensued in a smooth transition; for even the pupil, almost from the outset, in a certain sense already performed assistant duties at the same time. Within the assistant echelon the financial (as well as artistic) share in the total activity of the workshop could of course rise for older, especially gifted people to a third, in special cases up to half of the net profit taken in by the master.[57]

In citing such cash income of assistants it should not go unnoticed that a certain part of their work might have been paid for in the form of room and board or even through distribution of clothing. This corresponded to the general economic situation of the time, and to the nature and

---

after two years and then became a sculptor (Vasari-Milanesi, 2:108; 4:6:134-35; 7:10. See also the source citations in Hans Semper, *Donatello, seine Zeit und seine Schule*, Vienna, 1875, pp. 238-40).

[57] Thus Benozzo Gozzoli, as Ghiberti's assistant in the work on the second Baptistery door in 1444, drew an annual salary which rose from 60 florins in the first year to 80 florins in the third year of his collaboration. Michelozzo, however, was employed for the execution of the first door with 100 florins per annum (Milanesi, *Documenti*, p. 90). Compare also the notices on assistant compensation compiled by Hanna Lerner-Lehmkuhl in *Zur struktur und Geschichte des florentinischen Kunstmarktes im 15. Jahrhundert* (Wattenschied, 1936), pp. 51-52.

structure of an artistic workshop, often still much like a family artisan concern.[58]

In any case, we must imagine the collaboration and the personal bond between the head of the studio and his pupils and assistants in the form of a true "following" in a far more complete and real sense than this recent concept can actually be found embodied anywhere today (except perhaps in the smallest artisan households). And this close bond between the pupil and assistant and the master also explains the fact, in itself unusual, that certain artists came to be called, and so inscribed in the history of art, by a surname that came not from their biological father but rather from their first master or the studio chief of their assistant days.[59]

From the early sources we can conceive only approximately in what manner the young *garzoni* were able to advance their own artistic development during their years as assistants. They learned the most essential things in any case in the practical collaboration on commissions that the master was carrying out, in which they perhaps received a design drawing worked out by him to transfer into the full-size cartoon or later, after sufficient prior training, worked on the final execution of particular parts of a painting (see Vasari-Milanesi, 5:539, 590; 6:121).

One's own drawing studies were naturally pursued only incidentally during the student days, especially on Sundays and holidays when there was rest from service in the workshop.[60] More often, however, the master himself would probably also have made such additional private training in drawing for his apprentices a specific duty. This sort of master-pupil relationship, in this and generally in every respect a solicitous one, is for example very charmingly recognizable in the answering letter from Michelangelo's assistant Pietro Urbano, where in 1518 the latter reports to

[58] It is true that the tax declarations of Florentine artists published by Gaye and others (*Carteggio*, 2:103ff.) mention only the family members of the declarer and neither workshop personnel nor servants. On the other hand, Leonardo represented to the Duke of Milan that in his household he for years "had six mouths to feed," which must have meant primarily pupils or assistants (*JPK*, 1897, p. 111).

[59] Such was the case for Piero di Cosimo, as a pupil and later assistant of Cosimo Rosselli, for Andrea del Verrocchio, after his first teacher, the goldsmith Giulio Verrocchio, for Jacopo de' Tatti, generally called after his teacher and fatherly friend Andrea Sansovino; likewise for Perino del Vaga, formerly called Perino de' Ceri, after his first and second teachers. See Vasari-Milanesi (4:132; 7:487), in which this type of designation is related to spiritual paternity, although in the first of these cases this could hardly come into consideration (see further Vasari-Milanesi, 3:357, 379; 5:589-91).

[60] Vasari mentions such Sunday studiousness, for example, in his biographies of Andrea del Sarto and certain other artists of his own time. But Leonardo also takes occasion, in a paragraph of his book on painting (Section 74) to justify this holiday work against narrow-minded condemnation.

the master in Pietrasanta that he was working diligently in drawing every day, as he had promised him, and had even done some drawing after nature (Michelangelo Buonarroti, *Sammlung ausgewählter Briefe an Michelangelo Buonarroti*, ed. Karl Frey, Berlin, 1899, p. 93).

The journey at the end of the training years, almost universally required for German artists of the time, was not customary in Florence until the late Renaissance, when a stay in Rome for study began to be held as highly desirable and almost indispensable for all who wanted to advance.[61]

As to how the customary work management ran its course in the artistic workshops, on this some fairly dependably documented information could be given much sooner for the succeeding Mannerist epoch, for the time of Vasari and Cellini, than for the period that concerns us here. What Vasari and his nearest predecessors report, however, on artistic life and workshop management of the Renaissance century has only a very uncertain value as source material and touches also for the most part only on certain remarkable peculiarities in the working procedure of particular masters, which indeed on account of their singularity were noted by contemporaries, retold, and thus even passed into the written tradition. These are artist anecdotes to which we shall return below when we come to the representation of the artistic personality and its status, in its own society and in the eyes of immediate posterity.

Only a few features of the so-to-speak normal routine of an artistic workshop such as mark the customs and attitudes of that time as in many ways remarkably different from those prevalent today can be cited here. Thus (already mentioned repeatedly) there is the self-evident inclusion of the most varied and sometimes even humblest tasks of everyday applied arts within the scope of the work of famous, highly qualified ateliers. Vasari indeed on many occasions alluded to this practice as no longer consistent with the status-consciousness of the artist of his time.[62]

Then the use of preparatory drawings by other, more inventive masters was often practiced by the weaker artists, which at that time could not appear especially strange or even noteworthy, since originality and nov-

[61] Previously only a few artists of the early Renaissance, like Brunelleschi and Donatello, set out for Rome on personal initiative, with the conscious intention to study the artistic world of antiquity at the source. They earned a living, incidentally, by working as assistants for a goldsmith. See Manetti-Holtzing, *Vita di Filippo Brunelleschi*, p. 18; Eugene Müntz, *Les arts à la cour des Papes* (Paris, 1878-1882), 2:116.

[62] See especially his biography of Dello (Vasari-Milanesi, 2:148-49; 3:270; 5:629 concerning Ghirlandaio and Perino del Vaga). Such activity is confirmed by documents also for Benozzo Gozzoli, who in his later years, in Pisa, still allowed casual jobs like the decorative painting of processional banners, trumpet pennants, and a chest for wax offerings to be executed in his workshop, sometimes for nothing, sometimes for a very small consideration. (*ASA*, 7, 1894, pp. 233-34).

elty in invention of images were looked on as a special supplementary value, not as an indispensable property of an artistic work.[63] Occasionally, however, a more or less precise repetition, although unequal in value, of an esteemed masterwork by pupils or artists of lesser ability even seems to have been specifically desired, or in any case gladly accepted by the client.[64] The artistically unexceptionable use of certain elements from Dürer's graphics, especially by Andrea del Sarto, the young Pontormo, and others also belongs in the same category.

From the work contracts we can gain at least a theoretical point of reference for the average time of execution for painting and sculpture. In practice, however, very large transgressions of the deadline fixed in the contract sometimes occurred. It is true that this was sometimes occasioned by a cut-off of the supply of funds on the patron's part, perhaps on account of the considerable costs of material. The excessive delay of completion, occurring more often on account of the peculiar temperament and behavior of a particular artist, will be discussed below.

In general the employer believed himself able to determine and contractually enforce a normal date for delivery with the artist, just as with other craftsmen. In an atelier like Neri di Bicci's, by all means organized in an emphatically craftsmanly and commercial manner, it took no more than two or three months, for example, for the completion of a medium-sized altarpiece, as can be learned from the entries in the workshop journal (see Vasari-Milanesi, 2:74-75). This can stand as an approximate norm for the whole broad lower level of artistic workshops. For artists of finer quality, and in case of particular higher demands by the patron, however, considerably more generous periods for execution could be allotted.[65]

The deadline for delivery that we almost always find stipulated in the surviving contracts (with observance sometimes honored with a premium and transgression punished with a penalty for breach of contract), is

[63] Michelangelo's followers Bugiardini, Sebastiano del Piombo, and others frequently ventured to make use of the master's drawings for their works (Vasari-Milanesi, 5:22, 568, 634; 6:207-208, 267-70).

[64] For example, no less than eleven contemporary copies of one of the favorite half-length Madonnas of Pesellino are identified (see *RA*, 1938, p. 140). A free copy of Fra Filippo's *Adoration*, produced by Pier Francesco Fiorentino, now stands in the chapel of the Palazzo Medici; see further examples in *RA*, 1904, pp. 76ff. It is also probable that one or another lost work by an important master, unrecognized as such, has been handed down to us indirectly in some clumsy copy.

[65] Thus Ghirlandaio was given up to thirty months for the great *Adoration of the Magi* for the Innocenti. Two years were allotted for the painting of the Strozzi chapel; in fact, however, it was twelve years before Filippino, after long interruptions, completed his work (see Hanna Lerner-Lehmkuhl, *Zur Struktur und Geschichte des florentinischen Kunstmarktes im 15. Jahrhundert*, Wattenscheid, 1936, pp. 22-23).

explained by the conditions of the artistic life of that time: the patron, especially with an artist of rank and name, had constantly to fear that some competitor or other would thwart his plans with a more imposing or otherwise more attractive commission. At the granting of the commission he had, moreover, almost always already delivered a certain installment to the artist, whom he might on this account consider and treat as his debtor until the commissioned work was delivered.[66]

[66] Even Ghiberti was bound by the work contract for *St. Matthew* for Or San Michele to a very high fine (500 florins) in case of breach of contract, for which, if the occasion arose, he would have been liable with all his property. Bernardo Rossellino was threatened with a deduction of twenty florins at the time of the Beata Villana tomb in case of non-observance of the deadline. Conversely, in the case of a marble pulpit commissioned for San Pancrazio, the executing stonemason had a claim to a higher price if he completed his work before the contractual term. The clause of the fine for failure to meet the deadline is still found even in the work contract for Ghirlandaio's Innocenti altarpiece; yet in accordance with the position of a well-known artist in relation to the patron, which in the meantime had grown more secure, this contract also recognizes the obligation of an additional penalty charge in case of a delay in payment (see Lerner-Lehmkuhl, *Kunstmarktes*, pp. 17, 19, 20, 22). Deductions of two florins for each month after the deadline are provided for in the contract of the Ghirlandaio brothers with a Pratese convent (Milanesi, *Documenti*, pp. 118-19; 156-57).

CHAPTER 13

# BUSINESS PRACTICES IN THE
# WORKSHOP AND ART MARKET

## Price Formation and Forms of Payment

On the whole complex of questions concerning the Florentine art market
of the early Renaissance there exists a recent, solidly researched monographic study by Hanna Lerner-Lehmkuhl, which will be referred to
frequently in the following pages.

If we go through the payment figures for certain works of known
masters of the Quattrocento reported, sometimes in tabular surveys, in
this study, surprising conclusions result on the general price formation
within the different branches of art and on the factors involved in individual cases. In the sums paid for panel paintings we find, already in
the first period of the early Renaissance up to about 1470, certain dis-
crepancies in price range that at first glance are difficult to understand.[1]

To explain these extraordinarily sharp variations in prices, Lerner refers, probably correctly, to the already mentioned factors of picture size
and the more or less multipartite, elaborate picture composition. However, she also notes the expenditures, which in some cases had considerable weight in the total cost, for especially expensive materials like gold
leaf and ultramarine. In the especially low-priced panels, these materials
were used not at all or in very small quantity, or they were specially
charged to the patron, or furnished in kind.[2]

[1] On the one hand, there are works whose prices fall within a range from 20 to at most
40 florins. Such are the individual figures of the virtues by Pollaiuolo, now in the Uffizi,
at 20 florins each; Castagno's altarpiece of the Assumption of 1449, now in Berlin, at 24
florins, the Dante memorial picture of 1461 in the Duomo by Domenico di Michelino at
31 florins, and Fra Filippo Lippi's Barbadori altarpiece from Santo Spirito, now in the
Louvre, for which the painter received 40 florins.

Alongside this, however, are a series of much higher payments reported for the same
period: 89 florins for Baldovinetti's Trinitatis panel of 1469, now in the Accademia, 190
florins for the great Madonna tabernacle of 1433 by Fra Angelico for the Linaiuoli guild,
and finally, as a most extraordinarily higher item, 240 florins for *The Coronation of the
Virgin* of 1446-47 by Filippo Lippi, now in the Uffizi, that is, six times as much as the
same artist had received a mere ten years earlier for his Barbadori Madonna, which admittedly was not so large or rich in figures.

[2] We can, for example, survey very clearly the actual ratio of expenditure for these to
the other cost items in the account of specific costs for a Botticelli panel of somewhat later
origin in 1485, the Madonna with the two St. Johns now in Berlin, painted for the Bardi

The total cost of the Botticelli painting of the Madonna with the two St. Johns, as well as the specific work honorarium paid to the artist himself, appears remarkably low when we hear that around the same time Filippino received 240 florins for his *Vision of St. Bernard* now in the Badia, 250 florins for the altar of the Great Council Hall in the Palazzo della Signoria, even 300 florins for his *Adoration of the Magi* for San Donato a Scopeto, now in the Uffizi; and Pollaiuolo just as much for his altarpiece of the Martyrdom of St. Sebastian now in London.[3]

Prices of from one to two hundred florins are the general rule for altarpieces of the high classical period, with the standard that only pictures very rich in figures approach the upper price limit named.[4] We note that the prices generally set for the most highly respected masters of this generation were in no case higher, sometimes even considerably lower than the sums spent, for example, in the 1490s for certain panels of Filippino's. However, as Lerner also points out, this does not seem to mean a lesser valuation of artistic creation but rather the opposite: the external price-boosting factors of the painting style of the late Quattrocento with the luxurious material splendor and rich adornment with many realistic and decorative accessories had been abandoned on principle for the high classic style of portrayal.

For fresco work, for which I cite at least a few comparative prices, costly color materials generally did not even play a role (except for certain enterprises of the late Quattrocento, where the love of splendor of that time demanded a few gold ornaments and richly elaborated decorative work even in wall paintings, so that patrons must even have been prepared to make correspondingly increased expenditures). For individual frescoes

---

altar in Santo Spirito; namely 38 florins for gold and gilding work, 2 florins for ultramarine and only 35 florins as actual artistic honorarium for the master ("pel suo pennello"); to this was added as a special item 24 florins for the frame already carved by Giuliano da Sangallo before the painting was begun (Horne, *Botticelli*, p. 353, Igino Benvenuto Supino, *Sandro Botticelli*, Florence, 1900 [*Translator's note*: or Bologna, 1909 or Modena, 1911], p. 83).

[3] Thus we must certainly assume that the patrons in question had fixed high expenditures from the beginning and also that the rate of work for these large compositions, full of numerous figures and the richest scenic and decorative accessories, was especially highly valued. It remains noteworthy, however, that even the great *Coronation of the Virgin* of 1490 by Botticelli, now in the Uffizi, cost no more than 100 florins; the same price as the smaller and barer *Visitation* panel by Ghirlandaio of 1491, now in the Louvre. [*Translator's note*: The Ghirlandaio *Visitation* in the Louvre actually cost only 80 florins. See Cornelius von Fabriczy, "Memorie sulla Chiesa di S. Maria Maddalena de' Pazzi a Firenze . . . ," *L'Arte*, 9, 1906, p. 258.] Perhaps, however, for these last pictures there were later additional individual payments or supplies of material not specified in our documents.

[4] For his *Vision of St. Bernard* (1506-1508, Accademia) Fra Bartolommeo had initially wanted 200, then at least 160 florins; the arbiter called in, however, then appraised the picture at only 100 florins.

the prices in the middle decades of the Quattrocento range between 15 and 30 florins. It is accordingly noteworthy, as a symptom of the general price increase around mid-century, that of the two equestrian monuments in the Duomo, Uccello's was paid for with 15 florins, while the one painted by Castagno twenty years later earned a fee of 24 florins.[5]

The general price increase since the mid-Quattrocento, already mentioned above, became established in the payment for commissions for great cycles: Masolino in 1424 received a total remuneration of 74 florins for the painting (lost today) of a chapel in Empoli; this was probably approximately the payment that he and Masaccio together realized for the Brancacci chapel. On the other hand, Castagno in 1450 got 100 florins plus free lodging for his work in the choir of Sant' Egidio; and Baldovinetti took on the painting of the Trinita choir in 1471 for 200 florins.[6] Otherwise around this time, Gozzoli got no more than 1200 florins for the far more extensive cycle, eighteen murals in large format, in the Campo Santo of Pisa. And Filippino was paid only 300 florins for the painting of the Strozzi chapel in Santa Maria Novella by a contract of 1487, including the expenditure for gold and especially valuable ultramarine prescribed in the bargain by the commissioner (that is, exactly the same price for which Filippino had had to execute his Magi picture in 1494).[7]

In Florence it was only in the special case of a great state commission of the most significant subject and purpose that a price to match the higher ones in Rome at the time was set: 3000 florins for Michelangelo's Cascina fresco in the Great Council Hall (and probably just as much for Leonardo's counterpart in the same place). For the familiar church painting jobs the younger masters of the High Renaissance had to be content

[5] Around this time, in 1455, Neri di Bicci also already received 30 florins for his Gualbertus fresco in the cloister of San Pancrazio. The same amount, however, was promised to Fra Bartolommeo, admittedly less prominent at that time, for the very complicated representation of a Last Judgment, while a famous master like Perugino still received 55 florins for the *Crucifixion* in the chapter house of the Cestello convent, which had three parts but fewer figures.

[6] It is true that in the later final estimate for this work, evidently very carefully executed, the appraisers including Perugino, Gozzoli, Filippino, and Cosimo Rosselli in 1497 arrived at the figure of 1,000 florins, five times higher, probably with a view to the approximately equal sum that Ghirlandaio had been paid for his fresco cycle in Santa Maria Novella in 1490.

[7] Shortly after his acceptance of the commission for Filippo Strozzi, Filippino was assigned another fresco project of only slightly greater extent in Rome, the chapel of Cardinal Carafa in the Minerva. There, however, the honorarium was far higher, according to the more generous Roman standards: 2000 florins. No wonder that this commission received precedence over the Florentine one, and that the completion of the latter work dragged on so very long. See the work agreements in Alfred Scharf, *Filippino Lippi* (Vienna, 1935).

with payments that in no way exceeded the rates customary in the late Quattrocento.[8]

For a better understanding of these individual figures we must try to gain some sort of grasp of the real market and living value which the payments cited might actually have represented in the days of the early and High Renaissance.[9]

If we treat the florin as equal, for instance, to the English pound (before its recent devaluation), this corresponds in some measure to the meaning of this unit of currency in international finance at that time, but hardly to the actual purchasing power and practical value in daily market commerce. The immediate buying power of the florin in the life of that time could be most easily calculated or at least approximately imagined based on the price of basic necessities of life and the rates of payment for other, nonartistic trades, such as civil servants, etc.[10] Here I can only draw on the point of reference, by all means fundamental, of the rent and purchase prices of the houses inhabited by artists.

Thus Donatello, in his repeatedly changing dwellings, once paid 10 florins and at another time 14 or 15 florins annual rent, and most of his other declared expenses also fell within this range except for a few as little as 6 or 7 florins. Corresponding to the average rent price just mentioned, we hear of purchase sums for houses in a price range from 100 to 200 florins.[11]

[8] Andrea del Sarto was initially promised only a beginning honorarium of 98 florins for the whole Benizzi legend in the atrium of the Annunziata. This was subsequently raised to 140 florins to keep the artist from abandoning the work. For the individual scenes of the Marian cycle in the same place he also received no more than 15 to 16 florins per picture a few years later; and even for the great cenacolo fresco in San Salvi executed in 1519 he was paid only 38 florins, that is, nominally less than Perugino had received twenty years earlier for a similar work in the chapter room at Cestello. It is true that the buying power of the gold florin, somewhat increased in the meantime, must be considered in this context (on this compare Vasari-Milanesi, 5:13, 67-68; and further 5:93; 6:52, 258).

[9] With reference to Lerner's observations on this see Hanna Lerner-Lehmkuhl, *Zur Struktur und Geschichte des florentinischen Kunstmarktes im 15. Jahrhundert* (Wattenscheid, 1936), pp. 40, 41. A few summarizing and supplementary data may be briefly communicated here: the prices mentioned in our information and Lerner's tables are all converted, for better comparability, to the fixed gold unit of the Florentine ducat or florin, as far as the smaller denominations of the *libbre (lire)* and the small coins *soldi* and *denare* were put in the documents. The value of the *lira*, however, diminished progressively during the Renaissance century in relation to the rate for the florin, stable even in the international money market, from 4 *lire* which was equal to 1 florin around 1420 to approximately 6½ *lire* equal to 1 florin around 1520.

[10] On monetary matters consult the survey in Landucci-Herzfeld, *Tagebuch*, pp. 7-9, n.7 and p. 17, n.2. The tax declarations and testament protocols published by Gaye and others provide the main sources for the following.

[11] For example, Mino da Fiesole rented out a house he had acquired for 100 florins for

According to this, for bourgeois artisan needs, the monthly rent expenditure for dwelling and workshop in the early Renaissance would be set on the average at about 1.5 to 2 florins. And a medium-sized household needed an additional 2 to 3 florins for the daily necessities of life in a month. We shall return below to the whole standard of living and economic station of the artist class. But here, first, I shall give a little more information on sculpture prices. In this context the special estimation that fell to particular masters like Donatello and Michelangelo on account of their acknowledged superiority appears noteworthy. This is clearly discernible in the comparison of the price for similar commissions like the statues at the Duomo, where Donatello's works were appraised at a full 15 to 25 percent higher than those of his partners in a similar area of commissions (see the exact price quotations in Lerner). For Michelangelo, however, in the beginning of the sixteenth century the price distance from the standard of his contemporaries is still more significant. For the Christ-John group on the Baptistery, Sansovino received approximately the same price of 130 florins that had been set for the over-life-size evangelists on the Duomo facade one hundred years earlier. Michelangelo's colossal *David*, however, was paid for with 400 florins. For smaller reliefs in 1475 by Antonio Rossellino on the Prato pulpit, the same standard price of 20 to 22 florins paid around 1435 to Luca della Robbia for work on the Campanile still held good.

These sums concerned only the result of the sculptor's work. Along with this go the costs of work materials, which fell to the patron as separate, considerably higher cost items. For the Campanile statues these items—marble blocks and their procurement—made up on the average about a third of the total cost. The supplementary material costs for bronze works—for metal and casting—ran far higher.[12]

---

12½ florins per annum (*RA*, 3, p. 265). In 1518, however, Michelangelo acquired a piece of land on Via Mozza, where he erected his workshop for San Lorenzo, for 300 florins (Michelangelo-Milanesi, *Lettere*, p. 393). Desiderio bought himself a house in 1465 for only 65 florins, but on the other hand paid 13 florins workshop rent for a larger *casolare* near Santa Trinita (*RA*, 1930, pp. 250, 267, 270).

[12] For Ghiberti's St. Matthew at Or San Michele these costs came to almost half of the total cost of the figure, whose erection, including an item of 93 florins for the surrounding wall tabernacle, required the sum of 1039 florins. Even in this connection, then, one is struck by the proud readiness of the commissioning guild to take on an increase in execution costs amounting to about eight times as much as the same figure in marble would have cost in order to stand out among the others through a donation especially impressive even in the material.

Moreover, for Ghiberti's second bronze portals, the *Gates of Paradise*, the metal and casting costs alone at 1135 florins already ran to more than had been spent for the whole St. Matthew statue including the tabernacle. For various cost items for the purchase of metal, firewood, etc. for casting the bronze doors for the Duomo sacristy (1445-1465) see *l'Arte*, 21, 1918, pp. 197-201.

On the other hand, such supplementary costs in marble work carry a perceptible weight only in the case of the more extensive enterprises, because then even the procurement of the necessary quantities of blocks occasioned all sorts of expenses and difficulties.

Even the Duomo Opera, which since the late Trecento kept up a virtually uninterrupted flow of material from the marble mountains of the Ligurian coast, had in many cases to send its sculptors or stonemasons on a special mission to Carrara in order to choose the appropriate blocks there themselves, cut them properly, and direct them to Florence.[13]

One will thus well understand that in most cases the patrons, when they had to advance large sums for material, also desired a contractual guarantee that the work would be completed and wanted to have the artist's liability guaranteed by solvent citizens.[14] Through the method of payment in monthly installments, or even in fixed annual provisions, more often in use for the greater projects of long duration, the artist also found himself entangled in a kind of employee relationship that bound him, often under express contract provisions, to an uninterrupted, exclusive occupation with the commission taken on.[15]

Toward the end of the century we also find continuing monthly payments set for large painting projects: 3 florins for Ghirlandaio's painting of the Adoration of the Magi, and 30 florins a month for his painting in Santa Maria Novella. Andrea del Sarto, Franciabigio, and Pontormo still received that much monthly for their fresco work in Poggio a Caiano in 1520.[16] Such low rates were thought of, here as in general, as install-

[13] How and why even Michelangelo, for the Julius tomb as well as subsequently for the facade of San Lorenzo, took it on himself to supervise personally the marble procurement on the spot, and thus frequently had to stay for months in Carrara and the newly opened quarries of Seravezza, is already discussed above. The not inconsiderable advance payments that were placed at his disposal by his employers for this purpose proved in the end, in the matter of San Lorenzo in any case, to be a completely fruitless expenditure.

[14] It is true that this was not required of Michelangelo; it probably was, however, even of masters like Donatello and Ghiberti by their merchant-minded patrons who concluded contracts with them as operai of individual guilds.

[15] This was, for example, unambiguously imposed on Ghiberti in the work agreements for his two bronze portals; he was to receive the full amount of the considerable year's stipend of 200 florins promised to him only if he devoted his full working strength to this project daily through the whole year. Fra Angelico was assigned the paintings in Orvieto in 1447 under similar conditions and obligations. The head cathedral architect Brunelleschi, however, whose continual presence and activity at the construction workshop were not required, received accordingly only an initial salary of 36 florins per annum, which it is true subsequently rose to 100 florins. Donatello, during his work on the pulpit of San Lorenzo, took only as much payment each week as he himself and his four assistants needed to live (Vespasiano da Bisticci, *Vite*, p. 34).

[16] On the other hand, Michelangelo was entitled to only 2 florins cash per month, along with full board for himself and his assistants, in the commission for the marble apostles in the Duomo (1504; Vasari-Milanesi, 2:358; 5:195-96; 7:346).

ment payments on the whole honorarium, whose amount in many cases was still not finally established at the assignment of the commission. The patron rather reserved the right to have the artist's production appraised by an expert only on delivery of the work, according to quantity and quality, with advance payments already made taken into account.[17]

The arbiters appointed as nonpartisans either by the parties to the contract or by the guild (see above) could sometimes, so far as this was not ruled out a priori in the contract, decide on a higher amount than was originally foreseen (as for example the above-mentioned appraisal of the Baldovinetti frescoes in the Trinita). In the disagreement between Fra Bartolommeo and his patron Bernardo del Bianco in 1506 they finally confirmed the price recognized by the commissioner.[18]

It must still be noted, as a significant peculiarity of the circumstances of the time, that in many cases even well-known artists agreed to receive a part of their payment not in cash but in kind, that is in the form of constantly necessary articles such as grain, wine, or oil.[19] More frequently, particularly in the case of fresco work for convents, the artist and his assistants were given free room and board, to be calculated as part of the payment. It is true that dissensions and differences could result from this if the food offered was not satisfactory, and then, to cite only one relevant Vasari anecdote on Albertinelli's paintings in the Certosa, 1506, the young assistants compensated themselves by secret raids on the convent's pantry.[20]

[17] On this see the very characteristic excerpt from a work contract in Milanesi, *Documenti*, pp. 114-15. In a special case, for Fra Angelico in 1433, the stipulation is even found that the artist himself should decide, "according to his conscience," whether his work had turned out so well that he might really lay claim to the full price set for it. (It was a question of the great Madonna tabernacle of the Linaiuoli; see Hanna Lerner-Lehmkuhl, *Zur Struktur und Geschichte des florentinischen Kunstmarktes im 15. Jahrhundert*, Wattenscheid, 1936, p. 18).

[18] For the sculptor Francesco Ferrucci, whose sacrament tabernacle for Prato was appraised far too low in the artist's opinion, the Florentine Signoria interceded with the demand that two newly appointed experts, of which one had to be a sculptor from Florence, should appraise Ferrucci's work. In another case the artist Giovanni Francesco Rustici protested in 1510 against the personality of the appraiser appointed by the patrons. See Vasari-Milanesi, 6:605-606; and Milanesi, *Documenti*, pp. 143-44; 162-63, for a statement by Francesco del Tasso, ratified by a notary, on the mode of appraisal of choir stall work prevalent in Florence at that time, 1493.)

[19] And this is even still encountered in the beginning of the sixteenth century when, for example, Albertinelli received thirteen casks of wine as his payment claim for completing Fra Bartolommeo's *Last Judgment*. Likewise Andrea della Robbia in the settlement of accounts for his tympanum on the Duomo portal of Pistoia accepted a certain quantity of grain and wine from the Duomo building authorities instead of the corresponding amount of cash (*Rass. A*, 1909, p. 65; Pèleo Bacci, *Documenti toscani per la storia dell' arte*, Florence, 1910-1912, 2:167ff.).

[20] Vasari-Milanesi, 2:207; 6:221-22. Documentary records on the relation between sup-

## Economic Status of Artists

In the following we shall try to gain a conception, considering the income possibilities set forth above, of the form and variations of the artist's life style in economic and social terms during the Renaissance century.

In his testament of 1470 Luca della Robbia declared that since his nephew Andrea, as successor in the bottega, had already drawn rich profits from its operation up to that time ("satis superlucratus est"), the testator wanted in all fairness to bestow his cash legacy, which was fairly considerable, to the other nephew who had only learned the cobbler's trade. The enterprise of the Robbia workshop, with its extensive business, must indeed have proved a veritable goldmine. In the tax declarations and wills of Florentine artists of the Quattrocento published elsewhere (see below), only perhaps Ghiberti and Brunelleschi show a similarly high real capital; while Donatello, for example, still had no property in 1433 except perhaps some furniture and work tools to declare and never during his whole life went so far as to acquire a house of his own. So far as the anecdotes reported by Vasari and other chroniclers are in any measure historical, Donatello's outspoken artistic indifference to money and other possessions indeed already struck his contemporaries as remarkable. Almost all other artists of rank mention the possession of one or more houses (which they sometimes rented to someone else) in their *catasto* declarations and frequently also a yield from rent on agricultural real estate in the nearer or more distant environs of Florence. This was the case for Mino da Fiesole, Uccello, the Pollaiuoli, Botticelli, Ghirlandaio, and others.[21]

---

ply of provisions and cash payments can be found in the accounts of the hospital authorities of Santa Maria Nuova on the painting of the choir of Sant' Egidio. According to this, Castagno had first declared he set no store by free board, but subsequently during his work had constantly laid claim to room and board there with one or another of his assistants. On the other hand, Baldovinetti in 1461 had to venture into dealings for only a promise of free board for his work in the same choir chapel and to leave a supplementary cash remuneration up to the "beneficence" of the patrons, "la fatica sua . . . rimette a detto spedale per l'amore di Dio." (See *RA*, 3, pp. 207-208; Vasari-Milanesi, 4:221-22).

[21] See the tax declarations in Gaye (*Categgio*, 1:103ff.) for Ghiberti, Brunelleschi, Masaccio, Michelozzo, Pollaiuolo, Donatello; p. 142 for Buggiano, Uccello; p. 188 for Rossellino; p. 224 for Baldovinetti in 1470; pp. 263ff. for Pollaiuolo, Maiano, Mino da Fiesole, Gozzoli; and p. 343 for Botticelli in 1498. See *l'Arte*, 8, pp. 383-85 for Antonio Pollaiuolo; *l'Arte*, 22, p. 246 for Andrea della Robbia in 1480; *RA*, 3, p. 7 for Piero Pollaiuolo and pp. 265-66 for Mino da Fiesole. See *JPK*, 25, Beiheft, pp. 61ff. for Michelozzo.

For wills see Gaye, *Carteggio*, 1:147 for Uccello; p. 172 for Giovanni di Gaiuole; pp. 185ff. for Luca della Robbia; pp. 367ff. for Verrocchio, Lorenzo di Credi. See Milanesi, *Documenti*, p. 78 for Mariotto di Nardo; pp. 146ff., 167-68 for Fra Filippo Lippi, Cecca, Francione. See also *RA*, 1904, p. 43 for Mino da Fiesole; and Gualandi, *Memorie*, ser. 5, pp. 39ff. for Antonio Pollaiuolo.

Fra Filippo Lippi bought a double house from the yield of his work in Prato, in which Lucrezi Buti retained living rights after his death, while his son Filippino was able to acquire in addition a relatively expensive house (for 300 florins) in Florence. Benedetto da Maiano, besides his house in Florence (see above) possessed together with his brothers a large landholding in the vicinity of Pistoia, where he even occasionally stayed and where he had a field chapel set up with a Madonna of his own execution. The Pollaiuoli likewise owned several *poderi* in the Pistoia region; Botticelli, however, acquired a small country place before the Porta San Frediano with his brother Simone in 1494 (which Horne, *Botticelli*, pp. 267-68 would identify with the Villa !e Cave, below Montoliveto).

Accordingly we may say there was a fairly steady if not in fact quite sizeable income to be gained from artistic work, which often in the course of the years even made it possible to rise to a certain bourgeois affluence and to acquire some property in terms of capital and real estate.

To go beyond this within the Florentine market conditions of the fifteenth century with the constantly rather small net profit that the individual commission brought in, however, was not possible. Michelangelo was the first to attain finally to actual wealth, thanks to the unusually high payments conferred on him since the beginning of the sixteenth century, even in his parsimonious native city, but above all by the Roman popes. What Michelangelo saved from this money, by a very simple standard of living, was almost all invested in real estate, especially such as served to round out the inherited family holdings near Settignano.[22]

Within the stated general situation on the art market, it must not be overlooked that corresponding to the very extensive and continuous demand there was, however, also a very considerable supply of workers. And thus even many skillful artists had sometimes to make a considerable effort to get into the right place; an example is the almost pleading letter of Domenico Veneziano in 1439 to Piero de' Medici (Gaye, *Carteggio*, 1:136). There was for all practical purposes no other way to earn money except from commissions; and the individual commission rarely brought more than a moderate net profit. Thus anyone who was not provided with an uninterrupted flow of commissions could hardly lay by any financial reserves. We must surely not without exception take certain lamentations about bad business, the sad prospects of the trade, and the like all too tragically as they appear in artists' tax declarations. It is, however, certified by documents that Masaccio, whose life was admit-

---

[22] The tax declaration of 1534, which enumerates all these imposing landholdings, mentions in addition the patrician house on Via Ghibellina, bought by Michelangelo but lived in only by his heirs and afterwards rebuilt, as well as a still undeveloped lot on Via Mozza (*JPK*, 6, pp. 199ff.).

tedly cut short prematurely, as well as Castagno died in very needy circumstances and left debts (Gaye, *Carteggio*, 1:115-16; *RA*, 1932, pp. 503-504).

The generally customary advance installment payments on salary and material costs do indeed reflect the economic straits of the artist as closely as they do the shortage of cash on the part of most patrons, many of whom sometimes fell behind in the payments. Particularly in the crisis periods that occurred often, individual merchants or whole economic groups were temporarily crippled. This also explains the frequent remarkable halts and sometimes lengthy interruptions in the execution of artistic enterprises.[23]

In artists' tax declarations, references to outstanding debts for work delivered or begun are rarely lacking; sometimes with bitter comments on the dubiousness of their realization within a foreseeable time.[24] Sometimes, however, an artist's working strength finally failed due to illness or advanced age, and savings were used up. Even many masters who had been busily employed earlier came to such sad circumstances as the seventy-year-old Lippo di Corso represented in his tax declaration of 1427 (Carlo Pini and Gaetano Milanesi, *La scrittura di artisti italiani*, Florence, 1876, 1:15). Only one who had set by some property and had no family to care for could buy a place in a hospital for the security of his last years, perhaps even with a cash annuity, as Lorenzo di Credi did in Santa Maria Nuova in 1531, and before him, for example, Baldovinetti in the Ospedale di San Paolo.

---

[23] How very sharply the artist found himself hindered in his personal life, and often in the continuation of a work he had begun, by such delays in financial supplies is shown, for example, by two letters of Filippo Lippi and one from Gozzoli. In their moving tones, the precarious position of the respective writers can be very clearly recognized (Gaye, *Carteggio*, 1:141-42, 175, 192).

[24] In Giovanni del Monte's *denunzia* for 1427, for example, there is a long list of such credit items (*RA*, 4, p. 170). The excellent artistic metalsmith Niccolò Grosso also made it a principle, not without reason, in general never to take on a commission without a deposit and not to deliver any work before he had received the remainder. That he indeed did not deviate from this principle even for the powerful Parte Guelfa brought him the nickname Caparra, under which he lives on, with various anecdotes, in Vasari (Vasari-Milanesi, 4:455ff.).

CHAPTER 14

# THE ARTISTS

## CLASS STATUS AND CLASS CONSCIOUSNESS

According to the circumstances of his income as well as his form of work and life style, the artist, considered generally, belonged in the social scale to the middle or upper artisan class. His own personal and class self-estimation corresponded to this; as for example even a master of exceptional talent, Domenico Veneziano, in his letter to Piero de' Medici of 1439 expressly acknowledged, with subservient expressions, that his "bassa condizione" hardly allowed him to appeal in a letter to the "gentilezza" of his addressee (Gaye, *Carteggio*, 1:136). The continuous state of dependence, in work operations and daily life support, on the patron's small installment payments must indeed necessarily have stood constantly in the way of a freer self-assertion. Certain expressions in letters, such as in those of Filippo Lippi, give evidence of this.[1]

Yet already since the middle of the century, the newly awakened self-awareness of particular masters had begun to rebel against the all too lowly class status that in general still adhered for a long time to the artist.

One of the first manifestations of artistic pride of workmanship is the self-assured addition "mira arte fabricatum" in the artist's inscription that Ghiberti put on his second Baptistery doors.[2] Subsequently Ghiberti, likewise around 1450, emphatically set forth the worth and importance of creative artistry, including his own, in the artist biographies of his *Commentarii*. Thus he corroborated an attitude that had already been presaged earlier in Alberti's treatise on painting, here with reference to comparable testimony from the antique on the high status of the arts and their masters.[3]

---

[1] Alberti (Alberti-Janitschek, *Pittura*, p. 160) assumed without question that the artist in his work was seeking the approval of the general public ("l'opera del Pictore cerca esser grata alla moltitudine"). In a contract of the late Quattrocento the artist Giovanni di Gaiuole, who was to carve the choir stalls for San Pancrazio, declared his understanding that the price would be set only after the conclusion of the work. He also added candidly: "so that the work should praise the master," and the patron should pay for just what he had received (Milanesi, *Documenti*, pp. 114-15).

[2] Compare also Filarete's signature on a processional cross of 1445 in Bassano with the reference to his previous masterpiece: "Antonii . . . qui Romae Basil. S. Petrii portas aereas fecit" (*l'Arte*, 1906, p. 296), and Perugino's boastful completion inscription in the Cambio in Perugia, 1500 (Vasari-Milanesi, 3:582).

[3] See especially the dedicatory epistle and the passage, in Alberti-Janitschek, *Pittura*, pp.

I can cite no other corresponding statements by artists themselves. For what Vasari reports of such declarations from the late Quattrocento has an essential source value only for the point of view of the author who here, as at every other opportunity, was endeavoring to establish a high class standing for the artist among his contemporaries.[4] The extent to which Vasari's anecdotes, probably drawn from oral tradition, might actually contain a grain of truth, remains uncertain. But the situation that sparked the incidents is historically pertinent in any event: the conflict between the long traditional, yet by this time somewhat old-fashioned attitude of the patron on the one side and the newly strengthened self-esteem, nourished on Renaissance theory, of the artist, who had become conscious of his predestined gift. This conflict must certainly already have led to similar explosions in the late fifteenth century. Such rebellious artistic self-confidence is first expressly and directly proven in the case of Michelangelo and his repeated clashes with Pope Julius; and in the almost inconceivably blunt manner of expression that Michelangelo allowed himself with respect to the pope on such occasions.[5]

It is true that in this also Michelangelo, in the beginning of the sixteenth century, already anticipated much which otherwise was generally granted to him and his younger artist contemporaries only after the middle of

94-96. It has already been shown above how far humanistically educated contemporaries, likewise schooled by the study of antique authors, began consciously to appreciate the historical and cultural significance of the superior artistic personality.

[4] I may mention, for one thing, the anecdote concerning the preparatory work for the Colleoni. According to this, Verrocchio, in wrath over the subsequent limitation placed on his commission for the monument (that he should execute only the horse, while someone else did the rider), struck the head off his completed model of the horse and then left Venice. When the Signoria sent after him a threat that he would be beheaded if he was ever seen in Venice again, Verrocchio is supposed to have replied that the Venetians were certainly not in a position to put heads back on again once they had been cut off, at least heads like his, while for him, on the other hand, it would be easy to make his horse a new and perhaps a better one. Whereupon the Venetian government reconsidered and called the master back to complete the whole monument.

And then there is the no less drastic tale that is supposed to have taken place during the Ghirlandaio brothers' work in the Abbey of Passignano in 1476. Domenico's brother and collaborator Davide Ghirlandaio complained repeatedly to the abbot about the poor food the convent was offering the painters. It was not suitable that they should be treated like manual laborers (*manovali*). But when on the next evening the same poor quality food was dished up, the temperamental Davide thrashed the cook soundly with a loaf of bread and retorted to the reproaches of the abbot, who had hurried to the scene, in the greatest rage: "Che valeva più la virtù di Domenico che quanti porci abbati suoi pari furono mai in quel monastero!" (His brother Domenico's art was worth more than all the pigs of abbots like him who had ever governed this convent). Vasari-Milanesi, 3:272-73, 368.

[5] Such, for instance, was that brusque "quando potro" in answer to his patron's impatient question as to when he expected to finish the Sistine frescoes, and more (Condivi, *Michelangelo*, chap. 38). Noteworthy also is the conspicuously emphasized signing of his first Roman Pietà in 1499.

the century. This includes also the demonstrably noble origin of his forebears, affirmed by him, it is true, only in the later years, and Michelangelo's principle as a teacher, reported by his spokesman Condivi, to inculcate his art, if at all, by preference "in persone nobili e non plebei," and that on the basis: "come usavano gli antichi."[6]

### The Artist as a Person, his Social Circle, his Way of Life and Work

After the preceding indications on the artist's status within the social conditions of his surroundings, a sketch of the personal behavior of the individual in his more immediate living circle, among the family and professional associates, will now be attempted.

Many occasions for collegial exchanges in some congenial setting were already provided by the old, official, and sometimes obligatory assembly of the various artistic groups in their guilds and in the brotherhood of St. Luke. To determine how far and in what form these professional organizations still actually survived in the Renaissance period, however, the relevant documentary evidence would have to be sought out in the massive *inedita* of the Florentine archives. That a sociable note was also not lacking in guilds and brotherhoods may be assumed without question, although contemporary reports exist only on certain social gatherings of artists and art lovers in the early sixteenth century. Thus Baccio d'Agnolo's workshop must have been a kind of lecture hall where especially on winter evenings, "bellissimi discorsi e dispute d'importanza" sometimes went on. According to Vasari's account (Vasari-Milanesi, 5:350), such painters as Filippino, Granacci, and the young Raphael as well as such sculptors and architects as Sansovino, Cronaca, and Antonio and Giuliano da Sangallo came to such talks and dicussions here, "and occasionally, but only rarely, even Michelangelo attended."[7]

---

[6] Condivi, *Michelangelo*, chap. 1, 3, 67; Vasari-Milanesi, 7:136.

He himself in his early youth had been able to overcome his father's opposing, traditional view that the artistic calling was only for plebeians incapable of anything better only through the intervention of Lorenzo Magnifico. The same Magnifico, according to Vasari, is also supposed to have stressed, with reference to Pietro Torrigiani, that on the contrary, descent from a good family was an especially favorable precondition for the choice and development of an artistic career. On the other hand, Lorenzo once reassured Giuliano da Sangallo about the replacement of his old, respected family name Giamberti by the designation attached to him on account of his much admired convent construction at Porta San Gallo that he should rather be proud if he had become, by force of his own artistic merit, the founder of a new house named for it (Vasari-Milanesi, 4:256, 274). For the contrary see Fabriczy, *JPK*, 1902, suppl., p. 15, according to which the surname already appears in documents in 1483, probably on the basis of Sangallo's dwelling by that gate.

[7] Botticelli's atelier, according to one contemporary report, was a favorite meeting place

In addition, in the biography of Giovanni Francesco Rustici (Vasari-Milanesi, 6:609-16) we find a long, involved account of two clublike exclusive societies in which artists above all set the tone. The smaller of these societies usually met in Rustici's house and workshop, in the former Sapienza building; here this "Compagnia del Paiuolo" held its festive revels, for which the respective organizers had to come up with the most original possible form of setting and hospitality.[8] The whole activity of these societies half suggests a serious side line and half a burlesque travesty of the great public festivities and spectacles discussed above.

We infer from this how strongly, even in the last two decades of the Florentine Republic, in spite of—or rather precisely because of—the political situation, so tense due to external threats, the old Florentine joy in festivals and talent for festive ceremonies was determined to burst forth in its fullest intensity. And further, that here again the artists could prove themselves the indispensable directors and *maîtres de plaisir* and at the same time themselves go in for the most spontaneous collegial collaborations. Michelangelo's extensive correspondence in particular gives many examples of personal exchanges between individual artists and the comradely help that younger or weaker talents might receive from mature masters even outside the teacher-pupil relationship.[9]

Michelangelo was also occasionally pleased to frequent the company of the humblest artisans and to furnish them with helpful suggestions— such as the stonemason Topolino in Carrara and the eccentric minor

---

for idlers interested in art ("un academia di scioperati"), Horne, *Botticelli*, pp. 360ff. (doc. 46, 55).

Florentine colleagues often got together also at Perino del Vaga's after his return from Rome in 1523, for the purpose—"according to old artistic custom," as Vasari expressly noted—of conversing about artistic questions, learning about Roman novelties, or even going out together to visit and discuss local artistic monuments (Vasari-Milanesi, 6:103-104).

[8] It was similar in the larger "Compagnia della Cazzuola," founded in connection with an especially successful garden party in 1512. Rustici and Bugiardini were also there, and even Andrea del Sarto, as well as other less famous painters, sculptors, craftsmen, musicians, and various young people from the Florentine patriciate. The artists, however, were obliged to work out the kind of surprises described in detail by Vasari in the banquets, costume parties, theatrical productions, and other entertainments of both clubs, such as certain extraordinary food arrangements and centerpieces in the form of architectural monuments or figural images of antique subjects, fantastic masquerades, and dramatic games for the participants, etc. For one such production (Machiavelli's *Mandragola*) Andrea del Sarto and Aristotile da Sangallo painted the stage backdrop (Vasari-Milanesi, 6:437).

[9] Such are his solicitously friendly letters to Sebastiano del Piombo, which also contain many knowing words on the Venetian's artistic style; but also the letter of a Ferrarese to Michelangelo in 1508 asking him to receive the sculptor Antonio Lombardo, who was going to Rome, "as art and professional fellowship demand" (Michelangelo-Milanesi, *Lettere* [*translator's note:* or Milanesi, "Lettere"], pp. 413, 445-46, 458-59, etc.; Michelangelo-Frey, *Ausgewählte Briefe*, p. 11).

painter Menighella whom he assisted with designs for rustic pictures of saints. Thus such sympathy precisely for the primitive, rough simplicity of artisan professional colleagues must surely not have been far from the thoughts of other famous artists. It must only have been especially remarkable in Michelangelo—and even motivated Vasari to record these anecdotes in his biography of the artist—because Michelangelo otherwise usually treated the most important fellow artists of his time with such inimically harsh reserve.

It is true that in Vasari we come across much pertaining to this already in the artistic world of the fifteenth century. Some anecdotes indeed are not documented elsewhere or, like the horror story of the murder of Domenico Veneziano by his jealous rival Castagno, are certainly false. Yet it is not in itself to be doubted that within the closely interwoven relations of the artistic labor market in Florence there must often enough have arisen conflicts of interest and malicious talk and intrigues, even before Michelangelo's time. A note of such irritations and differences sounds frequently in the relationship between Brunelleschi and Donatello.[10] And Vasari speaks of the painters' mutually malicious tongues as of a traditional characteristic of Florentine artistic society (Vasari-Milanesi, 4:222; RA, 1906, pp. 134-35).

The whole embittered sharpness of feeling and language in the mutual antagonism of certain strong artistic personalities is, however, as stated, most immediately perceptible in Michelangelo's biography, especially in Condivi's exposition, inspired by Michelangelo himself. Here we find the intrigues that Bramante fomented against him, in which Michelangelo's bitter and certainly in many ways unjustly excessive animosity toward Raphael, originally Bramante's protégé, had its origins. Working contemporaneously with Raphael in the Vatican, as earlier with Leonardo in Florence, must however have almost necessarily led to all sorts of friction, considering the pronounced differences of temperament and working methods on both sides. Certain piquant taunts that are supposed to have been dropped in such clashes are recorded. How far they are true to the letter must remain uncertain. The mood that such snatches of dialogue bespeak is doubtless historically pertinent. And who knows how many similar verbal duels may have arisen between Michelangelo and his adversaries?[11]

---

[10] If later, in the guild regulations of 1470, it was expressly forbidden to the painter to take over a job that had already been assigned to another, this also indicates that such interference had probably often occurred; see the mocking sonnet on Donatello in Manetti's biography of Brunelleschi (Manetti-Holtzinger, Brunelleschi, pp. 49-50; 178), the controversy with the the presumptuous assistant Antonio Manetti.

[11] Truly Florentine in subject and tone is the small episode of about 1504, when Michelangelo on his way past Santa Trinita was invited, apparently quite harmlessly, by

It became apparent how very much Raphael's whole personal and artistic nature was generally repugnant to Michelangelo from various letters of the years 1517-1519—long before the later written portrayals of this illustrious artistic enmity by Condivi and Vasari. In the letters, some of the artists especially devoted to Michelangelo held forth with abusive comments on Raphael and the performance of his workshop, evidently well aware that they were thus telling Michelangelo something very welcome.[12]

On the other hand, the copious legacy of letters from and to Michelangelo also offers numerous insights into more sympathetic manifestations of his personal human nature, his family feeling. Unmarried himself and already from the earliest times remaining far away from his native city, often for periods of many years, he shows himself in the continuing exchange of letters with his father and brothers to be constantly interested and conscientiously concerned with all family affairs, sometimes intervening helpfully with suggestions and funds. Thus he later took responsibility for his orphaned nephew Leonardo in a thoroughly fatherly manner (and admittedly—like Beethoven in the similar relationship to his nephew—took upon himself almost nothing but vexation and disappointment from it).

Like Michelangelo, a whole series of other and indeed particularly noteworthy artist personalities remained unmarried: besides Masaccio, who died young, this holds true for Brunellesco, Luca della Robbia, Donatello, Alberti, Verrocchio, Botticelli, Leonardo, Piero di Cosimo, and Raphael. In connection with the old custom of monastic scholarship, nonmonastic scholars of the Renaissance also as a rule preferred to remain single. Thus it might also have seemed natural to many an artist to renounce marriage and a personal family life in the interests of the most undistracted pursuit of his professional goals. And instead of this, at most he might do as Brunelleschi did with Lazzaro Cavalcanti and take

---

Leonardo to state his opinion on a passage from Dante that Leonardo and his companions were discussing during their walk. Michelangelo abruptly cut the conversation short with a brusk taunt about Leonardo's uncompleted equestrian monument in Milan (Magliabecchiano-Frey, *Il codice*, p. 115). Another telling scene occurred in Rome a few years later: Michelangelo on the way to his workshop in the Sistina saw the young Raphael going by accompanied as usual by numerous friends and pupils and could not refrain from calling to him, with an ironic attitude of reverence: "Like a prince with his retinue." Raphael, however, parried sharply enough: "And you, solitary like the hangman!"

[12] See Michelangelo-Frey, *Ausgewählte Briefe*, pp. 58-59, 104-105, 132. The correspondents are Sebastian del Piombo, Baccio d'Agnolo, who called Raphael his "nemico capitale," Leonardo Sellaio, who spoke of the ceiling paintings of the Farnesina as a "cosa vituperosa." See also Michelangelo's dispute with Signorelli over a loan debt disavowed by the latter, 1518 (Michelangelo-Milanesi, *Lettere*, pp. 391-92), and his altercation with the old Francia in Bologna, 1507 (Vasari-Milanesi, 7:170).

an adoptive son into his house or care for younger relatives in case of need, as Luca della Robbia did for Andrea and his brother or Fra Filippo Lippi, who in his lamenting letter to Cosimo de' Medici cited above asserted that he had to provide the dowry for three marriageable nieces.

Yet it may be seen from Milanesi's genealogical tables to his Vasari edition that not a few artists also had wives and children. In his narrative text Vasari himself mentions only three wives of artists: Uccello's wife, who on many nights, troubled by her husband's tireless perspective studies, admonished him to come to bed and received only the ecstatic sigh: "Oh che dolce cosa è questa prospettiva!" (Vasari-Milanesi, 2:219).

On the other hand, there is Perugino's relationship, reminiscent of Rembrandt and Saskia, with his beautiful young wife (Vasari-Milanesi, 3:590) whom he loved to see dressed up as splendidly as possible and thus sometimes dressed her with his own hands. Finally comes the description, reading like a veritable novel, of Andrea del Sarto's marital sorrows, on account of which the artist broke off his glorious activity at the French king's court early and did many other foolish things, allowing himself to be disgracefully exploited by his wife and her clan.[13]

## THE ARTISTIC TEMPERAMENT AND RANGE OF INTERESTS

Here again it must be admitted at the outset that only very limited material in terms of trustworthy contemporary testimony exists for a sketch of the artist's personal character and attitudes. Statements in letters from the artists themselves, the most desirable evidence, are available only occasionally for the fifteenth and early sixteenth centuries, and other points of reference from other sources are almost completely lacking. What biographical and personal details Vasari and his most immediate predecessors Billi and the Magliabecchianus knew to report on artists of the past stemmed from a tradition that was often rather untrustworthy and altered to an unknown extent through oral transmission. In addition, as already noted once, it was naturally only the especially remarkable, anecdotally sharpened traits and comments that were seized on and passed down as material for stories. We shall accordingly have to settle for the fact that the sketches we take up here can in many points hardly be more than the repetition of such mental images as had been formed

[13] If Vasari, who in his youth was Andrea's pupil, dared to recount such details in the first as well as the second edition of his work—here admittedly shortened and toned down—even during the lifetime of Andrea's widow (Lucrezia died only in 1570), the picture he painted of this artist's marriage probably corresponded in some measure to the facts that were surely known to many older readers in Florence. Vasari-Milanesi, 5:19, 31, 55, with the more detailed version in the relevant section from the first edition of 1550, still more prejudicial to Lucrezia, also given in the commentary.

around the middle of the sixteenth century of the artists of earlier times.

With this reservation, a brief selection of data on the spiritual attitudes, the personal and generic peculiarities, the nature and temperament of the artist will be set forth below.

We begin with the question of religious and ecclesiastical views, to determine, according to the standard of the historical situation, whether and in what measure there is evidence for particular artists of an individually accentuated extreme of religiosity or else of a negative "free-thinking" alienation from the generally held opinions and way of life of contemporaries. The latter do indeed come to light in certain risky utterances and attitudes of many humanistically oriented literati of the fifteenth century. For the artists, however, even though they were in close relations with the literati or their patrons as employers, such departure from the normal religiosity of the period is nowhere confirmed.[14]

Rather there is evidence of occasional signs of a greater than average piety. Not only—where such attitudes would be naturally expected—in monastic artists like Fra Angelico, who followed the instruction and example of St. Antoninus almost to the point of his own canonization; or Fra Bartolommeo, who was moved by the violent impression of Savonarola's preaching and martyrdom to take monastic vows; but also in many other masters of the time, who were known expressly as followers of the Frate or at least showed religious stimuli received from Savonarola in their manner of artistic expression. It is true that I cannot cite unquestionable evidence of such religious transports and conversions. Unless literary expressions of more than generally customary religiosity and absorption in the church, unknown up to now, should be discovered, it would first of all have to be generally investigated how far an especially deep sympathy, independent of possible instructions from the patron, is evident in the artistic treatment by individual masters of the Mary theme, the Passion, and legends of saints in Savonarola's time and the succeeding period as well as in the preceding phase of the early Renaissance. In addition, the degree of harmony or of conflict between such an attitude and the formal aesthetic aspirations of the respective periods and schools would need to be examined.[15]

[14] Fra Filippo Lippi was certainly an unfortunate monk, being by nature unsuited for religious orders, yet surely never thought to break away from the general attitudes and precepts of the Church on account of this. And if Vasari asserts of Perugino that he was a man of "very little belief" (di assai poca religione) and stubbornly opposed the doctrine of immortality, he was thus probably only circulating a malicious insinuation that may have arisen from a general artistic discontent over Perugino's pious manner and its cheap public success (Vasari-Milanesi, 3:589). On religiosity and free-thinking among the literati see especially Ernst Walser, *Gesammelte studien zur Geistesgeschichte der Renaissance* (Basel, 1932).

[15] On concrete influences of important older members of the order on Fra Angelico, like

Many statements and actions that might appear to us as individual manifestations of church devotion probably simply correspond to general tradition and customs. Thus Ghirlandaio, Andrea del Sarto in 1529, and probably also many other artists belonged to a religious confraternity, and Benedetto da Maiano left his entire estate, including two completed works of art, to the Compagnia del Bigallo (Vasari-Milanesi, 3:277, n. 2; 344, n. 5; 5:71). Thus we find many pious expressions in the texts of artists' wills and the instructions for masses for their souls that are seldom lacking there. It is nevertheless surprising that even Leonardo da Vinci's testament (1518; Vasari-Milanesi, 4:48, n. 2) contains very extensive provisions in this direction. Somewhat unusual is the signature "Orate pro pictore" attached to an altarpiece of 1521 by Sogliani, in storage at the Uffizi.

On the other hand, it was more than mere traditional form when Michelangelo asked his closest relatives in many letters to pray for him and his affairs and once even to pray for the pope. He made such a request before an especially difficult artistic task, the casting of the statue of the pope in Bologna in 1507 after which he declared specifically: "I feel that someone's prayers (gli orazioni di qualche persona) have helped me and have preserved me against all expectation." Also characteristic of the importance Michelangelo attached to ecclesiastical duties is his letter of 1518 from Pietrasanta to his assistant Pietro Urbano in Florence whom he admonished, among other tasks, not to neglect to go to Easter confession. ("Confessati e attendi a imparare e abbi cura alla casa.") Pietro in his answering letter reassured his master on the performance of all these points.[16]

Many especially pronounced manifestations of religious feeling appear in Michelangelo's late Roman period in letters, poems, reports of third parties and not least in the passionate tenor of the religious works of his old age. These can only be referred to here as expressions confirming what has been observed about him earlier, but reaching beyond the scope of the time-period in question here.

What, however, is the situation with that other side of the mentality, the intellectual development and directions of interest among the artists? The antique attitude that the most extensive possible universal education was necessary or at least most desirable for artistic production was set forth prominently by Vitruvius. This opinion was also taken over by Renaissance theorists, particularly Alberti and Ghiberti, and represented

---

Fra Giovanni Dominici and St. Antonino, see Maione in *l'Arte*, 1914, pp. 281ff., as well as Padre Giuseppe Benelli in the Dominican journal *Il Rosario*, 1914, 1918.

[16] Michelangelo-Milanesi, *Lettere*, pp. 19, 21, 33, 40, 43, 62ff., 71, 88, and others; and Michelangelo-Frey, *Ausgewählte Briefe*, p. 93 (see p. 66).

as an ideal requirement.[17] That many artists lived up to this old humanistic theory in practice, especially in the first generation of the early Renaissance, is for example evidenced frequently for Brunelleschi and also for Donatello and Ghiberti.

In particular the problem of the rules of perspective, so important for the new realistic construction of painting, was studied in depth by Brunelleschi in intellectual exchanges with contemporary mathematicians as well as by Masaccio and Uccello.[18]

In addition, as a general intellectual, historical, and philosophical education, there was the study of Dante, the point of departure for any Florentine's aspirations to knowledge. Botticelli and Michelangelo in particular went into Dante studies in some depth. The latter, according to Condivi, is supposed to have known almost the whole *Divine Comedy* by heart and also to have enjoyed reading Boccaccio and other poets and "oratori volgari."[19]

On the other hand, the manner of expression and writing in many letters and tax declarations of artists, often not only very awkward but downright uneducated, seems somewhat striking. This is true, for instance, for Fra Filippo Lippi, who had moreover grown up in a convent. For him and probably also for many other young art students, enrollment in practical studio training took place very early, probably with a general renunciation of any other schooling.[20]

Vasari and the Magliabecchianus cite numerous proofs of the sharp wit of many artists. What concerns Botticelli and Michelangelo in this might well have been drawn from fairly trustworthy oral tradition (Magliabecchiano-Frey, *Il codice*, p. 104; Vasari-Milanesi, 3:319, 7:278-79). Certain utterances that point as much to nimble and keen wits as to an unconstrained, original freshness of the whole bearing will be illustrated

---

[17] On the supplementary education of the artist in general and the sculptor in particular, see Ghiberti in the introduction to his first and third commentary. Michelangelo's statement, already cited above in another context, "si dipinge col cervello, non con le mani" (1542; Karl Frey, ed. *Die Briefe des Michelangelo Buonarroti* [Berlin, 1907], p. 90) could also be associated in a broader sense with that conviction of the theorists that the complete artistic creation sprang only from a fundamentally spiritual essence.

[18] See Wolff in *ZKG*, 1936, pp. 47ff.; Kern in *JPK*, 1915, pp. 13ff.

[19] For Botticelli see Vasari-Milanesi, 3:317; for the information, probably somewhat exaggerated, concerning Michelangelo see Condivi, *Michelangelo*, chaps. 23, 64. Benedetto da Maiano's estate inventory (Cendali, *Giuliano e Benedetto da Maiano*, pp. 183-84), shows what books might be found in a Quattrocento sculptor's house. There is reference to a total of twenty-eight volumes in the *scrittoii* the brothers shared, including, besides a number of religious works, certain books of Livy, a history of Florence, a Dante, the *Cento-Novelle*, and others with uncertain designations.

[20] See Henriette Mendelsohn, *Fra Filippo Lippi* (Berlin, 1909), pp. 229ff., 235; and Gaye, *Carteggio*, 1:141, 175; 2:355-56 on Beccafumi and Francesco da Sangallo.

in more detail below as a particular characteristic of the genuinely artistic nature.

A range of ingenuity extending beyond purely manual, craftsmanly artistic activity also appears in artists who showed themselves gifted with poetic or musical abilities. This is true in the first respect for Brunelleschi as witness his polemical sonnet mentioned above, but also for Bramante and especially for Michelangelo in the most extensive and significant degree; see Luca Beltrami, *Bramante poeta* (Milan, 1884), with thirty-three sonnets by Bramante.[21] But the activity in artistic literature of Ghiberti, Filarete, Alberti, and Leonardo, as well as what we know of collecting interests of certain artists touches very closely on a profession in the figural arts.[22] The same close connection with artistic creation also explains the affectionate interest with which certain artists cared for some beautiful and remarkable animals in their own houses and gardens in order constantly to enjoy the sight of them and to be able to study their form and movements.[23] Of Sodoma, whom Vasari himself must have known, he says outright that his house "looked like Noah's ark," since Sodoma was constantly trying to obtain and surround himself with especially exotic or otherwise remarkable animal specimens: badgers, squirrels, small apes, Angora cats, bantams, turtledoves, etc., along with a talking raven that could imitate its master's voice deceptively.[24] It cannot be investigated here in more detail how far this passion of Sodoma's for animals, by all means unusually excessive, actually extended into erotic perversion, as his sinister nickname Sodoma suggests, and as certain contemporary epigrams that appeared in print in Siena in 1526, even

[21] The tradition that Domenico Veneziano and his later compatriot Sebastiano del Piombo were good lute players has admittedly been handed down only through an apocryphal anecdote in Vasari.

[22] On Ghiberti's antique collection see Julius von Schlosser, *Jahrbuch der Kunsthistorischen Sammlungen des Allerhöchsten Kaiserhauses* (Vienna, 1924), pp. 29ff. On other artists' collections see Burckhardt, *Beiträge:Die Sammler*, pp. 332ff. and Eugène Müntz, *I Precursori e propugnatori del rinascimento*, Florence, 1902, p. 200. Their information, however, deals chiefly with non-Florentine or later artists.

[23] If Vasari (Vasari-Milanesi, 3:36) asserts this of Pesello, it is admittedly based on unverifiable tradition. On the other hand, what he tells about Piero di Cosimo (Vasari-Milanesi, 4:134) along this line is probably based on eyewitness accounts (Vasari himself entered into training with Piero's pupil Andrea del Sarto not long after Piero's death). The story ran, for instance, that this eccentric, of such outlandish disposition in other respects as well, would run wherever there was any strange beast or other natural phenomenon to be seen, go into extravagant raptures over it and could hardly stop talking about it afterwards.

[24] Sodoma gave a complete inventory of this home menagerie in his tax declaration of 1531; likewise verified in documents are the race horses with which the painter won prizes in Florence and Siena. (See Vasari-Milanesi, 6:380, 388; and 6:60-69, for the account of the animals that Giovanni Francesco Rustici kept in his house: an eagle, a talking raven, a whole aquarium with various snakes, etc.)

during the master's lifetime affirm, or whether—as Vasari has it (Vasari-Milanesi, 6:389)—he only adopted this designation in frivolous bravado.

Finally, a few scattered observations on the nature of general sources of inspiration for artistic fantasy. Much on this can be found in Leonardo's notes for his book on painting. These deal primarily with inspiration from direct or indirect impressions from nature.[25]

However, still more surprising than such allusions to studies of physical nature through objective observation that belong as such to the general basic principles of artistic instruction of the Quattrocento are certain remarks that call attention to a more indirect stimulus to the artists' imaginative powers. Such is one observation, already made twice (by all means with opposite estimations) and thus probably more often, in the late Quattrocento. This was that the artist's eye could take all sorts of useful stimuli for the invention of lively compositions of battles on horseback, landscape scenes, and the like even from fortuitous, formless visual impressions such as a wall-surface weathered or sprinkled with water or the fleeting play of form in moving cloud masses.[26]

How the sculptor's imaginative powers could be kindled by the sight and touch of an uncut block of marble has already been mentioned above in connection with Michelangelo's relation to the material and to personal chisel work. During one of his long stays among the still unquarried marble masses of the mountains of Pietrasanta, he is supposed to have conceived the fantastic idea of forming one of the peaks rising above the coast into a nude giant, "which would be recognizable in the distance to those sailing past on the sea" (Condivi, *Michelangelo*, chap. 24).

## THE ARTISTIC TYPE IN CONTEMPORARY SOCIETY

The artistic person as a special, somewhat peculiar species of the *genus humanum* is a very familiar conception to us in recent and present times,

[25] Thus he recommends walks outdoors in the open air, in the rustic solitude of "lochi campestri" where "the soul can take in 'le specie de li allegri siti,'" the spectacle of shadowy valleys, with the playful motion of twisting streams, the variety of flowers whose bright-colored splendor fills the eyes with harmony" etc. (1:23 [*Translator's note*: probably referring to the Tabarrini edition]; Leonardo-Ludwig, *Das Buch von der Malerei*, p. 44).

[26] Leonardo makes such a statement, and mentions as an analogy the stimulus that many poets received from the sound of bells (Leonardo-Ludwig, *Das Buch von der Malerei*, 2:125). Vasari reports this as a method of inspiration consciously used by Piero di Cosimo (Vasari-Milanesi, 4:434). On the other hand, as Leonardo tells it, Botticelli is supposed to have placed little value on images of landscapes just for the reason that one could sometimes simulate something like a landscape picture by throwing a damp sponge against a wall. Botticelli's own landscapes, Leonardo adds, were thus very poor (fece tristissimi paesi) (Leonardo-Ludwig, *Das Buch von der Malerei*, 2:116-17). On Leonardo's pantheistic philosophy of nature and his landscape studies see Hans Hess, *Die Naturanschauung der Renaissance in Italien*, (Marburg, 1924), pp. 67ff.

thanks to numerous declarations by the artists themselves as well as those informants closest to them such as friends, employers, etc. But if from our present point of view we look for comparison even to the beginning of the nineteenth century at the numerous and frequently clearly recorded representatives of the group of artists, we find that the heterogeneity of the class, even among artists living at the same time, particularly over the generations from then until today, immediately stands out almost more strongly that the common points, which emerge only in closer examination going beyond the special individual types.

That common ground, however, founded on the special talent and professional activity of the artist, must surely also appear in the artistic sphere of the Florentine Renaissance; at least in the markedly creative personalities who confront us from among the great majority of crafts-men-representatives of the artistic branch of professions. Along with this it may appear doubly noteworthy in view of the artistic relationships of that time that long before any external separation according to social classes, it was already possible for certain powerful individual person-alities to stand out from the traditional class by virtue of impulsive thrusts of talent and formative powers inherent only to them. And such special figures were recognized and appreciated by certain perceptive contem-poraries of the same and succeeding generations.

The respect and appreciation for superior artistic mastery has already been discussed several times above. Here, however, it remains to examine as far as possible the traits and peculiarities that made the artistic per-sonality, the special character of the artist in a specific and higher sense, remarkable to contemporaries and to posterity.

At the outset we recall what has been said above about the very limited source value of the personality sketches of Quattrocento artists in Vasari and other informants of his time. Yet we do not want to overlook how closely these later artist anecdotes nevertheless match not only the sort that are already to be found in the novelists and other authors of the Trecento, but also the sparse information of this kind from the Renais-sance period itself.[27] From these come a series of images, traceable over the whole rich two-hundred year period from the mid-fourteenth to the mid-sixteenth century, of the artist type as he appeared to his contem-poraries at any given time and struck them, on account of peculiarities that deviated from general bourgeois characteristics, as worthy of re-cording. We may surely acknowledge the most constant characteristics of this image as a tradition whose content is at least in essence historically trustworthy. In the following I give a selection of the pertinent accounts,

[27] This whole stock of tales is brought together and discussed in a manner most deserving of gratitude by Hanns Floerke in his *Die fünfundsiebenzig italienischen Künstlernovellen der Renaissance* (Munich and Leipzig, 1913).

not too numerous, and begin with notices that relate to the artist's behavior in his professional activity, at the inception and execution of a work.

Here first of all the artists' undependability in adhering to agreed deadlines for completion appears often to have occasioned harsh remarks, particularly by patrons as the nearest party to the contract; this in contrast to the purely artisan receivers of commissions, with whom the artists were, however, habitually compared by tradition, sometimes into the sixteenth century.[28] "In what concerns works of painters and sculptors, as you know, it is difficult to promise anything with certainty," wrote the Signoria of Florence in December 1502 to the French Marshall de Cié, at whose desire they had commissioned a bronze David from Michelangelo. And a further letter on the same matter at the end of April 1503 has it that the master indeed had held out the most immediate prospects for the completion of the work, yet his promise must appear very uncertain "in view of the temperament of people of his class," as the chancery clerk pleased to express himself with the government official's time-honored arrogance toward the artist.

This is only one especially explicit testimony to the accusation of undependability that evidently stuck to artists in general; for this reason the clause of a fixed term of delivery was included in most contracts. It has been discussed above how little effect these stipulations admittedly proved to have in many cases. Reference has also been made to the material basis for such delays arising on the one side or the other. Not rarely, however, considerable extensions of the course of work must also have resulted from other, purely artistic causes, from the peculiar character of the artist himself. Consciously or unconsciously, certain early Quattrocento masters of more sensitive constitution already emancipated themselves from the artisan-like continuous working procedure of the broad cross section of their colleagues and took on themselves the freedom to let certain jobs lie idle for a while when they could not summon up the right mood and frame of mind; perhaps because other, extraartistic interests took precedence—as was frequently the case, much to the annoyance of his patrons, with Fra Filippo.

A solicitor for his patron Giovanni de' Medici tells in 1457 (Gaye, *Carteggio*, 1:176), how the latter spent a whole hour without moving from the painter's side to keep him at the easel. On the other hand, the old Cosimo de' Medici, again with relevance to this same painter but

[28] We already hear outraged complaints of this nature in the last years of the Trecento in the letter of a patron in Prato, Francesco di Marco Datini, who finally in sharpest irritation over the unsteady work and his painter's eternal demands for advance payments, announced: "Mai non piu farò dipingere" (see *RA*, 1929, 1930, p. 101 and passim).

with more judicious delicacy, refused to yoke up an artistic genius like a "pack-mule" (see above).[29]

Vasari expressly declares of his contemporary Granacci (Vasari-Milanesi, 5:345) that he seemed to practice his art not as a livelihood, but rather always as though it were a pastime and only with complete ease because he always had to have his "comodità." Likewise he represented Pontormo as an artist who would work only when and for whom it pleased him and thus not rarely made highly placed patrons wait in order to please some simple people (Vasari-Milanesi, 5:32; 6:279-80).

The artist's attitude toward the creative process can sometimes be more clearly recognized, however, in the patient, apparently inactive period of maturation he allowed for the conception of an image until the arrival of the fruitful moment that was then seized with lightning speed. There was thus an instinctive change of tempo in the execution process of a work as an eyewitness, the novelist Bandello, reported of Leonardo's creation in the Milan *cenacolo*. He saw the master sometimes spend hours without touching the brush, considering and reflecting before the half-finished work. Then again came times when Leonardo painted on without interruption from early morning until evening, or sometimes suddenly ran from his other work place, the sculpture studio in the Castello, to Santa Maria delle Grazie to add only a few decisive brush strokes to the Last Supper painting according to a pressing inspiration and then returned again to his equestrian monument.[30]

This inability to satisfy oneself and consequently to come to an end— "that you cannot finish makes you great"—viewed as the greatness and at the same time apparent weakness of the true artist was, of course, difficult for an expeditious virtuoso like Vasari to understand. It must have struck him as less admirable than strange and only for that reason as biographically noteworthy.[31] In view of this dissatisfaction it was only

[29] See Vasari (Vasari-Milanesi, 2:616) for another anecdote on Fra Filippo's indomitable propensity for amorous diversion from his work. See also a letter of admonition of 1444, as energetic as it is amiable, from a cardinal to an unknown artist about the completion of a long-promised image of the Madonna (Gaye, *Carteggio*, 2:74).

[30] See the introductory letter to the fifty-eighth novella of the first part of Bandello's tales. (Hanns Floerke, *Die fünfundsiebenzig italienischen Künstlernovellen der Renaissance*, Munich and Leipzig, 1913, p. 3).

Vasari reports quite similarly of Pontormo (Vasari-Milanesi, 6:264ff.) that during his work on the choir of San Lorenzo he sometimes would not come out of his brooding reflection for a whole day and therefore remained occupied with this fresco cycle for no less than ten years. Pontormo also would not call his frescoes in Castello finished even after work had gone on for five years, until finally the ducal patron lost patience and ordered the immediate unveiling of the work (Vasari-Milanesi, 6:282, 285, 289).

[31] He did by all means criticize Bugiardini for his overly quick self-satisfaction with his own production, for which Michelangelo, who was eternally dissatisfied with himself, sometimes ironically congratulated him; but he noted of the same Bugiardini that he would

natural that many artists anxiously hid their work from anyone's gaze during the slow process of execution, only in order not to be disturbed by any premature comments by a third party or uninvited advice from the patron.[32]

Vasari reports on the particularly intricate working procedure of certain early painters as something very remote from his own technique: with what pedantry, for instance, Lorenzo di Credi used to prepare his painting materials, how Albertinelli refined the color tones of his Annunciation panel for the confraternity of San Zanobi in 1510 with cautious testing, and finally even demanded the right to set the panel up in the confraternity's oratorio himself, in order to adapt the whole perspective as well as the distribution of light and shadow as perfectly as possible to the special conditions of the appointed place (Vasari-Milanesi, 4:223-24, 570-71).

In another place Vasari depicts (Vasari-Milanesi, 4:142) the temperamental passion for work of Piero di Cosimo who "without respect to expenditure of time and effort truly fell in love with his art, and forgot all bodily comforts on account of it." In Vasari's time, however (Vasari-Milanesi, 3:270) it was still told of Ghirlandaio's insatiable creative drive that he would not refuse even the humblest, purely utilitarian commission, such as for instance painting market baskets, and often said that as a fresco painter his only complaint was that he could not cover the whole circle of walls around Florence with murals.[33]

Finally Vasari reports of Michelangelo, whom he had the opportunity to observe at close range during his later years, that the master, when he was in the grip of a working frenzy, remained active in his studio even in the evening hours in order to lose no time and had devised a form of illumination as practical as it was cheap: a cardboard shell with a candle

---

not let an especially complicated composition, *The Martyrdom of St. Catherine* for Santa Maria Novella, out of his hands for a full twelve years because he was always finding something to change in it (Vasari-Milanesi, 6:202, 205).

[32] Such things were still known to Vasari concerning Piero di Cosimo, for example, and even Uccello; likewide on Pontormo, who during the endlessly drawn-out painting of the choir of San Lorenzo kept this area strictly closed off to everyone. He reports similarly of Rustici and especially of Michelangelo, who allowed no one to see his statue of David before it was completed, no more than the battle cartoon before its unveiling or the Sistine ceiling (Vasari-Milanesi, 2:216; 4:133, 140-41; 6:272, 600-601; 7:154, 160-68, 174-76). It will be reported how Franciabigio took revenge on the curious monks for the unveiling of his fresco in the forecourt of the Annunziata without his knowledge.

[33] Corresponding traits that Vasari could recount of artists of his own time show that such reports are more than pure fables; of Perino del Vaga, for instance, that he sometimes could not refrain, even when he had enough workshop personnel available, from executing odd jobs like pennants for trumpeters, decorative cloth painting, and the like with his own hand (Vasari-Milanesi, 5:629).

stuck on it that he wore on his head in order to be able to pursue his work everywhere with light without availing himself of his hands. Sometimes in the stress of work he did not even take time to change his clothes. When exhaustion overcame him he threw himself down, dressed as he was, on a resting place to sleep for a few hours (Vasari-Milanesi, 7:276).

For Michelangelo alone there is direct evidence—and for Leonardo in a less secure Vasarian tradition—that in a period that otherwise knew only art work originating on commission, he undertook a work in certain cases on his own choice and initiative, from a purely personal impulse.[34]

On the other hand, it conforms very well with this if Leonardo as well as Michelangelo later withdrew from certain commissioned work in spite of having received payments, because in the meantime he had met with another commission with stronger artistic appeal.[35] In such impulsive acts and ommissions, certain artists toward the end of the Quattrocento first emancipated themselves from the still somewhat craftsmanly situation, completely oriented toward the patron, of most colleagues of their generation. However, this self-liberation of certain self-assured personalities and their rise to a prominence above the average and traditional level is already recognizable in the trailblazers of the early Renaissance in the objectives and style of their work, which were in many ways completely new. In these they ventured, certainly not infrequently in opposition to a patron as well as to the broad mass of the contemporary public, to depart from the customary manner of expression.[36]

No less remarkable for contemporaries were the outbursts of temper, exceeding all usual measure even by southern and Florentine standards, that could occur in certain situations with certain artists and that were

[34] And indeed both already did this in early youth. Leonardo made an oil painting of a head of Medusa (Vasari-Milanesi, 4:25), "vennegli fantasia di dipingere . . . una testa di una Medusa." In addition, there is Michelangelo's lost but securely verified Hercules statue that he began in 1492 to console himself over Lorenzo Magnifico's death, and a marble figure, with no more precise designation, that he executed from a marble block he had obtained himself during the first Roman period.

[35] In addition, one may note in passing the no less unusual statement of Dürer, who, irritated by the many disagreements with his patron Jakob Heller in 1510, wrote to him: "So ich Euch nit zu sonderem Gefallen thäte, sollte mich niemand überreden, das ich etwas Verdingts mache; denn ich versäum mich an Besserem darum"; K. Lange and F. Fuhse, eds., *Dürers schriftlicher Nachlass auf Grund der Original handscriften und theilweise neu entdeckter alter Abschriften*, Halle, 1893, p. 47 (If I were not doing you a special favor, no one could persuade me to do a work on order; for I am missing out on better things on account of it.)

[36] This was true already of Nanni di Banco and the young Donatello among the other sculptors of the Duomo workshop, of Masaccio in the midst of contemporary painting of the 1420s, and also somewhat later, in his particularly delicate manner, of Fra Filippo Lippi, and so on up to the first leaders of the new stylistic movement around 1500, Leonardo and Michelangelo.

then retold up to Vasari's time as a striking expression of their identity as artists. A whole series of examples exists, for instance, for that most extreme fit of anger in which the artist was carried away to the point of destroying his own work.[37] Michelangelo's biographers report many oral expressions of his shockingly fiery nature and recount that even the pope had to reproach him expressly for this *terribilità* (Vasari-Milanesi, 7:189).

In the introduction to the biography of Raphael, however, Vasari (Vasari-Milanesi, 4:315) takes occasion to call sharp attention to the perfectly harmoniously balanced, constantly charming character of the master as a rare counterpart to the "extravagant, wild and obstinate nature of most artists before him."

Then certain manifestations are recorded of the artist's passionate sensitivity, no less extraordinary yet stemming from purely artistic impulses.[38] Vasari (Vasari-Milanesi, 3:370) recounts a charming example of the artistic sensitivity to style of Verrocchio's pupil Nanni Grosso, who in his last hour, in the hospital of Santa Maria Nuova, sent away the priest who had come to administer the sacraments for the dying until the latter at his request had the beautiful bronze cross by Donatello brought from the sacristy instead of his poor wooden crucifix; "otherwise he would die unconfessed, so offended was he by bad works of his art."

Michelangelo's biographer Condivi (*Michelangelo*, chap. 55) also considered it important to emphasize Michelangelo's powerful capacity to love and savor every kind of beauty in the works of nature, human bodies, animals, plants, and landscapes. And in this connection we may likewise remember Michelangelo's original lively characterizations, springing from a profound experience, of certain old architectural and

[37] Donatello threw a newly completed portrait bust to the ground and dashed it to pieces because the patron was trying to drive down the price (Vasari-Milanesi, 2:407-408). Then there are Verrocchio's similar enraged act in Venice, already recounted above, and the anecdote about Franciabigio (even confirmed by document) who in wrath over the unauthorized premature unveiling of his fresco in the Annunziata forecourt in 1513 severely damaged the almost completed work in several places and would not even restore it afterwards for any price (Vasari-Milanesi, 5:193). Finally there is Michelangelo, who abruptly gave his painting of Leda, executed for the Duke of Ferrara, to one of his shop assistants in anger over an insensitive remark by the Duke's envoy (Condivi, *Michelangelo*, chap. 47).

[38] There are two such anecdotes about Brunelleschi who, according to his anonymous biographer (Manetti-Holtzinger, *Brunelleschi*, p. 28) became so incensed with the skeptical Duomo foreman at the presentation of his vaulting project that he refused to be dismissed until the latter had him ejected by force twice in succession in order to have peace; in addition Vasari (Vasari-Milanesi, 2:340) tells of the occasion when Brunelleschi, on being told of a particularly beautiful antique relief found in Cortona, was immediately seized with such avid desire to see the work of art and to be able to sketch it that he set off on the spot. Piero di Cosimo could also sometimes talk endlessly about certain beauties and wonders of nature (Vasari-Milanesi, 4:134).

artistic works of Florence. He called Santa Maria Novella "his bride," compared San Salvatore al Monte with a "beautiful country girl" (*la bella Villanella*), praised Ghiberti's second bronze portals as worthy to be the gates of Paradise. However, he also branded certain unsuccessful works of his time with no less pertinent scathing formulations: the arcaded gallery under the cathedral dome as "a cricket cage," and others. With his own works in certain cases he felt himself to have grown so personally close that according to Condivi (*Michelangelo*, chap. 39) he "only with tears left off the work on the Julius tomb" ("piangendo lasciò la sepultura"), in order to undertake the facade of San Lorenzo, which had been forced on him.

All such behavior and manners of expression deviating from bourgeois custom evidently struck contemporaries as noteworthy peculiarities of the artistic personality, as it could be found embodied in its full distinctiveness not, by all means, in all members of the artistic professions, yet precisely in the masters who also stood out for their creations. What the sporadically noted individual traits of this type convey is first of all the wholly unconstrained uniqueness of the way of life, personal character, and tenor of relationships by which quite a few artists already in the fifteenth century must have presented themselves as decidedly original, not to say odd.[39] For example, there can often be found, to cite only the most striking, a very blunt willfulness, which often degenerated into whimsical caprices and precisely on this account made an impression as something special, probably belonging only to the artistic nature.[40]

[39] Vasari's biographies of Uccello and Piero di Cosimo in particular are veritable quarries of pertinent characteristics; to this may be added what he recounts of the sculptor and goldsmith Nanni Grosso, of Vecchietta, Sodoma, and of Pontormo's eccentricities, which by all means in the case of this last could probably have been so marked and extravagant as Vasari observed them only in his later years, perhaps after 1540. Precisely for this reason, however, his personality portrait of Pontormo may most readily be taken as an essentially authentic report because it is more immediately contemporary, which then gives Vasari's personal information on earlier artists at least an indirect support and confirmation. For the resulting characterizations, even considering all differences of detail, are in general fundamentally closely analogous.

[40] That Verrocchio pupil Nanni Grosso seems to have been a real exemplar of this. The beautiful torch holders of the Palazzo Strozzi, for example, are his work. Vasari (Vasari-Milanesi, 2:370; 4:445; once, it is true, with the first name Niccolò) tells amusing things about him in two places. He was a man of the strongest principles, who, for example, would never work for Jews, who rejected with indignation a commission to produce a crowbar or skeleton key—those were thieves' tools—who always executed all commissions in the order they came to him and consequently even let Lorenzo Magnifico wait until a work begun for some common people was finished. As a most esteemed master of his craft, he generally took the liberty of setting certain conditions, such as that he only undertook work outside his own shop when he was promised free access to the patron's wine cellar. His peculiarities included in particular, however, never to begin a work without a down payment from the commissioner—thence his nickname Caparra—and not to deliver any work before receipt of the remainder. He even sought to demonstrate this principle clearly

The nervously heightened sensitivity of Piero di Cosimo and also Pontormo to all outward disturbances is particularly remarkable. This, it is true, is generally comprehensible and familiar to us in view of the artist's particularly sensitive constitution. Thus Piero detested not only the cries of small children, the sound of bells, and the choir chants of monks, but could fly into a rage if he only heard someone cough or a fly buzz. He rejoiced at the sight of wild torrents of rain, but during any thunderstorm he hid himself, his cloak pulled over his head, in the furthest corner of the workshop. Already solitary by preference in his youth, indulging his fantasies, in his last years before he died in 1521 (thus shortly before Vasari's first Florentine period), he was so unsociable that he would not even have one assistant or servant around him.[41]

With reference to the exception of Raphael, Vasari felt bound to accept the characteristics of the "capriccioso," "stravagante," and "fantastico" as essential properties, scarcely laudable in themselves, of most artists of earlier times. Yet he also recognized their extreme development in Piero di Cosimo as the foundation of the latter's artistic fantasy, so peculiarly rich in ideas. And in fact Piero's art makes an impression that accords very clearly and convincingly with the picture, even if probably somewhat caricatured, of the man Piero in Vasari's biography.

Beyond this, however, we are generally inclined to look positively on many of the peculiarities, reported from Vasari's standpoint as strange oddities and weaknesses, as in some way necessary expressions of artistic behavior. Thus it is reported, again of Piero di Cosimo, that he combined the characteristics of the "malinconico" and the "fantastico"; that is, his brooding, solitary, eccentric, often immoderately detached and confused nature would suddenly change to downright bubbling loquaciousness, in which Piero came up with the most striking, sometimes paradoxical thought associations, and burst forth with an interminable torrent of words on all sorts of personal observations and reflections, to the point of boring the listener.[42]

---

by hanging a sign over his bottega with the representation of an account book consumed by flames. This image, he explained, meant that his books had burned up and thus he could record no credit. It was also he who, as already recounted above, would rather have expired without the sacrament than bring himself to make his last confession in the sight of a misshapen crucifix.

[41] For this reason and in order to lose no time himself, Piero sometimes lived only on hard cooked eggs that he boiled by the dozen when he cooked his glue. The setting for this singular existence, according to Vasari's account, was a house that could never be straightened up and cleaned and a consistently overgrown garden; for it was exactly such wholly uncultivated, free, and luxuriant natural growth that expressly suited Piero best.

Pontormo also lived similarly, as far as possible without servants, and, in order to be safe from uninvited visitors, chiefly in the upper story of his house, which was only accessible by a ladder that was usually pulled up (Vasari-Milanesi, 6:279).

[42] See Vasari-Milanesi, 4:133, 134, 143. Vasari also calls the painter and sculptor Vec-

In the meantime numerous cheerful figures can also be found among the artistic biographical material that has come down to us: thus the type of the humorous artist, who with his original brainstorms and witty tongue represented an especially popular, sociable element.

Such a one, for instance, in his younger years, was Piero di Cosimo, who later became such a hypochondriac. But all sorts of humorous and burlesque tales or expressions, sometimes coarse, are recorded by Vasari and the Florentine novelists about other masters such as Brunelleschi, Botticelli, and others. And even in Michelangelo's harsh grandeur and severity there was room for the humorous and comic, when—as already recounted above—he took the occasion to associate with primitive, rustic artisans as with equals.

Vasari represents Nunziata, an otherwise unknown assistant of Ridolfo Ghirlandaio (he lived from 1475-1525), as a pronounced wag, who, for instance, in order to tease certain peevish customers, produced all sorts of grotesque jokes, even in paintings of religious subjects (a bearded Madonna, a Crucified with long trousers; Vasari-Milanesi, 6:535-37). Along with the "persona burlevole" of this Nunziata there appears the "persona carnale," the character inclined predominantly toward sensual pleasures, such as Vasari (Vasari-Milanesi, 4:222) designates Mariotto Albertinelli. The latter—departing far from the way of life of his youthful comrade Fra Bartolommeo—even worked for a while as a publican and is supposed to have felt perfectly happy in such a trade.[43] In the introductory passage to the biography of Davide Ghirlandaio (Vasari-Milanesi, 6:531) the artist biographer also holds forth in general about the neglect of artistic aspirations in consequence of an excessively rich income and a correspondingly hedonistic way of life. The boundless generosity of certain artists—such as for instance Donatello (Vasari-Milanesi, 2:420) and Rustici (Vasari-Milanesi, 6:607-608)—and the absolute indifference to money and possessions on which it was founded appeared to him more sympathetic and in any case not detrimental to artistic creation. Many of Michelangelo's letters give us clear evidence of his extremely humble standard of living.

A master like Donatello would put on the fine clothes conferred on him by Cosimo de' Medici only once or twice, and then—as Vespasiano

---

chietta (Vasari-Milanesi, 3:78-79) a *persona malinconica e solitaria*; Pontormo, according to his representation (Vasari-Milanesi, 6:289) also lived "in incredible seclusion," though probably only in old age.

[43] Sodoma became a personality known throughout the city, in Florence as well as Siena, for his sometimes rather daring jokes and was even ridiculed in public satires (see above). Vasari found of Domenico Puligo (Vasari-Milanesi, 4:476) that he had missed out on his higher artistic fulfillment because of his inveterate laziness and his inclination toward *piaceri mondani*.

da Bisticci notes as a contemporary (*Vite*, p. 259)—preferred to resume his usual simple craftsman's garb. This was so repugnant to Vasari and his ideal of the artist courtier that he probably left this anecdote out of his Donatello biography on purpose. He also specifically reproached another artist of his time, Doceno, for neglecting his outward appearance so completely and putting on new clothes only with reluctance (Vasari-Milanesi, 7:241-43); he noted, however, with satisfaction Sodoma's need always to appear splendidly dressed (Vasari-Milanesi, 6:386-87).[44]

The preceding particulars of artistic biography and psychology are for the most part taken from Vasari, who for his part drew these details from a more or less uncertain tradition and who may probably in addition have altered them according to his own ideas and ideals. Reference has already been made to this above, but at the same time it was emphasized how often these Vasarian notations accord with artistic-biographical reports from older literature, as well as information from the contemporary circle of Vasari himself.

If we attempt, in review of all the particular traits, to bring to mind a total picture of the artist type of the Florentine Renaissance, the result is a harmony, recognizable at least in essential characteristics, of this image with that of the artistic type of yesterday and today as he is familiar to us partly through direct observation and partly through a large body of trustworthy testimony. To show this in detail here, however, would lead us too far afield.[45]

Only this much might still be added: the general artistic conditions of the Renaissance period in Florence were fundamentally determined by the existence of an uncommonly strong, multifaceted demand for art and an equally extensive body of patrons, encompassing all social levels. This condition and structure of the whole nature of art, so very different from those of the present, must naturally have had particular kinds of influence on the situation of the artist within his environment, as well as on his personal attitudes, behavior, and way of life. Thus the fact is all the more remarkable that in spite of all this certain basic characteristics of the human spirit that we still see today as decisive signs of the artistic person also appear here and there already in the midst of that very different period.

[44] Vasari reports also of Jacopo Sansovino (Vasari-Milanesi, 7:509) that he set great store by fine clothing and a well-groomed appearance, as a pronounced ladies' man even in his later years. And from his own youthful memories he depicts the old Signorelli, who appeared in carefully chosen garments and in general more like a *signore* and *gentiluomo* than a painter (Vasari-Milanesi, 3:693, 695-96).

[45] I refer to the book by Lucien Arréat, *La psychologie du peintre* (Paris, 1892), as well as the Münster dissertation by Wilm Arenhövel, *Die Künstlerpersönlichkeit in der zweiten Hälfte des 19. Jahrhunderts*, 1936, based on the writings of artists and the voluminous information reported in literature in connection with these.

According to this, the free development of artistic genius and of the artist's special way of life were in no way, or in any case not in any decisive measure, hindered by the admittedly much more limited right of self-determination that was allowed him by the attitudes and conditions of his time.

If, however, as the works that have come down to us testify, those personal living conditions existing for the Florentine Renaissance artist obstructed his creative calling as little as did his contemporaries' pertinent evaluation of him as peculiar, then we may be able to recognize the system of preconditions and factors of Florentine artistic life recorded in this book almost as an ideal picture of desirable artistic conditions in general. With reference to this picture, we may perhaps also accordingly consider whether at least a few of those foundations, so enviable in a material as well as theoretical sense, might not once again be regained for the artist of today or tomorrow.[46]

[46] More detailed statements on this were presented in my *Vier Aufsätze über geschichtliche und gegenwärtige Faktoren des Kunstlebens* (vol. 1 of the series of studies Lebensräume der Kunst, Wattenscheid, 1936).

# AUTHOR'S BIBLIOGRAPHY

Books and articles referred to only for specific points and cited in detail in those contexts are not listed here.

## SOURCES AND COLLECTIONS OF EARLY WRITINGS

### Individual Authors

Alberti, Leon Battista. *Della pittura e della statua.* Edited and translated by Hubert Janitschek. Quellenschriften für Kunstgeschichte, 11. Vienna, 1877. See also Pandolfini, Agnolo.

Albertini, Francesco. *Memoriale di molte statue e picture della citta di Firenze.* Florence, 1510. In J. A. Crowe and G. B. Cavalcaselle, *Geschichte der italienischen Malerei*, edited by M. Jordan, vol. 2, appendix. Leipzig, 1869-1871.

"Anonimo Magliabecchiano," *Il codice Magliabecchiano.* Edited by Karl Frey. Berlin, 1892.

Baldovinetti, Alesso. *Alesso Baldovinetti, pittore fiorentino con l'aggiunto dei suoi "Ricordi."* Edited by Emilio Londi. Florence, 1907. Also in *Frammenti inediti di vita fiorentina*, edited by Giovanni Poggi. Florence, 1909. See also Horne in *Burlington Magazine*, 2, 1903, pp. 22-32, 167-74 and Fabriczy in *Repertorium für Kunstwissenschaft*, 28, 1905, p. 540.

Billi, Antonio. *Il Libro di Antonio Billi.* Edited by Karl Frey. Berlin, 1892.

Bisticci, Vespasiano da. *Vite di uomini illustri del secolo XV.* Edited by Angelo Mai. Florence, 1859. German edition with selections, *Lebensbeschreibungen berühmter Männer des Quattrocento*, edited by Paul Schubring. Jena, 1914.

Cambi, Giovanni. *Istorie.* In *Delizie degli Eruditi toscani*, edited by Fra Ildefonso di San Luigi. Vol. 21. Florence, 1790.

Cennini, Cennino. *Das Buch von der Kunst* or *Traktat der Malerei.* Edited and translated by A. Ilg. Quellenschriften für Kunstgeschichte, 1. Vienna, 1871.
———. *Il Libro dell'Arte.* Edited by Gaetano Milanesi. Florence, 1859.

Condivi, Ascanio. *Vita di Michelangelo Buonarrotti.* Rome, 1553. Edited by Karl Frey. Berlin, 1887. German edition, *Das Leben des Michelangelo Buonarrotti geschrieben von seinem Schüler Ascanio Condivi*, translated by Valdeck. Quellenschriften für Kunstgeschichte, 6. Vienna, 1883.

Filarete, Antonio. *Traktat über die Baukunst.* Edited by W. von Oettingen. Quellenschriften für Kunstgeschichte, N. F. 3. Vienna, 1896.

Ghiberti, Lorenzo. *Lorenzo Ghibertis Denkwürdigkeiten.* Edited by Julius von Schlosser. 2 vols. Berlin, 1912.

Gori, Antonio Francesco. *La Toscana illustrata nella sua storia con vari scelti monumenti e documenti per l'avanti o inediti, o molto rari.* Vol. 1. Livorno, 1755.

Landucci, Luca. *Diario Fiorentino (1450-1516).* Edited by Jodoco del Badia. Florence, 1883. German edition, *Ein florentinisches Tagebuch 1450-1516*, edited and translated by Marie Herzfeld. 2 vols. Jena, 1912-1913.

Leonardo da Vinci. *Das Buch von der Malerei*. Edited and translated by H. Ludwig. Quellenschriften für Kunstgeschichte, 15-17. 3 vols. Vienna, 1882. Italian edition, *Trattato della pittura di Leonardo da Vinci, condotto sul codice Vaticano Urbinate 1270*, edited by M. Tabarrini. Rome, 1920.

Machiavelli, Niccolò. *Historie fiorentine*. Florence, 1556. German edition, *Florentinische Geschichten*, edited by Alfred von Reumont. Leipzig, 1846.

Manetti, Antonio. *Vita di Filippo Brunelleschi*. Edited by Holtzinger. Stuttgart, 1887.

Masi, Bartolommeo. *Ricordanze di Bartolommeo Masi, calderaio fiorentino, dal 1478 al 1526*. Edited by G. Odoardo Corrazzini. Florence, 1906.

Maso di Bartolommeo. *Ricordi*. French edition, *Journal d'un sculpteur florentin au XVe siècle*, edited by C. Yriarte. Paris, 1894.

Michelangelo Buonarroti. *Die Aufzeichnungen Michelangelo Buonarrotis im Brit. Mus. und im Vermächtnis Ernst Steinmann*. Edited by W. Maurenbrecher. Römische Forschungen der Bibliotheca Hertziana, 14. Leipzig, 1938.

———. *Die Briefe des Michelangelo Buonarroti*. Translated by Karl Frey. Berlin, 1907.

———. *Le lettere coi ricordi ed i contratti artistici*. Edited by Gaetano Milanesi. Florence, 1875.

———. *Sammlung ausgewählter Briefe an Michelangelo Buonarroti*. Edited by Karl Frey. Berlin, 1899.

Neri di Bicci. *Le ricordanze (1453-75)*. Extracts in Giorgio Vasari, *Le vite de' piu eccellenti pictori ecc.*, edited by Gaetano Milanesi, vol. 2, pp. 701ff. Florence, 1878-1885. Complete publication by Giovanni Poggi has begun in the journal *Il Vasari*, Arezzo, 1927ff. 1, pp. 317-38; 3, pp. 133-53; 4, pp. 189-202 etc.

Pandolfini, Agnolo. *Trattato del governo della famiglia*. Milan, 1802. By Alberti.

Rucellai, Giovanni. *Lo Zibaldone*. Extracts in *Un mercante fiorentino e la sua famiglia nel secolo xv*, edited by Giovanni Marcotti. Florence, 1881. *Autografo tolto dal Zibaldone di Giovanni Rucellai*, also edited by J. Temple Leader. Florence, 1871.

Rinuccini, Filippo. *Ricordi Storici*. Edited by G. Aiazzi. Florence, 1840.

Strozzi, Alessandra Macinghi degli. *Lettere di una gentildonna fiorentina nel secolo xv*. Edited by C. Guasti. Florence, 1877.

Strozzi, Lorenzo di Filippo. *Vita di Fil. Strozzi il vecchio*. Edited by G. Bini and P. Bigazzi. Florence, 1851.

———. *Le vite degli uomini illustri della casa Strozzi*. Edited by F. Zeffi. Florence, 1892. See also *Vite di alcuni della famiglia Strozzi*, edited by P. Stromboli. Florence, 1890.

Vasari, Giorgio. *Die Lebensbeschreibungen der berühmtesten Architekten Bildhauer und Maler*. Edited by Adolf Gottschewsky and Georg Gronau. Strasbourg, 1904ff. First section translated by Wackernagel.

———. *Le vite de' piu eccellenti pittori ecc.* Edited by Gaetano Milanesi. 9 vols. Florence, 1878-1885.

———. *Le vite de' piu eccellenti pittori ecc.* Edited by Karl Frey. 1 vol. Munich, 1911.

Verino, Ugolino. *De illustratione urbis Florentiae libri tres (c. 1510-12)*. Florence, 1636. Extracts in *Festschrift zu Ehren des Kunsthistorischen Institutes in Florenz*, edited by Heinrich Brockhaus. Florence, 1897.

Vespasiano da Bisticci. See Bisticci, Vespasiano da.

### Collections of Sources: Early Historical and Topographical Literature

Bacci, Peleo. *Documenti toscani per la storia dell'arte*. 2 vols. Florence, 1910-1912.

Bicchierai, Zanobi. *Alcuni documenti artistici non mai stampati (1454-1565)*. Florence, 1855.
Privately printed for the Gentile-Farinola Wedding.

Bocchi, Francesco. *Le bellezze della citta di Fiorenza*. Florence, 1591. Revised edition by Giovanni Cinelli. Florence, 1677.

Fabroni, Angelo. *Laurentii Medicis Magnifici vita*. 2 vols. Pisa, 1784.

———. *Magni Cosmi Medicei Vita*. 2 vols. Pisa, 1788-1789.

Fantozzi, Antonio, and Bughetti, Benvenuto. *Nuova Guida di Firenze*. Florence, 1842.

Gaye, Giovanni (Johann Wilhelm). *Carteggio inedito d'artisti dei secoli XIV, XV, XVI*. 3 vols. Florence, 1839-1840.

Gualandi, Michelangelo. *Memorie originali italiane risguardanti le belle arti*. 6 series. Bologna, 1840-1845.

———. *Nuova Raccolta di Lettere sulla pittura ecc*. Vol. 1. Bologna, 1844-1856.

Migliore, Ferdinando Leopoldo del. *Firenze citta nobilissima illustrata*. Florence, 1684.

Milanesi, Gaetano. "Lettere di artisti dei secoli XIV e XV." *Il Buonarroti*, April, 1869.

———. *Nuovi documenti per la storia dell'arte toscana dal XII al XV secolo*. Florence, 1901.

Passerini, Luigi. *Curiosità storico-artistiche fiorentine*. Ser. 1. Florence, 1866.

Pini, Cesare, and Milanesi, Gaetano. *La scrittura di artisti italiani*. 3 vols. Florence, 1876.

Poggi, Giovanni. *Il Duomo di Firenze, Documenti sulla decorazione ecc*. Italienische Forschungen herausgegeben vom Kunsthistorischen Institut in Florenz, 2. Berlin, 1909.

Richa, Giuseppe, S. J. *Notizie istoriche delle chiese fiorentine*. 10 vols. Florence, 1754-1762.

### MODERN RESEARCH AND PRESENTATIONS

del Badia, Jodoco. *Miscellanea fiorentina*. 2 vols. 1902. Periodical.

Baum, Julius. *Baukunst und dekorative Plastik der Frührenaissance in Italien*. Bauformenbibliothek, 11. Stuttgart, 1920.

Benelli, Giuseppe. *Firenze nei monumenti domenicani*. Florence, 1913.

Bock, Elfried. *Florentinische und venezianische Bilderrahmen aus der Zeit der Gotik und Renaissance*. Munich, 1902.

Bode, Wilhelm. *Bertoldo und Lorenzo de' Medici*. Freiburg im Breisgau, 1925.

———. *Florentiner Bildhauer der Renaissance*. 4th edition. Berlin, 1921.

Brockhaus, Heinrich. *Forschungen über florentiner Kunstwerke.* Leipzig, 1902.

Burckhardt, Jacob. *Beiträge zur Kunstgeschichte von Italien.* 3 vols. *Das Porträt in der malerei. Das Altarbild. Die Sammler.* Basel, 1898.

———. *Geschichte der Renaissance in Italien.* 4th edition. Stuttgart, 1904.

Carocci, Guido. *I dintorni di Firenze.* 2 vols. Florence, 1906-1907.

Cendali, Lorenzo. *Giuliano e Benedetto da Maiano.* San Casciano, 1926.

il Centro di Firenze. *Studi storici e ricordi artistici* (p. c. della Commissione communale). Florence, 1900.

Chiappelli, Alessandro. *L'arte del rinascimento.* Florence, 1926.

Cocchi, Arnaldo. *Le chiese di Firenze dal secolo IV al secolo XX.* Florence, 1903.

Crowe, J. A., and Cavalcaselle, G. B. *Geschichte der italienischen Malerei.* Edited by M. Jordan. Vols. 2-4. Leipzig, 1869-1871.

Cruttwell, Maud. *Antonio Pollaiuolo.* London, 1907.

Davidsohn, Robert. *Forschungen zur Geschichte von Florenz.* Vol. 4. Berlin, 1908.

Fabriczy, Cornelius von. *Filippo Brunelleschi.* Stuttgart, 1892.

Gabelentz, Hans von der. *Fra Bartolommeo und die Florentiner Renaissance.* 2 vols. Leipzig, 1922.

von Geymüller, H. A., and Stegmann, C. M. von. *Die Architektur der Renaissance in Toskana.* 11 vols. Munich, 1885-1908.

Horne, Herbert Percy. *Alessandro Filipepi, commonly called Sandro Botticelli, painter of Florence.* London, 1908.

Huth, Hans. *Künstler und Werkstatt der Spätgotik.* Augsburg, 1923.

Janitschek, Hubert. *Die Gesellschaft der Renaissance in Italien und die Kunst.* Stuttgart, 1879.

Kauffmann, Hans. *Donatello.* Berlin, 1935.

Knapp, Fritz. *Fra Bartolommeo della Porta und die Schule von San Marco.* Halle, 1903.

———. *Piero di Cosimo.* Halle, 1898.

Küppers, Paul Erich. *Die Tafelbilder des Domenico Ghirlandaio.* Strasbourg, 1916.

Lensi, Alfredo. *Palazzo Vecchio.* Milan, 1929. [*Translator's note*: Not appearing in original bibliography, but appearing frequently in the author's notes.]

Limburger, Walther. *Die Gebäude von Florenz.* Leipzig, 1910.

Mackowsky, Hans. *Verrocchio.* Bielefeld and Leipzig, 1901.

Marchese, Vincenzo, O. P. *Memorie dei piu insigni pittori, scultori e architettori Domenicani.* 4th edition. 2 vols. Bologna, 1878-1879.

Marle, Raimond van. *The Development of the Italian Schools of Painting.* Vols. 2-10. The Hague, 1925ff.

Martin, Alfred von. *Soziologie der Renaissance. Zur Physiognomik und Rhythmik bürgerlicher Kultur.* Stuttgart, 1932.

Mendelsohn, Henriette. *Fra Filippo Lippi.* Berlin, 1909.

Mesnil, Jacques. *Masaccio et les débuts de la Renaissance.* The Hague, 1927.

Moisè, Filippo. *Santa Croce di Firenze.* Florence, 1845. [*Translator's note:* Not appearing in the original bibliography, but appearing frequently in the author's notes.]

Müntz, Eugène. *Les Collections des Médicis au XVe siècle.* Paris, 1888.

————. *Histoire de l'art pendant la Renaissance.* 3 vols. Paris, 1889-1895.

————. *Les Précurseurs de la Renaissance.* Paris, 1882.

————. *I Precursori e propugnatori del rinascimento.* Florence, 1902.

Offner, Richard. *Italian Primitives at Yale University.* New Haven, Conn., 1927.

Pedrini, Augusto. *L'Ambiente, il mobilio e le decorazione del Rinascimento in Italia.* Turin, 1925.

Reumont, Alfred von. *Lorenzo de' Medici, il Magnifico.* 2nd edition. 2 vols. Leipzig, 1883.

Salmi, Mario. *Paolo Uccello, Andrea del Castagno, Domenico Veneziano.* Rome, 1935.

Scharf, Alfred. *Filippino Lippi.* Vienna, 1935.

Schiaparelli, Attilio. *La casa fiorentina ed i suoi arredi nei secoli XIV e XV.* Florence, 1908.

Schlosser, Julius von. *Die Kunstliteratur.* Vienna, 1924. See also *Quellenbuch zur Kunstgeschichte des abendländische Mittelalters,* edited by Schlosser. Vienna, 1896.

Schnitzer, Joseph. *Savonarola.* 2 vols. Munich, 1924.

Schottmüller, Frida. *Die Bildwerke in Stein, Holz, Ton und Wachs. Die italienischen und spanischen Bildwerke der Renaissance und des Barock.* 2nd edition. Berlin and Leipzig, 1933. Catalogue of the Berlin Museums.

————. *Wohnungskultur und Möbel der italienischen Renaissance.* Bauformenbibliothek, 12. 2nd edition. Stuttgart, 1928.

Schubring, Paul. *Cassoni. Truhen und Truhenbilder der italienischen Frührenaissance.* 2 vols. Leipzig, 1915.

————. *Die italienische Plastik des Quattrocento.* Handbuch der Kunstwissenschaft. Berlin, 1915.

Semper, Hans. *Donatello. Seine Zeit und Schule.* Quellenschriften für Kunstgeschichte, 9. Vienna, 1875.

Straelen-Conrad, Hildegard van. *Studien zur florentiner Glasmalerei des Trecento und Quattrocento.* Wattenscheid, 1938. [*Translator's note*: Not appearing in the original bibliography, but appearing frequently in the author's notes.]

Thode, Henry. *Michelangelo und das Ende der Renaissance. Kritische Untersuchungen über seine Werke.* 6 vols. Berlin, 1902-1913.

Tinti, Mario. *Il mobilio fiorentino.* Milan, 1928.
    With 320 plates.

Venturi, Lionello. *Pitture italiane in America.* Milan, 1931.

Walser, Ernst. *Gesammelte Studien zur Geistesgeschichte der Renaissance.* Basel, 1932.

Warburg, Aby. *Bildniskunst und florentinisches Bürgertum.* Leipzig, 1902.

————. "Francesco Sassettis letztwillige Verfügung." In *Kunstwissenschaftliche Beiträge August Schmarsow gewidmet zum fünfzigsten Semester seiner akademischen Lehrtätigkeit,* edited by H. Weizsäcker et al., pp. 129ff. Leipzig, 1907.

————. *Gesammelte Schriften.* Edited by Gertrud Bing and Fritz Rougemont. 2 vols. Leipzig, 1932.
    This includes the above essays and other pertinent essays, some expanded by supplements.

Weisbach, Werner. *Francesco Pesellino und die Romantik der Frührenaissance.* Berlin, 1901.

———. *Trionfi.* Berlin, 1919.

Wilder Weismann, Elisabeth; Bacci, Pèleo; and Kennedy, Clarence. *The unfinished monument by Andrea del Verrocchio to the Cardinal Niccolò Forteguerri at Pistoia.* Florence, 1932.

Yriarte, Charles. *Florence, L'histoire, les Médicis, les humanistes, les lettres, les arts.* Paris, 1881.

# TRANSLATOR'S BIBLIOGRAPHY

The Translator's Bibliography represents a survey of literature since 1938 (including several doctoral dissertations) on topics covered in Wackernagel's work. In rare cases a book published before his work and omitted by him is listed, as are some English translations and new Italian editions of important early sources. The criteria for selection of specialized studies included their relevance to the Florentine Renaissance, especially from 1420 to 1530, their treatment of recurring themes in Florentine art, and their importance for the study of relationships between Florentine art and its social context.

In general, monographs on individual masters are not listed here; the sheer number and wide range of quality made this impractical. For literature on specific artists the reader is referred to the bibliographies of books under the heading IB; to the *Encyclopedia of World Art*, 15 volumes (New York, 1959-1968); and to periodical literature, which may be traced through the *Art Index*, the *Répertoire d'art et archéologie*, and, beginning in 1975, the *Répertoire internationale de la littérature de l'art*. The *Répertoire* citations include new monographs on artists.

Architecture, omitted by Wackernagel, appears here in a list of general works and specific studies that deal with major Florentine monuments or, like James Ackerman's *Architecture of Michelangelo*, have a significance for the study of Renaissance architecture and patronage transcending their immediate subject.

An exhaustive compilation of early sources, guidebooks, and editions of treatises and artists' writings published up to 1964 is Julius von Schlosser's *La Letteratura Artistica*, 3rd Italian edition with additions by Otto Kurz (Florence and Vienna, 1967).

Collection catalogues are listed as such only for museums, collections, and sites in Florence itself. Again exceptions were made for a few catalogues that are basic references for a wider topic.

The bibliography is organized into the following parts:

I. General Studies
  A. Political, Social, and
    Intellectual History
  B. Art
  C. Life, Shop Practice, and
    Organization of Artists
  D. Early Sources and Documents,
    Recent Editions, and English
    Translations
  E. Art Historiography

II. Painting
  A. Surveys and Special Problems
  B. Fresco
  C. Stained Glass and Manuscript
    Illumination
  D. Textiles and Intarsia

III. Sculpture
  A. Surveys and Special Problems
  B. Medals, Small Bronzes, and
    Plaquettes

IV. Drawing and Graphic Arts

V. Architecture
  A. Surveys and Special Problems
  B. Florentine Buildings and Their
    Decoration
    1. Churches, Hospitals,
      and Libraries
    2. Palaces and Loggie
    3. Villas and Gardens

VI. Theater, Festival, and Spectacle

# I. GENERAL STUDIES

## A. Political, Social, and Intellectual History

Ady, Cecilia. *Lorenzo de' Medici and Renaissance Italy*. London, 1955.

Baron, Hans. *The Crisis of the Early Italian Renaissance*. 2 vols. Princeton, N.J., 1955. 2nd ed. rev. 1966.

Bayley, C. C. *War and Society in Renaissance Florence*. Toronto, 1961. Deals with the period before 1434.

Brucker, Gene. *The Civic World of Early Renaissance Florence*. Princeton, N.J., 1977.

————. *Renaissance Florence*. New York, 1969. Includes a valuable discussion of Florentine culture and highly useful bibliographic notes.

————, ed. *The Society of Renaissance Florence: A Documentary Study*. New York, 1971.

Burckhardt, Jacob C. *The Civilization of the Renaissance in Italy*. Translated by S.G.C. Middlemore. London, 1878. From *Die Cultur der Renaissance in Italien*. 3rd edition. Leipzig, 1877-1878. Various subsequent editions.

Conti, Elio. *I Catasti agrari della Repubblica Fiorentina*. Rome, 1966.

Davidsohn, Robert. *Storia di Firenze*. Translated by Giovanni Battista Klein. Florence, 1956-1965. From *Geschichte von Florenz*. Berlin, 1896-1927.

Garin, Eugenio. *Italian Humanism*. Translated by Peter Munz. New York, 1965. From *L'umanesimo italiano*. Bari, 1952.

Goldthwaite, Richard. *Private Wealth in Renaissance Florence*. Princeton, N.J., 1968. Concerns the Strozzi, Guicciardini, Gondi, and Capponi families.

Hay, Denys. *The Church in Italy in the Fifteenth Century*. Cambridge, 1977.

————. *The Italian Renaissance in its Historical Background*. Cambridge, 1961. 2nd edition. 1977.

Helton, Tinsley, ed. *The Renaissance. A Reconsideration of the Theories and Interpretations of the Age*. Madison, Wis., 1961.

Herlihy, David, and Klapisch-Zuber, Christiane. *Les Toscans et leurs Familles*. Paris, 1978. Based on years of analysis of *catasto* records.

Holmes, George. *The Florentine Enlightenment 1400-1450*. London, 1969.

Kent, Dale. *The Rise of the Medici: Faction in Florence 1426-1434*. New York, 1978.

Kent, F. William. *Household and Lineage in Renaissance Florence: The Family Life of the Capponi, Ginori, and Rucellai*. Princeton, N.J., 1977.

Kristeller, Paul O. *Renaissance Thought*. Paperback edition. New York, 1961.
*The Classics and Renaissance Thought*. 1st edition. Cambridge, Mass., 1955.
———. *Renaissance Thought II*. New York, 1965.
Martin, Alfred von. *Sociology of the Renaissance*. Translated by W. L. Luetkens. New York, 1963. From *Soziologie der Renaissance*. Stuttgart, 1932.
Martinelli, Giuseppe, ed. *The World of Renaissance Florence*. Translated by Walter Darwell. New York, 1968. From *Tutto su Firenze Rinascimentale*. Florence, 1964.
Its abundance of illustrations makes this perhaps the closest visual counterpart to Wackernagel's book, although illustration sources are often inadequately identified.
Martines, Lauro. *Lawyers and Statecraft in Renaissance Florence*. Princeton, N.J., 1968.
———. *The Social World of the Florentine Humanists 1390-1460*. Princeton, N.J., 1963.
Rochon, André. *La Jeunesse de Laurent de Médicis (1449-1478)*. Paris, 1963.
de Roover, Raymond. *The Rise and Decline of the Medici Bank 1397-1494*. Cambridge, Mass., 1963.
Rubinstein, Nicolai. *The Government of Florence under the Medici (1434-1494)*. Oxford, 1966.
———, ed. *Florentine Studies: Politics and Society in Renaissance Florence*. London, 1968.
Sapori, Armando. *Compagnie e mercanti di Firenze antica*. Florence, 1955.
Illustrated with fifteenth-century drawings of churches from the Rustici Codex, with commentary by Ugo Procacci.
Weinstein, Donald. *Savonarola and Florence. Prophesy and Patriotism in the Renaissance*. Princeton, N.J., 1971.

## B. Art

Blunt, Anthony. *Artistic Theory in Italy 1450-1600*. Oxford, 1940. Numerous subsequent editions.
Burke, Peter. *Culture and Society in Renaissance Italy 1420-1540*. London, 1972. Revised edition published as *Tradition and Innovation in Renaissance Italy: a Sociological Approach*. London, 1974.
Chastel, André. *Art et humanisme à Florence au temps de Laurent le Magnifique; études sur la Renaissance et l'humanisme platonicien*. Paris, 1959. 2nd edition. 1961.
A study of the late Quattrocento with detail and documentation on a level with Wackernagel's.
———. *The Flowering of the Italian Renaissance*. Translated by Jonathan Griffin. New York, 1965. Published as *The Golden Age of the Renaissance: Italy, 1460-1500*. London, 1965. From *Renaissance méridionale: Italie 1460-1500*. Paris, 1965.
———. *Italian Art*. Translated by Peter and Linda Murray. New York 1963; New York, 1972. From *L'art italien*. 2 vols. Paris, 1956.
———. *Marsile Ficin et l'art*. Geneva, 1954.

Chastel, André. *The Myth of the Renaissance, 1420-1520*. Translated by Stuart Gilbert. Geneva, 1969. From *Le mythe de la Renaissance, 1420-1520*. Geneva, 1969.

————. *Studios and Styles of the Italian Renaissance, 1460-1500*. Translated by Jonathan Griffin. New York, 1971. From *Le grand atelier d'Italie, 1460-1500*. Paris, 1965.

Chastel, André, and Klein, Robert. *The Age of Humanism*. Translated by Katherine M. Delavenay and E. M. Gwyer. London, 1963; New York, 1964. From *L'age de l'humanisme: l'Europe de la Renaissance*. Paris, 1963.

Decker, Heinrich. *The Renaissance in Italy: Architecture, Sculpture, Frescoes*. London, 1969. From *Renaissance in Italien*. Vienna, 1967.

Gilbert, Creighton. *History of Renaissance Art: Painting, Sculpture, Architecture Throughout Europe*. New York, 1973.

————, ed. *Renaissance Art*. New York, 1970.

Gombrich, E. H. *The Heritage of Apelles. Studies in the Art of the Renaissance*. Vol. 3. Ithaca, N.Y., 1976.

————. *Norm and Form. Studies in the Art of the Renaissance*. Vol. 1. London, 1966.

————. *Symbolic Images. Studies in the Art of the Renaissance*. Vol. 2. London, 1972.

Hartt, Frederick. "Art and Freedom in Quattrocento Florence." In *Essays in Memory of Karl Lehmann*, edited by Lucy Freeman Sandler, pp. 114-31. New York University, Institute of Fine Arts, *Marsyas Supplement I*. New York, 1964. Reprinted, abridged, in *Modern Perspectives in Western Art History*, edited by W. Eugene Kleinbauer, pp. 293-311. New York, 1971.

————. *History of Italian Renaissance Art*. New York, 1969. 2nd edition. 1979. Extremely valuable bibliography, including list of artist monographs, mostly in English.

Hauser, Arnold. *The Social History of Art*. Translated in collaboration with the author by S. Godman. Vol. 2. London, 1951.

Heydenreich, Ludwig H. *Italienische Renaissance*. 4 vols. Munich, 1972-1975. French edition, *La Renaissance italienne*. Paris, 1972ff.

Janson, H. W. *16 Studies*. New York, 1974.

Keller, Harald. *The Renaissance in Italy: painting, sculpture, architecture*. Translated by Robert E. Wolf. New York, 1974. Italian edition, *Il Rinascimento italiano*. Florence, 1969.

Krey, August C. *A City that Art Built*. Minneapolis, 1936. Reprinted in *History and the Social Web*. Minneapolis, 1955, pp. 135-74.

Larner, John. *Culture and Society in Italy 1290-1420*. New York, 1971. The closest counterpart to Wackernagel for the Trecento and early Quattrocento, though concerned with more than the visual arts; excellent bibliographic notes.

Lee, Rensselaer W. "Ut Pictura Poesis: The Humanist Theory of Painting." *Art Bulletin*, 22, 1940, pp. 197-269. Reprinted as a book with new preface. New York, 1967.

Levey, Michael. *Early Renaissance*. Harmondsworth, 1967.

————. *High Renaissance*. Harmondsworth and Baltimore, 1975.

Lopez, R. S. "Hard Times and Investment in Culture." In *The Renaissance: a Symposium*, edited by Wallace K. Ferguson, pp. 19-32. New York, 1953. Reprinted as *The Renaissance: Six Essays*, pp. 29-54. New York, 1962. Also in *Social and Economic Foundations of the Italian Renaissance*, edited by Anthony Molho, pp. 95-116. New York, 1969.

Meiss, Millard. *The Painter's Choice: Problems in the Interpretation of Renaissance Art*. New York, 1976.

———. *Painting in Florence and Siena after the Black Death*. Princeton, N.J., 1951; New York, 1964.

A classic study of the impact of cataclysmic social change on artistic style and content in the fourteenth century.

Murray, Linda, *The High Renaissance*. New York, 1967.

Murray, Peter, and Murray, Linda. *The Art of the Renaissance*. New York and Washingston, D.C., 1963.

Mutini, Claudio. *La cultura a Firenze al tempo di Lorenzo il Magnifico*. Bologna, 1970.

Paatz, Walter. *The Arts of the Italian Renaissance: Painting, Sculpture, Architecture*. New York, 1974.

Includes useful bibliography and some unusual illustrations.

Panofsky, Erwin, *Meaning in the Visual Arts*. Garden City, N.Y., 1955. Reprinted, Woodstock, N.Y., 1974.

———. *Renaissance and Renascences in Western Art*. 2 vols. Stockholm, 1960. Numerous subsequent editions.

Classic study on the definition of the Renaissance.

———. *Studies in Iconology: Humanistic Themes in the Art of the Renaissance*. New York, 1939. 2nd edition. 1962.

Plumb, J. H. et al. *The Horizon Book of the Renaissance*. New York, 1961. Extremely useful illustrations.

Procacci, Ugo. "L'uso dei documenti negli studi di storia dell'arte e le vicende politiche ed economiche in Firenze durante il primo Quattrocento nel loro rapporti con gli artisti." In *Donatello e il suo tempo. Atti dell' VIII Convegno internazionale di studi sul Rinascimento, Firenze-Padoua, 25 settembre-1 ottobre, 1966*, edited by Istituto Nazionale di Studi sul Rinascimento. Florence, 1968, pp. 11-39.

Singleton, Charles, ed. *Art, Science and History in the Renaissance*. Baltimore, 1967.

Smart, Alastair. *The Renaissance and Mannerism in Italy*. New York, 1971.

Steinberg, Ronald M. *Fra Girolamo Savonarola, Florentine Art, and Renaissance Historiography*. Athens, Ohio, 1977.

*Studies in Western Art: Acts of the 20th International Congress of the History of Art, vol. 2: The Renaissance and Mannerism*. Edited by Meillard Meiss. Princeton, N.J., 1963.

Trexler, Richard C. "Florentine Religious Experience: The Sacred Image." *Studies in the Renaissance*, 19, 1972, pp. 7-41.

Concerned especially with the public cult of "miraculous images."

Warburg, Aby. *La rinascita del paganesimo antico; contributi alla storia della cultura*. Translated by Emma Cantimori. Florence, 1966. From *Gesammelte Schriften*, edited by Gertrud Bing and Fritz Rougemont. Leipzig, 1932.

Wind, Edgar. *Pagan Mysteries in the Renaissance*. New Haven, 1958. Revised edition. New York, 1968.

Wölfflin, Heinrich. *Classic Art: An Introduction to the Italian Renaissance*. Translated by Peter Murray and Linda Murray. New York, 1952. Various subsequent editions. From *Die Klassische Kunst*. Munich, 1899.

Wundram, Manfred. Art of the Renaissance. Translated by Francisca Garvie. New York, 1972. From *Renaissance*. Stuttgart, 1970.

———. *Frührenaissance*. Baden-Baden, 1970.
Exceptionally valuable bibliography.

## C. Life, Shop Practice, and Organization of Artists

Camesasca, Ettore. *Artisti in bottega*. Milan, 1966.

Chastel, André. "Vasari économiste." In *Mélanges en l'honneure de Fernand Braudel*, vol. 1, pp. 145-50. Toulouse, 1973.

Fehm, S. "Notes on the Statutes of the Sienese Painters' Guild." *Art Bulletin*, 54, 1972, pp. 198-200.

Glasser, Hannelore. *Artists' Contracts of the Early Renaissance*. New York, 1977.

Goldstein, Carl. "Vasari and the Florentine Accademia del Disegno." *Zeitschrift für Kunstgeschichte*, 38, 1975, pp. 145-52.

Gombrich, E. H. "The Leaven of Criticism in Renaissance Art: Texts and Episodes." In *Art, Science and History in the Renaissance*, edited by Charles S. Singleton, pp. 3-42. Baltimore, 1967. Reprinted in *The Heritage of Apelles*, pp. 111-31. Ithaca, N.Y., 1976.
Concerns the question of art as problem-solving.

———. "The Renaissance Conception of Artistic Progress and its Consequences." In *Norm and Form*, pp. 1-10. London, 1966. First presented as a paper at XVIIe Congrès International d'Histoire de l'Art, Amsterdam, July, 1952.

Harris, Ann Sutherland, and Nochlin, Linda. *Women Artists: 1550-1950*. Los Angeles County Museum of Art and New York, 1977.
This exhibition catalogue includes a useful discussion of women artists in Italy before 1550.

Jack, Mary Ann. "The Accademia del Disegno in Late Renaissance Florence." *The Sixteenth Century Journal*, 7, 1976, pp. 3-20.
Useful also on earlier organizations. See also her doctoral dissertation, Mary Ann Jack Ward, *The Accademia del Disegno in Sixteenth Century Florence: a Study of an Artists' Institution*. University of Chicago, 1972.

Janson, H. W. "The Image Made by Chance in Renaissance Thought." In *De Artibus Opuscula XL. Essays in Honor of Erwin Panofsky*, edited by Millard Meiss, pp. 254-66. New York, 1961. Reprinted in *16 Studies*, pp. 53-74. New York, 1974.

Martindale, Andrew. *The Rise of the Artist in the Middle Ages and Early Renaissance*. New York, 1972.

Mather, Rufus. "Il primo registro della Compagnia di S. Luca." *L'Arte*, 9, 1938, pp. 351-57.

Petersen, Karen, and Wilson, J. J. *Women Artists: Recognition and Reappraisal from the Early Middle Ages to the 20th Century.* New York, 1977.

Pevsner, Nikolaus. *Academies of Art, Past and Present.* Cambridge and New York, 1940. With a new preface, New York, 1973.

Procacci, Ugo. "Di Jacopo d'Antonio e delle compagnie di pittori del Corso degli Adimari nel XV. secolo." *Rivista d'Arte,* 24, 1961, pp. 3ff.

Sheard, Wendy S., and Paoletti, John T., eds. *Collaboration in Italian Renaissance Art.* New Haven, 1977.

Thomas, Anabel. *Workshop Procedure of Fifteenth-Century Florentine Artists.* Doctoral dissertation, Courtauld Institute of Art, London, 1976.

Wittkower, Rudolf, and Wittkower, Margo. *Born Under Saturn. The Character and Conduct of Artists. A Documented History from Antiquity to the French Revolution.* London, 1963.

## D. Early Sources and Documents, Recent Editions, and English Translations

Alberti, Leon Battista. *De Re Aedificatoria.* Edited by G. Orlandi and P. Portoghesi. Milan, 1966. Annotated Latin and Italian versions.

———. *The Family in Renaissance Florence.* Edited and translated by Renee New Watkins. Columbia, S.C. 1969.

———. *On Painting.* Translated by John R. Spencer. London, 1956. Subsequent editions.

———. *On Painting and On Sculpture.* Edited and translated by Cecil Grayson. New York, 1972.

———. *Ten Books on Architecture.* Edited by Joseph Rykwert and translated by James Leoni. London, 1955. Reprint of 1755 edition.

Bacci, Pèleo. *Documenti e commenti per la storia dell'arte.* Florence, 1944.

Barocchi, Paola, ed. *Scritti d'Arte del Cinquecento.* Milan and Naples, 1971. Turin, 1977.

———. *Trattati d'Arte del Cinquecento fra Manierismo e Controriforma.* 3 vols. Bari, 1960-1962.

Castiglione, Baldassare. *The Book of the Courtier.* Translated by Charles Singleton. Garden City, N.Y., 1959.

Cellini, Benvenuto. *The Life of Benvenuto Cellini.* Translated by John Addington Symonds. London, 1888. Edited by John Pope-Hennessy. London, 1949. Various subsequent editions.

———. *Opere (vita, trattati, rime, lettere).* Edited by Bruno Maier. Milan, 1968.

———. *La Vita, I Trattati, I Discorsi.* Edited by P. Scarpellini. Rome, 1967.

Cennini, Cennino. *Il Libro dell'Arte.* Edited by F. Brunello. Vicenza, 1971.

———. *Il Libro dell'Arte; the Craftsmans' Handbook.* Edited and translated by D. V. Thompson. 2 vols. New Haven, Conn. and New York, 1933. Translated only, New York, 1954.

Chambers, David Sanderson, ed. and trans. *Patrons and Artists in the Italian Renaissance.* London, 1970. Columbia, S.C., 1971.

Condivi, Ascanio. *The Life of Michelangelo.* Edited by Helmut Wohl and translated by Alice Sedgwick Wohl. Baton Rouge, La., 1976.

———. *Vita di Michelangelo Buonarroti.* Edited by E. Spina Baretti. Milan, 1964.

Corti, Gino, and Hartt, Frederick. "New Documents Concerning Donatello [and 8 others]," *Art Bulletin*, 44, 1962, pp. 155-67.

Dolce, Lodovico. *Dolce's Aretino and Venetian Art Theory of the Cinquecento*. Edited and translated by Mark Roskill. New York, 1968.

Filarete (Antonio Averlino). *Trattato di Architettura*. Edited by Anna Maria Finoli Grassi and Liliana Grassi. 2 vols. Milan, 1972.

————. *Treatise on Architecture*. Edited and translated by John R. Spencer. 2 vols. New Haven, Conn., 1965.
Includes a facsimile of the Magliabecchiana manuscript in Florence (Bib. Naz., Magl. II, I, 140).

Francesco di Giorgio (Martini). *Trattati di Architettura, Ingegneria e Arte Militare*. Edited by C. Maltese. 2 vols. Milan, 1967.

Gauricus, Pomponius. *De Sculptura*. Florence, 1504. French edition with notes by André Chastel and Robert Klein. Paris and Geneva, 1969.

Ghiberti, Lorenzo. *I Commentarii*. Edited by Ottavio Morisani. Naples, 1947.

Gilbert, Creighton. *Italian Art, 1400-1500. Sources and Documents*. Englewood Cliffs, N.J., 1980.
This work includes numerous English translations of texts cited but not quoted at length by Wackernagel.

Guicciardini, Francesco. *History of Florence and History of Italy*. Edited by John Hale and translated by Cecil Grayson. New York, 1964.

Hollanda, Francesco de. *Four Dialogues on Painting*. Translated by Aubrey F. G. Bell. London, 1928.

Holt, Elizabeth Gilmore, ed. *A Documentary History of Art*: Vol. 1, *The Middle Ages and the Renaissance*. Garden City, N.Y., 1957. Vol. 2, *Michelangelo and the Mannerists. The Baroque and the Eighteenth Century*. Garden City, N.Y., 1957.

Klein, Robert, and Zerner, Henri. *Italian Art, 1500-1600. Sources and Documents*. Englewood Cliffs, N.J., 1966.

Landucci, Luca. *A Florentine Diary from 1450-1516*. Translated by Alice de Rosen. London. 1927.

Leonardo da Vinci. *Il Codice Atlantico. Edizione in facsimile dopo il restauro dell'originale conservato nella Biblioteca Ambrosiana di Milano*. Florence, 1973—.

————. *The Literary Works of Leonardo da Vinci*. Edited by Jean Paul Richter and Irma Richter. 2 vols. London, 1939. 2nd edition. London and New York, 1955. New edition with commentary by Carlo Pedretti. Berkeley and Los Angeles, 1977.

————. *The Notebooks*. Translated by Edward McCurdy. 2 vols. New York, 1938.

————. *The Notebooks of Leonardo da Vinci: A New Selection*. Edited by P. Taylor. New York, 1960.

————. *Treatise on Painting (Cod. Urb. Lat. 1270)*. Edited and translated by A. P. McMahon. 2 vols. Princeton, 1956.

*Leonardo da Vinci on Painting: A Lost Book (Libro A)*. Edited by Carlo Pedretti. Berkeley, 1964.

Lomazzo, Giovanni Paolo. *Idea del Tempio della Pittura*. Edited and translated by Robert Klein. 2 vols. Florence, 1974.

———. *Scritti sulle Arti*. Edited by Robert Paolo Ciardi. 2 vols. Florence, 1973-1974.

Machiavelli, Niccolò. *The History of Florence and Other Selections*. Edited by Myron P. Gilmore and translated by Julia A. Rawson. New York, 1970.

Manetti, Antonio. *The Life of Brunelleschi*. Edited by Howard Saalman and translated by C. Enggass. University Park, Pa., 1970.
English and Italian.

Martines, Julia, trans. *Two Memoirs of Renaissance Florence. The Diaries of Buonaccorso Pitti and Gregorio Dati*. Edited by Gene Brucker. New York, 1967.
Late fourteenth to early fifteenth century.

Maso di Bartolommeo. *The Notebooks of Maso di Bartolommeo*. Edited by Harriet Caplow. Forthcoming.

Mather, Rufus. "Documents, Mostly New, Relating to Florentine Painters and Sculptors of the Fifteenth Century." *Art Bulletin*, 30, 1948, pp. 20-65.
*Catasto* declarations for eighteen major Florentine artists and artist families.

Michelangelo. *Complete Poems and Selected Letters of Michelangelo*. Edited by R. N. Linscott and translated by Creighton Gilbert. New York, 1963. 2nd edition with foreward and notes by Creighton Gilbert. New York, 1965.

———. *The Letters of Michelangelo*. Edited and translated by E. H. Ramsden. 2 vols. Palo Alto, Calif., 1963.

Morelli, Giovanni. *Ricordi*. Edited by V. Branca. Florence, 1955.
Written from 1393-1421.

Neri di Bicci. *Le Ricordanze (10 marzo 1435 - 24 aprile 1475)*. Pisa and Leiden, 1977.

Piero della Francesca. *De Prospettiva Pingendi*. Edited by G. Nicco Fasola. Florence, 1942.

Pino, Paolo. *Dialogo della Pittura*. Edited by E. Camesasca. Milan, 1954.

Pontormo, Jacopo. *Jacopo Pontormo. Diario*. Edited by Emilio Cecchi. Florence, 1956.

Rucellai, Giovanni. *Il Zibaldone Quaresimale*. Vol. 1. *Giovanni Rucellai ed il suo Zibaldone*. Edited by Alessandro Perosa. London, 1960.
A second volume is due out shortly.

Vasari, Giorgio. *The Lives of the Painters, Sculptors and Architects*. Translated by Gaston De Vere. 10 vols. London, 1912-1915.

———. *Vasari on Technique*. Edited by G. Baldwin Brown and translated by Louisa L. Maclehose. From the *Lives*. London, 1907. Various subsequent editions.

———. *La vita di Michelangelo nelle redazioni del 1550 e del 1568*. Edited by Paola Barocchi. 5 vols. Milan and Naples, 1962.

———. *Le Vite de' piu eccellenti pittori, scultori e architettori nelle redazioni del 1550 e 1568*. Edited by Rosanna Bettarini and Paola Barocchi. Florence, 1966ff.

Vespasiano da Bisticci. *The Vespasiano Memoirs. Lives of Illustrious Men of the*

*XVth Century*. Translated by William George and Emily Waters. London, 1926. Reprinted as *Renaissance Princes, Popes and Prelates: The Vespasiano Memoirs*. New York, 1963.

### E. Art Historiography

Boase, T.S.R. *Vasari: The Man and the Book*. Princeton, N.J., 1978.

Burke, Peter. *Culture and Society in Renaissance Italy 1420-1540*. London, 1972.
The introduction contains a useful discussion of Renaissance historiography.

Castelnuovo, Enrico. "Per una storia sociale dell'arte." *Paragone*, 27, 1976, pp. 3-25, and 28, 1977, pp. 3-34.

Kallab, Wolfgang. *Vasaristudien*. Vienna and Leipzig, 1908.
Not mentioned in Wackernagel's work but crucial for the study of Vasari as a source of information on artists.

Kleinbauer, Eugene, ed. *Modern Perspectives in Western Art History*. New York, 1971.
Extremely useful introductions discussing approaches to art history and writers who followed them.

Kultermann, Udo. *Geschichte der Kunstgeschichte*. Vienna and Dusseldorf, 1966.

Prinz, Wolfram. *Vasaris Sammlung von Künstlerbildnissen*. Mitteilungen des Kunsthistorischen Institutes in Florenz, 12, supplement. Florence, 1966.

Ragghianti Collobi, Licia. *Il Libro de' Disegni del Vasari*. 2 vols. Florence, 1974.

Rud, Einar. *Vasari's Life and Lives: The First Art Historian*. Translated by Reginald Spink. London, 1963. From *Giorgio Vasari, renaissancens kunsthistoriker; en biografi*. Copenhagen, 1961.

Schlosser, Julius von. *Die Kunstliteratur*, Vienna, 1924. First Italian edition, *La Letteratura Artistica*, translated by Filippo Rossi. Florence, 1935. 3rd Italian edition. Florence and Vienna, 1964.
Crucial study of primary sources, writings by and about artists in their own time, and topographical literature.

*Studi Vasariani: atti del Convegno internazionale per il IV centenario della prima edizione delle "Vite" del Vasari, Firenze, Palazzo Strozzi, 16-19 settembre 1950*. Edited by Istituto Nazionale di Studi sul Rinascimento. Florence, 1952.

*Il Vasari storiografo e artista: Atti del Congresso internationale nel IV centenario della morte, Arezzo-Firenze 2-8 settembre 1974*. Edited by Istituto Nazionale di Studi sul Rinascimento. Florence, 1976.

## II. PAINTING

### A. Surveys and Special Problems

Alazard, Jean. *The Florentine Portrait*. Translated by Barbara Whelpton. London, 1948. New York, 1968. From *Le Portrait florentin de Botticelli a Bronzino*. Paris, 1924.

Antal, Frederick. *Florentine Painting and its Social Background; the Bourgeois Republic before Cosimo de' Medici's Advent to Power, Fourteenth and Early Fifteenth Centuries*. London, 1948. 2nd edition. Boston, 1965.

Baxandall, Michael. *Giotto and the Orators: Humanist Observers of Painting in Italy and the Discovery of Pictorial Composition 1350-1450*. New York, 1971.

Concerns art theory and terminology.

———. *Painting and Experience in Fifteenth Century Italy*. London, 1972.

Concerns various levels of perception of art by a Renaissance audience, including terminology of art criticism.

Berenson, Bernard. *Italian Painters of the Renaissance*. London, 1952. Revised edition, 1967.

———. *Italian Pictures of the Renaissance: Florentine School*. 2 vols. London, 1963.

Bergstrom, Ingvar. "Medicina . . . a study in van Eyckean symbolism and its influence in Italian art." *Konsthistorisk Tidskrift*, 26, 1957, pp. 1-20.

Birbari, Elizabeth. *Dress in Italian Painting, 1460-1500*. London, 1975.

Boskovits, Miklos. *Tuscan Painting of the Early Renaissance*. Budapest, 1969.

Callmann, Ellen, *Apollonio di Giovanni*. Oxford, 1974.

Useful for *cassone* painting and secular subject matter in general, especially mythology.

Covi, Dario A. "Lettering in Fifteenth-Century Florentine Painting." *Art Bulletin*, 45, 1963, pp. 1-17.

The meanings of various types of lettering, illustrated with numerous examples.

Cremer, Leo, and Eikemeier, Peter. *Italienische Bilderrahmen des 14-18 Jahrhunderts*, exhibition catalogue, Munich, Bayerische Staatsgemäldesammlungen, 6 May-31 October 1976. Munich, 1976.

Davies, Martin. *National Gallery Catalogues: The Earlier Italian Schools*. London, 1961.

Exceptionally thorough studies of the numerous important Florentine paintings in London.

Dewald, Ernest T. *Italian Painting 1200-1600*. New York, 1961.

Ettlinger, L. D. "A Fifteenth-century View of Florence." *Burlington Magazine*, 94, 1952, pp. 160-67.

Fahy, Everett. "Les cadres d'origine de retables florentins du Louvre." *Revue du Louvre*, 26, 1976, pp. 6-14.

Fiocco, Giuseppe. *La pittura toscana del Quattrocento*. Novara, 1941.

Fredericksen, Burton B., and Zeri, Federico. *Census of Pre-Nineteenth Century Italian Paintings in North American Public Collections*. Cambridge, Mass., 1972.

Freedberg, Sydney J. *Painting of the High Renaissance in Rome and Florence*. 2 vols. Cambridge, Mass., 1961. New York, 1972.

———. *Painting in Italy, 1500-1600*. Harmondsworth and Baltimore, 1971. Revised edition, 1975.

Fremantle, Richard. *Florentine Gothic Painters from Giotto to Masaccio: A Guide to Painting in and near Florence, 1300 to 1450*. London, 1975.

Gardner, Christa. *Studies of the Tuscan Altarpiece in the 14th and Early 15th Centuries*. Doctoral dissertation, Courtauld Institute of Art, London, 1976.

Gilbert, Creighton. "The Archbishop on the Painters of Florence, 1450." *Art Bulletin*, 41, 1959, pp. 75-87.

Gilbert, Creighton. "Peintres et menuisiers au début de la Renaissance en Italie." *Revue de l'Art*, 37, 1977, pp. 9ff.
Concerns panels and frames and relationships between painters' and carpenters' workshops.

Gombrich, E. H. "Apollonio di Giovanni: A Florentine Cassone Workshop through the Eyes of a Humanist Poet." *Journal of the Warburg and Courtauld Institutes*, 18, 1955, pp. 16-34. Reprinted in *Norm and Form*, pp. 11-28. London, 1966.

———. "Botticelli's Mythologies: A Study in the Neo-Platonic Symbolism of his Circle." *Journal of the Warburg and Courtauld Institutes*, 8, 1945, pp. 7-60. Reprinted, with updating introduction, in *Symbolic Images*, pp. 31-81. London, 1972.

———. "Tobias and the Angel." In *Symbolic Images*, pp. 26-30. London, 1972. Expanded from an essay in *Harvest*, 1, 1948, pp. 63-67.

Gould, Cecil. *An Introduction to Italian Renaissance Painting*. London, 1957.

Hager, Hellmut. *Die Anfänge des Italienischen Altarbildes: Untersuchung zur Entstehungsgeschichte des toskanischen Hochaltarretabels*. Munich, 1962.

Hale, John. *Italian Renaissance Painting from Masaccio to Titian*. Oxford and New York, 1977.

Hatfield, Rab. *Botticelli's Uffizi "Adoration": A Study in Pictorial Content*. Princeton, 1976.
The *Adoration of the Magi* theme in Florence.

———. "Five Early Renaissance Portraits." *Art Bulletin*, 47, 1965, pp. 315-35.

Kaftal, George. *Iconography of the Saints in Tuscan Painting*. Florence, 1952.
A copious and fundamental study, richly illustrated.

Kasper, Karl. *Der ikonographische Entwicklung der Sacra Conversazione in der italienischen Kunst der Renaissance*. Doctoral dissertation, Kunsthistorisches Institut der Universität, Tübingen, 1954.

Kocks, Dirk. *Die Stifterdarstellung in der italienischen Malerei des 13-15 Jahrhunderts*. Doctoral dissertation, Kunsthistorisches Institut der Universität, Cologne, 1971.

Lesher, Melinda. *The Vision of St. Bernard and the Chapel of the Priors: Private and Public Images of Bernard of Clairvaux in Renaissance Florence*. Doctoral dissertation, Columbia University, 1979.

Markowski, Barbara. "Eine Gruppe bemalter Paliotti in Florenz und der Toskana und ihre textilen Vorbilder." *Mitteilungen des Kunsthistorischen Institutes in Florenz*, 17, 1973, pp. 105-140.

Meiss, Millard. "Jan van Eyck and the Italian Renaissance," *Venezia e l'Europa. Atti del XVIII Congresso Internazionale di Storia dell' Arte, 1955*, pp. 58-69. Venice, 1956. Reprinted in *The Painter's Choice*, pp. 19-35. New York, 1976.

———. "A New Monumental Painting by Filippino Lippi." *Art Bulletin*, 55, 1973, pp. 479-93.
Useful for northern influence on Florentine painting.

———. "Scholarship and Penitence in the Early Renaissance; the Image of St. Jerome." *Pantheon*, 32, 1974, pp. 134-40. Reprinted in *The Painter's Choice*, pp. 189-202. New York, 1976.

Mode, Robert. "San Bernardino in Glory." *Art Bulletin*, 55, 1973, pp. 58-76.

van Os, H. W., and Prakken, Marian, eds. *The Florentine Paintings in Holland, 1300-1500.* Maarssen, 1974.
Useful for style, technique, function, iconography, bibliography.

Panhans, Gunter. "Florentiner Maler verarbeiten ein Eyckisches Bild." *Wiener Jahrbuch für Kunstgeschichte*, 27, 1974, pp. 188ff.

Preiser, Arno. *Das Entstehen und die Entwicklung der Predella in der italienischen Malerei.* Hildesheim, 1973.

Ressort, Claudie; Béguin, Sylvie; and Laclotte, Michel. *Retables italiens du XIIIe au XVe siècle*, exhibition catalogue, Paris, Musée du Louvre, 14 October 1977-15 Jan. 1978. Paris, 1978.

Ringbom, Sixten. *Icon to Narrative: The Rise of the Dramatic Close-up in Fifteenth-Century Devotional Painting.* Acta Academiae Aboensis, Ser. A, vol. 31, no. 2, Abo, 1965.
A well-documented study of the role of images in private devotion, concerned especially with the themes of Madonna and Child, suffering Christ, Man of Sorrows, and Salvator Mur.di.

Salvini, Roberto, and Traverso, Leone. *The Predella from the XIIIth to the XVI Centuries.* London, 1960. Translated from *Predelle del '200 al'500.* Florence, 1959.

Spencer, J. R. "Spacial Imagery of the Annunciation in Fifteenth-Century Florence." *Art Bulletin*, 37, 1955, pp. 273-80.

Strens, B. Hatfield. "L'arrivo del Trittico Portinari a Firenze." *Commentarii*, 19, 1968, pp. 315-19.
Documents dating the arrival in 1483.

Thiem, Gunther, and Thiem, Christel. *Toskanische Fassaden-Dekoration in Sgraffito und Fresko, 14. bis 17. Jahrhundert.* Munich, 1964.
Useful for the study of Florentine palaces and their owners.

Turner, A. Richard. *The Vision of Landscape in Renaissance Italy.* Princeton, 1966.

Vavala, Evelyn Sandberg. *Uffizi Studies: the Development of the Florentine School of Painting.* Florence, 1948.

Venturi, Lionello. *Italian Painting.* 3 vols. Geneva, 1950-1952.

Vertova, Luisa. *I Cenacoli Fiorentini.* Florence, 1965.

Watson, Paul. *The Garden of Love in Tuscan Art of the Early Renaissance.* Philadelphia and London, 1979.

Weiss, Roberto. "Jan van Eyck and the Italians." *Italian Studies*, 11, 1956, pp. 1ff; and 12, 1957, pp. 7ff.

Werner, Friederike. *Das italienische Altarbild vom Trecento bis zum Cinquecento. Untersuchung zur Thematik . . .* Doctoral dissertation, Kunsthistorisches Seminär der Ludwig-Maximilians Universität, Munich, 1971.

Zeri, Federico, and Gardner, Elizabeth C. *Italian Paintings. A Catalogue of the Collection of the Metropolitan Museum of Art: Florentine School.* New York, 1971.

### B. Fresco

Borsook, Eve. *The Mural Painters of Tuscany from Cimabue to Andrea del Sarto.* London, 1960.

Gombrich, E. H. *Means and Ends: Reflections on the History of Fresco Painting.* London, 1977.

*The Great Age of Fresco: Giotto to Pontormo; an exhibition of mural paintings and monumental drawings.* Catalogue of exhibition, Metropolitan Museum of Art, New York, 1968.

Meiss, Millard. *The Great Age of Fresco: Discoveries, Rediscoveries and Revivals.* London and New York, 1970.

Procacci, Ugo. *Sinopie e affreschi.* Milan, 1961.

## C. Stained Glass and Manuscript Illumination

Alexander, J.J.G. *Italian Renaissance Illuminations.* New York, 1977.

Levi d'Ancona, Mirella. *Miniatura e miniatori a Firenze del XIV al XVI secolo.* Florence, 1962.

Marchini, Giuseppe. *Italian Stained Glass Windows.* New York, 1956. Translated from *Le vetrate italiane.* Milan, 1955.

Salmi, Mario. *Italian Miniatures.* 2nd edition, revised, enlarged. Translated by Elisabeth Mann Borghese. New York, 1956. London, 1957. From *La miniatura italiana.* Milan, 1956.

## D. Textiles and Intarsia

Arcangeli, Francesco. *Tarsie.* Rome, 1943.
    Extremely brief text, 56 plates.

Garzelli, Annarosa. *Il Ricamo nella attivita artistica di Pollaiuolo, Botticelli, Bartolomeo di Giovanni.* Florence, 1973.

Johnstone, Pauline. "Antonio del Pollaiuolo and the Art of Embroidery." *Apollo,* 81, April 1965, pp. 306-309.

Santangelo, Antonio. *A Treasury of Great Italian Textiles.* Translated by Peggy Craig. New York, 1964. From *Tessuti d'arte italiani dal XII° al XVIII° secolo.* Milan, 1959.

Shoemaker, Innis Howe. *Il Recamo . . . Art Bulletin,* 58, 1976, pp. 621-22.
    A review of Garzelli; Good bibliography on textiles.

## III. Sculpture

### A. Surveys and Special Problems

Avery, Charles. *Florentine Renaissance Sculpture.* New York, 1970.

Bode, Wilhelm von. *Florentine Sculptors of the Renaissance.* Translated by Jessie Haynes. London, 1968. Freeport, N.Y., 1968. From *Florentiner Bildhauer der Renaissance.* Berlin, 1902.

Bush, Virginia. *The Colossal Sculpture of the Cinquecento.* New York, 1976.

Casalini, Eugenio. *La Ss. Annunziata di Firenze.* Florence, 1972.
    Deals in particular with wax votive images.

Caspary, Hans. *Das Sakramentstabernakel in der italienischen Renaissance.* Doctoral dissertation, Kunsthistorisches Seminär der Universität, Munich, 1962.

Dal Poggetto, M.G.C.D. *L'Oreficeria nella Firenze del Quattrocento.* Florence, 1977.

Catalogue of the exhibition. An important work on Quattrocento Florence and its craftsmanship in general.

Galassi, Giuseppe. *La scultura fiorentina del Quattrocento*. Milan, 1949.

Klapisch-Zuber, Christiane. *Les Maitres du Marbre, Carrare, 1300-1600*. Paris, 1969.
A Study of the marble industry.

Lavin, Irving. "Bozzetti and modelli. Notes on sculptural procedure . . ." In *Stil und Uberlieferung in der Kunst des Abendlandes. Akten des 21. Internationaler Kongresses für Kunstgeschichte, Bonn, 1964*, vol. 3, pp. 93-104. Berlin, 1967.

———. "On the Sources and Meaning of the Renaissance Portrait Bust." *Art Quarterly*, 33, 1970, pp. 212ff.

Lisner, Margrit. *Holzkruzifixe in Florenz und in der Toskana von der Zeit um 1300 bis zum frühen Cinquecento*. Munich, 1970.

Maggini, Enrichetta. *Le Tombe Umanistiche Fiorentine*. Florence, 1972.

Middeldorf, Ulrich. "On the Dilettante Sculptor." *Apollo*, 107, April 1978, pp. 310-22.

Panofsky, Erwin. *Tomb Sculpture: its Changing Aspects from Ancient Egypt to Bernini*. Edited by H. W. Janson. New York and London, 1964. New York, 1969.

Pope-Hennessy, John. *Catalogue of Italian Sculpture in the Victoria and Albert Museum*. 3 vols. London, 1964.

———. *Essays on Italian Sculpture*. London and New York, 1968.

———. *An Introduction to Italian Sculpture: Italian Gothic Sculpture*. London, 1955.

———. *Italian High Renaissance and Baroque Sculpture*. 3 vols. London, 1963. 2nd edition. London and New York, 1970-1972.

———. *Italian Renaissance Sculpture*. London, 1958.

Rossi, Filippo. *Italian Jewelled Arts*. Translated by Elisabeth Mann Borghese. New York, 1957. From *Capolavori di oreficeria italiana dall' XI al XVIII secolo*. Milan, 1956.

Schütz-Rautenberg, Gesa. *Kunstlergraber der italienischen Renaissance*. Doctoral dissertation, Kunsthistorisches Seminär der Ludwig-Maximilians Universität, Munich, 1971.

Schuyler, Jane. *Florentine Busts: Sculpted Portraiture in the Fifteenth Century*. New York, 1976.

Seymour, Charles, Jr. *Michelangelo's David: A Search for Identity*. Pittsburgh, 1967; New York, 1974.
Important for the David theme. See also the later literature on Florentine Davids cited in Translator's Introduction, note 5.

———. *Sculpture in Italy, 1400-1500*. Baltimore and Harmondsworth, 1966.

Webster, Ursula, and Simon, Erika. "Die Reliefmedallions im Hofe des Palazzo Medici in Florenz." *Jahrbuch der Berliner Museen*, 7, 1965, pp. 15-91.

Wittkower, Rudolf. *The Sculptor's Workshop. Tradition and Theory from the Renaissance to the Present*. Glasgow, 1974.

———. *Sculpture: Process and Principles*. New York, 1977.

### B. Medals, Small Bronzes, and Plaquettes

Hill, George F. *A Corpus of Italian Medals of the Renaissance before Cellini.* London, 1930.
Omitted in Wackernagel's work.

Pollard, Graham. *Renaissance Medals from the Samuel H. Kress Collection at the National Gallery of Art.* London, 1967. Based on G. F. Hill. *The Gustave Dreyfus Collection: Renaissance Medals.* Oxford, 1931. Revised and enlarged by Graham Pollard.

Pope-Hennessy, John. "Donatello and the Bronze Statuette." *Apollo,* 105, 1977, pp. 30-33.

———. "The Italian Plaquette." *Proceedings of the British Academy,* 50, 1964, pp. 63-85.

———. *Renaissance Bronzes from the Samuel H. Kress Collection: Reliefs, plaquettes, statuettes, utensils and mortars.* London, 1965.

### IV. Drawing and Graphic Arts

Berenson, Bernard. *The Drawings of the Florentine Painters.* 3 vols. Chicago, 1938. Reprinted 1973.

Chastel, André. *Florentine Drawings XIV-XVII Centuries.* Edited by André Gloeckner and translated by Rosamund Frost. New York and London, 1950.

Degenhart, Bernhard, and Schmitt, Annegrit. *Corpus der italienischen Zeichnungen 1300-1450.* Berlin, 1968.

———. *Italienische Zeichnungen des frühen 15. Jahrhunderts.* Basel, 1949.

Hind, Arthur M. *Early Italian Engraving: a critical catalogue.* 2 vols. in 7. London, 1938-1948.

Levenson, Jay; Oberhuber, Konrad; and Sheehan, Jacquelyn. *Early Italian Engravings from the National Gallery of Art.* Washington, D.C., 1973.

Phillips, John G. *Early Florentine Designers and Engravers: Maso Finiguerra, Baccio Baldini, Antonio Pollaiuolo, Sandro Botticelli, Francesco Rosselli.* Cambridge, Mass., 1955.
Concerns nielli, intarsia, drawing, and engraving.

Popham, Arthur E. *The Italian Drawings of the XV and XVI Centuries in the Collection of His Majesty the King at Windsor Castle.* London, 1949.

Popham, Arthur E., and Pouncey, Philip. *Italian Drawings in the Department of Prints and Drawings in the British Museum. The 14th and 15th Centuries.* 2 vols. London, 1950.

Ragghianti, Carlo, and Dalli Regoli, Gigetta. *Firenze 1470-1480: Disegni dal modello: Pollaiuolo/ Leonardo/ Botticelli/ Filippino.* Pisa, 1975.

Rushton, Joseph G. *Italian Renaissance Figurative Sketchbooks 1450-1520.* Doctoral dissertation, University of Minnesota, 1976.

### V. Architecture

#### A. Surveys and Special Problems

Ackerman, James S. "Architectural Practice in the Italian Renaissance." *Journal of the Society of Architectural Historians,* 13, 1954, pp. 3-11. Reprinted in

*Renaissance Art*, edited by Creighton Gilbert, pp. 148-71. New York, 1970.
———. *The Architecture of Michelangelo*. 2 vols. London, 1961. Catalogue revised London, 1964. Revised edition, New York and London, 1966. One volume paperback, Baltimore and Harmondsworth, 1971.
Concerned not only with Michelangelo, but with the whole nature of Renaissance architecture, patron relations, and building types.
Burns, Howard, "Quattrocento Architecture and the Antique: Some Problems." *Classical Influences on European Culture A. D. 500-1500, proceedings of an international conference held at Kings College, Cambridge, April 1969*, edited by R. R. Bolgar, pp. 269-87. Cambridge, 1971.
Fanelli, Giovanni. *Firenze. Architettura e città*. 2 vols. Florence, 1973.
An important, richly illustrated study on the city and its development.
Francastel, Pierre. "Imagination et réalité dans l'architecture civile de '400." In *Homagè a Lucien Febvre - Eventail de l'histoire vivante*, vol. 2, pp. 195-206. Paris, 1953.
Gilbert, Creighton. "The Earliest Guide to Florentine Architecture, 1423." *Mitteilungen des Kunsthistorischen Institutes in Florenz*, 14, 1969, pp. 33-46.
Heydenreich, Ludwig, and Lotz, Wolfgang. *Architecture in Italy, 1400-1600*. Harmondsworth, 1974.
Lotz, Wolfgang. *Studies in Italian Renaissance Architecture*. Cambridge, Mass., and London, 1977.
Lowry, Bates, *Renaissance Architecture*. New York, 1962.
Murray, Peter. *The Architecture of the Italian Renaissance*. New York, 1963.
———. *Renaissance Architecture*. New York, 1976.
Westfall, Carroll William. "Society, Beauty and the Humanist Architect in Alberti's *De Re Aedificatoria*." *Studies in the Renaissance*, 26, 1969, pp. 61-79.
Wittkower, Rudolf. *Architectural Principles in the Age of Humanism*. London, 1949. 3rd edition, revised, London, 1962. Various subsequent editions.

### B. Florentine Buildings and Their Decoration

#### 1. CHURCHES, HOSPITALS, AND LIBRARIES

Atanásio, M.C.M., and Dallai, Giovanni. "Nuove indagini sullo Spedale degli Innocenti a Firenze." *Commentari*, 17, 1966, pp. 83-106.
Bacchi, Giuseppe. *La Certosa di Firenze*. Florence, 1956.
Bargellini, Piero. *Orsanmichele a Firenze*. Milan, 1969.
Barolsky, Paul. "Toward an Interpretation of the Pazzi Chapel." *Journal of the Society of Architectural Historians*, 32, 1977, pp. 228-231.
Bartoli, Lando. "La 'Generazione' Albertiana dei rapporti ne 'la Bella Villanella' a Firenze." *L'Arte*, 13, 1971, pp. 66-81.
Benevolo, Leonardo; Chieffi, Stefano; and Mezzetti, Giulio. "Indagine sul Santo Spirito." *Quaderni dell'Istituto di Storia dell'Architettura*, 85-90, 1968. Published by the University in Rome.
Busignani, Alberto, and Bencini, Raffaello. *Le Chiese di Firenze*. 4 vols. Florence, 1974ff.
Casalini, Eugenio. *La Ss. Annunziata di Firenze*. Florence, 1972.
Connor, Louisa Bulman. *Artistic Patronage at the Ss. Annunziata until c. 1520*. Doctoral dissertation, Courtauld Institute of Art, London, 1972.

Cox-Rearick, Janet. "Fra Bartolomeo's St. Mark Evangelist and St. Sebastian with an Angel." *Mitteilungen des Kunsthistorischen Institutes in Florenz*, 18, 1974, pp. 329-354.
Includes study of the interior of San Marco.

Dezzi Bardeschi, Marco. "Il complesso monumentale di San Pancrazio a Firenze e il suo restauro." *Quaderni dell'Instituto di Storia dell'Architettura.* no. 13, 1966. Published by the University in Rome.

———. *La facciata di Santa Maria Novella a Firenze. Rilievo a cura dell'Instituto di restauro dei monumenti.* Pisa, 1970.

Goldthwaite, R. A., and Rearick, W. R. "Michelozzo and the Ospedale di San Paolo in Florence." *Mitteilungen des Kunsthistorischen Institutes in Florenz*, 21, 1977, pp. 221-306.

Haines, Margaret. *The Intarsias of the North Sacristy of the Duomo in Florence.* Doctoral dissertation, Courtauld Institute of Art, London, 1976.

Hall, Marcia B. "The Operation of Vasari's Workshop and the Designs for S. Maria Novella and S. Croce." *Burlington Magazine*, 115, 1973, pp. 204-209.

———. "Ponte in S. Maria Novella: the Problem of the Rood Screen in Italy." *Journal of the Warburg and Courtauld Institutes*, 37, 1974, pp. 157-73.

———. *Renovation and Counter-Reformation: Vasari and Duke Cosimo in Santa Maria Novella and Santa Croce, 1565-1577.* Oxford, 1978.

———. "Tramezzo in Santa Croce, Florence." *Art Bulletin*, 56, 1974, pp. 325-41.

Hartt, Frederick; Corti, Gino; and Kennedy, Clarence. *The Chapel of the Cardinal of Portugal, 1434-1459, at San Miniato in Florence.* Philadelphia, 1964.

Herzner, V. "Zur Baugeschichte von San Lorenzo in Florenz." *Zeitschrift für Kunstgeschichte*, 37, 1974, pp. 89-115.

Höger. A. *Studien zur Entstehung der Familienkapelle und zu Familienkapellen und Altären des Trecento in Florentiner Kirchen.* Bonn dissertation, 1976.

Hyman, Isabelle. *Fifteenth Century Florentiner Studies: the Palazzo Medici and a Ledger for the Church of San Lorenzo.* New York, 1976.

Kreytenberg, Gert. *Der Dom zu Florenz: Untersuchung zur Baugeschichte im 14. Jahrhundert.* Berlin, 1974.

Lang, Susanne. "The Programme of the Ss. Annunziata in Florence." *Journal of the Warburg and Courtauld Institutes*, 17, 1954, pp. 288-300.

Luchs, Alison. *Cestello: A Cistercian Church of the Florentine Renaissance.* New York, 1977.

Marcucci, Luisa. "Per gli 'armari' della sacrestia di Santa Croce." *Mitteilungen des Kunsthistorischen Institutes in Florenz*, 9, 1959-1960, pp. 141-58.

Markowski, Barbara. *Die pseudotextilen Paliotti von S. Spirito in Florenz.* Kunstgeschichtliches Seminär der Universität. Münster, 1971.

Micheletti, Emma. *Chiese di Firenze.* Novara, 1959.
Mostly illustrations of art works in eight major churches.

Morozzi, Guido. "Ricerche sull'aspetto originale dello Spedale degli Innocenti di Firenze." *Commentari*, 15, 1964, pp. 186-201.

O'Gorman, James F. *The Architecture of the Monastic Library in Italy 1300-1600.* New York, 1972.

Orlandi, Stefano. *Santa Maria Novella e i suoi chiostri monumentali.* Florence, 1956. Revised edition by Isnardo P. Grossi. Florence, 1972.

Paatz, Walter, and Paatz, Elisabeth. *Die Kirchen von Florenz.* 6 vols. Frankfurt am Main, 1940-1954.
The basic, encyclopedic study of Florentine churches and their contents, present and former.

Pampaloni, Guido. *Lo Spedale di S. Maria Nuova e la costruzione del Loggiato di Bernardo Buontalenti.* Florence, 1961.

Paolucci, Antonio. *Le Chiese di Firenze.* Florence, 1975
Attractive and wide-ranging pictorial survey, mostly in color.

Pietramellara, Carla et al. *Battistero di S. Giovanni a Firenze. Rilievo a cura dell'Istituto di Restauro dei Monumenti.* Florence, 1973.

Roselli, Piero et al. *Coro e cupola di Ss. Annunziata a Firenze. Rilievo a cura dell'Istituto di Restauro dei Monumenti.* Florence, 1971.

Rossi, Ferdinando. *Arte Italiana in Santa Croce.* Florence, 1962.

Ruda, Jeffrey. "A 1434 Building Programme for San Lorenzo in Florence." *Burlington Magazine,* 120, 1978, pp. 358-61.

Saalman, Howard. *The Church of Santa Trinita in Florence.* New York, 1966.

———. *Filippo Brunelleschi: The Cupola of Santa Maria del Fiore.* London, in press.

———. "San Lorenzo: the 1434 Chapel Project." *Burlington Magazine,* 120, 1978, pp. 361-64. Interpretation of a document discovered by Jeffrey Ruda.

———. "Santa Maria del Fiore, 1294-1418." *Art Bulletin,* 46, 1964, pp. 471-500.

Taucci, Raffaele. *Un santuario e la sua citta: la Ss. Annunziata di Firenze.* Florence, 1976.

Teubner, Hans. "Das Langhaus der Ss. Annunziata in Florenz. Studien zu Michelozzo und Giuliano da Sangallo." *Mitteilungen des Kunsthistorischen Institutes in Florenz,* 22, 1978, pp. 27-60.

———. *Zur Entwicklung der Saalkirche in der florentiner Frührenaissance.* Doctoral dissertation, Kunsthistorisches Institut der Universität, Heidelberg, 1975.

Toker, Franklin. "Baptistery below the Baptistery of Florence." *Art Bulletin,* 58, 1976, pp. 157-67.

———. "Excavations below the Cathedral of Florence, 1965-1974. *Gesta,* 14, 1975, pp. 17-36.

Trachtenberg, Marvin L. *The Campanile of Florence Cathedral: Giotto's Tower.* New York, 1971.

Ullmann, B. L. *The Public Library of Renaissance Florence.* Padua, 1972. San Marco.

Zeitler, Rudolf. "Uber den Innenraum von Santo Spirito zu Florenz." In *Idea and Form: Studies in the History of Art,* edited by Nils Gösta Sandblad, pp. 48-68. Figura, Uppsala Studies in the History of Art, n.s. 1. Stockholm, 1959.

## 2. PALACES AND LOGGIE

Bargellini, Piero. *Scoperta di Palazzo Vecchio.* Florence, 1968.
Richly illustrated, brief commentary.

Below, Irene. *Leonardo da Vinci und Filippino Lippi. Studien zu den Altartafeln für die Bernhardskapelle im Palazzo Vecchio und für das Kloster San Donato a Scopeto.* Doctoral dissertation, Kunsthistorisches Institut der freien Universität, Berlin, 1971.

Bucci, Mario, and Bencini, Raffaello. *Palazzi di Firenze.* 4 vols. Florence, 1971-1973.

Bulst, Wolfger A. "Die ursprungliche innere Aufteilung des Palazzo Medici in Florenz." *Mitteilungen des Kunsthistorischen Institutes in Florenz*, 14, 1970, pp. 369ff.

Buttner, Frank. "Der Umbau des Palazzo Medici Riccardi zu Florenz." *Mitteilungen des Kunsthistorischen Institutes in Florenz*, 14, 1970, pp. 393ff.

Forster, Kurt W. "Palazzo Rucellai and Questions of Typology in the Development of Renaissance Buildings." *Art Bulletin*, 58, 1976, pp. 109-113. Follow-up to Mack article, below.

Frommel, Christoph. *Der römische Palastbau der Hochrenaissance.* 3 vols. Tübingen, 1973.
Includes discussion of fifteenth-century development of palace types in Florence.

Ginori Lisci, Leonardo. *I Palazzi di Firenze nella Storia e nell'Arte.* 2 vols. Florence, 1972.
A richly documented catalogue, also useful for the study of patron families.

Goldthwaite, Richard. "The Building of the Strozzi Palace: the Construction Industry in Renaissance Florence." *Studies in Medieval and Renaissance History*, 10, 1973, pp. 99-194.
Of special interest for exploration of the architect's function.

————. "The Florentine Palace as Domestic Architecture." *The American Historical Review*, 77, 1972, pp. 977-1012.
Deals in particular with the Strozzi palace.

Guicciardini, Paolo, and Dori, Emilio. *Le antiche case ed il palazzo dei Guicciardini a Firenze.* Florence, 1952.

Hersey, George L. *Pythagorean Palaces: Magic and Architecture in the Italian Renaissance.* Ithaca, N.Y. and London, 1976.

Hyman, Isabelle. *Fifteenth Century Florentine Studies: the Palazzo Medici and a Ledger for the Church of San Lorenzo.* New York, 1976.

Kent, Francis William. "The Rucellai Family and its Loggia." *Journal of the Warburg and Courtauld Institutes*, 35, 1972, pp. 397-401.

Mack, Charles Randall. "The Rucellai Palace: Some New Proposals." *Art Bulletin*, 56, 1974, pp. 517-29.
See also Forster, above.

Pampaloni, Guido. *Il Palazzo Portinari-Salviati.* Florence, 1960.

————. *Palazzo Strozzi.* Florence, 1963.

Paul, Jurgen. *Der Palazzo Vecchio in Florenz. Ursprung und Bedeutung seiner Form.* Florence, 1969.

Poli, Oreste. *Il recupero di un monumento a Firenze.* Florence, 1973.
Palazzo Ricasoli.

Preyer, Brenda. *Giovanni Rucellai and the Rucellai Palace.* Doctoral dissertation, Harvard University, 1976.

————. "The Rucellai Loggia." *Mitteilungen des Kunsthistorischen Institutes in Florenz*, 21, 1977, pp. 183-95.
  Includes material on Rucellai palace and San Pancrazio.

Sinding-Larsen, Staale. "A Tale of Two Cities. Florentine and Roman Visual Context for Fifteenth-century Palaces." *Acta ad Archaeologiam et Artium Historiam Pertinentia*, 6, 1975, pp. 163-212.
  Deals in particular with forms and meaning of rustication.

Thiem, Gunther, and Thiem, Christel. *Toskanische Fassaden-Dekoration in Sgraffito und Fresko, 14. bis 17. Jahrhundert*. Munich, 1964.

Webster, U., and Simon, E. "Die Reliefmedallions in Hofe des Palazzo Medici in Florenz." *Jahrbuch der Berliner Museen*, 7, 1965, pp. 15-91.
  On Medici palace courtyard decoration.

Wilde, Johannes. "The Hall of the Great Council of Florence." *Journal of the Warburg and Courtauld Institutes*, 7, 1944, pp. 65-81. Reprinted in *Renaissance Art*, edited by Creighton Gilbert, pp. 92-132. New York, 1970.
  A fundamental study; for subsequent criticism and new interpretations see Grohn and Isermeyer articles cited in Translator's Introduction, note 5.

### 3. VILLAS AND GARDENS

Acton, Harold. *Tuscan Villas*. Photographs by Alexander Zielcke. London, 1973.

Coffin, David R., ed. *The Italian Garden*. Washington, D.C., 1972.

Foster, Philip. *A Study of Lorenzo de' Medici's Villa at Poggio a Caiano*. New York, 1978.

Lensi Orlandi, G. C. *Le Ville di Firenze*. 2 vols. Florence, 1955.

Masson, Georgina. *Italian Gardens*. New York, 1961.

————. *Italian Villas and Palaces*. New York, 1959.

Rusconi, A. J. *Le ville Medicee (Boboli, Castello, Petraia e Poggio a Caiano)*. Rome, 1938.

### VI. THEATER, FESTIVAL, AND SPECTACLE

Blumenthal, Arthur. *Italian Renaissance Festival Designs*. Madison, Wisc., 1973.
  Deals mostly with the Cinquecento, but bibliography useful for earlier period also.

Borsook. Eve. "Decor in Florence for the Entry of Charles VIII of France." *Mitteilungen des Kunsthistorischen Institutes in Florence*, 10, 1961-1963, pp. 106-122 and 217.

*Enciclopedia dello Spettacolo*. 9 vols. Rome 1954-1962.

Fabbri, Mario; Zorzi, E. B.; and Tofani, A.M.P. *Il Luogo teatrale a Firenze: Brunelleschi, Vasari, Buontalenti, Parigi*. Catalogue of the exhibition at the Museo Mediceo, Palazzo Medici Riccardi, Florence, 31 May to 31 October 1975. Milan, 1975.
  Valuable bibliography and interesting reconstructions of Brunelleschi's stagecraft inventions.

Jacquot, Jean, ed. *Le Lieu théatral à la Renaissance*. Paris, 1964.

Molinari, Cesare. *Spettacoli fiorentini del Quattrocento: Contributi allo Studio delle Sacre Rappresentazioni*. Venice, 1961.

Pochat, Götz. "Brunelleschi and the 'Ascensions' of 1422." *Art Bulletin*, 60, 1978, pp. 232-34.

Shearman, John. "The Florentine Entrata of Leo X." *Journal of the Warburg and Courtauld Institutes*, 38, 1975, pp. 136-54.

## VII. SPECIAL ARTISTIC PROBLEMS IN VARIOUS MEDIA

Bargellini, Piero. *Cento tabernacoli a Firenze*. Florence, 1971.

Clark, Kenneth. *The Nude: A Study in Ideal Form*. New York, 1956. Princeton, N.J., 1972.

Dacos, Nicole. *La Découverte de la Domus Aurea et la Formation des Grotesques à la Renaissance*. London, 1970.
Antique influences on late Quattrocento ornament.

Eisler, Colin. "The Golden Christ of Cortona and the Man of Sorrows in Italy." *Art Bulletin*, 51, 1969, pp. 107-18 and 233-46.

von Erffa, Hans Martin. "Judith, Virtus Virtutum, Maria." *Mitteilungen des Kunsthistorischen Institutes in Florenz*, 14, 1969-1970, pp. 460-65.

Ettlinger, L. D. "Hercules Florentinus." *Mitteilungen des Kunsthistorischen Institutes in Florenz*, 16, 1972, pp. 119-42.

Hatje, Ursula. *Der Putto in der italienischen Kunst der Renaissance*. Doctoral dissertation, Kunsthistorisches Institut der Universität, Tübingen, 1954.

Janneau, Guillaume. *Les styles du meuble italien*. Paris, 1973.
A chapter on the Renaissance has drawings of examples; no bibliography.

Lavin, Marilyn A. "Giovannino Battista: A Study in Renaissance Religious Symbolism." *Art Bulletin*, 37, 1955, pp. 85-107 and 43, 1961, pp. 319-26.

Malvern, Marjorie M. *Venus in Sackcloth: The Magdalen's Origins and Metamorphoses*. Carbondale, Ill., 1975.

Pedrini, Augusto. *Italian Furniture: Interiors and Decoration of the Fifteenth and Sixteenth Centuries*. London, 1949. From *Il mobilio, gli ambienti e le decorazione del Rinascimento in Italia, secoli XV e XVI*. Florence, 1948. 2nd edition revised, Turin, 1967.

Pope-Hennessy, John. *The Portrait in the Renaissance*. New York, 1966.

Reid, J. D. "True Judith: Botticelli's Judith." *Art Journal*, 28, 1969, pp. 378-80.

Romby, Giuseppina Carla. *Descrizioni e rappresentazioni della citta di Firenze nel xv secolo*. Florence, 1976.

Seznec, Jean. *The Survival of the Pagan Gods: the mythological tradition and its place in Renaissance humanism*. Translated by Barbara F. Sessions. New York, 1953. Princeton, N.J., 1972. From *La survivance des dieux antiques*. London, 1939.

Simon, Kathrin. "Dais and the Arcade: Architecture and Pictorial Narrative in Quattrocento Painting and Sculpture." *Apollo*, 81, April 1965, pp. 278ff.

Warnke, Martin. "Italienische Bildtabernakel bis zum Frühbarock." *Münchner Jahrbuch der bildenden Kunst*, 19, 1968, pp. 61-102.

Winner, Matthias. "Zum nachleben des Laökoon in der Renaissance." *Jahrbuch der Berliner Museen*, 16, 1974, pp. 83-91.
Includes Filippino's Poggio a Caiano fresco.

VIII. Patrons and Collectors

A. General

Borsook, Eve. "Fra Filippo Lippi and the Murals for Prato Cathedral." *Mitteilungen des Kunsthistorischen Institutes in Florenz*, 19, 1975, pp. 1-148.

Borsook, Eve, and Offerhaus, Johannes. "Storia e leggende nella Cappella Sassetti in Santa Trinita." In *Scritti di Storia dell'Arte in Onore di Ugo Procacci*, edited by Maria G.C.D. Dal Poggetto and Paolo Dal Poggetto, pp. 289-310. Milan, 1977.

Brown, A. M., and de la Mare, A. C. "Bartolomeo Scala's Dealings with Booksellers, Scribes and Illuminators, 1459-63." *Journal of the Warburg and Courtauld Institutes*, 38, 1976, pp. 237-45.

Clough, Cecil H. "Federico da Montefeltro's Patronage of the Arts, 1468-72." *Journal of the Warburg and Courtauld Institutes*, 36, 1973, pp. 129-44.

Connor, Louisa Bulman. *Artistic Patronage at the Ss. Annunziata until c. 1520*. Doctoral dissertation, Courtauld Institute of Art, 1972.

Covi, Dario. "Botticelli and Pope Sixtus IV." *Burlington Magazine*, 111, 1969, pp. 616ff.

Craven, Stephanie J. *Aspects of Patronage in Florence 1494-1512*. Doctoral dissertation, Courtauld Institute of Art, London, 1973.

Csapodi, Csaba; Csapodi-Gárdonyi, Klára; and Szántó, Tibor. *Bibliotheca Corviniana: The Library of King Matthias Corvinus of Hungary*. New York, 1970.

Ettlinger, L. D. "Pollaiuolo's Tomb of Pope Sixtus IV." *Journal of the Warburg and Courtauld Institutes*, 16, 1953, pp. 238-74.

———. *The Sistine Chapel before Michelangelo*. Oxford, 1965.

Geiger, Gale Louise. *Filippino Lippi's Carafa Chapel, 1488-1493, Santa Maria sopra Minerva, Rome*. Doctoral dissertation, Stanford University, 1975.

Gilbert, Creighton. "Fra Angelico's Fresco Cycles in Rome: Their Number and Dates." *Zeitschrift für Kunstgeschichte*, 38, 1975, pp. 245-65.

Hersey, George L. *Alfonso II and the Artistic Renewal of Naples*. New Haven, 1969.

Howard, Deborah. *Jacopo Sansovino: Architecture and Patronage in Renaissance Venice*. New Haven and London, 1975.

Janson, H. W. "Giovanni Chellini's Libro and Donatello." In *Studien zur Toskanischen Kunst. Festschrift für Ludwig Heinrich Heydenreich*, edited by Wolfgang Lotz and Lise Lotte Möller, pp. 131-38. Munich, 1964. Reprinted in *16 Studies*, pp. 107-16. New York, 1974.

Johnson, Eugene J. *Sant'Andrea in Mantua. The Building History*. University Park, Penn., 1975.

Johnson, William McAllister et al. *L'Ecole de Fontainebleau*. Catalogue of an exhibition at the Grand Palais, Paris, October 17, 1972-January 15, 1973. Paris, 1972.

Juřen, Vladimír. "Le projet de Giuliano da Sangallo pour le palais du roi de Naples." *Revue de l'Art*, 25, 1974, pp. 66-69.

La Coste-Messeliere, Marie Geneviève de la. "Battista della Palla Conspirateur, Marchand ou Homme de Cour." *Oeil*, 129, 1965, pp. 19-25.

Lightbown, R. W. "Giovanni Chellini, Donatello, and Antonio Rossellino." *Burlington Magazine*, 104, 1962, pp. 102-104.

Molho, Anthony. "The Brancacci Chapel: Studies in its Iconography and History." *Journal of the Warburg and Courtauld Institutes*, 40, 1977, pp. 50-98.

Origo, Iris. *The Merchant of Prato Francesco di Marco Datini*. New York, 1957. Revised edition, Harmondsworth, 1963.

Panofsky, Erwin. "The Early History of Man in Two Cycles of Paintings by Piero di Cosimo." In *Studies in Iconology*, New York, 1939: 2nd edition annotated, New York, 1962.
Concerns Pugliese and Vespucci patronage, domestic decoration.

Rotondi, Pasquale. *The Ducal Palace of Urbino: Its Architecture and Decoration*. London and New York, 1969. Abridged translation of *Il Palazzo Ducale di Urbino*. 2 vols. Urbino, 1950.

Sachs, Hannelore. *Sammler und Maezene. Zur Entwicklung des Kunstsammelns von der Antike bis zur Gegenwart*. Leipzig, 1971.

Schulz, Anne Markham. "The Tomb of Giovanni Chellini at San Miniato al Tedesco." *Art Bulletin*, 51, 1969, pp. 328ff.

Weil-Garris, Kathleen. *The Santa Casa di Loreto: Problems in Cinquecento Sculpture*. 2 vols. New York, 1977.

Westfall, Carroll William. *In this Most Perfect Paradise. Alberti, Nicholas V and the Invention of Conscious Urban Planning in Rome, 1447-55*. University Park and London, 1974.

### B. Medici

Barfucci, Enrico. *Lorenzo de Medici e la società artistica di suo tempo*. 2nd edition. Florence, 1964.

*Catalogo della Mostra d'Arte Antica: Lorenzo il Magnifico e le arti*. Florence, 1949.

Chastel, André. "Vasari et la légende médicéenne: l'école du jardin de Saint Marc." In *Studi Vasariani: Atti del convegno internazionale per il IV centenario della prima edizione delle "Vite" del Vasari, Firenze, Palazzo Strozzi, 16-19 settembre 1950*. Edited by Istituto Nazionale di Studi sul Rinascimento. Florence, 1952.

Dacos, Nicole; Giuliano, Antonio; and Pannuti, Ulrico. *Il Tesoro di Lorenzo il Magnifico: le Gemme*. Florence, 1973.

Elam, Caroline. "Lorenzo de' Medici and the Urban Development of Renaissance Florence." *Art History*, 1, 1978, pp. 43-66.

Gombrich, E. H. "The Early Medici as Patrons of Art: A Survey of Primary Sources." In *Italian Renaissance Studies: A Tribute to the Memory of the Late Cecilia M. Ady*, edited by E. F. Jacob, pp. 279-311. London, 1960. Reprinted in *Norm and Form*, pp. 35-57. London, 1966.

———. "Renaissance and Golden Age." *Journal of the Warburg and Courtauld Institutes*, 24, 1961, pp. 306-309. Reprinted in *Norm and Form*, pp. 29-34. London, 1966.

Hatfield, Rab. "The Compagnia de' Magi." *Journal of the Warburg and Courtauld Institutes*, 33, 1970, pp. 137-61.

Involves Medici patronage of the Confraternity of the Magi and its festival procession in Florence.

———. "Some Unknown Documents on the Medici Palace in 1459." *Art Bulletin*, 1970, pp. 232-45.

Includes a Milanese visitor's lavish description of Piero's chamber.

Heikamp, Detlef, and Grote, Andreas, eds. *Il Tesoro di Lorenzo il Magnifico: I Vasi*. Florence, 1974.

Jenkins, A. D. Fraser. "Cosimo dei Medici's Patronage and the Theory of Magnificence." *Journal of the Warburg and Courtauld Institutes*, 33, 1970, pp. 162-70.

Martelli, Mario. "I pensieri architettonici del Magnifico." *Commentarii*, 17, 1966, pp. 107-111.

Involves Lorenzo's interest in Alberti's *De Re Aedificatoria*.

Miarelli-Mariani, Gaetano. "Il disegno per il complesso mediceo di Via Laura a Firenze: un significativo intervento urbano prefigurato da Giuliano da Sangallo per Lorenzo il Magnifico." *Palladio*, 22, 1972, pp. 127-62.

Morassi, Antonio. *Il Tesoro dei Medici: oreficerie, argenterie, pietre dure*. Milan, 1963. American edition, *Art Treasures of the Medici*. Greenwich, Conn., 1963. English edition, *Art Treasures of the Medici: jewelry, silverware, hardstone*, translated by Paul Colacicchi. London, 1964.

Procacci, Ugo. "Cosimo de' Medici e la costruzione della Badia fiesolana." *Commentarii*, 19, 1968, pp. 80-97.

Raises the possibility that Cosimo himself in effect designed the building.

Shearman, John. "Collections of the Younger Branch of the Medici." *Burlington Magazine*, 117, 1975, pp. 12ff.

Newly discovered inventories that mention paintings possibly by Botticelli.

Smith, Webster. "On the Original Location of the 'Primavera.'" *Art Bulletin*, 57, 1975, pp. 31-40.

Deals with the same material as Shearman, discovered independently.

### C. Rucellai

Kent, Francis William "The Letters Genuine and Spurious of Giovanni Rucellai." *Journal of the Warburg and Courtauld Institutes*, 37, 1974, pp. 342-49. Some letters published in Perosa, including one on the Holy Sepulchre, are called into question.

Rucellai, Giovanni. *Il Zibaldone Quaresimale*. Vol. 1. *Giovanni Rucellai ed il suo Zibaldone*. Edited by Alessandro Perosa. London, 1960. A second volume is due out shortly.

### D. Strozzi

Borsook, Eve, "Documenti relativi alle cappelle di Lecceto e delle Selve di Filippo Strozzi." *Antichita Viva*, 9, 1970, pp. 3-20.

———. "Documents for Filippo Strozzi's Chapel in Santa Maria Novella." *Burlington Magazine*, 112, 1970, pp. 737-45.

Davisson, Darrell D. "The Iconology of the S. Trinita Sacristy, 1418-1435: A Study of the Private and Public Functions of Religious Art in the Early Quattrocento." *Art Bulletin*, 57, 1975, pp. 315-34.

    Concerned especially with Palla Strozzi and Gentile da Fabriano's *Adoration of the Magi.*

Fiocco, G. "La biblioteca di Palla Strozzi." In *Studi di bibliografia e di storia in onore di Tammaro de Marinis,* vol. 2, pp. 289-310. Verona, 1964.

Friedman, David. "The Burial Chapel of Filippo Strozzi in Santa Maria Novella in Florence." *L'Arte,* 9, 1970, pp. 108-331.

Kent, Francis William. "Piu superba de quella de Lorenzo": Courtly and Family Interest in the Building of Filippo Strozzi's Palace." *Renaissance Quarterly,* 30, 1977, pp. 311-23.

Sale, J. Russell. *Filippino Lippi's Strozzi Chapel in Santa Maria Novella.* New York, 1979.

## IX. Guidebooks and Collections of Florence

### A. Guidebooks

Borsook, Eve. *The Companion Guide to Florence.* New York and London, 1966. 3rd revised edition. 1974.

*Guida del Touring Club Italiano: Firenze e dintorni.* Milan, 1974.
    The most complete guide to Florence, its monuments, and collections.

Higson, John W., Jr. *A Historical Guide to Florence.* New York, 1973.

Kauffmann, Georg. *Florence: Art Treasures and Buildings.* Translated by Edith Köstner and J. A. Underwood. London and New York, 1971.

### B. Uffizi and Pitti

Becherucci, Luisa. *The Treasures of the Uffizi Gallery.* Milan, 1957.

Berti, Luciano, and Caneva, Caterina, eds. *Gli Uffizi: Catalogo Generale.* Florence, 1979.
    Comprehensive catalogue with extensive bibliography.

Chiarelli, Renzo. *Palatine Gallery in Florence.* Rome, 1960. From *La Galleria Palatina a Firenze.* Rome, 1956.

Dalli Regoli, Gigetta et al. *Uffizi, Florence.* New York, 1968.

Francini Ciaranfi, A. M. *Pitti. Firenze.* Novara, 1971.

————. *The Pitti Gallery (Galleria Palatina). Visitors' Guide and Catalogue of Paintings.* Trans. by Evelyn Sandberg Vavala. Florence, 1967. From *Pitti. Galleria Palatina.* Novara, 1955.

Fremantle, Richard. *Florentine Painting in the Uffizi: An Introduction to the Historical Background.* Florence, 1971.

Mansuelli, Guido A. *Galleria degli Uffizi: le Sculture.* Rome, 1958.

Micheletti, Emma. *The Uffizi and Pitti.* Florence, 1968.

Negrini, Sergio. *The Uffizi of Florence and its Paintings.* Edinburgh, 1974. From *Uffizi, Firenze.* Milan, 1974.

Piacenti Aschengreen, Cristina. *Il Museo degli Argenti a Firenze.* Milan, 1968.

Rossi, Filippo. *Art Treasures of the Uffizi and Pitti.* New York, 1957, 1966.

Salvini, Roberto. *Uffizi. Firenze.* Novara, 1970.

————. *The Uffizi Gallery: Visitors' Guide and Catalogue of Paintings.* Florence, 1965. From *Galleria degli Uffizi.* Florence, 1962.

## C. Accademia and San Marco

Biagi, Luigi. *L'Accademia di Belle Arti di Firenze*. Florence, 1941.

Chiarelli, Renzo. *La Galleria dell'Accademia e il Museo di San Marco*. Florence, 1968.

Procacci, Ugo. *La Galleria dell'Accademia di Firenze*. 2nd edition. Rome, 1951.

## D. Bargello and Palazzo Vecchio

Artusi, Luciano. *Palazzo Vecchio*. Florence, 1970.

Baldini, Umberto. *Palazzo Vecchio e i Quartieri Monumentali*. Florence, 1950.

Berti, Luciano. *Il Bargello: Museo Nazionale*. Florence, 1970.

Lensi Orlandi, Giulio. *Il Palazzo Vecchio di Firenze*. Florence, 1978.

Pucci, Eugenio. *Piazza della Signoria e Palazzo Vecchio*. Florence, 1969.

Sinibaldi, Giulia. *Il Palazzo Vecchio a Firenze*. Rome, 1934. 4th edition. 1969.

Rossi, Filippo. *Il Museo Nazionale di Firenze*. Rome, 1938.

## E. Other Collections

Baldini, Umberto, and Dal Poggetto, Paolo. *Firenze Restaura*. Florence, 1972.
Catalogue of the exhibition at the Fortezza da Basso, 18 March-4 June 1972.

Bargellini, Piero. *Il Palazzo Medici e gli Affreschi di Benozzo Gozzoli*. Florence, 1950.

Becherucci, Luisa, and Brunetti, Giulia. *Il Museo dell'Opera del Duomo a Firenze*. 2 vols. Venice, 1971.
Invaluable for the study of works in various media done for or associated with the Duomo and Baptistery.

Bellosi, Luciano et al. *Museo dell'Ospedale degli Innocenti a Firenze*. Florence, 1978.

Berti, Luciano. *Palazzo Davanzati*. Florence, 1958.

———. *Il Museo di Palazzo Davanzati*. Milan, 1971.
Deals both with architecture and artistic contents.

De Tolnay, Charles. *Casa Buonarotti. Le sculture di Michelangelo e le collezioni della famiglia*. Florence, 1970.

Gamba, Carlo. *Il Museo Horne*. Florence, 1961.

Modi, Amerigo. *Il Palazzo Medici-Riccardi e il Museo Mediceo*. Florence, 1960.

Procacci, Ugo. *La Casa Buonarotti*. Milan, 1965.

Righini Bonelli, Maria Luisa. *Il Museo di Storia della Scienza a Firenze*. Milan, 1968.

Robinson, Henry Russell. *Il Museo Stibbert a Firenze*. Milan, 1973.

Russoli, Franco. *La Raccolta Berenson*. Milan, 1962.

# INDEX

abbey, *see* Badia

academy, xviiin, 262

Accademia di Belle Arti, 216

Accademia Gallery, xxiii, 129, 132n, 278; *Adimari Wedding*, 157, 178n, 199n; *Annunciation* (Botticelli), xxiii, 183n; *St. Bernardino*, 136n; *St. Matthew* (Michelangelo), 35; *Pietà* (Sarto), 130n; *Trinity* (Baldovinetti), 114, 338n; *St. Vincent Ferrer*, 136n; household altarpiece (Andrea di Giusto), 174n; *Legends of Hermits* (Uccello), 138n

Acciaiuoli, Niccolò, 213n

Acciaiuoli family, 284

Acton collection, 175n

Acuto, *see* Hawkwood

Adam and Eve, 180

Adamantino, Manetto, 288n

Adimari family, 178n

*Adimari Wedding*, 157, 178n, 199n

Adoration, 41, 137n; of the Child, 149, 175-176; of the Magi, *see* Magi; of the Shepherds, 114, 125, 267, 268

advertising, 181

Aemilius Paulus, 196

Agatha, St., 139n

Agli, Barnaba degli, 213n

Agnus-Dei salver, 256

Agolanti, Alessandro, 47

Agostino di Duccio, 29, 73n, 78n, 210n, 281

air pollution, xxiii

*alari, see* andirons

Albert, St., 126n

Alberti, Gherardo degli, 246n

Alberti, Leon Battista, 317, 353; *De arte aeraria*, 315n; on public approval, 348n; *Del governo della famiglia*, 189; Rucellai chapel, 227; Rucellai patronage, 44; Santa Maria Novella facade, 29, 44; Santissima Annunziata, 247; treatise on painting, 316-317, 321, 326, 348, 356; writings, 358

Alberti, Piero degli, 162n

Alberti family, 241n

Albertinelli, Mariotto, xxiii, 128n, 130, 133n, 176, 279n, 310n, 320n, 328, 331, 344, 363, 368

Albertini, Francesco, 51, 68, 69, 287

Albizzi, Giovanna degli (Tornabuoni), 151, 158

Albizzi family, 191, 223

Aldobrandini family, 173n

Aldovrandi, Ulisse, 289

Alessandri, Jacopo degli, 110n

Alexander, 98n

All Souls' Day, 141n

allegories, 155n, 162n, 197n

Allori, Alessandro, 153n

Aloysius de Alemania, 303n

altar; decoration, 81, 82, 131, 149; distribution in churches, 131; position of celebrant, 135; private, 10, 241, 243, 274

altar frontal, *see* antependium

altarpiece, 87, 113; double-sided, 134; folding, 135, 276; form, 132; household, 174n, 175n; iconography, 133; inscriptions in, 241; with inset crucifix, 90, 134; majolica, 80; marble, 80; portable, 173; private associations, 243; reused, 235n; with statue at center, 134; sketch for, 319n; veiling, 135-136

Altenburg, 175

Altoviti, 82, 106n, 279; Stoldo, 214n

Ammanati, Bartolommeo, 53

Amsterdam, 158n

Anadyomene, 155

anatomical studies, 320, 321

Anderburg, Margrave of, 81, 82

andirons, 106, 164

Andrea di Giusto, 174n, 213n, 311n

Andrea di Piero, 34

Andrew, St., 36n, 92, 125n

Andromeda, 177n, 277

Angelico, Fra, 41n, 293, 307; assistant, 126n; as Dominican, 355n; in Orvieto, 343n; piety, 355; pupils, 145; at San Domenico, Fiesole, 126; at San Marco, 124, 126, 127, 129, 130, 230; at Santa Maria Novella, 40, 41, 119n; school of, 140n, 268

Works; Adoration of the Magi tondo,

LIBRARY OF CONGRESS CATALOGING IN PUBLICATION DATA

Wackernagel, Martin, 1881-
  The world of the Florentine Renaissance artist.

  Translation of Der Lebensraum des Künstlers in
der florentinischen Renaissance.
  Bibliography: p.
  Includes index.
    1.  Art, Italian—Italy—Florence.    2.  Art,
Renaissance—Italy—Florence.    3.  Artists—Italy—
Florence.    4.  Art patronage—Italy—Florence.
I.  Title.
N6921.F7W313        709'.45'51        80-39683
ISBN 0-691-03966-6
ISBN 0-691-10117-5 (pbk.)